NGRESS®

100%
CERTIFIED
EXAM OBJECTIVES

The Official
CHFI
Exam 312-49 Study Guide
for Computer Hacking Forensics Investigators

Dave Kleiman Technical Editor

Kevin Cardwell

Timothy Clinton

Michael Cross

Michael Gregg

Jesse Varsalone

Craig Wright

KEY	SERIAL NUMBER
001	HJIRTCV764
002	PO9873D5FG
003	829KM8NJH2
004	BPOQ48722D
005	CVPLQ6WQ23
006	VBP965T5T5
007	HJJJ863WD3E
008	2987GVTWMK
009	629MP5SDJT
010	IMWQ295T6T

PUBLISHED BY
Syngress Publishing, Inc.
Elsevier, Inc.
30 Corporate Drive
Burlington, MA 01803

The Official CHFI Study Guide (Exam 312-49) for Computer Hacking Forensic Investigators

ISBN 13: 978-159749-197-6

Publisher: Amorette Pedersen
Managing Editor: Andrew Williams
Technical Editor: Dave Kleiman
Cover Designer: Michael Kavish
Indexer: Nara Wood

Project Manager: Gary Byrne
Page Layout and Art: Patricia Lupien
Copy Editors: Audrey Doyle, Adrienne Rebello,
 Mike McGee

For information on rights, translations, and bulk sales, contact Matt Pedersen, Commercial Sales Director; email m.pedersen@elsevier.com.

Transferred to Digital Printing in 2010

Technical Editor

Dave Kleiman (CAS, CCE, CIFI, CISM, CISSP, ISSAP, ISSMP, MCSE, MVP) has worked in the information technology security sector since 1990. Currently, he runs an independent computer forensic company, DaveKleiman.com, which specializes in litigation support, computer forensic investigations, incident response, and intrusion analysis. He developed a Windows operating system lockdown tool, S-Lok, which surpasses NSA, NIST, and Microsoft Common Criteria Guidelines.

Dave was a contributing author for *Microsoft Log Parser Toolkit* (Syngress Publishing, ISBN: 1-932266-52-6), *Security Log Management: Identifying Patterns in the Chaos* (Syngress Publishing, ISBN: 1597490423), and *How to Cheat at Windows System Administration* (Syngress Publishing ISBN: 1597491055). Dave was technical editor for *Perfect Passwords: Selection, Protection, Authentication* (Syngress Publishing, ISBN: 1597490415); *Winternals Defragmentation, Recovery, and Administration Field Guide* (Syngress Publishing, ISBN: 1597490792); *Windows Forensic Analysis: Including DVD Toolkit* (Syngress Publishing, ISBN: 159749156X); and *CD and DVD Forensics* (Syngress Publishing, ISBN: 1597491284). He was also a technical reviewer for *Enemy at the Water Cooler: Real Life Stories of Insider Threats* (Syngress Publishing, ISBN: 1597491292)

He is frequently a speaker at many national security conferences and is a regular contributor to security-related newsletters, Web sites, and Internet forums. Dave is a member of many professional security organizations, including the Miami Electronic Crimes Task Force (MECTF), International Association of Counter Terrorism and Security Professionals (IACSP), International Society of Forensic Computer Examiners® (ISFCE), Information Systems Audit and Control Association® (ISACA), High Technology Crime Investigation Association (HTCIA), Association of Certified Fraud Examiners (ACFE), and the High Tech Crime Consortium (HTCC). He is also the Sector Chief for Information Technology at the FBI's InfraGard®.

Contributors

Kevin Cardwell (CEH, ECSA, LPT) works as a freelance consultant and provides consulting services for companies throughout the U.S., U.K., and Europe. He is an adjunct associate professor for the University of Maryland University College, where he participated in the team that developed the Information Assurance Program for Graduate Students, which is recognized as a Center of Excellence program by the National Security Agency (NSA). He is an instructor and technical editor for computer forensics and hacking courses. He has presented at the Blackhat USA Conference.

During a 22-year period in the U.S. Navy, Kevin tested and evaluated surveillance and weapon system software. Some of this work was on projects like the Multi-Sensor Torpedo Alertment Processor (MSTRAP), Tactical Decision Support System (TDSS), Computer Aided Dead Reckoning Tracer (CADRT), Advanced Radar Periscope Discrimination and Detection (ARPDD), and the Remote Mine Hunting System (RMHS). He has worked as both a software and systems engineer on a variety of Department of Defense projects and was selected to head the team that built a Network Operations Center (NOC) that provided services to the command ashore and ships at sea in the Norwegian Sea and Atlantic Ocean. He served as the leading chief of information security at the NOC for six years prior to retiring from the U.S. Navy. During this time he was the leader of a five-person Red Team.

Kevin wishes to thank his mother, Sally; girlfriend, Loredana; and daughter, Aspen, all of whom are sources of his inspiration. Kevin holds a master's degree from Southern Methodist University and is a member of the IEEE and ACM. Kevin currently resides in Cornwall, England.

Marcus J. Carey (CISSP, CTT+) is the president of Sun Tzu Data, a leading information assurance and infrastructure architecture firm based out of central Maryland. Marcus' specialty is network architecture, network security, and network intrusion investigations. He served over eight years in the U.S. Navy's cryptology field. During his military service Marcus engineered, monitored, and defended the U.S. Department of Defense's secure networks.

Marcus holds a master's degree from Capitol College, where he also serves as professor of information assurance. Marcus currently resides in central Maryland with his family, Mandy, Erran, Kaley, and Christopher.

Timothy Clinton has held multiple roles in the EDD/ESI vendor space. He is currently employed as forensics operations manager for the National Technology Center division of Document Technologies, Inc. (DTI), a major ESI service. Since joining the DTI team, Mr. Clinton has served in multiple roles, including EDD production manager, technical architect, and forensic investigator. He has conducted and managed investigations for numerous civil cases regarding matters for Fortune 50 of law. Mr. Clinton's most notable achievement while at DTI is being responsible for the design and implementation of a showcase data forensics laboratory in Atlanta, Georgia.

Edward Collins (CISSP, CEH, Security+, MCSE:Security, MCT) is a senior security analyst for CIAN, Inc., where he is responsible for conducting penetration tests, threat analysis, and security audits. CIAN (www.cian-center.com) provides commercial businesses and government agencies with all aspects of information security management, including access control, penetration testing, audit procedures, incident response handling, intrusion detection, and risk management. Edward is also a training consultant, specializing in MCSE and Security+ certifications. Edward's background includes positions as information technology manager at Aurora Flight Sciences and senior information technology consultant at Titan Corporation.

James "Jim" Cornell (CFCE, CISSP, CEECS) is an employee of Computer Sciences Corp. (CSC) and an instructor/course developer at the Defense Cyber Investigations Training Academy (DCITA), which is part of the Defense Cyber Crime Center (DC3) in Maryland. At the academy he teaches network intrusions and investigations, online undercover techniques, and advanced log analysis. He has over 26 years of law enforcement and over 35 years of electronics and computer experience. He is a member/coach of the International Association of Computer Investigative Specialists (IACIS) and a member of the International Information Systems Forensics Association (IISFA) and the International Information Systems Security Certification Consortium (ISC2). He is currently completing the Certified Technical Trainer (CTT+) process and is a repeat speaker at the annual Department of Defense Cyber Crime Conference.

He would like to thank his mother for more than he can say, his wife for her patience and support, and Gilberto for being the best friend ever.

Michael Cross (MCSE, MCP+I, CNA, Network+) is an internet specialist/programmer with the Niagara Regional Police Service. In addition to designing and maintaining the Niagara Regional Police's Web site (www.nrps.com) and intranet, he has also provided support and worked in the areas of programming, hardware, database administration, graphic design, and network administration. In 2007, he was awarded a Police Commendation for work he did in developing a system to track high-risk offenders and sexual offenders in the Niagara Region. As part of an information technology team that provides support to a user base of over 1,000 civilian and uniformed users, his theory is that when the users carry guns, you tend to be more motivated in solving their problems.

Michael was the first computer forensic analyst in the Niagara Regional Police Service's history, and for five years he performed computer forensic examinations on computers involved in criminal investigations. The computers he examined for evidence were involved in a wide range of crimes, inclusive to homicides, fraud, and possession of child pornography. In addition to this, he successfully tracked numerous individuals electronically, as in cases involving threatening e-mail. He has consulted and assisted in numerous cases dealing with computer-related/Internet crimes and served as an expert witness on computers for criminal trials.

Michael has previously taught as an instructor for IT training courses on the Internet, Web development, programming, networking, and hardware repair. He is also seasoned in providing and assisting in presentations on

Internet safety and other topics related to computers and the Internet. Despite this experience as a speaker, he still finds his wife won't listen to him.

Michael also owns KnightWare, which provides computer-related services like Web page design, and Bookworms, which provides online sales of merchandise. He has been a freelance writer for over a decade and has been published over three dozen times in numerous books and anthologies. When he isn't writing or otherwise attached to a computer, he spends as much time as possible with the joys of his life: his lovely wife, Jennifer; darling daughter Sara; adorable daughter Emily; and charming son Jason.

Michael Gregg is the president of Superior Solutions, Inc. and has more than 20 years' experience in the IT field. He holds two associate's degrees, a bachelor's degree, and a master's degree and is certified as CISSP, MCSE, MCT, CTT+, A+, N+, Security+, CNA, CCNA, CIW Security Analyst, CCE, CEH, CHFI, CEI, DCNP, ES Dragon IDS, ES Advanced Dragon IDS, and TICSA.

Michael's primary duties are to serve as project lead for security assessments helping businesses and state agencies secure their IT resources and assets. Michael has authored four books, including: *Inside Network Security Assessment, CISSP Prep Questions, CISSP Exam Cram2*, and *Certified Ethical Hacker Exam Prep2*. He also was the lead author for *Hack the Stack: Using Snort and Ethereal to Master the Eight Layers of an Insecure Network* (Syngress, ISBN: 9781597491099). He has developed four high-level security classes, including Global Knowledge's Advanced Security Boot Camp, Intense School's Professional Hacking Lab Guide, ASPE's Network Security Essentials, and Assessing Network Vulnerabilities. He has created over 50 articles featured in magazines and Web sites, including *Certification Magazine*, GoCertify, *The El Paso Times*, and SearchSecurity.

Michael is also a faculty member of Villanova University and creator of Villanova's college-level security classes, including Essentials of IS Security, Mastering IS Security, and Advanced Security Management. He also serves as a site expert for four TechTarget sites, including SearchNetworking, SearchSecurity, SearchMobileNetworking, and SearchSmallBiz. He is a member of the TechTarget Editorial Board.

Justin Peltier is a senior security consultant with Peltier Associates, with over 10 years of experience in firewall and security technologies. As a consultant, Justin has been involved in implementing, supporting, and developing security solutions, and he has taught courses on many facets of information security, including vulnerability assessment and CISSP preparation. His previous employment was at Suntel Services, where he directed the company's security practice development. Prior to that, Justin was with Netigy, where he was involved in the company's corporate training efforts.

Justin currently holds 10 professional certifications in an array of technical disciplines.

Justin has led classes across the United States, as well as in Europe and Asia, for Peltier Associates, Sherwood Associates, Computer Security Institute, ISC2, the Mark I. Sobell Training Institute, Netigy Corporation, and Suntel Services.

Sondra Schneider is CEO and Founder of Security University, a Vienna, VA-based Qualified Computer Security and Information Assurance Training Company. For the past 18 years Sondra has been traveling around the world training network professionals to be network and security professionals. In 2004 she was awarded Entrepreneur of the Year at the First Annual Woman of Innovation Awards from the Connecticut Technology Council. She sits on the advisory board for three computer security technology companies and is a frequent speaker at computer security and wireless industry events. She is a founding member of the NYC HTCIA and IETF, and she works closely with ISC2, ISSA, and ISACA chapters and the vendor community to provide qualified computer security training and feedback. Sondra holds the CISSP, CEH, ECSA, LPT, and CHFI credentials.

Jesse Varsalone (A+, Linux+, Net+, iNet+, Security+, Server+, CTT+, CIW Professional, CWNA, CWSP, MCT, MCSA, MSCE 2000/2003, MCSA/MCSE Security, MCSD, MCDBA, MCSD, CNA, CCNA, MCDST, Oracle 8i/9i DBA, Certified Ethical Hacker) is a computer forensic senior professional at CSC. For four years, he served as the director of the MCSE and Network Security Program at the Computer Career Institute at Johns Hopkins University. For the 2006 academic year, he served as an assistant professor of computer information systems at Villa Julie College in Baltimore, Maryland. He taught courses in networking, Active Directory, Exchange, Cisco, and forensics.

Jesse holds a bachelor's degree from George Mason University and a master's degree from the University of South Florida. He runs several Web sites, including mcsecoach.com, which is dedicated to helping people obtain their MCSE certification. He currently lives in Columbia, Maryland, with his wife, Kim, and son, Mason.

Craig Wright has personally conducted in excess of 1,200 IT security-related engagements for more than 120 Australian and international organizations in the private and government sectors and now works for BDO Kendall's in Australia.

In addition to his consulting engagements, Craig has also authored numerous IT security-related articles. He also has been involved with designing the architecture for the world's first online casino (Lasseter's Online) in the Northern Territory. He has designed and managed the implementation of many of the systems that protected the Australian Stock Exchange. He also developed and implemented the security policies and procedural practices within Mahindra and Mahindra, India's largest vehicle manufacturer.

He holds (among others) the following industry certifications: CISSP (ISSAP & ISSMP), CISA, CISM, CCE, GNSA, G7799, GWAS, GCFA, GLEG, GSEC, GREM, GPCI, MCSE, and GSPA. He has completed numerous degrees in a variety of fields and is currently completing both a master's degree in statistics (at Newcastle) and a master's degree in law (LLM) specializing in international commercial law (E-commerce Law). Craig is planning to start his second doctorate, a PhD in economics and law in the digital age, in early 2008.

Contents

Chapter 1

CHFI

Computer Forensics in Today's World

Exam objectives in this chapter:

- The History of Forensics
- The Objectives of Computer Forensics
- Computer-Facilitated Crimes
- Reasons for Cyber Attacks
- Computer Forensic Flaws and Risks
- Computer Forensics: Rules, Procedures, and Legal Issues
- The Computer Forensic Lab
- Laboratory Strategic Planning for Business
- Elements of Facilities Build-out
- Electrical and Power Plant Considerations
- Essential Laboratory Tools

Introduction

As is often the case with security compromises, it's not a matter of *if* your company will be compromised, but *when*.

If I had known the employee I hired was going to resign, break into my office, and damage my computers in the span of three days, hindsight being 20/20, I would have sent notification to the security guards at the front door placing them on high alert and made sure he was not granted access to the building after he resigned. Of course, I in hindsight, I should have done a better job of hiring critical personnel .He was hired as a computer security analyst and security hacker instructor; and was (or should have been) the best example of ethical conduct.

Clearly, we see only what we want to see when hiring staff and you won't know whether an employee is ethical until a compromise occurs. Even if my blinders had been off, I would have never seen this compromise coming. It boggles the mind to think that anyone would ruin or jeopardize his career in computer security for so little. But he did break into the building, and he did damage our computers; therefore, he will be held accountable for his actions, as detailed in the following forensic information. Pay attention when the legal issues are reviewed. You will learn bits and pieces regarding how to make your life easier by knowing what you really need to know "when" your computer security compromise occurs.

Computer forensics is the preservation, identification, extraction, interpretation, and documentation of computer evidence. In Chapter 9 of *Cyber Crime Investigations*, digital forensics is referred to as "the scientific acquisition, analysis, and preservation of data contained in electronic media whose information can be used as evidence in a court of law."[1]

In the case involving the Hewlett-Packard board of directors, seasoned investigators within HP and the primary subcontracting company sought clarity on an investigative method they were implementing for an investigation. The investigators asked legal counsel to determine whether the technique being used was legal or illegal. Legal counsel determined that the technique fell within a gray area, and did not constitute an illegal act. As a result, the investigators used it and were later arrested. This situation could befall any cyber crimes investigator.

In the Hewlett-Packard case, legal counsel did not fully understand the laws relating to such methodologies and technological issues. The lesson for investigators here is not to assume that an action you've taken is legal just because corporate counsel told you it was. This is especially true within the corporate arena. In the HP case, several investigators were arrested, including legal counsel, for their actions.

In this CHFI study guide, you will learn the concepts of computer forensics and how to prepare for the EC-Council's Computer Hacker Forensic Investigator exam. This chapter will review the objectives of computer forensics. It will also discuss computer-facilitated crimes, the reasons for cyber crime, the computer forensics flaws and risks, modes of attack, digital forensics, and the stages of forensic investigation in tracking cyber criminals. The chapter also covers various stages of building a computer forensics laboratory.

The History of Forensics

Forensics has been around since the dawn of justice. Cavemen had justice in rules set to protect home and hearth. Francis Galton (1822–1911) made the first recorded study of fingerprints, Leone Lattes (1887–1954) discovered blood groupings (A, B, AB, and 0), Calvin Goddard (1891–1955) allowed firearms and bullet comparison for solving many pending court cases, Albert Osborn (1858–1946) developed essential features of document examination, Hans Gross (1847–1915) made use of scientific study to head criminal investigations. And in 1932, the FBI set up a lab to provide forensic services to all field agents and other law authorities across the country. When you look back at these historic forensic events, you see patterns of confidence in the forensic information recovered and analyzed. You will see in this study guide, today's computer forensics is clearly a new pattern of confidence, acceptance, and analysis.

The Objectives of Computer Forensics

Cyber activity has become an important part of the everyday lives of the general public. According to the EC-Council, eighty-five percent of businesses and government agencies have detected a security breach. The examination of digital evidence (media) has provided a medium for forensic investigators to focus on after an incident has occurred. The ultimate goal of a computer forensic investigator is to determine the nature and events concerning a crime and to locate the perpetrator by following a structured investigative procedure.

Test Day Tip

Working as a team, computer forensic investigators secure systems and networks. Computer forensics is one of the three main functions of computer security: the TRIAD consists of vulnerability assessment and risk management, network intrusion detection, and incident response computer investigations.

What is forensic computing? A methodical series of techniques and procedures for gathering evidence, from computing equipment and various storage devices and digital media, that can be presented in a court of law in a coherent and meaningful format.

—Dr. H.B. Wolfe

Investigators must apply two tests for evidence for both computer forensics and physical forensics to survive in a court of law:

- **Authenticity** Where does the evidence come from?

- **Reliability** Is the evidence reliable and free of flaws?

Head of the Class...

Security Statistics of Cyber Crime

Here are some interesting statistics pertaining to cyber crime from the EC-Council:

- Intellectual losses from hacking exceeded $400 billion in 2003.
- Eighteen percent of companies whose systems were broken into or infected with a virus suffered losses of $1 million or more.
- A total of 241 U.S. organizations collectively reported losses of $33.5 million from theft of proprietary information.
- Approximately 25 percent of all organizations reported attempted break-ins via the Internet.
- An FBI survey of 400 companies showed only 40 percent reported break-ins.
- One of every five Internet sites have suffered a security breach.

Cyber crime includes the following:

- **Theft of intellectual property** This pertains to any act that allows access to patent, trade secrets, customer data, sales trends, and any confidential information.

- **Damage of company service networks** This can occur if someone plants a Trojan horse, conducts a denial of service attack, installs an unauthorized modem, or installs a back door to allow others to gain access to the network or system.

- **Financial fraud** This pertains to anything that uses fraudulent solicitation to prospective victims to conduct fraudulent transactions.

- **Hacker system penetrations** These occur via the use of sniffers, rootkits, and other tools that take advantage of vulnerabilities of systems or software.

- **Distribution and execution of viruses and worms** These are some of the most common forms of cyber crime.

Cyber crime comprises three things: tools to commit the crime, targets of the crime (victim), and material that is tangential to the crime.

Cyber crime is motivated by many different things. Often it's the thrill of the chase, and a desire for script kiddies to learn. Sometimes cyber crime is committed by psychologically motivated criminals who need to leave a mark. Other times such crimes are committed by a person or group that is out for revenge; perhaps it's a disgruntled employee or friend who wants to embarrass the target. Most likely, a cyber criminal is being paid to gain information; hackers involved in corporate espionage are the hardest to uncover and often are never seen.

Damage & Defense…

Curbing Computer Crime

According to *The Wall Street Journal*, computer crime happens more often than car accidents, and car accidents occur four times a minute in the United States. A defensive posture, security awareness training, and continuous good communication help keep insider threats to a manageable minimum.

Computer-Facilitated Crimes

Our dependency on the computer has given way to new criminal opportunities. Computers are increasingly being used as a tool for committing crimes, and they are posing new challenges for investigators, for the following reasons:

- The proliferation of PCs and Internet access has made the exchange of information quick and inexpensive.

- The use of easily available hacking tools and the proliferation of underground hacking groups have made it easier to commit cyber crimes.

- The Internet allows anyone to hide his identity while committing crimes.

- E-mail spoofing, creating fake profiles, and committing identity theft are common occurrences, and there is nothing to stop it, making investigation difficult.

- With cyber crimes, there is no collateral or forensic evidence, such as eye witnesses, fingerprints, or DNA, making these crimes much harder to prosecute.

Damage & Defense...

Bridging the Gaps

In *Cyber Crime Investigations: Bridging the Gaps Between Security Professionals, Law Enforcement, and Prosecutors* (Elsevier, Inc., 2007), the author discusses a case that occurred before any identity theft laws had been passed. The case involved a woman whose ex-boyfriend was impersonating her online. He created an online user profile using her personal information and her picture on a popular chat site. During his chats, while pretending to be her, he solicited sexual acts from several men and gave her contact information to them. This information included her home address. During several of these online chats, he described a rape fantasy she wanted to fulfill with the men he was chatting with. When discussing the case with the prosecutor's office, the police detectives brainstormed about the charges they would use. There were no identity theft laws in place at that time, so the detectives decided to use traditional charges, including reckless endangerment, aggravated harassment, and impersonation. Here is an outline of the detectives' justification for using these statutes:

- The detectives selected reckless endangerment because the men were visiting the victim's home expecting to engage in sexual acts with her. These acts included the rape fantasy that the suspect described during the online chats. The reckless endangerment aspect of this crime was the possibility of some male raping her because of the described rape fantasy the suspect spoke about. Someone could have really raped her.

- The detectives selected aggravated harassment because of the number of phone calls she was receiving day and night that were sexually explicit. In New York, it covered the annoying phone calls the victim was getting.

- The detectives chose the charge of impersonation because the ex-boyfriend was pretending to be her. This impersonation included more than him just pretending to be her online. It included giving out all of her personal information, along with her picture. Today, this would most probably be covered under an identity theft law.

Reasons for Cyber Attacks

Today, cyber attacks are committed by individuals who are more organized. Cyber crime has different connotations depending on the situation. Most of us equate cyber crime with what

we see on TV and in the news: porn, hackers gaining access to sensitive government information, identity theft, stolen passwords, and so on. In reality, these types of computer crimes include more often than not, theft of intellectual property, damage of company service networks, embezzlement, copyright piracy (software, movie, sound recording), child pornography, planting of viruses and worms, password trafficking, e-mail bombing, and spam.

Cyber criminals are taught to be more technically advanced than the agencies that plan to thwart them. And today's criminals are more persistent than ever. According to the EC-Council, *computer crime is any illegal act involving a computer, its system, or its applications.* A computer crime is intentional, not accidental (we discuss this in more detail in the "Legal Issues" section, later in this chapter).

Computer Forensic Flaws and Risks

Computer forensics is in its developmental stage. It differs from other forensic sciences as <u>digital</u> evidence is examined. There is a little theoretical knowledge to base assumptions for analysis and standard empirical hypothesis testing when carried out lacks proper training or standardization of tools, and lastly it is still more 'art" than "science.

Modes of Attack

There are two categories of cyber crime, differentiated in terms of how the attack takes place:

- **Insider attacks** These involve a breach of trust from employees within an organization.

- **External attacks** These involve hackers hired by either an insider or an external entity whose aim is to destroy a competitor's reputation.

Stages of Forensic Investigation in Tracking Computer Crime

A computer forensic investigator follows certain stages and procedures when working on a case. First he identifies the crime, along with the computer and other tools used to commit the crime. Then he gathers evidence and builds a suitable chain of custody. The investigator must follow these procedures as thoroughly as possible. Once he recovers data, he must image, duplicate, and replicate it, and then analyze the duplicated evidence. After the evidence has been analyzed, the investigator must act as an expert witness and present the evidence in court. The investigator becomes the tool which law enforcement uses to track and prosecute cyber criminals.

For a better understanding of the steps a forensic investigator typically follows, consider the following, which would occur after an incident in which a server is compromised:

1. Company personnel call the corporate lawyer for legal advice.

2. The forensic investigator prepares a First Response of Procedures (FRP).

3. The forensic investigator seizes the evidence at the crime scene and transports it to the forensic lab.

4. The forensic investigator prepares bit-stream images of the files and creates an MD5 # of the files.

5. The forensic investigator examines the evidence for proof of a crime, and prepares an investigative report before concluding the investigation.

6. The forensic investigator hands the sensitive report information to the client, who reviews it to see whether they want to press charges.

7. The FI destroys any sensitive client data.

It is very important that a forensic investigator follows all of these steps and that the process contains no misinformation that could ruin his reputation or the reputation of an organization.

TEST DAY TIP

Here are some great resources on computer incident handling and digital forensics:

NIST's "Computer Security Incident Handling Guide," SP800-61, http://csrc.nist.gov/publications/nistpubs/800-61/sp800-61.pdf

NIST's "Guide to Integrating Forensic Techniques into Incident Response," SP800-96, http://csrc.nist.gov/publications/nistpubs/800-96/sp800-96.pdf

National Institute of Justice's "Forensic Examination of Digital Evidence: A Guide for Law Enforcement," www.ojp.usdoj.gov/nij/pubs-sum/199408.htm

RFC 3227, "Guidelines for Evidence Collection and Archiving," www.faqs.org/rfcs/rfc3227.html

Computer Forensics: Rules, Procedures, and Legal Issues

A good forensic investigator should always follow these rules:

- Examine original evidence as little as possible. Instead, examine the duplicate evidence.

- Follow the rules of evidence and do not tamper with the evidence.

- Always prepare a chain of custody, and handle evidence with care.

- Never exceed the knowledge base of the FI.

- Make sure to document any changes in evidence.

- If you stay within these parameters your case should be valuable and defensible.

Digital Forensics

Digital forensics includes preserving, collecting, confirming, identifying, analyzing, recording, and presenting crime scene information.

Assessing the Case: Detecting/Identifying the Event/Crime

In any type of investigation, the computer forensic examiner must follow an investigation process. That process begins with the step of assessing the case, asking people questions, and documenting the results in an effort to identify the crime and the location of the evidence. Computer investigations are conducted on two types of computers: the computer used to commit a crime, and computer that is the target of the crime.

Preservation of Evidence: Chain of Custody

Preserving the chain of custody is the next step. Identification of the evidence must be preserved to maintain its integrity. A chain of evidence must be prepared to know who handled the evidence, and every step taken by the forensic investigator must be documented for inclusion in the final report. Sometimes a computer and its related evidence can determine the chain of events leading to a crime for the investigator as well as provide the evidence which can lead to conviction.

TEST DAY TIP

A chain of custody is the accurate documentation of the movement and possession of a piece of evidence, from the time it is taken into custody until it is delivered to the court. This documentation helps prevent allegations of evidence tampering. It also proves that the evidence was stored in a legally accepted location, and it documents who is in custody and control of the evidence during the forensic testing phase.

A bit-stream image is an exact duplicate of a computer's hard drive in which the drive is copied from one drive to another, bit by bit. This image is then authenticated to the original by matching a digital

signature, which is produced by a mathematical algorithm (usually the MD5 standard) to ensure that no changes have occurred. This method has become the de facto standard and is widely accepted by the industry and the legal system.

Collection: Data Recovery, Evidence Collection

Finding the evidence, discovering relevant data, preparing an Order of Volatility, eradicating external avenues of alteration, gathering the evidence, and preparing a chain of custody are the recommended CHFI processes for collecting data. After you collect data, you should create an MD5 hash of the evidence. Prior to collection, one should do preliminary assessment to search for the evidence. After the assessment is concluded, collect and seize the equipment used in committing the crime, document the items collected, such as floppy disks, thumb drives, CDs, DVDs, and external back up drives. A photo of the crime scene should be taken before removing the evidence.

Damage & Defense...

Hashes

Hashes use cryptographic algorithms to create a message digest of the data and represent it as a relatively small piece of data. The hash can be used to compare a hash of the original data to the forensic copy. When the hashes match, it is accepted as proof that the data is an exact copy. Although it has not been challenged yet, the traditional hashes of CRC, MD5, and SHA1 have been cracked. Also, there are limitations in the sheer volume of 128 bit hashing algorithms such as MD5. There are only 2^{128} possible MD5 hashes. If the large multi-terabyte file server being analyzed stores $2^{128} + 1$ files, there absolutely will be two different files with unique data with the same hash. Now it is understood that 2^{128} is about 340 billion, and it would be an extremely large storage array of tiny files, but this fact opens the door for doubt, which could ruin a criminal prosecution. Although 2^{128} is still a huge number, as storage grows, it is not unrealistic to believe that 128 bit hashes will become an increasing issue. It will probably be an issue on large storage systems long before it becomes as big an issue on single workstations. The future appears to be the use of the SHA-256 algorithm and other 256 bit hashes. For now, the National Software Reference Library Hashes use the SHA-1 and MD5 algorithms.

After collecting all the information, the investigator can then list the steps that can be taken during the investigation and then begin. Caution, it is not necessary to seize the entire system. Identify the relevant data and copy that, otherwise it can result in over collection.

Head of the Class...

Suggested Tool Kit Contents

Your tool kit should contain the following components:

Hardware Target hard drives, write blocker, and cables (network, IDE, and SCSI)

Software Boot disks and drivers for both your forensic system and any system you may encounter, especially for network cards

Tools Allen keys; large and small screwdrivers (standard, Phillips, and Torx)

Other content Labels , anti-static bags, pens and markers, blank media: (CDs, DVDs), and a camera

Test Day Tip

Sterilize all the media to be used in the examination process, enter the crime scene, take a snap shot of the scene and then carefully scan the data sources, Retain and document the state and integrity of items at the crime scene then transport the evidence to the forensic facility

Examination: Tracing, Filtering, Extracting Hidden Data

The examination process follows the collection process. The computer forensic investigator must trace, filter, and extract hidden data during the process. Some evidence cannot stay for long. Such evidence is called volatile evidence because it needs consistent power supply for storage. There is also evidence that contains the information that keeps changing. CHFI investigators must review registers and cache, routing tables, ARP cache, process tables, and kernel statistics and modules.

In *Windows Forensic Analysis DVD Toolkit,* Harlan Carvey looks at the order of volatility from a "live system" view (see Chapter 1 of *Windows Forensic Analysis DVD Toolkit,* Elsevier Inc., 2007). Volatile data must be preserved in order of volatility, with the most volatile data preserved first. This applies to live systems for the most part, but the way in which we approach live systems will become more important in the near future. An example of an order of recovery of system data according to volatility looks like this:

- **Virtual memory** Swap space or paging files
- **Physical disks** The physical hard disks of a system

- **Backups** Offline back-up media such as magnetic tape or other media: It is extremely possibly the data you are looking for may not be on the system today, but it was there yesterday and is on last night's backup.

TEST DAY TIP

It is essential there is minimal tampering with the evidence because it can alter the exact copy of the evidence.

Analysis

Analysis of the data is greatly different from retrieving the evidence and depends greatly on exactly how the copy is. There are various techniques to capture an exact forensic copy to copy the evidence disk so you can analyze the data. Analysis should be done on the duplicate copy so that the original evidence can be protected from alteration because the first rule of forensics is to preserve the original evidence. Once a copy is created, use the copy for further processes. Analysis can be carried out using various forensic analysis tools such Encase, Access Data etc.

Head of the Class...

Presentation: Investigation Report and Expert Witness

The investigator should include what was done and the results in the final report. Basic report includes: who, what, when, where, and how of the crime. In a good computer investigation the steps can be repeated and the result obtained is same every time. The report should explain the computer and network processes. An explanation should be provided for various processes and the inner working of the system and its various interrelated components. The report should include the log files generated by the forensic tools to keep track of all the steps taken. All the proceedings related to the investigation should be documented properly asp that it can be used as proof of findings in a court of law. Since there are various readers of the documents the inner workings of the system, and it's various interrelated components should be provided. Templates for report writing are on the internet and each organization uses one. The narrative part should precede the log in the report, as based on the facts that were found.

An expert witness is a person who investigates, evaluates, educates, and testifies in court. An expert witness can be a consulting expert or strategy advisor, court's expert, or testifying expert. The role of an expert witness is to assist the court in understanding intricate evidence, express an opinion in court, attend the entire trial in court, to aid lawyers to get to the truth and not obscure it, and lastly to be qualified to exhibit their expertise. According to federal rules, to be present as an expert witness in a court, the investigator must have four

Continued

years of previous testimony (indicates experience), ten years of any published literature and previous payment received when giving testimony. The investigators CV should include: Certifications/credentials/accomplishments, recent work as an expert witness or testimony log, expertise, list of books written, if any, any training undergone, referrals and contacts.

Digital Evidence

Damage & Defense...

When digital evidence is extracted from digital resources an investigator must:

Protect the subject computer system during the forensic examination from any possible alteration, damage, data corruption, or virus introduction.

Discovers all files on the subject system.

This includes existing normal files, deleted yet remaining files, hidden files, password-protected files, and encrypted files.

Recover all (or as much as possible) of discovered **deleted files.**

Reveal (to the extent possible) **the contents of hidden files as well as temporary or swap files** used by both the application programs and the operating system.

Access (if possible and if legally appropriate) the contents of **protected or encrypted files.**

Analyze all possibly relevant data found in special areas of a disk.

This includes 'unallocated' space on a disk, 'slack' space in a file and disk cluster.

Print out an overall analysis of the subject computer system, as well as a listing of all possibly relevant files and discovered file data.

Provides an opinion of the system layout, the file structures discovered, any discovered data and authorship information, any attempts to hide, delete, protect, encrypt information, and anything else that has been discovered and appears to be relevant to the overall computer system examination.

Provide expert consultation and/or testimony, as required.

Approach the Crime Scene

Due to the presence of a majority of electronic documents, and the skills necessary to search and identify data in a computer, combined with the fact that digital evidence is delicate in nature for recovering deleted, encrypted or, corrupted files from a system there is a growing need for Forensic Investigators to approach crime scenes.

An investigator, if trained properly, will ensure that no possible evidence is damaged, destroyed, or compromised by the forensic procedures used to investigate the computer. (Preservation of evidence).

No computer malware, or harmful software, is introduced to the computer being investigated. (Non-contamination of evidence). Any extracted or relevant evidence is properly handled and protected from later mechanical or electromagnetic damage (extraction and preservation of evidence). A continuing chain of custody is established and maintained (Accountability of evidence).and that normal operations are effected for a limited amount of time.(limited interference of the crime scene on normal life).

Where and When Do You Use Computer Forensics?

Use computer forensics when there is a need to provide real evidence such as reading bar codes, magnetic tapes and to identify the occurrence of electronic transactions and reconstruct an incidence with sequence of events. You use computer forensics when a breach of contract occurs, or if copyright and intellectual property theft/misuse happens or during employee disputes where there is damage to resources.

Legal Issues

It is not always possible for a computer forensics expert to separate the legal issues surrounding the evidence from the practical aspects of computer forensics (e.g.,the issues related to authenticity, reliability, and completeness and convincing). The approach of investigation diverges with change in technology. Evidence shown is to be untampered with and fully accounted for, from the time of collection to the time of presentation to the court. Hence, it must meet the relevant evidence laws

Damage & Defense…

Permission

When my company was broken into, I provided verbal permission to law enforcement to search my facility and locate the missing computers. I also gave permission to turn on one of the computers where we confirmed the x-employee had broken into the building, stolen the computers, accessed the computers, erased intellectual property and left the building hiding the computers.

There are legal concerns, not just technical concerns. For example, for some forensic monitoring activity a certain level of security may be legally required, or your ability to monitor certain kinds of activities may be restricted. Also, if you ever need to prosecute, your logs may not be admissible in court. Local and federal laws must be considered when devising a security policy.

The computer revolution has given way to white-collar crimes done on the Internet. Remote targets are compromised by malicious users daily. While investigating these crimes, international issues can be raised as the electronic evidence necessary to prevent, investigate, or prosecute a crime is located outside the borders of the country, and law enforcement must seek assistance from law enforcement authorities in the different country. Preservation of evidence or request for evidence can be made under mutual legal assistance agreements or if no assistance is forthcoming through the Letters Rogatory process.

Consistency with all legal systems, the ability to implant confidence in the integrity of evidence, allowances for the use of common language, and applicability at every level are confronted by investigators.

Computer law is a large field. Areas of concern to security administrators are what constitutes illegal use of a computer, what you can and can't do to detect or monitor it, the status of any evidence you may collect, and your exposure to civil liability suits in event of a security problem. Computer crime law is a new field. The statutes are quite recent, less than 10 years old with little case law for guidance. Interpretations may change, and the laws themselves may change, as legislators react to newer threats.

The Computer Forensic Lab

The process of implementing and operating a computer forensic laboratory could be the subject of an entire series of books. This section of the chapter, however, will attempt to share a few ideas regarding core concepts to be considered during the planning, construction, and operation of a data forensic facility. The material is intended for midsized operations (corporate installations and stand-alone facilities) to demonstrate a diversity of concepts relating to facilities planning, business operations, and service offerings.

Recent changes to the Federal Rules of Civil Procedure (FRCP) in December 2006 have impacted the manner in which digital information is managed in civil litigation. The FRCP formalized the role of digital information in a legal environment. The rules have formally identified the role of electronically stored information (ESI) and how it will be handled and presented in a judicial setting.

The advent of personal computing empowered individuals to create and manage information on a massive scale; the vast majority of information created now exists in digital form on some type of computing system. An entire field of data analysis and digital investigation has evolved in response to the threat of wrongdoing in this digital realm. The technology (laptops, desktops, cell phones, the Internet) empowering individual productivity and creativity is the

same technology used to conduct activity against company policy or in violation of the law. Corporate investigators and law enforcement officers need to be able to investigate these types of digital transactions by identifying, recovering, analyzing, and reporting on the digital facts. The role of data forensic analysis will be of increasing importance to the legal system as information continues to evolve into the purely digital and the systems upon which that information is stored become more technologically advanced. The need and demand for expert forensic examiners and forensic data investigation facilities will likewise be on the rise.

Laboratory Strategic Planning for Business

The topic of strategic planning for business development is a series of books unto itself.

In this section, we will touch on a few points of interest in developing a forensics practice: philosophy of operation, core mission and services, revenue definition, and Standard Operating Procedure (SOP) definition.

Philosophy of Operation

Every data forensic implementation will reflect four core modes of operation. From solo-practitioner operations to government investigative arms, forensic implementations will function according to a similar set of operating philosophies. The four core aspects of operation are the business operations aspect, the technology venue aspect, the scientific practice aspect, and the artistic expression aspect. Regardless of scope, a computer forensic initiative must pursue sound business practices, must function in the realm of high technology with high-technology talent as ongoing status quo, and must foster excellence of method and diverse, creative vision in solving technology investigation problems.

A Forensic Laboratory Is a Business Venue

Every computer forensic laboratory is a business venue. A 1099 contract solo investigator, a commercial forensic department in the civilian litigation support space, a city/state police crime lab, a law firm's internal digital investigation group, and a federal network of investigative facilities are all business venues that must behave according to the principles of sound business management, financial profitability, core service provision, and so on. A police crime lab may not be pursuing profit per se, but that lab has to demonstrate value of service and return on investment (ROI) to remain funded or acquire annual budget allocations and new technologies to continue fighting crime. A solo practitioner must remain competitive in the marketplace he or she serves with regard to cost, service provision, and continuing education. A corporate commercial forensic venture must demonstrate profitability and maintain high standards for customer service and product quality to remain competitive in the marketplace. A massive entity such as the U.S. government's network of nationally distributed forensic facilities and

allied investigative entities must still obey the principles of good business management, seek operational excellence, and demonstrate value for service and ROI to the U.S. Congress and Senate to remain funded. *Running a data forensic laboratory means running a good business at all levels of scope.*

A Forensic Laboratory Is a Technology Venue

A data forensic facility of any size is the embodiment of front-of-the-wave mastery of data and data storage technologies in all its various guises. Criminals often afford the newest toys and desire the most complex technologies to hide their crimes from prying eyes, so the data forensic community must always strive to master technology as fast as technology evolves. The commercial consumer marketplace is always rolling out a new wave of the newest, shiniest technologies available to keep up with consumer demand for progress; again, the forensic community is at the front of the line, dismantling and investigating every new gadget that hits the shelves reveal its secrets.

A Forensic Laboratory Is a Scientific Venue

Understanding and implementing technology isn't sufficient, however. The practice of any branch of forensics is a practice of science. Examiners strive to perform their duties according to reliable, repeatable, valid, objective, consistent, and accurate methodologies to reveal facts objectively via empirical observation, deductive reasoning, and conversion of hypothesis to demonstrable patterns, thereby empowering the presentation of findings of value to be put forth as facts of merit in the court of law.

A Forensic Laboratory Is an Artistic Venue

The investigative process is more than a rigid set of procedures. Intuition and creativity play as great a role for the forensic examiner as do sound methodologies. Fact-finding in a wildly diverse technological realm requires a great degree of technical prowess as well as a flexible mind; forensic examiners often must be artisans of technology creation and deconstruction. Raw technology skill does not empower an investigator to understand the interaction of man and machine: Intuitive awareness of how the tools of technology and human nature, human thought processes, and human frailties interact allows for much of the artistry and creativity of forensic investigation to be revealed.

Core Mission and Services

Foremost in the consideration of a forensic facility design plan, decide what services the facility is to provide and the scope at which it is to provide those services. A firm grasp of the prospective laboratory's core mission and scope of service will provide guidance on every aspect of building and operating that forensic facility, touching on everything from annual budget to furniture ergonomics. Based upon scope of service, a good forensic laboratory can reside in one

room or it may require an entire building with multiple teams of specialists executing diverse tasks across multiple disciplines in each of several geographic regions. A law enforcement agency will focus upon violations of criminal statutes; a governmental agency may focus on one or more aspects of civil litigation; a commercial venture will typically define a service package and then market that package to any number of audiences.

Revenue Definition

A very applicable adage applies to a data forensic facility's operational capability: "Anything is possible with enough money, manpower, and time." As always, knowing how to effectively address the five w's (who, what, when, where, why) of a business plan will dictate the completeness of the plan from concept to execution. Implement a five-year strategic plan. Plan for successful growth. Plan based upon the realities of the specific environment in which the facility will reside, and to which the facility will respond. Implement a realistic and generous budget: Justify it with a cost vs. reward argument. Define milestones to achieve and a growth track to follow. Ultimately, the budget implemented will need to fully serve the needs of the facility in both actual operation and realization of strategic vision.

Every forensic facility initiative, whether law enforcement, corporate, or for-profit, will require funds to function. Developing a strong business plan based upon costs of doing business versus profitability of work product is necessary regardless of the intended audience. Every operation will need to demonstrate ROI to prove the viability of the venture.

Costs of doing business will include line item tangibles such as hard dollar outlay to build, staff, stock, operate, maintain, and grow a facility. Costs will also include intangibles such as administrative overhead for policy and procedure creation, implementation, and ongoing process improvement. Buffer will need to exist for known business variables such as payroll fluctuation and increasing utility costs. Equipment requires maintenance and replacement. And so on.

Defining profitability in light of any given operational ROI will vary depending on the core service provision of the facility. A law enforcement laboratory may want to define profitability in terms of metrics addressing man hours expended and cases processed vs. convictions/pleas achieved; a nonprofit or government agency may want to define profitability in terms of an annual impact statement on its sector of influence. Commercial ventures will certainly define profitability in terms of billable professional hours, machine time, and/or line item service provision. Regardless of how profitability is qualified, profitability needs to be quantified in order to demonstrate the fitness of the venture.

"I Know How Expensive I Am. Now, How Do I Get Paid?"

A data forensic operation will position itself as either a cost center or a revenue generator. In most law enforcement and government agency scenarios, a forensic offering will be perceived as a cost center and will rely on departmental budget allocations, grants, and so on for funding.

ROI will generally be defined by demonstrating efficiency and operational excellence. Profitability will be defined in terms of ongoing results achieved.

Corporate implementations, likely to be cost centers, may define themselves as revenue generators by creating a "billback" or cross-charge system in which profitability is determined by revenue tracking demonstrated by billable units (either "credit-for-time-served" being equated to billable hours, or actual interdepartmental invoicing "billed back" to the requesting business unit).

Commercial forensic service providers will invoice for services provided and must demonstrate a net profit margin above operating costs.

SOP

Whether applied at the strategic, daily operations, or process-specific level, policy and procedure implementation will ultimately be the measure of operational excellence by which the caliber of a data forensic laboratory (and the product the laboratory produces) is defined. The 10k SOP should be defined while still in the planning stages of laboratory design. The ultimate goal of any work executed in a data forensic laboratory is to send valid, objective electronic evidence into a court of law. The laboratory itself must operate according to high professional standards; the employees of the laboratory must comport themselves professionally and ethically; and the tasks executed by the employees in the investigation and handling of potential evidence must be procedurally sound. "Soundness" of process should be demonstrated by testable, repeatable procedures generating predictable results. Evidence integrity must be defensible; the first defense against spoliation attacks is a defensible process. For all of these things to occur, a robust policy for procedure implementation and oversight is necessary. Workflow management, product testing, process analysis, and method execution all fall within the scope of need for SOP development. Figure 1.1 outlines the phases of data analysis.

Figure 1.1 Data Analysis Phase Diagram

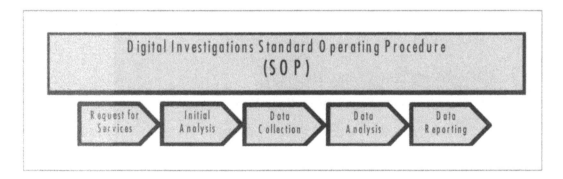

Quality Standards: Accreditation

Demonstration of operational excellence is important to any business operation. For a forensic facility of any discipline, demonstration of operational excellence is of utmost importance and independent certification of operational excellence is greatly desired. One route taken by many businesses is International Organization for Standardization (ISO) certification. A forensic laboratory could and should pursue ISO accreditations. An organization explicit to the universe of forensics (but not limited to data forensics) is the American Society of Crime Laboratory Directors/LAB (ASCLD/LAB) certifying body. ASCLD/LAB endorses a certification track for a data forensic facility that incorporates both ISO standard 17025 and a supplemental ASCLD requirement set explicit to laboratory operations. The certification itself includes both benchmark standards for operation and ongoing oversight for maintaining accreditation status.

The ASCLD/LAB model for facility operations focuses heavily on a number of areas deemed critical to quality laboratory performance:

- Leadership quality, hierarchy, and effectiveness

- Guidelines regarding policy and procedure creation and execution

- Interoffice and official communication protocols, both vertical and horizontal

- Definition of educational standards and skills testing

- Investment in human resources via training and development

- Physical plant design (security, infrastructure, fixtures)

- Locale ergonomics (personal and shared workspace)

- Implementation of business process control systems and audit methodology

- Explicit requirements at the level of business processes specific to the realm of evidence handling and forensic data examination

Both the ISO 17025 and ASCLD/LAB documents are very useful to review when planning both the physical plant and the operational function of a data forensic laboratory. You can contact ASCLD/LAB-International at www.ascld-lab.org.

Quality Standards: Auditing

Demonstration of operational excellence includes the need for multiple audit channels:

- Individual procedures must be tested for validity of method and adherence to process.

- Hardware and software tools require testing to prove function.

- Individual competency levels need to be performance-tested.

- Workflow requires an audit to guarantee operational excellence.

- Inventory control and chain of custody require ad hoc demonstration of 100 percent competency.

- Overall business SOP and mid-level operating procedure require constant reassessment.

A robust audit system is required to achieve the level of process rigor required of any forensic facility.

Human Talent

A forensic examination environment is only as good as the talent associated with the initiative. The best hardware purchasing plan in the world won't matter if the human element does not receive the same quality of investment. Experience gathering, knowledge sharing, continual education, and a serious investment in human resources development are essential to the overall success of a data forensic laboratory.

Education and Continuing Education

Bachelor's level and master's level degree programs exist that focus on forensic investigation; several universities offer a criminal justice degree with a specialty in digital forensics. Multiple certifications exist for the forensic examiner. Certification programs demonstrate both the breadth of knowledge and the hands-on proficiency of the examiner. Maintaining certification means routine retesting and accrual of classroom training hours on a regular basis.

Available certifications include:

- **Law enforcement** Certified Forensic Computer Examiner, or CFCE (www.cops.org) IACIS

- **Civilian and law enforcement** Certified Computer Examiner, or CCE (www.certified-computer-examiner.com) ISFCE; GIAC Certified Forensic Analyst, or GCFA (www.sans.org); and Certified Hacker Forensic Investigator, or CFCI (www.eccouncil.org)

- **Software-specific** Access Data Forensic Tool Kit, or ACE (www.accessdata.com) and Guidance Software EnCase Certified Examiner, or EnCE (www.guidancesoftware.com)

Elements of Facilities Build-out

In general, addressing any element of facilities build-out includes budgeting for construction and operation, provision of service based upon normal operations, provision based upon adverse events and subsequent disaster recovery, and provision based upon a roadmap for expansion, growth, and future modernizations. These topics can tailor the design of facility ele-

ments such as electrical or HVAC provision, or they can apply to business operations and workflow on an ongoing basis. Size of implementation and budget constraint always delimits a facility's complexity. Small facilities may not need to address many of the listed concepts addressed herein, but the average corporate, law enforcement, or stand-alone facility will likely address all of them, plus more.

Space Planning Considerations

In conceptualizing the overall layout of a forensic laboratory, attention should be given to at least four functional areas: administrative area, examination space, network facilities, and evidence storage. Figure 1.2 is a simple model of a facilities plan.

Figure 1.2 Forensic Laboratory Environment

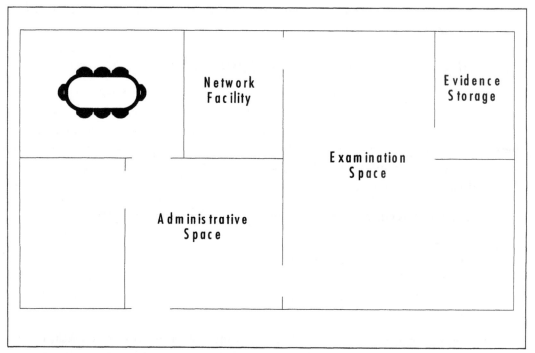

Administrative Area

Administrative space comprises office space for personnel associated with the forensic team (project management, executive staff, investigators, etc.), a general meeting space for internal personnel and clientele, and "privacy" or guest areas. This environment should provide adequate room for team meetings and a comfortable environment for customer-facing activities. The forensic investigation team will likely spend a lion's share of their time in the examination space (often a shared environment with little "personal space"). Consideration should be given

to adequate private workspace where individuals can hold confidential conversations, make telephone calls, and engage in general corporate communications.

Examination Environment

The examination space is the "lab proper," that is, all space devoted to the technical and investigative aspects of the forensic examination process. This environment is the home area for all of the technical equipment associated with the examination process and will likely be the functional area of the laboratory in which the forensic technical staff members spend a vast majority of their time. Access to the examination space should be restricted to relevant personnel and traffic to and from the examination space should be logged. Provide plenty of surface area and dedicate significant square footage per investigator (a good starting metric is 100 square feet, or the measure of a 10 ? 10-foot office space). Provide significant square footage for the location of forensic equipment (both shared and individual assets).

Evidence Storage

Evidence storage is dedicated storage space existing for the sole purpose of warehousing digital evidence and other evidentiary items. The evidence storage area is the physical embodiment of chain of custody functionality. Evidence storage should be the most secure/demanding environment to access, the most rigorously controlled area for any type of entry/egress/activity, and the most physically segregated area of a forensic build-out. The "evidence locker" must be constructed to defeat forced/unauthorized entry. It should be designed such that its contents survive environmental events. All access to this environment should be controlled with the highest rigor and restricted to key personnel, often to a single Custodian of Evidence. Multiple challenges to entry and identity should be employed. The evidence storage environment will require, in many cases, customized abatements (such as EMI shielding). A robust information management system should accompany an evidence storage environment: Automated security systems should be in place challenging all accessors and logging all accesses. Inventory should be controlled via both ink-signature and automated electronic management systems. Information management systems employed should have a robust audit methodology that guarantees the completeness and accuracy of the information maintained. Any and all components of the Evidence Storage Facility should ensure that the "who, what, when, where, and why" of every object considered "evidence" is always known and documented.

Network Facilities

This space is the environment in which data network, security, and telecommunications equipment serving the laboratory space resides. Ideally, this space should be protected from compromise to the same degree that evidence storage is protected. The physical elements of data networking and security technology warehousing, transmitting or otherwise accessing evidentiary data materials, or examination process work product should be dedicated and stand-alone

infrastructure. This rule applies to data cabling, servers, switches, routers, and any other physical element of the networked technology systems serving the forensic space. Steps should be taken to ensure that any inbound or outward-facing day-to-day business protocols (i.e., corporate e-mail, telephony, Internet access, etc.) provision across a completely separate physical network architecture.

Fire Protection/Suppression

A forensic laboratory, especially a larger facility, requires a well-thought-out fire protection plan. With regard to overall fire code, the local fire marshal can provide specifics regarding local standards and ordinances; if the laboratory is to be built out in preexisting space, the property may have its own supplemental fire protection requirements, especially if the need to tie into existing infrastructure exists. Fires are classified based on the material serving as fuel for the fires. The fire suppression methods employed will generally be determined via understanding cost constraints, habitation zones of personnel, and the technology venue residing in the space. In many ways, the ideal fire suppression system for a forensic facility will model after data center or disaster recovery data co-location facility design plans. Of special concern are Class C fires, which involve both some flammable fuel substrate and the presence of electricity. A new facility will be presented with multiple fire protection options, and the choices made regarding fire suppression implementation can have cost, timeline, and design impact on every other aspect of the build-out.

Fire classification varies worldwide with regard to accepted "classes" of fire. In the United States, fire ratings fall into five main classifications.

- **Class A** Common (solid) combustibles
- **Class B** Liquids and gases
- **Class C** Fires involving electricity
- **Class D** Combustible metals
- **Class K** Cooking fluids/oils

In the forensic laboratory environment, the most common fire classes are likely to be Class A (infrastructure materials) and Class C (electrical fires involving powered-up technology). To protect against a Class A/C hazard, multiple options are available regarding suppression system:

- Water dispersion systems (air-pressurized water systems)
 - Wet pipe system
 - Dry pipe system
 - Preaction system
- Gaseous suppression (clean agents)

- Inert gas
- Flourine compound
- Chemical suppression
 - Foam
 - Dry chemicals

Water Dispersion Systems

The three most common water dispersion system designs are wet pipe, dry pipe, and preaction.

Wet Pipe System

This system employs a piping scheme that maintains a constant water load. This system is generally the most cost-effective and low-maintenance of all fire protection options, but it does have drawbacks in an environment where significant electronics and high technology reside. Inadvertent failure or impact damage means water leaks (small or large). Typically, wet pipe systems are easy to repair and maintain, and they have a fast recovery window after activation.

Dry Pipe System

This system employs a piping scheme that maintains a pressurized air load. The pressurized air holds back liquid flow under normal circumstances. This system relies on deployment (sprinkler) head events to trigger gas release, which then allows water to flow into the pipes as the gas bleeds out. Typically, dry pipes are significantly more expensive than wet pipe systems, taking more hardware to deploy, having a higher space requirement (for the gas storage and pump equipment), and offering the same ultimate drawbacks as wet pipe. Additionally, dry pipe offers maintenance complexities and higher maintenance costs. Dry pipe does offer protection from pipes bursting in cold environments.

Preaction System

Preaction systems are typically the second level of fire protection implementation to be considered in a facility build-out. This system is a modified dry pipe arrangement; the advantage of a preaction system is the use of two triggers to release the liquid suppressant. A valve, typically an electronic valve, acts as the release inhibitor; water is not held back by gas pressurization. The valve will be controlled by a discrete fire sensor (i.e., one that operates independently of any sprinkler heads, etc.). If the valve releases, the pipes fill with liquid and the system then behaves like wet pipe. A second event must occur at the level of the delivery heads to release water into the environment. Pipe impact damage and head failures offer less threat to the surrounding environment given the fact that the pipes are in a no-load state under normal circumstances. The potential time delay between valve sensor engagement and sprinkler engagement could

also benefit the environment, presuming some intervention is able to resolve a sensor-perceived threat prior to head discharge. The cost factor step from wet pipe to preaction pipe can be a significant increase as the size of the planned facility increases. Preaction systems have the increased complexity level and maintenance disadvantages of dry pipe.

Water Damage

Wet pipe, dry pipe, and preaction systems usually utilize water as the liquid suppressant. In any environment where computer equipment, specialized electronics, and especially evidentiary-grade electronic devices are present, due consideration should be given to the potential for water damage to technology and evidence during an event. Another consideration might be secondary Class C electrical fires spawned from a primary suppression event. In any environment that utilizes water dispersion for fire control, thought should be given to "waterproofing" concepts for certain fixtures, such as primary evidence storage. Utilizing a waterproof fire-rated safe inside the evidence locker as the primary storage container for evidence is a good countermeasure against the use of water-based fire suppression systems. A fire-rated, waterproof lockbox storage system is another option for critical-to-survive evidentiary items.

Gaseous Suppression

Gas agent suppression systems, also known as clean agent or total flooding systems, provide a high-end option for laboratory fire control. This class of suppressants functions in one of two ways. One group removes heat faster than it can be generated during combustion, thereby suppressing combustion. The second group depletes oxygen to deprive combustion of oxygen fuels. Gas agent suppression systems offer advantages over water-based systems in that they can achieve total permeability in the environment. They offer advantages over chemical suppression systems because they tend to leave no chemical residues behind, lowering business recovery costs. A final positive characteristic is that these materials are, in general, nonconductive and they leave no conductive materials behind, making them ideal for areas with electronics. Gas suppression systems can include very complex delivery systems, and the gas storage systems generally have a large footprint. Cost for implementation and maintenance will be high. Total flooding systems tend to require sealed environments for best effect, so other facility costs also increase when this class of system is utilized. Although these suppressants can be used in occupied space, facilities utilizing gaseous suppression should have rapid evacuation capability.

Two main classes of gas agents exist: inert gases and fluorine compound gases.

Inert Gas Suppressors

Inert gas suppressors include a number of carbon dioxide, argon, and nitrogen blend gases. Inert gas suppressors are generally oxygen reducers. They tend to displace oxygen and prevent combustion via fuel deprivation. Pure CO_2 suppression should never be used for laboratory fire suppression (CO_2 suppression makes air completely deoxygenate and it is an active death risk to people). Branded suppressants such as Inergen and Pro-Inert are argon/nitrogen blends that

are sold in conjunction with proprietary delivery system deployments. They can be used in populated environments. They decompose into naturally occurring atmospheric gases and they are environmentally friendly.

Flourine Compound Suppressors

Flourine compound suppressors are widely utilized and they tend to be used as Halon replacements when Halon systems are upgraded. Flourine gas suppressors leach heat at a very high rate, acting as a combustion inhibitor. Branded suppressants such as Novec, FM-200, and FE-227 are common examples of suppressors in this class. They can be used in populated environments. They are environmentally friendly.

Chemical Suppression

Moving away from water dispersion and clean agent systems, several options for chemical suppression exist. Most chemical suppression methods require a significant facility investment to implement and significantly increase costs in many other areas of build-out. For instance, hermetically sealed environments may be required when certain area chemical suppression systems are utilized. Both foam and dry chemical suppression systems are available, but both classes tend to be "messy" and inappropriate for a populated environment; such systems are generally not implemented in a data-center-style facility.

Electrical and Power Plant Considerations

Any high-tech facility is going to have an above average power demand to run, cool, and keep stable all of its various technologies. In general, the cost of power provision to a forensic facility will be higher per square foot than in a "regular" corporate environment. In terms of the largest laboratory implementations, stand-alone power generation facilities and stand-by fuel tank resources may be part of the power provision plan; dedicated water provision may also be feasibly within scope for power, HVAC, and even site security. In the laboratory build-out, three main categories of need should be assessed, and those categories should all be interpreted in light of both day one and growth curve demands: regular facility load, LAN/WAN specific load, and local examiner workspace load.

The first category is the facility load considered during every facility build-out, that is, the electrical demand of all general infrastructure-level technology, including lighting, emergency lighting, HVAC, security systems, automatic doors/windows, audio/visual implementations, telephony and communication systems, corporate equipment, general electrical consumption per employee, and so on. Power provision should be generous and be cognizant of future growth as the built facility reaches 100 percent utilization and eventually physically expands.

The second category is the LAN/WAN load, which in any data center/forensic laboratory setting should be given independent consideration from a power perspective. Approaching the network plant according to data-center-grade power provision and management standards is a

good base thought process. Server rooms are generally given special consideration in any build-out, but electrical provision to any network technology needs to recognize that the forensic laboratory will have two fully disparate LAN provisions (a business operations LAN and an examination environment LAN) and that the examination environment LAN will need to be isolated from the general environment in terms of power provision, UPS/generator contingency planning, and so on. The examination environment LAN may also need a more robust failure/DR and redundancy plan with regard to power provision so that it is the first environment to recover from outage and the last environment to degrade. The examination LAN environment should, at a minimum, be equipped with enough primary and secondary power for a structured, intentional safe shutdown, even under the worst external conditions. The components of power provision to the examination LAN (and possibly all power provision) may even require special security and anticompromise considerations, depending on the security level at which the forensic laboratory may operate.

The third category is the examination "local workspace" load. This category applies to the examination space in general and the individual examiner's functional workspaces specifically, giving special consideration to the unusually high power consumption demands per capita the forensic technical team will incur. The average corporate user group may function on a shared 20 amp circuit, powering a single workstation/monitor or laptop and a few small-load items per person. A forensic investigator may well be able to max out a 30 amp circuit powering one investigation's worth of equipment, and that investigator may have numerous technology processes running concurrently in different workspaces. The examination environment of a mid-size laboratory facility is likely to be "always-on" in terms of power consumption, so both environmental and equipment power consumption in the examination space will draw three times the demand experienced in the administrative portions of the facility.

Examination space needs must be assessed in terms of more than raw power consumption as well. The density and number of electrical sockets may need to be much higher in the examination space to account for the number of devices that may be active per square foot or per examination. For example, the task of cloning one hard drive may require the following devices: one forensic workstation (socket #1), the workstation monitor (socket #2), one write blocker (socket #3), one external USB hard disk (socket #4), and the original external evidence hard disk (socket #5). An investigator may have multiple cloning processes ongoing in parallel (which could double or triple the number of needed sockets). The ergonomics of accessing those sockets also needs consideration, favoring ease of accessibility from work surfaces. When this many devices are involved, it is important to consider not only the physical frequency of socket placement, but also the density of circuit provision. It is important to prevent evidence-grade materials from experiencing under-voltage or over-voltage conditions. Significant technical or machine time investments can be lost to a sudden power outage. Consider using a higher rated circuit in the evidence space than would be implemented in a standard corporate environment. Consider dedicated circuits per single work area. Line quality may need to be conditioned to guarantee the best integrity of the evidence hardware items.

Electrical conduits in the walls may need to be shielded to prevent electromagnetic fields from compromising magnetically stored data in the evidence-handling lanes. Transformer placement and other major electrical units need to be carefully placed on the facility plan, shielded as necessary to abate adverse electrical fields, and so on.

LAN/WAN Planning

Modeling the core technology implementation of a forensic environment on data center design is a good starting point regarding the basic requirements for a forensic laboratory technology build-out. Additional consideration needs to be given to the global and personal workspace elements of technology provision explicit to the demands of a data forensic operation.

We have already mentioned the need to segregate the examination environment network components from the general corporate network; in addition to the functional separation of services a number of absolute physical boundaries should also be considered. If corporate and examination hardware is to reside in the same server room, consider a locking cage around the examination architecture or build internal divider walls and place the examination architecture behind a secure door: Severely limit human access levels to physical space. Apply all the same security restrictions and chain-of-custody protocols to the examination architecture as are applied to the evidence room. Consider placing the examination servers and data storage inside the examination laboratory space proper such that all servers, data warehouses, physical cabling, switches/routers, and so on are physically protected by the same security measures restricting laboratory accesses. Route all examination traffic through network switches dedicated to and connected physically to only examination servers and workstations. Don't rely on virtual segregations; deploy physical segregations.

When you are planning the data storage needs for the laboratory facility, emphasize disaster recovery, redundancy, and sustainability concepts. Keep in mind that the facility needs to support large data volumes. A typical small laboratory can encounter terabytes of data on a routine basis. Implementation of data storage for even a moderately sized facility may require an online examination environment data storage capacity of tens or hundreds of terabytes; this architecture will consume a significant footprint in a server room. It will be tied to other high-footprint items such as large tape backup jukeboxes, near-line storage solutions, and so on. Systems will need to be put in place that can handle the overhead required to maintain and preserve these enormous data volumes.

HVAC

Large numbers of computers result in enormous BTU generation (British Thermal Units, a standard measure of heat generation). Perform very conservative calculations when determining how many tons of AC cooling is required for the technology spaces in which large amounts of heat-generating equipment reside. Make certain that cooling calculations are made from the actual equipment purchasing plans and individual device specifications, as opposed to hypothet-

ical estimates. Keep in mind that human bodies also generate BTUs. Consider overcooling maximum capacity by a factor of 2–3x across the total HVAC design. Plan for hardware growth, and factor future hardware purchases when implementing day-one cooling services. Consider fully redundant units in areas that cool the examination environment technology, and make sure either/or can provide for the entire cooling burden for the space in question. Make certain that ventilation requirements are sufficient for the spaces being cooled, and that active and passive returns are located in effective placements. If an advanced fire suppression system is in place that utilizes gas suppression, for instance, provide an active exhaust system to recover the environment once a fire event has been suppressed. Consider the water and coolant provision to any HVAC units that serve various areas; is the pipe work and pump system redundant, and does a failover system exist that guarantees the AC units will continue to be fed water? Are these feed lines protected from compromise? Are the HVAC units serving the examination space to be located over the examination space, or housed elsewhere? Placing HVAC units above the lab space adds security against physical compromise, but also adds adverse risk in the form of potential leakage and water line breakage. Environmental HVAC concerns should include noise abatement measures: An AC unit placed above the examination space may provide positive white noise in certain laboratory designs and unwelcome noise pollution in others.

Abatements

In any environment where mission-critical computing systems and magnetic/tape/optical data storage reside, a number of abatement strategies need to be considered. In the forensic laboratory, most, if not all, of the following should be reviewed during the planning phase and then monitored after build-out is compete.

Temperature

All equipment has a desired temperature operating range. A typical data center will maintain an ambient temperature of 68–70°F. Make sure the overall HVAC system can provide temperature stability within the desired ranges, even during possible HVAC equipment failures. Consider a portable cooling device standby plan. Make certain temperatures are not held at a low point that would encourage electrostatic buildup and discharge in dry air.

Humidity

Install a humidity management system that has the ability to control humidity measure to within +/-1 percent. Humidity control is an important factor in abating electrostatic buildup and discharge. When assessing correct local operating values to maintain, you need to determine standards with respect to specific details regarding tolerances of the equipment to be utilized in the environment and to general factors such as geographic location, elevation, and so on.

Static Electricity

As mentioned previously, temperature and humidity are two major environmental factors to regulate to avoid static electricity concerns. Consider workspace elements such as antistatic flooring and actively dissipative counter surfaces and drawer linings; also, ground all metal furniture to earth. An operation of any size should make liberal use of portable antistatic mats and gloves. Provide antistatic spray to employees wearing charge-generating fabrics.

Electromagnetic Interference

Plan the electrical plant carefully to minimize electromagnetic field generation in any data storage/handling areas. Shield main power plant components such as transformers as required. Consider electromagnetic interference (EMI) shielding in and around the examination laboratory space. Give strong consideration to shielding the evidence locker, at a minimum. Maintain a gauss meter or series of gauss meters in the functional laboratory space, and check them regularly for anomalies. EMI regulation should speak directly to ISO planning and competency levels for any operation that specializes in electronic data handling.

Acoustic Balancing

Ambience abatements are also important in laboratory planning. Many workspaces intentionally pipe white noise into their environments to create acoustic masking for privacy reasons and to prevent an environment from being "too quiet"; a forensic laboratory is very likely to have many acoustically reflective surfaces, necessitating some surface texture applications, baffling, or other acoustically absorptive abatements.

Security

Security is of paramount concern to any forensic operation. Campus-level access, environment-level access, and object-level access protocols must all be implemented. Video surveillance and live surveillance by internal security are strongly recommended. With regard to general security, the entire facility should have at a minimum a two-challenge system in place such that every entrant will be providing at least one validator at an automated checkpoint (i.e., biometric entry, external security card swipe, etc.) and one other independent manual or automatic validator (sign-in at security desk, internal security card swipes, etc.).

Higher levels of access control should be applied to any infrastructure or workspace related to the examination environment or to any other environment in which evidentiary grade materials may be stored or examined. Each access attempt to the examination environment should be challenged by dual-authentication and the access points should be under constant independent monitoring (i.e., cameras and access logging).

Dual authentication refers to two-factor identification methodology. Two-factor identification presumes that any two personal identification factors will be challenged and that both challenges must be successfully responded.

Challenge factors fall into the following identification categories:

- **Something you are** Biometric keys such as a fingerprint or retinal scanner
- **Something you know** Password, PIN, and so on
- **Something you have** Security card, digital token, bingo card, and so on

Dual authentication across two categories of factors is recommended.

A physical sign-in/out log is a useful supplemental tool for physical plant security even if a dual-authentication protocol is in place; providing an ink-signature audit trail is useful for independent audit of security system performance and original handwriting can be used to investigate identity during security audit and review phases.

Evidence Locker Security

A good, locking, fire-rated safe in a locked room coupled with accurate hand-written access logs may prove sufficient security for a small (e.g., solo-practitioner) environment. Other evidence storage environments implement a shelf-and-cage methodology with a single portal of entry that is key-locked and monitored for access. Depending on the needs of the facility and other factors, such as level of national security, the build-out of an evidence locker can become an expensive and complex endeavor.

The main security criteria to fulfill are the following:

- Is access truly restricted to the custodian(s) of evidence?
- Is all access to the evidence locker documented completely and without exception?
- Is all item-level access (i.e., chain of custody) maintained correctly and without exception?
- Does an independent method of audit exist to confirm that the preceding criteria have been met?

Considering security design at the corporate departmental and dedicated facility level, the highest and most restrictive levels of access control should be applied to the evidence storage environment. Dual challenge is mandatory. Access to the evidence storage locker must be extremely limited. Only those persons with personal responsibility for evidence integrity should be allowed access. In many environments, a single custodian of evidence is assigned master access and only that person can execute chain of custody check-ins and check-outs from the locker itself. The evidence storage environment should have dedicated security protocols for access to that environment and all accesses should be logged with 100 percent accuracy. Chain-of-custody procedures on any item entering or exiting this space should be upheld

without fail. Video surveillance of the evidence storage environment is recommended with cameras on both the entry view and exit view of the door as well as coverage of the storage systems where evidence items are physically stored. An alarm should be in place to expose incursion attempts. The alarm should be robust enough to expose catastrophic entry through ceiling, walls, floor, and so on, as well as unauthorized entry through the main door. The evidence storage environment should have security features built into the infrastructure itself. The walls, floor, and ceiling should be hardened to discourage entry via tunneling or destruction by force; the core construction should have features such as floor-to-ceiling walls (no plenum or raised flooring, therefore no "crawl-over" or "crawl-under" unauthorized access). Fixtures such as fire suppression and air provision should be independently controlled such that adverse events elsewhere in the facility do not cause unwanted effects inside the evidence locker itself. Air ducts need to be of a size too small for human egress and weld-grated to prevent objects from passing. No openings should be left in floor, wall, or ceiling space that could allow unwanted items to be inserted into or evidence items to be removed from the space.

General Ambience

As in any other professional space, the general ambience of a data forensic laboratory should be free of major distractions, providing employees an opportunity to work without disruption. The laboratory space should be a low-foot-traffic environment. It should be physically separated from other environments. The examination space should be well lit. The environment should promote personal comfort and positively support both standing tasks in common areas and seated tasks in personal space.

Spatial Ergonomics

A data forensic laboratory will in some ways function like a warehouse operation. The computer hard disks the forensic examiners peruse will often be provided with the rest of the computer in tow; these chassis, monitors, and other associated items will require handling and storage. Monitors, workstations, servers, and other technology packages are often bulky, relatively heavy pieces of equipment. Moving bigger items to and from evidence lockdown, lifting and bending concerns surrounding transporting such items to workspaces, and temporary rack system holding areas should be considered during workspace design. Safety equipment such as lumbar harnesses should be made available to employees expected to execute the physical labor of lifting/carrying tasks. The traffic areas of the lab should be economized to maximize the safe execution of such tasks. Any work surface and staging area provisions should accommodate heavy vertical lifting concerns.

A Note on "Common Office Technology"

Any evidence-handling facility needs to pay special attention to potential data repositories to guarantee that privileged information stays confidential. A forensic laboratory should include

scope of such consideration to include common office technologies such as copiers and fax machines. Modern copiers and fax machines commonly have the ability to store data in memory for long periods, and either technology may have a hard disk on board! Maintenance plans for such devices should consider the possibility of privileged information being resident, and security and audit methodology should be applied to guarantee proper handling/destruction of any storage medium's contents.

Personal Workspace Design

Each laboratory inhabitant should be provided a significant amount of operating space. Work surface area should be bountiful, especially digital work surface areas (i.e., monitor footprint). Electricity supply should be robust. The personal space of each examiner should be considered a "mini laboratory" and that mini lab should be stocked with all the hardware and software necessary for an examiner to perform common investigative tasks and to maintain the work product. A dedicated investigation platform, a complete kit of write blockers and accessories, a separate system for corporate/business communications, a workspace-level data management system, and a close-at-hand library of reference materials are all desired elements for an active and useful personal investigation workspace.

Common-Area Considerations

Consider providing multiple units of every technology. Multiple sets of write blockers and multiple investigation machines allow for several parallel forensic tasks to occur. Design workspaces with a template design to allow multiple individuals to execute similar tasks concurrently in different workspaces, or to allow one individual to rotate between several stations to manage multiple machine-time-intensive tasks. Design work areas to support the execution of multiple tasks with minimal foot traffic. Deploy sufficient "shared resources" to effectively serve the needs of staff without causing workflow bottlenecks. For example, when scoping DVD production capability make sure the DVD burning tower has a job scheduling capability to capitalize on a full 24-hour production cycle regardless of staffed shift availability. Determine how many DVD burning towers are required to fully serve departmental needs. Is one large central unit the best choice, or are four smaller units located in different areas the most effective option?

Essential Laboratory Tools

The tools of the trade: essential and specialized technology for both field and laboratory (see Table 1.1).

NOTE

The author is not attempting to endorse the use of any specific product, or to be exhaustive in the description of capability or utilization of any product listed herein. This chapter hopes simply to expose the reader to a wide selection of readily available hardware and software tools.

Table 1.1 Vendor Reference Matrix

Vendor	Product Examples	Web Site
Tableau	Write block devices	www.tableau.com
Intelligent Computer Solutions	Hardware, write block devices	www.ics-iq.com
WiebeTech	Write block devices, hardware	www.wiebetech.com
Digital Intelligence	Write block devices, hardware, software	www.digitalintelligence.com
MyKey Technology	Write block devices	www.mykeytech.com
Guidance Software	Write block devices, software	www.guidancesoftware.com
Paraben Corporation	Write block devices, hardware, software	www.paraben-forensics.com
Forensic Computers	Hardware, software, systems	www.forensic-computers.com
LogiCube Forensics	Hardware, software	www.logicubeforensics.com
VOOM Technologies	Hardware	www.voomtech.com
DIBS USA	Hardware, software, systems	www.dibsusa.com
Fernico	Software/hardware	www.fernico.com
Primera Technology	Software/hardware	www.primera.com
Project-A-Phone	Hardware	www.projectaphone.com
Rimage	Hardware	www.rimage.com
Ashby	Hardware	www.ashbyind.com
CopyPro	Hardware	www.copypro.com

Write Blockers

No laboratory or field forensic tool kit would be complete without write block methodology and devices. Prevention of *data spoliation* (the compromise of data integrity by intentionally or inadvertently altering the state of the data from its "original" form) is a prime directive for forensic examiners. The courts will challenge forensic work product to leverage spoliation concerns; one of the most common attacks on forensic work product focuses on the methodologies employed when handling digital evidence. Was the evidence maintained in an original state? Were the conclusions drawn based on uncompromised materials? Were the proper tools used in the process? In a vast number of circumstances, when an unprotected writable data device is connected to a computer, it will incur change. Computer boot sequences, volume mounts, and a plethora of other events can modify some component of the evidence data store if it is not explicitly protected from write-to events. A forensic examination environment, therefore, will host a broad range of methodologies and devices ensuring write block capability (see Figure 1.3).

Figure 1.3 Write Blockers

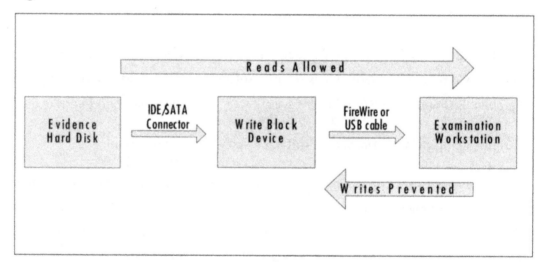

In certain circumstances, utilizing the proper methodology, it is possible to achieve a no-write status at a software level. Certain Windows Registry edits can protect USB devices from write events; Linux volumes can be mounted in a certain way as to make data stores read-only. Microsoft DOS and Linux operating systems can both be modified to be forensically sound with regard to data stores, and they can be packaged as a self-contained bootable environment from diskette, CDR, DVD, thumb drive, and so on. Of course, an investigator implementing these techniques must repeatedly test his methodology and be able to both demonstrate and explain proofs that the methods truly are forensically sound to defeat the inevitable court challenges to the method that will arise.

Hardware write block devices (aka write blockers, forensic bridges) are a flexible, extremely useful, and core component of the forensic tool kit. They have the advantages of portability, broad application, ease of use, and ease of function testing. It is a simpler task to visually and conceptually demonstrate the function of a hardware write block device than to explain the esoteric technical specifics of a Linux operating system forensic recompile to a jury of average (and often nontechnical) citizens.

A number of major write block devices are readily available for purchase. Common write block brands include Tableau, WiebeTech, and Intelligent Computer Solutions DriveLock. Digital Intelligence carries the complete line of Tableau products under the brands UltraBlock and FireFly. Guidance Software has FastBloc, based upon WiebeTech firmware. Paraben Corporation vends LockDown. MyKey Technology vends NoWrite. A majority of these write blockers are designed to be portable, allowing them to have equal value on a laboratory bench or in the field.

Multiple form factors exist to serve different environmental needs. Hard-disk technology has multiple interface types (IDE, SATA, SCSI, etc.). Write block technology therefore integrates multiple interface types to attend to the diverse connectivity needs an investigator may encounter. Many write blockers are designed to support the IDE hard disk interface and will have an adapter/cable kit that allows the device to also support SATA. Tableau has an explicit forensic bridge model for each interface type: SATA (T3u and T15), IDE (T5 and T14), SCSI (T4 and adaptor kit), USB (T8), and so on. There are advantages to both design scenarios. USB and FireWire form factors are common interface types utilized to connect external write blockers to examination machines. Most write blockers will be packaged with the appropriate power supplies and cabling to support that device.

Forensic bridges can also be acquired for permanent installation into workstations. Although not portable (unless the entire workstation is portable), the internal forensic bridges usually have the advantage of being space-efficient, often providing several evidence drive interfaces while consuming only one device bay on the workstation. The Tableau T35i Combination Bridge is an example of a permanent mount device.

Write block technology also exists to support examination of non-hard-disk media. A number of multiformat forensic card readers exist to handle SD, SDC, xD, MMC, CF, and so on. Examples include the Tableau TDA8-M 12-in-1 reader, the Addonics DigiDrive 12-in-1 Flash Media Reader, and the UltraBlock Forensic Card Reader from Digital Intelligence. In addition to the core write block device, passive format-to-format adapters can be purchased from retail and specialty outlets that can adapt a nonsupported card format to a supported card format, further enhancing the interface capability of the multicard readers. (When adapting formats, always test the adapter to ensure that it is indeed a passive, non-change-inducing device.)

Write Block Field Kits

Forensic Bridge field kits are an excellent addition to the forensic laboratory inventory. Aside from the obvious (field use), a field kit can be fully functional on an examiner's laboratory

desktop, and as such, they help reduce inventory purchase costs by minimizing the amount of hardware per examiner required to execute data acquisition and investigation in diverse environments. Field kits tend to be lightweight, ruggedized, designed to meet air transport criteria, and packed with device, adapter, and cabling options to address as many of the "unknowns" of field work as possible. The Digital Intelligence UltraKit and the Ultimate Forensic Write Protection Kits from Forensic Computers are excellent examples of single-package systems; they include a majority of the Tableau devices referenced earlier as well as numerous supporting parts. Field kits also commonly supply a basic multifunction hand tool kit, bit/driver set and a digital camera to help support other aspects of field work. A good core field kit can be substantially fleshed out with cabling, adapters, extra devices, and so on to create a very powerful and economical portable laboratory system. Always include redundancy for high-use/fragile components: multiple AC adapters, power cords, and interface cabling units are a must. Convenience items such as the Tableau in-line power switch (T2) add a level of protection to the examination equipment assembly process and help protect against damage to evidence media via pilot error.

One major implementation of write block methodology focuses on protecting original media from change during examination. Another implementation is protecting original media from change during duplication. In many instances, field investigation practices will require the acquisition of data from the wild for later study. This acquisition often occurs via the creation of a forensic duplicate of original evidentiary materials for transport of evidence back to a laboratory environment for analysis. In such cases, the need for write blocking will be conjoined to the need for a duplication platform.

Hardware Duplication Platforms

A number of handheld and desktop forensic duplication systems are available. The core functions they provide include write-blocking the original evidence media, performing a data duplication process to secondary media, and measuring the correctness/completeness of the duplication process via some measurement criteria (almost always via utilizing a hash algorithm such as MD5 or SHA1 or both) to validate that the entire original was duplicated to the forensic copy. Several devices of this class also integrate reporting capability (see Figure 1.4).

Figure 1.4 Hardware Duplication Devices

A number of popular models are readily available. The Logicube Forensic Talon, boasting a data duplication rate of up to 4GB per minute, provides multiple media adapter kits and possesses extensive reporting capability. Intelligent Computer Solutions' ImageMASSter Solo-III forensic duplication device handles several interface types and has the ability to write to two output hard drives concurrently. Voom Technologies' Hardcopy II provides a simple interface and handles IDE hard-disk duplication (expandable to SATA duplication with adapters). Voom Technologies also produces a SCSI HardCopy for SCSI platform acquisitions. Some vendors package multiple hardware duplication devices and accessories into a field kit: the DIBS RAID: Rapid Action Imaging Device is an example. Many of these devices also provide the output options of bit-for-bit duplication, one or more forensic image format acquisitions, and transport media sterilization. Hardware-based duplication platforms tend to have much faster data transcription rates than software-based duplication solutions.

Duplication hardware is a valuable addition to the examiner's toolbox, but duplication tools generally provide no environment in which an examiner can investigate the data being duplicated. Portable forensic computer systems provide an examiner with an investigation environment, expanding the examiner's field capability one step further.

Portable Forensic Systems

When the need to take the entire investigation process into the field arises, a forensic examiner must have access to not only the protective and duplication tools available, but also fully interactive examination environments. Specialized portable forensic computing systems provide a highly mobile, equipment-intensive and methodology-sound platform for the forensic examiner. Complete field examination systems allow the examiner the ability to duplicate digital evidence and analyze said evidence on one robust platform. "By-hand transport" level portable forensic systems will generally be provided in the form of ruggedized, feature-packed laptops or custom "suitcase-style" workstations. A second tier of "portable" forensic systems includes a class of machines and mini networks that are heavily ruggedized for mobility but are not intended for day-to-day high mobility. All of these investigation systems tend to have fast processor capability, copious amounts of memory, and high-volume data storage space. Most will be optimized for running specific forensic software packages. Implementation of multiple operating systems on one workstation is common.

Every examiner will need a personal field kit inventory that is easily manageable for loading/unloading into vehicles and for air travel. High-mobility portable systems are often designed to rely on external field kits such as the write blocker field kit and supplemental cable and adapter solutions to make the core system smaller and more transportable. Table 1.2 references a number of such systems and examples of core features.

Table 1.2 Laptop-Style Portable Forensic Solutions

Vendor	System	Class	Feature Examples
Forensic Computers	Forensic Air-Lite VI MKIII	Forensic Laptop plus external bridge kit	2GB memory; supplied with write blocker accessory kit; 25-in-1 media card reader; ruggedized hard-shell case; extra external HD storage supplied
LogiCube	"PFL" Portable Forensics Lab	Forensic Laptop plus external duplicator kit	2GB memory; supplied with a Forensic Talon drive duplicator; bundled with the forensic investigation software suite FTK from Access Data; ruggedized hard-shell case
DIBS USA	DIBS Mobile Forensic Workstation	Forensic Laptop Plus external accessories	1GB memory; supplied with an inkjet printer in a hard-shell case; bundles with preinstalled forensic software including Access Data FTK, CD/DVD analysis tools, and other forensics utilities; digital camera; write block accessories
Digital Intelligence	FRED-L	Forensic Laptop plus external bridge kit	2GB memory; multiple bootable operating systems onboard; supplied with UltraKit write block kit; forensic card reader; ruggedized hard-shell case

"Workstation-in-a-box"-style computers can offer a few flexibilities to field personnel that may not be available in the laptop-style kits, such as a higher number and/or friendlier form factor of available slots for add-on devices. The suitcase-style workstations often have a detachable monitor/keyboard/mouse set that can be used to work with evidence workstations (presuming those components are not available at the field site) for boot-up procedures such as BIOS checks and verifying proper suspect system reassembly (see Table 1.3).

Table 1.3 Suitcase Workstation-Style Portable Forensic Solutions

Vendor	System	Class	Feature Examples
Forensic Computers	Forensic Air-Lite IV MKII	Forensic workstation (suitcase type)	Pentium IV 4.3GHz; 2GB memory; external keyboard and mouse; ruggedized hard-shell case; LCD monitor; upgradeable
Digital Intelligence	FREDDIE	Forensic workstation (custom design)	4GB memory; multiple bootable operating systems onboard; two removable hard disk bays; multiple onboard write block formats; supplemental toolbox including hand tools and camera; optional hard-shell case; multiple accessories and several onboard software utilities

Portable Enterprise Systems

In some instances, field portability concerns address the need for a robust, temporary laboratory facility at an examination location. Forensic portability can be extended to "network-in-a-box" solutions. "Half-rack" solutions can fill this need. A portable enterprise system will offer core components such as the examination system(s) plus integrated write block bridges plus robust examination hard-disk storage space (multiterabyte RAID-level storage, etc.) plus all add-on hardware such as monitors, kvm, and so on wrapped into one ruggedized cage. This type of portable environment is usually high durability but low mobility, quite weighty, and meant to be transported crated and packed (i.e., setup and breakdown time) as opposed to the more "plug-and-play" high-mobility equipment (see Table 1.4).

Table 1.4 Digital Intelligence's FRED-M Portable Forensic System

Vendor	System	Class	Feature Examples
Digital Intelligence	FRED-M	Forensic environment	Rack-mount enclosure; high-end forensic processing workstation including rack-mount monitor, keyboard, and mouse assembly; networked within enclosure; complete write blocking system onboard; onboard tape backup system; up to 6TB of RAID 5 examination drive space; onboard uninterruptable power supply (UPS); highly customizable.

Laboratory Forensic Systems

In many instances, the high-mobility equipment that accompanies the field examiner on excursions can also be utilized on the desktop. Small operations, especially solo practitioners, will find great economy in purchasing their primary gear with both field and desktop implementation in mind. For facilities that can support a permanent lab installation of desktop investigative gear plus field support equipment, numerous "nonportable" investigative powerhouse systems are available. These systems tend to offer all the various field hardware solutions found in portable kits for write blocking and hard-disk management combined into one desktop chassis. A solo practitioner or cost-conscious operation may find value in a "white box" approach, building a desktop system from scratch to suit specific needs; all-in-one devices such as the Tableau T35i Combination Bridge and Tableau T335 Drive Bay Controller are economical options for implementing multiple write-block and multiple hard-disk solutions in a single chassis.

Prebuilt desktop forensic systems (see Table 1.5) will often have the best computing power available at the time of purchase (portable technology historically tends to lag behind desktop technology in terms of "bigger-better-faster-more").

Table 1.5 Desktop Forensic Systems

Vendor	System	Class	Feature Examples
DIBS USA	DIBS Advanced Forensic Workstation	Forensic full-tower desktop plus accessories	1GB memory; Pentium 4 processor; one operating system hard drive and one removable hard-drive bay; multiple forensic applications installed; onboard write block capability; external supplemental USB drive bay; DVD writer; custom search engine software
Digital Intelligence	FRED	Forensic full tower desktop plus accessories	4GB memory; dual core processor; onboard write block capability; dual RAID-capable SATA drive controllers; multiple removable hard disk bays; onboard forensic card reader; optional tape backup system; optional 2TB RAID 5 subsystem; supplemental toolbox including hand tools, camera, and adapter kits; multiple bootable operating systems; onboard SCSI controller
Forensic Computers	Original Forensic Tower II	Forensic full tower desktop plus write blocker field kit plus accessories	2GB memory; dual core processor; multiple external device bays including Tableau T335 forensic bay controller, two read-only hard-disk bays, one writable hard-disk bay, DVD writer; supplemental Write Blocker field kit; onboard SCSI controller; upgradeable; optional forensic examination software preloads available

Continued

Table 1.5 continued Desktop Forensic Systems

Vendor	System	Class	Feature Examples
Forensic Computers	Forensic Tower II	Forensic full tower desktop plus write blocker field kit plus accessories	4GB memory; dual core processor; multiple external device bays including Tableau T335 forensic bay controller, two read-only hard-disk bays, one writable hard-disk bay, DVD writer; supplemental Write Blocker field kit; onboard SCSI controller; available expansion slots for add-ons; optional forensic examination software preloads available; upgradeable

When you are choosing the specifications for a desktop laboratory processing system, always target the fastest processing, largest memory allocation, and largest possible hard-disk drive volume available at the time of purchase, subject to any budget constraints. Hardware ages quickly, and maximizing the point of purchase processing capability of new systems maximizes the useful lifespan of the equipment. Given the process-intensive needs of most forensic software application suites, a fast, powerful CPU, and a large amount of RAM are critical.

Typical data storage space requirements for the forensic examiner are astronomical. As of this writing, a single hard disk of 1TB is readily available in the retail consumer marketplace and a 1TB hard disk is commonly available in home and corporate computers at point of sale. Encountering hard disks of 500GB or 750GB is commonplace. Current prebuilt forensic systems offer BASE storage of 2–6 TB per system. Make maximizing storage space a priority and consider the relatively short span of any volume's sufficiency when allocating resources to acquire forensic computing equipment. Evaluate hardware-level redundancies and robust backup systems for managing data volumes of this volume.

Provide considerable monitor real estate. Forensic examiners have to visualize enormous amounts of data during an examination, and the viewable area of the computer monitors upon which they work can have notable impact on investigation speed and efficiency. Many forensic systems are sold with dual-head video cards, such that two or four monitors may be attached to one system. Large (22–30-inch) flat-panel monitors are space-efficient, readily available and reasonably priced.

The ability to operate under multiple operating systems is greatly desired. The forensic examiner will use both cutting-edge and "old-school" investigation tools, requiring multiple operating systems to support those tools. From an investigative standpoint, the investigator will routinely analyze evidence derived from (and will therefore require access to) multiple operating system environments. Provision of multiple operating systems extends across version levels

(such as multiboot options for Microsoft DOS 6.22, Windows 98 SE, Windows 2000, and Windows XP) and platforms (Windows and Linux boot options). The more powerful prebuilt forensic systems will provide four or more bootable operating systems.

Media Sterilization Systems

Spoliation challenges to evidence integrity include challenges to the duplicate evidence copy; often an argument will be made charging evidence could experience spoliation due to data artifacts preexisting on hard drives used as duplication destination. To help prevent questions of this type from arising, a solid policy for work product media sterilization should be in place for any forensic practice. Any hard drive to be utilized as a substrate for an evidence duplicate should be sterilized prior to use and documented as sterile. Furthermore, the sterile state of such media should be validated by some post-sterilization procedure. Some forensic hardware and software duplication tools sterilize in conjunction with data acquisition by hash-validating written sectors and subsequently zeroing out all other writable space; they will validate the acquired evidence data stream via hash methodology, then "wipe" any remaining writable data space to a random or zero value via data overwrite methods. Relying on this process is more complicated from an "explain-to-jury" standpoint than confirming all new substrate media as clean and viable for use, prior to use.

Software solutions such as Guidance Software's EnCase forensic examination suite include the capability to sterilize and subsequently validate hard-disk media; retail products such as White Canyon Software's WipeDrive (www.whitecanyon.com) can destroy data according to a number of data overwrite patterns. (Many retail "drive wiping" programs are ineffective at complete data destruction. If any software data destruction method is utilized, make certain to test results and validate any destruction attempts case by case.) Hardware sterilization devices exist that can bulk-overwrite hard disk media.

If any evidentiary or sensitive data needs destruction after its value expires, a sterilization process and validation process should be applied to the media to destroy data. Both hardware and software sterilization tools exist that can destroy data. A forensic laboratory environment will often need to demonstrate adherence to commonly accepted practice. Data destruction practices are no exception. One of the most popular courtroom attacks on digital evidence centers around spoliation; it behooves a forensic practice to not only practice good methods but also adopt commonly defined "industry standard" practices with regard to work product media consumption. Although an argument can be made that no truly "industry-standard" definition for data destruction exists, several published standards do serve as common reference materials for most forensic practitioners on the topic of data destruction practices.

By far the most referenced document is Department of Defense (DoD) 5220.22-M. Commercial practices especially, in order to lend market credence to their vended product, will claim adherence to "DoD grade" destruction practices. This document, reissued in February 2006 as the NISPOM ("National Industrial Security Program Operating Manual"), is, in its current incarnation, a high-level document and it does not speak to actual technical specifics of

sanitization method. Prior to 2007, the DoD CSM ("Clearing and Sanitization Matrix") directly defined the term *sanitize*, and it included specific technical processes for n-pass overwrite techniques on magnetic media as viable sterilization techniques (including a three pass-plus-verification data overwrite technique commonly cited as the DoD 5220.22-M standard). In June 2007, an updated CSM was published by the Defense Security Service of the DoD explicitly disavowing the process of data overwriting as a valid method of sanitization for classified materials; the new matrix endorses degaussing and physical total destruction techniques (incineration/chemical abrasion) of magnetic media to truly "make data gone" (www.dss.mil/isp/odaa/documents/clearing_and_sanitization_matrix.pdf).

Other U.S. government-derived "industry standards" include the 1993 NAVSO (Navy Security Operations) P-5239-26 MFM/RLL standard for dealing with data remanence on hard disks using MFM/RLL encoding schema. This standard continues to endorse degaussing and data overwrites, but it is currently best interpreted in light of DoD 2007 CSM.

The U.K. governing body standard "HMG Infosec Standard No 5" is another storage device disposition standards document gaining popular citation; various other data overwrite standards and protocols are frequently cited, including GOST P50739-95 (Soviet) and Gutmann-35 (New Zealand). Data destruction services may also include references to procedural HIPAA (Health Insurance Portability and Accountability Act) compliance regarding data storage media that also happens to hold content falling under the scope and provisions of the Act.

Ultimately, a forensic laboratory should have data destruction tools on hand to address the real needs of that facility; a solo practitioner may never need access to an incinerator or hardware shredder. Environments engaging in data destruction practices as a vended or self service should consider a bulk data wiping hardware device for new media preparation and a degauss chamber or physical destruction device for any disposal sterilization needs.

Data Management (Backup, Retention, Preservation)

Forensic operations have a significant need for data storage and preservation. When considering implementation of a forensic environment, consider the many touch points for data storage and data transactions that typically exist. Forensic examiners require high volumes of digital workspace; examination workstations may have terabytes of onboard storage, and high volumes of data may transact across that environment on a regular basis. This workspace needs to be managed as part of the examiner's workflow. Common network data stores will also be in the terabyte (or higher) storage measures. Networked storage may have data content requiring long-term preservation, rapid workflow turnaround to archive, or extended presence in on-line storage. A robust policy of data-handling strategies will need to be developed to accommodate these different levels of need. A forensic facility, given the evidentiary nature of original and work product data and hardware, will require far more stringent policy and procedure for oversight, auditing, and reporting on data management activities as compared to the typical corpo-

rate or data center operation. Data management solutions provided at both the "per-machine" and enterprise level guarantee flexible options for efficient data handling, potentially minimizing workflow-based bottlenecks.

Modern hard-disk sizes indicate the need for high-volume data storage solutions. Even a solo practitioner can reasonably expect to have a need to manage terabytes of information. A forensic environment may want to consider a number of options to ameliorate the need for constant, rapid, and high-volume data management. Possible components for data management include various hardware and software solutions for data storage and movement. Tape backup systems deployed at a "per-machine" and enterprise level provide the ability to back up and store large volumes of work product via "clone-validate-delete" methodology. Near-line storage in the form of redundant or low-speed disk storage or tape jukeboxes can help serve the offloading and retrieval needs of high-volume data management by providing "standby" access levels to low- or intermittent-use work product. Offline storage (tape, optical disk, and offline hard disk arrays) allow multiple options for long-term preservation. Hot-swappable/external storage devices add value to the overall data management proposition by providing "instant access" or "instant storage" methods for data repository refreshes and fast data offlining.

Various magnetic tape and DVD formats are readily available and cost-effective form factors for evidence preservation. Magnetic storage such as hard disk or tape can provide high-volume storage solutions when environmental factors are tightly controlled; both media formats are magnetic and subject to limitations regarding data degradation over time.

Magnetic tape offers the benefit of tamper resistance: to add or delete data results in obvious physical signs (splicing) or electronic signs (readability/nonreadability.) Downsides to tape use include backup software versioning changes adversely impacting tape readability, relatively little recourse for restoration when a tape span media tapes fail, and simple media degradation over time. Tape hardware tends to be expensive and can be a significant investment at an enterprise level. Installation and licensing for backup software at an enterprise level also tends. to be a significant cost. Even so, tape systems—even high-end hardware rotary jukeboxes and advanced library software systems—tend to be more cost-effective than full hardware storage redundancies such as parallel storage area networks (SANs).

CD/DVD Hardware Solutions

Many long-term evidence preservation and storage needs are addressed via the use of optical media such as DVD or CD. Optical media tends to be very inexpensive and readily available. Use of CD media as a long-term storage medium was commonplace prior to hard-disk space and magnetic tape hardware becoming cost-effective to purchase and utilize; CD and DVD media still have practical application as backup or unitized evidence storage, especially with newer DVD format storage capacity improvements. High-grade optical media tends to have a life span measured in decades, making it ideal for long-term evidence preservation (caveat: Make sure your hardware standard will survive as long as the media needs to survive!). For instance, one common evidence acquisition methodology involves the creation of "image file

sets" of a specific format and size: Most forensic software and hardware offerings supporting image set creation also allow the size of image files to be dictated by the examiner. Default image segment file sizes tend to reflect the anticipated use of CD as the ultimate storage unit (i.e., 650MB per image file, allowing one image segment to be written to one CD media).

Data and media duplication hardware has been developed to support the special needs of a forensic environment. One example of such technology is the Fernico FAR system. The FAR system is based on CDR/DVD burning technology from Primera Technology and is augmented by specialized forensic data archiving software written by Fernico. The combined system provides a robust data management and archival tool that provides several services to the forensic examiner that are explicit to evidence management needs. The system provides the benefits of automation to a typically tedious and manpower-intensive series of tasks. The FAR system will burn DVDs or CDRs, label the media, intelligently manage the spanning of data across disks, and apply forensically desired validators such as robust hashing options to the data burned to disk. The device is network-capable, and it is able to automate activities utilizing a calendar and job-based scheduling system. The system is designed to not only archive data to disk, but also restore data from archive libraries of disks. A FAR system may also be utilized to correctly duplicate CD/DVD original evidence media. Multiple FAR systems are available, each catering to a specific scope of media capacity and disk production. Other robust optical media production systems exist for high-volume CDR and DVD production, provided by vendors such as Rimage. Whether designed explicitly to serve forensic needs or simply to serve as a vehicle for work product duplication and publication, an optical media production platform is a valuable addition to the forensic laboratory tool set.

Disk duplication systems are not limited to optical media. Forensic laboratories must be prepared to process older storage technologies as well; floppy diskettes are still a viable medium to encounter and evidence duplication services for this type of media can be automated by bulk duplication machines as well. Vendors such as Ashby and CopyPro provide floppy diskette duplication systems that auto-feed bulk diskette media and bit-for-bit validate copies.

Portable Device Forensics: Some Basic Tools

In this section we'll discuss basic forensic tools that you can use.

Faraday Devices As Applied to Forensics

From both an information privacy and data integrity standpoint, the science of portable device forensics embraces the use of various configurations of the Faraday enclosure to preserve data integrity and/or prevent data transmission.

A Faraday enclosure is simply an enclosure capable of blocking electromagnetic fields and energy waveforms. A Faraday enclosure is composed of *conductive materials* (e.g., layers of variously composed wire mesh) that allow electrical induction to occur across the surface of the materials when energy is applied to that surface. When a Faraday enclosure is introduced to a

penetrating electromagnetic field or a waveform of a particular frequency or range of frequencies, the applied field/waveforms will not penetrate the enclosure surface; they will instead travel across the conductive surface(s) of the enclosure.

If a signal generator is placed inside a Faraday enclosure, that signal can be "kept inside the box."

If a signal receiver is placed inside a Faraday enclosure, the enclosure can prevent the receiver from "hearing the signal."

Real-World Examples

Radio Frequency Identification (RFID) tags that actively transmit information are becoming widespread in actual/planned implementations of personal data management. Faraday systems have been designed specifically to defeat RFID scanners picking up signals from active RFID tags inside the Faraday enclosure. Conversely, the enclosure can also prevent active RFID scanners from successfully "pinging" a passive RFID tag. Paraben Forensics sells forensic products that explicitly address RFID data management. (See www.paraben-forensics.com for an applied example of the Paraben Passport StrongHold Bag product referencing RFID technology applied to future versions U.S. passports.)

Cell telephones are ubiquitous, protocol chatty data storage repositories. Forensic acquisition methodology focuses not only on the data they may directly harbor, but also on the air gap protocol channels via which they communicate. External signals capable of compromising data integrity (spoliation via inbound signals modifying/deleting data) are blocked, and internal signals are prevented from reaching intended destinations. To isolate a device that may be actively in communication with cellular towers, other proximate devices, and so on, the use of a Faraday enclosure is paramount. Another product in the Paraben StrongHold line, the StrongHold Bag, is designed for convenient and highly portable field isolation, transportation, and storage of cell phones and other transmission/receipt-capable portable devices. Guidance Software offers WaveShield bags, a similar signal blocking solution (www.guidancesoftware.com).

Other applications of Faraday enclosures include both portable tent and sealed box environments that can be used for field analysis, isolation, and portage of suspect devices. The Paraben Wireless StrongHold Tent and Wireless StrongHold Box are both designed to be fully portable Faraday environments enabling the isolation and examination of portable devices in the field. Even an entire forensic laboratory environment can be shielded inside a Faraday enclosure! Specialized environmental abatement companies cater to this facet of facilities build-out, designing anti-electromagnetic shielding for many industries, including medical, military, and of course, data forensic environments.

Portable Devices and Data Storage

Data on portable devices can reside in many storage forms: SIM cards and other types of card media, chip-based storage, and so on are common, and modern portable devices will typically have more than one of these storage mechanisms in place. In addition to the multiplicity of data storage form factors, the form factor may predispose either static data storage (e.g., phone numbers stored on a SIM card) or volatile data storage (recently dialed phone numbers stored in the battery powered, chip-based memory).

Power

The first rule of securing portables for forensic examination is that if the device is off, leave it off (but keep the battery charged); if the device is on, do everything feasible to keep the device powered on until a full examination can be performed. To help power management and "limited time to respond" portable device research, a number of tools can be added to the examiner's tool kit.

Multipurpose power devices such as Paraben's Remote Charger and Handheld First Responder Kit (which includes a power device, Faraday bags, and portable device flash cards) supply power to a device to significantly extend its data preservation window, giving the forensic examiner time to transport the device to a laboratory environment for detailed analysis.

For assistance in documenting a live review process in lab or field, tools such as the Project-A-Phone device analysis platform and the Fernico ZRT Mobile Device Screen Capture Tool help examiners do rapid video examination and preservation of "power-on" screen states, menu system function, and other live-system processes that are difficult to recover by a data export process or to document for examination and later presentation purposes.

Readers, Readers, Readers!

Many of the card types inherent to cell phone technology (notably SIM) are proprietary; to decipher SIM contents, custom forensic software/hardware packages are usually required. For the more common data storage card types (common form factors for PDAs, cameras, cell phones, etc., such as SD, MMC, and CF formats), a good 15-in-1 card reader is a good tool to add to the tool kit; forensically sound card media readers are distributed via forensic vendors such as Digital Intelligence (see UltraBlock Forensic Card Reader on the Digital Intelligence Web site).

Cables, Cables, Cables!

A good portable device forensic tool kit will include many, many portable device power and data cables. Many of the all-in-one forensic cell phone and PDA examination suites provide an extensive cable selection for both powering and linking to the multitude of data interface formats found on portable devices. Don't discount the retail cell phone outlets, retail electronics

stores, and Web sites for supplemental cables and adapters to augment your mobile device field kit! In addition to cables, cables, cables, a good tool kit also includes adapters, adapters, adapters!

Several expansive portable device forensic tool kits are available, including:

- The Paraben Device Seizure Toolbox (www.paraben-forensics.com)
- LogiCube CellDEK (www.logicube.com)
- Guidance Software Neutrino (www.guidancesoftware.com)
- Secure View Forensics (www.datapilot.com)

NOTE

For an up-to-date general principles guide to mobile forensics, and an excellent listing of supplemental resources, terms, and tools, refer to the National Institute of Standards and Technology (NIST) Special Publication 800-101, "Guidelines on Cell Phone Forensics," released in May 2007 (http://csrc.nist.gov/publications/nistpubs/800-101/SP800-101.pdf).

Forensic Software

The realm of forensic software selection is broad. A forensic examiner will require a diverse array of applications to effectively address the myriad investigative scenarios encountered during the course of business. It is important to understand that no one tool is all-inclusive; therefore, having multiple tools on hand is desired. Many of the tools may have overlapping functions, but each application will have unique strengths that add value to an overall investigative process. Having multiple tools on hand that perform similar functions allows processes and methods to be validated. The unique strength of each tool applied to a given problem will allow for a diverse and thorough investigation to take place. When provisioning software services to an investigative team, it is important to consider a few main areas of focus:

- Operating systems
- File systems
- Main investigative platform
- Special focus tools
- Tools in the enterprise
- Ad hoc scripts and programs

Operating Systems

Operating systems are software implementations. Miriam Webster Online (www.m-w.com) defines *operating system* as follows: "software that controls the operation of a computer and directs the processing of programs (as by assigning storage space in memory and controlling input and output functions)." When considering any forensic laboratory implementation, consider the need for possessing a software library containing a large number of operating systems, including any available version levels of each operating system retained.

A forensic examiner will want to leverage multiple operating systems as his or her production environment, that is, the platform upon which he or she conducts an investigation. There are many reasons to want a good library of operating systems in a forensic laboratory. From a provision of services standpoint, the ability to work with multiple Microsoft Windows versions, Linux/UNIX flavors, and Apple/Mac OS versions should be standard. Numerous other operating systems exist as well.

Leveraging multiple operating systems allows the examiner to use software applications written for specific operating system platforms. For instance, a 20-year-old software application may provide an examiner with a needed function that no newer software provides, and to run that special program the use of an operating system from the same era may be required.

The decision regarding which operating system to use for a given examination may be strategic. A forensic examiner may want to examine a New Technology File System (NTFS) format hard disk from a Windows operating system suspect computer while working on an examination system running one of the Linux operating system flavors to defeat a spoliation argument such as "your Windows examination computer made those Windows artifacts, changing the evidence". A plethora of other proper handling best practices aside, the examiner's response to such a challenge could subsequently be "Linux doesn't create Windows artifacts".

A forensic examiner may be called upon to examine suspect computers configured with a diverse spectrum of operating systems: Having a library of installable operating systems allows the investigator to create a test environment and/or reconstruct events in the same software universe as the suspect computer.

File Systems

Different operating systems support different file systems; to examine file systems of certain types, it may be necessary to have a compatible operating system available.

File systems are not software per se; a file system is a method for storing and organizing data content in/on a given medium. The most common application of the term *file system* in computer forensics usually refers to the organizational structure of electronic computer data stored on computer media such as hard/floppy/optical disks, thumb drives, and so on. A large number of file systems exist. A forensic examiner will want to be prepared to work on as many different file systems as possible: An examiner will need access to multiple operating systems, multiple hardware devices, and various software applications to attack a broad scope of file systems.

Investigative Platforms

Multiple software applications fill the role of "main investigative software platform" for a forensic examiner (see Table 1.6). Common characteristics of the main investigative tool suite include the ability to create an "image file set" or "bit-for-bit clone" copy of suspect media, analyze live or imaged data streams, search and cull suspect data content, generate reports on contents and findings, and export data of interest for subsequent use external to the software. Investigative software suites are available for multiple operating systems (Windows, Linux, and Mac). Some investigative software is restricted to law enforcement (iLook) whereas other application suites are available to the general public (EnCase Forensic, Forensic Tool Kit, S.M.A.R.T., and MacForensicsLab).

Table 1.6 Vendor Reference Matrix

Vendor	Product	Web Site
Guidance Software	EnCase Forensic, EnCase Enterprise	www.guidancesoftware.com
AccessData Corporation	Forensic Tool Kit (FTK), Password Recovery Toolkit (PRTK), Registry Viewer	www.accessdata.com
IRS-CI Electronic Crimes Pgm	iLook ** (law enforcement only)	www.ilook-forensics.org
SubRosaSoft	MacForensicsLab	www.subrosasoft.com
ASR Data Acquisition & Analysis	S.M.A.R.T. for Linux	www.asrdata.com
Paraben Corporation	Chat Examiner, Email Examiner, Device Seizure	www.paraben.com
Hot Pepper Technology	EMail Detective	www.hotpepperinc.com
Wetstone	Gargoyle Investigator; LiveWire Investigator	www.wetstonetech.com
TechPathways	Prodiscover Forensic/IR	www.techpathways.com

Each investigative suite in Table 1.6 has a unique set of strengths. A forensic examiner often possesses several software suites and leverages more than one investigative suite during an investigation. EnCase Forensic by Guidance Software has a robust scripting language empowering custom investigation. Forensic Tool Kit from AccessData has a very intuitive user interface and the ability to integrate password-breaking software from the same vendor. MacForensicsLab is currently the only major forensic investigative suite developed to run on an Apple OS X

system; S.M.A.R.T. is a robust tool suite developed for the Linux operating system. ProDiscover Forensic by Techpathways is capable of performing examinations on Sun Solaris UFS media.

Other/Specialty Tools

Many software packages have been developed to attend to specific data analysis needs. E-mail analysis tools, password-breaking tools, decryption tools, portable hardware analysis tools, artifact-specific identification and analysis tools, and *many* other types of data identification, conversion, and analysis tools have been developed, all of which may prove valuable to the forensic data examiner. AccessData's Password Recovery Toolkit executes password-breaking and certain decryption tasks. Access Data Registry Viewer enables Windows Registry examinations. Paraben's Chat Examiner, Email Examiner, and Device Seizure all provide specific realm analysis capability. Hot Pepper Technology's EMail Detective AOL e-mail analysis provides product-specific e-mail analysis. Wetstone's Stego Suite provides steganographic investigation capability; Wetstone's Gargoyle Investigator provides malware detection. These products and many other special-focus tools can supplement an investigator's digital toolbox. An examiner's digital toolbox should be as robust as, if not more robust than, his physical toolbox.

Tools in the Enterprise

Forensic examination may also be executed against LAN and WAN resources in the enterprise. Whether responding to an acute need for examination across a corporate wide area network or functioning as a forensic service permanently attached to a corporate security group, investigation tools have been developed to address forensic-grade data harvesting and reporting in widely dispersed environments. Enterprise forensic tools often possess the capability to investigate live systems remotely and analyze volatile memory contents and network metrics as well as local machine activities in situ.

Guidance Software's EnCase Enterprise Edition has all the functional aspects of EnCase Forensic regarding data collection, analysis, and reporting: the enterprise version allows those functions to be driven across networked resources via the use of local application connector clients and centralized investigative resources. Wetstone Live Wire Investigator also allows data collection, analysis, and reporting over a network of distributed resources. Live Wire is an "agentless" investigation tool that pushes its application software packet across network resources directly into the memory space of suspect systems. Live Wire is designed for either permanent installation to a corporate network or ad hoc investigation. EnCase Enterprise is intended for permanent corporate implementation; a special version called the Field Intelligence Model (FIM) is available to law enforcement only for ad hoc investigation. Prodiscover IR by TechPathways performs collection and analysis tasks and may be utilized ad hoc or via in situ implementation.

Ad Hoc Scripts and Programs

Even with the plethora of prebuilt tools available to the forensic examiner, many circumstances may arise in which a custom solution may need to be created to fully address investigative needs. Code writing, scripting, and resource fabrication skills are a welcome addition to the forensic examiner's toolbox! Of course, any ad hoc implementation still requires full validation and testing of mechanics and process to guarantee that the tool performs as expected and preserves the integrity of the evidence upon which it acts.

Software Licensing

Quite simply, an examiner's entire software environment (encompassing operating system(s) and applications) must be license legal at all times. Utilizing unlicensed software is effectively an act of software piracy (illegal). Any evidence gathered during the commission of a crime may prove inadmissible. Software licensing is a main cost factor for laboratory scope of service provision, initial purchasing targets, and ongoing laboratory operations. Maintaining, auditing, documenting, and demonstrating license compliance should be integrated into the laboratory SOP.

Tool Validation

Tool testing is a mandatory and ongoing process for both a forensic examiner and a forensic laboratory. Both software and hardware need to be tested to ensure that they perform as expected. Repeat testing validates methods and guarantees equipment integrity over time. It is critical to demonstrate and document proof of any given tool's ability to preserve the integrity of any data under examination. Testing and documentation of testing are the foundation of a very important line of process defensibility: An examiner needs to be able to say with certainty (i.e., provide test results) that the tools utilized in evidence examination do not spoliate the evidence. No examiner wants to be on the witness stand and be unable to provide proof of the competency of his methodology and tools. The best way to prevent this unfortunate circumstance is to consistently and repeatedly test every hardware and software tool, document the test methodology, results, and theory surrounding the test design, and be able to state that testing was performed personally as well as departmentally. The best defense toward methodology attacks is to be able to state "I *personally* tested this tool/method/process. Here is a copy of my test results. Let me explain why my testing is valid proof of the soundness of my method. Would you care to see a demonstration?" The exact methodology of tool testing needs to be tailored to the tool. Testing must be specific and exhaustive enough to prove the underlying function of the tool valid. For instance, most examiners will create a specific test script for their write block devices, create "gold standard" test media, and perform a set number of procedures (attempt to write data to media, attempt to delete data from media, attempt to access media via X method, etc.) to demonstrate tool function integrity. NIST has an entire Web site dedicated to the testing of computer forensic tools (www.cftt.nist.gov/). Of note on the NIST Web site are a general framework for tool testing and a list of several specific tool test documents.

Summary of Exam Objectives

After reading this chapter, you should be familiar with forensics in today's world, the history of computer forensics, and its objectives. You should also understand what computer-facilitated crimes are as well as the reasons for cybercrime. You will be challenged to know computer forensic flaws and risks, modes of attack, and the stages of forensic investigation in tracking cyber criminals. You also learned about the rules of computer forensics, how to approach the crime scene, and the legal issues surrounding computer forensics.

In the second part of this chapter, you learned about the core concepts to be considered during the planning, construction, and operation of a data forensic facility.

Exam Objectives Fast Track

The History of Forensics

- ☑ Francis Galton (1822–1911) made the first recorded study of fingerprints, and Leone Lattes (1887–1954) discovered blood groupings (A, B, AB, and 0)

- ☑ Calvin Goddard (1891–1955) allowed firearms and bullet comparison for solving many pending court cases, Albert Osborn (1858–1946) developed essential features of document examination, and Hans Gross (1847–1915) made use of scientific study to head criminal investigations.

- ☑ In 1932, the FBI set up a lab to provide forensic services to all field agents and other law authorities across the country.

The Objectives of Computer Forensics

- ☑ The objective of a computer forensic examiner is to examine digital evidence (media).

- ☑ The ultimate goal of a computer forensic investigator is to determine the nature and events of the crime and to locate the perpetrator by following a structured investigation procedure.

- ☑ Application of physical sciences to law in the search for truth in civil, criminal, and social behavioral matters to the end that injustice shall not be done to any member of society.

Computer-Facilitated Crimes

- ☑ Computers are used as a tool for committing crimes, and they are posing new challenges for investigators.

☑ Speed, the proliferation of personal computers, and access to the Internet have made the exchange of information very quick and inexpensive.

☑ The use of easily available hacking tools and underground groups has increased cybercrimes. The Internet allows anyone to hide his or her identity while committing crimes.

Reasons for Cyber Attacks

☑ Cyber attacks in today's world is made up of individuals who are more organized in crime.

☑ Types of computer crime include theft of intellectual property, damage of company service networks, embezzlement, copyright piracy (software, movie, sound recording), child pornography, planting of viruses and worms, password trafficking, e-mail bombing, and spam.

Computer Forensic Flaws and Risks

☑ The field of forensic is in the developmental stage.

☑ There is no standardization of tools, and forensic investigations are more an art than a science.

Computer Forensics: Rules, Procedures, and Legal Issues

☑ Digital forensics is preserving, collecting, confirming, identifying, analyzing, recording, and presenting crime scene information.

☑ Good forensic rules minimize the damage to original evidence.

☑ Always prepare a chain of custody and make sure to document any change in evidence.

The Computer Forensic Lab

☑ The need and demand for expert forensic examiners and forensic data investigation facilities are on the rise; this demand is fueled by mankind's ever increasing leverage of and reliance on digital technology for communication, productivity, and knowledge management (for purposes both benign and malign).

☑ Digital forensic analysis plays an increasingly important role in modern civil and criminal investigation; contemporary legal precedent has validated electronically stored information (ESI) as a discrete class of evidential entity and has created new standards for ESI discovery and ESI as evidence in judicial settings.

Laboratory Strategic Planning for Business

☑ A digital forensics facility is a business venue, technology venue, scientific venue, and artistic venue.

☑ Define a core mission statement and scope of service; build manpower, architecture, and asset bases with the intent to achieve operational excellence and successful growth.

☑ An investigative operation is only as good as the investments in human talent and equipment allow. Invest wisely and often.

Elements of Facilities Build-out

☑ A data forensics facility should accommodate administrative space and examination space. It should have room for a significant and expanding technology footprint and a secure, hardened environment dedicated to evidence storage.

☑ A data forensics facility will have many of the same architectural attributes as a data colocation facility: emphasis should be placed on redundancies, specialized abatements, and robust implementation of core services, such as electricity and specialized fire control systems.

Electrical and Plant Considerations

☑ A strategy for provision of electricity, in terms of both amount and ease of access, should be defined in terms of general facility consumption, examination environment consumption, and personal workspace consumption.

☑ Customized abatement strategies will include aggressive temperature and humidity control, antistatic measures, electromagnetic interference shielding, and acoustic balancing.

☑ Robust facilities security is mandatory: a robust mechanism for access control and the ability to completely document all activity within the system must exist.

Essential Laboratory Tools

☑ One main mission of any forensic data-handling process is to preserve the integrity of electronic evidence: write prevention technologies, including both hardware and software forms, are essential tools in any forensic data toolkit.

☑ Data duplication, publication, and destruction technologies are required for evidence replication and digital work product processing.

☑ Multiple vendors offer integrated investigations platforms that combine the availability of multiple write block devices, numerous device interface options, multiple operating systems, and high-volume data storage. These investigation platform options scale from "carry-on" portable systems to permanent, immobile enterprise-level solutions.

Exam Objectives
Frequently Asked Questions

The following Frequently Asked Questions, answered by the authors of this book, are designed to both measure your understanding of the Exam Objectives presented in this chapter, and to assist you with real-life implementation of these concepts.

Q: What is data spoliation?

A: Merriam-Webster.com defines spoliation as "the act of injuring especially beyond reclaim." With regard to data spoliation, such injury may take the form of introduction of change to the physical media or to the digital content stream so as to alter any element of accessibility, completeness, or content. In fact, failure to document proper custodianship of the digital evidence may be sufficient to introduce a claim of spoliation, even if all other protective methodology is executed properly.

Q: What measures should a data forensics laboratory have in place to prevent spoliation of evidence?

A: A forensics operation will have many defenses against spoliation. Specific hardware and software tools, rigorous documentation of chain of custody, well-defined and trained methodologies, and continuing education of forensic personnel are all ways to combat the possibility of evidence spoliation.

Q: What are some of the abatement strategies a specialized electronics environment may want to consider during build-out?

A: Temperature control, humidity control, static electricity reduction, electromagnetic shielding, and acoustic balancing are all possible considerations during laboratory design.

Q: What is the most important resource associated with any digital investigations practice?

A: Human talent.

Q: Is it important to maintain the licensing on products utilized during investigations?

A: Yes. If any hardware, software, or services utilized are subject to licensing agreements, those licensing agreements must be valid. Installing, distributing, or utilizing unlicensed tools may be in violation of the law; evidence procured as a result of an illegal act may be deemed inadmissible (and the investigator may be held accountable for illegal acts).

Q: When I am utilizing hardware and software tools to execute forensic analysis, is it sufficient to have mastered the mechanics of the tools?

A: No. It is also necessary to be able to describe and demonstrate how the tools achieve their results and to test the tools to prove that they work as expected.

Notes

1. *Cyber Crime Investigations: Bridging the Gaps between Security Professionals, Law Enforcement, and Prosecutors* (Elsevier Inc., 2007).

CHFI

Systems, Disks, and Media

Exam objectives in this chapter:

- **File Systems and Hard Disks**
- **Digital Media Devices**
- **Image File Forensics**

Exam Objectives Review:

- ☑ **Summary of Exam Objectives**
- ☑ **Exam Objectives Fast Track**
- ☑ **Exam Objectives Frequently Asked Questions**

Introduction

Data is the driving force of any system that uses computers. Data availability is the reason the Internet became popular, and the ability to modify, store, process, and retrieve data is a major reason why computers are used in homes and businesses around the world. The term *storage media* usually refers to a means of storing data permanently, and numerous methods can be used to store data more or less permanently on several different media types. These methods include storing data magnetically on a disk or using optical disks.

In this chapter, we'll look at various types of fixed and removable media, and learn how they store (and sometimes lose) data. We'll also look at one of the most common data types that is saved to media and analyzed in computer forensic examinations: images. *Image files* comprise digital photos, line art, and other graphical representations of people, places, and objects that can be saved to a storage device or other medium. As we'll see, these files can be created in a variety of different formats, and numerous techniques and tools can be used to view and recover damaged files.

File Systems and Hard Disks

Hard disks are nonvolatile storage devices that are used to store and retrieve data quickly. *Nonvolatile storage* is physical media that retains data without electrical power. This means that no data is lost when the computer is powered off, making hard disks suitable for permanent storage of information. As we'll discuss in the sections that follow, a hard disk drive (HDD) writes digital data as magnetic patterns to rigid disks that are stored inside the HDD. Because the HDD is installed in the computer, it is able to access and process the data faster than removable media such as floppy disks.

File systems are used to organize and locate data stored on a hard disk. Although many file systems have been developed over the years, they all perform the same basic tasks of controlling how directories and files are stored and organized on physical media. To put it another way, the hard disk is like a library that contains books, whereas the file system is comparable to the Dewey Decimal System that's used to determine where those books are placed on the shelves.

Although hard disks have been used for decades in computers, their use has expanded to other forms of technology. Today you can find camcorders, game systems, and digital video recorders that use hard disks to store data, instead of magnetic tapes or other media. Regardless of their use, hard disks and their related file systems perform the same tasks of storing data so that it can be retrieved, processed, and viewed at a later time.

Overview of a Hard Disk

Although removable hard disks exist, most HDDs are designed for installation inside a computer, and for that reason they were referred to as *fixed disks*. To avoid having to purchase custom or proprietary hard disks to fit inside different brands of computer, standards were developed early in the PC's history. These standards dictate the size and shape of the hard disk,

as well as the interfaces used to attach it to the computer. These standards are called *form factors*, and they refer to the physical external dimensions of the disk drive. The most common form factors that have been used over the past few decades are:

- **5.25-inch** These were the first hard drives that were used on PCs, and they were commonly installed in machines during the 1980s.

- **3.5-inch** This is the common size of form factor used in modern PCs.

- **2.5-inch** This is the common size of form factor used in laptop/notebook computers.

NOTE

The two most common sizes of hard disk are the 2.5-inch form factor (used for laptops) and 3.5-inch form factor (used for PCs). The numbers are generally but not always associated with the width of the drive's platter (or sometimes the drive itself). The 3.5-inch drives are generally 4 inches wide and use a platter that's 3.74 inches wide. They're called 3.5-inch form factor drives because they fit in the bay for a 3.5-inch floppy drive. Similarly, the obsolete 5.25-inch form factor was named as such because it fit in the 5.25-inch floppy drive bay.

The 5.25-inch disk drive is obsolete, although you still can find some in legacy machines. The first of these drives appeared on the market in 1980, but were succeeded in 1983 when the 3.5-inch drives appeared. When these became available, they were either mounted into the computer case's 3.5-inch floppy drive bays, or screwed into frames that allowed the 3.5-inch form factor to fit into the larger 5.25-inch bays.

Even though the 3.5-inch form factor has been around for more than two decades, it continues to be the common size used in modern desktop computers. The other popular form factor is the 2.5-inch disk, which is used in laptop computers. Figure 2.1 shows a 3.5-inch form factor hard disk on the left, and a 2.5-inch form factor drive on the right. When comparing the two, you can immediately notice the difference in size, and see that both encase the internal mechanisms of the disk drive inside a sturdy metal case. This is to prevent dust and other foreign elements from coming into contact with the internal components, which (as we'll see later) would case the disk to cease functioning.

Figure 2.1 Hard Disks

In looking at the 3.5-inch hard disk depicted on the left of Figure 2.1, you can see that it has several connections that allow it to be installed in a computer. The 2.5-inch hard disk doesn't have these components because it is installed differently in a laptop; a cover is removed from the laptop (generally on the back of the computer), where the 2.5-inch HDD is inserted into a slot. The 3.5-inch HDD needs to be installed in the computer using the following components on the outside of the HDD:

- Jumpers
- Hard disk interface
- Power connector

A *jumper* is a connector that works as an on/off switch for the hard disk. A small piece of plastic with metal connectors inside is placed over two of the metal pins to create an electrical circuit. The existence of the circuit lets the computer know whether the hard disk is configured in one of the following two roles:

- **Master** This is the primary hard disk that is installed on a computer. The master is the first hard disk that the computer will attempt to access when booting up (i.e., starting), and it generally contains the operating system that will be loaded. If only one hard disk is installed on a machine, that hard disk is the master drive.
- **Slave** This is the secondary hard disk that is installed on a computer. Slave drives are generally used for additional data storage, and as a place to install additional software.

TEST DAY TIP

The terms *master* and *slave* for hard disks have undergone some criticism in recent years, due to the political incorrectness of the terms. In reading material and on questions in exams, you may see them referred to as *primary* and *secondary* hard disks instead.

The *power connector* on a hard disk is used to plug the hard disk into the computer's power supply. A power cable running from the power supply is attached to the hard disk, allowing it to receive power when the computer is started.

The *hard disk interface* is used to attach the hard disk to the computer so that data can be accessed from the HDD. The hard disk interface shown in Figure 2.1 is an IDE hard disk interface, which is one of the most popular interfaces used on HDDs. A thin, flat cable containing parallel wires called a *ribbon cable* is inserted into the interface on the HDD, and the other end of the ribbon cable is plugged into the disk drive controller. In doing so, the computer can communicate with the HDD and access its data. (We'll discuss hard disk interfaces in greater detail later in this chapter.)

Head of the Class...

The Evolution of Hard Disks

The hard disk is usually the primary permanent storage medium in a PC. However, the earliest PCs didn't have hard disks. In fact, early computers (prior to the PC) didn't have any sort of data storage medium. You had to type in every program that you wanted to run, each time you ran it. Later, punched cards or tape was used to store programs and data. The next advancement in technology brought us magnetic tape storage; large mainframes used big reels of tape, whereas early microcomputers used audiocassette tapes to store programs and data. By the time the IBM PC and its clones appeared, computers were using floppy disks (the 5.25-inch type that really was floppy). More expensive models had two floppy drives (which we'll discuss later in this chapter)—one for loading programs and a second for saving data—but still no hard disk.

The first hard disks that came with PCs provided 5 megabytes (MB) of storage space—a huge amount, compared to floppies. The IBM PC XT came with a gigantic 10MB hard disk. Today's hard disks are generally measured in hundreds of gigabytes (GB), at prices far lower than those first comparatively tiny disks, with arrays of them measured in terabytes (TB). Despite the fact that they're much bigger, much faster, less fragile, and more reliable, today's hard disks are designed basically the same way as those of years ago.

Disk Platter

Although there are a number of external elements to a hard disk, the major components are inside the HDD. As shown in Figure 2.2, hard disks are composed of one to several platters, which are flat, round disks that are mounted inside the platter. The platters are stacked one on top of another on a spindle that runs through a hole in the middle of each platter, like LPs on an old-time record player. A motor attached to the spindle rotates the platters, which are made of rigid material (often aluminum alloy, glass, or a glass composite) and are coated with a magnetic substance. Electromagnetic heads write information onto the disks in the form of magnetic impulses and read the recorded information from them.

Figure 2.2 Internal Components of a Hard Disk

Data can be written to both sides of each platter. The information is recorded in tracks, which are concentric circles in which the data is written. The tracks are divided into sectors (smaller units). Thus, a particular bit of data resides in a specific sector of a specific track on a specific platter. Later in this chapter, when we discuss computer operating systems and file systems, you will see how the data is organized so that users can locate it on the disk.

The spindles of a hard disk spin the platters at high speeds, with the spindles on most IDE hard disks spinning platters at thousands of revolutions per minute (RPM). The read/write head moves over the platter and reads or writes data to the platter. When there is more than one platter in the hard disk, each platter usually has a read/write head on each of its sides.

Smaller platter sizes do more than save space inside the computer; they also improve disk performance (seek time) because the heads don't have to move as far.

To read and write the magnetic information on the hard disk, the read/write head of the HDD is positioned incredibly close to the platter. It floats less than 0.1 microns over the surface of the platter. A *micron* (or *micrometer*) is one-millionth of a meter, meaning that the read/write head is less than $1/10^{th}$ of a millionth of a meter from the platter's surface. To illustrate this, Figure 2.3 shows a comparison of the sizes of a read/write head, an average dust particle (which is 2.5 microns), and an average human hair (which is 50 microns). In looking at the differences in size, it is easy to see how a simple piece of dust or hair on a platter could cause the hard disk to crash, and why the internal components are sealed inside the hard disk assembly.

Figure 2.3 Comparison of Objects to a Read/Write Head's Distance from the Platter

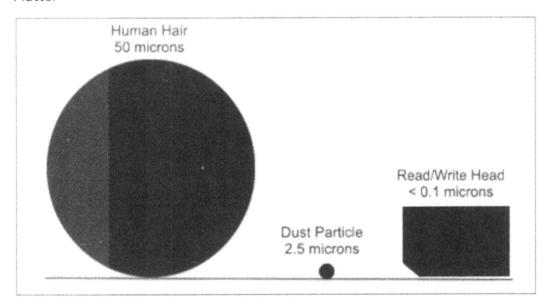

Hard Disk Sizes

IBM introduced its first hard disk in 1956, but the real "grandfather" of today's hard disks was the Winchester drive, which wasn't introduced until the 1970s. The standard physical size of disks at that time was 14 inches (the size of the platters that are stacked to make up the disk). In 1979, IBM made an 8-inch disk, and Seagate followed that in 1980 with the first 5.25-inch hard disk, which was used in early PCs. Three years later, disks got even smaller when the 3.5-inch disk was introduced. This became a standard for PCs. Much smaller disks (2.5 inches) were later developed for use in laptop and notebook computers. The IBM "microdrive" shrunk the diameter of the platter to 1 inch, connecting to a laptop computer via a PC Card (also called PCMCIA, for the Personal Computer Memory Card International Association that created the standard).

Tracks

While the platters in a hard disk spin, the read/write head moves into a position on the platter where it can read data. The part of the platter passing under the read/write head is called a track. *Tracks* are concentric circles on the disk where data is saved on the magnetic surface of the platter. These thin concentric rings or bands are shown in Figure 2.4, and although a full number of tracks aren't shown in this figure, a single 3.5-inch hard disk can have thousands of tracks. The tracks hold data, and pass beneath the stationary read/write head as the platter rotates.

Figure 2.4 Track on a Hard Disk

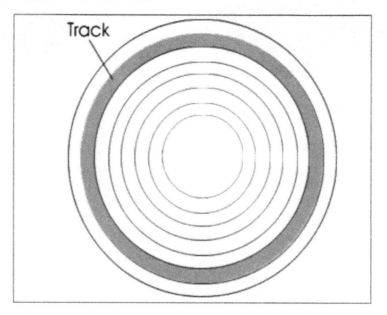

Tracks and sectors (which we'll discuss in the next section) are physically defined through the process of low-level formatting (LLF), which designates where the tracks and sectors are located on each disk. Although in the 1980s people would perform an LLF on their hard disks themselves, today this is typically done at the factory where the hard disks are made. It is necessary for the tracks and sectors to be present so that the areas where data is written to are visible to the disk controller, and the operating system can perform a high-level format and generate the file structure.

Because there are so many tracks on a platter, they are numbered so that the computer can reference the correct one when reading and writing data. The tracks are numbered from zero to the highest numbered track (which is typically 1,023), starting from the outermost edge of the disk to the track nearest the center of the platter. In other words, the first track on the disk is the track on the outer edge of the platter, and the highest numbered disk is close to the center.

NOTE

Although we discuss tracks and sectors on hard disks here, other media also use these methods of formatting the surface of a disk to store data. For example, a 1.44MB floppy disk has 160 tracks.

Sector

Sectors are segments of a track, and the smallest physical storage unit on a disk. As mentioned previously, a hard disk is composed of predefined tracks that form concentric rings on the disk. As seen in Figure 2.5, the disk is further organized by dividing the platter into pie slices, which also divide the tracks into smaller segments. These segments are called sectors, and they are typically 512 bytes (0.5KB) in size. By knowing the track number and particular sector in which a piece of data is stored, a computer is able to locate where data is physically stored on the disk.

Figure 2.5 Sectors on a Hard Disk

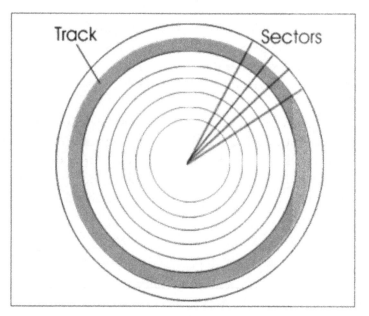

Just as tracks on a hard disk are numbered, an addressing scheme is associated with sectors. When a low-level format is performed at the factory, a number is assigned to the sector immediately before the sector's contents. This number in this header identifies the sector address, so it can be located on the disk.

Bad Sectors

At times, areas of a hard disk can be damaged, making them unusable. *Bad sectors* are sectors of a hard disk that cannot store data due to a manufacturing defect or accidental damage. When sectors become unusable, it means that only those areas of the disk cannot be used, not the entire disk itself. When you consider that an average 3.5-inch disk will have more than a thousand tracks that are further segmented into millions of sectors, it isn't surprising that over the lifetime of a disk, a few sectors will eventually go bad.

Because bad sectors mean that damage has occurred at the surface of the disk, the disk cannot be repaired, and any data stored in that area of the hard disk is lost. That area can, however, be marked as bad, so the operating system or other software doesn't write to this area again. To check and mark sectors as being unusable, special utilities are used. Programs such as ScanDisk and CheckDisk (*CHKDSK* in DOS 8.3 notation) have been available under versions of Windows, whereas Badblocks is a tool used on Linux systems. Each can detect a sector that has been damaged and mark it as bad.

EXERCISE 2.1

CHECKING FOR BAD SECTORS ON WINDOWS XP

In this exercise, we'll check a system for bad sectors using CheckDisk, a tool used on Windows NT, 2000, 2003, XP, and Vista machines. Older versions of Windows use another tool called ScanDisk to check for bad sectors.

1. Click on the Windows Start menu.

2. Select Programs | Accessories and then click on the Command Prompt menu item. Alternatively, you can click on the Run menu item, and when the Run dialog box appears, you can type CMD in the field labeled Open and then click OK.

3. When the Command Prompt appears, type CHKDSK /R /F to check the current drive and fix any errors on the disk. Alternatively, you can use any combination of the switches listed in Table 2.1 with the CHKDSK command.

Table 2.1 Switches Used with the *CHKDSK* Command

Switch	Description
Volume	The drive letter followed by a colon, which specifies the drive to check. For example, *CHKDSK C:* would check the C: drive for errors.
Filename	The filename to check for fragmentation. For example, *CHKDSK C:\autoexec.bat* would check the autoexec.bat file for fragmentation. This switch is used only on FAT and FAT32 file systems.
/F	Specifies that any errors found should be automatically fixed.
/V	On NTFS file systems, any cleanup messages are displayed. On FAT/FAT32 file systems, the full path of every file checked is displayed.
/R	Specifies that bad sectors are to be located and any readable information should be recovered.
/L:size	On NTFS file systems, this switch is used to specify the size of the log file in kilobytes. If the size isn't specified, the current log file size is displayed.
/X	Forces the volume to dismount if necessary.

Continued

Table 2.1 continued Switches Used with the *CHKDSK* Command

Switch	Description
/I	On NTFS file systems, this indicates that a less vigorous check of index entries should be performed.
/C	On NTFS file systems, this skips checking cycles within the folder structure.

4. If an error message displays stating that the current volume is being used, press the **Y** key on your keyboard so that CHKDSK will check the disk the next time the operating system is started.

Disk Capacity

Disk capacity is the amount of data that a hard disk is capable of holding. The capacity is measured in bytes, which is 7 or 8 bits (depending on whether error correction is used). A *bit* is short for binary digit (where the first two letters of *binary* and the T in *bit* are used to create the name), and it is the smallest unit of measurement for data. It can have a value of 1 or 0, which respectively indicates on or off. A bit is abbreviated as *b*, whereas a byte is abbreviated as *B*. Because bits and bytes are incredibly small measurements of data, and the capacity of an HDD or other medium is considerably larger, capacity is measured in increments of these values.

A *kilobyte* is abbreviated as KB, and although you might expect this to equal 1,000 bytes, it actually equals 1,024 bytes. This is because a kilobyte is calculated using binary (base 2) math instead of decimal (base 10) math. Because computers use this function to calculate the number of bytes used, a kilobyte is calculated as 2^{10} or 1,024. These values increase proportionally, but to make it easier for laypeople to understand, the terms associated with the number of bytes are incremented by thousands, millions, and larger numbers of bytes. The various units used to describe the capacity of disks are as follows:

- Kilobyte (KB), which is actually 1,024 bytes
- Megabyte (MB), which is 1,024KB or 1,048,576 bytes
- Gigabyte (GB), which is 1,024MB or 1,073,741,824 bytes
- Terabyte (TB), which is 1,024GB or 1,099,511,627,776 bytes
- Petabyte (PB), which is 1,024TB or 1,125,899,906,842,624 bytes
- Exabyte (EB), which is 1,024PB or 1,152,921,504,606,846,976 bytes

- Zettabyte (ZB), which is 1,024EB or 1,180,591,620,717,411,303,424 bytes

- Yottabyte (YB), which is 1,024ZB or 1,208,925,819,614,629,174,706,176 bytes

To put these monumental sizes in terms that are fathomable, consider that a single terabyte can hold roughly the equivalent of 1,610 CDs of data, or approximately the same amount of data stored in all the books of a large library.

TEST DAY TIP

Although you shouldn't expect to see any questions dealing directly with differences in file size (e.g., "Which is larger, an exabyte or a zettabyte?"), it may be useful to refresh your memory regarding which of them *is* larger. Questions may indirectly address the size of a particular storage medium, and understanding what is being said could help you to determine a correct answer.

Calculating Disk Capacity

Hard disk capacity is determined by elements of the disk, including the number of tracks, sectors, and surfaces on which data can be written. As we've seen, these elements determine how the HDD accesses data, and the amount of data that can be written to a disk. The capacity of a hard disk drive can be calculated using the following formula:

Capacity = (bytes/sector) * (sectors/track) * (tracks/surface) * # of surfaces

If we were to look at the specifications of the following hard disk, we could use the information to calculate the disk capacity of the drive:

- Bytes per sector: 512

- Sectors/track (avg): 426

- Total tracks: 43,152

- Total cylinders: 14,384

- Number of heads: 3

In looking at these specifications of an actual hard disk, you will notice that the tracks/surface is not provided, but we are given the total tracks and number of physical heads. This is common to many hard disk specifications. However, because each head reads the surface of the disk, this gives us the number of surfaces on the HDD. Using this information, we could divide the total tracks by the number of heads (i.e., 43,152 / 3) to get the tracks/surface, or we could simply revise the formula to:

Capacity = (bytes/sector) * (sectors/track) * total tracks

Using the preceding formula, we would find the disk capacity as follows:

512 bytes/sector * 426 sectors/track * 43,152 total tracks = 9411969024 or 9.4GB

Hard Disk Interfaces

The *hard disk interface* is one of several standard technologies used to connect the hard disk to the computer so that the machine can access data stored on the hard disk. The interface used by an HDD serves as a communication channel, allowing data to flow between the computer and the HDD. Over the years, a number of different interfaces have been developed, allowing the hard disk to be connected to a disk controller that's usually mounted directly on the computer's motherboard. The most common hard disk interfaces include:

- IDE/EIDE/ATA
- SCSI
- USB
- Fibre Channel

IDE/EIDE/ATA

IDE is an acronym for Integrated Drive Electronics, and *EIDE* is an acronym for Enhanced IDE. Integrated Drive Electronics is so named because the disk controller is built into, or integrated with, the disk drive's logic board. It is also referred to as Advanced Technology Attachment (ATA), a standard of the American National Standards Institute (ANSI). Almost all modern PC motherboards include two EIDE connectors. Up to two ATA devices (hard disks or CD-ROM drives) can be connected to each connector, in a master/slave configuration. One drive functions as the "master," which responds first to probes or signals on the *interrupt* (a signal from a device or program to the operating system that causes the OS to stop briefly to determine what task to do next) that is shared with the other, "slave" drive that shares the same cable. User-configurable settings on the drives determine which will act as master and which as slave. Most drives have three settings: master, slave, and cable-controlled. If the latter is selected for both drives, the first drive in the chain will be the master drive.

SCSI

SCSI (pronounced "skuzzy") is an acronym for Small Computer System Interface. SCSI is another ANSI standard that provides faster data transfer than IDE/EIDE. Some motherboards have SCSI connectors and controllers built in; for those that don't you can add SCSI disks by installing a SCSI controller card in one of the expansion slots. There are a number of different

versions of SCSI; later forms provide faster transfer rates and other improvements. Devices can be "chained" on a SCSI bus, each with a different SCSI ID number. Depending on the SCSI version, either eight or 16 SCSI IDs can be attached to one controller (with the controller using one ID, thus allowing seven or 15 SCSI peripherals).

USB

USB is an acronym for Universal Serial Bus. As we'll discuss later in this chapter, USB is used for a variety of different peripherals, including keyboards, mice, and other devices that previously required serial and parallel ports, as well as newer technologies such as digital cameras and digital audio devices. Because these devices are based on a bus topology, they can be daisy-chained together or connected to a USB hub, allowing up to 127 devices to be connected to the computer at one time.

In addition to peripherals, USB provides an interface for external hard disks. Hard disks can be mounted in cases that provide a USB connection which plugs into a USB port on the computer. Once the connection is plugged into the port, the computer detects the device and installs it, allowing you to access any data on the external hard disk. The current standard for USB is USB 2.0, which is backward-compatible to earlier 1.0 and 1.1 standards, and supports bandwidths of 1.5Mbps (megabits per second), 12.5Mbps, and 480Mbps. Using an external USB hard disk that supports USB 2.0 provides a fast exchange of data between the computer and the HDD.

Fibre Channel

Fibre channel is another ANSI standard that provides fast data transfer, and uses optical fiber to connect devices. Several different standards apply to fibre channels, but the one that primarily applies to storage is Fibre Channel Arbitrated Loop (FC-AL). FC-AL is designed for mass storage devices, and it is used for Storage Area Networks (SANs). A SAN is a network architecture in which computers attach to remote storage devices such as optical jukeboxes, disk arrays, tape libraries, and other mass storage devices. Because optical fiber is used to connect devices, FC-AL supports transfer rates of 100Mbps, and is expected to replace SCSI for network storage systems.

File Systems

File systems or *file management systems* are systems that the operating system uses to organize and locate data stored on a hard disk. File systems may manage storage media such as hard disks, and control how sectors on the drive are used to store and access files. In doing so, it will keep track of which sectors are used to store files, and which are empty and available for use. In the complex world of networks, however, this isn't always the case. Network file systems aren't used to manage the HDD, but instead provide a way to present a client with access to data on a remote server.

Many file systems are *hierarchical file systems* in which the data is organized as a tree structure. As seen in Figure 2.6, a hierarchical file system looks like an inverted tree. At the base of the structure is a root directory, and directories (or *folders*, as they're now called in Windows) branch out from the root. These directories are containers that can be used to store files or other directories. These directories within directories are called *subdirectories* (or subfolders). As we'll see later in this chapter, the file system will keep track of how this organization translates to directories and files that are stored on the disk so that when a particular directory is opened, the files in that directory are displayed properly and can be located on the hard disk.

Figure 2.6 Hierarchical Directory Structure

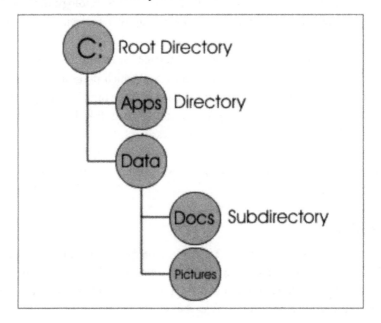

File systems keep track of this structure (the directories and the files contained within those directories) using different methods. As we'll discuss in the next section, the FAT file system uses a File Allocation Table that will manage where the file is stored on the hard disk, as well as other aspects of how you name and can access the file. In earlier operating systems, such as MS-DOS, the FAT file system allowed files to be named with only eight characters, with a period separating the name from a three-character extension. For example, a document might be named DOCUMENT.DOC using this 8.3 notation. When Windows 95 was developed, long filenames were supported that allowed files to have names of up to 255 characters. The file system stores this and other information within the file, along with properties identifying the owner of a file, when it was created, and attributes that control access to the file (such as whether it is read-only or can be modified).

Microsoft File Systems

Different operating systems use different file systems, and some operating systems support more than one file system. The most familiar are those used by the Microsoft operating systems:

- FAT12
- FAT16
- VFAT
- FAT32
- NTFS

In the following sections, we will look at some of the characteristics of each file system, along with some less commonly encountered file systems used by networks and non-Microsoft operating systems.

FAT12

FAT stands for File Allocation Table; the FAT file system was developed for use by the DOS operating systems. The first version of FAT was called FAT12 because its allocation tables used a 12-digit binary number (12 bits) for cluster information (which we'll discuss later in this chapter). FAT12 was useful for the very small hard disks that came with the original IBM PC (less than 16MB in size). It is also used to format floppy diskettes.

FAT16

FAT16 was developed for disks larger than 16MB, and for a long time it was the standard file system for formatting hard disks. As you can probably guess, it uses 16-bit allocation table entries. FAT16 (often referred to as just FAT) is supported by all Microsoft operating systems, from MS-DOS to Windows XP. It is also supported by some non-Microsoft operating systems, including OS/2 and Linux.

This support makes it the most universally compatible file system. However, it has many drawbacks, including the following:

- FAT16 doesn't scale well to large disks; because the cluster size increases as the disk partition size increases, a large disk (larger than about 2GB) formatted with FAT16 will have a lot of wasted space.

- FAT16 doesn't support file-level compression; the compression scheme used with FAT16, such as that implemented by DriveSpace, requires that the entire logical drive be compressed.

- FAT16 doesn't support *file-level security* (assignment of permissions to individual files and folders).

NOTE

You may read in some sources that FAT16 is limited to 2GB in size, but that's not really the case (although it does become inefficient at larger disk sizes). MS-DOS will not allow you to create a FAT16 partition larger than 2GB, but you can create larger FAT16 partitions (up to 4GB) in Windows NT/2000. These larger FAT16 partitions are not supported and recognized by MS-DOS or Windows 9x.

VFAT

Virtual FAT, or *VFAT*, is a file system driver that was introduced in Windows for Workgroups 3.11 and supported by Windows 95. Its advantages are that it operates in protected mode and enables you to use long filenames with FAT16. VFAT is not a file system; rather, it is a program extension that handles filenames over the 8.3 limitation imposed by the original FAT16.

FAT32

FAT32 uses a 32-bit allocation table. It was first supported by the OSR 2 version of Windows 95 (95b) and was designed to improve on the functionality of FAT16 by adding features such as the following:

- More efficient use of space with large hard disks by using smaller cluster sizes

- Support for larger partitions, up to 2TB in size, in theory (Windows supports FAT32 partitions of up to 32GB)

- Greater reliability, due to the inclusion of a backup copy of important data structure information in the boot record

FAT32 also has its disadvantages, including the fact that it is incompatible with MS-DOS, Windows 3.x, Windows 95a, Windows NT, and some non-Microsoft operating systems (although FAT32 drivers are available from third-party vendors for Windows 95, NT, and even non-Microsoft operating systems such as Linux). Additionally, the overhead used by FAT32 can slow performance slightly.

NTFS

NTFS is an acronym for *New Technology File System*, and it is the most secure file system offered for computers running Microsoft Windows operating systems. Since a technology can be "new" for only a limited amount of time and NTFS was first released in 1993, today it is referred to by its initials rather than the full name. NTFS was designed as a replacement for the

FAT file system on Windows NT operating systems, including successive releases such as Windows 2000, 2003 Server, XP, and Vista.

NTFS was designed to be more robust and secure than other Microsoft file systems. You can see this in part by how it handles partitions. As we'll see later in this chapter, partitions are logical divisions of a hard disk, allowing you to divide the space on a hard disk so that it functions as separate drives. For example, you could partition a hard disk to appear as a C: drive, D: drive, and so on, on the computer. NTFS supports very large partition sizes (up to 16EB, in theory) and allows you to create volumes that span two or more partitions.

NTFS is also more reliable because it supports a feature called *hot fixing*, a process by which the operating system detects a bad sector on the disk and automatically relocates the data stored on that sector to a good sector, and then marks the bad sector so that the system won't use it. This process is done on the fly, without the awareness or intervention of the user or applications.

TEST DAY TIP

You can expect to see a number of questions directly or indirectly dealing with file systems. Because Microsoft manufactures the most widely used operating and file systems, you should review the various Microsoft file systems before taking the exam.

Metadata and the Master File Table (MFT)

Metadata is information about a particular set of data, and can include such information as who created a file, its size, and other technical information hidden from the common user. In other words, metadata is data about data. It can be used to describe a file, its format, when it was created, and other information. NTFS stores data about files, users, and other information used by the system in the form of special files that are hidden on the system. When a disk is formatted to use NTFS, these files are created, and their locations are stored in one of these files, called the *Master File Table* (MFT). Table 2.2 lists the special system files that NTFS creates to store metadata, and their location in the MFT.

Table 2.2 Special Files Created by NTFS, and Metadata Stored About Them in the Master File Table

MFT Record	System File	Filename	Description
0	Master File Table	$Mft	Stores information on files and folders on an NTFS volume
1	Master File Table 2	$MftMirr	Mirror of the first four records in the MFT
2	Log file	$LogFile	Transaction log that can be used for file recovery
3	Volume	$Volume	Stores information about the volume, including its label and version information
4	Attribute definitions	$AttrDef	Table of names, numbers, and descriptions of attributes used in NTFS
5	Root filename index	$	Root folder
6	Cluster bitmap	$Bitmap	Representation of which clusters are used on the volume
7	Boot cluster file	$Boot	Stores information needed to mount the volume. If the volume is bootable, it also contains bootstrap loader code.
8	Bad cluster file	$BadClus	Stores information on bad clusters on a volume
9	Security file	$Secure	Stores unique security descriptors of files
10	Upcase table	$Upcase	Stores information used to convert lowercase characters to uppercase Unicode characters
11	NTFS extension file	$Extend	Stores information for optional extensions, such as quotas and object identifiers
12–15	Unused/reserved for future use		

Whereas the FAT file system uses a File Allocation Table to keep track of files, NTFS uses a Master File Table to perform similar (albeit more complex) functions. When a disk is formatted to use the NTFS file system, an MFT is created to keep track of each file on the volume. As seen in Table 2.2, the first record of the table describes the MFT itself, and a mirror of this information is stored in the second record in case the first record is corrupted. The third record in the MFT is a log that is used to recover files, and the bulk of the remaining records are used to keep track of each file and folder in the NTFS volume, as well as the attributes of those files. Keeping track of the files in a table enables you to access them quickly from the hard disk.

NTFS Attributes

One of the records stored in the MFT deals with NTFS attributes. NTFS views each file and directory as a set of file attributes, consisting of such information as its name, data, and security information. *Attributes* are data that define a file, and are used by the operating system and other software to determine how a file is accessed and used. In the MFT, a code is associated with each attribute, and may contain information on the attribute's name and description. In NTFS, two different kinds of attributes can be used:

- **Resident attributes** These can fit in an MFT record. The name of the file and the timestamp are always included as resident attributes.

- **Nonresident attributes** These are allocated to one or more clusters elsewhere on the disk. These are used when information about a file is too large to fit in the MFT.

As seen in Table 2.3, a number of attributes can be associated with files and directories stored on an NTFS volume. To identify the location of all of the records associated with file attributes, NTFS uses an attribute list. The list contains attributes defined by NTFS, and allows additional attributes to be added later.

Table 2.3 Common NTFS File Attributes

Attribute	Description
Attribute List	Location of records which are not stored in the MFT record
Bitmap	Contains the cluster allocation bitmap, which is used by the $Bitmap file
Data	Contains data associated with the file. By default, all data is stored in a single attribute, even if it is split into separate pieces due to its size.
Filename	Name of the file. This includes its 8.3-character short name, 255-character long name, and other names or links required to identify the file.

Continued

Table 2.3 continued Common NTFS File Attributes

Attribute	Description
Index Root	Index of files contained in a directory. If the index is small (i.e., a few files in a directory), the entire index will fit in this MFT attribute. If the index is large, an external index buffer may be used to store additional information.
Index Allocation	When an index is too large, this attribute is used to store pointers to index buffer entries. This allows the MFT to access the remaining index information for a directory.
Security Descriptor	Identifies the owner of the file, and who can access it. This attribute contains security information that controls access to a file or directory. Information on ownership, auditing, and access control lists (ACLs) is stored in this attribute.
Standard information	Basic information about the file, including whether a file is read-only, hidden, and so on, as well as timestamps showing when a file was created, modified, and last accessed
Object ID	Used to identify the file. The Object ID is a volume-unique file identifier, meaning that no two files on a volume will have the same Object ID.
Volume Name	Used to store information about the NTFS volume's name. Used by the $Volume file.
Volume Information	Attributes used to store information about the NTFS volume. Used by the $Volume file.
Volume Version	Attributes used to store version information about the NTFS volume. Used by the $Volume file.

From the administrator's and user's point of view, these attributes can be modified on the file or folder by using the file or accessing its properties. For example, by modifying the filename, you are modifying the Filename attribute. Similarly, opening a file will change timestamp information regarding when the file was last accessed. By accessing the properties of a file, you can set access permissions at the file level to control who can read, change, or otherwise access a file. This applies to users accessing the file from the local machine as well as over the network and is in addition to network share permissions that are set at the folder/directory level.

NTFS Compressed Files

NTFS allows files to be compressed to save space by compressing an entire NTFS volume, or on a file-by-file basis. With NTFS compression, individual folders or files can be compressed, or everything on a particular drive can be compressed using the NTFS file system. In doing so, a file is decompressed automatically when it is read, and compressed when it is saved or closed. Compressing data allows you to save disk space and archive folders, without having to rely on additional software to compress and decompress files.

When data is compressed on an NTFS drive, only the file system can read it. When a program attempts to open a file that's been compressed, the file system's compression drive must first decompress the file before making it available.

NTFS Encrypting File Systems (EFS)

Encryption is the process of encoding a file so that it can't be read by anyone other than those who are authorized to open and view the data. Users who aren't authorized will be denied access to the file, and will be unable to open, copy, move, or rename a file or folder that's been encrypted. Encryption may be used on a single file or on an entire disk.

Disk encryption refers to encrypting the entire contents of a hard disk, diskette, or removable disk. *File encryption* refers to encrypting data stored on a disk on a file-by-file basis. In either case, the goal is to prevent unauthorized people from opening and reading files that are stored on the disk. Support for disk/file encryption can be built into an operating system or file system. NTFS v5, the native file system for Windows 2000, 2003 Server, XP, and Vista, includes the Encrypting File System (EFS), which can be used to protect data on a hard disk or large removable disk. EFS can't be used to protect data on floppy diskettes because they cannot be formatted in NTFS format, but allows encryption of individual files and/or folders. Because EFS is integrated with the operating system, the processes of encryption and decryption are invisible to the user.

EFS relies on public key cryptography and digital certificates. Public key cryptography involves two mathematically related keys, one called the *public key* and another called the *private key*, which are generated to be used together. The private key is never shared; it is kept secret and used only by its owner. The public key is made available to anyone who wants it. Because of the time and amount of computer processing power required, it is considered "mathematically unfeasible" for anyone to be able to use the public key to re-create the private key, so this form of encryption is considered very secure.

Each file has a unique file encryption key, which is used to decrypt the file's data. Like the encrypted file or folder, the key is also encrypted, and must be decrypted by the user who has a private key that matches the public key. Because these keys match, the system can determine that the person is authorized to view the data, and can then open the file.

Whether a person is permitted to access the data is based on the user account that is being used when opening the file. A digital certificate is used to identify the person logged into the computer, and to provide credentials showing that the person is authorized to access certain

data. EFS uses digital certificates that are associated with the user account. Although this requires less user interaction, it does have its drawbacks. It might not be possible to share encrypted files with others without decrypting them in cases where only one particular account is allowed access. In addition, there is a security risk if the user leaves the computer while logged on; then anyone who sits down at the machine can access the encrypted data.

Linux File Systems

Linux is an open source operating system that is based on the UNIX operating system. It supports multiple file systems through the use of a *Virtual File System* (VFS). VFS works as an abstract layer between the kernel and lower-level file systems. For a file system to work on Linux, it has to conform with and provide an interface to VFS, so the upper levels of the operating system can communicate with the file systems used on the machine. Using VFS, Linux has been able to support a number of file systems, including the following:

- ext, the first version of the Extended File System, and the first file system created specifically for Linux. It was also the first file system to use the VFS that was added to the Linux kernel. It was replaced by ext2 and xiafs, both of which were based on the older Minix system and are not found in current systems because of their obsolescence. Minix was a file system originally used by Linux, but it was replaced by ext because of shortcomings such as a 14-character limit in naming files, and a 64MB limitation on partition sizes.

- ext2, the Second Extended File System. This offers greater performance, supports file sizes of up to 2TB, and continues to be a file system used on many Linux machines. This file system implemented a data structure that includes *inodes*, which store information about files, directories, and other system objects. ext2 stores files as blocks of data on the hard disk. As we'll see when we discuss clusters later in this chapter, *blocks* are the smallest unit of data used by the file system, and data is stored to one or more blocks on the HDD. A group of blocks containing information used by the operating system (which can contain such data as how to boot the system) is called a *superblock*.

- ext3, the Third Extended File System, which supersedes ext2. A major improvement to previous versions is that ext3 is a *journaled* file system, which makes it easier to recover. A journal is similar to transaction logs used in databases, where data is logged before being written. On ext3, the journal is updated before blocks of data are updated. If the computer crashed, the journal could be used to restore the file system by ensuring that any data that wasn't written to blocks before the crash is resolved so that the blocks are marked as being used when they are actually free (a concept we'll discuss later when we talk about clusters). On ext2, if a problem occurred, you would need to run Filesystem Check (fsck) to resolve issues with files and metadata on the system.

- ext4, which (as you'd expect by this point), is short for Fourth Extended File System. In addition to improvements in performance, this version of the file system supports volumes of up to 1EB.

Mac OS X File System

Apple's *Macintosh* line of computers has used several different file systems over the years. When the original Macintosh was released January 24, 1984, it used the *Macintosh File System* (MFS), which was used to store data on 400KB floppy disks. Although archaic by today's standards, MFS offered a number of innovations, as is common with technology developed by Apple.

MFS saved files to hard disks in two parts. A *resource fork* was used to store structured information, and a *data fork* was used to store unstructured data. Whereas data used in a file would be stored in the data fork, information related to the file (including icons, menus, menu items, and other aspects of the file) was stored in the resource fork. The resource fork allowed files to be opened by the correct application, without the need for a file extension, and could also be used to store metadata.

A year after MFS was released the *Hierarchical File System* (HFS) replaced it. HFS continued to use multiple forks when storing data, but was designed to organize and manage data on both floppy disks and hard disks. Like its predecessor, it also supported filenames that were 255 characters in length, but where it was exceptional over MFS was in performance. MFS was designed for use on floppy disks, so it performed slowly on larger media. HFS was designed to perform well with hard disks, and it used a hierarchical design through a Catalog File to replace the flat table structure used by MFS.

In 1998, Apple introduced a new version of HFS called *HFS Plus*. In addition to better performance, improvements were made in how HFS Plus handled data. Like Linux machines, HFS and HFS Plus both store data in blocks on the hard disk, with volumes divided into logical blocks that are 512 bytes in size. HFS used 16-bit block addresses, but this was improved in HFS Plus, where 32-bit block addresses were supported. The 16-bit blocks used in HFS meant that only 65,536 blocks could be allocated to files on a volume. Although this wasn't an issue when hard disks were smaller, it resulted in a considerable amount of wasted space on larger volumes.

Sun Solaris 10 File System: ZFS

Sun Solaris is an open source operating system developed by Sun Microsystems. Although previous versions of Solaris have used different operating systems, the ZFS file system was first used in Solaris 10. ZFS is an acronym for *Zettabyte File System*, and is designed to handle large amounts of data.

ZFS uses virtual storage pools called *zpools*, which are composed of virtual devices (*vdevs*). Pools can consist of various vdevs, which in turn can consist of one or more storage devices, including those using RAID (Redundant Array of Inexpensive Disks). ZFS is also a 128-bit storage system, meaning that it supports more data, and supports variable sized blocks of up to

128KB. If the file system can compress data to fit into smaller blocks, it will do so to improve I/O throughput.

Network File Systems and File Sharing Protocols

Network file systems and *file sharing protocols* allow users to access and update files on remote computers as though they were on the local computer. They can make different file systems on the remote machine irrelevant when accessing that machine's resources across the network. This is why a Windows 9x computer, which does not support NTFS and can't access NTFS files locally, is able to read and write to NTFS files that are stored on a remote computer running Windows NT, 2000, XP, or Vista. Popular mechanisms for file sharing across a network include the following:

- **Server Message Block (SMB)** Microsoft uses this protocol to allow client applications to access and write to remote files and request services from server applications on remote systems. SMB is included with Windows operating systems. SAMBA is an implementation of SMB and the Common Internet File System (CIFS) that can be installed on UNIX computers to allow Windows clients to access their files as though they were SMB servers.

- **Common Internet File System (CIFS)** CIFS is a protocol proposed as an Internet standard for allowing access to remote files across the Internet. CIFS is considered an open (nonproprietary) version of SMB. Both SMB and CIFS run on top of the TCP/IP protocol stack.

- **NetWare Core Protocol (NCP)** NCP is actually a set of protocols that provide file and printer access, among other services, between clients and remote servers on NetWare networks. NCP runs over IPX or IP.

- **Network File System (NFS)** NFS is a client/server application developed by Sun Microsystems that runs on TCP/IP to allow remote file access. NFS uses the Remote Procedure Call (RPC) communication method. NFS is used for remote file access by UNIX/Linux machines and can be installed on Windows and Macintosh computers.

Damage & Defense…

NFS Exploits

The Network File System (NFS) allows users to remotely mount disks on other computers in order to access the files on the remote system. This makes the files on the remote disk available across the network. A program called nfsbug can be used to try out different methods of mounting an NFS disk to determine whether the remote computer is configured in such a way as to allow remote mounting. If it works, this allows the attacker to gain full access to the remote file system. The attacker can then read or write to all the files.

CD-ROM/DVD File System

Not all file systems are developed for hard disks or for accessing data over a network. File systems also exist that are specifically designed for organizing and accessing files stored on CDs and DVDs. CD is an acronym for Compact Disc, and DVD is an acronym for Digital Video Disc or Digital Versatile Disc. As we'll discuss later in this chapter, although both are 5-inch optical discs that visually appear identical, CDs can contain up to 700MB of data whereas DVDs are able to store from 4.7GB to 17GB of data. Although CDs were designed to store an entire album of music and DVDs were designed to store an entire movie on one disc, both CDs and DVDs are capable of storing various kinds of data.

Universal Disk Format (UDF) is a file system that is used by both CDs and DVDs. It is a standard format developed by the Optical Storage Technology Association (OSTA). UDF is based on the International Organization for Standardization (ISO) 13346 standard, and it uses a file structure that's accessible by any computer or CD/DVD system. UDF was not initially supported by Microsoft operating systems, which was why Microsoft released a format called UDF Bridge with Windows 95 to provide support until the next release of Windows. Although UDF is compatible with ISO-9660 (which we'll discuss next), UDF was developed as a hybrid of both UDF and ISO-9660 standards. To allow DVDs to be played and burned (i.e., recorded) on Windows computers, DVD-ROM vendors had to include support for both UDF and UDF Bridge.

ISO-9660 was introduced as a standard for CD-ROM media in 1988, and is commonly referred to as CDFS (Compact Disc File System). It allows CDs created on different operating systems to be accessed by other OSs. Using this standard, CD data is stored as frames on the disc, with each frame being 24 bytes in length. Using ISO-9660 for recording, three different modes may be available in disc creation software:

- CD-ROM Mode 1, which is generally used to record computer data. Filenames are limited to eight characters with three additional characters for the extension (i.e., standard 8.3 format).

- CD-ROM Mode 2 Form 1, which is also generally used for recording computer data. Although it uses the same format as Mode 1, it isn't compatible across all systems. It allows filenames of up to 180 characters (depending on how many extended attributes are used).

- CD-ROM Mode 2 Form 2, which allows data to be fragmented so that it can be written in increments to the CD. It is commonly used for video CDs, and other fault-tolerant data, where any errors that occur would happen so fast that they would generally not be detected by a person viewing the media.

Because technology changed, extensions to the ISO-9660 standard were developed to address issues that the initial standard didn't address. These extensions include the following:

- Joliet, which addresses limitations in the filenames as ISO-9660 didn't support long filenames. Joliet is still supported by disc creation software and all Windows operating systems since Windows 95, and allows filenames that are 64 characters in length.

- Apple ISO9660 Extensions, which Apple developed to address limitations in the properties of files stored on CDs. Because HFS supports more properties than the FAT file system and uses a resource fork and data fork to save files, Apple developed an extension that allows non-Macintosh systems to access data saved by Macintosh computers and view the properties of these files.

- Rock Ridge Interchange Protocol, which is abbreviated as RRIP and corresponds to IEEE P1282. RRIP is used for storing information that's specific to UNIX machines, and supports filenames of 255 characters.

- El Torito, which was developed by Phoenix Technologies (which manufactured the BIOS of computers) and IBM to allow computers to be booted from a CD. If a CD has already been inserted in a CD-ROM when the computer starts up and it has a boot code on it, the BIOS assigns a drive number to the CD-ROM and allows the computer to boot from that device.

Disk Partition

Before a hard disk can be formatted to use a particular file system, the hard disk drive needs to be partitioned. A *partition* is a logical division of the hard disk, allowing a single hard disk to function as though it were one or more hard disks on the computer. Even if different partitions aren't used, and the entire disk is set up as a single partition, a partition must be set so that the operating system knows the disk is going to be used in its entirety. Once a partition is set, it

can be given a drive letter (such as C:, D:, etc.) and formatted to use a file system. When an area of the hard disk is formatted and issued a drive letter, it is referred to as a *volume*.

If more than one partition is set, multiple file systems supported by the operating system can be used on a single HDD. For example, on one volume of a Windows computer, you could have C: formatted as FAT32 and D: formatted as NTFS. Similarly, one partition of a Linux computer could be formatted as ext and another could use ext2. This allows you to use features that are unique to different file systems on the same computer.

On computers running Linux, DOS, or Windows operating systems, different kinds of partitions may be used. The two types of partitions are:

- Primary partition
- Extended partition

A *primary partition* is a partition on which an operating system can be installed. A primary partition with an operating system installed on it is used when the computer starts to load the OS. Although a primary partition can exist without an operating system, on older Windows and DOS operating systems, the first partition installed had to be a primary partition. Modern versions of Windows allow up to four primary partitions, or three primary and one extended partition (which we'll discuss next) on a single disk.

An *extended partition* is a partition that can be divided into additional logical drives. Unlike a primary partition, you don't need to assign it a drive letter and install a file system. Instead, you can use the operating system to create an additional number of logical drives within the extended partition. Each logical drive has its own drive letter and appears as a separate drive. Your only limitations to how many logical drives you create are the amount of free space available on the extended partition, and the number of available drive letters you have left on your system.

System and Boot Partitions

When partitions are created, a partition may be designated as the boot partition, system partition, or both. A *system partition* stores files that are used to boot (start) the computer. These are used whenever a computer is powered on (cold boot) or restarted from within the operating system (warm boot). A *boot partition* is a volume of the computer that contains the system files used to start the operating system. Once the boot files on the system partition have been accessed and have started the computer, the system files on the boot partition are accessed to start the operating system. The *system partition* is where the operating system is installed. The system and boot partitions can exist as separate partitions on the same computer, or on separate volumes.

EXAM WARNING

Don't get too confused about the purposes of the boot and system partitions. The names are self-explanatory if you reverse their actual purposes. Remember that the system partition is used to store boot files, and the boot partition is used to store system files (i.e., the operating system). On many machines, both of these are on the same volume of the computer.

Boot Sectors and the Master Boot Record

Earlier in this chapter, we discussed how sectors are used to store data on the HDD. Although many sectors may exist on an HDD, the first sector (sector 0) on a hard disk is always the *boot sector*. This sector contains codes that the computer uses to start the machine.

The boot sector is also referred to as the *Master Boot Record* (MBR). The MBR contains a partition table, which stores information on which primary partitions have to be created on the hard disk, so it can then use this information to start the machine. By using the partition table in the MBR, the computer can understand how the hard disk is organized before actually starting the operating system that will interact with it. Once it determines how partitions are set up on the machine, it can then provide this information to the operating system.

NOTE

At times, you'll hear about boot viruses that infect your computer when it's started, which is why users have been warned never to leave a floppy disk or other media in a bootable drive when starting a machine. Because the MBR briefly has control of the computer when it starts, a boot virus will attempt to infect the boot sector to infect the machine immediately after it's started, and before any antivirus software is started.

NTFS Partition Boot Sector

Because NTFS uses a Master File Table that's used to store important information about the file system, information on the location of the MFT and MFT mirror file is stored in the boot sector. To prevent this information from being lost, a duplicate of the boot sector is stored at

the disk's logical center, allowing it to be recovered if the original information in the boot sector was corrupted.

Clusters

Clusters are groups of two or more consecutive sectors on a hard disk, and are the smallest amount of disk space that can be allocated to store a file. As we've mentioned, a sector is typically 512 bytes in size, but data saved to a hard disk is generally larger than this. As such, more than one sector is required to save the data to the disk. To access the data quickly, the computer will attempt to keep this data together by writing the data to a contiguous series of sectors on the disk. In doing so, the read/write head can access the data on a single track of the hard disk. As such, the head doesn't need to move from track to track, increasing the time it takes to read and write data.

Unlike tracks and sectors of the hard disk, clusters are logical units of file storage. Clusters are managed by the operating system, which assigns a unique number to each cluster, so it can keep track of files according to the clusters they use. Although the computer will try to store files in contiguous clusters on the disk, this isn't always possible, so data belonging to a single file may be split across the disk in different clusters. This is invisible to the user of the computer, who will open the file without any knowledge of whether the data is stored in clusters that are scattered across various areas of the disk.

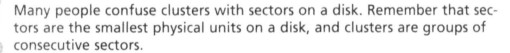

Exam Warning

Many people confuse clusters with sectors on a disk. Remember that sectors are the smallest physical units on a disk, and clusters are groups of consecutive sectors.

Cluster Size

Because clusters are controlled by the operating system, the size of the cluster is determined by a number of factors, including the file system being used. When a disk is formatted, the option may exist to specify the size of the cluster being used. For example, in Windows XP, right-clicking on a drive in Windows Explorer displays a context menu that provides a **Format** menu item. When you click on this menu item, the screen shown in Figure 2.7 is displayed. As seen in this figure, the dialog box provides the ability to choose the file system in which the disk will be formatted; it also provides a drop-down list called **Allocation unit size**. This drop-down list is where you choose what size clusters will be created when the disk is formatted.

Figure 2.7 Specifying Cluster Size When Formatting a Disk

The dialog box in Figure 2.7 provides options to allocate clusters in sizes of 512 bytes, 1,024 bytes, 2,048 bytes, and 4,096 bytes. If a cluster size isn't specified, Windows will use the option of a default allocation size. Table 2.4 lists the default cluster sizes on computers running Windows 2003 Server.

Table 2.4 Cluster Sizes on Windows 2003 Server

Volume Size	FAT File System	FAT32 File System	NTFS File System
7MB–16MB	2KB	Not supported	512 bytes
17MB–32MB	512 bytes	Not supported	512 bytes
33MB–64MB	1KB	512 bytes	512 bytes
65MB–128MB	2KB	1KB	512 bytes
129MB–256MB	4KB	2KB	512 bytes
257MB–512MB	8KB	4KB	512 bytes
513MB–1,024MB	16KB	4KB	1KB
1,025MB–2GB	32KB	4KB	2KB

Continued

Table 2.4 continued Cluster Sizes on Windows 2003 Server

Volume Size	FAT File System	FAT32 File System	NTFS File System
2GB–4GB	64KB	4KB	4KB
4GB–8GB	Not supported	4KB	4KB
8GB–16GB	Not supported	8KB	4KB
16GB–32GB	Not supported	16KB	4KB
32GB–2TB	Not supported	Not supported	4KB

NOTE

When converting a FAT file system to NTFS, you can use the CONVERT.EXE program. Because FAT file systems typically use 512KB clusters, you are not given the option of changing the cluster size. Therefore, when you convert from FAT to NTFS file systems, the cluster size is always 512KB.

Slack Space

Because clusters are a fixed size, the data stored in a cluster will use the entire space, regardless of whether it needs the entire cluster. For example, if you allocated a cluster size of 4,096 bytes and saved a 10-byte file to the disk, the entire 4KB cluster would be used even though 4,086 bytes of space is wasted. This wasted space is called *slack space* or *file slack*. Slack space is the area of space between the end of a file and the end of the last cluster used by that data.

Because an operating system will track where a file is located using the clusters used to store the data, clusters will always be used and potential storage space will always be wasted. Essentially, slack space is the same as pouring a bottle of cola into a series of glasses. As the bottle is emptied, the first glasses are filled to the top, but the final glass will be only partially filled. Because the glass has already been used, it can't be filled with something else as well. In the same way, once a cluster has been allocated to store a file, it can't be used to store data associated with other files.

Because extra space must be allocated to hold a file, it is better that the sizes of the clusters are smaller. When clusters are smaller, the amount of space in the final cluster used to store a file will have less space that is unused. Smaller clusters will limit the amount of wasted space and will utilize disk space more effectively.

On any system, there will always be a certain amount of disk space that's wasted. You can calculate the amount of wasted space using the following formula:

(Cluster size / 2) * number of files

Although this formula isn't exact, it does give an estimate of how much disk space is wasted on a particular hard disk. The number of files includes the number of directories, and this amount is multiplied by half of the allocated cluster size. Therefore, if you had a cluster size of 2,048 bytes, you would divide this in half to make it 1,024 bytes (or 1KB). If there were 10,000 files on the hard disk, this would be multiplied by 1KB, making the amount of wasted space 10MB, that is, (2,048 / 2) * 10,000 = 10,000KB or 10MB.

Any tool used to acquire and analyze data on a hard disk should also examine the slack space. When a file is deleted from the disk, data will continue to reside in the unallocated disk space. Even if parts of the file are overwritten on the disk, data may be acquired from the slack space that could be crucial to your investigation.

EXAM WARNING

Slack space and unallocated disk space are areas that should always be examined in a computer forensic examination. Make sure you understand each of these, and how they relate to storage media.

Lost Clusters

As we mentioned, each cluster is given a unique number, and the operating system uses these to keep track of which files are stored in particular clusters on the hard disk. When you consider the thousands of files stored on a hard disk, and that each may be assigned to one or more clusters, it isn't surprising that occasionally a cluster gets mismarked. From time to time, an operating system will mark a cluster as being used, even though it hasn't been assigned to a file. This is known as a *lost cluster*.

Lost clusters are also known as *lost allocation units* or *lost file fragments*. In UNIX or Linux machines that refer to clusters as *blocks*, they are referred to as *lost blocks* or *orphans*. According to the operating system, these clusters don't belong to any particular file. They generally result from improperly shutting down the computer, loss of power, shutting down the computer without closing applications first, files not being closed properly, or ejecting removable storage such as floppy disks while the drive is reading or writing to the media. When these things occur, data in the cache may have been assigned a cluster but was never written because the machine lost power or shut down unexpectedly. Even though the cluster isn't actually used by a file, it isn't listed as being free to use by the operating system.

Although lost clusters are generally empty, such as when a cluster is allocated to a program but never released, lost clusters may contain data. If the system was incorrectly shut down (or some other activity occurred), the cluster may have had data written to it before the event occurred. This data may be a fragment of the file or other corrupted data.

Just as bad sectors can be marked as unusable using programs such as ScanDisk and CheckDisk, these same programs can be used to identify lost clusters. These tools will find lost clusters, and can recover data that may have been stored in the cluster. The data is stored as files named *file####.chk*, and although most of the time they are empty and can be deleted, viewing the contents using Notepad or other tools to view text may reveal missing data that is important. In UNIX, another program called Filesystem Check (fsck) can be used to identify and fix orphans. With this tool, the lost blocks of data are saved in a directory called *lost+found*. If the data contained in these files doesn't have any useful information, it can simply be deleted. In doing so, the lost cluster is reassigned and disk space is freed up.

Windows XP

Although Windows XP is composed of thousands of different files that are installed with the operating system, a number of files are essential to starting the operating system. Without these files, the computer couldn't boot properly and XP would be unable to start. The following files are the core components of XP, and must exist for the operating system to function:

- **Ntoskrnl.exe** The executive and kernel of the OS. It is critical to the boot process of the computer. It provides the microkernel and executive layers of the operating system, and provides system services such as memory management and hardware virtualization.

- **Ntkrnlpa.exe** On systems with Physical Address Extension (PAE) support, it is the executive and kernel components of the operating system. It allows addressing of more than 4GB of memory.

- **Hal.dll** The hardware abstraction layer of the operating system. This allows the kernel to run on different systems without needing to change the code in the kernel.

- **Win32k.sys** The kernel-mode portion of the Win32 subsystem that handles the Graphics Device Interface (GDI) service calls.

- **Ntdll.dll** The "NT Layer" that provides internal support functions. It is responsible for system service dispatch stubs to executive functions.

- **Kernel32.dll** Handles memory management, I/O operations, and interrupts.

- **Advapi32.dll** Part of the API services library that supports APIs, including those involving security and Registry calls.

- **User32.dll** The Windows User API Client Library.

- **Gdi32.dll** Handles functions used by the GDI, which allows Windows to generate graphics.

In addition to these files, a number of additional files are used to boot the computer. Each of these files is located in the root directory (e.g., C:), and is loaded in a specific order each time you start Windows XP. These startup files are:

- **Ntldr** Reads the Boot.ini file, presents a menu, and then loads Ntoskrnl.exe, Bootvid.dll, Hal.dll, and boot-start device drivers.

- **Boot.ini** An initialization file that contains options on how Windows starts.

- **Ntdetect.com** Used to query the computer for information on devices and their configuration.

- **Pagefile.sys** Used to store data that can't fit into physical memory.

- **Ntbootdd.sys** Used instead of the boot code functions for disk access if SCSI devices are used on the system.

Booting Computers

Now that we've looked at the core files that Windows XP uses, let's look at how they work together when Windows XP is first started. Anytime you start a computer running XP, a number of steps must be completed between the time you've pressed the power button and the time the logon screen appears:

1. Regardless of the operating system and file system, whenever you turn on your computer, it undergoes a *Power On Self Test* (POST). This tests the computer's memory and subsystems, as well as any devices installed on the computer that are listed in the BIOS. This includes hard disks recognized by the BIOS, and may include network cards or other devices.

2. The BIOS will then read the MBR, which as we mentioned earlier is the first sector of the hard disk installed on the machine.

3. The MBR will then take over the boot process, and look at the boot sector of the hard disk.

4. Ntldr will load ntoskrnl.exe and Hal.dll. These are located in %SystemRoot%System32.

5. Ntoskrnl.exe will then start Winlogon.exe, which in turn loads Lsass.exe to display the logon screen where you will enter your username and password.

Boot disks

On older operating systems such as MS-DOS, you could fit your entire operating system on a floppy disk and start the computer from that. Because modern operating systems take up so much hard disk space, this isn't possible anymore. *Boot disks* are bootable floppies or CDs that contain essential files that are needed to start the computer. If something is wrong with the operating system, a bootable floppy disk or CD with the files needed to start the machine can be created.

BootDisk.com (www.bootdisk.com) is a Web site that provides bootable floppy disks and CDs that can be used to start a machine. It provides boot disks for DOS, various versions of Windows, Linux, and other operating systems. By downloading the compressed file containing the boot disk for your system from this site, you can decompress the file and copy it to a bootable disk.

The Registry

The Windows Registry in Windows 9*x*, ME, NT, 2000, XP, and Vista (i.e., all Windows operating systems later than Windows 3.*x*) is a database in which critical system and application configuration and initialization information is stored. The Registry contains information on hardware, the operating system, other software, user preferences, and other elements of the system. When you make changes to programs available through the Control Panel, Windows Explorer, and other tools in Windows, these settings are reflected and stored in the Registry.

The Registry can also be modified directly using the Registry Editor program seen in Figure 2.8. In looking at this figure, you can see from the left pane of the program that information is organized into several groups called *hive keys* or HKEYs. The following HKEYs are found in the Registry:

- **HKEY_CLASSES_ROOT** Contains information on registered applications, associations to file extensions, and other information needed by software. It is derived from the HKEY_CURRENT_USER\Software\Classes and HKEY_LOCAL_MACHINE\Software\Classes.

- **HKEY_CURRENT_USER** Contains information on the user currently logged on to the machine. This information is derived from a subkey of HKEY_USERS that's related to the user account currently used.

- **HKEY_LOCAL_MACHINE** Used to store settings that are common to all users who log on to the machine.

- **HKEY_USERS** Contains settings for each user who has an account on the machine.

■ **HKEY_CURRENT_CONFIG** Contains information that's compiled when the computer is booted. Information in this key is generated each time the computer starts, and isn't stored permanently.

Figure 2.8 Registry Editor

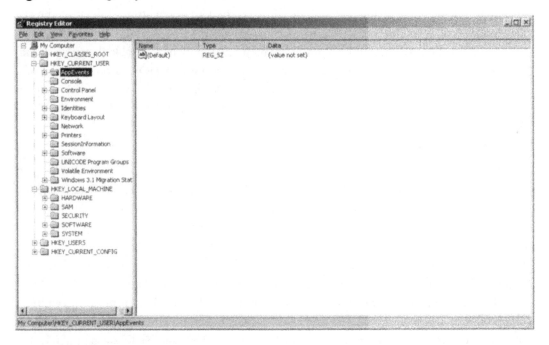

Each key appearing in the Registry may contain additional subkeys, similar to directories containing subdirectories on a hard disk. The similarities don't end here either, as the path to a particular subkey is written the same way. For example, you can see in Figure 2.8 that the AppEvents subkey is selected, which appears under the HKEY_CURRENT_USER key. To write this path, it would appear as HKEY_CURRENT_USER\AppEvents. Beyond the keys and subkeys are entries that correspond to the computer or user account, which are called *values*. Numerous values may exist under the various keys of the Registry, but all will use one of the following types:

■ String Value

■ Binary Value

■ DWORD Value, which is a 32-bit unsigned integer

■ Multi-String Value

■ Expandable String Value

Notes from the Underground…

Registry Hacks

Although having all the information stored in one centralized location instead of scattered in multiple initialization and configuration files offers many benefits, it also makes the Registry vulnerable to hackers and attackers. The Regedit and Regedt32 tools in Windows allow the user to connect to the Registry on a remote system across the network and make changes to Registry settings. A hacker can exploit this ability and alter important information that could bring down the system. Administrative privileges are needed to edit remote registries, and you cannot edit a Windows 95/98 computer's Registry unless remote administration has been explicitly enabled by installing the remote Registry service. Administrators can do this using a batch file during the rollout of a number of Windows 9x machines.

It can be difficult to detect Registry attacks, because the system accesses the Registry often, complicating the monitoring process. However, utilities such as RegMon can be used to track Registry access data, which can be compared with common attack models.

Forensic Tools

Forensic tools will often feature the ability to acquire evidence from the hard disk. By duplicating data, the information from a machine can be acquired and then analyzed for any information that is applicable to your case. In situations where an investigation isn't necessary, but data simply needs to be recovered, these same tools can assist in retrieving information that was previously lost. In the sections that follow, we'll look at two tools that were developed by X-Ways Forensics, and are available from www.x-ways.net.

Evidor: The Evidence Collector

Evidor is a tool that is used to search hard disks for textual information. When you select the disk to examine and enter a list of keywords, Evidor will search every file on the disk, including any data located in slack space. As we mentioned earlier in this chapter, data may continue to reside on the computer even after it has been deleted from the machine. The data may still be accessed despite the fact the information has been deleted, and partially overwritten.

Because Evidor searches a computer using keywords that you've entered, it will only provide results that contain these words. This can be useful in situations where you don't want to display results that may be unrelated to the case, and contain confidential or proprietary information. After entering names, e-mail addresses, filenames, account numbers, or other facts you know about the data you're searching for, any occurrences of these words will be returned through an output file. This output file is formatted in HTML or plain text, and can then be imported into other applications for analysis.

WinHex

Winhex is a hexadecimal editor that can be used to examine files that have been acquired for analysis. This may include any file fragments, recovered deleted files, or other data that may have been corrupted. If you don't have an application to open a particular document that has been retrieved from a hard disk, you can use this tool to examine the contents of a file and view the data inside. Similarly, if packets of data were captured from a network, you could view the data using Winhex to identify passwords and other data.

Winhex also provides a feature that allows you to clone a hard disk, thereby making a duplicate of the data for you to work with. In doing so, you can then work with the data, without fear of damaging the original. Although Winhex can be used to access and edit files on a hard disk, it can also provides a RAM editor feature that allows you to access the physical RAM and any processes running in virtual memory. This allows you to access any data on a system, regardless of whether it's been saved.

Another benefit of this tool is that it can be set to run in a write-protected mode, which will open any file as read-only and prevent any accidental or intentional modification. This allows you to examine the contents of a file without fear that it may be altered or damaged.

Digital Media Devices

Although to this point we've focused on the most common method of storing data, it is important to realize there are other data storage methods besides hard disks. There are several popular types of removable media, so called because the disk itself is separate from the drive, the device that reads and writes to it. There are also devices that attach to a computer through a port, allowing data to be transferred between the machine and the storage device. In the sections that follow, we'll look at a number of different digital media devices, including:

- Magnetic tape
- Floppy disk
- Compact disc
- Digital video/versatile disc
- Blu-Ray
- iPod
- Zune
- Flash memory
- USB

EXAM WARNING

Removable media refers to media that can have a disk or other storage method removed from a drive or port. This isn't the same as hard disks or other devices that can be removed from the computer. Removable disk racks and bays allow you to easily slide an IDE or SCSI hard disk drive (mounted in a carrier rack) in and out of a docking bay that remains attached to the computer's ATA or SCSI interface. Hard disk drives can also be inserted into external bays that are easily plugged into and removed from the computer's USB port. The distinction is that in these cases, you are removing the entire drive, not just the disk itself, whereas with true removable storage media, the drive stays attached to the computer and only the media—disk, tape, or card—is removed.

Magnetic Tape

Early in this chapter, we discussed how in the early days of computing, magnetic tapes were one of the few methods used to store data. *Magnetic tapes* consist of a thin plastic strip that has a magnetic coating on which data can be stored. Early systems throughout the 1950s to 1970s used 10.5-inch magnetic tape, whereas home computers in the early 1980s used audiocassette tapes for storing programs and data. Today, magnet tape is still commonly used to back up data on network servers and individual computers.

Magnetic tape is a relatively inexpensive form of removable storage, especially for backing up data. It is less useful for data that needs to be accessed frequently because it is a sequential access medium. You have to move back and forth through the tape to locate the particular data you want. In other words, to get from file 1 to file 20, you have to go through files 2 through 19. This is in contrast to direct access media such as disks, in which the heads can be moved directly to the location of the data you want to access without progressing in sequence through all the other files.

Floppy Disk

In the early days of personal computing, floppy disks were large (first 8 inches, then 5.25 inches in diameter), thin, and flexible. Today's "floppies," often and more accurately called diskettes, are smaller (3.5 inches), rigid, and less fragile. The disk inside the diskette housing is plastic and coated with magnetic material. The drive into which you insert the diskette contains a motor to rotate the diskette so that the drive heads, made of tiny electromagnets, can read and write to different locations on the diskette. Standard diskettes today hold 1.44MB of data; SuperDisk technology (developed by Imation Corporation) provides for storing either 120MB or 240MB on diskettes of the same size.

Compact Discs and DVDs

CDs and DVDs are rigid disks a little less than 5 inches in diameter, made of hard plastic with a thin layer of coating. CDs and DVDs are called optical media because CD and DVD drives use a laser beam, along with an optoelectronic sensor, to write to and read the data that is "burned" into the coating material (a compound that changes from reflective to nonreflective when heated by the laser). The data is encoded in the form of incredibly tiny pits or bumps on the surface of the disc. CDs and DVDs work similarly, but the latter can store more data because the pits and tracks are smaller, because DVDs use a more efficient error correction method (that uses less space), and because DVDs can have two layers of storage on each side instead of just one.

CDs

The term *CD* originates from "Compact Disc" under which audio discs were marketed. Philips and Sony still hold the trademark to this name. Several different types of CDs have been developed over the years, with the first being CD Audio or Compact Disc Digital Audio (CDDA).

CD Audio are the first CDs that were used to record audio discs. Little has changed in CD physics since the origin of CD Audio discs in 1980. This is due in part to the desire to maintain physical compatibility with an established base of installed units, and because the structure of CD media was both groundbreaking and nearly ideal for this function.

CD-ROM

Until 1985, compact discs were used only for audio, when Philips and Sony introduced the CD-ROM standard. CD-ROM is an acronym for Compact Disc–Read Only Memory, and refers to any data compact disc. However, the term has grown to refer to the CD-ROM drive used to read this optical storage medium. For example, when you buy software, the disc used to install the program is called an installation CD. They are capable of holding up to 700MB of data, and remain a common method of storing data.

DVD

Originally, *DVD* was an acronym for *Digital Video Disc* and then later *Digital Versatile Disc*. Today it is generally agreed that DVD is not an acronym for anything. However, although these discs were originally meant to store video, they have become a common method of storing data. In fact, DVD-ROM drives are not only able to copy (rip) or create (burn) data on DVD discs, but are also backward-compatible and able to copy and create compact discs as well.

Digital Versatile Discs (DVDs) are an evolutionary growth of CDs with slight changes. Considering the development of DVD follows the CD by 14 years, you can see that the CD was truly a revolutionary creation in its time. It is important to understand that both CDs and DVDs are electro optical devices, as opposed to nearly all other computer peripherals which are electromagnetic. There are no magnetic fields in the reading or recording of these discs; therefore, they are immune to magnetic fields of any strength, unlike hard drives.

Due to their immunity to magnetic fields, CD and DVD media are unaffected by Electromagnetic Pulse (EMP) effects, X-rays, and other sources of electromagnetic radiation. The primary consideration with recordable CD media (and to a lesser extent, manufactured media) is energy transfer. It takes a significant amount of energy to affect the media that the writing laser transfers to the disc. Rewritable discs (which we'll discuss later) require even more energy to erase or rewrite data.

This is in direct contrast to floppy discs and hard drives, which can be affected by electromagnetic devices such as Magnetic Resonance Imaging (MRI) machines, some airport X-ray scanners, and other devices that create a strong magnetic field. CDs and DVDs are also immune to EMPs from nuclear detonations.

It is important to understand that CD and DVD media are *read with light*, and recordable discs are *written with heat*. Using an infrared (IR) laser, data is transferred to a CD or DVD onto a small, focused area that places all of the laser energy onto the target for transfer. It should be noted that all CD and DVD media are sensitive to heat (i.e., above 120°F/49°C), and recordable media is sensitive to IR, ultraviolet (UV), and other potential intense light sources. Some rewritable media are affected by Erasable Programmable Read-Only Memory (EPROM) erasers, which use an intense UV light source. Various forensic alternative light sources can provide sufficient energy to affect optical media, especially if it is focused on a small area. It is not necessarily a question of heat but one of total energy transfer, which can result in heating.

Both CD and DVD media are organized as a single line of data in a spiral pattern. This spiral is more than 3.7 miles (or 6 kilometers [km]) in length on a CD, and 7.8 miles (or 12.5 km) for a DVD. The starting point for the spiral is toward the center of the disc, with the spiral extending outward. This means that the disc is read and written from the inside out, which is the opposite of how hard drives organize data.

With this spiral organization, there are no cylinders or tracks like those on a hard drive. The term *track* refers to a grouping of data for optical media. The information along the spiral is spaced linearly, thus following a predictable timing. This means that the spiral contains more information at the outer edge of the disc than at the beginning. It also means that if this information is to be read at a constant speed, the rotation of the disc must change between different points along the spiral.

As seen in Figure 2.9, all optical media are constructed of layers of different materials. This is similar to how all optical media discs are constructed. The differences between different types of discs are as follows:

- **CD-R** The dye layer can be written to once.

- **CD-ROM** The reflector has the information manufactured into it and there is no dye layer.

- **CD-RW** The dye is replaced with multiple layers of different metallic alloys. The alloy is bi-stable and can be changed many times between different states.

- **DVD** DVDs are constructed of two half-thickness discs bonded together, even when only one surface contains information. Each half disc contains the information layer 0.6 millimeter (mm) from the surface of the disc.

Figure 2.9 CD-R Construction

DVD media consists of two half-thickness polycarbonate discs, and each half contains information and is constructed similarly to CD media. DVD write-once recordable media uses a dye layer with slightly different dyes than those used for CD-R media, but otherwise they are very similar physically. Manufactured DVD media have the information manufactured into the reflector and no dye layer is present. Rewritable DVD media use bi-stable alloy layers similar to those for CD rewritable media. The differences between manufactured, write-once, and rewritable media are physically similar between CD and DVD media.

The key to all recordable media types is the presence of a reflector with the ability to reflect laser energy. Data is represented by blocking the path to the reflector either by dye or by a bi-stable metallic alloy. The bottom of a CD is made of a relatively thick piece of polycarbonate plastic. Alternatively, the top is protected by a thin coat of lacquer. Scratches on the polycarbonate are out of focus when the disc is read, and minor scratches are ignored completely. It takes a deep scratch in the polycarbonate to affect the readability of a disc. However, even a small scratch in the lacquer can damage the reflector. Scratching the top of a disc can render it unreadable, which is something to consider the next time you place a disc on your desk top-down "to protect it." A DVD has polycarbonate on both sides; therefore, it is difficult to scratch the reflector.

Types of DVDs

Just as there are several types of CDs that may be used for various purposes, there are a wide variety of DVDs available. As mentioned previously, the storage capacity of a DVD is immense compared to a CD, and can range from 4.5GB on a single-layer, single-sided DVD to 17GB on a dual-layer, double-sided DVD. The various types of DVDs on the market include the following:

- **DVD-R** This stands for DVD minus Recordable. A DVD-R disc will hold up to 4.5GB of data, and is a write once-read many (WORM) medium. In other words, once it is written to, the data on the DVD cannot be modified.

- **DVD+R** This stands for DVD plus Recordable. A DVD+R disc will also hold up to 4.5GB of data, and is similar to the DVD-R. Choosing between DVD-R and

DVD+R discs should be guided by the intended use of the disc. There is some evidence that DVD-R discs are more compatible with consumer DVD recorders than DVD+R discs; however, there are consumer players that will only read DVD+R discs. DVD-R discs are often the best choice for compatibility if the disc being produced contains data files. Early DVD-ROM drives can generally read DVD-R discs but are incapable of reading DVD+R discs. DVD writers that only write DVD+R/RW discs will read DVD-R discs.

- **DVD-RW** This stands for "DVD minus Read Write." This, like CD-RW discs, allows an average of 1,000 writes in each location on the disc before failing. A DVD-RW disc will hold up to 4.5GB of data and is recordable.

- **DVD+R DL (dual layer)** This is an extension of the DVD standard to allow for dual-layer recording. Previously, the only dual-layer discs were those manufactured that way. This allows up to 8.5GB of data to be written to a disc. Most current DVD drives support reading and writing DVD+R DL discs.

- **DVD+RW** This stands for "DVD plus Read Write." This, like CD-RW discs, allows an average of 1,000 writes in each location on the disc before failing. A DVD+RW disc will hold up to 4.5GB of data and is recordable.

- **DVD-RAM** This is a relatively obsolete media format, which emphasized rewritable discs that could be written to more than 10,000 times. There were considerable interoperability issues with these discs and they never really caught on.

TEST DAY TIP

Expect to see questions that deal directly or indirectly with DVDs, CDs, and other storage media on the exam. Before taking the exam, familiarize yourself with the features of different media, and know aspects of storage media such as which can be written to only once.

HD-DVD

HD-DVD is an acronym for High Definition DVD, and is the high-density successor to DVD and a method of recording high-definition video to disc. Developed by Toshiba and NEC, a single-layer HD-DVD is capable of storing up to 15GB of data, whereas a dual-layer disc can store up to 30GB of data. Although developed for high-definition video, HD-DVD ROM drives for computers were released in 2006, allowing them to be used as optical storage media for computers.

HD-DVDs require so much storage space because of the amount of data required to record high-density television (HDTV) and video. A dual-layer HD-DVD can record eight hours of HDTV or 48 hours of standard video. The difference between the two is that HDTV uses 1,125 lines of digital video, which requires considerably more storage space. HD-DVD ROM drives are used in much the same way that VCRs were used to record video onto VHS tapes, and have a transfer rate of 36Mbps, which is 12Mbps more than HDTV signals are transmitted at.

Blu-Ray

The main competitor for HD-DVD is Blu-Ray. Like HD-DVD, *Blu-Ray* is a high-density optical storage method that was designed for recording high-definition video. The name of this technology comes from the blue-violet laser that is used to read and write to the discs. A single-layer Blu-Ray disc can store up to 25GB of data, whereas a dual-layer Blu-Ray disc can store up to 50GB of data.

Although there are standalone Blu-Ray and HD-DVD players and recorders, ones that will play either technology are also available. There are also Blu-Ray drives that allow users to record and play data on computers. In 2007, Pioneer announced the release of a Blu-Ray drive that can record data to Blu-Ray discs, as well as DVDs and CDs. In addition to this, Sony has also released its own rewritable drive for computers.

iPod

iPod is the brand name of portable media players that was developed by Apple in 2001. iPods were originally designed to play audio files, with the capability to play media files added in 2005. Apple introduced variations of the iPod with different capabilities. For example, the full-size iPod stores data on an internal hard disk, whereas the iPod Nano and iPod Shuffle use flash memory, which we'll discuss later in this chapter. Although the iPod is a device created by Apple, the term has come to apply in popular culture to any portable media player.

iPods store music and video by transferring the files from a computer. Audio and video files can be purchased from iTunes, or can be acquired illegally by downloading them from the Internet using peer-to-peer (P2P) software or other Internet sites and applications, or by sharing them between devices.

Unless you're investigating the illegal download of music or video files, where iPods become an issue during an investigation is through their ability to store other data on the devices. iPods can be used to store and transfer photos, video files, calendars, and other data. As such, they can be used as storage devices to store any file that may be pertinent to an investigation. The "Enable Disk Use" option in iTunes activates this function, and allows you to transfer files to the iPod. Because any media files are stored in a hidden folder on the iPod, you will need to enable your computer to view hidden files to browse any files stored on the iPod.

iPods use a file system that is based on the computer formatting the iPod. When you plug an iPod into a computer, it will use the file system corresponding to the type of machine it's connecting to. If you were formatting it on Windows XP, it would use a FAT32 file system format, but if it were formatted on a machine running Macintosh OS X, it would be formatted to use the HFS Plus file system. The exception to this is the iPod Shuffle, which uses only the FAT32 file system.

Zune

Entering late in the portable digital media market is Microsoft, which developed its own version of the iPod in 2006. *Zune* is a portable media player that allows you to play both audio and video, as well as store images and other data. Another feature of this device is that you can share files wirelessly with others who use Zune. In addition to connecting to a computer, Zune can also be connected to an Xbox using USB. Ironically, although it is only compatible with Xbox 360 and Windows, it was incompatible with Windows Vista until late 2006.

Flash Memory Cards

Flash memory cards and sticks are popular for storing and transferring varying amounts of data. Memory cards have typically ranged from 8MB to 512MB, but new cards are capable of storing upward of 8GB of data. They are commonly used for storing photos in digital cameras (and transferring them to PCs) and for storing and transferring programs and data between handheld computers (Pocket PCs and Palm OS devices). Although called "memory," unlike RAM, flash media is nonvolatile storage; that means the data is retained until it is deliberately erased or overwritten. PC Card (PCMCIA) flash memory cards are also available. Flash memory readers/writers come in many handheld and some laptop/notebook computers and external readers can be attached to PCs via USB or serial port. Flash memory cards include:

- Secure Digital (SD) Memory Card
- CompactFlash (CF) Memory Card
- Memory Stick (MS) Memory Card
- Multi Media Memory Card (MMC)
- xD-Picture Card (xD)
- SmartMedia (SM) Memory Card

USB Flash Drives

USB Flash Drives are small, portable storage devices that use a USB interface to connect to a computer. Like flash memory cards, they are removable and rewritable, and have become a common method of storing data. However, although Flash Memory Cards require that a reader

be installed, USB Flash Drives can be inserted into the USB ports found on most modern computers. The storage capacity of these drives ranges from 32MB to 64GB.

USB Flash Drives are constructed of a circuit board inside a plastic or metal casing, with a USB male connector protruding from one end. The connector is then covered with a cap that slips over it, allowing the device to be carried in a pocket or on a key fob without worry of damage. When needed, the USB Flash Drive can then be inserted into the USB port on a computer, or into a USB hub that allows multiple devices to be connected to one machine.

USB Flash Drives often provide a switch that will set write protection on the device. In doing so, any data on the device cannot be modified, allowing it to be easily analyzed. This is similar to the write protection that could be used on floppy disks, making it impossible to modify or delete any existing data, or add additional files to the device.

Although USB Flash Drives offer limited options in terms of their hardware, a number of Flash Drives will come with software that can be used to provide additional features. Encryption may be used, protecting any data on the device from being accessed without first entering a password. Compression may also be used, allowing more data to be stored on the device. There are also a number of programs that are specifically designed to run from a USB Flash Drive rather than a hard disk. For example, Internet browsers may be used that will store any history and temporary files on the flash drive. This makes it more difficult to identify a person's browsing habits.

USB Flash in a Pen

USB flash drives have been known by many other names over the years, including ThumbDrive and USB Pen Drive. Because these devices are so small, they can be packaged in almost any shape or item. There are USB flash drives that are hidden in pens, making them unidentifiable as flash drives, unless someone pulled each end of the pen to pop it open and see the USB connector. The pen itself is completely usable, but it contains a small flash drive that is fully functional. This allows the device to be hidden, and it can be useful for carrying the drive around with you … unless you tend to forget your pen in places, or you work in a place where others walk off with your pens.

Image File Forensics

One of the most common types of media acquired in a computer forensic examination is image files. The Internet and computers in general are graphical in nature, so you are bound to gather a considerable number of files that are inherent to the suspect computer's operating system and other software, or images stored as temporary files on the machine. Added to this are the various pictures that people will import from digital cameras and other devices, download or share with others over the Internet, or create and modify using graphics programs. When analyzing a computer, it isn't uncommon to come across thousands of image files that are innocuous and unrelated to a case.

Of course, not all graphics on a computer are innocent. According to Internet Filter Review (http://internet-filter-review.toptenreviews.com/internet-pornography-statistics.html), in 2006, $2.84 billion was spent in the U.S. on pornography over the Internet. In addition to this, according to statistics reported by the Computer Crime Research Center (www.crime-research.org/news/01.08.2005/1398/), more than 70 percent of child pornography worldwide is distributed over the Internet, and is requested by 15 percent of U.S. customers who pay for porn sites. Because of the volume of pornography that is downloaded and shared over the Internet, it is often wise to include searches for image files when conducting a computer forensic examination. Although possessing child pornography is a criminal offense, even possession of pornographic images depicting adults can result in disciplinary actions if stored on a business's computer.

Image Files

An *image file* is any picture or graphical depiction that has been stored in digital format. Generally, this refers to photographs, drawings, or other graphics that don't include any motion or animation. However, as we'll see later in this chapter, a wide variety of image file formats support different features. One of these is the ability to store images as part of a presentation or as individual frames that display movement when the image is displayed. Using this format, you can see that images can be different from one another, beyond the subject depicted.

A primary component of an image's characteristics is how the image was created. Different types of images can be created, which determine how the graphic is displayed, its resolution when it is expanded or reduced in size, the colors displayed, and other elements that make up the overall presentation of the graphic. In the following sections, we'll look at three types of graphics:

- Raster images
- Vector images
- Metafile images

Raster Images

Raster images are graphics that are created or captured as a set of pixels that are mapped to a grid. A *pixel* is an abbreviation of the words "picture element" and it comprises the smallest element of a digital image. Basically, a pixel is simply a dot on the screen that is illuminated in color or monochrome. Each pixel contains programmable information that defines its color, size, and location in the image. When enough pixels appear on the screen, mapped to x (horizontal) and y (vertical) coordinates, an image appears. Because a raster graphic is mapped pixel by pixel to a page, it is also referred to as a *bitmapped* image.

The term *raster* is derived from the Latin term *rastrum* for "rake," which accurately describes how the image is displayed on a screen. The image is rendered pixel by pixel in a vertical or hor-

izontal motion, similar to a rake scraping lines in dirt, until the entire image is displayed. You've probably seen this sweeping motion of a graphic slowly loading when you've gone on the Internet and viewed an image being transmitted and slowly displayed on the screen.

Pixels are used to measure the size and resolution of raster images. Size is measured by the number of pixels that are aligned horizontally and vertically on the image. For example, an image that is 640 x 480 would be 640 pixels wide and 480 pixels high. *Resolution* is the sharpness of an image, which is determined by the number of pixels used in the graphic. The more pixels used in an image, the higher the resolution. Resolution is measured in *dots per inch* (dpi), which refers to the number of pixels that are used in a 1-inch space of the document. For example, an image that is 71 dpi would use 71 dots (pixels) in every inch of the image. Because relatively few pixels are used for such a graphic, it would be considered low-resolution, making its file size smaller and good for use on the Internet. However, images can also be high-resolution, using 300 dpi or more if the image will be used in print.

Unfortunately, when resizing a raster image, the resolution of the image doesn't change. This can dramatically affect the appearance of the graphic, making its edges look jagged as the size increases. As the size of the image increases, the pixels making up the image become more visible, making the edges blockier. This doesn't occur when an image is reduced in size.

Another aspect that will determine the quality of an image is the level of color. *Color depth* is a term used to describe the number of bits (binary digits) used to represent the color of a pixel, which is measured as *bits per pixel* (bpp). The more bits used for a pixel, the more colors can be represented. To explain this further, consider that each color is a combination of red, green, and blue (RGB) and the more possible combinations of these, the wider the spectrum that can be used to define a particular shade or hue. Raster graphics can use up to three bytes of data to specify a pixel's color, with each byte representing one of the three RGB combinations. Because of this, if a graphic uses 8-bit color, 256 colors are available in the graphic. Similarly, if 16 bits (High Color) are used, approximately 65,000 colors are used in the image. If 24 bits (True Color) are used, the image will be able to contain 16 million colors.

Exam Warning

Remember that most images used on computers and the Internet are raster images. Such images are bitmapped images and are rendered to a display using *x* and *y* coordinates.

Vector Images

Vector graphics are generated from mathematical information stored in the graphic, which instructs the program opening the image how to display the position, width, length, direction,

and other aspects of objects used to create the picture. Drawing programs such as Adobe Illustrator and Corel Draw can be used to create structured or vector graphics. Another common use is in CAD (computer-aided design) programs that are used for drafting and design, and to make diagrams, blueprints, or 3D renderings of objects. These programs create images using shapes (circles, squares, lines, etc.) that are independent objects in the graphic being created, instead of individual pixels that are used to create a raster image.

Vector images are commonly used in print and advertising because they don't lose resolution when they're enlarged or reduced. Because of this, a logo created as a vector graphic could be used on a bumper sticker or a billboard without getting the jagged quality of a raster image that's been expanded. However, eventually, almost any vector image is *rasterized*, meaning that it is rendered into pixels. Vector images are converted into raster graphics so that they can be used on other systems. For example, you may create a graphic using Adobe Illustrator, but then save it as a raster image that can be displayed on a Web site, or used in a file format commonly used in printed documents.

Scalable Vector Graphics

Although files created as vector graphics aren't supported by a number of programs, the inclusion of an XML specification and file format called *Scalable Vector Graphics* (SVG) enables the use of vector graphics on Web pages. SVG images are images that incorporate vector graphics, raster images, and text to create an image that is portable and resizable. SVG images can be scaled indefinitely without any loss of quality. Using XML, an SVG file can be included in a Web page as a simple graphic, or incorporating scripts that make the image interactive.

Metafile Graphics

Metafile graphics are images that can contain a combination of raster, vector, and type data. Because they contain multiple types of data, they can be enlarged or reduced without any loss of resolution, making the image appear the same regardless of resizing. Some types of metafile graphics include:

- Encapsulated PostScript, which have the file extension .eps
- Computer Graphics Metafile, which have the file extension .cgm
- Windows Metafile, which have the file extension .wmf
- Enhanced Metafile, which have the file extension .emf

Image File Formats

Anyone who's looked at digital pictures is well aware that a wide number of file formats are available in which images can be saved. Each format has its own benefits and drawbacks, and

can impact the quality of the image, and how it should be used. In the sections that follow, we'll look at the following raster graphics, and look at the features of each:

- BMP (Bitmap) files
- GIF (Graphics Interchange Format)
- PNG (Portable Network Graphics)
- JPEG (Joint Photographic Experts Group)
- JPEG 2000
- TIFF (Tagged Image File Format)

BMP

Because each file format we'll discuss here is a raster graphic, which is a bitmapped image, it should come as no surprise that bitmaps are included here. BMP is a Bitmap file that has been used for years in operating systems such as Windows and OS/2. They support a color depth of up to 24 bits, allowing for 16.7 million colors. You will see BMP files as the logo that appears when Windows starts up, and may have used them as wallpaper for your desktop. Another common use for BMP files is when pictures or other documents are scanned and saved in a BMP file format.

Because BMP files aren't compressed, they are often large, and generally not suitable for the Internet. Despite this, Internet browsers such as Internet Explorer do support BMPs, and will load them from Web pages or downloads. Because of this, when examining a computer, you shouldn't necessarily assume that a BMP file is a system file and not an image that is worth further analysis.

GIF

GIF is an acronym for *Graphics Interchange Format*, and is one of the most popular file formats used for images on the Internet. GIF is an image format developed by CompuServe that allows images to be saved using an 8-bit palette, limiting the number of possible colors used in the image to 256. Due to the limitation in color, GIFs are commonly used for line art, cartoons, logos, and other images that aren't detailed and use a limited number of colors.

Although GIFs were first introduced in 1987, another version of the format was released two years later that provided additional features. The two versions of GIF that continue to be used today are:

- **GIF87A** Developed in 1987, and provides basic features and the ability to interlace graphics.
- **GIF89A** Developed in 1989, and has all the features of 87A in addition to support for transparency, inclusion of comments in the file, and animation.

NOTE

GIF is generally pronounced as *jif* (with a soft G) although so many people pronounce it with a hard G that either is considered acceptable.

Interlacing

When a GIF or other image loads in an Internet browser or other programs, it isn't shown until the entire image has been completely downloaded. An *interlaced GIF*, on the other hand, will display as it is being transmitted. Whereas a noninterlaced GIF will display by scrolling from the top of the screen to the bottom, much like a blind being pulled down, an interlaced GIF displays the image like a Venetian blind. As seen in Figure 2.10, the image first appears fuzzy, but becomes clearer as more lines of data are received and the image is filled in. Because of the way the image becomes progressively clearer as data is received, interlacing is also referred to as *progressive encoding*.

Figure 2.10 Interlaced GIF Loading

Transparency

A *transparent GIF* is an image that has one of up to 256 colors set as being fully transparent. When transparency is set on a particular color, any areas of the image using that color become invisible, and the background of the Web page or document is seen through the image. All of the other colors that aren't transparent remain opaque, and are fully visible on the document.

A common use of this is with a logo or other image that has transparency set on a background color. When you consider that an image is generally square or rectangular, a simple logo or graphic will appear as though it's on a block of color, because the background color of the

image is fully visible. By setting the background color as transparent, the rest of the image appears as though it's printed on the page.

Animation

Animated GIFs are images that have individual images embedded in them. When the GIF is loaded, these individual images, called *frames*, are displayed in sequence, providing movement to the series of pictures displayed. This is the essentially the same method used by films, where individual frames of a filmstrip are played to give motion to the pictures.

Because the animation is a series of individual images, other data can also be inserted into the image file. Textual information can be added to these files as comments, which aren't visible when the image is played, but can be used to provide information regarding who created the file.

PNG

PNG is an acronym for Portable Network Graphics, and was developed as an open source successor to the GIF format. When it was developed, a number of improvements to the old GIF format were added. PNG supports 24-bit color, allows areas of the image to be made transparent, supports interlacing, and uses a variety of compression methods (which we'll discuss later in this chapter).

Another difference between PNG and GIF is that PNG doesn't support animation. Instead, a companion format was created, called Multiple Image Network Graphics (MNG). Animation is not incorporated in the PNG format because animated GIFs were rarely used, were considered distracting on a Web page, and often were used for only a short time until the novelty wore off. As other dynamic content such as Shockwave and Flash gained in popularity, however, interest in animation also grew.

NOTE

PNG is pronounced *ping*, or is often discussed by stating the letters of its abbreviation: P-N-G. Similarly, the animated companion file format to PNG, called MNG, is pronounced *ming* or simply stated using the letters M-N-G.

Even though the first specification for PNG was developed in 1996, it took a considerable amount of time before Internet browsers supported this format. Although Internet browsers could display GIFs or JPEGs (which we'll discuss next), PNG graphics were initially supported by a small number of browsers, which increased over time. With the release of Internet Explorer 7, however, all major Internet browsers now support this file format.

JPEG

JPEG images are another of the most popular file formats on the Internet. *JPEG* is an acronym for *Joint Photographic Experts Group*, which is the also the name of the committee that developed this file format. JPEG images support 24-bit color and use compression to make the files smaller. Because the color depth is better than GIFs, while remaining at a manageable size, JPEG is often used to transmit images over the Internet.

This file format also allows you to save the file using interlacing. A JPEG using interlacing is called a *progressive JPEG*, and displays a picture in a series of passes that starts as a blocky, low-resolution image that progressively improves. Even though the JPEG is interlaced, it retains the same color depth and quality as a noninterlaced JPEG.

> **NOTE**
>
> JPEG is the pronounced *jay-peg*.

JPEG 2000

JPEG 2000 was designed as a successor to the JPEG format, which had been accepted as a standard in 1994. The JPEG 2000 standard provides the same features as JPEG (such as compression, 24-bit color, etc.), but also supports transparency. Because the compression in JPEG 2000 is improved and doesn't result in the same loss of image quality, JPEG 2000 files are used in digital cameras and software.

TIFF

TIFF is an acronym for Tagged Image File Format, an image format that has been commonly used for print since its introduction. TIFFs are often used for desktop publishing and graphic design, although the format was originally developed in the 1980s as a standard file format in which scanned images could be saved. The goal was to avoid proprietary file formats when a picture or document was scanned, with the assumption that all scanners would eventually support the TIFF format. As scanners grew more powerful, the TIFF file format evolved to support grayscale and color images. Because the image quality was so high, even images that weren't scanned were saved in this format and used in printed materials.

TIFFs support a wide range of colors, and can be exported as 8-bit, 16-bit, 24-bit, or 32-bit color modes. Because higher-quality images are also larger, this affects its portability to other systems, and its use on the Internet. When TIFFs are saved, they are generally high-resolution graphics that are larger in size than JPEGs or other file formats. As such, Internet browsers generally don't support this format. However, in addition to images created or modified in graphics programs, many digital cameras support TIFF as a format in which photos are stored on the camera.

Data Compression

Image files can be considerably large, with many photos, drawings, or other graphics being measured in megabytes. Such graphics can take minutes to transfer across the Internet or networks, and can even take awhile when loaded from a local hard disk. Because their size can make them unusable for many purposes, images often use compression to make them smaller. *Image compression* makes files smaller by reducing the amount of redundant information in the image. To achieve this, one of two compression methods may be used:

- Lossy compression, in which the original image is approximately re-created
- Lossless compression, in which the original image is exactly re-created

Lossy Compression

Lossy compression is a method of data compression in which the size of the file is reduced by eliminating data in the file. In doing so, image quality is sacrificed to decrease file size. Any data that the compression algorithm deems expendable is removed from the image, thereby reducing its size. Although the file doesn't have the same data as it did before compression was used, often this won't be noticeable, even though the resolution of the image has suffered.

Where lossy compression does become noticeable is when a file is modified and resaved multiple times. In comparing the two images in Figure 2.11, you will see that the image on the left is of higher quality. This is because the image on the right has been saved as a JPEG several times. Each time it was saved, lossy compression was used, and details of the image were sacrificed. Although the first number of times an image is saved won't result in noticeable differences, Figure 2.11 shows that multiple saves of an image using lossy compression will eventually degrade the image so that the sacrifice in quality becomes recognizable.

Figure 2.11 Lossy Compression

Saying that lossy compression sacrifices data doesn't mean it removes data arbitrarily. After all, it would be noticeable if someone in a JPEG photo was suddenly missing an eye. Rather, lossy compression removes data from an image using one or more of several techniques:

- **Chroma subsampling** Decreasing the color (chroma) information stored in the image rather than the brightness in the image decreases the size of the file. Because the human eye sees luminance more sharply than colors, colors used in the image can be sacrificed if the brightness of the picture is adjusted accordingly.

- **Color reduction** Colors that are saved in the image take up space, but many times the number of colors used can be reduced without being noticeable. For example, you might see the sky as merely being blue, but if you looked at it closely, you would notice that it is numerous shades of blue. Taking a picture of the sky would capture these variations in color. When you reduce the number of colors used to the most common ones, the pixels in the image reference a single color or group of colors.

- **Fractal compression** Because a fraction of one image may resemble another, parts of an image that are similar to one another are located, and a fractal algorithm is used to duplicate those parts.

- **Transform coding** This method involves averaging the colors used in an image so that fewer colors are used in total. Because the human eye perceives certain colors more vividly than others, the use of this method isn't perceptible to most people.

- **Vector quantization** Rather than representing individual values for data stored in an image, an algorithm will approximate the data as a smaller set of data. It does this by using a codebook that contains a limited number of values that resemble the original data. The algorithm uses these choices to create an approximation of the original image using the smaller subset of data. For example, to use our earlier example of a blue sky, the blues in a 24-bit color image could be reduced to a smaller 8-bit set of colors. A vector quantization algorithm would approximate what colors in the image could be replaced with the smaller set of data. Although data in the image has changed, the approximation of data would be similar enough that it wouldn't be readily identifiable.

Lossless Compression

Lossless compression is a method of data compression in which the size of the file is reduced without sacrificing image quality. Unlike lossy compression, no data is lost when this method is used. Because the data is preserved, the technique will decompress the data and restore it exactly to its original state.

Because no data is removed from the file, it can't be compressed to the same degree as lossy compression. On average, files are reduced by a maximum of 50 percent, whereas lossy

compression can surpass this and provide a greater reduction in file size. To achieve compression without losing data, several methods can be used:

- **Adaptive dictionary algorithms** Dictionary-based algorithms shrink files by finding common elements that match a catalog of data. One method that is used by GIFs and TIFFs is LZW. When the compression algorithm is run, it will compare data in the file to data that is stored in the dictionary, and then replace values in the image with those in the dictionary. To illustrate this with a simple example, let's say the dictionary contained the values 1-my, 2-is, 3-stupid. If the file contained the words "my job is stupid," it could replace the words with values from the dictionary index, making it "1 job 2 3" in the file. To decompress the file, it would then use the dictionary to revert the compressed data back to its original form. The more words that are used in the file that will match those in the dictionary, the greater the reduction in size when the file is saved.

- **Deflation** This method uses a combination of Huffman Coding (which we'll explain next, when we discuss entropy coding) and LZ77 (Lempel-Ziv) Coding algorithms. Deflation is used by PNG, MNG, and TIFF formats as well as by compression programs such as ZIP, PKZIP, and GZIP. *Lempel-Ziv* coding works by finding sequences of data that have been repeated, and then replaces the repeated data with information regarding where to find it before. A "sliding window" is used to keep track of data that appeared previously in a file so that a repetition of the data can be replaced with information concerning how far back that sequence resides in the data, and the length of the repeated data.

- **Entropy encoding** This method compresses images by looking for patterns in the data, and replacing those that occur frequently in the image with codes that are smaller in size. *Huffman Coding* is an example of entropy encoding. It assigns variable-length codes to a known set of values. Values that occur the most frequently in a file are assigned the shortest codes, and patterns that occur infrequently are assigned longer codes. In doing so, the bulk of data is replaced by the shortest possible code, which means less data is used to create the file.

- **Run-length encoding** Data will often contain sequences of the same data occurring repeatedly in a file; run-length encoding finds these repetitive patterns and stores them as a count of how often the pattern repeats and the value. For example, if we looked at the line AAAABBC, we would see that it consists of four As, two Bs and one C. Using run-length encoding, we could convert this to 4A2BC.

Remember that image compression will be either lossy or lossless. Lossy compression will compress/decompress the image as an approximation of the original data. Lossless compression is a re-creation of the original data. With lossless compression, no data is permanently modified or lost.

Locating and Recovering Image Files

Although occasionally you may be asked to look at an image stored on a single floppy disk, or an image that was e-mailed to a particular account, more often you're required to examine the contents of a hard disk, and accompanying DVDs, CDs, or other larger media. As we'll see in the sections that follow, to examine images on a computer, you may need to extract them, repair them, and perform other tasks before they can even be viewed.

Image File Headers

An *image file header* is a portion of a file that contains data about the image's size, resolution, number of colors, and other facts that a program will need to display it properly. File headers provide information on the unique characteristics of files, which make it possible to identify the type of file simply by a few bytes in the beginning. For example, all BMP files have the characters BM in the first two positions of the file data. When an application opens a file, it will read the header to ensure that the image isn't damaged and can be opened by the program. Such information can be viewed by using a hexadecimal editor such as WinHex or a binary file viewer.

If a header is missing or damaged, the file may not open properly (if at all) and may appear corrupted. You can restore headers manually by replacing the missing header of one file on another. For example, if you were dealing with a Microsoft Word document, you could open another document in a hex editor, copy the header from it, and then paste it onto the document that has a missing header. With images, however, this can result in the picture appearing odd. As we mentioned, the image header will provide information regarding the height, width, and other factors that determine how the image is displayed. If you replaced the header of a file with incorrect information, this could make an image unrecognizable.

File Fragments

Even though a file has been deleted, part of the data may still be found in unallocated space or slack space on the hard disk. Even though part of the data is missing from the file, it is still possible to view the information using a Hex Editor or other tools, and reconstruct the file so that it is restored. In restoring the file, the image may not be an exact re-creation of its original

state, but it can be close enough to view the contents of the file, or see what was depicted in the image.

Reconstructing file fragments is easier when dealing with text files or other documents and files that can be read and easily understood. If you found a fragment of a text file or Word document, for example, you might be able to view what was written in the document, and determine which other file fragments are a part of the document. By piecing the fragments together, you can completely or approximately restore the original document to its original condition.

Unknown Files

When analyzing a computer, it is possible that you will discover fragments or entire files that you're unsure about. These files may have file extensions that you're unfamiliar with, and may not be associated with any programs on the suspect's computer or on the computer that's being used to analyze the data. In such cases, you will need to identify what the file is for, and what program may be used to open it.

One of the most useful tools to determine what a particular file is for is a Web site called FILExt (www.filext.com). Using FILExt is straightforward, as you simply enter the file extension you want to learn about into a search box on the Web page, and then click a Submit button. The online database is then searched, providing you with the following information about the file:

- Name of the extension.

- Function, which explains such information as whether the file is a graphic, is an executable for a particular program, or is used by a particular program (such as a .doc being a Microsoft Word document.

- Notes, which may provide additional information. For example, if you looked up information on a .cbr extension, you'd find that it is actually a renamed RAR file that can be decompressed using the RAR utility.

- MIME type, which may provide MIME information.

- Company, which may identify who has proprietary ownership of the file type.

- Identifying characters, which may provide header data which may be used to identify the file type.

- Associated links, which may provide links to sites providing programs that will open files with that extension.

Image File Forensic Tools

As we'll see in Chapter 14 of this book, forensic software such as EnCase provides the ability to make a bitstream image of a hard disk (including deleted files, data in slack space, and file fragments found on the lost clusters or other areas of the disk). EnCase and many other forensic

tools also have a component that will allow you to view photos and other graphics that were found on the disk, showing them in a manner similar to that of a normal picture viewer. In addition to such software, tools are available that are specifically designed to deal with images found on disks. You can use image file forensic tools to extract data from an existing image file (i.e., a duplicate of data) so that you can view them. Some of these tools also have built-in image viewers, allowing you to view images without modifying them. Some of the more popular image file forensic tools available include the following:

- **GFE Stealth** GFE stands for Graphics File Extractor, and it is designed to be used with SafeBack bitstream backup files. SafeBack has been marketed to law enforcement agencies since 1990 and has been used by the FBI and the Criminal Investigation Division of the IRS to create image files for forensic examination and evidentiary purposes. It is capable of duplicating individual partitions or entire disks of virtually any size, and the image files can be transferred to SCSI tape units or almost any other magnetic storage media. The product contains CRC functions to check the integrity of the copies, as well as the date and timestamps to maintain an audit trail of the software's operations. The vendor provides a three-day computer forensic course to train forensic specialists in the use of the software. (In fact, the company does not provide technical support to individuals who have not undergone this training.) SafeBack is DOS-based and you can use it to copy DOS, Windows, and UNIX disks (including RAID drives) on Intel-compatible systems. You can save images as multiple files for storage on CDs or other small-capacity media. To avoid legal concerns about possible alteration, no compression or translation is used in creating the image. Once you have created a duplicate of the data using SafeBack, you can use GFE Stealth to automatically extract photos and other images. You can examine files output by GFE Stealth using any of the picture viewers discussed in the next section. GFE Stealth is available from www.forensics-intl.com.

- **P2 eXplorer** This tool allows you to view an image created with SafeBack, as well as other forensic software such as EnCase and Paraben's Forensic Replicator. After you mount these image files, the software then allows you to view what data was acquired when the evidence files were created, and the bitstream copy of the data was created. P2 eXplorer is available from www.paraben-forensics.com.

- **ILook** With this tool, you can analyze an image acquired from a suspect computer with other software. Using a GUI similar to Windows Explorer, you can examine evidence by moving through a directory structure as it appeared on the original machine. Once you find photos and other evidence that you'd like to extract, you can extract all or part of the file system, and then view the file through built-in features. It also has a built-in hex viewer and reporting features. ILook is available from www.ilook-forensics.org.

Picture Viewers

Once you've extracted images from a suspect's machine, people other than those using the forensic software may need to view the images you've found. This not only includes defense lawyers, prosecutors, investigators, and others in law enforcement, but also employers in cases of internal investigations. Because forensic software is expensive, access to the same software you used to acquire the evidence may be limited. It's for this reason that picture viewers may be used to view the data. Many picture viewers are on the market, including the following:

- IrfranView, www.irfanview.com

- ACDSee, www.acdsee.com

- ThumbsPlus, www.cerious.com

- AD Picture Viewer, www.abroaddesign.com

- Picture Viewer Max, www.accessoryware.com/PictView.htm

- FastStone Image Viewer, www.faststone.org

- XnView, www.xnview.com

As shown in Figure 2.12, XnView provides a listing of directories in the left pane, and shows what images are in a particular directory in the upper-right pane. When you select an image, it appears in the lower **Preview** pane. In addition to this, clicking on the **Properties** tab will display information on a particular image, including its file format, timestamps, size, compression used, and other attributes. By clicking on the **EXIF** tab, you can display extra information, which could include the type of camera used to take the image, the exposure, the date the picture was taken, and other facts.

Figure 2.12 XnView

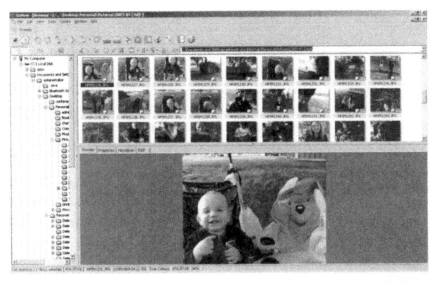

A problem with picture viewers is that there is no guarantee that they will not modify the image. As such, picture viewers are primarily designed for viewing personal photos and other images that have been saved. Generally, when such programs access a file, the timestamp showing when it was last accessed is updated. Other features may also be included in the software for directly modifying images. Such issues can affect the credibility of the images as evidence.

When providing copies of evidence to investigators and other individuals, you should store them on DVD-R or CD-R discs that are Write Once-Read Many. Because data can't be added or modified once it's written to the disc, any images that are viewed with a picture viewer will be safe from any damage or modification.

Steganography in Image Files

Steganography is a process of hiding one form of data within another. Because of the way data is stored in files, there are often unused (empty) bits in a file such as a document or graphic. A message can be broken up and stored in these unused bits, and when the file is sent it will appear to be only the original file (called the *container file*). The hidden information inside is usually encrypted, and the recipient will need special software to retrieve it (and then decrypt it, if necessary). Messages can be concealed inside all sorts of other files, including executables and graphics and audio files. Another form of steganography is the hidden watermark that is sometimes used to embed a trademark or other symbol in a document or file. We'll take a close look at hiding data in Chapter 7, which specifically deals with this subject.

Copyright Issues Regarding Graphics

Copyright is a form of legal protection to prevent unauthorized use and copying of a person's work. Although this is often associated with written work, music, software, and other forms of work, it also extends to photographs, logos, and other graphics that may be created. If you've ever had your picture taken by a professional photographer, you're already aware that although you paid for the pictures to be taken, you don't actually own them. The photographer owns the photos, and you simply pay for copies of them. Because of copyright laws, the photographer has the right to reproduce, sell, or display those images, whereas you would need expressed permission to do the same.

Copyright laws vary between countries, and are enforced internationally through treaties. Since 1989, copyrights in the United States are automatic, and don't require any official patent or registration. In other words, as soon as a photograph, drawing, or graphic is created, it is the property of the creator, and thereby protected by copyright. The key to this is that the image is in a tangible form, and not simply an idea.

This isn't to say that a copyright can't be officially registered with the government. You can use the U.S. Copyright Office (www.copyright.gov) to register creative works, providing proof of when a particular image or logo was created. In doing so, you have proof that the image is your work and that it has been protected by copyright since a particular time. If the copyright was violated, you could use this as evidence and pursue civil litigation.

Summary of Exam Objectives

In this chapter, we looked at a number of issues dealing with file systems, hard disks, other media, and image files. We saw that hard disks are the most common media for storing data, and that data is stored to a disk on tracks and in sectors. Operating systems may use a variety of different file systems to format the drive, organizing the files into a logical system, and storing data in logical clusters or blocks on the disk. Even when data is deleted or corrupted, it may continue to exist in lost clusters, slack space, and other areas of the file system.

Storage media aren't limited to hard disks, and we saw how floppy disks, CDs, DVDs, USB flash drives, and other removable media and devices can provide a way to make data portable and safe. Unlike in the early days of computers, a considerable amount of data can be saved to such media today. In some cases, this can provide a useful alternative for storage, whereas in others (such as magnetic tape), it is best used for backing up data.

A common form of data stored on various media and devices is images. Pictures may be stored in a variety of formats and compressed in different ways to make the files easier to transfer across such as like the Internet. Digital photos may also use compression and specific file formats on disks, and (as with other graphical images created by a person) may be protected by copyright. If such data is being recovered using forensic software, various programs are available to work with the forensic software and extract the pictures from evidence files. Once this is done, features in the program may be used to examine the graphical images, or picture-viewing software may be used to look at them.

Exam Objectives Fast Track

Understanding File Systems and Hard Disks

- ☑ Storage media are physical devices and items that store data permanently.

- ☑ Hard disks are nonvolatile storage devices that are used to store and retrieve data quickly.

- ☑ Nonvolatile storage is physical storage media that retain the data without electrical power. This means that no data is lost when the computer or device is powered off.

- ☑ Form factors define the physical dimensions of a device, and refer to the width of a disk drive.

- ☑ Jumpers are connectors that works as on/off switches for the hard disk, and are used to configure the hard disk as either a primary or secondary hard disk.

- ☑ In a master/slave configuration, the master is the primary hard disk installed on a computer, and the slave is the secondary hard disk.

☑ A platter is a rigid disk inside the hard disk, on which data is written and read.

☑ Tracks are concentric circles on the disk where data is saved on the magnetic surface of the platter.

☑ Sectors are segments of a track, and the smallest physical storage unit on a disk.

☑ Disk capacity is the amount of data that a hard disk is capable of holding.

☑ SCSI is a standard that allows devices to be connected in a daisy-chain fashion.

☑ USB allows up to 127 devices to be connected in a daisy chain or through a USB hub to a computer.

☑ Fibre Channel uses optical fiber to pass data at high speeds. It is commonly used on SANs.

☑ File systems control how data is organized and stored on storage devices.

☑ FAT stands for File Allocation Table; the FAT file system was developed for use by the DOS operating systems. FAT16 was developed for disks larger than 16MB, and for a long time it was the standard file system for formatting hard disks, whereas FAT32 is the common version of FAT used today. It uses a 32-bit allocation table, and supports larger volumes.

☑ Virtual FAT, or VFAT, is not a file system, but a file system driver that handles long filenames to deal with the 8.3 limitation imposed by the original FAT16.

☑ NTFS is the New Technology File System, and is designed to be more robust and secure than other Microsoft file systems.

☑ Encryption is the process of encoding a file so that it can't be read by anyone other than those who are authorized to open and view the data.

☑ Disk encryption refers to encrypting the entire contents of a hard disk, diskette, or removable disk.

☑ File encryption refers to encrypting data stored on disk on a file-by-file basis.

☑ EFS is used to protect data on a hard disk or large removable disk. EFS can't be used to protect data on floppy diskettes because they cannot be formatted in NTFS format, but allows encryption of individual files and/or folders.

☑ Linux is an open source operating system that is based on the UNIX operating system. It supports multiple file systems through the use of a VFS. Some of the operating systems supported include versions of EXT.

☑ MFS is a file system used to store data on 400KB floppy disks. It uses a resource fork to store structured information, and a data fork to store unstructured data.

☑ HFS superseded MFS, supporting larger storage media (i.e., hard disks) and allowing long filenames of up to 255 characters.

☑ HFS Plus is the latest file system used by Macintosh computers, and supports larger storage media.

☑ ZFS is an acronym for Zettabyte File System, and is designed to handle large amounts of data on computers using the Sun Solaris 10 operating system.

☑ Network file systems and file sharing protocols allow users to access and update files on remote computers as though they were on the local computer.

☑ UDF is a file system that is used by both CDs and DVDs, and is a standard format from the Optical Storage Technology Association (OSTA). It is based on the ISO-13346 standard.

☑ ISO-9660 was introduced as a standard for CD-ROM media in 1988, and is commonly referred to as CDFS.

☑ Partitions are used to divide areas of the disk so that the operating system can format the partition and assign it a drive letter. Primary partitions can be used to store the operating system, whereas extended partitions can be used to create logical drives that can also have their own drive letters.

☑ The first sector on a hard disk is the boot sector or MBR, which contains a partition table with information on partitions used on that disk.

☑ Clusters are groups of two or more consecutive sectors on a hard disk.

☑ Slack space is the area of space between the end of a file and the end of the last cluster used by that data.

☑ A lost cluster is a cluster that has been marked as being used, even though it hasn't been assigned to a file.

☑ Boot disks are bootable floppy disks or CDs that contain essential files that are needed to start the computer.

☑ The Windows Registry is a database in which critical system and application configuration and initialization information is stored.

Understanding Digital Media Devices

☑ Magnetic tapes consist of a thin plastic strip that has a magnetic coating, on which data can be stored. Tapes are commonly used to back up data on network servers and individual computers.

☑ Floppy disks have been a common method of storing data since the early days of personal computers; 3.5-inch floppy disks are disks that are coated with a magnetic material and are housed in plastic. They are capable of storing 1.44MB of data.

☑ CD is an acronym for Compact Disc and is a 5-inch optical disc that can contain up to 700MB of data.

☑ DVD is an acronym for Digital Video Disc or Digital Versatile Disc. It is a 5-inch optical disc that is able to store from 4.7GB to 17GB of data.

☑ HD-DVD is the high-density successor to DVD that was developed for recording high-definition video to disc. A single-layer HD-DVD is capable of storing up to 15GB of data, and a dual-layer disc can store up to 30GB of data.

☑ Blu-Ray is a high-density optical storage method that was designed for recording high-definition video. A single-layer Blu-Ray disc can store up to 25GB of data, and a dual-layer Blu-Ray disc can store up to 50GB of data.

☑ iPod is the brand name of portable media players that was developed by Apple, and can be used to store audio, video, and other files.

☑ Zune is a portable media player that was developed by Microsoft. It has similar features to the iPod and can share files wirelessly.

☑ Flash memory cards and sticks are storage devices that are commonly used for storing photos in digital cameras (and transferring them to PCs) and for storing and transferring programs and data between handheld computers (Pocket PCs and Palm OS devices).

☑ USB flash drives are storage devices that can store any type of data, including photos, video, documents, and various other types of data. They come in a range of storage sizes (up to 64GB), and can be used with almost any system that supports the USB version of the device.

Image File Forensics

☑ Image files are digital photos, line art, and other graphical representations of people, places, and objects that can be saved to a storage device.

☑ Raster images are graphics that are created or captured as a set of pixels that are mapped to a grid.

☑ *Pixel* is an abbreviation for the words *picture element* and is the smallest element of a digital image. Each pixel contains programmable information that defines its color, size, and location in the image

☑ Resolution is the sharpness of an image, which is determined by the number of pixels used in the graphic. The more pixels used in an image, the higher the resolution.

☑ Resolution is measured in *dots per inch* (dpi), which refers to the number of pixels that are used in a 1-inch space of the document.

☑ Color depth is a term used to describe the number of bits (binary digits) used to represent the color of a pixel, which is measured as *bits per pixel* (bpp).

☑ Vector graphics are generated from mathematical information stored in the graphic, which instructs the program opening the image how to display the position, width, length, direction, and other aspects of objects used to create the picture.

☑ Scalable Vector Graphics (SVG) are images that incorporate vector graphics, raster images, and text to create an image that is portable and resizable. Using XML, an SVG file can be included in a Web page as a simple graphic, or incorporating scripts that make the image interactive.

☑ Metafile graphics are images that can contain a combination of raster, vector, and type data.

☑ BMP (Bitmap) files are bitmapped images that are commonly used by Windows and OS/2 operating systems for system graphics, and for wallpaper images.

☑ GIF (Graphics Interchange Format) is an image format that uses an 8-bit palette, allowing the image to be saved in 256 colors.

☑ Interlaced GIFs are displayed on a screen through a series of passes, where the image becomes progressively clearer as more data is received.

☑ Animated GIFs are images that have individual images embedded in them that are shown in sequence when the graphic is loaded.

☑ PNG is an acronym for Portable Network Graphics, and was developed as an open source successor to the GIF format. PNG supports 24-bit color, allows areas of the image to be made transparent, supports interlacing, and offers multiple compression methods.

☑ JPEG (Joint Photographic Experts Group) is an image format that supports 24-bit color, and uses compression to make the files smaller.

☑ JPEG 2000 is a file format that was designed as a successor to the JPEG format, and provides improved compression and supports transparency.

☑ TIFF (Tagged Image File Format) is an image format that has been commonly used for print.

☑ Image compression makes files smaller by reducing the amount of redundant information in the image.

☑ An image file header is a portion of a file that contains data about the image's size, resolution, number of colors, and other facts that a program will need to display it properly.

☑ Steganography is the process of hiding one form of data within another.

☑ Copyright is a form of legal protection to prevent unauthorized use and copying of a person's work.

Exam Objectives Frequently Asked Questions

The following Frequently Asked Questions, answered by the authors of this book, are designed to both measure your understanding of the Exam Objectives presented in this chapter, and to assist you with real-life implementation of these concepts.

Q: As I understand it, any data that's examined in a computer forensic examination should be duplicated first. Does this apply only to hard disks, or does it apply to other media that can't be modified, such as CD-Rs and DVD-Rs?

A: Because CD-Rs and DVD-Rs are Write Once-Read Many (WORM), data on such media can't be modified once it's been written. However, the original discs can still be damaged, making any data irretrievable. Because the original evidence is now lost, anything you found on the discs could be brought into question. After all, the process isn't repeatable if the original evidence hasn't been destroyed. To protect the evidence from possible damage, you should duplicate the data on the discs and then work from these duplicate images. The original discs can then be placed in a safe location.

Q: Which of the file systems for Microsoft system provides the most security?

A: NTFS is the most secure of the file systems used on Microsoft operating systems. In supports permissions on files and folders, as well as encryption using the Encrypting File System (EFS).

Q: It seems as if Blu-ray and HD-DVD are about the same. Which one is better?

A: There are arguments on both sides for which is better. HD-DVD can store up to 15GB of data, whereas a dual-layer disc can store 30GB. Blu-ray can store 25GB, whereas dual-layer can store up to 50GB. Both provide high-definition video, and movies are distributed on both types of discs. However, the popularity for both formats is great enough that players and recorders are available that support both formats.

Q: I am searching for pictures that may have been exported from a digital camera's memory card to a location on the hard disk. Are there any particular file formats that I should watch for?

A: Many cameras will store images in either TIFF or JPEG 2000 format. Both of these formats support high color depth, and can be compressed for better storage on a memory card.

CHFI

The Computer Investigation Process

Exam objectives in this chapter:

- **Investigating Computer Crime**
- **Investigating Company Policy Violations**
- **Conducting a Computer Forensic Investigation**

Exam Objectives Review:

- ☑ **Summary of Exam Objectives**
- ☑ **Exam Objectives Fast Track**
- ☑ **Exam Objectives Frequently Asked Questions**

Introduction

The word *forensics* is derived from a Latin term meaning a forum in which legal disputes are settled, but no one in ancient Rome could have ever imagined how the term would apply to today's legal system. As with other areas of forensics, *computer forensics* refers to an investigative process of gathering and examining evidence to establish facts so that accurate testimony and evidence can later be presented in court or other hearings. The key to this definition being that any work an investigator performs may be scrutinized and used as evidence in court.

Where computer forensics differs from other forensic sciences is that electronic evidence is collected and examined. Although fingerprints or other evidence may also be obtained from the devices collected at a crime scene, a computer forensic technician will use specialized methods, techniques, and tools to acquire data stored on hard disks, USB Flash Drives, or other devices. Once the data is acquired from a device, the computer forensic technician will then examine it to identify which files, folders, or information may be useful as evidence, and can provide facts about the case.

Although computer forensics is commonly used in criminal cases, it may also be used in civil disputes or corporate investigations, such as when internal policies have been violated. When an employee is suspected of using a computer to perform some action that violates policies, the files, e-mail, and other data on the computer may be inspected. Because there is the possibility that the violations could lead to criminal charges or civil actions against the employee, it is important that forensic procedures are followed.

Collecting such evidence requires following established procedures, and can take considerable amounts of time to ensure it is collected correctly. Because it may reveal the identity of a culprit and be used to establish the guilt or innocence of people, it is vital that the data aren't modified as they are acquired, or altered afterwards when the data are examined. In addition to this, any actions and results are documented in case this information is required in court. By following such methodologies, the investigation of a computer crime can be conducted effectively and with a higher degree of success in collecting and processing evidence.

Investigating Computer Crime

Computer forensics may be employed in any crime that involves a computer. Because computers are so commonly used in homes and business, they are increasingly a source of evidence. Files stored on computers are often used in place of other record systems, and may contain a significant amount of information that can be employed to convict a suspect or prove their innocence. For example, in a homicide investigation, a suspect may have written about their plans in a diary on the computer, or a blog on the Internet. Conversely, if a student were accused of bullying a classmate via e-mail, a simple check of the messages on his or her machine could establish whether the accusations were false. Almost any type of crime may result in some type of evidence being stored on a computer, but a number of cybercrimes commonly require a computer forensic examination. These include:

- Threatening e-mail

- Harassment

- Fraud

- Hacking and/or the dissemination of viruses

- Theft of intellectual property

- Child pornography

When crimes are committed using computers, often the only evidence available to prosecute the person who committed the offense resides in a digital format. Illegal images will only be stored on a hard disk or other media, proof of an intruder's activities may be stored in logs, and documents containing evidence of the crime are only available by investigating computers used in the crime or those subjected to the crime. By examining the digital contents of these computers, an investigation can reach a successful conclusion: prosecuting the culprit and using information acquired from the investigation to make existing systems more secure.

Damage & Defense...

Using a Bad Situation to Improve Current Systems

When a computer system is hacked or used in the commission of a crime, the victim is often unaware of the vulnerabilities in their systems that left them open to attack. A person who had malicious software installed might not know of antivirus or antispyware software, or the need to update signature files regularly. Similarly, a company might not know that their current firewall failed to prevent certain kinds of intrusions, or was configured incorrectly. To prevent future intrusions or attacks, victims of computer crime can learn from the experience and help improve current systems.

An example of this is a crime that occurred against a major university in October of 2006. Brock University experienced the embarrassment of their systems being hacked and the personal information of nearly 70,000 alumni and other donors being stolen. Information on possibly every person who had ever donated to the university was accessed, including the individuals' credit card and banking information. The university contacted police to investigate the incident and then notified those people whose information may have been stolen. Within 24 hours, people were contacted via telephone, and thousands of letters were sent to inform donors of this breach in security. The university followed up by having the security of their systems reviewed and improvements made. Damage control also involved responding to the media and informing the public that steps were being taken to repair vulnerabilities and improve security. Although the university was caught in a bad situation, the handling of it is a textbook case on how to properly respond to an incident and use the situation to review and revise current systems.

How an Investigation Starts

Investigations always start with a crime being committed and someone noticing it. As basic as this sounds, if these two aspects are not a valid part of the equation, an investigation will never occur. To illustrate this, let's look at a situation where a man has downloaded pornography to his computer. If the people posing in these images are of legal age, it is not illegal to save them to his hard disk and view them later, but if the images depict minors engaged in sex, then the pictures are illegal and a crime has occurred. However, even though a crime has been committed, this doesn't mean he'll ever be investigated. For an investigation to begin, someone must notice the crime has happened and report it to the appropriate authorities. If no complaint is made, the person gets away with the crime.

The complainant plays a key role in any investigation. In addition to making authorities aware of the criminal activity, they provide essential information about what they've discovered. They may have seen a threatening e-mail or other illegal materials displayed on a co-worker's computer and can identify which computer contained the evidence. If they were repairing a computer and found illegal files in a particular directory, they can quicken an investigation by indicating where the files are stored. The statements made by a complainant can also be used to acquire search warrants (as we'll discuss later in this chapter) and act as the basis for further testimony in court. As the catalyst of an investigation, the role of a complainant is vital.

Who the complainant contacts often depends on the environment in which the crime took place and the computer(s) involved. In a computer crime, the computer may play one of two roles:

- It may be the target of a crime.
- It may be used to commit a crime.

If the complainant notices his or her home computer has been involved in a criminal act, chances are the complainant is the victim and the computer was a target of a crime. After all, few people confess to their involvement, or would subject themselves to being suspected. In situations involving home computers, the police are generally called first. This is also the case when someone notices illegal content on another person's home computer, or in small business environments that have limited staff. In larger companies, a complainant may first contact their supervisor or the Information Technology department. This is especially true if the crime involves a person's ability to work, such as when a server is compromised or a workstation has been infected by a virus or been hacked. If the organization's IT staff has someone who has been trained to properly respond to incidents, they may take some actions themselves before eventually contacting police.

What Your Role Is

Even when police have been called in to investigate a crime, a number of people may be involved. In a corporate environment, members of an Incident Response Team will generally be

the first people to respond to the incident. An Incident Response team is made of members of IT staff, and has the training and expertise to respond to various types of incidents. Members of this team may work with police investigators to provide access to systems and expertise, if needed. Senior staff members should be notified to deal with the effects of the incident and any inability to conduct normal business. In some cases, the company's Public Information Officer may be involved if the incident becomes known to the media and is deemed newsworthy.

If police aren't called in and the matter is to be handled internally, then the Incident Response team will deal with a much broader range of roles. Not only will team members handle the initial response to the incident, but will conduct the investigation and provide evidence to an internal authority. This authority may be senior staff, or in the case of a law enforcement agency, an Internal Affairs department. Even though no police may be involved in the situation, the procedures used in the forensic examination should be the same.

When conducting the investigation, a person must be designated as being in charge of the scene. This person should be knowledgeable in forensics and be directly involved in the investigation. In other words, just because the owner of the company is available, that person should not be in charge if they're computer illiterate and/or unfamiliar with procedures. The person in charge should have the authority to make final decisions on how the scene is secured, and how evidence is searched, handled, and processed.

People typically perform three major roles when conducting an investigation. These roles are:

- First Responder
- Investigator
- Crime Scene Technician

As we'll see in the paragraphs that follow, and as shown in Figure 3.1, each of these roles has specific duties associated with them, which are vital to a successful investigation. In certain situations, such as those involving an internal investigation within a company, a person may perform more than one of these roles.

EXAM WARNING

The primary roles in an investigation have specific duties associated with them. Although a person may play more than one role in an investigation, it is important you understand what is expected from each role, both for the exam and for real-world applications.

Figure 3.1 Primary Roles in an Investigation Involving Computer Forensics

The First Responder

The *First Responder* is the first person to arrive at a crime scene. However, while a first responder may be a complainant to a computer crime and notify police, this role should not be confused with someone without sufficient computer skills to deal with the problem. In other words, the first responder would not be a janitor who notices a server is making funny noises and calls someone else to begin an investigation. While someone like this is still important, as they could become the complainant if they notify appropriate parties, a first responder is someone who has the knowledge and skill to deal with the incident. This may be an officer, security personnel, a member of the IT staff or Incident Response Team, or any number of other individuals. The first responder is responsible for identifying the scope of the crime scene, securing it, and preserving volatile evidence.

Identifying the scope of a crime scene refers to establishing its scale. What is affected and where could evidence exist? When arriving on the scene, the first responder must identify what systems have been affected since these will be used to collect evidence. If these systems were located in one room, then the scope of the crime scene would be the room itself. If it were a single server in a closet, then the closet would be the crime scene. If a system of networked computers were involved, then the crime scene could extend to several buildings.

Once the crime scene has been identified, the first responder must then establish a perimeter and protect it. As we'll discuss in greater detail later in this chapter, protecting the

crime scene requires cordoning off the area where evidence resides. Until it is established what equipment may be excluded, everything in an area should be considered a possible source of evidence. This includes functioning and nonfunctioning workstations, laptops, servers, handheld PDAs, manuals, and anything else in the area of the crime. Until the scene has been processed, no one should be allowed to enter the area, and the existence of people in the area at the time of the crime should be documented.

The first responder shouldn't touch anything at the crime scene. Depending on how the crime was committed, traditional forensics may also be used to determine the identity of the person behind the crime. In the course of the investigation, police may collect DNA, finger-prints, hair, fibers, or other physical evidence. In terms of digital evidence, it is important for the first responder not to touch anything or attempt to do anything on the computer(s) since it may alter, damage, or destroy data or other identifying factors.

Preserving volatile evidence is another important duty of the first responder. As we'll discuss later in this chapter, *volatile data* is any data that may be lost once power is gone. If a source of evidence is on the monitor screen, they must take steps to preserve and document such evidence so it isn't lost. For example, a computer that may contain evidence can be left on and have programs opened on the screen, but if a power outage occurred, the computer would shut down and any unsaved information in memory would be lost. Photographing the screen or documenting what appeared on it would provide a record of what was displayed that could be used later as evidence.

The Investigator

When investigators arrive on the scene, it is important that the first responder provide as much information to them as possible. If the first responder touched anything, the investigator should be notified so this information can be added to a report. Any observations should be mentioned, as this may provide insight into resolving the incident.

An *investigator* may be a member of law enforcement or the Incident Response Team, and is responsible for investigating the crime or incident that has taken place. If a member of the Incident Response Team arrives first and collects some evidence, and the police arrive or are called later, then it is important that the person in charge of the team hand over all evidence and information dealing with the incident. If more than one member of the team was involved in the collection of evidence, documentation must be provided to the investigator dealing with what each person saw and did.

A chain of command should be established when the person investigating the incident arrives at the scene. The investigator must make clear that they are in charge so that important decisions are made or presented to them. Documentation should also be created to show who handled or possessed evidence during the course of the investigation, and provide details about how evidence is transferred to someone else's possession. Once the investigation begins, anyone handling the evidence is required to sign it in and out so there is a clear understanding of who possessed the evidence at any given time.

Even if the first responder has conducted an initial search for evidence, the investigator will need to establish what constitutes evidence and where it resides. If additional evidence is discovered, the perimeter securing the crime scene may be changed. The investigator will either have crime scene technicians begin to process the scene once its boundaries are established, or the investigator will perform the duties of a technician. The investigator or a designated person in charge remains at the scene until all evidence has been properly collected and transported.

Crime Scene Technicians

Crime Scene Technicians are individuals who have been trained in computer forensics, and have the knowledge, skills, and tools necessary to process a crime scene. The technician is responsible for preserving evidence, and will make great efforts to do so. The technician may acquire data from a system's memory, make images of hard disks before shutting them down, and ensure that systems are properly shut down before transport. Before transporting, all physical evidence will be sealed in a bag and/or tagged to identify it as a particular piece of evidence. The information identifying the evidence is added to a log so that a proper inventory of each piece exists. Evidence is further packaged to reduce the risk of damage, such as from electrostatic discharge or jostling during transport. Once transported, the evidence is then stored under lock and key to prevent tampering, until such time that it can be properly examined and analyzed.

As you can see, the roles involved in an investigation have varying responsibilities, and the person in each role requires special knowledge to perform it properly. While the preceding paragraphs provide an overview of what's involved, we still need to look at the specific tasks to understand how certain duties are carried out.

The Role of Evidence

The primary purpose of computer forensics is the collection, examination, preservation, and presentation of digital evidence. This course of action begins at the crime scene and ends in court or another type of inquiry, such as military or disciplinary tribunals where the process of hearing evidence is somewhat different from a criminal court. If evidence is collected, examined, preserved, or presented in a less than adequate manner, the evidence can be called into question and possibly deemed inadmissible in court.

Collection is a practice consisting of the identification, processing, and documentation of evidence. When collecting evidence, a crime scene technician will start by identifying what evidence is present, and where it is located. For example, if someone broke into the server room and changed permissions on the server, then the room and server would be where you would find evidence. When establishing this, the crime scene technician will then ensure that the crime scene has been secured, and that others have been prevented from entering the area and accessing the evidence. If the area wasn't secured, then suspects could enter the area and alter or contaminate evidence. For example, if fingerprints were being taken to determine who broke into the server room, then merely touching the door and other items would distort any find-

ings. Maybe the perpetrator left the fingerprints while in the process of breaking in, or maybe someone else left them before the crime scene was secured.

Once the crime scene technician has identified what evidence is present, the next step is identifying how the evidence can be recovered. Evidence on computers may be obtained in a variety of ways, from viewing log files to recovering the data with special forensic software, such as Encase or other tools that we'll discuss in Chapter 4. If data recovery is needed, the computer's operating system should be identified, and/or the media used to store the evidence. Once you've determined this, it is then possible to decide on the techniques and tools needed to recover the data.

In addition to photographing the screen of a computer to record any volatile data displayed, photographs should also be made of how the equipment is set up. When you've transported the equipment and are ready to begin examining it, you will need to set it up exactly as it was at the crime scene. After the case is completed, setup may also be required if the equipment is returned to the owner. To ensure the equipment is set up properly, you should photograph the front and back of the machine upon seizing it. Photographs or diagrams should be made showing how cables and wires were attached.

Backup media should also be collected since analyzing any backup tapes may show that an incident began earlier than expected. In some cases, you may find that data that were backed up days or even weeks before show that an intruder entered a system, or a virus infected data on hard disks. If this went undetected, it is possible you could unknowingly restore a virus to the system as part of the recovery process and thus repeat the initial incident.

Head of the Class…

Forensic Procedures

Forensics is a science in which the evidence is what may identify or convict a culprit. Because of the weight this evidence may present in a trial or internal investigation, you must ensure that the evidence hasn't been compromised in any way. If evidence is compromised, it can mean that someone whom you're certain committed a crime cannot be convicted, and an employee who threatened security will go unpunished.

A standard requirement in forensics is practicing due care. You need to be extremely careful as to how evidence is handled, and that every action is documented and accountable. At no time should there be any confusion as to who had possession of evidence, or what was done to it during that time. By taking precautions to protect the data, you will ensure it isn't compromised in any way.

Investigation Methodology

Investigation methodology is the practices, procedures, and techniques used to collect, store, analyze, and present information and evidence that is obtained through a computer forensics investigation. While the individual steps to perform these tasks may vary from case to case and depend on the types of software and equipment used, many common practices will always be

consistent. The methodology of a computer forensics investigation can be broken down into three basic stages:

- Acquisition

- Authentication

- Analysis

Acquisition is the act or process of gathering information and evidence. However, in computer forensics, the evidence not only pertains to a computer that's been seized, but the data stored on that computer. After all, in most computer forensic investigations, it is the data on a computer that will be used to provide insight into the details of a crime or other incident, and be used as evidence to convict a suspect. As we'll discuss later in this chapter, computer forensic software can be used to acquire data from a machine, and make an exact copy of everything stored on the hard disks. By studying this image of the computer's data, the machine's original data are unaltered during later examination. The computer forensic technician can then study the suspect computer's contents through an image of the data, leaving the original data untouched.

To guarantee that the data acquired from a computer is a correct duplicate, it must be authenticated. *Authentication* is a process of ensuring that the acquired evidence is the same as the data that was originally seized. If the data that's been acquired from a computer were corrupted, modified, or missing from the imaging process, it would not only affect your ability to accurately examine the machine's contents, but could also make all of the evidence you find on the computer inadmissible in court. After all, if it is not a perfect duplicate, how would the court know that anything you found was really on the original machine? To authenticate the data acquired from a suspect computer, features included in forensic software can be used to compare the data duplicated in the imaging process to the original data on a suspect's computer.

Once these steps have been completed, the content of the computer can then be inspected for individual pieces of evidence that will later be used in court or other disciplinary processes. When a duplicate is made of a computer's data, an image is created of everything on the machine. This includes system and configuration files, executable programs, and other files installed with the operating system and other software. In addition to this, you'd find innocuous documents and pictures that the computer's users have saved, but that wouldn't be useful to an investigation. Needless to say, most of what you'd find on any computer would not be evidence. The person examining the machine must sift through these files to find evidence related to their investigation, or that are illegal and may result in additional charges.

Analysis is the process of examining and evaluating information. When examining computer files, it is vital that they aren't modified in any way. This not only refers to changing the information in the file itself (such as by accidentally changing the values entered in a spreadsheet), but also modifying the properties of the file. For example, opening a JPG or other picture could change the date and time property that shows when the file was last accessed. If you wanted to prove when a suspect last viewed this image, that information would be lost to you,

and a suspect could then argue he or she never saw the file. It is important to use tools that won't modify data in any way, and that analysis occurs after the data are acquired and authenticated by imaging the hard disk. If any data duplicated is damaged or modified, the original data on the suspect computer can still be used to create another duplicate.

Securing Evidence

If data and equipment are to be used as evidence, you must ensure their integrity hasn't been compromised. Preservation of data involves practices that protect data and equipment from harm, so that original evidence is preserved in a state as close as possible to when it was initially acquired. If data are lost, altered, or damaged, then you may not be able to even mention it in court. This means such evidence might as well have never existed. Worse yet, the credibility of how evidence was collected and examined may be called into question, making other pieces of evidence inadmissible as well.

Evidence must be secure throughout the investigation. Securing evidence is a process that begins when a crime is first suspected, and continues after the examination has been completed. If a trial, civil suit, or disciplinary hearing has ended, the evidence must remain secure in case of an appeal or other legal processes. Because of this, a retention date should be set for all equipment and data retained as evidence. For example, the police may retain evidence files acquired from forensic software for many years after a person has been convicted. Similarly, a company may retain such files for a few years after firing an employee, in case the person attempts to sue for wrongful dismissal. The retention date provides a guideline as to how long a forensic technician should retain the data before deleting it or allowing equipment to be released or destroyed. To determine specified dates, a company should consult legal counsel, and keep in contact with the investigator to determine if the data acquired from an examination can be deleted or may still be needed.

Securing the Crime Scene

As mentioned earlier in this chapter, the first responder is responsible for establishing the scale of the crime scene and then securing that area. In some situations, this may be as simple as securing a server closet or server room, while in others it may be as complex as dealing with computers and devices spread across a network. Once the suspected systems have been identified, it is important to prevent individuals from entering the area and to protect systems so equipment isn't touched and data are not manipulated or lost.

At face value, it may seem difficult to prevent others from accessing systems. However, in many cases, people will respect the difficulty of the situation, or not want to get involved for fear of having to testify later. The fact is that anyone who does have access to effected systems may be required to testify or at least explain their presence at the scene. In worst-case scenarios, they may even be considered suspects. As part of securing the crime scene, a list of anyone attempting or achieving access to the area should be developed. This should include the name of the person, the time they entered and left the area, and the purpose of their presence.

To protect information appearing on monitors or other display devices, volatile evidence should be preserved. As we'll discuss in the next section, *volatile evidence* is any data or other evidence that may be lost once power is lost, and may exist on equipment other than computers. If pagers, cell phones, or other equipment that contains possible evidence and that runs on batteries is involved, you should ensure it is also preserved for immediate examination. Phone numbers, pages received by the person, and other evidence could be lost once the battery power runs out. Document anything that's visible through the display of a device, and photograph it if possible.

Nonvolatile data also needs special consideration so it isn't accidentally lost. If a system has power, it is advisable an image be made of the computer's hard disk before powering it down. Criminals sometimes "booby trap" their systems so that malicious programs residing on the hard disk can damage or erase data when it is shutdown or started up again later. To prevent such situations, forensic software can be used to make an exact bit stream duplicate of the disk's contents, including deleted data that haven't been overwritten. In some cases, even partially overwritten data can be recovered using these tools. However, certain data can be modified by simply powering a system on or off, such as temporary files and logs that are written to at system startups and shutdowns. If the system doesn't have power when you arrive on the scene, *do not* start it up. A duplicate of the hard disk's contents can be created using such software by booting the system safely from a floppy, preventing any malicious programs from damaging data.

EXAM WARNING

Securing a scene is important to both criminal investigations and internal incidents, which both use computer forensics to obtain evidence. The procedures for investigating internal policy violations and criminal law violations are basically the same, except that internal investigations may not require the involvement of law enforcement.

Volatile Evidence

The data that is held in temporary storage in the system's memory (including random access memory, cache memory, and the onboard memory of system peripherals such as the video card or NIC) are called *volatile data* because the memory is dependent on electric power to hold its contents. When the system is powered off or if power is disrupted, the data disappears. According to the IEEE Internet draft titled *Guidelines for Evidence Collection and Archiving,* the most volatile evidence should be collected first. This makes sense because the most volatile evidence is the most likely to disappear before it can be documented or collected. The draft lists the "order of volatility" as:

1. Registers and cache

2. Routing tables, ARP cache, process tables, and kernel statistics

3. Contents of system memory

4. Temporary file systems

5. Data on disk

Collecting volatile data presents a problem because doing so changes the state of the system (and the contents of the memory itself). Some experts recommend that investigators or crime scene technicians capture such data as running processes, the network status and connections, and a "dump" of the data in RAM, documenting each task or command they run to do so. Some of this work can be done by running such commands as *netstat* (on both Windows and UNIX systems) and *nbtstat* (on Windows only) to view current network connections. The *arp* command will tell you what addresses are in the ARP cache (and thus have recently connected to the system). The *dd* command can be used to create a snapshot of the contents of memory on UNIX machines, and the *ps* command can be used to view the currently running processes. On Windows machines, the downloadable *pslist* utility can be used to list running processes, or they can be viewed in Task Manager. Other commands such as *ipconfig* (Windows) or *ifconfig* (UNIX) can be used to gather information about the state of the network. These programs should be run from a special forensics CD that you bring with you (instead of running the same commands from the hard disk of the suspect computer) and should not require any programs or libraries from the computer's hard disk to run.

During Investigation of a Machine

As we'll discuss in greater detail later in this chapter disk imaging software will create an exact duplicate of a disk's contents, and can be used to make copies of hard disks, CDs, floppies, and other media. Disk imaging creates a bit stream copy, where each physical sector of the original disk is duplicated. To make it easier to store and analyze, the image is compressed into an image file, which is also called an evidence file.

Once an image of the disk has been made, you should confirm that it's an exact duplicate. As we mentioned earlier in this chapter, authentication is vital to ensuring the data acquired are identical to that of the suspect or victim's computer. Many computer forensic programs that create images of a disk have the built-in ability to perform integrity checks, while others require you to perform checks using separate programs. Such software may use a cyclic redundancy check (CRC), employing a checksum or hashing algorithm to verify the accuracy and reliability of the image.

When you're ready to perform an examination, copies of data should be made on media that's *forensically sterile*. This means that the disk has no other data on it, and has no viruses or defects. This will prevent mistakes involving data from one case mixing with other data, as can happen with cross-linked files or when copies of files are mixed with others on a disk. When

providing copies of data to investigators, defense lawyers, or the prosecution, the media used to distribute copies of evidence should also be forensically sterile.

While the situations in each case involving computer equipment will be different, you can follow a number of common steps to protect the data's integrity and prevent a loss of evidence. These procedures assume the computer has been shut down when you encounter it.

1. Photograph the monitor screen(s) to capture the data displayed there at the time of seizure. Be aware that more than one monitor can be connected to a single computer; modern operating systems such as Windows 2000/XP support spreading the display across as many as 10 monitors. Monitors attached to the computer but turned off could still be displaying parts of the desktop and open applications.

2. Take steps to preserve volatile data.

3. Make an image of the disk(s) to work with so that the integrity of the original can be preserved. This step should be taken *before* the system is shut down, in case the owner has installed a self-destruct program to activate on shutdown or startup.

4. Check the integrity of the image to confirm it is an exact duplicate, using a cyclic redundancy checker or other program that uses a checksum or hashing algorithm to verify the image is accurate and reliable.

5. Shut down the system safely according to the procedures for the operating system that is running.

6. Photograph the system setup before moving anything, including the back and front of the computer showing any cables and wires attached.

7. Unplug the system and all peripherals, marking/tagging each piece as it is collected.

8. Use an antistatic wrist strap or other grounding method before handling equipment, especially circuit cards, disks, and other similar items.

9. Place circuit cards, disks, and the like in antistatic bags for transport. Keep all equipment away from heat sources and magnetic fields.

EXAM WARNING

Remember that copies of data made for examination should be created on forensically sterile media. If other data resides on the disk or CD storing the image file (or copy of the original data), it can be argued that the evidence was compromised by this other data. When CDs that can be rewritten (CD-RW) are used, it could be argued that the evidence was actually preexisting data or that it corrupted the evidence in some manner.

When the Computer Is Not Being Examined

Anytime a computer is not being examined, it must be stored in a secure location. Once the computer has been transported from the original crime scene, it should be stored in a locked room or closet that has limited access. In police departments, this may be a property room or an area of the lab in which electronic evidence is acquired and examined. For internal investigations conducted in a corporate environment, it should be treated with the same level of respect, and also stored in a location with limited access.

Data acquired from a computer should be stored on a server or another computer that has limited access. Because any images of the computer that have been acquired using forensic software will be used to examine the computer's contents, and will be used in court as evidence, it is important that few people ever have access to these files. If an unauthorized individual were able to access the files, it could be argued that the files were tampered with, and this could result in the case being thrown out of court or being seriously undermined.

However, in any organization, there are those who will need to access a room that contains evidence. Lawyers, police investigators, and members of the IT staff may all need to access the secure location from time to time. To keep track of those entering the room, you should maintain a log showing who entered the room or secure area, the dates and times they were there, and any other information (such as their purpose for being there). By having people sign in and sign out, you can keep track of who had access should it ever come into question.

From the time an incident or crime has been identified, it is important that any evidence that may exist in an area be protected from tampering, accidents, or other potential damage. By keeping the crime scene, evidence, and any items transported to another location secure, you are preventing the validity of evidence from coming into question, and protecting any devices in your care from coming to harm.

Head of the Class…

Treating Every Investigation as if It Were Going to Court

Every case must be treated as if it would eventually go to court and be subject to the scrutiny of lawyers and others involved in the trial process. Although it may seem that a computer isn't part of a criminal case, examination of the computer may present materials that are illegal. In addition, those who are suspected of breaking the law or policies may eventually sue the company and others involved in the investigation. By following computer forensic procedures, keeping detailed documentation on what was done, and maintaining a log of who had access to the computer and its data, you can protect the integrity of the case and protect those involved in the investigation from civil litigation.

Chain of Evidence Form

Because of the importance of evidence, it is essential that its continuity be maintained and documented. A *chain of evidence*, also known as a *chain of custody*, must be established to show how evidence made it from the crime scene to the courtroom. It proves where a piece of evidence was at any given time and who was responsible for it. By documenting this, you can establish that the integrity of evidence wasn't compromised.

If the chain of evidence is broken, it could be argued that the evidence fell into the wrong hands and may have been tampered with, or that other evidence was substituted. This brings the value of evidence into question, and could make it inadmissible in court. To prevent this from happening, it is important we adhere to the policies and procedures dealing with the management of evidence.

Evidence management begins at the crime scene, where it is bagged and/or tagged. When the crime scene is being processed, each piece of evidence should be sealed inside an evidence bag. An evidence bag is a sturdy bag with two-sided tape that allows it to be sealed shut. Once sealed, the only way to open it is to damage the bag, such as by ripping or cutting it open. The bag should then be marked or a tag should be affixed to it, showing the person who initially took it into custody. The tag would provide such information as a number to identify the evidence, a case number (which shows what case the evidence is associated with), the date and time, and the name or badge number of the person taking it into custody. A tag may also be affixed to the object, providing the same or similar information to what's detailed on the bag. However, this should only be done if it will not compromise the evidence in any manner.

Information on the tag is also written in an evidence log or chain of evidence form, which is a document that inventories all evidence collected in a case. In addition to the data available on the tag, the chain of evidence form will include a description of each piece of evidence, serial numbers, identifying marks or numbers, and other information that's required by policy or local law.

The chain of evidence form will also have a log that provides details about who had custody of the evidence. This document will be used to describe who had possession of the evidence after it was initially tagged, transported and locked in storage. To obtain possession of the evidence, a person will need to sign in and sign out evidence. Information is added to a chain of evidence form to show who had possession of the evidence, when, and for how long. The form will specify the person's name, department, date, time, and other pertinent information.

In many cases, the investigator will follow the evidence from crime scene to court, documenting who else had possession along the way. Each time possession is transferred to another person, it is written on the form. For example, the chain of evidence form would show the investigator had initial custody, while the next line might show that a computer forensic examiner took possession at a particular date and time. Once the examination is complete, the next line would show the investigator again took custody. Even though custody is transferred back to the investigator, this is indicated in the log so there is no confusion over who was responsible on any date or time.

Before Investigating

Contrary to what's seen in the movies and television, a significant amount of work goes into investigating computer crimes before they occur. The training and tools used in this type of investigation must be in place prior to examining any computer. Because it is so specialized, the person examining the computer must be knowledgeable in computer forensics and different areas of Information Technology, and the equipment and software used to perform the examination of a machine must already be available to him or her.

When a crime does occur, certain actions must also be taken before attempting to acquire evidence from a machine. Interviews must be conducted and search warrants may need to be obtained. If this isn't done, time may be wasted searching for evidence that doesn't exist, or is located in other areas of a hard disk or even a different computer. Worse yet, if certain steps aren't followed, any evidence that is acquired may be inadmissible in court, making the entire process a waste of time.

Preparing for an Investigation

Preparation is one of the most important aspects of any investigation. Regardless of whether it is the police or part of an Incident Response Team performing the investigation, it is important that a proactive approach be taken. Those involved in investigations must be properly trained and have the resources and tools they need. The more that is done before an investigation, the fewer problems you'll have when conducting it.

Training is crucial to every part of an investigation. Computer forensics requires knowledge of procedures, along with expertise in the forensic software and hardware used to acquire and study the data. This cannot only be obtained through courses, but also by studying under those with more experience in performing investigations. Additional experience with network components and technologies such as TCP/IP are also essential, as is knowledge of computer hardware since its common to remove hard disks or other devices before connecting it to the investigator's computer to duplicate the data. As you might expect, certification in these various areas are often useful, especially when providing testimony as an expert witness in court (which we'll discuss in Appendix A of this book). The more training a person has in various aspects of computers, the better.

Because no one can know everything about computers, it is important to maintain reference materials that can be consulted as needed. A library of manuals and other books dealing with common software and hardware can be useful in looking up infrequently used commands or features, but resources can also include maintaining hyperlinks and electronic documents. Links to the manufacturers of computers, cell phones, hard disks, and other devices will enable you to look up information on how to properly remove a hard disk from a particular make and model of computer, how to access the BIOS Setup, bypass certain security features, or access information stored in the device. These links will allow you to refer to manuals, knowledge bases, and other online resources quickly during an investigation.

Other resources that should be maintained are prepared documents that may be used during an investigation. As we discussed earlier, chain of custody forms may be used to keep track of who had possession of evidence at any given time, while property forms may be used to maintain information on who is ultimately responsible for evidence that's stored in a secure location. Contact lists are also useful, providing a listing of individuals with specific skills (such as the hardware technician in the company where you work, or an expert in Linux or Macintosh machines that can be contacted as needed). Such lists should also contain information on how to contact certain legal departments or individuals who respond to the abuse of services at certain web sites or companies. For example, if a case involved a free e-mail account at Hotmail, it would be useful to keep a request form that can be completed when requesting information on a particular account, as well as phone numbers to contact Hotmail during the investigation. In many cases, these documents can be stored on a computer or server that's used for forensic examinations, so that the information is always handy in an electronic format.

As we discussed in Chapter 1, it is important to have a computer forensic lab set up prior to any investigations. The lab should be of adequate size, and have a server or media (such as CDs and DVDs) to store evidence files on, with storage facilities that allow computers to be locked in a secure location when not being examined. In addition to this, you will need to outfit the lab with equipment that can be used in the facility or taken in the field to locations where the crime has taken place. This would include such items as:

- **Laptop computers** The laptop should have forensic software installed on it and include additional hardware that may be used to acquire data. For example, if Encase forensic software is used, FastBloc might also be included in a field kit. FastBloc is hardware that is attached to the examiner's computer and a suspect's hard disk, enabling the two to be connected together while preventing writes to the disk. In addition to this, adapters to connect to laptop hard disks and ribbon cables to connect hard disks to your laptop should also be included.

- **Boot disks and CDs of tools** The boot disk is used to start a computer from a floppy disk or CD so files aren't modified when the computer starts. A floppy disk or CD of various utilities can also be useful in acquiring data from a machine. Any tools included should not unknowingly modify data.

- **Digital cameras** These can be used to photograph what's displayed on a computer screen, and also to photograph the scene of the crime. Before taking the computer from the crime scene, the back of the computer should be photographed to show where cables were plugged into the machine so it can be set up the same way once the investigation is over.

- **Evidence and antistatic bags, tags, and stickers** Evidence bags are tamperproof bags that items can be stored in to prevent unauthorized handling or contamination by fingerprints, DNA, or other taint evidence. Once sealed, the bag must be ripped open to access the contents. To safely transport hard disks and any circuit boards, they

should also be stored in anti-static bags. Tags and stickers can also be used to identify the contents of the bag, showing the incident number or other information that associates items with a particular criminal case or incident.

- **Pens, notepad, and masking tape** It is important to document the actions taken in removing keyboards, monitors, and other peripherals attached to the computer prior to transporting it. To label any cables that were attached to the machine, masking tape can be used to mark which cables were attached to the suspect computer and where they were connected.

Interviewing

As we mentioned early in this chapter, a complainant can provide a wealth of information necessary to the successful investigation of an incident. It is important to identify and document who had access to affected systems, what they observed, and any other information they can provide. When you are interviewing people at a crime scene, it is important to record their names and contact information, in case they need to be contacted at a later time. Not only can their information be useful in identifying what the problem is, and which systems were effected, but their statements can be used to obtain search warrants and provide testimony in court if criminal charges are made against a suspect.

Search Warrants

A *search warrant* is a legal document that permits members of law enforcement to search a specific location for evidence related to a criminal investigation, and possibly seize that evidence so it can be analyzed and possibly used in court. For the warrant to be legal, it must be signed by a judge or magistrate, such as a Justice of the Peace or another type of judicial officer. To obtain this signature, the police officer or government agent must present good reasons as to why a search warrant should be granted. This requires law enforcement officials to provide a sworn statement in which the location to be searched is identified and which may list the type of property being sought. The statement may also be accompanied by documentation on the complaint that initiated an investigation, and other written information that would validate the request. The key point of this process is to protect the rights of the individual and provide reasonable grounds for why permission should be given to invade a person's privacy and property.

Many countries use search warrants to protect the privacy of its citizens by requiring authorities prove the necessity for the search and seizure of a person's property. An example of legislation that's used to prevent unreasonable searches and seizures of property is the Fourth Amendment of the United States Constitution, which states:

> The right of the people to be secure in their persons, houses, papers, and effects, against unreasonable searches and seizures, shall not be violated, and no Warrants shall issue, but upon prob-

> able cause, supported by Oath or affirmation, and particularly
> describing the place to be searched, and the persons or things to
> be seized.

In looking at this quote, you will notice that probable cause is the primary basis for issuing a search warrant. *Probable cause* is a standard of proof that must be shown, in which a cautious person would find reasonable grounds for suspicion. This places the burden of proof on the government so investigations aren't conducted in an authoritarian or oppressive manner. Without probable cause, the request for a search warrant is denied.

If the search warrant is issued, its use is limited. After all, it would go against the philosophy of protecting the individual's rights if a warrant allowed police to search a person's home indefinitely, as many times as they like. The warrant can only be executed within a set amount of time (generally three days), so if it wasn't a search warrant wasn't used in that time, a new one would need to be obtained. Also, an officer may only search areas outlined in the court order, and generally cannot seize items not included in the document. For example, if the warrant specified a person's home could be searched, the police could not search other properties (such as a cabin) also owned by the person. By being specific in what can be searched, the conditions of the warrant protect both the rights of the individual and the integrity of the investigation.

Searching without Warrants

Warrants are not necessary in every situation where evidence could be obtained. Despite appearances at times, legislation is often constructed from common sense needs and well thought out arguments, balancing the needs of society against the government's ability to manage its citizens. Requesting a search warrant to acquire every piece of evidence in every criminal and civil case would become an administrative nightmare, so exclusions to needing a warrant are provided in statutes that address investigative procedures and requirements.

For law enforcement, there are a number of exceptions regarding when a search warrant is needed, although few apply to computer forensics. For example, an officer can frisk a suspect, checking his clothes for weapons or contraband, but there is no way this search would include an examination of the person's computer. In terms of computer forensics, a primary reason why a search warrant could be excluded is when the evidence is in plain view, and an officer can see it from a reasonable vantage point. For example, if an officer approached a car and saw the passenger viewing child pornography on a laptop computer, the laptop would be seized for later analysis. Similarly, let's say an officer had a warrant to search the home of a suspect and seize computer equipment believed to contain child pornography. If the officer saw a collection of photographs displaying naked children in various acts, the officer could then seize the pictures as evidence even though they may not have been specifically mentioned in the warrant. When illegal items or other evidence is in plain view, it is often reasonable for the officer to seize the item immediately, rather than leave it and take the risk of it being hidden, altered, or destroyed.

The need for a search warrant is also excluded when consent is given by the owner, or by an authorized person in charge of the area or item being searched. In other words, if the victim of a cybercrime wanted to have his or her own computer searched for evidence, a search warrant wouldn't be necessary. Similarly, the senior staff of a company or the manager of an IT department could give permission to have servers and workstations in a company examined. The key is whether the person owns the property or has proper authorization, which can sometimes be less than clear. For example, on a college campus, a student in residence might be able to give permission to search the room he occupies, but wouldn't be able to give permission to search his roommate's computer. Similarly, a parent would be able to give permission to search a family computer, but may not have the authority to permit a search of an adult child's personal computer. Because a search conducted on a computer without a warrant or proper permission could make any evidence collected inadmissible in court, it's vital to determine who can give permission before seizing or examining a computer.

Legal differences exist between how a private citizen and law enforcement can gather evidence. There are stricter guidelines and legislation controlling how agents of the government may obtain evidence. Because of this, evidence collected prior to involving law enforcement is less vulnerable to being excluded in court. If the IT staff of a company acquired files from a server or workstation before calling the police, it would probably be admitted as evidence in a trial, even though the same actions taken by law enforcement without permission or a warrant could make it inadmissible.

Constitutional protection against illegal search and seizure applies to government agents (such as the police), but may not apply to private citizens. Before a government agent can search and seize computers and other evidence, a search warrant, consent, or statutory authority (along with probable cause) must be obtained. This does not apply to private citizens, unless they are acting as an "agent of the government" and working under the direction or advice of law enforcement or other government parties. However, although fewer restrictions apply to private citizens, forensic procedures should still be followed. Failing to follow them may result in lost or unusable evidence. The procedures outlined in this section will help preserve evidence and ensure it is considered admissible in court.

Preparing for Searches

Because search warrants aren't required in all situations, you should try to identify whether one is needed early in the investigation. In doing so, you should ask the following questions:

- Does the company or complainant own the computer? If so, then permission can be given to search the machine.

- Does the company have a legitimate reason for searching the computer? If not, the employee using the computer could have reason for civil litigation.

- Have employees been warned that the company has the right to search the machine? As we'll discuss later in this chapter, by warning employees that computers may be

searched at any time, the employee has little to no recourse if anything has been found on his or her machine.

If there are no legal grounds to search the computer without a warrant, then statements and any documented evidence pertaining to the incident should be collected. As seen in Exercise 3.1, statements should include as many details as possible, providing a timeline of when events took place and what occurred. Statements should be gathered from anyone associated with the incident, and this should be done as soon as possible while memories of the event are still fresh. Gathering statements in this manner provides information that can be used to obtain a search warrant and can be used as evidence later if the case goes to trial.

EXERCISE 3.1

WRITING A STATEMENT

Statements are required to obtain search warrants so a judge or magistrate can evaluate the reasons a search warrant has been requested, and determine whether one should be issued based on the merit of existing evidence and observations. To write a statement, follow these steps:

1. Ensure that each page and line of the statement is numbered. This makes it easier to refer to in court or when discussing the contents of the document.

2. Include the date the document was written.

3. Begin the statement by stating who you are and that you are stating what follows in the document. If you are part of the investigation, you should also include your position and employment (that is, whether you are part of the company where the investigation took place, a member of the police, and so on). For example, "I <insert name> will say that I am an employee of <insert company> in the position of <insert position> since <insert date>."

4. Include any additional information that provides credibility to your statement such as providing information on any certifications or other qualifications you might have. This may indicate whether you could be used later as an expert witness, and should be included in the opening or first couple of paragraphs of the statement.

5. After introducing who you are, begin relating, in chronological order, the events that have occurred, stating the dates and times

where available. For example, "On January 1, 2007, at approximately 10:30 a.m., I noticed an increased amount of network traffic. Upon checking the mail server, I saw that a significant amount of e-mail was being sent to e-mail addresses on the Internet."

6. Provide as much detail as possible, inclusive to references to logs or other evidence that can be included with the statement. Include only facts, not unfounded speculation of what you personally believed to have occurred and why. At all times, try to relay the events in plain English, explaining any technical terms used.

7. Close the document by signing your name.

Professional Conduct

At all times in an investigation, it is important to maintain professional conduct. Whether you are working as a member of police or an employee of a company, you are acting as a representative of the organization, and the level of ethical behavior that's displayed will indicate how you're handling the case as a whole. By reflecting the ethics adopted by the organization, you are also showing that the investigation will be handled with integrity.

A balance of morality and objectivity must be maintained through the investigation. If potentially offensive materials are found on the computer, showing interest in the material is both unprofessional and could be used to undermine the findings in court. In the same way, you should also display objectivity and not make judgments on what is found during an examination of evidence or when interviewing those involved in the investigation. You should avoid making any kinds of jokes or comments about what is found, and focus on the tasks involved in performing the investigation with professionalism.

In performing these tasks, it is important to remain somewhat detached from the incident. While it is important to display a level of compassion toward any victims in the case, you should remain disconnected from anything but the tasks that must be performed. Showing disgust or other negative emotions toward what has occurred could be perceived that you are being judgmental, or have a vendetta against the person who committed the crime or other violations. Professional detachment involves placing all of your attention on the work rather than the emotional or psychological stress factors that may be involved.

Confidentiality is another important component of professional conduct. Throughout the investigation, it is important to keep information about the case private and not reveal information to those who aren't directly involved in the investigating the incident. Information should not be shared with witnesses, co-workers, or others outside of the case, especially if they show

interest in what has occurred. This can be difficult since friends or family may often ask about higher profile cases being reported in the media. However, it is important that information is limited to those who need it. You don't want to accidentally reveal what's going on to someone who may later be a suspect or will pass information on even further.

Classifying what materials can be revealed to certain individuals in an organization and/or the public can help in maintaining confidentiality. Document classification involves developing categories for materials to identify who can have access to the information, so that confusion doesn't develop as to who may and may not view the information. Classifications may include:

- *Top secret*, which is considered the highest level of security associated with a document, and could cause an exceptionally high level of damage to the organization or security if the information is released to the public.

- *Secret*, which limits the information to only those who have been specifically authorized to view it, and which could cause serious damage if released.

- *Confidential* or *For Internal Use Only*, which limits information to a specific group or organization, such as members of law enforcement or the company effected by the investigation. Such information is not to be shared with the public.

- *Restricted*, which limits the information to only those who have been specifically authorized to view the information, and could cause undesirable repercussions to the company or security if the information was released.

- *Unclassified* or *For Public Release*, which allows information to be viewed by anyone, inclusive to allowing it to be disseminated to media outlets and the public.

The investigator may also work with public relations or a media representative in the company or police to determine what will be revealed to the public. In such situations, crime technicians and anyone else involved in the investigation should limit their comments to information that has been approved for public release, and keep any additional facts to themselves.

Investigating Company Policy Violations

Corporate investigations are often different from other types of investigations. When criminal activity occurs on a home computer, generally the police are called to conduct an investigation. In companies where an IT staff is available, policies may exist that designate a person or team of people with specialized skills to initially respond to the incident. The Incident Response team may contact police eventually, but this will often depend on the type of incident and what is found in their investigation.

Investigations in corporations can also be different from others that involve computer forensics since a crime might never have been committed even though an investigation is required. Anyone who has worked for a company knows that employers will impose certain rules and practices that must be followed by employees as conditions of their employment. For

example, a dress code may be compulsory, stating that employees must wear a uniform or dress clothes while working. In the same way, a number of regulations may be implemented to address how computers and other equipment are to be used in the workplace, and breaking these rules could result in an investigation and having computers and other devices used by the employee undergo a forensic examination.

Policy and Procedure Development

A *policy* is used to address concerns and identify risks to a company, while *procedures* are used to provide information on how to perform specific tasks and/or deal with a problem. For example, a policy may be created to deal with the potential threat of unauthorized access to restricted areas of a building, and procedures may be implemented that state how a visitor should be signed into a building and escorted to a particular department. Through the policy, an issue that is pertinent to the organization is explained and dealt with. Through the procedure, people are shown how to abide by policies by following specific instructions.

When you consider the sheer number of issues an organization may face, you can see that many different types of policies and procedures may be implemented. Regardless of the type, however, each should have the following features:

- They should be straightforward, stating points clearly and understandably. If areas of a policy can be interpreted in different ways, it can be disputed when attempting to enforce it.

- It must define what actions should be taken. Procedures must lay out the steps needed to complete a task, while policies must outline the actions that may be taken if the policy is violated.

- They cannot violate any applicable law. If policies do violate any existing legislation, then they cannot be adequately enforced. In addition, the company may face civil or criminal charges, because they implemented policies that forced employees to break the law.

- They must be enforceable. If a policy isn't enforced each time it is violated, or can't be enforced for some reason (perhaps because it violates contractual agreements with individuals or unions), then the policy becomes worthless to the company. Policies must be fairly and equally enforced whenever they are violated, otherwise any disciplinary actions dictated in the policy can be disputed.

When implementing policies, you should also devise methods to confirm that employees have read and agreed to comply with them. One method is to have employees read and sign copies of certain policies when they are hired. However, if there are changes to the policy, then each person already hired must be approached, and reread and sign the policy. Another method is to implement one policy that employees sign upon being hired, which states that part of their employment relies on reading and acknowledging compliance with all policies. You can

then post the policies on the corporate intranet, enabling employees to read them at their convenience. Still another method is to e-mail copies of policies to all of the employees' internal e-mail addresses, and requesting them to respond stating they have read and agree with the terms of the policy. Whatever method you implement, it is important that some process is in place. If employees are unaware of the policies, they can't realistically be expected to comply with them.

Acceptable Use Policy

One such policy employees should be required to acknowledge reading and complying with is an acceptable use policy. This type of policy establishes guidelines on the appropriate use of technology. It is used to outline what types of activities are permissible when using a computer or network, and what an organization considers proper behavior. Acceptable use policies not only protect an organization from liability, but also provide employees with an understanding of what they can and cannot do using company resources.

Acceptable use policies will restrict certain actions, including what types of Web sites or e-mail an employee is allowed to access on the Internet at work. You may have read news articles about employees who access pornography over the Internet. Not only does this use up bandwidth and fill hard disk space on non-work-related activities, but having others see the employee view the material can create an uncomfortable work environment. Worse yet, a company can be liable for creating or allowing a hostile work environment under the Civil Rights Act of 1964 or other legislation. For these reasons, businesses commonly include sections in their Acceptable Use Policies that deal with these issues.

TEST DAY TIP

Remember that policies protect not only corporations, but also the individuals who work there. A hostile work environment is one that a reasonable person would find abusive, whether it is because of harassment that a person finds humiliating or physical threats. Because such an environment will affect an employee's performance, it is in the company's best interest to take such problems seriously. When computers, BlackBerry devices, cell phones or other devices owned by the company are involved in such activities, it goes against acceptable use policies and can result in a forensic examination of any machines or devices involved in creating this atmosphere.

Beyond handling potentially offensive materials, acceptable use policies also deal with other online activities that can negatively impact network resources or sidetrack users from their jobs. For example, having a stock ticker on their desktop, watching streaming media, and installing game software or other technologies will often distract an employee from their hired duties.

For this reason, restrictions on installing software and other technologies on company computers can be found in *acceptable use policies*.

Acceptable use policies would also specify methods of how information can be distributed to the public, thus avoiding sensitive information from being "leaked." Imposing rules on the dissemination of information might include:

- Specifications that prohibit classified data from be transmitted via the Internet (for example, e-mail or FTP)

- Provisions on how content for the Web site is approved

- Rules on printing confidential materials

- Restrictions on who can create media releases

Through this, important information is protected, and employees have an understanding of what files they can or cannot e-mail, print, or distribute to other parties.

Incident Response Policy

Incident response policies are implemented to provide an understanding of how certain incidents are to be dealt with. The policy should identify an incident response team, who is to be notified of issues and who have the knowledge and skills to deal with them effectively. Members of the team should be experienced in handling issues relating to unauthorized access, denial or disruptions of service, viruses, unauthorized changes to systems or data, critical system failures, or attempts to breach the policies and/or security of an organization. If the incident is of a criminal nature, the policy should specify at what point law enforcement should be contacted to take control of the investigation.

A good incident response policy will outline who is responsible for specific tasks when a crisis occurs. It will include such information as:

- Who will investigate or analyze incidents to determine how an incident occurred and what problems are faced because of it

- Which individuals or departments are to fix particular problems and restore the system to a secure state

- How certain incidents are to be handled, and references to other documentation

Including such information in the Incident Response Police will ensure that the right person is assigned to a particular task. For example, if the Webmaster was responsible for firewall issues and the network administrator performed backups of data, you would assign tasks relating to these responsibilities in your incident response policy. By determining who should respond and deal with specific incidents, you will be able to restore the system to a secure state more quickly and effectively.

Incident response policies should also provide clearly defined steps regarding what users are supposed to do when identifying a possible threat. Upon realizing an issue exists, users should notify their supervisor, a designated person, or a department, who can then contact the Incident Response Team. While awaiting the team's arrival, the scene of the incident should be vacated and any technologies involved should be left as they are. In other words, those on the scene shouldn't touch anything since this could alter the evidence. The users should also document what they observed when the incident occurred, and list anyone who was in the area at the time.

To address how a company should handle intrusions and other incidents, it is important that the incident response policy includes a contingency plan. The contingency plan will address how the company should continue to function during the investigation, such as when critical servers are taken offline during forensic examinations. Backup equipment may be used to replace these servers or other devices so employees can still perform their jobs and (in such cases as e-commerce sites) customers can still make purchases. A goal of any investigation is to avoid negatively impacting the normal business practices as much as possible.

Policy Violations

When policies are violated, it doesn't necessarily mean a full police investigation is required. In many situations, the violation may require disciplinary actions against the employee, whether it is a reprimand, fine, demotion, or termination. The severity of actions will often depend on the past performance and current conduct of the person. Despite the end result, computer forensics may still be incorporated. Using forensic procedures to investigate the incident creates a tighter case against the employee, thereby making it difficult for them to argue the facts.

In any investigation, it is important to treat the case as if it were going to court since you never know what you'll find. For example, an employee may have violated a company's acceptable use policy by viewing questionable Web sites during work hours. However, if it was found that the person was downloading child pornography, the internal investigation becomes a criminal one. Any actions taken in the investigation would be scrutinized, and anything found could be evidence in a criminal trial.

Policy violations can also extend beyond the machines owned by a company. Many people have their own blogs or personal Web sites, or enjoy social networks such as Facebook (www.facebook.com), Friendster (www.friendster.com), and others. On such sites, people can publish text and pictures to the Internet. If the person mentions where they work, and makes derogatory comments about co-workers or portrays the company in a negative manner, it may seem that there is little that can be done. After all, the information isn't on a corporate computer, but on another server entirely. However, depending on policies implemented in the organization, this may not always be the case. In 2007, a Grade 11 student in Abbotsford, British Columbia named Amanda Bunn created a page on Facebook entitled "If 200 people sign this, I'll kick (teacher Pat Mullaney) in the box." Because the threat was made to her teacher, the student was suspended for three weeks before ultimately being expelled from the school. Other

schools have taken similar actions against students in cases of cyberbullying. Because school policies exist in many schools that prohibited threatening teachers and students, the students are held accountable for their actions, even though the incidents never occurred on school property.

Regardless of whether you're a student or working for an establishment, fewer and fewer organizations are tolerating hostile working environments. *Hostile working environments* are workplaces where a person fears intimidation, harassment, physical threats, humiliation, or other experiences that create an offensive or oppressive atmosphere. One common example of a hostile working environment is sexual harassment. If a person had to view sexual images displayed on a computer, or received messages sent through e-mail, SMS, or instant messaging that had undertones or blatant sexual remarks, they could feel objectified and humiliated by the atmosphere. In such cases, internal disciplinary tribunals, criminal charges, or civil suits may be the only way to stop such actions. When these activities are received, transmitted, or displayed using technologies issued by the company, it is simple to acquire evidence by looking at information stored on the devices or on hard disks.

One of the most devastating types of policy violation is industrial espionage, which is also a criminal act. *Industrial espionage* is the selling of trade secrets, intellectual property, or other classified information to competitors. If the wrong person has access to such information, it could be detrimental to the organization, as releasing it to the public or competitors could undermine confidence in the organization, and even jeopardize its ability to remain solvent. Source code for programs, secret recipes, and other knowledge that is often limited to the most trusted insiders could be devastating if released. Information must be kept secure, and any suspected leaks must be dealt with swiftly.

Notes from the Underground...

The Cola Wars and Industrial Espionage

When you think of Coca-Cola and Pepsi, you probably think of staunch competitors in the Cola Wars, with each trying to get an advantage over the other in the marketplace. The last thing you'd imagine is the two of them working together to stop a Coke employee from selling secrets to Pepsi. However, because such companies rely on secret recipes and other trade secrets to remain in business, the threat of industrial espionage is one that can't be tolerated and is considered one of their greatest risks to security.

In May 2006, PepsiCo Inc. received a letter offering to sell them trade secrets of the Coca-Cola Co. Pepsi immediately contacted Coke, who in turn contacted the FBI. The FBI worked with both companies to create a sting operation that led to the arrest of Joya Williams, a secretary who worked at Coca-Cola, and two others working with her to sell the secrets. Williams had not only stolen confidential information, but also a sample of a new soft drink the company was developing, which she, Ibrahim Dimson, and Edmund Duhaney tried to sell to Pepsi for $1.5 million.

In 2007, Williams was convicted and received a prison sentence of 8 years, while Dimson who entered a guilty plea was sentenced to 5 years in prison. Both were also sentenced to an additional 3 years of supervised release, and ordered

Continued

to each pay $40,000 in restitution. Although Duhaney also entered a guilty plea, he had not been sentenced at the time of this writing.

Warning Banners

Warning banners are brief messages used to inform users of policies and legislation regarding the use of a system and the information it contains. They are generally displayed at the startup of programs and operating systems, or when accessing the default page of intranets and public Web sites. Because the warning banner advises a user about key elements of proper usage, and may even provide references to existing laws and policies, they serve as a legal notice to users of the system.

Warning banners can come in different formats, inclusive to splash screens or message boxes that pop up when software is started, or information appearing in graphics or other content on Web sites. As seen in Figure 3.2, the Goddard Space Flight Center (webmaster.gsfc.nasa.gov/warning.html) has a simple textual warning that outlines the purpose of the site, and that any attempts to modify the site may be punishable under the Computer Fraud and Abuse Act of 1986. It also informs the user that any activities on the site may be monitored to the degree that keystrokes may be recorded. By using the Web site, the user agrees to these actions, so anyone committing a criminal act has consented to having information gathered in logs, which could then be used against them as evidence.

Figure 3.2 Warning Banner on a Web Site

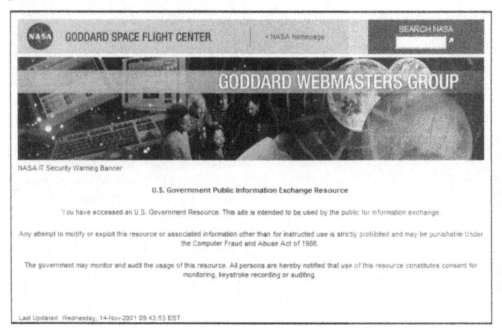

Warning banners should be implemented at any access point to a system in the event an organization seeks to discipline an employee or prosecute an unauthorized user. By providing a clear and strong message, the warning banner essentially dissolves any excuse of not knowing what he or she did was wrong. The user is given a warning, so any violations can be proven as being intentional. The message should provide the following points of information and correspond with any security policies the user may have read and agreed to as part of his or her employment:

- A brief outline of what is considered proper usage of the system

- Expectations of privacy, and that the system may be monitored for illegal or improper activity

- Any penalties or possible punishment that may result from noncompliance

Adding such messages when users log on to an operating system is relatively simple, and should be implemented on any computers that are part of a corporate network. As we'll see in Exercise 3.2, computers running Windows can have information added to the Registry that will cause a message box to appear with a warning before the user logs on. This feature has been included in Windows operating systems since Windows 95 and Windows NT 3.1 and presents the warning banner after pressing **Ctrl + Alt + Del** and before being presented with a login dialog box. It requires the user to agree to the warning by clicking an OK button before they are able to use Windows.

TEST DAY TIP

Expect the possibility of seeing a question dealing with warning banners on your exam. Warning banners are an important prerequisite of having the ability to perform a search without the need of a search warrant. They also limit a user's ability for legal recourse since they are warned upon accessing the system.

EXERCISE 3.2

CREATING A WARNING BANNER AT WINDOWS LOGON

1. From the Windows Start menu, click the **Run** menu item.

2. When the Run dialog box appears, type **REGEDIT** into the Open field, and then click the **OK** button.

3. When the Registry Editor appears, expand the HKEY_LOCAL_MACHINE node in the left pane of the program and navigate to the SOFTWARE\Microsoft\Windows NT\CurrentVersion\Winlogon subkey. In doing so, you should see a screen similar to that shown in Figure 3.3.

Figure 3.3 The Registry Editor

4. In the right pane, double-click **LegalNoticeCaption** and enter the caption that will appear as the title of a message box displayed when a user logs on. For example, you might enter Important Notice as the caption for the message box. Click the **OK** button to save your caption.

5. Double-click **LegalNoticeText** and modify the value so it contains the warning you would like users to see in the message box. Click the **OK** button to save your warning.

6. From the File menu, click the **Exit** menu item to close the Registry Editor. When you next press Ctrl + Alt + Del to log on to the system, the warning banner will be presented to users before they log in.

Conducting a Computer Forensic Investigation

While investigations will often vary in the type of incident or crime that's occurred, the evidence that's available, and the environment in which evidence is collected, many elements are common to any investigation. As we've seen throughout this chapter, it is important you assume that any investigation will invariably wind up in court, where the evidence and process in which it was collected may be challenged. Because of this, it is important the procedures in the investigative process are always followed.

Once you've gone through the process of securing a crime scene and interviewing witnesses, evidence must be collected, preserved, and transported. Each piece of evidence must then be assessed, with digital evidence acquired from hard disks and other media before being examined. Throughout this process, documentation is essential since any actions taken should be included in a statement and/or final report. As we'll see in the sections that follow, this can be a lengthy process with procedures that must be followed to prevent any evidence from becoming inadmissible or being overlooked altogether.

The Investigation Process

The process of conducting a computer forensic investigation can be a hectic experience, especially in a business environment where it is essential that systems are online to maintain the business. For example, if the company used an e-commerce site to make sales, making the system down to perform an examination could cost thousands upon thousands of dollars. During such instances, you want to ensure that you follow forensic procedures, but not waste time wondering which steps should be performed next.

To perform an investigation properly, it is important to follow set procedures, which detail the steps to be taken. Following these guidelines will help you meet the goals of an incident investigation, and provide information that can be used to handle the incident so it doesn't escalate into a more significant problem. In the investigation process, six steps should be followed:

- Preparation
- Detection
- Containment
- Eradication
- Recovery
- Follow-up

TEST DAY TIP

The CHFI exam focuses on not only criminal investigations but also ones that occur as part of an internal investigation within an organization. As such, you should be familiar with the different roles you can play in an investigation, and the process of investigating an incident.

Preparation

As with anything dealing with security, it is important that threats are dealt with proactively, with safeguards and other measures in place before problems occur. If the necessary policies, procedures, and tools aren't available when responding to an incident, then valuable time can be wasted trying to get organized. Preparation is the key to handling and investigating incidents.

Training is an important part of properly managing how an incident is handled and investigated. Those performing the investigation should have a thorough understanding of the tasks they're expected to perform, where reference material and other information is located, and expertise in using any tools needed. Management and users should also be trained in identifying and reporting problems, inclusive to procedures for contacting the necessary people in an emergency.

Earlier in this chapter, we discussed the importance of an Incident Response Policy to provide information that can be used in responding to incidents. Part of this policy should include or reference a communications plan that provides contact information on who must be called when problems are first identified. This includes members of the Incident Response Team, other IT staff, third-party vendors and support, senior management, department managers, public relations people, and anyone else who may need to be conferred with. The contact list should include the names of anyone who may need to be called during an incident, along with their phone numbers, pager numbers, addresses, and any other relevant information.

In an emergency, you don't want people scrambling to find contact information, so it should be left with a centralized source of information. Some options might be the company switchboard, dispatch, the Help Desk, or other departments of the company. If an incident needed to be reported, employees could notify the switchboard operator or dispatcher, who in turn could contact Incident Response Team members.

In some cases, notifying the appropriate parties may be automated, allowing network administrators and other parties to be alerted when certain events occur. Systems may be configured to send out alerts via e-mail or to a pager number, notifying the person of such things as low disk space, errors, loss of power, or other events that may indicate a significant problem. When automated alerts are used, notified personnel may arrive to fix problems before users are even aware of the incident.

Because every member of an Incident Response won't be sitting by their phone and may otherwise be unavailable, you will need to ensure important knowledge is still available. Documentation on specific procedures should be available to team members through files on the network, the corporate intranet, or other methods. Printouts of this material should also be available, in case the areas where electronic versions are held are the targets of a particular incident. After all, if the server storing this information fails due to a virus, other malicious software, or an intrusion, no one will be able to access the electronic documents that explain how to deal with the problem.

Passwords are another piece of information that should be available in emergencies. Members of IT staff or the Incident Response Team may have varying levels of security, and may be unable to get into certain areas of the network or certain systems. For example, they may not have passwords to access administrative functions in certain systems, or workstations and servers may be locked down and inaccessible without an administrator password. To allow them entry in extreme situations, copies of passwords should be written down, sealed in an envelope, and stored in a locked container (such as a safe). Any encrypted keys needed to access critical data should also be stored with these passwords. In an emergency, if the person who knows the passwords is unavailable, then a member of the team can access the passwords and keys and use them to fix issues requiring them.

In some incidents, data may be altered, corrupted, or deleted. When this happens, the data may be irrevocably lost, unless backups have been regularly performed beforehand. By performing regular backups, the data on a server or workstation can be restored as needed. This is especially important if a particular machine is seized as evidence or data prior to the investigation date needs to be reviewed. To make it easier for members of the team to restore the data, recovery procedures should be documented thoroughly, allowing members to follow the understandable steps to restore systems to their previous state.

To aid in the detection process of an incident investigation (which we'll discuss next), preparation also requires that logging be activated on systems. Logging information to a file is a feature that's commonly provided for operating systems, and certain software and equipment. Logs can provide a great deal of information, revealing indicators that may show whether an incident has occurred. The more information that's provided in these logs, the more evidence you'll have for discovering incidents and dealing with them accordingly.

Baselines should also be created by recording data about how the system behaves normally. The metrics recorded in a baseline would include measurements of network traffic, memory usage, and other information that provides a clear understanding of how systems normally run. The Incident Response Team can compare the baseline to measurements taken when a problem is suspected, and thereby detect whether an incident has occurred.

Detection

Determining whether an incident has actually occurred is the next step of the incident investigation process. After all, just because someone reported that something doesn't seem right,

doesn't mean the company's at risk or that a crime has occurred. A user could report that files have been deleted, and although it could be indicative of hacking, it could just mean the user is too embarrassed to admit he deleted them by accident. The detection phase of incident investigation examines such reports, and determines what further actions (if any) are required.

Detection requires looking at the safeguards and auditing controls that have previously been set up, and determining whether anomalies exist. For example, logs may provide a great deal of information that can confirm or discard any notions of unwanted activity. Members of the IT staff or information security should check logs on a regular basis and determine if indications of problems have been recorded. System logs may show errors related to security violations, impending hardware failure, or other potential problems. Firewall logs should also be analyzed to identify attempted hacking from the Internet, policy breaches, or other damaging events. By not checking logs regularly, an incident may be avoided early, preventing more significant problems from occurring.

Software specifically designed to deal with certain incidents, or elements of an incident, can be used in the detection process. Antivirus software packages can be used to detect viruses, and can be configured to automatically deal with them upon detection. Intrusion detection systems can also be used to identify whether system security has been violated, systems have been misused, or accounts have been used or modified. Implementation of such software not only aids in protecting the network, but also allows you to detect incidents early.

In addition to the logs created by systems on the network, you should also keep a manual logbook. This will provide a record of dates, times, observations, system names, error messages, actions taken, and other details that may be considered valuable. The name of the person who reported the incident and the names of people who had access to systems should also be recorded. Creating a log should be done as early as possible. Information recorded in the log may be vital to solving problems, and may be needed for reference purposes if you're later required to testify in court.

Another reason for maintaining a logbook is that it can reveal patterns. Hackers may make several attempts to hack into a network, and being able to reference information on these previous occurrences can be valuable in identifying vulnerabilities and uncovering who is making these attempts, and may be used in the prosecution of that person. It can also be useful in identifying training issues, such as when multiple mistakes by the same person result in damaged data, invalid data entry, or the erroneous reporting of incidents. Without a log of previous incident investigations, such patterns may be unidentifiable.

When an incident is confirmed, it is important that an image of the effected system be made as soon as possible. As we mentioned earlier and will discuss further later in this chapter, computer forensic software can be used to generate an image of the data, creating an exact duplicate of a hard disk. This allows you to examine data on the disk, while leaving the original computer untouched. This is important because examinations of the original computer's data could modify data on the disk. Even opening a file can alter information (such as the date/time of when it was last opened), and negatively affect any further investigation or future prosecu-

tion. It is important to make an image of the system as soon as possible, because further intrusions into the system or the activation of malicious programs could delete evidence used to identify a suspect. Rather than giving the suspect a chance to cover their tracks, it is important to preserve that evidence quickly.

Containment

It is important to limit the extent and significance of an incident so it doesn't spread to other systems and continue doing damage. It makes no sense to identify a hacker's entry into a server, and then allow him or her to continue entering other servers on the network. In the same light, letting viruses spread across the network increases the level of damage, and defeats the purpose of even having an Incident Response Team. Containment limits the scope of such incidents, preventing the damage from spreading.

How an incident is contained will depend on the type of incident that's occurred, what's affected, and the importance of systems to the business. If someone had hacked into a network file server, it might be prudent to remove that server from the network, such as by unplugging the network cable from the adapter. In doing so, the hacker would be unable to do further harm and be unable to modify or delete any evidence they left behind. In other situations, such as an employee breaching policy, it might be overkill to prevent everyone from using network resources. In this case, having a member of the Incident Response Team stay with that person, and preventing them from using a computer would probably suffice.

EXAM WARNING

As important as it is to obtain evidence, it is also vital that a crime scene be secure. Not only does this require limiting physical access, but also remote access through machines. To contain access to a crime, you must also detach computers from networks (inclusive to the Internet) since a suspect or intruder may alter data before you can acquire evidence from the machine.

Eradication

Just as it's important to prevent further damage by containing an incident, it is equally important to remove its cause. Eradication removes the source of a threat so that further damage isn't caused or repeated. In doing so, the system is left more secure, and further incidents may be prevented.

Eradication may occur through a variety of methods. For example, if a virus were detected on systems, eradication would require removing the virus from all media and systems by using

antivirus software. In situations involving violations of law or policy, the eradication phase of incident investigation might require disciplinary action (such as terminating the employee) or pressing criminal charges. As you can see by this, the appropriate method of eradicating an incident depends on what or who is being dealt with.

Recovery

Once an incident has been handled, you will need to ensure that any data, software, and other systems are back to normal. The recovery phase is where these are restored to a normal state. It is here that you ensure the incident did not permanently affect elements of the network, and everything is as it was previous to the incident.

Recovery is important because data may be modified, deleted, or corrupted during incidents, and configurations of systems may be changed. Other problems that may result include malicious code that was planted on systems. Such code may be triggered by certain events, or activate at a later date when everything is presumed to be okay. Because of the possibility of future threats, you must determine whether any remnants of an attack exist, and what may have been damaged by the incident.

Systems may be restored in a variety of ways. Certain systems may need to reconfigured to the way they were before the incident, data may need to be validated to verify it is correct, or in other cases, the system may need to be completely restored from backups. If data has been modified or destroyed, and a backup is restored, then any work that took place since the backup was performed will need to be redone.

Follow-up

The follow-up to an incident investigation is where you determine whether improvements can be made to incident handling procedures. At this point, you examine the previous phases of the investigation, and review what was done and why. The follow-up requires an analysis of such details as:

- Preparation for the investigation, and whether additional preparation is needed

- Whether communication was effective, or if information was not conveyed in a timely fashion

- Steps taken during the investigation, and problems identified

- Determining whether the incident was detected quickly and accurately

- Whether the incident was adequately contained or spread to different systems

- Evaluating tools used in the investigation and whether new tools would result in improvements

It is also important to establish how much the incident cost, so changes to budgets can be made to effectively manage the risks associated with certain incidents. This not only includes

the cost of downtime, but personnel costs, the value of data lost, the hardware damaged, and other costs related to the investigation. By determining the financial costs associated with an incident, insurance claims can then be filed to reimburse the company, and cost/benefit analyses can be updated.

Evidence Assessment

Earlier in this chapter, we discussed how the crime scene technician is responsible for processing digital evidence that is collected during an investigation. While this may involve the technician being called directly to a crime scene and forced to deal with the situation on-the-fly, often this role will be involved in assisting in obtaining a search warrant and assisting in technical aspects of the case before any evidence is ready to be searched and seized. As we'll see in the sections that follow, processing evidence is a four-part set of procedures consisting of assessment, acquisition, examination, and documentation.

Evidence assessment is the first part of this process, and involves evaluating issues related to the case and the digital evidence that's being sought. It requires reviewing the search warrant or details of legal authorization to obtain the evidence, the details of the case, hardware and software that may be involved, and the evidence you hope to acquire for later evaluation. In doing so, you are able to determine the best course of action to take in obtaining the evidence, based on the scope of the case.

Case Assessment

When an incident occurs that requires a computer forensic investigation, the investigator for the case will request the services of the crime scene technician. The request for forensic services should not be taken at face value so the technician simply walks blindly into the case. It is important that the technician reviews the request and identifies the legal authority for his or her participation. This request for assistance should be in writing and include such information as:

- Who is making the request for service, and the contact information necessary to call, page, and/or e-mail this person

- The incident or case number

- The name and other information regarding the suspect

- Who owns the machine

- Whether the data has been viewed or accessed by anyone prior to your examination

- What kind(s) of forensic services are being requested

A request for service form that allows an investigator to provide this information is useful for several reasons. First and foremost, it provides an easy reference that connects evidence to a particular case. The form will provide information on whether a search warrant is required (based on who owns the computer), and can be useful in identifying information to search for.

For example, if you were interested in searching for documents containing the suspect's name, you could simply refer to the form to get the correct spelling. If you were unsure whether all of the services requested have been fulfilled, they can be quickly checked by looking at the list of services the investigator wanted you to perform. Also, if the request for services was illegitimate and the request was made for personal reasons, you have an official form that will protect you from disciplinary actions.

Because the computer may have been accessed prior to your acquiring the data and examining it, you should also request the complete chain of evidence documentation. This is especially important if a computer has already been seized and is being delivered to the forensic lab. If there are any questions regarding data, you can then contact any parties who previously had custody of the machine to determine if they accessed any files or performed any actions with the machine.

Although an investigator may be adept at interviewing suspects, following leads, and performing other tasks necessary to an investigation, he or she may not fully understand what is involved with computer forensics. It is important to discuss what you can and cannot do in an investigation, and what may or may not be discovered. In addition to this, you should discuss whether other attempts to acquire evidence or certain avenues of investigation have already been acted upon, such as:

- Is there a need for the use of other types of forensics? Has the evidence been checked for fingerprints, DNA, trace evidence, or other forensic evidence? If there is a need for this, you should wait before touching the computer until this has been completed.

- Has an attempt been made to acquire evidence from noncomputer sources? Because evidence is so often found on computers, it is possible other sources of evidence have been overlooked. For example, digital cameras and cell phones that take pictures can be useful in child pornography cases, while check paper, paper files, and other items may be useful in financial crimes.

- Is there a need to acquire evidence from other systems? In cases involving the Internet, you may wish to obtain logs and account information from Internet service providers, which may have logged when the person connected to the Internet, what sites they visited, e-mails that were sent and received, remote storage locations, and other information.

You should also discuss specific details of the case that can be used to narrow your search for information on a computer. If you have an understanding of why a person is being investigated, and the type of evidence the investigator is searching for, it can decrease the amount of time required in finding that evidence. For example, fraud cases will often involve searching for spreadsheets and financial records, child pornography cases will require looking for photographs, and hacking cases will often require looking at source code and specific applications. In addition to this, certain information about the suspect should be available to you, such as

their name, e-mail address, aliases, and user account information. By having this information beforehand, you will spend less time attempting to identify it when examining the computer.

In identifying aspects about the suspect who uses or owns a machine being examined, you should try to determine the person's computer skills. Different suspects will have varying levels of expertise with computers, with more advanced users possibly incorporating encryption or booby traps that will delete data if certain actions are performed. The more you know about a suspect and the case prior to dealing with the evidence, the better position you'll be in to successfully acquire and evaluate pertinent evidence.

Processing Location Assessment

While the thought of where you'll collect or examine evidence may not be the first thought in an investigation, it is important to identify this early in the investigation. In many cases, the evidence will be examined in a forensic lab, where you'll be working with equipment in your own work area. In other situations, you'll have to visit the scene of the crime. Sometimes this will be an easily controlled environment, such as a server room that limits the number of people who can enter and have access to evidence. Other situations may require you to collect evidence from a kiosk, a computer in a public Internet café, or the scene of a homicide where other forensic professionals are still gathering their own evidence. By understanding where the evidence needs to be gathered, you'll be better prepared to determine the type of equipment you'll need to bring, or if other personnel (such as police officers) will need to be present.

When assessing the location, you should consider a number of factors. Collecting evidence from certain scenes may take considerably longer than others might, so an estimate should be provided to the investigator. If it will take a lengthy period, you should try to determine the impact on the business by being there. In some situations, it is better to remove a hard disk from a server and allow members of the company's IT staff to restore systems as swiftly as possible. However, even in the best of circumstances, a computer may be unavailable for some time, requiring personnel at the company to use other systems. If you will be onsite for a long period, consideration should be given as to who will perform other forensic examinations while you're unavailable.

Equipment and training may also be an issue in certain circumstances. In our previous example of a homicide scene, it's possible you may be exposed to blood and other biological matter. In such cases, you may need to work in a suit that will protect you from biological hazards, or at the very least wear a mask and latex or vinyl gloves. By understanding the location where an investigation will take place, you can better prepare for factors that will impact your ability to collect and examine evidence.

Legal Considerations

As we discussed earlier in this chapter, a number of considerations must be taken into account prior to a search. Search warrants may or may not be required in certain situations, and there may be issues regarding the extent of your authority to search for evidence. Federal legislation,

state statutes, and local policies can all provide information that is specific to how and when a search may be conducted.

The U.S. Privacy Protection Act (PPA) covers the search and seizure of items that fall under First Amendment (freedom of speech and freedom of the press) protections. The Privacy Act was intended to protect journalists, publishers, and other such people who might have evidence of criminal activity but are not suspected of having committed any criminal act. This law applies to materials created for the purpose of disseminating information to the public (which could apply to writings intended to be posted to Web sites, because this is a form of publishing to a public forum).

If there is reason to suspect that the person who has the materials is committing the crime that the materials pertain to or if there is a danger to some person of physical injury or death that could be prevented by seizing the evidence, search and seizure is not a violation of the Privacy Act. Violation of the act is a civil rather than a criminal matter. Violators of the act are subject to civil lawsuits, but a violation does not mean the evidence will be thrown out of court, as is the case with violations of constitutional rights.

The Electronic Communications Privacy Act (ECPA) was passed to protect the privacy rights of customers of ISPs when their personal information is disclosed. Penalties for violation include civil damages and, in some cases, criminal charges. The ECPA provisions are laid out in Title 18 of the U.S. Code. However, the passage of the U.S. Patriot Act made changes to some of the provisions of the ECPA.

The U.S. Patriot Act went into effect in October 2001 in response to the continued threat of terrorism in the United States. Its passage resulted in several changes to federal law regarding computers and digital data as evidence. For example:

- Previously, under the Computer Fraud and Abuse Act, government investigators were not allowed to intercept voice wire communications as evidence in cases. The Patriot Act adds U.S. Code Title 18, Section 1030 (Computer Fraud and Abuse Act), as one of the offenses for which a wiretap order can be obtained.

- Previously, investigators had to get a wiretap order to seize and listen to unopened voice-mail messages stored with a third-party provider. The Patriot Act rewords the definition of *wire communication* so that stored messages are not included and investigators can obtain voice-mail evidence under a search warrant rather than undergoing the more difficult process of obtaining a wiretap order.

- Previously, investigators could not subpoena certain records such as credit card numbers of customers from ISPs. The Patriot Act added to the types of records that could be subpoenaed such items as credit card numbers and other payment information, temporarily assigned network (IP) addresses, and records of session times and durations.

- Previously, records could not be subpoenaed or obtained by search warrant from cable companies. Notice had to be given to the customer if the government wanted to examine the records, and the customer had to be given the opportunity to appear

in court for a hearing to determine whether the government was justified in examining the records. The Patriot Act changed this stance so that these requirements apply only to records regarding cable TV programming, not Internet services provided by cable companies.

- Previously, ISPs were not authorized to disclose information about customers in emergency situations (for example, when the customer was suspected of planning a terrorist attack), nor was there any provision that permitted ISPs to voluntarily disclose non-content information (for example, login records) when their networks were attacked. The Patriot Act permits ISPs to disclose both content and non-content information in emergency situations where there is an immediate risk of death or serious bodily injury or to protect their own property and rights. (ISPs are not required by the act to review records for dangers, nor are they required to disclose records in these situations.) The act also provides a defense against civil lawsuits for ISPs and others who provide information relying in good faith on the request of a government agent to preserve evidence.

- The Patriot Act expanded the scope of pen register and "trap and trace" devices to apply to information used in processing and routing electronic communications, such as e-mail header information, IP addresses, and port numbers. (Pen/trap orders can't be used to intercept the contents of a message—only the routing, addressing, and signaling information can be used.) The authority of the federal courts was expanded to allow issuance of pen/trap orders anywhere in the United States (previously limited to the court's particular district or jurisdiction).

- Previously, law enforcement officers were limited in their legal ability to assist owners of computers and networks in monitoring activity to protect against and detect intrusions and attacks. The Patriot Act specifically authorizes victims of network attacks to allow law enforcement officers to monitor their systems as part of an ongoing investigation (civil or criminal).

- The Patriot Act extends the scope of search warrants for e-mail communications to a nationwide basis so such warrants can apply to records not in the district in which the issuing court is located.

- The Patriot Act increases penalties and modifies sentencing guidelines for offenses that involve intentionally damaging protected computers (under Title 18, Section 1030) and extends the scope of the law to apply to computers that are located in other countries, if U.S. interstate or foreign commerce is affected. The act also clarifies the culpable mental state (*mens rea*) required to charge a hacker under Section 1030; only intent to cause damage must be proven, rather than intent to cause a specified dollar amount of damage. Enhanced penalties are provided when the damage is to computers that are used for national security or criminal justice purposes.

TEST DAY TIP

The Patriot Act has had a major effect on the government's ability to monitor activities and seize property. Because of the impact this has had on computer investigations, you should review the information previously presented on this act before taking the test.

Evidence Assessment

The final step in evidence assessment specifically deals with the evidence itself. You should identify the stability of evidence, and collect the most volatile evidence first before moving on to nonvolatile evidence. In doing so, the collection and acquisition of evidence should be prioritized so that the evidence most likely to contain what you're searching for is examined first. For example, if a border guard discovered that someone had child pornography as the wallpaper on a laptop, you would obviously want to acquire evidence from the laptop and examine it first, before moving on to any CDs, DVDs, and other media that may also have been collected. Throughout this process, you should document any actions taken, and determine the best methods of relating that information. This may include taking notes, making diagrams, photographing items, or utilizing features available in forensic software.

When evidence needs to be transported, you should evaluate the condition and vulnerability of the items. Certain devices like PDAs, cell phones, or laptops could simply be packaged in an evidence bag, while circuit boards and individual hard disks should first be stored an antistatic bags. In some cases, an investigator may also need to provide continuous electric power to battery-operated devices like laptops that are low in power so any volatile evidence isn't lost before it is delivered to you. Once the evidence has been acquired, you should then place it in a secure location free of electromagnetic interference.

Acquiring Evidence

The next phase of processing evidence is acquisition. As we mentioned earlier in this chapter, acquiring evidence is the process of obtaining digital evidence from its original source. In doing so, it is vital that the original data isn't altered, damaged, or destroyed in making a copy that the forensic technician can work from.

The first step in acquiring evidence from a computer is to document as much information about the machine as possible. You should note the serial number and any identifying information on the computer so you can prove that the computer taken from a crime scene was actually the one that evidence was acquired from at a later time. This is especially important when there is a backlog of cases, and the computer may have been stored for a period of time until the examiner had time to work on the machine. In documenting information, you should also

review information on any hardware and software configurations that were noted when the machine was seized, in case this needs to be duplicated on the examiner's machine.

If you are dealing with a hard disk that has already been removed from a computer, the tasks in acquiring evidence are considerably easier. You would simply attach the hard disk to the examiner's workstation in a forensic lab, or to a device like FastBloc (used with Encase software), and then use forensic software to acquire its contents. However, generally you will be dealing with an entire computer or laptop, not individual components that have been seized. In such cases, you'll need to take steps to remove storage devices yourself. Disassembling the computer case will provide you with physical access to these devices, so you should ensure you have taken precautions against static discharge and have not placed the equipment close to any strong magnetic fields. Either of these can seriously damage computer components, so during the disassembly you should wear an anti-static wristband or stand on an anti-static mat.

Once the case has been opened, you can identify what hard disks and other components (for example, PC card, network card, and so on) are installed, and begin taking steps to remove the storage devices. Before removing any storage devices, you should note how they are installed and configured so they can later be reinstalled exactly as they were before. This could include taking a picture of the inside of the computer so a visual reference is available for later. Once you've noted this, you should then remove the power connector or data cable from the back of the drive or motherboard. Doing so will prevent the destruction, damage, or modification of any data stored on the device in the steps that follow. After disconnecting the storage device, you should make a note of the make, model, size, jumper settings, location, drive interface, and any other information you can see that will identify the hard disk and its settings.

Once you've removed the power connector or data cable from the hard disk, you can then take steps to retrieve information stored on the computer through a series of controlled boots. To perform a controlled boot and capture data stored in the CMOS/BIOS, you would start the computer and press the particular key on the keyboard that allows you to access the BIOS Setup for that particular machine. This is often displayed on the screen when the computer is first powered on, and is generally the **Del** or **F10** key that accesses this program. However, you should check the manufacturer's Web site if it's not evident which key to press since it can vary from system to system. Once you've entered the BIOS Setup, you can view the configuration information for that machine. You should note the date and time of the system, whether power on passwords has been set up, and the boot sequence of the machine. If the boot order of the machine isn't configured to first try and boot from a floppy disk or the CD-ROM, you may need to change this. However, before modifying these settings, document what the original settings were, and what you changed them to afterwards.

After ensuring that the system is configured to first boot from a floppy or CD-ROM, you would then test your forensic boot disk to make sure the computer will boot from that drive properly. With the power connector or data cable still removed from storage devices, you would insert the boot disk, and then boot the computer. If it boots from the floppy, you would then

reconnect the storage devices to prepare for a third boot. When the computer boots this time, document the drive configuration information, inclusive to logical block addressing (LBA), large disk, cylinders, heads, and sectors (CHS), and whether the computer is configured to auto-detect any hard disks installed. Once this is documented, power the system down.

If possible, it is best to physically remove the hard disk from the computer that's been seized and connect it to a workstation in a forensic lab, or a device like FastBloc that prevents disk writes and works between the examiner's computer and the hard disk. If it is attached to the machine that will perform the acquisition, you can then use information acquired earlier from the CMOS/BIOS to properly configure the storage device so it will be recognized. In some situations (like those that follow), it may be easier, or only possible, to read the hard disk by leaving it installed on the suspect's machine:

- Laptop computers use different hard disks from desktop computers; although adapters can be purchased that will connect the hard disk to a desktop system. In some cases, removing the disk from the laptop may be difficult, and reading the disk may not be possible if the appropriate adapter to connect the drive to a ribbon cable is unavailable.

- Sometimes equipment requirements, such as when the disk is used for network storage and when network equipment is needed to access the data, make it necessary to leave a disk in the suspect's machine. It is also necessary to leave the disk in a suspect's machine when other equipment (such as the adapters mentioned previously) is not available to the technician performing the examination.

- RAID (Redundant Array of Inexpensive Disks) may need to be left in an array since attempting to acquire data from them individually may not provide results that are usable.

- In some cases, older drives (legacy equipment) may not work with newer systems, making it impossible to read the data.

If the hard disk isn't going to be connected to the examiner's machine, you will need to leave it installed on the suspect's machine. Depending on the forensic software used, the examiner could then attach a CD-RW or other storage device to the machine, or connect to the machine using a network cable, null modem cable, or other method of allowing communication between the two machines. Regardless of the method used to connect the machines, the data that's acquired and saved as image files should be stored on forensically clean media.

As we'll discuss later in this chapter, write protection is an important part of acquiring data since it will prevent any data from being written to the suspect hard disk. If hardware-based write protection is used, it should be installed prior to starting the computer, while software-based write protection should be activated immediately after booting the system with the examiner's operating system or boot disk. Once started, you should then attempt to capture and document any electronic identifiers the disk might have, such as its electronic serial number.

Once these facts about the disk have been recorded, you are then ready to begin acquiring the data using methods that won't modify data on the disk, such as by using disk-imaging software to duplicate the data.

Disk Imaging

Disk imaging is accepted as standard practice in computer forensics to preserve the integrity of the original evidence. Disk imaging differs from creating a standard backup of a disk (for fault-tolerance purposes) in that ambient data is not copied to a backup; only active files are copied. Because a backup created with popular backup programs (such as the Windows built-in backup utility, BackupExec, ARCserve, or the like) is not an exact duplicate (in other words, a physical bitstream image), these programs should not be used for disk imaging. Programs such as Norton Ghost include switches that allow you to make a bitstream copy, but these programs were not originally designed for forensics use and do not include the features and analysis tools included with imaging programs and stand-alone imaging systems designed especially for forensics examination.

Bitstream Copies

Digital evidence is, by its nature, fragile. Some data is *volatile*—that is, it is transient in nature and, unlike data stored on disk, will be lost when the computer is shut down. Data on a computer disk can be easily damaged, destroyed, or changed either deliberately or accidentally. The first step in handling such digital evidence is to protect it from any sort of manipulation or accident. The best way to do this is by immediately making a complete bitstream image of the media on which the evidence is stored.

A *bitstream image* is a copy that records every data bit recorded to the original storage device, including all hidden files, temp files, corrupted files, file fragments, and erased files that have not yet been overwritten. In other words, every binary digit is duplicated exactly onto the copy media. Bitstream copies (sometimes called *bitstream backups*) use CRC computations to validate that the copy is the same as the original source data. The "mirror image" should be an exact duplicate of the original, and the original should then be stored in a safe place where its integrity can be maintained. The copy is made via a process called *disk imaging*. In some cases, evidence could be limited to a few data files that can be copied individually rather than creating a copy of the entire disk. In the following sections, we discuss both disk-imaging and file-copying techniques. We also look at the importance of ensuring the integrity of disks used for imaging or copying, and we consider environmental factors that can affect the integrity of evidence, as well as preservation concerns related to specific types of storage media.

Using Disk Imaging to Create Duplicate Copies

Disk imaging refers to the process of making an exact copy of a disk. Imaging is sometimes also called *disk cloning* or *ghosting*, but the latter terms usually refer to images created for purposes other than evidence preservation. Disk imaging differs from just copying all the files on a disk

in that the disk structure and relative location of data on the disk are preserved. When you copy all the data on a disk to another disk, that data will usually be stored on the new disk in contiguous clusters as there is room to store it. That way, all the data on the two disks will be identical, but the way the data is distributed on the disks will not. When you create a disk image (a bitstream copy), each physical sector of the disk is copied so the data are distributed in the same way, and then the image is compressed into a file called an *image file*. This image is exactly like the original, both physically and logically. A bit-level duplicate of a disk can be created in a number of different ways, including:

- Removing the hard disk from the suspect computer and attaching it to another computer (preferably a forensic workstation) to make the copy

- Attaching another hard disk to the suspect computer and making the copy

- Using a stand-alone imaging device such as the DIBS Rapid Action Imaging Device (RAID)

- Using a network connection (Ethernet connection, crossover cable, null modem cable, USB, or the like) to transfer the contents of the disk to another computer or forensic workstation

Which of these methods you choose will usually depend on the equipment you have at hand. A portable forensic workstation or stand-alone imaging device is probably the best solution, but it's also the most expensive.

Write Protection

Write protection prevents any data from being written to storage media, so in the case of a computer forensic investigation, the data on the original hard disk isn't modified or deleted. Write protection is important in forensics, because even the slightest modification to a file could destroy information that might be important in an investigation, and bring the validity of the data into question in court.

Probably one of the easiest examples of showing how write protection works is a floppy disk. As seen in Figure 3.4, when looking at the back of a 3.5-inch floppy disk, a tab on the upper left corner can be switched to an open or closed position. When slid to a bottom position where the hole is closed, the disk can then be written to. If you were to open a file saved on the disk, the LastAccessed Date property of the file would be modified, showing it was last accessed at the current date and time. To avoid modifying the disk, the tab could be slid to the top position, creating a hole in the disk, and thus write protecting the disk. In doing so, if the file was opened, the file and its properties could not be modified, so the date the file was last accessed would still show a previous date.

Figure 3.4 Write Protection on a Floppy Disk

Other media may not even require worrying about modification to data. For example, when a CD-R or DVD-R is being examined, it cannot be modified because once the data has been stored on the disk, it cannot be written to again. This may not, however, be the case if you were accessing rewritable optical disks, such as a DVD-RW or CD-RW, which can be written to and modified multiple times.

When you are dealing with hard disks and other storage devices that can be written to over and over again, simple measures like flipping a tab aren't available, so other methods must be used. To ensure write protection, hardware or software-based solutions can be used. Some forensic software provides write protection so that any data suspect's computer isn't modified as an image is being created on another storage device. An even better solution is hardware-based write blockers. The hard disk is connected to the hardware, while a USB cable, FireWire, serial or parallel cable is used to connect the write blocker to the examiners computer. The forensic software connects to the hard disk through this device, which passes data from the hard disk to the examiner's computer, where an image of the disk is created. In doing so, no data are modified on the original drive.

Retaining Data and Timestamps

The time and date of creation or modification of a file can be an important issue in a criminal case. Remember that the timestamp on the files will be in accordance with the time and date set on the system clock. Some systems default to a particular time zone (usually Greenwich Mean Time, or GMT). If the user set up the system without configuring the proper time zone, or if the user deliberately changed the date and time settings, the timestamps on the files might not correlate to "real-world" occurrences regarding when the files were created. This can be a problem if, for example, the system records show that a file was created on a particular date and the suspect is able to prove they were nowhere near the computer on that date. For this reason,

you should note the system time and date settings before shutting down the computer and document them with a photograph, if possible; otherwise, do so with written notes. Opening a file changes the file's time and date records. Thus, it might be prudent to photograph the screen showing the file access or modification times prior to opening the file. You should be prepared to testify as to your actions and provide expert testimony that the actions you took changed the timestamps but did not modify the contents of the file in any way. When you do all your work on an image rather than the original, the original times and dates will be on the original disk. You can create a second copy of the original to illustrate this fact.

Evidence Examination

The examination is evidence that occurs after it has been acquired using forensic software. Working from an image of the original machine, files and other data can be extracted from the image to separate files, which can then be reviewed by the examiner. For example, a Word document found in the image of the suspect machine could be extracted, allowing it to be opened and viewed in Microsoft Word without modifying the original data or that available through the disk image. As seen by this example, the file is first extracted and then analyzed to determine what value it holds as evidence. While every file may not be individually examined in this manner, the process of analyzing data does require a repeated process of extracting data stored in different areas of the machine, and then determining its value to the investigation.

Extracting data from the machine isn't only limited to files available to the operating system, file system, or other software that may have been installed on the machine. By viewing various areas of the disk, file fragments and data that have been corrupted or deleted can be accessed and examined. Extraction of evidence from a hard disk can occur at either of two levels:

- Logical extraction
- Physical extraction

A *logical extraction* is used to identify and recover files based on the operating system(s), file system(s) and application(s) installed on the computer. This type of extraction allows you to identify what data is stored in active files, deleted files, slack space, and unallocated file space. Any data found with this type of examination would find information that is available to the operating system, and/or visible to the file system on the suspect's computer. When this type of extraction occurs, any or all of the following actions might be performed:

- Extraction of file system information. This is done to identify the structure of folders, as well as the names, locations, sizes, attributes, date, and timestamps of files.

- Extraction of files relevant to the investigation, which would be based on the name, extension, header/footer, content and/or location of the file on the drive.

- Extraction of data that is encrypted, password protected, and/or compressed.

- Extraction of data in the file slack. As we discussed in Chapter 3, a cluster is a group of disk sectors where data are stored, which the operating system assigned a unique number to keep track of files. Because the cluster is a fixed size in operating systems like Windows, the entire cluster is reserved for a file even if the file doesn't fill that amount of space. This unused space is referred to as slack space.

- Extraction of data in an unallocated space. Unallocated disk space is part of a hard disk that is not part of any partition. For example, if you had a single 1GB partition that was assigned a drive letter (such as C:), this would be allocated space. However, if the drive were larger than 1GB, the remaining space on the drive would be unallocated space. Even though it hasn't been allocated to a partition, it may still contain damaged or deleted data.

- Recovery of deleted files. As we'll see in Chapter 4, various techniques and tools can be used to recover data that have been deleted.

- Reduction of data, which would reduce the number of files returned by eliminating known files.

A *physical extraction* is used to identify and recover files and data across the entire physical hard drive. Because it occurs at the physical level, the file system used on the hard disk doesn't matter. A physical extraction may involve a number of different methods to find data stored on the computer, including:

- Keyword searching. Extracting data in this way involves searching for specific data using specific keywords. Because the search occurs at a physical level, it can find data stored anywhere on the hard disk.

- File carving, in which utilities will recover files or file fragments by looking for file headers/footers and other identifiers in the data. This is particularly useful when attempting to find data that have been damaged or deleted, were located in corrupt directories on the disk, or stored on damaged media.

- Partition table and unused space examinations. Examining the partition structure can help you identify the file system being used and determine whether the physical size of the hard disk is accounted for.

Once the data have been extracted from the computer, they can then be analyzed. This involves looking at the data and determining whether their relevance and significance to the case. While an investigator may analyze data like pictures that have been found on the machine, or perform subsequent analysis on various files that have been recovered, the person examining the machine will perform a significant amount of this work to limit the amount of information later provided to the investigator of the case. Various types of analysis include:

- Timeframe analysis

- Data-hiding analysis

- Application and file analysis

- Ownership and possession

Timeframe Analysis

Timeframe analysis is used to determine when files were downloaded, viewed or modified on a machine. It can be useful in constructing a sequence of events, or associating a particular user to a time period. Using the date and timestamps on files, which show when a file was created, last accessed, or modified, a timeframe can be established that shows when particular events occurred. In addition to this, dates and times stored in logs and other system files can show when a particular user logged on to a system or performed some action.

TEST DAY TIP

Different types of analysis may be used together to obtain specific types of data. Be sure to read the specific elements of a question carefully so you understand what information the question is trying to obtain from you.

Data–Hiding Analysis

Data-hiding analysis involves looking for data that may be hidden on the hard disk. By concealing the information, the person who hid the information hopes it will avoid detection from casual or forensic detection. While some techniques for hiding data may require special tools, others may be simple to detect if you're aware of the methods to use.

Files can be hidden in a number of ways on a system. On DOS/Windows file systems, setting the hidden attribute (*-h* at the command line, or set in the File Properties dialog box in the GUI) will prevent the file from showing up in response to the *DIR* command at the command line or in the files list in Explorer *if* the default settings are in place in Folder Options | View. However, if the Show Hidden Files And Folders option button is enabled, these hidden files will still be displayed. On UNIX systems, files and directories with names that begin with a dot are hidden and are not displayed in response to the *ls* command unless you use the *−a* switch.

Another method for hiding files is known as *hiding in plain view*. Using this method, a cybercriminal gives a file a name that makes it appear to be something it isn't—and something that the investigator would not be interested in. For example, a graphic file containing child

pornography could be renamed to something like window.sys and stored in the Windows system directory. To the casual observer, it looks like just another operating system file. When the criminal wants to access it, he merely has to change the file extension back to .jpg or .gif and open it in any graphics viewer program.

Although it might seem obvious to technical experts that moving a file to the Recycle Bin or Trash does not even remove the file's pointers as deleting it does, many cybercriminals are *not* technical experts and could think they have deleted evidence when in fact it is still intact in the Recycle Bin. Of course, this is more likely to be true in the case of "nontechnical" cyber-crimes such as child pornography or con-artist scams than network intrusions and other hacker activities. However, considering the level of technical knowledge required (or rather, *not* required) to launch attacks using the script- and click-kiddie methods, it never hurts to check. The evidence you need could be sitting right there waiting for you, easily restored with a single click of the mouse.

The *host protected area* or *hidden protected area* (HPA) is an area of the hard disk that normally isn't visible to an operating system. An HPA may be used to store utilities, diagnostic tools, or programs used when the computer is first powered up. Although it may seem insidious, many computer manufacturers use this space to store software. For example, IBM and LG notebooks both use an HPA to store system restore and recovery software. If this hidden partition of the hard disk exists, and is known to the user of the computer, then it may be used to store illegal or sensitive materials that may be relevant to your case.

Steganography

Steganography (from the Greek word for *covered writing*) refers to a method of hiding data—not just concealing its contents as encryption does, but concealing its very existence. Steganography is usually used in conjunction with encryption for the added protection of sensitive data. This method ameliorates one of the biggest problems of encrypting data—the fact it is encrypted draws the attention of people who are looking for confidential or sensitive information. For more information on steganography, see Chapter 7.

Application and File Analysis

Application and file analysis is used to identify what kinds of programs the suspect is using, recognize common file types used for specific purposes relevant to the investigation, and associate files that have been located on the drive with a particular software. Often, people will use certain patterns to name files or directories, whether it is to be as specific and detailed as possible (for example, TaxReturn2007.q07) or to hide the contents by using a specific code (for instance, cp13yf.jpg to indicate child pornography depicting a 13-year-old girl). By identifying these patterns and their relevance, you can expand your search to look for other files with these features.

Some files can be associated with specific applications to identify what programs are commonly being used. For example, you could identify files in a Temporary Internet Files directory

to those used with Internet Explorer, while other files could be associated with e-mail programs. In doing so, you can determine what programs are being used. Similarly, by reviewing the Internet history and messages in the e-mail software, you could correlate files that have been saved to those sent or received via e-mail, or those downloaded from a particular Web site.

The most direct method of determining what's in a file is of course to examine the contents. To identify what is depicted in an image, or the data in a spreadsheet or document, you will need to view the contents and determine the relevance to the case. To reduce the amount of files you'll need to review, you should perform other actions mentioned in previous sections to narrow down what needs to be viewed.

Ownership and Possession

Ownership and possession analysis is used to identify who created, modified, or accessed files on a computer. By identifying the individual who created, viewed, or downloaded a particular file, you can associate the existence of a file to the actions of a person. For example, if a person said they hadn't seen a file, you could show that the file's ownership belonged to their user account, and by identifying the last time it was accessed, show the person had reasonable knowledge of its existence. In this example, you can see that this type of analysis can easily be used with timeframe analysis to show when a particular person used the computer and had access to a particular file.

As seen in Exercise 3.3, ownership of a file can be displayed through the properties of a file. In looking at the properties of a file, you can view who the current owner of a file is. If multiple users are on a machine, you can associate who owns the file with the person who uses that particular account. In knowing this, you can then pursue firewall logs or other resources to obtain additional information about the user's actions.

EXERCISE 3.3

VIEWING OWNERSHIP OF A FILE ON A WINDOWS XP COMPUTER

1. From the Windows Start menu, select Programs | Accessories and then click the Windows Explorer menu item.

2. When Windows Explorer opens, right-click a file located on your C drive. On the context menu that appears, click the Properties menu item.

3. When the Properties dialog box appears, click the Security tab.

4. On the Security tab, click the Advanced button.

5. When the Advance Security Settings dialog appears, click the Owner tab.

6. On the Owner tab, you will see a field labeled Current owner of this item:, followed by the username of the file's current owner.

7. Click Cancel to exit the dialog.

8. Click Cancel to exit the Properties dialog box.

Documenting and Reporting of Evidence

Because any evidence may be used in possible criminal proceedings, thorough documentation cannot be stressed enough. Documentation provides a clear understanding of what occurred to obtain the evidence, and what the evidence represents. No matter what role you play in an investigation, you must document any observations and actions made. Information should include the date, time, conversations pertinent to the investigation, tasks that were performed to obtain evidence, names of those present or who assisted, and anything else relevant to the forensic procedures that took place.

According to Digital Evidence Standards and Principles, developed by the SWGDE and IOCE in 1999 and published in the April 2000 issue of *Forensic Science and Communications* (a publication of the FBI), "[C]ase notes and observations must be in ink, not pencil, although pencil (including color) may be appropriate for diagrams or making tracings. Any corrections to notes must be made by an initialed, single strikeout; nothing in the handwritten information should be obliterated or erased. Notes and records should be authenticated by handwritten signatures, initials, digital signatures, or other marking systems."

Documentation may also be useful as a personal reference, should the need arise to testify in court. Because of the technical nature involved, you may need to review details of the evidence before testifying at trial. Without it, your memory may fail you at a later time, especially if a case doesn't go to court until months or years later. These notes may also be referred to on the stand, but doing so will have them entered into evidence as part of the court record. As the entire document is entered into evidence, you should remember not to have notes dealing with other cases or sensitive information about the company in the same document since this will also become public record.

In addition to the documents you create, it is important that procedures used for incident investigation and handling are also available to investigators, members of an Incident Response Team and other IT staff. Documented procedures allow incident responses to be more organized and effective. They provide a methodical approach, allowing those investigators to perform necessary tasks step by step. This can be particularly important during investigations, as investigators aren't required to rely on memory when dealing with unexpected events.

Investigators can simply move through the documented process, completing each of the necessary tasks in a set order.

EXAM WARNING

Documentation plays a vital role in any investigation. You should remember that documentation must be maintained throughout an investigation, and may be used in court. As we'll discuss in Appendix A, documentation may be referred to, whether it be to challenge what you did, or may be used by you in providing testimony as a personal reference.

Evidence Logs

The *evidence log* is a document that lists all evidence collected in a criminal case, with a description of each piece of evidence, who discovered and collected it, the date and time of collection, and the disposition of the evidence. The description should be detailed enough to differentiate the item from others like it and should include serial numbers and other identifying numbers when possible. The log should show all transfers of custody of the evidence from one person to another. This process of logging the transfer of evidence is tangible proof of the preservation of the chain of custody.

Documenting Evidence Analysis

When the bit-stream image of the suspect computer's disk(s) is analyzed, a log should be kept documenting the evidence analysis. This log should show each step of the analysis process, including who was present, what was done (for example, running a software utility to remove binary data from a swap file), the result of the procedure, and the time and date. As the data on the disk are assessed for their evidentiary value, you should document all potential evidence found. For example, if you open a .jpg that appears to be a pornographic photo of a child, document the filename, where on the disk it was located, date and timestamps, and other file properties. In addition to the volatile data and obscure areas on the disk where data hides that we discussed earlier (slack space, unallocated space, partition gaps, and so forth), some of the data that should be examined for evidence, depending on the type of cybercrime offense, includes:

- List of URLs recently visited (obtained from the Temporary Internet Files or Web cache and History folders).

- E-mail messages and lists of e-mail addresses stored in the suspect's address book. The filename depends on the e-mail program in use—for example, the .pst file for

Outlook. (In some cases, this information will be stored on an e-mail server, such as an Exchange server.)

- Word-processing documents; the file extension is dependent on the program used to create them—common extensions are .doc, .wpd, .wps, .rtf, and txt.

- Spreadsheet documents; the file extension is dependent on the program used to create them—examples include .xls, .wg1, and .wk1.

- Graphics, in the case of child pornography cases; file extensions include .jpg, .gif, .bmp, .tif, and others.

- Chat logs; the filename depends on the chat program.

- The Windows Registry (where applicable).

- Event viewer logs.

- Application logs.

- Print spool files.

The Final Report

Once evidence has been examined, the documentation that has been compiled is used to create a final report that outlines what actions have been taken, and what has been found on the suspect's machine. The final report will include a statement on what occurred during the investigation process, information you acquired and generated during the analysis of a suspect machine, and printouts of pertinent data. For example, in an Internet luring case (where an online predator seduces a child into having sex), the chat logs from their conversations would be included in the final report. Excerpts from the chat may be included to indicate important parts of the document the investigator should be aware of, as well as the complete log. In situations where pornography was found on a machine, printouts of thumbnails would also be included in the report, with information on the filename, the full path to its location on the suspect's hard drive, the file size, and the time and date information. As you can see from this, the specific information included in the final report can depend on what the case involved, and what was found on the machine.

Closing the Case

Regardless of what the investigation entails, there comes a time when every case must be closed. Once the analysis has been completed, and a sufficient amount of time has passed, you will need to accept what has been found and move on to another case. If certain evidence has been found, it may even be decided that additional evidence on the computer isn't necessary for the case. For example, if you've found the smoking gun in the case (such as dozens of child pornography pictures), additional evidence may be unnecessary if enough has been found to

pursue a conviction. Once you're satisfied that, based on the search parameters you have, the analysis you've performed is complete and there's little to nothing else to find, it is usually time to stop. After all, no one makes a career of a single case.

After a final report has been prepared and submitted to the investigator and/or prosecutor, you should follow up to identify what actions (if any) are being taken regarding the case. In some situations, new information that can be used to search for evidence may become available, and you may be asked to revisit the machine or examine new sources of data (such as other machines, devices, or storage sites) and try to find more. Other times, you will find that the person has taken a plea bargain (ending your role in the process), or that a trial will get underway at some point in the future. By following up with investigators, you will be able to determine what will occur next in the case.

At some point, any evidence you've acquired and analyzed will no longer be needed. Policies dealing with the destruction and disposal of evidence should be in place to provide a guideline as to how long you should keep property that's been seized, as well as disk images acquired from machines, media, and devices. When the date approaches, you should contact the investigator since he or she will be able to inform you whether the evidence should be retained longer. In some situations, evidence will be retained in the event of an appeal or delays in hearing the case in court or other hearings.

Summary of Exam Objectives

Computer forensics involves collecting, examining, preserving, and presenting evidence that is stored or transmitted in an electronic format. This branch of forensics uses scientific methods to retrieve and document evidence located on computers and other electronic devices. Using specialized tools and techniques, digital evidence may be retrieved in a variety of ways. Such evidence may reside on hard disks and other devices, even if it has been deleted so it's no longer visible through normal functions of the computer or hidden in other ways. Forensic software can reveal data that are invisible through normal channels, and restore the same to a previous state. Because the purpose of computer forensics is uncovering evidence for possible use in court, strict procedures must be followed for evidence to be admissible.

Computer forensics may be used in criminal and civil cases, as well as for internal corporate investigations. When certain incidents occur in a company, not only does the immediate problem need to be fixed but also the person causing the problem has to be investigated. Companies may find their Web sites or networks hacked by outside parties, receive threats via e-mail, or fall victim to any number of cyber-crimes. Once systems are secure from further intrusion, the next step is to acquire information useful in finding and prosecuting the person(s) responsible. In other cases, an administrator may discover that people internal to the organization are committing crimes or violating policies, such as by using a computer for non-work-related use or to download and store images and other files prohibited by the organization. These actions can result in disciplinary actions (up to and including termination of employment). To protect the company from a lawsuit for wrongful termination, discrimination, or other charges by the disciplined employee, any actions taken by the company must be based on sound evidence. Because any facts acquired may become evidence in court, standard computer forensics techniques must be used to protect the integrity of potential evidence.

To ensure the evidence can be used in court, numerous standards must be met to ensure it isn't compromised and that information has been obtained correctly. If you don't follow forensic procedures, judges may deem evidence inadmissible, defense lawyers may argue its validity, and the case may be damaged significantly. In many cases, the only evidence available is that which exists in a digital format. This could mean that the ability to punish an offender rests with the quality of evidence you've acquired, authenticated, examined, and presented to the court through thorough documentation and testimony.

Exam Objectives Fast Track

Investigating Computer Crime

☑ Computer forensics is the application of computer skills and investigation techniques for the purpose of acquiring evidence. It involves collecting, examining, preserving, and presenting evidence stored or transmitted in an electronic format.

☑ A first responder is the first person to respond to an incident who has the knowledge and skill to deal with the situation and preserve evidence. This may be an officer, security personnel, a member of the IT staff or Incident Response Team, or any number of other individuals.

☑ An investigator may be a member of law enforcement or the Incident Response Team and is responsible for investigating the crime or incident that has taken place.

☑ Crime Scene Technicians are individuals who have been trained in computer forensics, and have the knowledge, skills, and tools necessary to process a crime scene.

☑ The primary purpose of computer forensics is the collection, examination, preservation, and presentation of digital evidence.

☑ The methodology of investigating computer crime can be broken down into three components: acquisition, authentication, and analysis. Acquisition is the act or process of gathering information and evidence. Authentication is the process of ensuring the acquired evidence is the same as the data originally seized. Analysis is the process of examining and evaluating information.

☑ Volatile evidence is any data or other evidence that may be lost once power is lost.

☑ Computer forensic software should be used to make an image of the disk(s) to work with so the integrity of the original can be preserved. Disk imaging software will create an exact duplicate of a disk's contents and can be used to make copies of hard disks, CDs, floppies, and other media.

☑ Copies of data should be made on media that is forensically sterile. This means the disk has no other data on it, and has no viruses or defects.

☑ Any computers, devices, or data associated to a case must be kept secure throughout the investigation. This includes securing the crime scene, ensuring evidence is kept safe during transport, and storing evidence in a secure location that has limited access.

☑ A chain of evidence\chain of custody form is used to monitor who has had possession of evidence at any point in time, from the crime scene to the courtroom.

☑ A search warrant is a legal document that permits members of law enforcement to search a specific location for evidence related to a criminal investigation, and seize that evidence so it may be analyzed and possibly used in court.

Investigating Company Policy Violations

☑ A policy is used to address concerns and identify risks to a company, while procedures are used to provide information on how to perform specific tasks and/or deal with a problem.

☑ Acceptable use policies are used to establish guidelines on the appropriate use of technology.

☑ Incident response policies are implemented to provide an understanding of how certain incidents are to be dealt with.

☑ Hostile working environments are workplaces where a person fears intimidation, harassment, physical threats, humiliation, or other experiences that create an offensive or oppressive atmosphere.

☑ Industrial espionage is the selling of trade secrets and classified information to competitors.

☑ Warning banners are brief messages used to inform users of policies and legislation regarding the use of a system and the information it contains.

Conducting a Computer Forensic Investigation

☑ Processing evidence is a four-part set of procedures consisting of assessment, acquisition, examination, and documentation.

☑ Evidence assessment involves evaluating digital evidence to determine the best course of action to take based on the scope of a particular case.

☑ Acquiring digital evidence is the process of obtaining a duplicate copy that can later be studied from its original source. Data can then be extracted from the disk image and examined without modifying the original data.

☑ The examination of evidence occurs after it's been acquired so that the forensic technician can analyze an exact duplicate of the data from the suspect's machine.

☑ Disk imaging refers to the process of making an exact copy of a disk.

☑ A bit-stream image is a copy that records every data bit recorded to the original storage device, including all hidden files, temp files, corrupted files, file fragments, and erased files that have not yet been overwritten.

☑ When the bit-stream image of the suspect computer's disk(s) is analyzed, a log should be kept documenting the evidence analysis. This log should show each step of the analysis process, including who was present, what was done (for example, running a software utility to remove binary data from a swap file), the result of the procedure, and the time and date. Information from this log can be used in a final report on the case.

☑ Write protection prevents any data from being written to storage media. It can be software- or hardware-based.

☑ A logical extraction is used to identify and recover files based on the operating system(s), file system(s), and application(s) installed on the computer.

☑ A physical extraction is used to identify and recover files and data across the entire physical hard drive.

☑ Timeframe analysis is used to determine when files were downloaded, viewed, or modified on a machine.

☑ Data-hiding analysis involves looking for data that may be hidden on the hard disk.

☑ Steganography is a method of hiding data to conceal its existence, such as by hiding data inside other data.

☑ Application and file analysis is used to identify what kinds of programs the suspect is using.

☑ Ownership and possession analysis is used to determine who created, modified, or accessed files.

☑ Documentation provides a clear understanding of what occurred to obtain the evidence, and what the evidence represents.

Exam Objectives
Frequently Asked Questions

The following Frequently Asked Questions, answered by the authors of this book, are designed to both measure your understanding of the Exam Objectives presented in this chapter, and to assist you with real-life implementation of these concepts.

Q: A system used by my company doesn't support electronic warning banners being displayed at startup. What should I do to ensure people adhere to proper usage?

A: Any information that would be contained in a warning banner should be included in a security policy that employees have read, understood, and signed. In addition to this measure, you can also print warnings on posters or large pieces of paper and post them in locations where the system is used. For example, in a school library or computer lab, printouts of a warning on large pieces of paper can be posted on walls by the computers.

Q: How should I prepare evidence to be transported in a forensic investigation?

A: Before transporting evidence, you should ensure it is protected from possible damage. Hard disks and other components should be packed in anti-static bags, and other components should be packaged to reduce the risk of damage from being jostled. All evidence should be sealed in a bag and/or tagged to identify it as a particular piece of evidence, and information about the evidence should be included in an evidence log.

Q: My company is planning to assign someone the duty of performing forensic investigations for internal violations of policies, and to work with the Incident Response Team when incidents occur. What qualifications should this person have?

A: A person conducting computer forensic investigations and examinations should have expert computer skills, including an understanding of hardware, network technologies, programming skills, and forensic procedures. It is also a good idea for the forensics investigator to have a good knowledge of applicable local, state, and federal laws regarding computer crimes and rules of evidence.

CHFI

Acquiring Data, Duplicating Data, and Recovering Deleted Files

Exam objectives in this chapter:

- **Recovering Deleted Files and Deleted Partitions**
- **Data Acquisition and Duplication**

Exam Objectives Review:

- ☑ **Summary of Exam Objectives**
- ☑ **Exam Objectives Fast Track**
- ☑ **Exam Objectives Frequently Asked Questions**

Introduction

Before data can be analyzed, it needs to be acquired. This means that the data needs to be duplicated so that the person performing the analysis can work from it without modifying the data. This means using any number of tools to duplicate the data so that an exact sector-by-sector mirror image of the disk is generated. This enables the forensic analyst to view any data that is hidden, fragmented, or deleted. Whether data is being duplicated as part of a computer forensic investigation or to acquire a backup of the data for other purposes, it is important that the original data is not modified or corrupted during the duplication process.

Deleted data can be an issue in any situation dealing with computers. A file may be deleted on purpose or by accident, as a normal process of an application, or as the result of a virus, intrusion, or malicious software. In some cases, an entire partition may be lost, causing everything on a volume to appear unrecoverable. However, this is not necessarily the case. When data is deleted, various tools may be used to recover the data from a hard disk or other storage media. In some cases, the files may be corrupted or damaged in some way, and additional software may be needed to repair the file. As discussed in the following sections, regardless of the cause, there are many ways to recover data.

Recovering Deleted Files and Deleted Partitions

At the company where you work, there is probably an inventory of company assets. It may be as simple as a typed list for insurance purposes or as detailed as a database containing records of every desk, computer, printer, and every other asset owned by the company. On your computer, a similar table of records is used to maintain information about the files saved on your hard disk. In the same way that deleting a record from an inventory does not make your desk disappear, deleting a file on your hard disk does not necessarily make the data disappear.

In Chapter 2, we discussed how files are stored on hard disks and other media. *Clusters* are two or more sectors of a hard disk, and they are the smallest unit of disk space that can be allocated to store a file. When a file is saved, information on which clusters are used to store the file is kept in another kind of table. A *file allocation table* is used to keep track of files on FAT and FAT32 file systems, whereas on NTFS volumes a *Master File Table* (MFT) is used. Using such tables, the operating system can maintain where files are located. When a file is deleted, the record of the file is removed from the table, thereby making it appear that it does not exist anymore. The clusters used by the file are marked as being free and can now be used to store other data. However, although the record is gone, the data may still reside in the clusters of the hard disk.

Also in Chapter 2, we discussed how *partitions* are used to create a logical division of a hard disk. Even if multiple partitions are not used, the entire disk can be set as a single partition, formatted to use a particular file system (such as FAT or NTFS), and given a drive letter (such as

C: or D:). Information about how partitions are set up on a machine is stored in a *partition table*, which is stored in the Master Boot Record (MBR). When the computer is booted, the partition table allows the computer to understand how the hard disk is organized and then passes this information to the operating system when it is started. When a partition is deleted, the entry in the partition table is removed, making the data inaccessible. However, even though the partition entry has been removed, the data still resides on the hard disk.

As discussed in the following sections, there are many different tools that can be used to recover deleted files and deleted partitions from a hard disk. Depending on how the data was deleted, and whether it was overwritten before it could be recovered, there is the possibility that files and partitions can be restored.

Deleting Files

Every operating system (OS) provides a way of removing data from a hard disk. If it did not, a hard disk would fill up quickly from all of the temporary files, backup files, and other data written to a disk by the OS or other software installed on a computer. Although the OS and applications on a machine will generally clean these when they are no longer needed, this is not always the case (as discussed later). In addition to all the files created and deleted by programs on your computer, there are also the ones that you have created and no longer need. These can be old to-do lists, documents that are out of data, and other files that serve no purpose to you anymore. In cases involving computer forensics, it can also be files that contain incriminating evidence.

A *deleted file* is any file that has been logically erased from the file system but may still remain physically on storage media. How a file is deleted can vary. Although for many people, deleting a file means selecting a file and pressing the **DEL** or **Delete** button on their keyboard, there are other ways in which a file may be deleted.

Command Line Delete

In the days before the graphical user interface, the only way to delete a file was from a command prompt. When DOS was one of the major operating systems of choice, you would enter textual commands from a prompt, which was generally a symbol following the drive letter you were currently using. In Windows, the **Command Prompt** is a window that provides an interface to enter the commands to perform certain actions. As shown in Figure 4.1, the **Command Prompt** allows you to enter commands that can be used to delete files and directories from a partition.

Figure 4.1 Command Prompt Delete

```
Command Prompt                                              _ □ x

C:\>dir file*.*
 Volume in drive C has no label.
 Volume Serial Number is 68E6-C099

 Directory of C:\

08/01/2007  07:21 AM          1,454,166 filefragment
              1 File(s)      1,454,166 bytes
              0 Dir(s)  66,324,168,704 bytes free

C:\>del filefragment

C:\>
```

There are two commands that can be used to delete files or directories from the command line:

- *DEL*
- *ERASE*

Each of these commands has been available on Microsoft operating systems since DOS and is used to remove a file from any writable storage media. They perform the same function and have the same *switches*, which are options that control what actions are taken by a command. The switches available on systems running Windows 2000, XP, and later are shown in Table 4.1.

Table 4.1 DEL/ERASE Switches

Switch	Description
/p	Prompts you for confirmation as to whether you want to delete the file
/f	Forces the deletion of read-only files
/s	Deletes the specified files from the current directory and any sub-directories
/q	Specifies not to prompt for confirmation before deleting files. This is called quiet mode.

Continued

Table 4.1 continued DEL/ERASE Switches

Switch	Description
/a:	Deletes files based on the following attributes:
	■ r read-only
	■ a archive
	■ s system
	■ h hidden
	■ - prefix used with any of the above attributes, indicating "not"
/?	Displays help

In using this command, you can specify a particular filename or use wildcards. For example, if you wanted to delete a file called filename.txt in the root directory of C:, you would type **DEL C:\filename.txt**. However, if you wanted to delete all files in the current directory, you could type **DEL *.***, which indicates to delete files with any filename or extension.

As previously discussed, the FAT file system uses a file allocation table to keep track of files, whereas NTFS uses an MFT. In using this command, the file that is deleted will have the pointer to that file removed from the table, but the data will remain on the hard disk. This gives you the opportunity to acquire the data using file recovery or forensic tools that are discussed later in this chapter.

Moving Files

Another method of deleting a file involves moving it. If the file is moved from one directory to another on the same partition, the table used to keep track of where files are stored is updated. Because the file still resides on the same partition, a pointer to the file's location is updated. The record showing the file's location is modified to reflect that it is now in another directory, but nothing else about the file changes. Any attributes on the file (such as whether the file is compressed) remain the same.

However, when a file is moved from one hard disk or partition to another, it is actually a multistep process of copying and deleting the file. First, a new copy of the file is created on the target partition. After the file has been copied, the original file is then deleted. This process also requires some housekeeping in the FAT or MFT tables. A new entry is created in the table on the partition where it has been copied, whereas the record for the deleted file is removed from the table on its partition.

When a file is moved from one partition to another, it can offer greater possibilities for recovering a file that has been deleted. If a file is moved to another partition and then deleted

later, the file has essentially been deleted twice. As such, you may be able to recover it from the partition on which it was deleted, and you may also be able to recover it from the partition from which it was moved.

Disk Cleanup

Another way in which files are deleted is when software does it for you. Software will generally clean up after itself by deleting old setup, temporary, and backup files when they are no longer needed. However, sometimes files are not properly removed, and a considerable number of files may continue to reside on a hard disk. This is the reason for tools such as Disk Cleanup, which removes files and programs from a Windows XP computer. Disk Cleanup will check for files that can be safely removed so that more disk space is available for use and performance is improved. The Disk Cleanup utility can be run by clicking on the Windows **Start** menu, selecting **Programs | Accessories | System Tools**, and then clicking the **Disk Cleanup** menu item. Once started, the utility will analyze your hard disk to determine what files can be safely deleted, and then it will display a screen similar to that shown in Figure 4.2. As seen in this figure, there are a number of different types of files that may be removed, including the following:

- **Temporary Setup Files**, which are files created by setup programs and no longer used

- **Downloaded Program Files**, which are ActiveX controls and Java programs that were used on certain Web pages you visited

- **Temporary Internet Files**, which are Web pages, images, and other content that are stored on your hard disk so an Internet browser can display them

- **Old *CHKDSK* Files**, which are file fragments that were saved when *CHKDSK* was run to check for disk errors

- **Recycle Bin**, which, as discussed later, is a repository for deleted files

- **Temporary Files**, which are programs temporarily stored in a Temp folder by a program but weren't properly removed by the software. Any temporary files that haven't been modified in the last week are considered safe for deletion.

- **Temporary Offline Files**, which are copies of recently used network files that have been cached, so you can use them after disconnecting from the network

- **Offline Files**, which are local copies of network files that you wanted to have available for use after disconnecting from the network

- **Compress Old Files**, which will compress any files that haven't been recently used

- **Catalog Files for the Content Indexer**, which are files left over from a previous indexing operation, used by the Indexing service

Figure 4.2 Disk Cleanup

Once you select the types of files you want to delete and press **OK**, the files related to the selected categories are removed from your hard disk. As we saw with previous methods, the entry related to the file is removed from the file allocation table or MFT, and the clusters are marked as free to use for storage of other files.

Permanently Destroying Data

In considering the previously discussed methods, you can see that data can be deleted in a number of ways, but this may not necessarily mean the data is destroyed. If data is deleted, any number of data recovery or computer forensic tools can be used to restore the data. Even formatting the hard disk is not a suitable solution, when you consider that certain tools and data recovery methods can still access the data. The only way to be certain that data cannot be recovered using software solutions is to overwrite it with other data.

Disk erasing software wipes the disk clean by erasing all the files and overwriting the disk space with a series of ones and zeros. In doing so, every sector of the disk is overwritten, making the data unrecoverable. If anyone attempted to recover data on the disk, they would not be able to retrieve anything because the data is completely destroyed.

A *degausser* or *bulk demagnetizer* is hardware that can be used to destroy data stored on magnetic media such as floppy disks and backup tapes. A degausser is a powerful magnet that erases all data from magnetic media so that no one can retrieve information from it. Hard disks can also have data erased with a degausser, performing a low-level format that erases all data from the disk. If there are concerns regarding particularly sensitive information being seen by outside

sources, an additional measure of security is physically scarring or destroying the media. For floppy disks and backup tapes, this involves shredding the media into pieces. For hard disks, you would open the hard drive, remove the platter inside, and physically scar or destroy it. Acid can also be used to destroy magnetic media.

EXAM WARNING

Remember that if a file is deleted, the data isn't necessarily gone. Until it is overwritten by another file, software that overwrites the file with other data, or is erased using tools such as a degausser or bulk demag-netizer, the data may still be recovered.

Recycle Bin

So far, we've examined various ways of deleting files by using commands, utilities, and performing actions such as moving files. With each of the methods, the files are no longer visible to the operating system and are considered "permanently" deleted. However, this doesn't mean that the data is completely gone. Until the data is overwritten or destroyed using the methods discussed previously, it may still be recovered. The files are considered permanently deleted by the operating system because there are no programs native to the OS that will allow you to restore the files. For most people, this means the files are simply gone.

To give users a second chance to restore a file before permanently deleting it, a number of operating systems provide an easy-to-use method of restoring deleted files. A *Recycle Bin* or *Trash Can* is a repository where files are temporarily stored after they are deleted. On machines running Windows 95 and later, this container for deleted items is called a Recycle Bin, whereas Macintosh OS uses a Trash Can.

Macintosh OS X allows items to be dragged and dropped into the Trash Can icon on the desktop. By opening the Trash, you can browse previously deleted items, manually drag and drop items out of the trash, or delete all of the items you want to get rid of. Macintosh OS X doesn't provide the ability to delete individual items in the trash; it can only empty everything.

The Recycle Bin has been available in every Microsoft operating system since Windows 95, and it also allows items to be dragged and dropped into the Recycle Bin icon on the desktop. When a file is deleted from the desktop or using Windows Explorer, the file is moved to the Recycle Bin with a record of its original location. The file hasn't actually been deleted; its pointer has simply been changed to show that it now resides in the Recycle Bin. Whereas with Macintosh OS X you must remember where a file was deleted from, Windows will auto-matically restore an item to its original location.

Another similarity between the two is that you can open the Recycle Bin and browse previously deleted files and directories. Unfortunately, you can't browse the contents of deleted directories in the Recycle Bin. If a file or directory was deleted and you tried to open it in the Recycle Bin to view its contents, double-clicking on it would only display the properties of the deleted item. The option of double-clicking on an item to view its properties isn't available in the Trash Can, nor is the ability to delete individual items from the Trash Can. In the Recycle Bin, however, you can restore or permanently delete individual items so that space can be made available for storing other files.

TEST DAY TIP

Don't confuse the Trash Can in Macintosh OS X with the Recycle Bin in Windows operating systems. Although they are both containers for deleted items, the Trash Can will only allow you to remove everything from the trash, whereas the Recycle Bin allows you to empty everything or delete individual files. Also, by double-clicking on items in the Recycle Bin, you can view the properties of those items. Whereas the Recycle Bin will automatically restore items to their original location, the Trash Can requires you to remember where the files were located and manually move them out of the trash to their original locations.

What Gets Deleted

Although the Recycle Bin is a repository for deleted items, not everything that is deleted will wind up in it. Any items stored on local hard drives that were deleted using Windows Explorer or the desktop will appear in the Recycle Bin. In addition, any items you delete using software that is Windows compliant will send the deleted items to the Recycle Bin. For example, if you were opening a file using Microsoft Word and noticed a file listed in the **Open** dialog box that you wanted to get rid of, selecting the item and pressing the **Delete** key on your keyboard would send the item to the Recycle Bin. However, many programs are not compliant and will simply delete the item, never to be seen again without the use of data recovery or forensic software.

As discussed in previous sections, when you use utilities such as Disk Cleanup, or the *DEL* and *ERASE* commands, the files bypass the Recycle Bin and are simply deleted. The same may occur if software on your machine was cleaning up files after an installation or shutting down. The reason for this is because there are so many files that may be deleted by these programs that it would quickly fill the Recycle Bin. For example, if you used Windows Update to apply a number of fixes or upgrades, the files used to install programs, patches, and service packs would be deleted and never appear in the Recycle Bin. If they did, you would have a difficult time finding the files you mistakenly deleted when browsing the Recycle Bin.

Files are also not deleted if they are not on the local hard drives. If you were to delete a file on a mapped network drive, a compressed folder, a floppy disk, or any other removable storage media, the file would not be sent to the Recycle Bin. The same may occur if a file that is too large for the Recycle Bin is deleted. If there isn't enough space in the Recycle Bin for a file or directory that is deleted, a warning message will appear informing you that it will be deleted. If you agree to the deletion, it bypasses the Recycle Bin and is deleted from the system.

Exam Warning

Only files deleted from the local hard drive are stored in the Recycle Bin. Any files on a network or removable storage will not appear in the Recycle Bin after they are deleted.

Configuring the Recycle Bin

The Recycle Bin can be configured by right-clicking on the Recycle Bin icon that appears on the Windows desktop and then selecting **Properties** from the context menu that appears. In doing so, a dialog box similar to that shown in Figure 4.3 will appear. Looking at this figure, you can see there is a **Global** tab and an additional tab for a drive letter. This is because there is one Recycle Bin folder allocated for each partition on a hard disk. In other words, for each hard disk or partition setup on your machine, there is a different Recycle Bin that can be configured and used to store deleted items. By opening the **Properties** of the Recycle Bin, you can either configure all of the Recycle Bins together using the **Global** tab or configure each Recycle Bin separately by using the tab associated with each drive letter. Whether the controls are enabled on each of the drive letter tabs is set using the following options on the **Global** tab:

- **Configure drives independently**
- **Use one setting for all drives**

Figure 4.3 Recycle Bin Properties

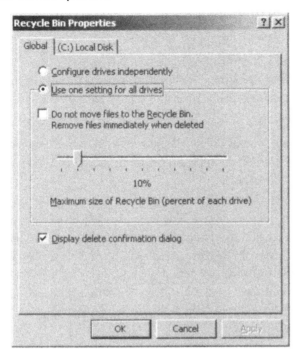

The **Global** tab also provides the ability to disable the Recycle Bin so that deleted files are not moved to it but are simply deleted instead. By checking the **Do not move files to the Recycle Bin. Remove files immediately when deleted**, no files that are deleted will be sent to the Recycle Bin.

You can also configure how much space is used to store files in the Recycle Bin using this dialog box. The slider bar on this tab allows you to configure the percentage of disk space that will be used to store deleted files in a Recycle Bin. If you have configured the option of configuring drives independently, then you can set the percentage using a slider that is available on each of the drive letter tabs. On systems prior to Windows Vista, the Recycle Bin is allocated 10% of the disk space for recycled files. This default value can be changed using the slider bar, allowing up to 3.99 GB of space to be used. In Windows Vista, 10% of the disk space can be used on drives up to 40 GB, but above that, Windows Vista allows a maximum of 4 GB plus 5% of the disk capacity. If the amount of data stored in the Recycle Bin exceeds this amount, then the oldest files are removed (permanently deleted) from the Recycle Bin first so that newly deleted files can be stored there. This is referred to as FIFO, or *first in, first out*.

Storage Locations of the Recycle Bin

When files are deleted, they are stored in a special hidden directory, which is located in the root directory. Because one Recycle Bin is allocated for each partition on a computer, there is

one of these folders on each partition of a hard disk. The name of this folder depends on the file system and operating system being used:

- On FAT file systems, the folder is named *Recycled*. For example, on your C: the storage location of the Recycle Bin would be C:\RECYCLED.

- On NTFS file systems used by Windows NT, 2000, and XP, this folder is named *Recycler*. For example, on your C: the storage location of the Recycle Bin would be C:\RECYCLER.

- On NTFS file systems used by Windows Vista, this folder is named *$Recycle.Bin*. For example, on your C: the storage location of the Recycle Bin would be C:\RECYCLE.BIN.

If you were to search these directories on a partition of your hard disk, you might be surprised to find that none of these appear. The reason is probably because they are hidden folders. To view these directories, you would need to configure the View settings in Windows Explorer. In Windows Explorer, click on the **Tools** menu, and then click on the **Folder Options** menu item. When the **Folder Options** dialog box appears, click on the **View** tab, and uncheck the **Hide protected operating system files (Recommended)** checkbox. Once this box is unchecked, you should be able to view the hidden folders through Windows Explorer or My Computer.

On NTFS partitions, a Recycle Bin is created in the Recycler folder for each user who logs onto the computer. Because the Recycler directory contains Recycle Bins for each user of the computer, a number of subdirectories will exist under this folder. Each of the subdirectories is named after the Security ID (SID), which is a unique number that identifies users and groups in Windows, appearing similar to S-1-5-21-191058668-193157475-1542849698-500. Although opening the Recycle Bin will automatically show the contents of a directory related to the account you logged in with, looking at the subdirectories in the Recycler folder will require you to find which SID corresponds to your account.

NOTE

For a listing of well-known security identifiers in Windows, you can visit support.microsoft.com/kb/243330. This will provide you with information on SIDs associated with particular groups and users. For example, if you were analyzing the Administrator account, this would be a well-known SID and could be identified as S-1-5-*domain*-500.

Undeleting or Permanently Deleting a File

Before we discuss how to undelete or remove a file from the Recycle Bin, let's review exactly what happens when the file is deleted. When you delete a file from the desktop or using Windows Explorer, My Computer, or a compliant application, the entry in the file allocation table or MFT is removed, and the file is indicated as being located in the Recycle Bin directory in the root drive of the partition on which it was deleted. The file is then renamed using the following syntax:

D*<original drive letter><#>.<original extension>*

To illustrate how the renaming works, let's say you deleted C:\myfile.txt, and this was the second file that was deleted and residing in the Recycle Bin. In using the previous syntax, the file would be renamed Dc2.txt. By examining this, you can see that it starts with the letter D, followed by the original drive letter (c), that it was the second file deleted, and that it uses a .txt extension. Its original name and location are stored in a hidden index file named INFO, which is located in the Recycle Bin folder in the root directory. On Windows 95 machines and partitions using NTFS, this file is called INFO2.

The information stored in the INFO file is important because it allows the file to be automatically restored to its original location. You can view information on the files that have been deleted and stored in the Recycle Bin by double-clicking on the Recycle Bin icon on the Windows desktop. In doing so, a screen similar to that shown in Figure 4.4 will appear. This figure shows that the Recycle Bin allows you to view information such as when a file was deleted and its original location. By right-clicking on a file, you can then click on the **Restore** menu item in the context menu that appears. Restoring a file enables the original path to be read from the INFO file. The file can be renamed and restored to its original path and filename.

Figure 4.4 Recycle Bin

Deleting or emptying files from the Recycle Bin permanently deletes them from the system, so they can be recovered only with data recovery or forensic software. To delete a file from the Recycle Bin, you can select the file and then press the **DEL** or **Delete** key on your

keyboard. You could also delete all of the files from the Recycle Bin by right-clicking on the desktop icon and then clicking **Empty Recycle Bin** from the context menu that appears.

Although the Recycle Bin can be configured so that files are immediately deleted, you can also delete a file and not have it go to the Recycle Bin on a file-by-file basis. If you wanted to bypass the Recycle Bin and simply delete the file, you would select the file you want to delete and then hold down **Shift +DEL** (that is, the **Shift** key and **Delete** key at the same time). When doing this, a prompt will appear asking you to confirm the deletion, and upon choosing **Yes**, the Recycle Bin is bypassed and the file is deleted.

Damaged Recycle Bins

As with any other software, there are times when the Recycle Bin might not function correctly and needs to be repaired. If you have deleted files and the Recycle Bin appears to be empty, it could mean that something is wrong with the INFO file. As we discussed, the INFO file maintains information on files stored in the Recycle Bin. If this is damaged or deleted, no files will appear in the Recycle Bin, but this doesn't mean that anything has happened to the deleted files. Although the files were renamed when they were put in the Recycle Bin folder, they contain the same data and will appear under the Recycled folder. To restore the file, you could simply rename the file to its original name.

Repairing a deleted INFO file is one of the easiest repairs you'll encounter because it will be re-created when you restart Windows. If it is damaged, however, you will need to delete the INFO file from the Recycled folder. Once deleted, you would then restart Windows so it can be re-created. To delete an INFO file, you would follow these steps:

1. From the Windows **Start** menu, select **Programs | Accessories** and then click on the **Command Prompt** menu item.

2. Type **cd recycled** if it is a FAT partition or **cd recycler** if it is NTFS. On an NTFS partition, you will also need to navigate into the directory named after the SID related to the user account you logged in with. Press the **Enter** key.

3. Type **attrib –h inf*** and the press the **Enter** key.

4. Type **del info** (or **del info2** on NTFS partitions) and then press the **Enter** key.

5. Restart your computer.

Another problem that may occur with the Recycle Bin is that the Recycled\Recycler directory may be damaged. When the folder is damaged, no files appear in the Recycle Bin. When this occurs, you would create a copy of the DESKTOP.INI file, which is located in the Recycled directory or in the Recycler subdirectory that matches the SID of the user who is currently logged on. After copying this file, you would then delete the contents of the Recycled directory or the appropriate subdirectory in the Recycler directory. Doing so deletes all files in the Recycle Bin. Once this is done, you would then copy the DESKTOP.INI file back to its previous location.

The final part of the Recycle Bin that may possibly be damaged is the Recycled\Recycler folder. When this happens, the Recycle Bin icon on the desktop will appear full, but the contents cannot be viewed and the **Empty Recycle Bin** command (which appears on the context menu when you right-click on the Recycle Bin icon) will be disabled. To fix this problem, you would perform the following steps:

1. From the Windows **Start** menu, select **Programs | Accessories** and then click on the **Command Prompt** menu item.

2. Type **attrib –s –h recycled** if it is a FAT partition or **attrib –s –h recycler** if it is NTFS. Press the **Enter** key.

3. Type **del recycled** if it is a FAT partition or **del recycler** if it is NTFS. Press the **Enter** key.

4. When prompted as to whether you are sure, press the **Y** key.

5. Restart your computer.

Data Recovery in Linux

Just as files can be removed in Windows and Macintosh operating systems by selecting a file and pressing the **Delete** key on the keyboard, Linux files can also be deleted from a hard disk in this way. Files can also be deleted in Linux and UNIX machines by using commands. To delete a file in Linux or UNIX, you would use the *rm* command. Deleting a file with this command won't prompt you for any confirmation by default, so once it is deleted, you will have to rely on data recovery software to restore the file. Like the *DEL* and *ERASE* commands discussed previously, there are a number of switches that can be used with the *rm* command (Table 4.2).

Table 4.2 *rm* Switches

Switch	Description
-f	Forces deletion of files, and ignores nonexistent files, without prompting
-i	Interactive mode in which confirmation is required before files are deleted
-r	Contents of a directory removed recursively
-v	Verbose; provides details of what is done

A more secure way of deleting files in Linux and UNIX is to use the *shred* command. With this command, the file is deleted and overwritten to ensure that it can't be recovered. As mentioned previously, by overwriting the data on a disk, the file cannot be recovered. As such, it is

important that this command is only used when you are absolutely sure that you want the file to be destroyed. There are a number of options that can be used with this command, as shown in Table 4.3.

Table 4.3 *shred* Switches

Switch	Description
-f	Forces deletion of files and will change permissions to allow writing if necessary
-n	Iterations in which the file will be overwritten. By default, it is over-written 25 times, but with this command, you can specify a number.
-s	Shreds a specific number of bytes
-u	Truncates and removes the file after writing
-v	Verbose; provides details of what is done
-x	Indicates not to round file sizes to the nearest block
-z	Adds a final overwrite with all zeros to hide that the file was shredded

There are also a number of desktops that can be used on Linux that provide a Recycle Bin that can be used to restore files that were deleted by selecting a file and pressing the **DEL** key on your keyboard. As mentioned previously, Recycle Bins are part of the desktop environment, and on Linux and other operating systems, a number of desktop environments can be used, such as GNOME and Xfce. These desktop environments provide a Recycle Bin, allowing files to be restored or permanently deleted. However, any files deleted using the *rm* or *shred* command bypass the Recycle Bin. Whereas the *shred* command overwrites the data so it cannot be restored, the *rm* command does not modify the data after deleting it. This means that any files deleted using the *rm* command could have data restored using recovery tools.

Recovering Deleted Files

When a file is deleted, it doesn't necessarily mean that the data cannot be completely or partially recovered. Data written on a hard disk generally stays there unless or until it is either overwritten by more data or physically erased by a magnet. Simply deleting the data using operating system file management utilities does not get rid of the data. It only removes the pointer used by the file system to locate that data physically on the disk. The data itself (in the form of the physical changes to the disk's magnetic surface) is still there and can be recovered using special recovery software.

Many people also think that formatting a hard disk erases all its data, but this isn't necessarily so. *Formatting* defines the structure of the disk. *Low-level formatting* (LLF), which physically defines where the tracks and sectors are on the disk, does erase data. However, modern disks are

formatted at the low level at the factory; users do not perform LLF on today's IDE and SCSI disks. Thus, when we discuss formatting, we are generally talking about *high-level formatting*. This term refers to the process of defining the file system structure. Thus, we say a disk is formatted in FAT or formatted in NTFS.

If a file has not been overwritten or damaged in some way, there is always the chance that tools can be used to restore the data. The question that will determine which tools you use is, *Why am I recovering it?* This question in itself will decide whether you will need to perform data recovery or computer forensics.

Although the two terms are often used interchangeably, there is a difference. *Data recovery* is a process of salvaging data that was lost or deleted. *Computer forensics* is a process of gathering and examining evidence to establish facts so that accurate testimony and evidence can later be presented in court or other hearings. In considering these definitions, you will notice that there is a difference in why the data is being acquired: Data recovery seeks to restore the data, whereas computer forensics seeks to obtain data to be used as evidence in court.

Mistakes happen, and its common for a person to accidentally delete a file needed for work or personal use. Ask any network administrator, and they'll tell you that there are many occasions when they need to restore a file that a user has deleted. On personal computers, workstations, and laptops, you can restore the data from the Recycle Bin or Trash Can. If the file has been deleted from removable media or has been emptied from the Recycle Bin, then data recovery software can be used to retrieve the data.

Such software is not suitable in other situations. Standard data recovery software may not guarantee that the file won't be modified when it is recovered, or the software may generate temporary files that could damage other data on the disk. To preserve data, computer forensic software is necessary.

As discussed in Chapter 3, if you are investigating an incident, always assume that the case will eventually go to court. If you used software that was not designed for forensic use, you could alter or damage data on the disk and compromise the investigation. In addition, any data that you retrieved could be deemed inadmissible in court. In any situation in which you are investigating an intrusion, policy violations, cybercrimes, or other incidents in which data could be used as evidence, you should always take the side of caution and use computer forensic tools.

Regardless of which type of tool you use, you should never install the software on the drive containing the data you wish to recover. For example, if you accidentally deleted a file on your C: and then downloaded and installed data recovery software to your C:, you could over-write the data that you were trying to recover in the first place. Computer forensic software may use bootable disks to access the drive or connect to the machine using a network cable. By sharing the drive and connecting to it over a network or using a network cable to connect two machines, you could restore the data without worrying about corrupting data on the disk. If the computer has two drives and you are performing data recovery, you could also install the software on another drive. However, if you deleted the file on a boot partition, files may be installed in your operating system's directory or other directories used to store common files.

When you are using these tools, remember that the integrity of the data you are seeking to recover is paramount, and take whatever actions necessary to keep it from being damaged or destroyed.

Head of the Class...

Deleted Files

An occasional but recurring problem in network administration is recovering data deleted by users. Often, a user will accidentally delete a file and then complain that it is missing. They may say "someone deleted or moved my file," accuse the IT department of doing something, or come up with any number of excuses. Occasionally, someone will actually admit they made a boo-boo. The funny thing is that it's so common for someone to accidentally delete a file, network administrators and IT staff are used to performing various degrees of data recovery.

If a file is deleted from a computer, the user can generally restore it him- or herself because it is usually sent to the Recycle Bin before actually being deleted. If the Recycle Bin has been emptied, the person held down **Shift + DEL** when deleting the file, or the person used a noncompliant program to delete the file (which bypassed the Recycle Bin), then the data may still be recoverable. The important point is that time isn't wasted before contacting someone to restore the data and nothing else is written to the hard disk (since this may overwrite the data).

When data is deleted from a network, it is often easier to restore the data. Network operating systems such as Novell NetWare provide Salvage features, which can undelete a file that was deleted on a network drive. Even if it can't be recovered in this way, nightly backups are often made of network drives so that a file can be restored from a recent backup. If the backup was made the previous night, the file will contain all of the data from when the backup occurred. This may mean that, at worst, the user will have lost a day's work.

Deleted File Recovery Tools

Data recovery tools are designed to restore data that has been deleted or corrupted from any number of sources, including hard disks, CDs, DVDs, Blu-ray, HD-DVD, floppy disks, memory cards used in digital cameras, and other storage media. Depending on the capabilities of the software, it will scan the media and search for any damaged, corrupted, or deleted files and display which ones are available for recovery, allowing you to choose which ones will be restored. In some cases, the tools will even repair damaged files so that data can be accessible again.

EXAM WARNING

Although many tools are available on the Internet, the ones discussed in the following sections are those that you are expected to know about

for the CHFI exam. Although it is impossible to remember every specific feature and functionality of the programs that follow, you should have a basic understanding of what these tools are used for. For each of the tools, a link to where you can acquire additional information and download a copy of the software is provided.

Undelete Tools

As mentioned previously, using commands such as *DEL* and *ERASE* from the command line or holding down the **Shift** key when deleting a file will bypass the Recycle Bin. To restore the file, you need to use tools that will search the hard disk for deleted files and allow you to undelete them. Fortunately, there are a number of tools available that perform this task, with various features that make undeleting files easier. They should be used as soon as possible, however, to avoid any other data overwriting the file.

Undelete

In discussing tools that undelete files, we start with one of the most basic ones used in MS-DOS 5.00 to 6.22. *Undelete* is a command-line tool that can be used on these old systems, allowing you to simply type **UNDELETE** followed by the path to the file you wish to restore. For example, if you wanted to undelete a file named mytext.txt from your root directory, you would simply type **UNDELETE C:\MYTEXT.TXT**. Doing so would restore the file. In addition, there are a number of switches that can be used (Table 4.4).

Table 4.4 UNDELETE Switches

Switch	Description
/all	Automatically restores all of the specified files
/list	Lists all files that are available to be restored
/DOS	Limits recovery to files that meet the file specifications in the disk directory table
/DR	Limits recovery to files in the Delete Tracking File
/DS	Limits recovery to files in the SENTRY directory
/load	Loads UNDELETE.EXE into memory using information in the UNDELETE.INI
/unload	Unloads UNDELETE from memory
/purge	Deletes contents of the SENTRY directory

Continued

Table 4.4 UNDELETE Switches

Switch	Description
/status	Displays the type of delete protection on the computer
/S	Loads the memory resident portion of UNDELETE and enables the Delete Sentry level of protection
/T	Loads the memory resident portion of UNDELETE and enables the Delete Sentry level of protection. Optional entries may be used to specify the maximum number of entries found in the PCTRACKR.DEL file.

People who have been using computers since the days of MS-DOS tend to automatically think of this program when mentioning *Undelete*. However, it was designed to work only on systems running MS-DOS 5 to 6.22, and it can cause problems when run on systems running Windows 9*x* or later. There are, however, a number of other programs that use this name but are designed for newer operating systems.

Active@ Data Recovery Software

Active@ Data Recovery Software is a company that has developed a number of tools used to recover lost or deleted files from storage media. Two of these are

- Active@ UNDELETE
- Active@ UNERASER

Active@ UNDELETE is data recovery software available from www.active-undelete.com. Using this tool, you can recover data from basic and dynamic volumes, including RAID volumes, and large hard disks that are more than 500 GB in size. It also supports recovery from removable storage media such as USB flash drives, ZIP drives, and memory sticks and cards.

Active@ UNERASER is another data recovery product available from www.uneraser.com, and it will run on Windows or DOS. Using this tool, you can access deleted files before Windows even starts, and it supports local files, compressed files, MBR backups and can access sectors of the disk drive with a disk viewer feature. The Active@ UNERASER tool can run from either a bootable floppy disk or a CD. It also provides a Bootable ISO CD Image and Bootable Floppy Creator to create the disk or CD that can then be used to recover files.

R-Undelete

R-Undelete from r-Tools Technology (www.r-undelete.com) is a tool that restores deleted files, but it also provides an easy-to-use wizard that takes you through the steps of recovering a file. In addition, it provides features that allow you to reconstruct damaged graphics, audio, and video files. Before recovering a file, you can preview the file to determine if you actually want to restore it or leave it deleted.

Easy-Undelete

Easy-Undelete (www.easy-undelete.com) is a tool that will not only restore files from hard disks using FAT12, FAT16, FAT32, and NTFS file systems but also restore files from non-Microsoft partitions such as Linux and Macintosh OS X. It also supports other storage media, such as memory cards used in digital cameras, including a preview feature that allows you to view images before restoring them. In addition, it provides a hexadecimal preview feature that allows you to view the contents of clusters.

WinUndelete

WinUndelete is a popular recovery tool that is available from www.winundelete.com. It allows you to recover files from Microsoft file systems with the original create and modified storage dates. It provides a search feature to scan for specific files, and it allows you to filter results by extensions and file types. It also allows you to preview certain types of data before restoring them, such as Microsoft Office documents, images, and plain text.

Restoration

Restoration is a free tool that was written by Brian Kato and is available for download from software distribution sites such as www.snapfiles.com. It is a fast and easy-to-use tool, which is small enough to run from a floppy disk. As shown in Figure 4.5, it allows you not only to view any deleted files on a hard disk but also to search for specific files by entering all or part of the filename into a search box. Exercise 4.1 discusses how to acquire this tool and use it to undelete any files on your local hard disk.

Figure 4.5 Restoration

EXERCISE 4.1

USING RESTORATION TO UNDELETE A FILE

Before beginning this exercise, you will need to acquire a copy of Restoration. Visit www.snapfiles.com/get/restoration.html, and click on the **Download** button. When the download completes, run the executable and specify where you would like the files to be extracted (by default this is C:\RESTORATION).

1. Using Windows Explorer, navigate to the directory where you extracted the files and double-click on **Restoration.exe**.

2. When the program opens, select the drive you want to analyze for deleted files using the **Drives** dropdown list.

3. Press the **Search Deleted Files** button. Restoration will search the selected drive and list all deleted files on the drive.

4. Type all or part of the filename into the field labeled **All or part of the file**. This could be part of the file name or an extension. In using this, remember that wildcards (such as *) are not allowed.

5. Press the **Search Deleted Files** button. Restoration will search the selected drive for any files matching the text you entered.

6. Click on the **Include used clusters by other files** checkbox and then click on the **Search Deleted Files** button again. In doing this, you may notice additional files listed. However, because the clusters are used by other files, any deleted files have been overwritten by another file.

7. Click on the **Include even if the file size is zero** checkbox and then click on the **Search Deleted Files** button again. In doing this, you may notice additional files listed. However, because the file size is zero, restoring the file will create an empty file.

8. Select a file from the listing, and then click the **Restore by copying** button.

9. When the **Save As** dialog box appears, select where you want to save the file, and then click Save.

10. Click **Exit** to close the program.

Mycroft V3

Mycroft V3 is computer forensic software developed by Dibs USA and is available at www.dib-susa.com. The software runs from a bootable floppy disk, and it provides a search engine that is used to scan a computer for data on the disk. Using this tool, an investigator can determine if there is evidence on the computer. By using this tool to provide a cursory search of a computer's hard disk, you can determine if additional investigation and acquisition of evidence is necessary.

Recover My Files

Recover My Files is a tool created by GetData Software Development (www.getdata.com) and is available for download at www.recovermyfiles.com. It provides an easy-to-use interface that allows you to recover data from hard disks and removable storage media such as floppy disks, Zip drives, USB, and camera cards. As discussed later, this is just one of the tools available from GetData that can be used for data recovery.

eData Unerase

eData Unerase is a free tool developed by Octanesoft and is available at www.octanesoft.com. It allows you to restore any files that have been deleted from the Recycle Bin or using other methods that make it otherwise unrecoverable without data recovery software. It provides an easy-to-use interface with a wizard that takes you through the steps of recovering your data, and it allows you to specify whether you want to search for all deleted files or just specific types of files (for example, pictures, multimedia, documents, and Web pages). If you know the filename, you can also enter all or part of the name to search for. As shown in Figure 4.6, once the wizard is complete, you simply select which files you'd like to restore and then click the **Save Files** button to specify where the recovered data should be saved.

Figure 4.6 eData Unerase

Recover4all Professional

Recover4all Professional is a tool for recovering data from FAT12, FAT16, FAT32, NTFS, and RAID volumes, and it is available at www.recover4all.com. It also allows recovery from encrypted drives that have not been encrypted with EFS, compressed drives, and Windows ME/XP protected files. Its interface is easy to use, appearing similar to Windows Explorer; folders appear in the left pane, and selecting a folder will allow you to view deleted files in the right pane. By selecting a file and clicking the **Recover** button, you can specify where on the disk you want to restore the file.

File Scavenger

File Scavenger is a tool developed by QueTek Consulting Corporation and is available at www.quetek.com. It allows data to be recovered from hard disks formatted as FAT12, FAT16, FAT32, and NTFS. It can also recover data from floppy disks, ZIP disks, memory sticks, flash cards, RAID volumes, compressed drives, and other media. It provides data recovery features using an interface similar to Windows explorer, and it allows you to search for specific files using search strings and wildcards.

VirtualLab

VirtualLab is data recovery software designed for use on Windows 9x or later, as well as Apple Macintosh computers running OS 9 or later. It is available at www.binarybiz.com, and it allows you to recover files from drives using FAT12, FAT16, FAT32, NTFS, HFS, or HFS Plus partitions. It can also be used to recover data from other media, such as Apple iPods, digital camera cards, and removable storage. Using an exhaustive scan, it can locate lost files and will also locate lost partitions. Using this tool, you can not only undelete files but also unformat partitions to restore data from a formatted, damaged, or lost partition. Once the files you want to retrieve are found, they can be saved to another location (such as a network drive or another local disk).

File Recover

File Recover is a tool developed by PC Tools Software that is available at www.pctools.com/file-recover/. It supports FAT16, FAT32, and NTFS file systems and also IDE/ATA/SCSI hard drives, including drives larger than 8 GB. It provides an easy-to-use interface that allows you to quickly scan for files and also advanced features that allow you to search by all or part of the filename, specific extensions, or file size and scan either the logical drive or the physical hard disk.

As shown in Figure 4.7, once a scan is complete, it will provide a listing of deleted files, with information on the condition of each file that was found. Double-clicking on an image file will provide a preview of the image, allowing you to view the picture before restoring it. The left pane of the interface also allows you to view different files that were found based on

file type. Clicking on items in the left pane will display only HTML documents, PNG images, JPEGs, or files in other file formats.

Figure 4.7 File Recover

Badcopy Pro

Badcopy Pro is another popular data recovery tool that was developed by Jufsoft and is available at www.jufsoft.com/badcopy/. It can restore data from hard disks, damaged or defective CDs and DVDs, floppy disks, USB flash drives, as well as Iomega Zip, Jas, and MO disks and other storage media. It has features to repair damaged floppy disks, recover photos from memory cards used in digital cameras, and data recovery on UDF and packet-writing disks. One of the benefits of this tool is that it doesn't write data to the disk or media where data is being recovered, and it saves recovered data to a location that you specify. This prevents overwriting any data on the disks, which could prevent further recovery.

Zero Assumption Recovery

Zero Assumption Recovery is a recovery tool available at www.z-a-recovery.com. It provides support for FAT16, FAT32, and NTFS, RAID0 and RAID5 hardware recovery, as well as limited support for the Linux ext2 file system. To perform recovery, it uses a wizard-style interface that will take you through the process of determining how and where data is to be recovered. Recovery can take a considerable amount of time, as it can scan the physical disk, locating bad

sectors and data fragments in addition to complete files that have been deleted. As discussed later, it also provides features that allow you to recover images from memory cards used by digital cameras.

SUPERFileRecover

SUPERFileRecover is another easy-to-use tool to recover files, which is available at www.superfilerecover.com. It allows you to search for all files on a partition, or specific filenames, supporting wildcards. You can also specify to search only for music, movies and video, pictures and photos, or documents. Once a deleted file is selected in the interface, you can view the file in a preview pane.

DiskInternals Uneraser and NTFS Recovery

DiskInternals (www.diskinternals.com) provides a number of data recovery solutions, each of which provides an easy-to-use intuitive interface that provides wizards for restoring data. Two of the tools available from DiskInternals are

- NTFS Recovery, which restores data on NTFS drives that are corrupted, formatted, or otherwise inaccessible. It will also recover data if the partition table has been corrupted or damaged. It provides a wizard that will scan the disk and then restore the original structure of folders and files.

- Uneraser, which is designed to recover files that have been deleted from FAT/FAT32 and NTFS drives, and it will also recover encrypted files. It supports recovery from compressed drives, USB flash drives, digital cameras, as well as other storage media.

PC Inspector File Inspector

PC Inspector File Recovery is a free tool developed by CONVAR that can be used to restore files from partitions formatted in FAT12, FAT16, FAT32, and NTFS. It will restore files with their original timestamps, and it allows recovered files to be saved on a network. It is available at www.pcinspector.de/file_recovery/uk/welcome.htm.

Search and Recover

Search and Recover is a data recovery tool from Iolo Technologies (www.iolo.com) that is designed to restore documents, images, music files, and other data from a variety of storage media. The tool provides wizards that take you step by step through the recovery process, and it allows you to preview documents and multimedia before restoring them. To prevent any data loss from installing the software, Search and Recover can run from the installation CD, and it provides features to make a disk image that will duplicate any data on the hard disk, CDs, or DVDs.

Additional features in the software also allow you to permanently delete the data by having files overwritten by other data. You can configure Search and Recover to overwrite the files up

to 100 times, making these files unrecoverable with any data recovery software. It also provides features to recover deleted e-mails from Netscape, Thunderbird, Eudora, Microsoft Outlook Express, and Microsoft Outlook. In addition, you can restore deleted e-mail, tasks, notes, and other elements in Outlook.

O&O Unerase

O&O Unerase is a tool developed by O&O Software to recover data from hard disks, floppy disks, digital cameras, memory cards, and other media. It provides an easy-to-use interface that simplifies finding and recovering files. Using the search options in this tool, you can search for deleted files by name, type, size, or date of last change. It is available at www.oo-software.com/en/products/oounerase/.

Filesaver

Filesaver, available at www.file-saver.com, is a tool that can recover data from FAT and NTFS drives, floppy disks, memory cards used with digital cameras, and other storage media. It provides different modes, including one that allows you to view deleted files through a Windows Explorer-style interface, and allows you to preview images before restoring them. Using this tool, you can not only restore individual files but also restore entire folders of data.

Stellar Phoenix

Stellar Phoenix is a data recovery tool from Stellar Information Systems and is available at www.stellarinfo.com. It supports FAT and NTFS file systems, and it will analyze the hard disk for damage and corrupted data before offering you a listing of files available to restore. It will also allow you to recover data from hard disks that have been formatted, even after an operating system has been installed, and provides features for recovering data from repartitioned and lost hard drives.

Restorer 2000

Restorer 2000 is a data recovery tool available at www.restorer2000.com that supports recovery from hard disks using FAT12, FAT16, FAT32, and NTFS file systems, as well as floppy disks, memory cards used in digital cameras, and other storage media. It will recover data from IDE, ATA, SATA, and SCSI hard drives and will recover and reconstruct data from RAID5, damaged volume sets, stripe sets, and mirrored volumes. It will also recover data from damaged partitions and hard disks that have been formatted, and it will search for deleted files by name, date, mask, size range, attributes, and other search parameters. If a graphic, audio, or video file is being recovered, you can preview the file before restoring it and use a built-in hexadecimal editor to view and edit files. If the network version of this software is used, then you can also connect to remote computers, scan their hard disks and partitions, and restore data across the network.

R-linux

R-linux is a free data recovery tool developed by r-Tools Technology and is available at www.data-recovery-software.net/Linux_Recovery.shtml. Unlike the other tools discussed in this section, R-linux is specifically designed for the ext2 file system used on Linux and UNIX machines. It can recover data from local disks, but it is unable to reconstruct damaged RAID or stripe sets. In acquiring data from a disk, it can create an image file of the entire disk or partition and allow data to be acquired from the image file as if it were a regular disk. Once a file is recovered, it can be saved to a local or network drive that you specify.

PC ParaChute

PC ParaChute is a backup tool developed by UniTrends and is available at www.unitrends.com. It is used to perform a backup of the first physical disk and partitions on the computer. In doing this, it writes your system's boot drive and creates an image of the computer on a server backup tape, ensuring that any data that is lost can be recovered by restoring the backed up image. Restoring the data involves booting from a recovery disk and then choosing a restore option from a menu. PC ParaChute automatically backs up the image file and restores the machine.

Although most of the tools in this section deal with restoring deleted files from data on the disk, it is important to realize that backing up data is the easiest and most reliable method of restoring data. By making a copy of any data on a hard disk or other media, you can then restore it as needed. Regular backups will ensure that recent versions of files are ready as needed so that if there is a hard disk failure or some other problem, the data can be quickly restored to its previous state.

Recycle Bin Replacements

An ounce of prevention is worth a pound of cure, and if users have a way of recovering their own files, it means you won't have to do so. Although the Recycle Bin is a wonderful tool to give users a second chance before permanently deleting a file, it isn't without its flaws. As previously mentioned, not all files are sent to the Recycle Bin, so some files aren't recoverable by the common Windows user. Because developers found ways to improve the security of the Recycle Bin, and allow better opportunities to restore files, there are a number of products that can be installed on Windows machines to replace the existing Recycle Bin.

Diskeeper Undelete

Undelete from Diskeeper Corporation (www.undelete.com) is a tool that runs on Windows XP and 2000, and it replaces the Recycle Bin with a *Recovery Bin*. Once installed, files that are deleted are sent to the Recovery Bin, allowing you to search the bin and restore any files that were accidentally deleted. It even provides the ability to view versions of files that were deleted in order to select the correct version to restore. If you had a Microsoft Word, Excel, or PowerPoint file that was overwritten, you could use the Recovery Bin to restore a previous

version. Versions of the Undelete software can be used to protect local files, whereas the server edition can be used to protect and restore files deleted by network clients.

Fundelete

Fundelete is a tool that replaces the Recycle Bin on systems running Windows NT, ME, 2000, and XP so that any files that are deleted from the **Command Prompt**, using the **Shift + DEL** command, or within a program can be recovered. It also provides filter options so that files with specific file extensions are not sent to the Fundelete Bin.

Fundelete was created by Sysinternals, which was acquired by Microsoft in 1996. As such, visiting their Web site will redirect you to Microsoft's Web site. Information on the Sysinternals products can be fount on Microsoft's TechNet Web site at www.microsoft.com/technet/sysinternals/default.mspx, whereas copies of Fundelete are still available from sites such as http://fundelete.en.softonic.com.

CD/DVD Data Recovery

As you are well aware at this point in the book, not all data is stored on hard disks, so it follows that there would be data recovery software that is specifically designed to restore damaged and deleted files stored on CDs and DVDs. When data is stored on CDs and DVDs, the data can not only be deleted from rewritable discs but also be damaged by scratches, other damage, and defects in the media. The following are some of the more popular programs used to restore data:

- CDRoller
- IsoBuster
- CD Data Rescue
- InDisk Recovery

CDRoller

Despite its name, CDRoller recovers data written to both CDs and DVDs and is available at www.cdroller.com. It not only allows you to recover data from CD-ROM, CD-R, and a variety of other CD and DVD formats but also allows you to recover data recorded directly onto the discs, such as that written by stand-alone DVD recorders, camcorders, and other products. It provides the ability to split recovered VOB and VRO files into separate clips, and it can convert raw video into MPEG files, allowing you to create a new video from damaged data.

This tool also provides software to burn data onto CDs and DVDs, allowing you to back up any data before there is a problem or once its been recovered. It supports the ISO 9660 file system, Joliet extensions for long file name support, and discs formatted in the UDF file system.

IsoBuster

IsoBuster is another tool that supports a wide range of discs, and it is available at www.iso-buster.com. It recovers data from not only CDs and DVDs but also Blu-ray and HD-DVD discs. It also supports ISO 9660, Joliet, and UDF; will scan for IFO, BUP, and VOB file systems on audio and video DVDs; and supports Mount Rainier CD-RW and DVD+RW discs. IsoBuster is also one of the few tools that provide support for discs created using Macintosh file systems. It has an HFS Reader to support HFS and HFS Plus file systems and a built-in support for Resource Fork extenstions in ISO 9660 and UDF file systems.

CD Data Rescue

CD Data Rescue is a tool developed by Naltech Software (www.naltech.com) that is designed to recover data from damaged, scratched, and defective CD-ROM, CD-R, and CD-RW disks. It supports Mount Rainier/EasyWrite MRW discs, and it can recover data created by CD writing software in ISO and UDF formats.

InDisk Recovery

InDisk Recovery is a tool developed by Octanesoft and is available at www.octanesoft.com. It is designed to recover data from damaged, scratched, defective, or otherwise unreadable CD and DVD discs. It supports the ISO-9660, UDF, and Joliet file systems.

Microsoft Office Repair and Recovery

Data recovery does not just mean restoring deleted files. Occasionally, any previously deleted data may be incomplete or corrupt once it is recovered. Even if a file has not been deleted and restored, the file may be corrupted from improperly shutting down the application or computer, or records within a database may be deleted accidentally. To restore the data within these files, you can use any of the following products:

- OfficeFIX
- Repair My Excel
- Repair My Word

OfficeFIX

OfficeFIX is a suite of products from Cimaware Software (www.cimaware.com) that is designed to repair and recover data from damaged files that were created with Microsoft Office products. The following tools are included in the suite:

- AccessFIX is a tool with features to recover, repair, and undelete Access databases. It recovers not only the data stored in tables but also forms, reports, macros, and other data and elements of the database. It has functions that will restore deleted records

from tables and restore password-protected files regardless of whether or not you have the password.

- ExcelFIX is a tool used to recover corrupted Excel files. It will extract the information from a damaged Excel spreadsheet and store it in a new file, complete with any data, formulas, and other content.

- WordFIX is a tool used to recover Word files. This not only includes files created with the PC version of Microsoft Word but also those created with any version of Word for Macintosh. Not only can it recover the text but also higher editions of this tool can recover formatting, tables of contents, embedded images, and other data.

- OutlookFIX is a tool used to repair files used in Microsoft Outlook, and it provides the ability to recover damaged or deleted e-mail, calendars, notes, attachments, and other elements in Outlook. It also provides an inbox repair tool and has the ability to split large files into smaller ones to solve the 2GB limitation on Personal Folders files (pst).

Repair My Excel and Repair My Word

There are also a number of other products that are designed to repair Microsoft Office products. GetData Software Development (www.getdata.com) provides a number of recovery tools, including the following:

- Repair My Excel (www.repairmyexcel.com) is used to recover spreadsheets created in Excel, including formulas, formatting, and other elements of the file's contents.

- Repair My Word is a free tool available from www.repairmyword.com that is used to recover text from corrupt or damaged Word files. Once recovered, it can then be saved in another Word document.

Compressed Files

Compressed files are files that have had a compression algorithm used to make the files smaller. Because the compressed file may be damaged, any files stored inside of it are inaccessible. This means that before you can recover a Word document, image, or other file, you must first repair the compressed file created with tools such as PKZIP, WinZip, RAR, or other compression software.

Zip Repair

Zip Repair is another tool developed by GetData Software Development (www.getdata.com) and can be downloaded from www.ziprepair.com. It is used to repair corrupted Zip files that have been compressed using WinZip or other software. It supports large file sizes of 2 GB or more, and it can even repair and extract data from spanned Zip volumes that have been split into smaller sets of data. Spanned Zip files are often used to make large Zip files into smaller pieces, allowing them to be e-mailed without worry of any e-mail size limitations.

Deleted Images

Of the various types of data you will try to recover, deleted images are common. If they are personal photographs, losing this data can be particularly devastating since pictures of events and special occasions are something that can never be replaced. Images may be corrupted or deleted from hard disks or directly from the memory card used in a digital camera. At times, the image may have been damaged, and repair of the file is necessary. A number of different tools are available that can be used to recover lost images.

eIMAGE Recovery

eIMAGE Recovery is another tool developed by Octanesoft and is available at www.octane-soft.com. It is designed to recover any digital images or media that may have been lost or deleted from memory cards used by digital cameras. It can restore files from any number of different media, including compact flash, smartmedia, memory sticks, mmd, XD, multimedia, or secure digital memory cards.

Canon RAW File Recovery Software

Canon RAW File Recovery Software (CRW Repair) is another free tool developed by GetData Software Development (www.getdata.com) and can be downloaded at www.crwre-pair.com. Canon cameras usually store images in a JPEG format, with RAW images stored inside of a file with a .CRW extension. The CRW file is generally used for processing photos, and it allows a photo's exposure, white balance, and other elements to be manipulated. The CRW file also allows users of the camera to access the JPEG quickly. Unfortunately, because it is a complex file, it can be easily corrupted by such things as a change in file size. CRW Repair will examine the file size to ensure it is correct, and it has the ability to access and extract the JPEG image.

ImageRecall

ImageRecall Software (www.imagerecall.com) provides several editions of software that can be used to retrieve corrupted or deleted files. The *Don't Panic – Photo Edition* allows you to recover pictures and video that have been damaged or deleted from digital cameras. Using this software, you can obtain and restore data from memory cards, USB storage devices, and other storage media. The tool also provides a thumbnail viewer that allows you to view small images of the pictures available to recover. The software is available only for Windows 2000, XP, and Vista, but support for Macintosh OS X is forthcoming.

RecoverPlus Pro

RecoverPlus Pro is a tool that allows you to recover digital images that may have been damaged or deleted, and it is available at www.arcksoft.com. It provides recovery of a wide variety of graphic formats and will attempt to adjust the image to improve it during recovery. It will

attempt to repair any images that are unreadable, including RAW files such as Canon CRW, CR2, and Nikon NEF. It provides a preview pane, which allows you to view a full-size image as well as thumbnails that are rendered from the image file. RecoveryPlus Pro also provides a number of options for scanning and undeleting files, including performing a deep-level scan on damaged media.

Zero Assumption Digital Image Recovery

Zero Assumption Digital Image Recovery was a free stand-alone digital image recovery tool developed by Zero Assumption Recovery (www.z-a-recovery.com). However, the stand-alone version of this tool was discontinued because its features are included in the trial and full versions of ZAR. As part of ZAR, the Digital Image Recovery is designed to restore pictures from digital memory cards. The types of images it can restore are GIF, JPEG, TIFF, CRW, CR2, MOV, and WAV files.

DiskInternals Flash Recovery

As discussed previously, DiskInternals (www.diskinternals.com) provides a number of data recovery solutions including DiskInternals Flash Recovery, which is designed to recover deleted or corrupted pictures from memory cards, including those that have been reformatted or lost due to a hardware malfunction. It provides an easy-to-use interface that allows images to be recovered using a wizard that takes the user step by step through the recovery process.

PC Inspector Smart Recovery

PC Inspector Smart Recovery is a free tool developed by CONVAR that can be used to restore files from memory cards and memory sticks used with digital cameras. It acquires read-only access to the memory card, ensuring that the data is not altered. Once recovered, you can specify where you would like the files to be saved. It is available at www.pcinspector.de/smart_media_recovery/uk/welcome.htm.

Recovering Deleted Partitions

Partitioning a hard disk involves dividing the disk into volumes, which generally appear to the operating system as logical drives, identified by different drive letters. The disk is divided into logical drives for the purposes of performance and organization of the data. Each logical drive can be formatted separately so that each one uses a different file system. Of course, you can partition the disk as a single partition. Partitioning schemes and tools differ depending on the operating system and file system.

Contrary to popular belief, partitioning utilities do not erase the data on a disk; they only delete and manipulate the partition tables. Although tools such as Partition Magic warn that their use will erase the data on a disk, this is not true; the warning is intended for the average user who will not be able to recover the data after using the utility. Generally, partition utilities

will delete the entry for that partition in the partition table so that any space associated with the partition becomes unallocated. Even if the tool overwrites the first sector (sector 0) of the partition before removing it, a backup of the boot sector may still be available and can be restored. Professional data recovery techniques can still recover the data, although the data might be fragmented—that is, the contents of a file could be spread out in different areas of the disk and recoverable in bits and pieces.

Deleting Partitions Using Windows

Partitions can be created and deleted in Windows using the *Computer Management (Local)* console, which is used to control various aspects of your computer. To open the console, you can right-click on the **My Computer** icon on your desktop, and then click the **Manage** menu item on the context menu that appears. Alternatively, you can open the console through the Control Panel. From the Windows **Start** menu, select **Settings** and click the **Control Panel** menu item. When the Control Panel opens, you would then double-click **Administrative Tools**, and then double-click **Computer Management**. It is important to note, however, that to access this tool, you need to use an Administrator account or be a member of the Administrators group.

As shown in Figure 4.8, the Computer Management console provides access to a variety of tools that can be used to manage your computer. By expanding the **Storage** node in the left pane, you can then click on the **Disk Management** item in the console tree. By selecting this item, information about the hard disks and other storage (such as DVD or CD-ROM drives) installed on your computer is shown in the right portion of the screen.

Figure 4.8 Disk Management in the Computer Management Console

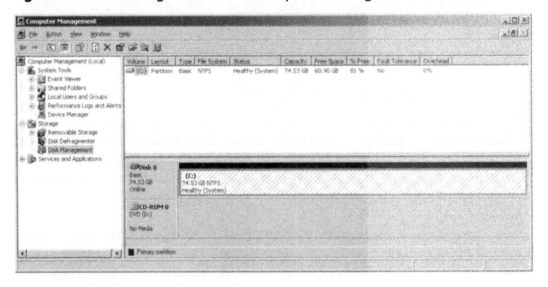

By right-clicking on a partition, logical drive, or volume in the lower right pane of the console, a context menu will appear with a **Delete Partition** menu item. If this item is enabled, clicking it will delete the partition. However, the **Delete Partition** menu item will not be enabled in certain circumstances, in which case it is impossible to delete the partition:

- A system volume (which contains files to boot the computer), boot volume (which contains system files), or a volume with an active paging file or crash dump (memory dump)

- An extended partition that is not empty. Before deleting an extended partition, all of the logical drives in that partition must be deleted first.

Deleting Partitions from the Command Line

Partitions can also be deleted from the command line using disk partitioning utilities that require you to type commands from a prompt. There are two commands that may be used on different versions of Windows:

- FDISK

- DISKPART

Using either of these tools, you can view a listing of partitions, determine the number or drive letter of the disk, and delete any existing partitions. It does, however, have the same limitations described previously when we discussed deleting a partition with the Computer Management console. You must be an Administrator or member of the Administrators group, and you can't delete a system volume, boot volume, or a volume with an active paging file or crash dump. In addition, any logical drives need to be deleted before deleting an extended partition.

FDISK

FDISK is a command line interpreter that is used to create and delete partitions on computers running MS-DOS, Windows 9*x*, Windows NT, or Windows ME. As shown in Table 4.5, there are a number of switches that can be used with this command to view information and perform various actions on a hard disk.

Table 4.5 FDISK Switches

Switch	Description
/MBR	Rewrites the MBR
/CMBR <disk>	Re-creates the MBR on a specific disk
/PRI: <size>	Creates a primary partition

Continued

Table 4.5 continued FDISK Switches

Switch	Description
/EXT: <size>	Creates an extended partition
/LOG: <size>	Creates a logical drive
/Q	Prevents rebooting the computer automatically after exiting FDISK
/STATUS	Shows current status of hard drives
/ACTOK	Forces FDISK not to check disk integrity
/FPRMT	Disables prompt for FAT32 support

When you are typing **FDISK** without any of these switches, the first screen that appears will prompt as to whether you want to enable large disk support. This will determine whether FAT32 is used on the drive. If a hard disk is larger than 512 MB, FAT32 is needed if you want to format a disk over 2 GB as a single drive. Once you press the **N** or **Y** key on your keyboard to indicate whether FAT32 should be used, a menu screen will appear with a number of options:

1. **Create DOS partition or Logical DOS Drive**
2. **Set active partition**
3. **Delete partition or Logical DOS Drive**
4. **Display partition information**
5. **Change current fixed disk drive**, which only appears if you have multiple hard disk drives on your computer

To delete a partition, you would press **3** on your keyboard, which would give you another menu that asks what kind of partition or logical drive you want to delete. The options are

1. **Delete Primary DOS Partition**
2. **Delete Extended DOS Partition**
3. **Delete Logical DOS Drive(s) in the Extended DOS Partition**
4. **Delete Non-DOS Partition**, which is used to delete partitions using NTFS

Upon choosing the type of partition you want to delete, you may be presented with a list of drives that are available to delete. For example, choosing the third menu item will present you with a listing of logical DOS drives in the extended partition. Upon choosing what you will delete, a prompt will appear warning you that all of the data will be lost and asking if you're sure that you want to proceed with the deletion. By pressing the **Y** key on your keyboard, the partition or drive is deleted.

DISKPART

DISKPART is a command line interpreter that is used to create and delete partitions on computers running Windows 2000, Windows XP, or Windows Vista. Unlike FDISK, it doesn't provide a series of menus that can be navigated to delete partitions. Instead, as shown in Figure 4.9, typing **DISKPART** at the prompt will activate the command line interpreter, allowing you to enter different commands.

Figure 4.9 DISKPART

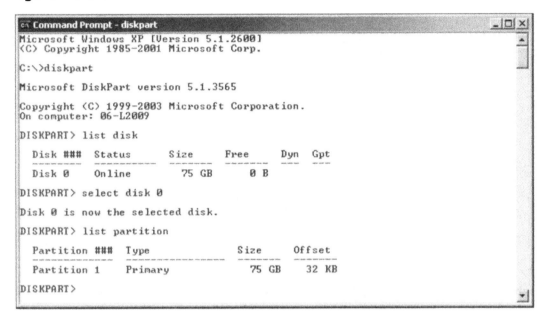

A number of commands can be used to view information on disks and partitions on your hard disk, as well as perform tasks such as creating and deleting partitions. The commands available through DISKPART are shown in Table 4.6.

Table 4.6 DISKPART Commands

Switch	Description
ADD	Adds a mirror to a simple volume
ACTIVE	Marks the current partition as being the active boot partition
ASSIGN	Assigns a drive letter or mount point to the selected volume
BREAK	Breaks a mirror set
CLEAN	Clears the configuration information or all information off the disk

Continued

Table 4.6 continued DISKPART Commands

Switch	Description
CONVERT	Converts the disk from one format to another. This will allow you to convert the disk from dynamic to basic, basic to dynamic, MBR to GPT, or GPT to MBR.
CREATE	Creates a volume or partition
DELETE	Deletes a missing disk, selected volume, or a selected partition
DETAIL	Provides details about a disk, partition, or volume
EXIT	Exits the program
EXTEND	Extends a volume
HELP	Prints a listing of Help commands
IMPORT	Imports a disk group
LIST	Prints a list of disks, partitions, or volumes
INACTIVE	Marks the current partition as an inactive partition
ONLINE	Online a disk that is currently marked as offline
REM	Used to comment scripts
REMOVE	Removes a drive letter or mount point
REPAIR	Repair a RAID-5 volume
RESCAN	Forces DISKPART to rescan the computer for disks and volumes
RETAIN	Places a retainer partition under a simple volume
SELECT	Moves the focus on an object

Using a combination of these commands, you can delete a partition from a computer, allowing you to later create and format in a particular file format. These steps are outlined in Exercise 4.2, but they should not be performed on any production computer.

EXERCISE 4.2

DELETING A PARTITION FROM A WINDOWS XP COMPUTER USING DISKPART

The following exercise will delete a partition. Do not use it on any production computer.

1. From the Windows **Start** menu, select **Programs | Accessories**, and then click on the **Command Prompt** menu item.

2. When the Command Prompt appears, type **DISKPART** and then press the **Enter** key.

3. From the DISKPART prompt, type **LIST DISK** and then press the **Enter** key. When the listing of disks appears, note the disk number of the disk from which you want to delete the partition.

4. Type **SELECT DISK *n***, where n is the number of the disk from which you want to delete the partition. Press the **Enter** key.

5. Type **LIST PARTITION** and then press the **Enter** key. When the listing of partitions appears, note the partition number you wish to delete.

6. Type **SELECT PARTITION *n***, where n is the number of the partition you want to delete. Press the **Enter** key.

7. Type **DELETE PARTITION** and then press the **Enter** key.

8. Type **EXIT** and then press the **Enter** key to exit DISKPART.

9. Type **EXIT** and then press the **Enter** key to exit the Command Prompt.

Deleted Partition Recovery Tools

When a partition is deleted, its entry in the partition table is removed. Although it can appear quite imposing that an entire partition of information is no longer visible, the data hasn't been destroyed from the disk. Essentially, deleting the partition is similar to removing the table of contents from a book; none of the information outside of the table is missing, it just requires other methods to find it. This is where partition recovery tools come into play.

Partition recovery tools perform a number of automated tasks that will attempt to restore a damaged or deleted partition and/or restore data from that partition. The following are some of the automated tasks these tools will use to locate and recover data:

■ Determining the error on the disk and allowing the user to choose another partition and make it active

■ Scanning the disk space for a partition boot sector or damaged partition information, and then attempting to reconstruct the partition table entry. By finding the partition boot sector, it will have all the information necessary to reconstruct the entry in the partition table. Because both NTFS and FAT32 volumes maintain backup boot sectors, you can recover the volume by restoring the boot sector.

- Scanning the disk space for a partition boot sector or data from deleted partition information, and then attempting to reconstruct the partition table entry

A number of tools are available for partition recovery, each of which has various features that can make it easier to restore data that may have been lost from accidental deletion or damage to the partition. Damaged partitions can occur from power or software failure, the root directory being damaged by a virus, formatting, and from being deleted with tools such as FDISK, DISKPART, or the Disk Management tool in the Computer Management console. Problems can also occur when the partition table, MFT, root directory, or boot record is lost or corrupt. Each of these can cause Windows not to recognize the hard disk, requiring partition recovery tools to be used to recover the partition and data.

Test Day Tip

You are expected to know about various tools used to restore deleted and damaged partitions for the CHFI exam. On the day of the exam, it is wise to quickly review the basic features and functionality of the programs that follow. A link is provided for each of the tools so you can acquire additional information and download a copy of the software while studying for the exam.

Active@ Partition Recovery

Previously in this chapter, we discussed a number of other tools developed by Active@ Data Recovery Software, so it should come as no surprise that this company also has a utility for deleted or damaged partitions. Active@ Partition Recovery is a tool that is available at www.partition-recovery.com, and it will recover FAT12, FAT16, FAT32, and NTFS partitions and logical drives. It also provides the ability to create an image file of the drive to back up data on a disk, as well as back up MBR, partition table, and boot sectors, which can be restored after a problem occurs.

Active@ Partition Recovery will scan the hard disk to locate deleted partitions and logical drive. In doing so, a SuperScan (which does an extensive scan of the hard disk) may even detect partitions after new ones have been created. Even if you've formatted and used these new partitions, the old ones may still be detected. Once detected, you can then undelete primary and extended partitions or logical drives to restore the data. If you're unsure whether the data on the partition is something you want to recover, this tool provides the ability to preview files and folders located on the deleted partition or drive before its recovered.

There are different versions of Active@ Partition Recovery software available to use, including

- Active@ Partition Recovery for DOS, which is a DOS-based version of the tool and is used if the system partition has been lost or if the computer doesn't boot in Windows. It can't recover a partition if it has been overwritten. It is small enough to run from a bootable floppy, and it supports IDE, ATA, and SCSI hard drives.

- Active@ Partition Recovery for Windows, which is the Windows-based version of the tool and is used if a nonsystem partition is lost or when the computer boots in Windows. It can also be used to restore a deleted partition on a USB flash drive or memory card. It supports IDE, ATA, SATA, and SCSI drives.

The Active@ Partition Recovery Professional and Active@ Partition Recovery Enterprise Toolkit both include each of these versions. As shown in Figure 4.10, the interface for the Windows version of this tool is easy to use. By clicking on the **QuickScan** or **SuperScan** buttons, the hard disk is scanned and any partitions are detected. You can preview files and folders detected on the partition and recover the partition. By clicking on the **Image** button, you can create a copy of the logical drive or physical device. Items in the **Tools** menu can also be used to repair the MBR, back up or restore partitioning information, recover the partition, or delete an invalid partition.

Figure 4.10 Active@ Partition Recovery

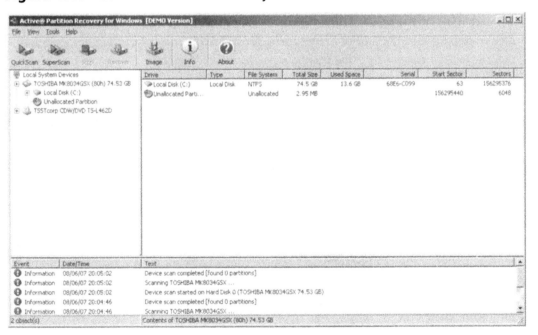

Active@ Disk Image

Whereas Active@ Partition allows you to create a raw image of a logical or physical drive, Active@ Disk Image is a DOS-based tool designed to completely back up and restore an image of your entire hard disk, FAT12, FAT16, FAT32, and NTFS partitions and logical drives. This tool allows you to create both compressed and uncompressed images that contain a mirror of the drive's surface or compressed data images that contain data stored in the clusters. As with other tools from this developer, you can preview the data stored in one or more image files before restoring them. It is available at www.disk-image.net.

DiskInternals Partition Recovery

DiskInternals is another company whose tools were previously discussed. DiskInternals Partition Recovery is a tool that is used to recover deleted and damaged partitions, and it is available at www.diskinternals.com. It supports FAT12, FAT16, FAT32, and NTFS volumes, and it provides features to recover deleted files. Even if files were deleted before the partition was lost, they can still be recovered.

DiskInternals Partition Recovery also provides the ability to create snapshot files of logical drives, allowing any data on a drive to be stored in files that can be kept on another machine until needed. By creating an image of the drive, the data can be restored in case of a problem.

DiskInternals Partition Recovery also provides features to recover the MBR and unformat NTFS and FAT drives. In addition, it can provide recovery for other storage media, such as USB flash drives, memory cards, and other media.

One of the major features of this tool is that it provides a number of wizards that take you step-by-step through the process of recovering partitions. Because it walks you through the process, you can recover a partition without any previous experience.

GetDataBack

GetDataBack is a partition recovery tool developed by RunTime Software, and it is available at www.runtime.org. It will restore data from a variety of sources, including hard disks, memory cards, USB flash drives, iPods, and other media. There are two versions of this software available from this site:

- GetDataBack for NTFS, which is used to recover data from an NTFS file system
- GetDataBack for FAT, which is used to recover data from a FAT file system

Each of these tools can be used on a remote computer, allowing you to connect over a network or serial cable to restore a damaged or deleted partition. This can be useful if you don't want to remove the drive and attach it to another computer or use DOS-based tools to recover the partition.

It provides a wizard-like interface that allows you to specify settings to optimize the recovery process, selecting whether to use default settings, that damage was caused by partitioning software such as FDISK or formatting the drive, or if a new operating system was installed. If there is no problem with the partition, you can also set the tool to simply recover deleted files.

NTFS Deleted Partition Recovery

NTFS Deleted Partition Recovery is a tool that is designed to recover partitions and perform other tasks to restore data that may have been lost. It can retrieve data from formatted, corrupted, or otherwise damaged partitions, as well as from other storage media such as Zip drives, USB flash drives, and memory cards. It is available at www.techddi.com.

Handy Recovery

Handy Recovery is a tool for recovering deleted, damaged, and formatted partitions that is available at www.handyrecovery.com. Using this tool, you can search for files by names or by using a mask, and you can restore entire folders and their contents. You can browse data on the disk, allowing you to see deleted files and folders in addition to ones that have not been deleted. It supports FAT12, FAT16, FAT32, and NTFS file systems and will recover compressed and encrypted files stored on drives formatted as NTFS. It can also recover data from memory cards and other media. Each file that is displayed provides information on the probability that it can successfully be recovered.

Acronis Recovery Expert

Acronis Recovery Expert is another easy-to-use tool that recovers deleted or lost partitions, and it is available at www.acronis.com. It provides a series of wizards that take you step-by-step through the process of recovering data, and it supports FAT16, FAT32, NTFS, HPFS, Linux ext2, ext3, ReiserFS, and Linux Swap file systems. It also provides features that allow you to work from bootable CDs and floppy disks so you can recover system partitions or systems that fail to boot.

TestDisk

TestDisk is a free tool that can be used to recover data and partitions that have been deleted or lost. It can run on a number of different systems, including Windows NT, Windows 2000, Windows XP, Windows 2003, Linux, FreeBSD, NetBSD, OpenBSD, SunOS, and Macintosh OS X. It has features to fix partition tables, recover FAT32 and NTFS boot sectors from a backup, and rebuild FAT12, FAT16, FAT32, and NTFS boot sectors. It can also locate ext2 and ext3 backup SuperBlock, fix MFT using an MFT mirror, and provide other features that make it possible to recover partitions from a number of different systems. It is available at www.cgsecurity.org.

Scaven

Scaven is a partition recovery tool that can perform unattended multistring searches on hard disks and recover deleted and lost data. It can recover data from accidentally formatted drives, drives with bad sectors, damaged MBRs, and lost partitions. It is available at http://pjwalczak.com/scaven/index.php.

Recover It All!

Recover It All! is a tool developed by DTIData available at www.dtidata.com/recover_it_all.htm. It is designed to restore data lost from accidentally formatting the disk, deleted files, and deleted or damaged partitions and boot sectors. It also provides an executable that will run from a floppy disk allowing you to restore the partition even if the computer's operating system won't start and will prevent overwriting data on the disk by installing the software.

Partition Table Doctor

Partition Table Doctor is a partition recovery tool that checks and repairs the MBR, partition table, and boot sector and recovers damaged or deleted data from FAT16, FAT32, NTFS, ext2, ext3, and Linux Swap partitions on IDE, ATA, SATA, SCSI, and removable hard disk drives. It provides features to browse the contents of a disk, and it allows you to back up and restore the MBR, partition table, and boot sector. It is available at www.ptdd.com.

Data Acquisition and Duplication

Electronic evidence is fragile by nature and can easily be modified, damaged, or destroyed. Even booting a computer can erase temporary files, modify timestamps, or alter other data in addition to writing data and creating new files to the drive using the boot process. In addition, a computer could be booby trapped so that if a set of keys weren't pressed at bootup or an incorrect password was entered, a program or script could run to reformat the hard disk or overwrite certain data making retrieval of evidence more difficult or impossible. It is because of this that data must be acquired or duplicated from a hard disk before any analysis takes place.

As discussed in Chapter 3, *data acquisition* is the act or process of gathering information and evidence. In computer forensics, this means using established methods to acquire data from a suspect computer or storage media to gain insight into a crime or other incident and potentially use it as evidence to convict a suspect. The goal of data acquisition is to preserve evidence, so any tools that are used should not alter the data in any way and should provide an exact duplicate. To prevent contamination, any data that is duplicated should be stored on forensically sterile media, meaning that the disk has no other data on it and has no viruses or defects.

Duplication of data is a critical part of any computer forensic investigation. As discussed in the following sections, a number of tools are available that can create a copy of data. To effectively examine data on a suspect machine, a person performing a forensic examination of the machine needs to create an *image* of the disk. As discussed in Chapter 3, when you create a disk image (a bitstream copy), each physical sector of the disk is copied so that the data is distributed in the same way, and then the image is compressed into a file called an *image file*. This image is exactly like the original, both physically and logically. As an exact duplicate of the data on a suspect machine or storage media, the mirror image includes hidden files, temp files, corrupted files, file fragments, and erased files that have not yet been overwritten. In other words, every binary digit is duplicated exactly.

Exam Warning

To ensure that all data is acquired, a bitstream image needs to be made of the suspect hard drive or other media. This will acquire any deleted files, file fragments, slack space, and other data on the disk. If a standard image is created that does not acquire this data, then potential evidence may be unavailable to you. Standard images or clones of a machine can, however, be useful for backing up data or creating a duplicate of the operating system, applications, and data on the machine in case a disaster occurs.

This is different from other methods that may be used to duplicate data for disaster recovery or other purposes for which every scrap of data isn't necessary. For example, when you use tools to back up a hard disk, the only data duplicated are those that are visible to the file system. Similarly, a disk image may be created as a method of backing up a system, including only files that haven't been deleted. The backup or clone of the disk contents wouldn't include any data that was hidden, deleted, or lost on the disk. If a disaster occurred and/or data needed to be restored, the backup or image could be used to recover data and get systems back online quickly.

From the perspective of someone performing an investigation, backups on magnetic tape or image files stored to disks can be a useful source of evidence. Most organizations will have a regimen of nightly backups, in which data stored on servers and certain other computers on the network will be copied to magnetic tape or other storage media. Even individuals may back up important data to a disk or location on the network, creating an image of any data that was saved to the disk over a period of time. This can be important to an investigation because it can provide a timeline of what data was saved to certain files at what time. For example, if someone was embezzling from a company, you could see what entries he or she added, deleted, and modified in a spreadsheet or database on a given day by restoring versions of the file from

different backups. As discussed later, a number of tools can be used to duplicate data stored on magnetic tapes, and others that can mount an image file created with various types of software. By analyzing a duplicate of the image or backup, you may find important evidence without altering the original media or file.

In an investigation however, most of the time you'll need to use software to create an image of a hard disk, CDs, DVDs, floppy disks, USB flash drives, memory cards from digital cameras, and other storage media. The bitstream copy will contain all of the data stored on the device or removable media and can later be analyzed for potential evidence.

Because you don't boot from the hard disk of a computer you're investigating, you need to connect the computer you're using (with forensic software installed) to the suspect's machine via a network cable or serial cable. Once you've created a physical connection to the computer, you can then run the forensic software and create an image of the machine's hard disk.

Forensic software may include a special program that can run from a bootable floppy or be small enough to fit on a bootable CD or floppy. Upon booting from the CD or floppy, the program on the floppy or CD is run. Depending on the program, it may connect to the forensic software on your computer so that it can then make an exact image of the disk, or it may simply write the image file to your computer.

Alternatively, you could also remove the hard disk from a suspect computer and connect it to your computer or a device that provides write protection. Write protection prevents data from being written to the disk that you're duplicating. When using any forensic software, it is always advisable to use hardware-based write-blocking software. The hardware prevents the forensic software and the operating system you're using from altering data on the suspect hard disk when you attach the hard drive to your computer. Once the hard disk is connected to your computer in this way, you can then begin running the forensic software so that a duplicate of the data is written to an image file on your machine.

Once the image is created, you can then use the forensic software or other tools that we'll discuss in this chapter to mount the image. This allows the software to display the contents of the machine and will allow you to view any data that exists on the machine from which it was acquired. Any software being used should mount the image as a read-only volume so there is no way that any changes can be made to the data. This allows you to view data in areas of the disk, inclusive to partition information, sectors, files stored on the machine, directory structure, and other information. Because it is read-only, any files you view won't be altered, inclusive to retaining their original timestamps and other attributes.

Because the data you're analyzing is a duplicate of the original source, the original hard disk or storage media is preserved in its original state. If a situation occurred in which the image file or duplicated magnetic media was damaged or destroyed, you could reacquire the data as you did the first time. Of course, any machine used to store forensic image files should be backed up regularly. This will ensure that if a problem does occur that damages or deletes the image file you're working from, you can restore it from an existing backup.

Notes from the Underground…

Booby Traps

Booby trap is military slang for a trap that is set off by a foolish or unsuspecting person. In computers, there are many different kinds of traps that can be set for people whom you do not want to have access. A simple trap is to create an icon on the desktop that someone may want to activate. For example, if a suspect created an icon named "Kiddie Porn," an investigator might be tempted to double-click on it. The trap is that the shortcut actually points to a script or program that will overwrite selected files, encrypt the hard disk, or perform other actions that make analyzing the disk impossible. If you didn't want to use an icon, you could configure your computer to run a particular script or program at startup or shutdown. This could be as simple as adding a batch file to the Windows Startup menu or adding a few lines to an AUTOEXEC.BAT file.

There are many applications on the Internet designed to wipe data from your computer by overwriting deleted files. A simple batch file could delete a folder and then invoke such a program that would overwrite any deleted files with a series of ones and zeros or other data. It could even initiate a low-level format that would erase everything on the disk sector by sector.

The danger of booby traps is another reason why it's very important to analyze a computer using an image of its data. By working from an image file, you won't need to worry about such programs executing and damaging evidence on a machine. The original data remains preserved, and because the forensic software mounts the image as a read-only file, there is no chance that such scripts or programs will modify any data in the image file.

Data Acquisition Tools

Whereas years ago the number of tools that could be used for forensic acquisition and analysis was limited, today there are quite a few options. As mentioned previously, in choosing which tools to use, you should ensure that they do not modify data. You should also evaluate the reputations of these tools and whether they have previously been accepted in court. For example, if you are using a tool such as Encase, which has been widely accepted, there would be less of a chance of it being heavily scrutinized. Since testifying in court can be stressful enough, you don't want to waste time justifying the tools you used to acquire evidence. Although you may still need to validate the tool that was used, using tools that are widely accepted can make the process easier.

In the following sections, we'll discuss a number of data acquisition tools and how their features may be useful. These tools may consist of software used to duplicate data, create image files that may be mounted and analyzed afterward, or hardware-based solutions that can acquire data from a suspect machine. We'll also discuss a number of native commands and tools that can be used to duplicate data on computers and transfer them to another machine.

FTK Imager

The Forensic Tool Kit (FTK) is a product developed by AccessData (www.accessdata.com) and is a fully integrated forensic data acquisition and analysis program. It provides a number of features, such as supporting full text indexing of image files without needing to extract them to a hard disk, and includes a file viewer to preview files. It also has an imaging component (derived from the shareware ISOBuster product) that does a good job of collecting data from CDs and DVDs with any of the commonly supported file systems.

FTK Imager is an imaging tool that allows you to preview data and assess potential evidence on a machine. Using this tool, you can make a forensic image of the data, duplicating everything on the machine so that there is no chance of modifying the original data. By previewing the contents of the image and reviewing the duplicated data, you can then determine if additional analysis is required using FTK.

You can view forensic images of hard disks, floppy disks, CDs, DVDs, and other storage media created with FTK Imager, or you can view images created with other tools. FTK Imager will read image files created with ICS and SafeBack. It also reads uncompressed images created with Ghost. FTK Imager will read or write image files in Encase, dd Raw, SMART, and FTK image formats. This means that even if another organization or person with different software created a forensic image, you could still view the image file and determine if there was any evidence on media. This is particularly useful in a situation such as when an internal investigation was conducted, a forensic image was created from a suspect computer, and police now need to view the evidence that was acquired.

In addition to the image file formats that can be made for analyzing disks, there are also a number of file formats that can be read and created for CD and DVD forensics, including ISOBuster CUE, CloneCD, Alcohol, PlexTools, and Virtual CD.

As shown in Figure 4.11, FTK Imager provides an easy-to-use interface. Once an evidence file is opened, you can view the folder structure in the **Evidence Tree**, located in the upper left pane. By selecting a folder, you can then view files stored in that folder in the **File List**, located in the upper right pane. To preview a particular file, you can select it in the upper pane and view an image of pictures, hexadecimal data, text, and previews of other data in the lower right pane. Additional information on the file, including any DOS attributes the file might have, can be viewed in the **Properties** pane in the lower left side of the screen.

Figure 4.11 FTK Imager

Now that we've discussed a number of the features of this product, let's try it out and create a forensic image using the tool. Instructions for how to create an image file are outlined in Exercise 4.3.

EXERCISE 4.3

CREATING AN IMAGE FILE WITH FTK IMAGER

Before you can do this exercise, you will need to visit www.accessdata.com and download a copy of FTK Imager. You can download a copy of this and other products from www.accessdata.com/common/pagedetail.aspx?PageCode=downloads.

1. Insert floppy disk into your floppy disk drive. If your computer doesn't have a floppy disk drive, insert a CD into the CD-ROM drive.

2. From the Windows **Start** menu, select **Programs | AccessData | FTK Imager** and then click on the FTK Imager menu item.

3. When the programs open, click on the **File** menu, and then click on the **Add Evidence Item** menu item.

4. When the **Select Source** dialog box appears, click on the option labeled **Logical Drive**. Click the **Next** button.

5. When the **Select Drive** dialog box appears, select the drive containing your floppy disk or CD. Click **Finish**.

6. When the **Create Image** dialog box appears, click **Add**.

7. When the **Select Image Destination** dialog box appears, specify where the image file will be stored by entering a path into the field labeled **Image destination folder**.

8. In the field labeled **Image filename**, enter the name you'd like to give the file without an extension. Click **Finish**.

9. When the **Create Image** dialog box appears again, click **Start**.

10. Wait while FTK Imager creates a forensic image file of the data on the drive you specified. This may take several minutes. Once the **Status** field indicates *Image created successfully*, click the **Close** button.

SafeBack

As mentioned in Chapter 2, SafeBack was one of the earliest DOS-based tools for acquiring evidence from a computer sector by sector. It was developed by NTI and is available at www.forensics-intl.com/safeback.html. SafeBack has been marketed to law enforcement agencies since 1990 and has been used by the FBI and the Criminal Investigation Division of the IRS to create image files for forensics examination and evidentiary purposes. Booting from a floppy disk, it can make a duplicate image of everything on a hard disk, preserving its integrity and allowing you to analyze evidence without worry of modifying it.

SafeBack is capable of duplicating individual partitions or entire disks of virtually any size, and the image files can be transferred to SCSI tape units or almost any other magnetic storage media. The product contains CRC functions to check integrity of the copies and date and timestamps to maintain an audit trail of the software's operations. The vendor provides a 3-day computer forensics course to train forensics specialists in the use of the software. (In fact, the company does not provide technical support to individuals who have not undergone this training.) Although it is a DOS-based tool, it can be used to copy DOS, Windows, and UNIX disks (including Windows NT/2000 RAID drives) on Intel-compatible systems. Images can be saved as multiple files for storage on CDs or other small-capacity media. To avoid legal concerns about possible alteration, no compression or translation is used in creating the image.

DriveSpy

DriveSpy is another DOS-based data acquisition tool developed by Digital Intelligence Forensic Solutions and is available at www.digitalintelligence.com. If you are familiar with DOS commands, it is an easy-to-use tool because it uses a DOS prompt and many of the commands used in DOS to navigate through the directory structure of a system being analyzed. In addition to these commands, special commands are used to invoke features of DriveSpy.

Although it is a DOS-based tool, it can acquire evidence from partitions using FAT, non-DOS partitions, and hidden DOS partitions. This not only includes files that are visible to the file system but also data that has been deleted or that exists in slack space and unallocated space on the disk. It supports acquisition from hard drives larger than 8.4 GB as well as floppy disks and other storage media. It provides a built-in sector and cluster Hex Viewer to view data, and it has the ability to create and restore compressed forensic images of partitions.

A beneficial feature of this tool to an investigation is its logging capabilities. You can configure DriveSpy to document how the acquisition of evidence is conducted, including logging every keystroke that you made. These are written to a log file and can be used later for inclusion in a report of what actions you took to acquire the evidence.

Mount Image Pro

Mount Image Pro is a tool developed by GetData Software Development (www.getdata.com) that allows you to mount and view forensic image files created by EnCase, Unix and Linux DD images, SMART, and ISO images of CDs and DVDs. It is used by a variety of organizations, including the FBI, state and federal law enforcement, and various other investigative agencies and firms. Once an image is mapped to a drive letter, you can explore the data acquired through the image and use third-party tools discussed previously (such as Recover My Files) to restore files.

Because Mount Image Pro can mount different types of forensic image files, you don't need additional copies of software or dongles used by software such as EnCase to view evidence acquired in the image. This can save a considerable amount of money because machines used to analyze the image don't require the original software used to acquire the evidence. Additionally, if an EnCase image file is password protected, you can still open it even if you don't have the password. It is available at www.mountimage.com.

DriveLook

DriveLook is a free forensic search tool developed by Runtime Software and is available at www.runtime.org/drivelook.htm. It is designed to index all of the text that was written to a hard disk or other media. The drives searched can be physical or logical drives, or remote drives to which you connect using a serial cable or network connection using TCP/IP. You can also use this tool with image files, such as those created with Runtime's DiskExplorer or GetDataBack, allowing you to search for words that were stored on a suspect machine. Once it

has indexed the words on the media and saved them to a table, you can search by keywords or browse the table to view the location of where these words are stored.

When DriveLook first opens, it provides an easy-to-use wizard that takes you through the steps of indexing a drive. When it first starts, you configure where you'd like to store a log file, words to include in the search and other settings, or accept the defaults before DriveLook scans the drive. Once the scan is finished, you click the **Next** button to begin indexing the drive. Once complete, clicking the **Next** button to view the screen shown in Figure 4.12. As shown in this figure, by selecting a word from the left pane, you can view the sector in which it is located on the drive in the upper right pane and view how it appears in the lower right pane. The interface also allows you to filter the results using a search field on the bottom of the screen.

Figure 4.12 DriveLook

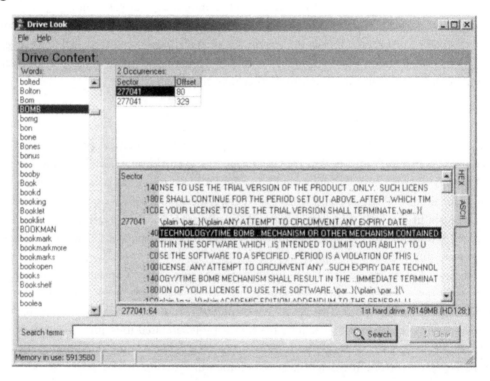

Although it is free, when you initially install DriveLook, it installs as an evaluation copy. Before using it, you need to click in the **Help** menu, and then click on the **Register** menu item. Upon doing so, a dialog box appears in which you enter the following information:

- Name: Runtime Software
- License key: BKZSBKFTUPYEK

Upon clicking **OK**, the program is then registered, and you can use it as a fully licensed version.

DiskExplorer

DiskExplorer is another tool that allows you to browse the contents of a hard disk. Developed by Runtime Software and available at www.runtime.org/diskexpl.htm, there are two versions of this tool available to use:

- DiskExplorer for NTFS
- DiskExplorer for FAT

Both of them are disk editors, which are used to respectively browse NTFS and FAT file systems and recover data stored on a disk. They allow you to view the contents of a physical or logical drive or image files. As shown in Figure 4.13, when viewing information on a disk, you can analyze the partition table, MFT, boot record, and index buffers. Using back and forward buttons, you can navigate through data on the disk, or you can use items on the menu to go to a particular sector or area of the disk to view its data. DiskExplorer also features search capabilities that allow you to search for text, view files and their properties, and identify to which file a cluster belongs. Using this tool, you can edit sectors of the disk and also recover files that may have been lost or deleted.

Figure 4.13 DiskExplorer

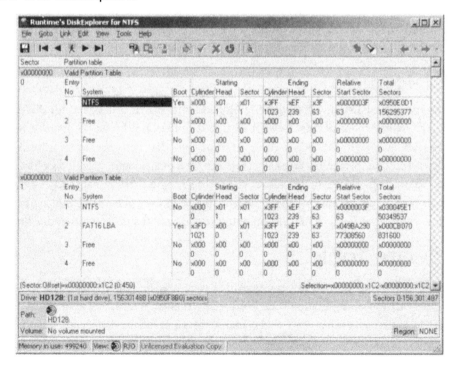

This tool can also duplicate data on a hard drive by creating an image file. After creating an image file, you can preserve data on the disk for later analysis. Once the image file is created, you can then open it again with DiskExplorer and analyze its contents or use other tools to restore it on another machine.

SnapBack DatArrest

DatArrest is a suite of data duplication and forensic tools developed by SnapBack and is available at www.datarrest.com. One of the benefits of this tool is that data can be acquired from a machine using a program on a bootable floppy. Images created not only include files that can be seen by the file system but also those that have been deleted, encrypted, or that are in slack space on the disk. Even CMOS settings used by the computer are captured as part of the image. Using the modules and utilities included with this product, you can acquire data and create images to and from hard disks, removable media, and magnetic tapes.

SCSIPAK

SCSIPAK is a suite of tools developed by Vogon and is available at www.vogon.co.uk/data-conversion/scsipak.htm. It provides data recovery and data conversion between Windows NT4 or Windows 2000 and other systems such as UNIX, DEC, ICL, and IBM Mainframe. When attempting to view a backup tape created by one of these systems on a Windows NT or 2000 tape drive, the Windows machine may be unable to read it and view it as blank. SCSIPAK extends the capabilities of the Windows tape drive so that this data is now readable. You can download data from tapes or optical discs and write them to up to seven drives simultaneously. Using SCSIPAK, you can copy tapes, transfer data from one system to Windows NT or Windows 2000, or transfer data between disk, tape, or optical disc.

IBM DFSMSdss

Data Set Services (DFSMSdss) is a utility developed by IBM that is designed for disaster recovery and management of data. Developed as part of the Data Facility Storage Management Subsystem (DFSMS), DFSMSdss is used to move or copy data between different types of storage media so that storage on various servers can be managed and space won't fill up on one particular volume of a server. It also allows you to back up and restore data and copy backups to other storage media, regardless of whether it is between the same or different types of media. It is available at www-03.ibm.com/systems/storage/software/sms/dss/index.html.

Hardware Tools

Although to this point we have discussed how software may be used for data acquisition, this is not the only method of duplicating data. Using these tools in a forensic lab or in the field, you can create forensic images that can later be analyzed for potential evidence. In some cases, these

tools serve as portable forensic labs, allowing you to perform acquisition and analysis before the computer is even removed from the crime scene.

A number of these tools will store data directly on a hard disk inside of the device, provide the ability to transfer image files from the device to another computer in a forensic lab, and can then wipe the device's drive to make it forensically sterile. This ensures that there is no contamination from other data on the drive each time data is acquired from a new machine.

Test Day Tip

Remember that all methods of acquiring data don't strictly involve software-based solutions. Hardware used in data acquisition may only provide write blocking (to prevent data being written to a suspect drive) or may be full systems that are used to acquire and analyze data in the field or a forensic lab.

ImageMASSter Solo-3 Forensic

ImageMASSter Solo-3 Forensic is a hardware tool developed by Intelligent Computer Solutions and is available at www.icsforensic.com. It is a portable, hand-held device that can acquire data from suspect machines at speeds exceeding 4 GB per minute. By connecting the hard disks directly to the machine using a drive-to-drive interface or external Firewire/USB interface, you can create an exact replica of data from one or two drives simultaneously without any reduction in speed. Specifically designed for computer forensic purposes, it can acquire data from IDE, SATA, and SCSI hard drives.

LinkMASSter-2 Forensic

LinkMASSter-2 Forensic is another hardware tool developed by Intelligent Computer Solutions and is also available at www.icsforensic.com. The device attaches to a computer through a Firewire or USB port and can then create an image of any data on the machine. Software is used to boot the machine and connect to the LinkMASSter, allowing it to acquire data using the Firewire or USB ports. Data on the original machine is protected during acquisition due to write-blocking features in the device.

ImageMASSter 6007SAS

ImageMASSter 6007SAS is a powerful tool for creating images of data from suspect machines, and it is a useful part of any forensic lab. It was developed by Intelligent Computer Solutions and is available at www.icsforensic.com. It duplicates IDE, SAS, SATA, and IDE hard drives, and it can migrate server data from SCSI to SAS/SATA. ImageMASSter can also acquire data

from multiple hard disks and store multiple images on one hard drive. It is the only duplication system on the market that supports SAS (Serial Attach SCSI) hard drives and can copy multiple drives simultaneously at high speeds. It also includes a 1GB network connection that can be used to transfer files to and from a network drive. To acquire and analyze data, the system provides a Windows XP-based interface that allows you to copy data from Windows, Macintosh, and UNIX file systems.

RoadMASSter-3

Whereas many tools are developed for use inside of a forensic lab, the RoadMASSter-3 is a data acquisition and analysis tool designed for use in the field. The RoadMASSter-3 is developed by Intelligent Computer Solutions and is available at www.icsforensic.com. It is designed to create an image and analyze data acquired from suspect hard drives. It can connect to an unopened computer using Firewire and USB ports, and it can connect directly to IDE, SATA, SAS, and SCSI hard drives. It can also acquire data from multiple drives to a single target drive, making acquisition faster.

The RoadMASSter-3 also allows you to analyze data immediately. It has a 15-inch color display in its case that allows you to view the data stored in the image file so that you can determine whether any evidence exists on the machine while you're still in the field.

Disk Jockey IT

Disk Jockey IT is a portable, hand-held hardware tool developed by Diskology and is available at www.diskology.com. It is the smallest write-blocking and disk copy device available for computer forensics. It can be used as a write-blocking device for data acquired using Firewire and USB connections to a suspect computer. The device can then be connected to a Macintosh or Windows computer in write protect mode to analyze the data without fear of altering the data.

Backing Up and Duplicating Data

Although the previously discussed tools are used for investigations in which there is a need to acquire an exact duplicate of data for the purpose of analyzing and potentially using certain data as evidence in court, this is not the only reason why data is duplicated. Many tools are used to create backups of data so that systems can be restored in the event of a virus or other malicious software, catastrophic failure of a hard disk, intrusion, or other events that could result in the corruption, loss, or deletion of data.

Images are also made of computers when there is a mass deployment of a system. For example, on a network, most of the workstations will have the same operating systems, applications, and other software installed and configured the same way. By setting up one computer and making an image of it, you can then restore the image on other computers being deployed. You would only need to change the computer's name, IP address, and a few other settings on the machine to make it unique on the network. Because the operating system and other soft-

ware are only installed once, and every other computer has an image restored on it, this saves time and money in setting up machines being deployed on the network.

Backups and duplicates of data are particularly useful during investigations. Because a computer may be seized during an investigation, a new computer can quickly be deployed with a clean image restored to it. This minimizes the impact of losing a computer for any length of time because a replacement computer can be deployed in its place almost immediately.

R-Drive Image

R-Drive Image is a data duplication tool developed by r-Tools Technology and is available at www.drive-image.com. It is designed for backing up and duplicating data, and it creates a byte-by-byte copy of data on hard drives, partitions, and logical disks. These files can then be stored on another hard disk, network drive, or other storage media and restored as needed.

Save-N-Sync

Save-N-Sync is a tool designed by Peer Software to synchronize data stored in a directory on a laptop or desktop computer with data stored on another storage device or location, such as a network server. The data can be backed up to a location you specify, or you can synchronize it so that any changes on either the source or the target folder will be reflected in both directories. You can manually or automatically have the data on a computer backed up or synchronized, ensuring that if a problem occurs, the data can be restored from another location. It is available at www.savensync.com.

The standard version of this tool allows you to choose a single directory to synchronize with another directory, whereas the corporate version allows up to 15 directories to be synchronized. Although this may sound like a small number of directories, you can select for all subdirectories below each directory to be included in the synchronization process. For example, if you choose your C: as the source folder, and had any subdirectories included in the synchronization, then your entire C: drive would be synchronized.

QuickCopy

QuickCopy is a tape duplication system developed by Shaffstall Corporation that is designed to make tape-to-tape copies of backups. When data from a server or other computer is backed up to magnetic tape, copies may be required for offsite storage. When a nightly backup is made, QuickCopy can be used to make a duplicate of this data, providing a backup of the backup tape.

Although useful in disaster recovery situations, it can also be useful in making duplicates of tapes so they can be analyzed for potential evidence. QuickCopy verifies the data byte-for-byte and also provides the ability to copy a single tape to an image file that can be stored on a hard disk. It is available at www.shaffstall.com/products/software/qctsw/.

Acquiring Data in Linux

In addition to the data recovery and forensic tools that run or can be used on machines running Linux, UNIX, and other Posix operating systems, certain commands can be used on these operating systems to copy data on a machine and transfer it across a network. Versions of these same tools are also available for Windows operating systems but have their roots in Linux/UNIX machines. These commands are

- *dd*, which is a convert and copy command
- *Netcat*, which is used to transfer data and for other functions

DD

The *dd* command is a common UNIX command that is also used in Linux; it is used to convert and copy data. A version of DD is also available for systems running Windows, which is available at either http://unxutils.sourceforge.net or www.cygwin.com. It allows you to copy a hard disk to another disk drive or magnetic tape, or vice versa. In doing so, data is transferred byte-for-byte, creating an exact mirror image. The syntax for using this command is

```
dd <options>
```

As you can see from this syntax, there are options used with this command to specify different aspects of converting and copying data. For example, if you wanted to copy the contents of one disk to another, you would use the command with the *if* (input file) and *of* (output file) options:

```
dd if=/dev/hda of=/dev/hdy
```

Similarly, if you were going to back up the disk to an image on a hard disk, you could use the following:

```
dd if=/dev/hda of=/path/to/image
```

Additional options can be used with the *dd* command to specify the size of blocks to copy, whether data is to be converted when copying, and other options shown in Table 4.7.

Table 4.7 *dd* Options

Option	Description
if=*inputfile*	Specifies where to input data from (file or device)
of=*outputfile*	Specifies where to output data (file or device)
ibs=*bytes*	Number of bytes to read at a time
obs=*bytes*	Number of bytes to write at a time

Continued

Table 4.7 continued *dd* Options

Option	Description
bs=*bytes*	Number of bytes to read and write. This is used instead of ibs and obs, and it specifies the same number of bytes to use for both input and output.
bs=*bytes*	Number of bytes to convert at a time
skip=*blocks*	Specifies to skip blocks in the input file before copying
seek=*blocks*	Specifies to skip blocks in the output file before copying
count=*blocks*	Copy blocks from the input file, instead of everything at the end of the file
conv=*conversion*	Specifies to convert the input file before copying to an output file. Conversion methods include ■ ascii, which converts EBCDIC to ASCII ■ ebcdic, which converts ASCII to EBCDIC ■ ibm, which converts ASCII to alternate EBCDIC ■ block, which replaces the input newline with a padding of spaces to fit the size of cbs ■ unblock, which replaces trailing space characters in datasets of size cbs with newline characters ■ lcase, which converts uppercase characters to lowercase ■ ucase, which converts lowercase characters to uppercase ■ swab, which swaps every pair of input bytes ■ noerror, which ignores read errors ■ notrunc, which specifies not to truncate the output file ■ sync, which pads every input block to the size of *ibs* with null bytes if its shorter than the specified size

Using the *dd* command, you can even extract the MBR from a disk. Remember that the MBR and partition table are located in the first bytes of the disk. As such, by specifying to only acquire the first few bytes of data from the disk, you can acquire a backup of this data. For example, if we were going to acquire the file from the disk we previously used as an example, we would use the following command:

```
dd if=/dev/hda of=/path/to/image count=1 bs=512
```

To later restore this data to the disk in the event of a problem, we could reverse the input and output file information and instruct dd to put the data back:

```
dd if=/path/to/image of=/dev/had
```

EXAM WARNING

Remember that DD is a Linux/UNIX tool that is used to copy and convert data. A version of this tool is also available for Windows systems.

Netcat

Netcat is a tool that is available on all Posix operating systems, including Linux and UNIX, used to transfer data across a network using Transmission Control Protocol (TCP) and User Datagram Protocol (UDP). A version of Netcat is also available to use on systems running Windows 9*x*, Windows NT, Windows ME, Windows 2000, and Windows XP. Using this tool, you can create an image of the partition and send it to a machine or transfer files between remote computers. It also provides port scanning capabilities and the ability to connect via Telnet.

Netcat is run in server mode on one machine and client mode on another machine to communicate with one another. Netcat in server mode listens on a port you specify and sends data to the client that connects to that port number. To run Netcat from the server, the following syntax would be used, where *port number* is the port that you want the server to listen on and that clients will connect to:

```
nc -l <-options> <port number>
```

From the client, you would use the following syntax, where *ip address* is the IP address of the server, *options* are the options you can use, and *port number* is the port that the client will use to connect to the server:

```
nc <-options> <server ip address> <port number>
```

As shown in Table 4.8, Netcat provides a number of additional options that can be used for listening on a network and connecting to computers.

Table 4.8 Netcat Options

Option	Description
-d	Background mode. Detach from console
-e *program*	Inbound program to execute
-g	Source routing flags
-h	Help
-i *seconds*	Delay interval for lines sent, ports scanned
-l	Listen for inbound connections
-n	Numeric only IP addresses (no DNS)
-o	Hex dump of traffic to a file
-p	Local TCP/IP port to listen to. This is used in server mode with –l.
-r	Random local and remote ports
-s *addr*	Local source address
-t	Answer TELNET negotiation
-u	Use UDP to listen on port. This is used in server mode with –l.
-v	Verbose. –v-v will put it into ultra verbose mode.
-w *seconds*	Timeout for connects and final net reads, before Netcat will automatically quit
-z	No I/O mode. Used for scanning ports

Netcat can also be used with other tools to create a compressed image of the disk and allow others to download the file. In the following example, the *dd* command is used to create an image of a disk, with gzip used to compress it. Netcat is then used to listen to port number, making the file available:

```
dd if=/dev/hdb | gzip -9 | nc -l 4321
```

Damage & Defense...

Netcat as a Hacking Tool

Netcat is a useful tool for simple file transfers and sending backups of data across a network, but it is also referred to as the "hacker's Swiss army knife." It is a powerful tool, and in the wrong hands it could be devastating to a system. In fact, Symantec lists Netcat as a hacking tool on its Web site and provides information on how to remove it from a system (www.symantec.com/security_response/writeup.jsp?docid=2005-120115-5633-99). It is an incredibly useful and possibly dangerous tool on networks. Although network administrators commonly use it for debugging and transferring files, it could be used by a hacker to obtain unauthorized access to a Web site, execute programs remotely, and transfer data from a machine to an intruder's computer.

Summary of Exam Objectives

As discussed in this chapter, there are a number of ways in which data may be deleted from a system. Operating systems provide commands to remove data from a hard disk or other media, such as menu items or commands used from a command prompt. When a file is deleted using the **DEL** key or commands in compliant programs, it will generally be sent to the Recycle Bin. When this occurs, the user can recover the file him- or herself. If the file has been emptied from the Recycle Bin or deleted using other methods, then you may need to use tools to recover the file. Even if an entire partition is deleted, and the volume is formatted, this doesn't mean that the data is gone. As we discussed, data recovery and computer forensic tools may still be able to retrieve the data from a system.

In this chapter, we saw that computer forensics requires specialized tools to duplicate data from a hard disk or other media. In some cases, the tools may be software, whereas hardware may also be used to acquire evidence from suspect machines. The hardware and software-based solutions will create bitstream images of the disk and include any data that is visible to the file system, as well as hidden, deleted, and fragments of files, the MBR, partition table, and any number of other items on a disk. Software can then mount these images and view the data in a variety of ways. Many tools will even allow you to preview the data without extracting it from the forensic image file.

Exam Objectives Fast Track

Recovering Deleted Files and Deleted Partitions

- A deleted file is any file that has been logically erased from the file system but may still remain physically on storage media. When a file is deleted, it doesn't necessarily mean that the data cannot be completely or partially recovered.

- *DEL* and *ERASE* are command line utilities that remove a file from any writable storage media, and they have been available on Microsoft operating systems since DOS.

- When a file is deleted from storage media, the pointer to that file is removed from the file allocation table (on FAT/FAT32 file systems) or MFT on NTFS volumes.

- Moving a file from one hard disk or partition to another is a process of first copying the file to a new location and then deleting the file in the original location.

- Disk Cleanup is a Windows XP tool used to remove files that are safe to delete.

- Disk erasing software wipes the disk clean by erasing all of the files and overwriting the disk space with a series of ones and zeros.

- A degausser or bulk demagnetizer is hardware that can be used to destroy data stored on magnetic media such as floppy disks and backup tapes.

- A Recycle Bin or Trash Can is a repository where files are temporarily stored after they are deleted.

- Only files deleted from the local hard disk are placed in the Recycle Bin. Files deleted from a network drive or removable storage are not placed in the Recycle Bin, nor are files deleted from compressed folders, files deleted using commands from the Command Prompt, or those that you delete using noncompliant software.

- A Recycle Bin folder is allocated for each partition on a hard disk. For each hard disk or partition setup on your machine, there is a different Recycle Bin that can be configured and used to store deleted items.

- By default, 10% of the Recycle Bin (up to 3.99 GB) can be allocated for use by the Recycle Bin. For Windows Vista, this amount is increased. In Windows Vista, 10% of the disk space can be used on drives up to 40 GB, but above that, Windows Vista allows a maximum of 4 GB plus 5% of the disk capacity.

- Any file that is too large to be stored in the Recycle Bin is permanently deleted.

- The Recycle Bin automatically removes files on the basis of first in, first out (FIFO). If the amount of data stored in the Recycle Bin exceeds the maximum storage capacity, then the oldest files are removed so that newly deleted files can be stored.

- Information on a deleted file is stored in a hidden index file named INFO. On Windows 95 machines and partitions using NTFS, this file is called INFO2. This file keeps track of a deleted file's original name and location.

- The Recycle Bin's storage location varies between file systems and operating systems. On FAT file systems, the folder is named *RECYCLED*. On NTFS file systems used by Windows Vista, this folder is named *$Recycle.Bin*. On NTFS file systems used by Windows NT, 2000, and XP, this folder is named *RECYCLER*. There is one Recycle Bin for each user who logs onto the computer using NTFS, and these are sorted under the RECYCLER folder by each user's Security Identifier (SID).

- Desktop environments can be used on Linux machines that provide a Recycle Bin. Commands can also be used to delete files, but these will require data recovery to restore the data.

- Data recovery is a process of salvaging data that was lost or deleted, whereas computer forensics is a process of gathering and examining evidence.

- Data recovery tools are designed to restore data that has been deleted or corrupted from any number of sources, including hard disks, CDs, DVDs, Blu-ray, HD-DVD, floppy disks, memory cards used in digital cameras, and other storage media.

- Partitioning a hard disk involves dividing the disk into volumes, which generally appear to the operating system as logical drives, identified by different drive letters.

- When a partition is deleted, partitioning utilities do not erase the data on a disk; they only delete and manipulate the partition tables.

- Partitions can be created and deleted in Windows using the Computer Management (Local) console.

- FDISK is a command line interpreter that is used to create and delete partitions on computers running MS-DOS, Windows 9*x*, Windows NT, or Windows ME.

- DISKPART is a command line interpreter that is used to create and delete partitions on computers running Windows 2000, Windows XP, or Windows Vista.

- Partition recovery tools perform a number of automated tasks that will attempt to restore a damaged or deleted partition and/or restore data from that partition.

Data Acquisition and Duplication

- Computer forensics requires that a bitstream image is created. The image is an exact duplicate of the suspect's computer or other storage media, and it allows a copy of the data to be analyzed so that the original data is preserved.

- Data duplication may involve duplicating hard disks, magnetic tapes, optical disks, or other storage media.

- Write protection devices prevent data from being written to the disk that's being duplicated.

- Hardware tools may also be used to acquire data from a suspect machine. Some of these tools are designed for use in the field, are portable, and provide capabilities to duplicate and analyze data.

- *dd* is a command used on Linux/Unix machines to convert and copy data. A version of this tool is also available for computers running Windows.

- Netcat is a tool used on Linux/Unix machines to transfer data and perform other functions. A version of this tool is also available for Windows. Although it is a useful tool for network administrators, it is considered a hacking tool.

Exam Objectives
Frequently Asked Questions

The following Frequently Asked Questions, answered by the authors of this book, are designed to both measure your understanding of the Exam Objectives presented in this chapter, and to assist you with real-life implementation of these concepts.

Q: I have restored a deleted file, but when I open it, the file is empty. What happened?

A: The file is probably zero length. Because the file size is zero, an empty file is created. If clusters were used by other files, it was overwritten. Because so much data was overwritten by another file, there was nothing to recover.

Q: I am preparing to back up data on my hard disk using a partition recovery tool. What data should I back up?

A: You should make an image of all data on the disk so that this can be restored in the event of a problem. The image file could be stored on a network server or another disk, where it will be safe until you need it. You should also back up the MBR, partition table, and boot sectors, which can be restored after a problem occurs.

Q: If software is available to create a forensic image of a hard disk or other media, what is the benefit of forensic hardware?

A: Different types of forensic hardware are available. Write-blocking tools may be used to prevent data from being written to a suspect hard disk or other media. Forensic tools are also available, which can be connected to an unopened computer or hard disk and acquire data from it. In some cases, they even provide the ability to perform analysis of the acquired data in the field. Many of these tools are portable, allowing you to carry them to a crime scene, and can provide the ability to acquire data from multiple hard drives at high speeds.

Q: Why is it important that all the software used by law enforcement officers be licensed and registered? Law enforcement budgets are often tight; why not use freeware as much as possible?

A: Some freeware and shareware tools available on the Internet are good tools, and the price is certainly right. However, there are some dangers in using these programs for forensic purposes. First, you never know exactly what you're getting when you download a free program (and you certainly can't ask for your money back if it doesn't work properly). Downloads can be infected with viruses or Trojans that can damage the systems on which you use them. Using unlicensed software (illegal copies) is even worse. The opposing attorney(s) will have a field day if he or she discovers that the police used pirated or "borrowed" software in the investigation. This behavior can destroy the credibility of the people who conducted the forensic examination and even result in losing the case. In addition, with properly purchased and registered software, you will be able to get technical support from the vendor if necessary. Makers of computer forensics software often offer discounts to law enforcement agencies, making it easier to afford the proper tools for the job. After all, officers and agencies probably wouldn't suggest saving money by buying their duty weapons from a pawnshop; that's because these are essential tools of the trade and must be as reliable as possible. For the cybercrime investigator or technician, the same is true of the forensics software that is used to collect and preserve evidence that can make or break a criminal case.

CHFI

Windows, Linux, and Macintosh Boot Processes

Exam objectives in this chapter:

- The Boot Process
- The Macintosh Boot Process
- Macintosh Forensic Software

Exam Objectives Review:

- ☑ Summary of Exam Objectives
- ☑ Exam Objectives Fast Track
- ☑ Exam Objectives Frequently Asked Questions

Introduction

In this chapter we will look at the startup process that most computers go through and how the fundamental operating systems get loaded and started. You will see that computers start with tiny steps that build on each other, getting larger until the entire system is loaded and running. Only then can you, the end user, issue commands that the computer interprets and understands.

One of the most popular analogies for how a computer starts up is the amnesia scenario. For a moment look around you at the things you use everyday: telephones, pencils, coffee cups, and so on. Now imagine that you closed your eyes and when you opened them you didn't recognize any of those things, and didn't know how they worked. That is what happens inside a computer when you press the reset or the power button.

At the most fundamental level, computers understand only two things: true and false. The process of getting the computer from being a completely blank state to a fully running operating system is one of the fundamental items that every investigator should understand.

After looking at how a Macintosh boots, we will look at some of the tools that are available for analyzing Macintosh systems using both the Macintosh and Windows operating systems.

The Boot Process

The term "boot," depending on whom you talk to, came either from the old phrase, "Pulling one's self up by the bootstraps," or just from the word "bootstrap," meaning the leather tabs you use to pull on your boots. Either way it is a part of computer history and lore and is commonly used as the computer term for the initial startup of the system. All systems that are able to run Microsoft or Linux operating systems use the same boot up process. Once the computer completes this initial startup the specific operating system will load what it needs to continue. First we will look at the boot process in detail.

System Startup

When the computer power is first applied, a series of very small programs are executed in series leading to the eventual fully running system. Each small program builds on the previous until the entire operating system is loaded and operational.

Much like the character in the movie where the person with amnesia wakes up every morning not knowing what happened the day before, the computer needs to rediscover the world every time it is awakened.

When the power switch is engaged, circuits in the power supply go through an initial surge and then settle to a smooth output of 5 and 12 volts typically. When the voltage and amperage are within specifications, a power-good signal is generated and sent to the microprocessor. Think of this as the computer's wake-up call.

POST: Power On Self Test

The microprocessor then goes through a reset that clears its registers and memory and begins to execute the program stored in the Read-only Memory (ROM) Basic Input-Output System (BIOS) starting at address hF000. This small program tests the basic motherboard functions and will report any errors with audio beep codes. This small program is known as the Power On Self Test (POST).

In addition to the audio beeps, most modern computers also send a diagnostic code to internal port h80 if an error occurs. Diagnostic cards are available that plug into the ISA/PCI/AGP slots on motherboard that read these codes and give more comprehensive error reports.

The next step is for the BIOS to search for a video display adapter that has its own ROM. After verifying the checksum of the video ROM the BIOS will execute that ROM code to initialize the video adapter. Successful completion of the video ROM test and load usually produces a blinking cursor on the screen at a minimum. Different video ROMs do different things on completion, including flashy rainbow colored logos, for example.

The BIOS then checks the value at memory location h0472 for the existence of h1234, which is the indicator of a warm start, meaning that the computer is being restarted. Any other value indicates the computer is coming up from a cold start or powered off state.

If the computer is being cold started then the complete BIOS POST is performed, otherwise an abbreviated POST is done. In most modern computers the BIOS settings will let you skip things like full memory testing if you are just restarting the machine.

If a cold start is being performed the computer will read and write to every memory location in Random Access Memory (RAM) to verify that it is working properly. On most computer systems, you will see a counter or progress bar on the screen at this stage showing the status of this memory test.

It is at this point that the POST looks for the existence of a keyboard, and checks for any key press actions. If keys have been pressed, the program stores that information for action at the completion of the POST process. The keys pressed may be requests for access to the BIOS setup menu or the key command to boot from the network.

The computer then checks for the existence of any floppy or hard disk drives. Any devices found are compared to the contents of the configuration information stored in the CMOS memory chip on the motherboard. This chip has a small battery attached to it, keeping the data stored inside active when the computer is powered off.

The BIOS then scans memory for any other ROMs in the range of hC800 to hDF80 that may contain any additional code needing to be executed for other adapter cards like sound cards, RAID arrays, and such. If a ROM is found then the checksum is tested and programs found are run for each device in order.

If new devices are found during this stage the system may display the BIOS Setup screen, allowing you to make the modifications permanent.

Traditionally, if you hear a single beep, the system has completed the POST and is proceeding with Operating System Load.

The Master Boot Record

The BIOS will then search for a volume boot sector at cylinder 0, head 0, and sector 1 of the default boot drive. Historically the default boot drive was the first floppy disk drive. Modern configurations allow you to designate any drive, or external device like a USB thumb drive or even the network interface card as a boot device.

If there doesn't appear to be bootable code at the first sector, then the BIOS will look for a Master Partition Record at that location. If there is no Master Partition Record then the system will display an error similar to:

Non-System disk or disk error

Replace and strike any key when ready

DISK BOOT FAILURE, INSERT SYSTEM DISK AND PRESS ENTER

If a volume boot record is found, the program is loaded and tested to ensure that the last two bytes are h55AA, and then the program is run. This program is very small since it must stay within a 512 byte sector. The actual program can only be 444 bytes long.

The Master Boot Record (MBR) is traditionally the first 512 bytes, or the first sector (sector 0), of a storage device like a hard disk drive that is bootable.

The 512 bytes are broken down as shown in Figure 5.1; the first 444 bytes are allocated for any boot program, end of code marker of two nulls (h00), four 16 byte master partition records, and the end of MBR marker of h55AA.

Figure 5.1 The MBR Layout

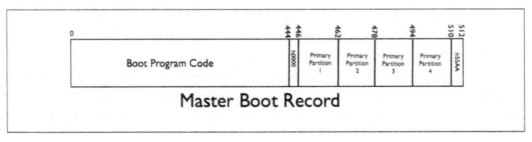

The Master Partition Table entries are broken down as shown in Table 5.1. There can be up to four entries in this area of the MBR.

Table 5.1 Master Partition Table Entries

Byte Offset/Length	Contents	Value
0 (I byte)	Boot Indicator Byte	h80 = Bootable h00 = Nonbootable
1 (3 bytes)	Cylinder/Head/Sector (CHS) of Partition Start	(Variable)
4 (1 byte)	Partition Type	h00 = No Partition h01 = DOS 12 bit FAT h04 = DOS 16 bit FAT h05 = Extended DOS h06 = Primary DOS h07 = OS2 h08 = AIX (File Sys) h09 = AIX (boot) h64 = Novell NetWare hFF = Unix Bad Block Table
5 (3 bytes)	Cylinder/Head/Sector (CHS) of Partition End	(Variable)
8 (4 bytes)	Relative Sector Offset of Partition	(Variable)
12 (4 bytes)	Partition size in sectors	(Variable)

The Partition Type values shown are some of the more common found; different operating systems can use different values.

Damage & Defense…

The Worst Place to Get a Virus

In the days of bootable floppy disks, Master Boot Record (MBR) viruses were much more prevalent. With fewer people using or even having a floppy disk drive in their computer, MBR attacks are harder to accomplish. This does not mean that they can't be done!

It is a very good practice to scan boot media that is from a less than obvious source. Placing MBR viruses on bootable USB media or copied CDs and DVDs is still a very real threat.

Since MBR code runs well before any antivirus program it can infect and rootkit your machine before you even realize it.

Loading MSDOS

The volume boot record program has only two things it must do: look for the existence of the files, IO.sys and MSDOS.sys (or in some cases IBMDOS.com); and then load and run IO.sys. Once IO.sys is running, the boot record program is no longer needed.

IO.sys contains a routine called SYSINT, which facilitates the loading of additional drivers and settings that the system will need in order to complete loading the operating system.

Part of the SYSINT process loads the MSDOS.sys program that resets the disk system, resets and initializes attached devices, and sets the system to the default parameters.

If SYSINT finds a CONFIG.sys file in the root directory of the default boot device, it passes the contents to MSDOS.sys for processing. The CONFIG.sys file contains directives that define the number of files and file buffers to allocate for this system, and may contain more device drivers to be loaded for special attached devices.

Then the SYSINT routine loads COMMAND.com, which is referred to as a shell program. It contains the last of the device extensions to the base operating system. It also contains the standard command line programs like ECHO, DIR, and FORMAT.

The last thing that COMMAND.com has SYSINT do is look for a file in the root directory of the default drive called AUTOEXEC.bat, which may contain programs and commands that the user wants executed each time at startup. If this file is found, COMMAND.com executes the directives in the file and when that is complete the user is presented with the command prompt. The default command prompt is the default drive letter, a colon, and the greater than sign (example: "A:>"). This prompt can be changed by the Prompt command in the AUTOEXEC.bat file.

Loading Windows XP

On disks that are configured to boot Windows XP, the volume boot record program looks for a program called NT Loader, or NTLDR for short. This program determines the file system of the default boot drive, which should be either FAT or NTFS.

If the operating system had been put to sleep or placed in hibernate mode, and the NTLDR finds a HIBERFIL.sys file, it will reload the contents of the file to RAM and resume operations at the point the system went to sleep.

Otherwise, the NTLDR looks for the BOOT.ini file in the root directory of the default drive.

NTLDR will display the versions of the operating system in a "boot menu" and waits a specified number of seconds before loading the first in the list (see Figure 5.2).

Figure 5.2 The Windows Boot Menu

```
Please select the operating system to start:

    Microsoft Windows XP Professional
    Microsoft Windows 98

Use the up and down arrow keys to move the highlight to your choice.
Press ENTER to choose.
Seconds until highlighted choice will be started automatically: 26

For troubleshooting and advanced startup options for Windows, press F8.
```

Once the operating system version has been selected, NTLDR runs the NTDETECT.com program to gather and verify the configuration of the computer.

After verifying the computer configuration the Hardware Abstraction Layer linked library HAL.dll is read into memory and then the Windows kernel NTOSKRNL.exe is loaded. Only after a series of driver checks and verifying that nothing has changed since the last run, or if the system was shut down improperly, does the NTLDR pass control to the kernel. If all goes well the end user sees the familiar login screen and is prompted to enter a username and password.

The number and types of checks that are run during this last phase of the boot process can be many depending on the configuration of the system, the version of the operating system, and the options that the administrator of the system has enabled. For more information on this exact process, see the Microsoft TechNet article *Troubleshooting the Startup Process* at http://technet.microsoft.com/en-us/library/bb457123.aspx.

Loading Linux

If the system to be loaded is a Linux-based system, then the volume boot record program will find the existence of either Grand Unified Boot Loader (GRUB) or the older Linux Loader (LILO). Both programs are boot loaders with LILO being the smaller and less feature-driven version for smaller systems. GRUB is the boot loader of choice on most modern systems since it allows for more interactive choices during the boot process.

LILO Booting

LILO is known as a Two Stage Loader, and stage one is stored in the 444 bytes of the MBR. Its primary functions are to gather the disk geometry information and load the second stage. The second stage is then loaded into memory and the Linux version is displayed on the screen. If there is more than one Linux kernel available in the LILO configuration file (/boot/boot.b) a menu of the available OS versions is displayed.

Either the menu choice or the default operating system version kernel and the contents of INITRD are loaded into RAM and LILO gives control to the kernel. Typically, LILO gives a command line login prompt only at completion.

The important files to LILO are:

- /sbin/lilo (the kernel installer)
- /boot/boot.b (the bootloader)
- /boot/map (tells LILO where the kernel is on the drive)
- /etc/lilo.conf (LILO configuration file)

GRUB Booting

GRB is *technically* also a two-stage loader as we will see. Like LILO, GRUB starts with the stage one loaded in the 444 bytes of the MBR. Stage one will load either stage 1.5 or 2 as required when the boot drive uses LBA mode or if the /boot partition is located beyond cylinder 1024. The stage 1.5 program code typically is found in the /boot partition.

The stage two boot loader is then read into memory and in turn loads the operating system kernel and the contents of INITRD. If multiple versions of the operating system are found in the configuration file GRUB will display a menu of those available and wait for a choice before loading that configured version of the OS. GRUB gives control of the system to the kernel and a login prompt either on the command line or via GUI window is presented to the end user.

The GRUB configuration file may be in several locations depending on the version of Linux, it can also be located on a removable USB drive! Some possible locations and names are:

- /boot/grub/menu.lst (SUSE and Debian)
- /boot/grub/grub.conf (Fedora uses this and the menu.lst above for compatibility.)

The Macintosh Boot Process

In this section, we will briefly examine the way an Apple Macintosh computer boots. The information here is for the Mac OS X version of their operating system using Intel based microprocessors. Older Motorola chipset Macintosh computers use a much different boot process.

OS X uses Open Firmware that is very much like the BIOS noted earlier. The Open Firmware that Apple uses in the Macintosh is based on the IEEE-1275 standard.

EFI and BIOS: Similar but Different

Just like any other computer on the market, when the power switch is activated on a Macintosh, the system goes through a Power On Self Test (POST), resets the microprocessor, and starts the execution of initialization code, which is the Open Firmware instead of BIOS.

Like the BIOS, Extensible Firmware Interface (EFI) checks the configuration of the machine and loads any device ROMs that it finds into memory. It then looks for a default boot device… and here is where it gets interesting. There are numerous optional startup functions that EFI can perform based on user input. Single keys, known as "snag keys," can be pressed that will allow the system to boot from specific devices.

- Pressing the C key will attempt to boot from the CD/DVD-ROM drive.
- Pressing the D key will attempt to boot from the first hard disk drive.
- Pressing the N key will attempt to boot from the Network Interface Controller (NIC).
- Pressing the Z key will attempt to boot from the ZIP drive.

It is also possible to enter the EFI interactive console mode by pressing the cmd-opt-O-F key combination during power up. (Note: If you are like me and just tried this before reading on, typing mac-boot at the prompt will let the Macintosh finish booting.) You should read a good source of Open Firmware/EFI commands before trying the console mode. An excellent mirror of the Open Firmware Working Group is at http://bananjr6000.apple.com/1275/.

The EFI program is located in the BOOT.efi file. This is the portion of the boot loading process that loads the OSX kernel and starts the user interface.

DARWIN

To many die-hard Macintosh users the move to OS X wasn't immediately seen as a move to the open source Unix environment. It wasn't long before they realized their beloved Mac was now a Unix machine. When you look at the roots of OS X, a large number of open source modules and programs were obtained from other groups including Carnegie Mellon, FreeBSD, GNU, Mach, Xfree86, NEXTSTEP, and OPENSTEP.

The OS X Kernel

In a nutshell the real OS X is when the combination of several components come together. XNU is the actual OS X kernel name on the boot drive. It is comprised of the following modules:

- Mach – Provides the service layer to the kernel

- BSD – Provides the primary system program interface

- I/O Toolkit – Provides driver support

- LIBSA & LIBKERN –Kernel libraries

- The Platform Expert – A motherboard-specific hardware abstraction layer

- Apple I/O components – The unique Mac interfaces

Apple uses proprietary components to invoke the Macintosh look and feel to the open source products listed. Carbon, Cocoa, Quartz, OpenGL, QuickTime, and the Aqua interfaces are just a few of the unique interfaces that make the Macintosh so special.

Notes from the Underground…

Bad Guy Won't Give You The Password? No Problem!

If you need to investigate a Macintosh that is running OS X and you need to access a program on a booted forensic copy of the subject's drive, and he won't give you his login password, don't worry. If you have any version of the Macintosh OS X boot CD or DVD, place that in the examination system and hold down the C key to boot from the CD/DVD drive.

When the system asks if you want to install/reinstall OS X, choose the Password Reset Utility from the drop-down menus at the top of the screen. You will be shown a list of users and you can pick one or all of them and change the password of the accounts to something you know. Problem solved!

Macintosh Forensic Software

Only recently has the Macintosh begun to be accepted in the forensic community. Listed next are just a few of the tools that can make forensics of OS X systems easier.

As with all forensic tools, the examiner should have a solid understanding of how tools work and should be able to prove by demonstration that each finding produced by the tool can be duplicated in a court of law.

BlackBag Forensic Suite

BlackBag Technologies, Inc. is one of the few providers of forensic software for the Macintosh platform. Its *Macintosh Forensic Suite* is a collection of 26 modules that can be launched individually or from the *Forensic Suite Toolbar* (see Figure 5.3).

Figure 5.3 The Forensic Suite Toolbar Is a Fast Way to Launch Programs in the Suite

Directory Scan

The Directory Scan utility allows you to view all the files and folders on a Macintosh volume (see Figure 5.4). A volume can be any mounted storage device including USB or Firewire

devices. All files, including invisible files, can be examined to include Data Fork/Resource Fork data sizes, Creator and Type codes, and all important date/time stamps.

You can select individual files and folders for export to a new directory for further examination as well as printing a comprehensive report on all the files viewed or selected in the main window.

Figure 5.4 A Fully Expanded Directory Scan Window Can Be Quite Large

Data and Resource Forks

The Macintosh file system is unique in that every file contains two parts known as Forks. The Resource Fork typically contains program components like preferences for the file, special menus or icons, special controls or buttons and the last window position.

The Data Fork typically contains the data that the user supplied or created as part of the file. It is not uncommon to find that one fork is empty. Knowing how these two forks interact can be of great benefit during tough investigations of Macintosh computers.

More information can be found at the Apple Developer Connection: The Data Fork and the Resource Fork: http://developer.apple.com/documentation/mac/MoreToolbox/MoreToolbox-11.html.

Head of the Class…

FileSpy

When you need to take a quick look inside of a file that has forks, FileSpy is a good tool (see Figure 5.5). This utility allow you to view either fork in a file, see the relative sizes of each fork, and move to any sector of a file directly. The utility even includes an ASCII filter to aid in file viewing.

Figure 5.5 FileSpy Allows You to See the Raw EXIF Data in a JPG File

HeaderBuilder

Because the header is a calculated portion of Macintosh files, changing the header or repairing one can be time and math intensive using a traditional hex editor. HeaderBuilder makes this an easy task by allowing you to make the changes and then generate the CRC32 checksum and the MD5 hash of the file immediately (see Figure 5.6).

Figure 5.6 HeaderBuilder Makes Changing Headers Easy and Shows MD5 Hashes Quickly

Other Tools

Other utilities in the Forensic Suite include:

- Breakup – Splits large folders or files into more manageable sizes.

- Comment Hunter – Looks in the Comment fields of Mac files for keywords.

- DCFLDDassistant – Launches the Macintosh version of DCFLDD.

- File Searcher – Looks for specific filenames or Type/Creator codes.

- GraphicView – Uses the QuickTime engine to view files or movies.

- HFS Extractor – Converts image file formats (Safeback, Linux, DD, FWB).

- ImageBuster – Searches image files for keywords.

- ListBuilder – Allows you to create keyword lists in native languages (Spanish, Russian, etc.).

- LockMaster – Allows you to quickly lock or unlock a large number of files/folders.

- MacCarver – Lets you carve image files from within a container.

- PhantomSearch – Allows you to capture all the invisible files of a volume.

- Typer – A very fast little utility that shows/changes the Type/Creator for a given file.

- VolumeExplorer – HFS partition analyzer.

Carbon Copy Cloner

Mike Bombich has created a handy utility called Carbon Copy Cloner (CCC) for making backups or copies of important data on your Macintosh. It is a front-end for several less than intuitive utilities that are part of OS X.

As the name implies CCC can clone one hard disk to another when you use its default options. This copy can also be made to an image file on another drive, but it should be noted that this is not a forensic copy of the original (see Figure 5.7).

Documentation is available at the Bombich Software site: www.bombich.com/software/ccc.html.

Figure 5.7 Selecting the Source and Destination Drive Is a Simple Matter

Only Macintosh formatted volumes can be "cloned" using CCC; any other DOS or Unix formats are not recognized in the drop-down menus. If you do not have psync installed, you can install it from the Preferences menu (see Figure 5.8).

Figure 5.8 The Preferences Menu

Note the list of files that are not copied in the Advance Settings Dialog (see Figure 5.9).

Figure 5.9 The Advance Settings Dialog

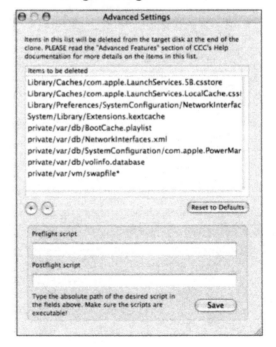

The CCC documentation goes into more detail on the list of files that are not copied during the clone process. This can be because of PowerMac to Intel Macintosh copying causing problems. When in doubt check the reference material or the online forum.

MacDrive6/7

Technically Mediafour MacDrive 6 or 7 is not Macintosh software; it really is a Windows program that lets you mount and read Macintosh formatted volumes. MacDrive 6 is for Windows 2000 and 98SE; MacDrive 7 is for Windows XP (see Figure 5.10), Vista, and Server 2003.

If you have a Windows-based workstation and need to quickly view some files on a Macintosh volume, this utility can be very helpful.

Figure 5.10 The Main MacDrive7 Screen (Windows XP Version)

From the main menu you have the quick choices of Exploring a Macintosh volume, burning a Macintosh formatted CD or DVD, and formatting or repairing a Macintosh formatted volume. Mounted Macintosh volumes are shown with a small red Apple logo (see Figure 5.11).

Figure 5.11 Macintosh Options

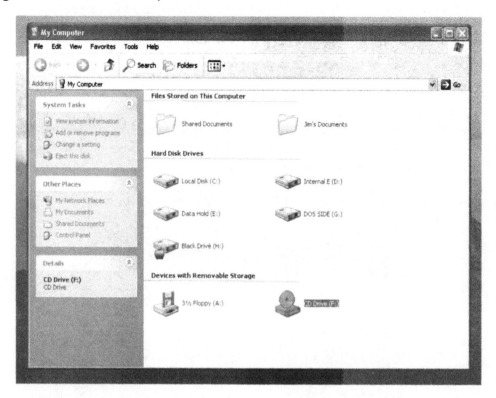

Summary of Exam Objectives

Now you can see how the computer progresses through the steps of booting up. The power supply generates the Power-Good signal that resets the microprocessor and starts the loading of the BIOS from the Boot ROMs. Then the computer checks all its basic functions during the Power On Self Test (POST). If the POST is successful the computer then progresses through the different phases of loading the necessary drivers and initialization code that eventually leads to the computer finding the Boot Loader for a given operating system, which it then loads and runs. Finally the kernel of the operating system is loaded and the computer completes the boot process when the login prompt or command prompt is displayed and the computer is waiting for input.

You should also be familiar with the Master Boot Record (MBR) and how it is used in the boot process. The LILO and GRUB boot loaders for the Linux operating systems should be familiar now along with the Extensible Firmware Interface for the Macintosh OS.

Exam Objectives Fast Track

The Boot Process

- ☑ Know that POST stands for Power On Self Test
- ☑ Know that the Power-Good signal comes from the power supply.
- ☑ Know what port the POST error codes are sent to.
- ☑ Know where the MBR is on a boot device.
- ☑ Know the layout of the MBR.
- ☑ Know the end of file marker of the MBR.
- ☑ Know what files are needed for MSDOS to load properly.
- ☑ Know what files are needed for Windows to load properly.
- ☑ Know what files are needed for Linux to load properly.
- ☑ Know what files are needed for Mac OS X to load properly.
- ☑ Know the locations of the files listed for each OS.

The Macintosh Boot Process

☑ Know that Macintosh OS X uses a form of Open Firmware known as Extensible Firmware Interface.

☑ Know that there are special "snag keys" that allow for different boot options.

☑ Know that Macintosh files have two forks—a data fork and a resource fork.

☑ Be aware of the various sources of the modules that make up the OS X Kernel.

Macintosh Forensic Software

☑ Be aware of the forensic tools that make up the BlackBag Forensic Suite.

☑ Know that using Carbon Copy Cloner is good for copying Mac OS X files, but does not make forensic copies of media.

☑ Be aware of the MacDrive 6/7 tool to read Macintosh OS X formatted media in a Windows environment.

Exam Objectives Frequently Asked Questions

The following Frequently Asked Questions, answered by the authors of this book, are designed to both measure your understanding of the Exam Objectives presented in this chapter, and to assist you with real-life implementation of these concepts.

Q: Where is the Master Boot Record located?

A: The Master Boot Record is always located at Cylinder 0, Head 0, Sector 0 of a boot device or disk.

Q: How large is the Master Boot Record?

A: The Master Boot Record (MBR) is 512 bytes long and always ends with the end-of-file marker of h55AA.

Q: Do all Power On Self Test programs send error codes to port h80?

A: No. Some vendors of BIOS programs send error codes to other port numbers. This is typically a function of the card interface type. ISA uses port h80, EISA

can use port h30, and so on. Most vendors have the error code ports listed on their web support sites.

Q: Is it true that the MSDOS command FDISK can refresh the Master Boot Record?

A: Yes! It is an undocumented feature of the FDISK command. FIDSK /MBR is the command.

Q: If I don't want the versions of Windows that are listed in the Boot menu , can I edit BOOT.ini manually to remove the ones I don't want?

A: The answer here is yes and no. It is possible to simply remove the lines for the Windows versions you don't want; however, they will still exist and take up room on the disk. It is better to follow Microsoft's guidance on removing these properly.

Q: If Macintosh OS X is for Intel-based processor systems, will it run on my PC?

A: There has been a lot of discussion on some of the hacker sites about a "hacked "version of Mac OS X running on regular Intel boxes. Using one of these modified versions is a violation of licensing with Apple Computers.

CHFI

Windows and Linux Forensics

Exam objectives in this chapter:

- **Windows Forensics**
- **Linux Forensics**

Exam Objectives Review:

- ☑ **Summary of Exam Objectives**
- ☑ **Exam Objectives Frequently Asked Questions**

Introduction

In this chapter we introduce the reader to both Windows and Linux-based forensic tools. The chapter is split into two sections which reflect Module 10: Windows Forensics and Module 11: Linux Forensics respectively. The forensic analyst should be conversant with both Windows and Linux. In the course of a career you will be expected to work with both fairly regularly. Although it is likely that you will have personal preferences, a thorough understanding of the strengths and weaknesses of each type of system will aid you in understanding both of them and also provide you with a wealth of additional tools.

By limiting the choices to a single operating system you are severely restricting your options. As such the best choice is to become familiar with the complete range of options available and this means gaining an understanding of both Windows and Linux.

Often, the most fruitful process for gathering evidence involves the use of both Windows and Linux-based tools. There are a number of Windows tools that enable the collection of data from live systems. Many Linux-based tools, on the other hand, provide a depth of analysis rarely found in any Windows-based tool. The combination of both Windows and Linux allows for the introduction of the strengths of both tool sets while removing many of the weaknesses.

Windows Forensics

The first section of this chapter is designed to introduce the reader to the forensic process under Windows. Even the most diehard Linux enthusiast will occasionally come across a live Windows system. Rather than shutting the system down, a large amount of volatile evidence may be collected on a live system. The section objectives include:

- Locating and gathering volatile evidence on a Windows host
- Investigating Windows file slack for evidence
- Interpreting the Windows registry and memory dump information
- Analyzing Internet trace data and events
- Investigating the system state backups

Where Can You Locate and Gather Evidence on a Windows Host?

The term "evidence location" refers to the process of investigating and gathering information of a forensic nature and particularly of legal importance. This evidence aids in the investigation of both criminal investigations and civil suits.

The Windows operating system contains a number of locations that can act as a rich source of evidence. Information gathering through investigating hidden files can be extremely helpful to any investigation.

Even file attributes and time stamps are valuable. Often, a perpetrator may attempt to change a file's attributes in order to either cover their tracks or hide important data that may be present in the system. Collating time stamps, for instance, can aid in reconstructing the actions taken by the suspect.

Some of the more important sources of electronic evidence on a Windows host include:

- Files
- Slack space
- Swap file
- Unallocated clusters
- Unused partitions
- Hidden partitions

TEST DAY TIP

Remember the order in which you should search for data on a Windows system. Start with collecting the volatile data and work through to check the Internet traces (see Figure 6.1). Don't forget the steps in the middle!

How Can You Gather Volatile Evidence?

One of the most crucial aspects of digital forensics is one of the most often overlooked. This is the gathering of volatile data as evidence. When investigating a Windows-based operating system for possible evidence or information and facts relevant to the case, it is important to ensure that you have collected all relevant volatile data. Volatile data maintains current information about the system, the registry, cache, and memory. As such, if the system is powered down, valuable information is lost and may not be recovered. With nonvolatile memory, however, the data is not lost when the power is cycled.

Figure 6.1 Steps for Searching for Data on a Windows-Based System

Some of the most crucial areas to check for evidence within volatile data include: registers, cache, physical and virtual memory, network connections, running processes, and disk (for instance, the page file). Any external device associated with the system should also be considered and checked for evidence (floppy disk, tape, CD-ROM, and printers). Captured data must then be gathered and saved in external devices so that it may be safely removed and kept offline at another location.

RFC 3227 lists the order of volatility in a Windows-based system as:

- Registers, cache
- Routing table, ARP cache, process table, kernel statistics
- Memory

- Temporary file systems

- Disk

- Remote logging and monitoring data that is relevant to the system in question

- Physical configuration, network topology

- Archival media

EXAM WARNING

It is important to understand the different sources of volatile data and how to capture them. RFC 3227 (Guidelines for Evidence Collection and Archiving) provides the best practice guidelines for how to collect volatile evidence.

This document is available from: www.faqs.org/rfcs/rfc3227.html

The Features and Advantages of Windows Forensics Tools

It should be clear that with the majority of systems running Windows throughout the world, a large percentage of all incidents and thus forensic analysis will be conducted against Windows hosts. The ability to gather data on a live Windows system is incredibly valuable. Although offline imaging and searching through disk images is the standard fare of a computer forensic analyst, the value of volatile information should never be overlooked.

Further, there are times when it may not be feasible to take a system offline for imaging. In the case of a large e-commerce site (such as eBay) where any downtime is calculated in the millions of dollars, when critical infrastructure is a factor, or when a system must be maintained online, the ability to capture, image, and analyze a system while it is live can be of immense value.

The tools listed in this section not only provide a means of forensically capturing images of drives, but also enable the capturing and analysis of critical volatile data that would be lost if the system was powered down. In fact, these tools may be used to determine not only the nature of an incident but also whether an incident occurred. When something appears to be wrong, the cause is not always clear.

TEST DAY TIP

Helix Live Acquisition can capture an image of the system's physical memory (RAM). This can be of great eventual value as many programs retain data in memory long after they have closed. It is important to remember that all changes on a live system have an impact. As such, remember to capture physical memory prior to capturing a disk image or running other tools as these will change the memory and possibly destroy critical evidence.

Helix Live on Windows

Helix runs on Windows as a standard application. In this mode it is used to collect evidence from active or live Windows systems. Remember: the state of a live system is in constant flux—it is constantly changing. Working on a live system will disturb the system state. Even if you do "nothing," you change the state of the system by running an application, changing the virtual memory, and so forth. Alternatively, turning off the system will result in the destruction of the same evidence; that is, the loss of potentially important forensic information. Tools such as Helix may be used to collect volatile information. There are also situations where the system cannot be turned off. Critical infrastructure, medical devices, or even financial markets systems often have to be maintained in a live state and thus imaged in that manner. To aid in this process, Helix presents a portable forensics environment which provides access to many Windows-based tools. Helix presents these tools and options together in a forensically sound manner.

Helix Live Response is really about the tools. The CD contains static binaries for Linux, Solaris, and Windows using GNU utilities and Cygwin tools. These tools include Sysinternal's tools, Garners Forensic Acquisition Utilities suite, Foundstone's open source tools, the Windows Debugger, and the Windows Forensic Toolchest, amongst others. All these tools are accessible from the Helix.exe application.

The Helix.exe graphical application only operates in a live Windows environment. It has been tested and successfully runs on Windows 98SE, Windows NT4, Windows 2000, Windows 2003, Windows XP, and even Windows Vista. The Helix.exe application will vary slightly on each of these operating systems. Remember that as Windows is live, a number of DLL files are used by Helix and the operating system during this process.

The Windows Live function of Helix is basically a GUI interface (called the Incident Response screen) to a number of tools and a Windows command-line interface. The key benefits are that Helix will be your actions and maintain the integrity of the command line by ensuring that built-in Windows tools (such as netstat or ipconfig) are not run from the compromised system itself, risking evidence corruption or data corruption. This is because Helix

maintains known safe versions of these tools. It is common practice for an attacker to replace system tools (such as ipconfig).

The majority of Windows command-line tools that you will need are available and may be accessed from the Helix.exe application on the CD. These include:

- .cab extractors
- ipconfig
- kill
- netstat
- process explorers and much more

Some of the other valuable tools and applications on the CD that you should become familiar with include:

- An inclusive file attributes browser
- The Rootkit Revealer from Sysinternals
- A screen-capture application
- The PC Inspector data recovery tool

These are the tools that will be most useful. These tools are found in the Helix CD Windows module, which is also useful for a variety of ordinary network tasks. Of course, Helix is a forensics tool first and foremost; thus powerful tools for imaging disks for analysis are included (as well as tools to direct the image files to remote analysis systems).

TEST DAY TIP

These are the tools that will be most likely referred to during the CHFI exam. Remember also that Helix is a forensic suite. It contains powerful tools for both the imaging and analysis of drives. It also allows images to be captured and sent to remote systems

Damage & Defense...

Keep a Log of Your Actions!

Many forensic tools enable you to record your actions. The Helix Live CD allows you to save a log of what you did while using the program. Upon exiting Helix, you will be presented with the option to save your actions as a PDF log file (see Figure 6.2). Always save this file!

This log is your protection. Not only does it provide you with evidence of what you have done, saving on documentation, but it may also be used to validate your actions if they are disputed. Without this file it is just your word. Remember, logs are there for your protection too!

Figure 6.2 The Helix Live CD's Audit Log Option

The Tools Present in Helix CD for Windows Forensics

The following tools are all available from the Windows Live side of Helix. You should become familiar with their use.

EXAM WARNING

Please ensure that you're familiar with these tools. It is likely that you'll be questioned about them on the exam. Take special care to familiarize yourself with both Secreport and the Windows Forensic Toolchest (WFT).

Access PassView This application reveals the database password of password-protected MDB files created using Microsoft Access 95/97/2000/XP or with Jet Database Engine 3.0/4.0.

Astrick Logger This utility can reveal the passwords stored behind the asterisks in standard password text-boxes.

Drive Manager Drive Manager will identify drives which are of the same type. It displays the volume label as well as vendor information so that multiply CD/DVD drives and removable drives such as USB thumb drives can be differentiated by their manufacturer's name, version, and revision date. The serial number can be seen as a unique ID for each drive.

FAU This is an Incident Response tool that can be used to image a system's memory as well as any attached devices.

Forensic Server Project The Forensic Server Project (FSP) is a proof of concept tool for retrieving volatile (and selected non-volatile) data from potentially compromised systems. The FSP consists of several Perl scripts and third-party utilities. The server component of the FSP is run on an investigator or administrator's system, and handles all data storage and activity logging. The client components of the FSP are on the CD so they may be run on the compromised system and connect to the remote server. Data is copied to the server component via TCP/IP.

FTK Imager FTK Imager can acquire physical device images and logically view data from FAT, NTFS, EXT 2 and 3 as well as HFS and HFS+ file systems. It also provides the ability to create multiple images from a single source and/or multiple images simultaneously. FTK Imager generates DD, SMART, and Encase® images and reads several other industry standard formats. Using Isobuster technology, FTK Imager provides ready access to CDFS and DVD file systems and allows access to include multi and open session CDs.

Galleta Galleta parses the information in a cookie file and output the results in a field-delimited manner so that it may be imported into a spreadsheet program.

HoverSnap HoverSnap is a snapshot tool with JPG, PNG, BMP, and GIF support. HoverSnap can take snapshots of the full screen, active window, or a selected area. It

also captures layered windows (alpha-blended ones under 2K/XP). It enables the setup of a capture folder or filename and format. It will reduce the capture size. It allows an auto-generate filename option that will add the time stamp (date/time) to your filename so you can take several captures without having to change the filename.

IECookiesView IECookiesView is a small and handy utility that displays the details of all cookies that IE has stored on a computer. It will also sort the cookies, delete selected ones, view detailed information about each, and even save the cookies to a readable text file. Over a network, it can watch the cookies of other computers. If it has read permission on the cookies folders of other users it can view their cookies (admin rights). IECookiesView also allows the viewing of references to deleted cookies that are still stored in the index.dat file.

IEHistoryView IEHistoryView allows the viewing and modification of the history of visited websites in Internet Explorer. In addition it also may be used to export all or selected items to HTML reports, view detailed properties for selected entries, and sort. The program allows you to access the history of other user accounts or network computers as well, provided that it is run with the proper access rights.

IRCR The Incident Response Collection Report is a script to call a collection of tools that gathers and/or analyzes data on a Microsoft Windows system. It provides a snapshot of the system. The tools are generally oriented towards data collection rather than analysis.

Mail PassView Mail PassView is a small password-recovery tool that reveals the passwords and other account details for Outlook Express, Microsoft Outlook 2000 (POP3 and SMTP Accounts only), Microsoft Outlook 2002/2003 (POP3, IMAP, HTTP, and SMTP Accounts), IncrediMail, Eudora, Netscape 6.x/7.x, Mozilla Thunderbird, Group Mail Free, and Yahoo! Mail email clients.

MEMDump The MEMDump utility is designed to dump or copy any part of 4GB linear memory address space under MS-DOS and Windows 9x DOS to a console, text, or binary file.

MessenPass MessenPass allows the recovery of passwords from a wide variety of popular Instant Messenger programs, including MSN Messenger, Windows Messenger, Yahoo Messenger, ICQ Lite 4.x/2003, AOL Instant Messenger, AOL Instant Messenger/Netscape 7, Trillian, Miranda, and GAIM. When run, it will recover both the username and passwords. The list can be exported to HTML or saved as text file. MessenPass can only be used to recover the passwords for the current logged-on user on your local computer.

MozillaCookiesView MozillaCookiesView is an alternative to the standard "Cookie Manager" provided by Netscape and Mozilla browsers. It displays the details

of all cookies stored inside the cookies file (cookies.txt) in one table, and allows you to save the cookies list into text, HTML, or XML file, delete unwanted cookies, and backup/restore the cookies file.

Network Password Recovery Network Password Recovery can retrieve all network passwords stored on a system for the current logged-on user; this includes any .NET Passport accounts that are stored locally.

Pasco Pasco parses the information contained within an index.dat file and outputs the results in a field delimited manner so that it may be imported into a spreadsheet program.

PC Inspector File Recovery PC Inspector File Recovery is a data recovery program that supports the FAT 12/16/32 and NTFS file systems. It can discover partitions automatically even where the boot sector or FAT has been erased or damaged. It recovers files with the original time and date stamp.

PC On/Off Time This application is a time tracking tool that shows the times a computer has been active during the last 3 weeks. It requires no previous setup.

Process Explorer The Process Explorer display consists of two sub-windows. The top window displays a list of the currently active processes, including the names of their owning accounts. The lower window displayed depends on the mode that Process Explorer is in. When the application is in handle mode you'll see the handles that the process selected in the top window opened. If it is in DLL mode you'll see the DLLs and memory-mapped files that the process has loaded. Process Explorer includes a powerful search capability that will quickly show which processes have particular handles opened or DLLs loaded.

Protected Storage PassView Protected Storage PassView is a small utility that reveals the passwords stored on a computer by Internet Explorer and Outlook Express. The passwords are revealed by reading the information from the Protected Storage. These include all email and web site passwords where you chose "remember password" (not cookie passwords) as well as auto-complete passwords. This utility only shows the passwords of the currently logged-on user and cannot reveal the passwords of other users.

PsTools Suite These tools allow the management of remote systems as well as the local one. PsList is a tool that lets you view detailed information about processes, and the suite is continually growing. The following tools are included in the PsTools suite:

- **.PsExec** Execute processes remotely.
- **.PsFile** Show files opened remotely.
- **.PsGetSid** Display the SID of a computer or a user.

- **.PsKill** Kill processes by name or process ID.

- **.PsInfo** List information about a system.

- **.PsList** List detailed information about processes.

- **.PsLoggedOn** See who's logged on locally and via resource sharing.

- **.PsLogList** Dump event log records.

- **.PsPasswd** Change account passwords.

- **.PsService** View and control services.

- **.PsShutdown** Shut down and optionally reboot a computer.

- **.PsSuspend** Suspend processes.

Pst Password Viewer Password encryption over a PST file is very fragile. For each password-protected PST file, there are many passwords that can open it. PstPassword provides three different passwords for each password-protected PST file. All three passwords provided by PstPassword will open the PST file without problems.

PTFinder PTFinder searches a memory dump of a system running Microsoft Windows for traces of processes and threads. Some functional checks are also applied.

PuTTY SSH Client PuTTY is a free implementation of Telnet and SSH for Win32, with an xterm terminal emulator.

Reg Adds, changes, and displays registry subkey information and values in registry entries, for the Local User.

RegScanner RegScanner is a small utility that allows you to scan the Registry, find the desired Registry values that match to the specified search criteria, and display them in a list. It can also export the found Registry values into a REG file that can be used in RegEdit.

ReSysInfo ReSysInfo is a system information viewer for Windows. The tool has 25 total information modules: BIOS information, CMOS, desktop, DirectX, drives, environment, fonts, keyboard, locale, machine and APM, mainboard, MCI, memory, mouse, multimedia, network, OpenGL, passwords, ports, printers and fax, processes, processor, video system, general information about Windows, and a summary. ReSysInfo also includes a Report Wizard, which can export the information to plain text, HTML, or XML format.

Rifiuti Rifiuti will parse the information in an INFO2 file and output the results in a field delimited manner so that it may be imported into a spreadsheet program.

Rootkit Revealer Rootkit Revealer is an advanced rootkit detection utility. Its output lists Registry and file system API discrepancies that may indicate the presence

of a user-mode or kernel-mode rootkit. Rootkit Revealer successfully detects all persistent rootkits published at www.rootkit.com, including AFX, Vanquish, and HackerDefender.

SecReport This app is a small suite of two command-line tools. SecReport will collect security-related information from Windows-based systems. Delta will compare any two reports either from two systems or from the same system after some time. It produces XML-based reports that may be viewed with IE 6.0 browser, and automatically creates an MD5 hash file for reports.

WinAudit WinAudit is easy to use; no special knowledge is required to use the program. It is a self-contained single file that needs no installation or configuration. It reports on most aspects of computer inventory and configuration. Results are displayed in a web-page format that is categorized for ease of viewing and text searching.

Windows Forensic Toolchest Windows Forensic Toolchest (WFT) was written to provide for automated incident response on a Windows system and collect security-relevant information from the system. It is a forensically enhanced batch processing shell capable of running other security tools and producing HTML-based reports in a forensically sound manner. WFT is designed to produce output that is useful to the user, but is also appropriate for use in court proceedings. It provides extensive logging of all its actions along with computing the MD5 checksums along the way to ensure that its output is verifiable. The primary benefit of using WFT to perform incident responses is that it provides an easy method of scripting responses using a repeatable methodology for data collection.

EXERCISE 6.01

USING HELIX LIVE FOR WINDOWS

1. Begin by starting Helix Live for Windows.
 If the CD autorun feature is enabled, a Helix license Window should appear. If autorun is disabled, you can run Helix by double clicking on the helix.exe file on the CD.

Figure 6.3 Helix Terms of Use Window

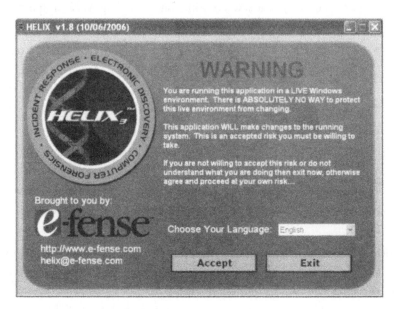

2. Now accept the Terms of Use.

 The default language that Helix will use via the drop-down box is English. French and German are also available. To use Helix, read the agreement and then press **I Agree** to continue (see Figure 6.3). Once the terms have been accepted, the main screen will appear (see Figure 6.4).

Figure 6.4 Helix Main Screen

3. After Helix's main screen appears, select any of the options by clicking on the associated icons (see Figure 6.4).

 The Helix Main screen doesn't behave as a standard window. Helix does not show up in the taskbar, and it is not possible to **Alt + Tab** to it. Helix places an icon in the system tray, which can be used to access the program (see Figure 6.5).

Figure 6.5 Helix Icon

By double-clicking or right-clicking on the icon and selecting "Restore," the main Helix window is brought to the front of the screen. Other options on the right-click menu include Minimize and Exit.

The main screen provides access to three main examination options in Windows:

■ **Preview System Information** This option displays the basic information of the system. Information obtained includes the Operating system version, network information, owner information, and a summary of the drives on the system. There is also a second page that will show a list of running processes.

■ **Acquire a "live" image of a Windows System using dd** This enables the imaging of hard drives, floppy disks, or memory, and allows storage on local removable media or over a network.

■ **Incident Response tools for Windows Systems** There are a large number of tools (including the Windows Forensic Toolkit) that can be run directly from the CD-ROM. After clicking this icon, a small triangle will appear (see Figure 6.6).

Figure 6.6 Selecting Tools within Helix Live for Windows

4. Clicking on the triangle gives access to the other tools pages. Explore all the following pages and try the tools:

- **Documents pertaining to Incident Response, Computer Forensics, Computer Security, and Computer Crime** This option accesses a number of reference documents in PDF format. These documents include a chain of custody form, preservation of digital evidence information, forensic examination for digital evidence guide, and Linux forensics guide for beginners. These documents are a great introduction to conducting a forensic examination.

- **Browse contents of the CD-ROM and Host OS** This option takes the user to a file browser that provides basic information about the selected files. It displays the filename, dates (created, accessed, and modified), file attributes, CRC, MD5, and file size.

- **Scan for Pictures from a live system** This option accesses a tool that can scan the system to find any suspect graphic images. Many different graphic formats are recognized, and these are displayed as thumbnails.

- **Investigative Notes** This is a small notepad to make notes while working on the system.

WARNING

The first time a file is selected, Helix will display the access date of the last access. If the same file is selected again, it will show the date and time of the preceding access. This is due to the nature of the Windows operating system. It cannot be prevented while in Live Mode (This is not an issue when booting into Linux Mode). When examining a live system remember that your actions may modify the system.

5. Helix's Quick Launch option provides access to a number of tools. Try them all and become familiar with their use (see Figure 6.7).

Figure 6.7 Helix's Quick Launch

MD5 Generators

An MD5 generator is a means of ensuring the integrity of a file, application, or file system. These applications create a cryptographic hash of the bit-wise information in the data. This hash is practically impossible to replicate. As a result, if you run the utility again at a later time and it returns the same value on the data, you may be assured that it remains unaltered.

This added layer of protection is essential in digital forensics. To maintain the value of the chain of custody and to ensure the admissibility of evidence, you need to ensure that the data has not been tampered with or altered. An MD5 generator can aid in achieving this end.

Chaos MD5 Chaos MD5 is a free MD5 generator for Windows. Input a file into it to generate an MD5 checksum for that file. That means that it generates a unique signature for each and every file. Chaos MD5 does not require installation. Just copy it to the hard drive or USB device to run. The MD5 checksum that is generated is used for file identification or integrity checks.

Secure Hash Signature Generator The Secure Hash Signature Generator creates signatures that are unique to the data stored on a disk drive. These signatures are used to verify intentional or accidental tampering with the drive image. The software has the ability to scan any secondary or slave drives attached to a computer running a Windows operating system. It does not write to the drive. It includes three different algorithms used to generate the signature: MD5 (128-bit signature), SHA1 (160-bit signature), and CRC (32-bit signature).

MD5 Generator: Mat-MD5 Mat-MD5 is designed to check the MD5 value for each file processed and compare it with other MD5 strings. It can process one or more files and add the result value to a list. You can add your MD5 value to compare by typing it or by copying it from an external file.

MD5 Checksum Verifier 2.1 MD5 Checksum Verifier is a file integrity checker which uses the MD5 algorithm. It can create checksums of files and verify their integrity. Operation involves two steps: make check file and verify check file.

Pslist

Pslist displays process, CPU, and memory information or thread statistics for all processes that are presently running on the system. The information listed for each process includes the time the process has executed, the amount of time the process has executed in kernel and user modes, and the amount of physical memory that the OS has assigned the process. Command-line switches allow the viewing of memory-oriented process information, thread statistics, or all three types of data. Here is an example of the syntax:

```
pslist [-?] [-d] [-m] [-x] [-t] [-s [n] [-r n]] [\\computer [-u username] [-p password]] [name | pid]
```

Some common parameters include:

- **-d** Shows statistics for all active threads on the system, grouping threads with their owning process.

- **-m** Shows memory-oriented information for each process, rather than the default of CPU-oriented information.

- **-x** Shows CPU, memory, and thread information for each of the processes specified.

- **-t** Shows the tree of processes.

This tool can be downloaded from www.microsoft.com/technet/sysinternals/default.mspx.

TEST DAY TIP

Ensure that you are familiar with pslist and the various command line options.

fport

fport displays all open TCP/IP and UDP ports and maps them to the application that owns the port. The application is similar to netstat except that it maps those ports to running processes with the PID, process name, and path. It is very useful in locating unknown open ports and their related applications. The switches may be utilized by making use of either a / or a - prior to the switch.

The command-line switches are as follows:

- **/?** Usage help
- **/p** Sort by port
- **/a** Sort by application
- **/i** Sort by pid
- **/ap** Sort by application path

This tool can be downloaded from www.foundstone.com.

Psloggedon

Psloggedon displays both locally logged on users and users logged on through resources for either the local or a remote computer. It ascertains which users are logged on by examining the keys under the HKEY_USERS key. For each key that has a name that is a user SID (Security IDentifier), Psloggedon finds the corresponding user name and displays that particular user name. Psloggedon utilizes NetSessionEnum API to ascertain who is logged onto a computer via resource shares. Here is an example of the syntax:

```
psloggedon [-?] [-l] [-x] [\\computername | username]
```

Some common parameters:

- **.-?** Displays the supported options and the units of measurement used for output values.
- **.-l** Shows only local logons instead of both local and network resource logons.

What Is File Slack? How Can You Investigate Windows File Slack?

A Windows disk cluster is a fixed length block of data which is used to store files. File size will never match the size of one or more clusters; this is where slack space occurs. File slack is the space that exists on a Windows disk (or other data device) between the end of the file and the end of the last cluster. It may contain data from the system's memory. It is possible to find user names, passwords, and other sensitive information associated with the system in slack. Larger cluster sizes relate to an increase in the volume of file slack leading to a waste in storage space. This is a vital source of evidence to the forensic investigator.

The Windows operating system provides for the difference between the end of the file and the end of a cluster by filling the leftover space with data from its memory buffers if there is no space available. This data, which is chosen randomly from the system's RAM is called RAM slack since it is obtained from the memory of the computer. RAM slack contains information

related to files that are created, viewed, modified, or copied since the system was last booted. If the system has not been powered down for a period of time, then the data stored in file slack can come from past sessions.

Encase software provides a number of tools to conduct complex investigations with precision and effectiveness. Encase enables a methodical approach to digital forensic investigations. This approach allows the forensic analyst to manage large volumes of digital evidence and view computer drive contents, including files and artifacts such as operating system, file system, and deleted files or file fragments located in file slack or unallocated space.

How Do You Examine File Systems?

Examining the file system is an indispensable component of forensically analyzing a computer based on the Windows operating system. Simple commands such as *dir /O:d* (which sorts files in a directory based on the date order) play a significant role during the investigation of a Windows-based system. This simple command enables the forensic investigator to ascertain the time and date of the installation of the operating system. The service packs, patches, sub-directories, drivers, and other eventual files may be examined by using this command. When checking a file system, the analyst must give more regard to those files that have been updated most recently and develop a timeline of activities. Being able to sort files into time and date order makes the creation of a timeline a far simpler process.

Built-in Tool: Sigverif

Sigverif.exe can analyze a system and report on any unsigned drivers found. To run the tool:

- Click **Start | Run**, type **Sigverif**, and click **OK**.
- Click the **Advanced** button (see Figure 6.8).
- Click **Look for other files that are not digitally signed**.
- Select the **WINNT | System32 | Drivers** folder, and then click **OK**.

After Sigverif.exe has completed the process of its checks, it displays a list of all unsigned drivers installed on the system. The list of all signed and unsigned drivers found by Sigverif.exe may be viewed in the Sigverif.txt file in the *Windir* folder, typically the *Winnt* or *Windows* folder. All unsigned drivers are marked as Unsigned.

Figure 6.8 Sigverif Is Included with Windows and Helps to Verify Digitally Signed Programs

The Word Extractor Forensic Tool

Word Extractor is an application that extracts human understandable interpretation from the computer binary format. It is similar to the UNIX command, *strings*. It offers users the following features:

- Replaces non-human words with spaces or dots for better visibility.
- Supports drag and drop and wrap text.
- Multitasks by responding to commands and processing large files.
- Saves results as TXT or RTF.
- Does not thwart registry or system with unwanted DLLs.

How Can You Interpret the Windows Registry and Memory Dump Information?

The Registry is an important component that should be examined during an investigation of a Windows system. Selected keys must always be checked and given more importance as they supply evidence for what services have been running, what services are presently running, and who had logged on to the system over a certain period of time. The primary keys that you will need to know for the exam include:

HKEY_LOCAL_MACHINE

- \Software\Microsoft\Windows\CurrentVersion\Run
- \Software\Microsoft\Windows\CurrentVersion\RunOnce
- \Software\Microsoft\Windows\CurrentVersion\RunOnceEx
- \Software\Microsoft\Windows\CurrentVersion\RunServices
- \Software\Microsoft\Windows\CurrentVersion\RunServicesOnce
- \Software\Microsoft\WindowsNT\CurrentVersion\Winlogon

The same keys must also be checked for the following:

- HKEY_CURRENT_USER
- HKEY_USERS\.DEFAULT

EXAM WARNING

You will be examined on your knowledge of the Windows registry. Make sure you know the purpose for each of the registry keys listed above.

Registry Viewer Tool: RegScanner

There are a variety of registry tools that either augment or supplant the Windows' Registry Editor Application (regedt32). Although it is simple to use, regedt32 does not come with a mass search function. It is not possible to find and display all instances of a given string in the registry. The utility RegScanner from NirSoft provides this additional functionality. It provides a search function that can search for any value in the registry and display all the available instances of that value in a single view. From that view it allows a simple selection and jump function that takes you to the particular registry key for editing. It also provides a means to export results to a REG file so that they can be saved or loaded onto another computer.

RegScanner doesn't require installation. It may be unpacked from the distribution.zip file to any directory and run from there. When launched it provides an option to choose which base key to start a search from. It provides a dropdown menu with a number of common base keys. The search string can be case-sensitive or case-insensitive, and the match can be exact or within certain parameters. For instance, you can match against the data and the values, but not the key names themselves.

The application also provides a function to search for Unicode strings in binary values. RegScanner reports its results in a grid-type list, which can be saved as a REG file or exported to an HTML-format.

Microsoft Security ID

The Microsoft Security IDs are obtainable in the Windows registry key:

`HKEY_LOCAL_MACHINE\SOFTWARE\Microsoft\Windows NT\CurrentVersion\ProfileList`

The ProfileList key holds the SIDs, on selecting individual ID value entry, and an associated user name is possible. There are some specific IDs enclosed under Microsoft Security that are viewed as follows:

- Encrypted File System Information
- Event Logging Utility
- Retrieve MAC Address
- Retrieve Security ID
- GUID to object
- Processor.vbs
- Registry Dump
- Registry Reference
- Registry Restoration
- Registry Scan

Summary of the Features and Importance of Memory Dump

Windows often creates a memory dump file when it crashes. This file contains valuable information that can aid in determining why the system stopped. For a memory dump to be produced in Windows the system requires a paging file that is at least 2 megabytes (MB) on the boot volume. Even if there is a large paging file on another disk but none on the boot volume, a memory dump will not function. Memory dumps are useful in aiding the diagnosis of system bugs and in analyzing memory contents during a program failure. They can contain information in binary, octal, or hexadecimal forms.

Where the system is running Microsoft Windows 2000 or later, a new file is originated every time the system stops abruptly. The Microsoft tool, dumpchk.exe, is designed to check memory dump files for information. The **systemroot | Minidump** folder contains a list of all small memory dump files. When conducting a forensic analysis of a Microsoft Windows system,

always check for and obtain any memory dumps on the system. A memory dump file generally contains:

- The stop message and its parameters

- A list of loaded drivers

- The processor's context (PRCB) for the processes that stopped a regular normal operation of Windows

- The processor information and kernel context (EPROCESSES) for the processes that have been stopped

- The process information and kernel context (ETHREAD) for the thread that stopped

- The kernel-mode call stack for the thread that stopped the process from execution

Pagefile.sys and PMDump

Windows XP Professional uses paging file information to create a memory dump file in the systemroot directory. This dump file can be analyzed to supply some information as to the cause of a crash during offline analysis. It may also be analyzed using tools running on another computer. Post Mortem Dump or PMDump is a tool that performs the dumping of the memory contents related to any process to a file having its process stopped. This tool can be used for performing forensics analysis of a dump file.

What Is Virtual Memory?

Virtual memory is an imaginary memory location supported by the Windows operating system. It acts as an alternate set of memory addresses and expands the range of available memory. In this way slow hard drive memory is used to supplement physical RAM. Programs use these virtual addresses for data that does not need to be addressed quite so often, to store instructions and data. When these memory address locations are called, virtual memory is converted into RAM.

In order to copy virtual memory into RAM, the operating system divides virtual memory into pages. Each page contains a fixed number of addresses that are stored on disk until called by the operating system. When pages are called by the operating system they are copied from disk memory to RAM, a process which translates virtual addresses into real addresses. This process is known as mapping. The process of copying virtual pages from disk to main memory is known as paging or swapping.

System Scanner

System scanner (available from www.codeproject.com/w2k/system_scaner.asp) is designed as a replacement to the Task manager (see Figure 6.9).

Figure 6.9 System Scanner Provides a Visual Map of a System's Virtual Memory

The Windows task manager lacks the ability to fetch more specific info about the processes; that is supplied using the System Scanner (such as the IDs of all the threads, handles to DLLs, ability to suspend specific threads of a specific process, and, finally, an ability to view a process' virtual memory map—see Figure 6.9).

When the program is started, you are shown the main window, which shows all the currently running processes in your system, the number of threads per process, and the executable path. The status bar will show you the overall number of running processes. The list will be updated (by default) every 5000 milliseconds. Pressing **Enter** will force the update of the list.

From the main menu it is possible to force an update of the process list and enter **Options**, where you can customize the refresh time, turn hot track on\off (on by default) and customize the colors of the memory regions in the virtual memory map.

Right-clicking on any of the processes brings up a context menu which will uncover all the features of the program. This uncovers information about the process' threads, DLLs, virtual memory, and set process' priority, and offers a kill process function.

Integrated Windows Forensics Software: X-Ways Forensics and its Features

Based on WinHex, X-Ways Forensics is an advanced work environment for the digital forensic analyst. It provides a number of features such as:

- Forensically sound disk cloning and imaging

- Examining the complete directory structure inside raw image files, even if spanned over several segments

- Native support for FAT, NTFS, Ext2/3/4, CDFS, and UDF file systems

- Built-in interpretation of RAID 0 and RAID 5 systems and dynamic disks

- Viewing and dumping physical RAM and the virtual memory of running processes

- Various data recovery techniques and file carving

- File header signature database, based on flexible GREP notation

- Hard disk cleansing to produce forensically sterile media

- Gathering slack space, free space, inter-partition space, and generic text from drives and images

- File and directory catalog creation for all computer media

- Easy detection of and access to NTFS alternate data streams (ADS), even where other programs fail

- Mass hash calculation for files (CRC32, MD5, SHA-1, SHA-256)

- Manual NTFS decompression

- Support for the file systems HFS, HFS+, ReiserFS, Reiser4, UFS, UFS2

- Supported partitioning types: MBR, Windows dynamic volumes, GUID (GPT), Apple, unpartitioned (Floppy/Superfloppy)

- Gallery view for pictures

- Calendar view

- File preview, seamlessly integrated viewer component for 400+ file types

- Ability to examine e-mail extracted from Outlook (PST)*, Outlook Express (DBX), Mozilla (including Netscape and Thunderbird), generic mailbox (mbox, Berkeley, BSD, Unix), Eudora, PocoMail, Barca, Opera, Forte Agent, The Bat!, Pegasus, PMMail, FoxMail, *maildir* folders (local copies)

- Automated file signature check

- Ability to tag files and add them to customized report tables of notable items

- Automatic identification of encrypted MS Office and PDF documents

- Finds pictures embedded in documents (such as MS Word, PDF, and PowerPoint) automatically

- Internal viewer for Windows Registry files (all Windows versions); automated Registry report

- Viewer for Windows event log files

- Lists the contents of archives directly in the directory browser, even in a recursive view

- Logical search, in all or selected files/directories only, following fragmented cluster chains, in compressed files, optionally decoding text in PDF, WPD, and more

- Searches in both Unicode and various code pages

- Skin color detection (for example, a gallery view sorted by skin color percentage greatly accelerates a search for traces of child pornography and obscene images)

- Detection of host-protected areas (HPA), or ATA-protected areas

X-Ways Forensics also has the capability to write protect data to ensure authenticity and integrity. The product has a case management function integrated with automated activity logging (audit logs) and automated reports that can be imported and further processed by any other application that understands HTML, such as MS Word. It couples this with the ability to associate comments about files for inclusion in the report or for filtering.

How Can You Investigate Internet Traces?

Internet Explorer has several locations that should be checked for evidence. The following are the files and folders that should be investigated when analyzing Web browser activity:

- Cookies: In Windows 2000/XP, cookies can be found at the following location:

 1. <c:\Documents and settings\%username%\Cookies

 2. In Windows 95/98/ME, cookies can be found in the following folder: *C:\Windows\Cookies*

- History

- Typed URLs

- Temporary Internet files

Internet Explorer saves the record of all the sites visited by a user in a separate folder called the History folder. The URLs of all the websites visited by the user are present in this folder.

There is another folder in the Documents and Settings folder, usually present in the C:\ drive, which stores cookies visited by the user under the folder of each user. These cookies are generally stored in the Cookies folder. These files are present in the Temp folder. The location of temporary Internet files gives the name and number of sites visited by the user. The Temp files are important because they contain information about the user's activities in the various TMP files.

Traces Viewer

Traces Viewer as a tool that allows you to view all images, flash movies, pages, and other media files cached by the Internet Explorer browser. It also has a function that removes any web-traces made by Internet Explorer on a system. It doesn't wipe the evidence and it may be uncovered. It is available from www.bytescout.com/freeware.html.

IECookiesView

IECookiesView is a forensic utility that is used to display the details of all cookies that are stored by Internet Explorer. It provides the capability to sort cookies according to name and date. Additionally, it provides a search function that can find a cookie in the list by just specifying the name of a website. It will also copy cookie information onto the clipboard, and through remote login, can display cookies of other users of the same system or a different system.

IE History Viewer

Any URL that is typed into the address bar or any link that is followed in Internet Explorer automatically causes the address to be stored in the history index file. The IE History Viewer parses all data from the history file, and prints the list of all visited URLs. This application provides the ability to save the list of addresses as a text, HTML, or XML file.

Cache Monitor

Cache monitor offers a real-time view of the present state of the systems cache. It can also verify the configuration of dynamic caches. This tool can prove helpful to the forensic analyst in verifying the cache policies and monitoring cache statistics. Few other tools provide the ability to monitor data flowing through cache and even the data present in the edge cache. The following cache statistics are available through Cache Monitor:

- **ESI Processors** Number of processes configured as edge caches.
- **Number of Edge Cached Entries** Number of entries currently cached on all edge servers and processes.
- **Cache Hits** Number of requests that match entries on edge servers.
- **Cache Misses by URL** Cache policy that do not exist on the edge server for the requested template.

How Do You Investigate System State Backups?

A system state backup is in effect a backup of the complete system. Everything that is present within the system will be copied as backup so that no data or information is lost when there is a system crash, a corruption of the driver files, or if certain system files stop the system from functioning properly. To perform a forensic analysis of evidence on a Windows system, backing up a system's registry is insufficient. An extensive backup of data is essential so that the system can be secured against any malfunctions.

A full system state backup saves the:

- Active Directory (NTDS)
- Windows Boot files
- COM+ class registration database
- Registry
- System volume (SYSVOL)
- The IIS metabase

The process to create a System State Backup is simple:

1. Go to Start | Programs | Accessories | System Tools | Backup
2. In the **Backup** tab, check the **System State** box.
3. Select the **Schedule Job** tab and select the **Add Job** button.
4. Select **Yes** and choose **media options**:
 1. Media type
 2. Location
 3. Backup name
5. Select **Next** and check that the **Normal** option is selected, and then select **Next** again.
6. When backing-up to disk there is no need to verify data. Select **Next**.
7. Choose if you want to append to or replace an existing backup. Select **Next**.
8. Schedule the backup. Select **Next**.
9. Set the account with which the backup has the required permission to run.
10. Select **Finish**.

Investigating ADS Streams

A relatively unheard-of compatibility feature of NTFS is the Alternate Data Streams (ADS). These can provide an attacker with a method of hiding root kits or hacker tools on a compromised system which allows them to be executed without being detected by the systems administrator. Alternate Data Streams are strictly a feature of the NTFS file system. They may be used as a method of hiding executables or proprietary content.

Alternate Data Streams are simple to create and entail little or no skill to use. Common DOS commands such as **type** can be used to create Alternate Data Streams (ADS). These commands are used in conjunction with a redirect [>] and colon [:] to fork one file into another.

For example, the following command may be used to fork the common Windows calculator program with an ADS "malicious.exe":

```
type c:\malicious.exe > c:\winnt\system32\calc.exe:malicious.exe
```

Files with an ADS are almost impossible to detect using native file browsing techniques like command line or Windows Explorer. A third-party file checksum application can be used to effectively maintain the integrity of an NTFS partition against unauthorized Alternate Data Streams.

ADS Tool?LADS (List Alternate Data Streams):

- **Syntax** {file name}:{stream name}
- **Create** type textfile > visible.txt:hidden.txt
- **View** more < visible.txt:hidden.txt

EXAM WARNING

Become familiar with the tool LADS (List Alternate Data Streams) from www.heysoft.de/nt/ep-lads.htm. This program lists all alternate data streams of an NTFS directory including the ADS of encrypted files, even when these files were encrypted with another copy of Windows 2000. Try using the /S switch to walk through subdirectories recursively and the /A switch to show the total of all bytes.

Creating a CD-ROM Bootable for Windows XP

There are a number of tools such as the "Ultimate Boot CD-ROM" and "Bart's PE Builder" that are designed to assist you in creating a bootable Windows CD-ROM. These tools are appropriate for PC maintenance tasks and yield a complete Win32 environment with network

support, a graphical user interface (800x600), and FAT/NTFS/CDFS file system support. All details of these tools are supplied below.

Bart PE (Bart Preinstalled Environment): Screenshot

Bart's PE Builder assists in building a "Bart Preinstalled Environment" (BartPE) bootable Windows CD-ROM or DVD from the original Windows XP or Windows Server 2003 installation/setup CD. This can restore any DOS boot disk. Supported Windows versions are:

- Windows XP Home Edition
- Windows XP Professional
- Windows Server 2003, Web Edition
- Windows Server 2003, Standard Edition
- Windows Server 2003, Enterprise Edition

Ultimate Boot CD-ROM

The Ultimate Boot CD-ROM allows floppy-based diagnostic tools to be executed from CD-ROM drives on Intel compatible machines. This does not require a separate operating system. This tool holds a number of diagnostic utilities that provide for sharing Internet access or surfing the web. Modifying NTFS volumes, restoring deleted files, scanning hard drives for viruses, and creating new NTFS volumes are possible with network support. This tool is available from www.ultimatebootcd.com/index.html.

The Ultimate Boot CD includes CPU Tests, memory tests, and peripherals tools.

CPU Tests

- .CPU Burn-in
- .Mersenne Prime Test
- .StressCPU

Memory Tests

- .Memtest86
- .Memtest86+
- .Windows Memory Diagnostic
- .DocMem RAM Diagnostic
- .TestMem4

Peripherals Tools

- .Parallel port detection and test utilities

- ■ .ATAPI CD-ROM Identification

- ■ .CHZ Monitor-Test

The compilation contains tools in the following additional categories:

- ■ CPU Information
- ■ System Information
- ■ Benchmarking Tools
- ■ System Information
- ■ Benchmark Tools
- ■ BIOS Tools
- ■ Hard Disk Installation Tools
- ■ Hard Disk Diagnostic Tools
- ■ Hard Disk Device Management Tools
- ■ Hard Disk Wiping Tools
- ■ Hard Disk Cloning Tools
- ■ Hard Disk Low-Level Editing Tools
- ■ Partition Tools
- ■ Boot Managers
- ■ File Tools
- ■ Anti-Virus/Malware Tools
- ■ Network Tools

The disk also supplies both DOS and Linux Boot Disks. A complete listing of the tools found on the Ultimate Boot CD-ROM is available from their website.

TEST DAY TIP

You don't need to memorize all the tests contained within the Ultimate Boot CD for the exam; however, you do need to know the basic functions.

Linux Forensics

In this section of the chapter we will introduce the reader to computer forensics from the perspective of the Linux operating system. The objectives of the section are:

- Introduce Linux as a forensic tool
- Enable you to recognize the file systems and partitions in Linux
- Enable you to understand the challenges involved when using Linux
- Introduce you to the wide range of forensic tools that are freely available under Linux

Why Use Linux as a Forensic Tool?

With the wide range of Windows-based forensic tools, both in the open-source and commercial realm, it is easy for one to ask: Why learn Linux?

One of the key advantages of using Linux for forensics is the greater levels of control that it provides. Linux treats every device, from the hard drive to the monitor, as a file. One key benefit provided by Linux (and in fact UNIX in general) is its ability to mount drives in read-only mode. This capability means that Linux does not require a separate right blocker to ensure that data is not altered on the disk.

Another benefit of Linux is its flexibility. There are a wide range of Linux file systems and specialist forensic compilations designed to boot from a CD. Linux also has support for a large number of operating systems and is capable of mounting a large variety of file systems. Of particular benefit, the open source nature of Linux has resulted in the ability to access and image a large range of commercial file systems for little or no cost.

The availability of the Linux code coupled with this flexibility has resulted in a number of very powerful forensic distributions. Distributions such as F.I.R.E, Sleuth, Auditor, and Helix provide the forensic analyst with a wide range of choice coupled with a minimal capital outlay. These CDs provide file system support, platform support, recognize numerous file systems, and contain a large range of both command-line tools and GUI applications.

File System Description

Linux treats all devices as a file. As such, an entry is created in the file system for each hardware device recognized by the operating system. For instance, if a standard IDE hard drive is connected to the system, it will be listed under */dev/hdx*. These listings start from the letter "a" (or */dev/hda*) and increase in alphabetical order.

In a similar fashion, each partition of the drive is numbered from "1" on (starting with */dev/hda1*, for instance). To see a list of all the partitions that are available for a drive, type the following command: **fdisk –l /dev/hdx**.

The partitions are identified by their Linux terminology. A "★" indicates that it is a boot partition. The *if this* command also outputs the start and end cylinders for each of the partitions, as well as the number of blocks used by each partition. The output of the *fdisk* command also displays the file system type and partition identifier (ID).

Devices Under Linux

Linux treats all devices as files. These devices are available as "files" under the */dev* directory. This capability to directly access hardware devices allows the forensic analyst to redirect both input and output to a device. This capability allows for the redirection of text to the screen, or the capture of keystrokes from keyboard.

Head of the Class…

The Primary Linux Directories

The majority of Linux distributions have a very similar directory structure. An example directory structure that will apply to most Linux systems and a description of the directory is supplied in Table 6.1.

Table 6.1 The Major Linux Directories and Their Functions

Linux directory path	Description of the Linux directory
/	The root directory is the lowest level directory in the Linux file system.
/bin	The bin directory contains executable programs which are needed in single user mode. These programs help boot the system or repair it.
/boot	The boot directory contains a static foals knitted by the boot loader. This directory should hold only files which are needed during the boot process.
/dev	This directory contains special or device files. These files refer to physical devices.
/etc	The *etc* directory contains consideration files which are local to the machine. Certain larger packages such as X11 have their own subdirectories with consideration files under */etc*.

Continued

Table 6.1 continued The Major Linux Directories and Their Functions

Linux directory path	Description of the Linux directory
/etc/opt	This directory contains host-specific configuration files for add-on applications which are installed in /opt.
/etc/sgml	This directory is used to contain the configuration files for SGML and XML.
/etc/skel	The files contained in this directory are copied to a user home directory whenever a new account is created.
/etc/X11	This directory contains configuration files for the X11 windowing system.
/home	This directory is often configured as a root directory to place user home directories.
/lib	The /lib directory holds shared libraries that are ne commands found in the root Filesystem.
/mnt	The /mnt directory contains mount points to which file systems may be temporarily mounted.
/opt	The /opt directory contains add-on packages in the form of static files.
/proc	The /proc directory is a mount point for the proc file system. The proc pseudo-file system provides information about running processes and the Linux kernel. More detail is provided by proc(5).
/root	The /root directory is commonly the home directory for the root user.
/sbin	The /sbin directory holds system commands which are not usually executed by normal users.
/tmp	The /tmp directory contains temporary files.
/usr	The /usr directory generally contains local software, system libraries, games, and other applications. It is common for this directory to be mounted on a separate partition.
/usr/games	This directory commonly holds binary files associated with games.
/usr/include	Include files for the C compiler.
/usr/lib	This directory contains object libraries, including dynamic libraries, and some executables that are not generally invoked directly.

Continued

Table 6.1 continued The Major Linux Directories and Their Functions

Linux directory path	Description of the Linux directory
/usr/lib/X11	This directory contains data files associated with X programs, and configuration files for the X system.
/usr/local	Programs in consideration files which are local to the particular system are generally installed in or under this directory.
/usr/local/bin	This directory generally contains binaries for programs that are local to the host.
/usr/local/doc	This directory is for local documentation.
/usr/local/etc	This directory contains configuration files associated with the locally installed programs.
/usr/local/info	This directory contains the *info* pages associated with the locally installed programs.
/usr/local/man	This directory contains the *man* pages associated with the locally installed programs.
/usr/local/sbin	This directory contains binaries used for local system administration.
/usr/local/src	This directory contains the source code for locally installed software.
/usr/sbin	This directory contains program binaries for system administration. The binaries in this directory are not generally essential to the boot process and are not required for mounting */usr*. System files required for system repair should not be in this directory.
/usr/share/locale	This directory contains locale information.
/usr/share/man	The system's *man* pages are arranged in subdirectories according to their main page sections under this directory.
/usr/share/zoneinfo	Files containing data time-zone information are maintained under this directory.
/usr/src	This directory contains source files for the system.
/usr/src/linux	This directory was the traditional location to store the Linux kernel source.
/var	The *VAR* directory contains variable files which are expected to change in size. This includes spool and log files.
/var/lib	This directory maintains variable state information for the programs running on the host.

Continued

Table 6.1 continued The Major Linux Directories and Their Functions

Linux directory path	Description of the Linux directory
/var/local	District ridges to hold variable data files and programs located under *lusrllocal*.
/var/log	The standard log directory.
/var/mail	Location in many systems of user mailboxes.
/var/run	This directory contains run-time variable files such as files holding process identifiers (PIDs). Logged user information (such as *utmp*) is also maintained in this directory. Most file systems clear this directory on a reboot.
/var/spool	The spool directory contains queued files; *at, cron, lpd*, and *mqueue* will all create subdirectories to spool jobs underneath this directory.
/var/tmp	This directory is similar to */tmp* and stores temporary files for an unspecified length of time.
/var/yp	This directory contains database files for NIS.

Mount Command

Before a file system can be used under Linux it needs to be mounted (this statement also applies to the Mac and other UNIX variants). Linux will mount any file systems defined in */etc/fstab* at each system boot. It is important to note however that Linux will write to devices even when they are not mounted.

Head of the Class…

Mount Command Options

Using the -*t* flag on the mount command allows the user to set the file system type:

- *auto* is for user-mounted floppies, allowing ext2, ext3, and vfat (DOS / Windows)
- *iso9660* is used for CD-ROMS and is the default type
- *nfs* is for files that are mounted over the network
 The mount options are delineated by the -o flag on the mount command and include:

- *noauto* means that the file system is not automatically mounted at boot time, but may be mounted later using mount -*a* <*path*>

Continued

- *auto* (as an option) causes a file system to be mounted at boot time
- Default options are *rw, suid, dev, exec, auto, nouser,* and *async*
- *ro* allows the file system to be mounted read-only
- *rw* allows read-write
- Multiple options may be selected (for example, *–o ro,noauto*)

The mount command also has a number of file system-specific options such as the following options that are used when mounting NFS partitions:

- *bg* after an unsuccessful attempt, causes subsequent tries to be made in the background
- *soft* causes an error to be returned if the server does not respond
- *timeo* sets the NFS time-out period to tenths of a second
- *intr* allows interrupts to be made in programs running over NFS, and the program can then resume where it left off, once the NFS server is back online

A common location to situate mount points is in the directory */mnt*. Only the *superuser* (or *root*) account can create directories in */mnt*. Redhat and several other flavors of Linux come with mount points already set up for a floppy, a CD-ROM, and a parallel port Zip drive. To export a file or directory from a server over a network, it may need to be explicitly specified by root account in the */etc/fstab* file.

Table 6.2 lists common mount points and their options.

Table 6.2 Common Settings Used with the Mount Command

Node:Mount_dir	Mount Point	File Type	Mount Options
/dev/fd0	/mnt/floppy	auto	noauto 0 1
/dev/cdrom	/mnt/cdrom	iso9660	ro, noauto 0 1
/dev/zip	/mnt/zip	Vfat	auto, exec 0 1
server:/exported	/mnt/server	Nfs	Defaults

EXAM WARNING

Whenever you are working on a drive image or physical drive, ensure that it is mounted so that you cannot change the file's last access times. It is important to remember to mount any evidence that you're working with using the *-o ro* options of the mount command.

Linux will allow you to analyze file systems from several different operating systems. All that is required is to mount the file system with the proper type and options. For example, using Sun UFS:

```
# mount -r -t ufs -o ro,ufstype=sun /dev/hdc2 /mnt
```

Always use the *noexec* and *nodev* options to prevent accidentally running programs from the partition being analyzed, and to ignore any device files it may contain. This is an example of a typical mount command:

```
# mount -o ro,noexec,nodev /dev/hdc1 /t
```

The Linux kernel can support a large number of file system types (the following information is taken from the command *man mount*):

> The file system types which are currently supported are listed in linux/fs/filesystems.c: adfs, affs, autofs, coda, coherent, devpts, efs, ext, ext2, hfs, hpfs, iso9660, minix, msdos, ncpfs, nfs, ntfs, proc, qnx4, romfs, smbfs, sysv, udf, ufs, umsdos, vfat, xenix, xiafs. Note that coherent, sysv and xenix are equivalent and that xenix and coherent will be removed at some point in the future—use sysv instead.

For this reason Linux makes an excellent forensic analysis platform. The ability to use a single set of utilities to access file contents and i-node information from a large number of system types for little cost is a key feature of all Linux forensic applications. Another benefit of Linux is the inclusion of "loopback" devices. Loopback devices provide the ability to mount a file containing an image copy (such as that obtained using *dd*) with your forensic analysis host.

Loopback devices allow the use of a file system within a file. This method is used for bootdisks, burning CD-ROMS, and for encrypted file systems. Further information may be found in the following commands and Linux FAQs:

- man losetup

- man mount

- Laptop-HOWTO

- Bootdisk-HOWTO

- Loopback-Encrypted-Filesystem-HOWTO

TEST DAY TIP

Install NASA enhanced loopback drivers on your system. The driver allows you to mount a complete disk image as a loopback device instead of the standard single partition at a time. There are currently different kernels for *i386*, *i686*, *p4*, and *athlon* architectures. The NASA enhanced loopback drivers simplify the process of mounting evidential drives. More importantly, if you only have to mount a single file you are less likely to make a mistake than if you run multiple commands.

These drivers are available from ftp://ftp.hq.nasa.gov/pub/ig/ccd/enhanced_loopback/.

The Linux Boot Sequence

Linux starts the boot process by loading the kernel. Generally, the Linux kernel image will be contained in the boot directory (*/boot*). Either LILO or GRUB may be queried by viewing their consideration files (*/etc/lilo.conf* or */etc/grub.conf*) using the command **less**. The boot loader specifies the location of the "root device," which is in effect the boot drive and the kernel version which is to be booted.

Next, the Linux boot process starts initialization. In this stage *run level* and *startup* scripts are initialized and the terminal process is controlled. Initialization is controlled through the file */etc/inittab*. The *file/sbin/init* starts the initialization process. In Linux (like other UNIX variants), *runlevel* is used as a description of the system state. In Red Hat Linux some of the startup scripts of interest are:

- **/etc/rc.d/rc.sysinit** This script controls system initialization, file system mount, and checks, amongst other things.

- **/etc/rc.d/rc.*** For each value of ★ (0-6), the *runlevel* passed as an argument by the *init* process. This script calls the specified script for the *runlevel* as it starts.

- **/etc/rc.d/rc.local** This script is called from within the specific runlevel scripts. The script, rc.local, is a general purpose script that is modified to include commands needed at bootup and to customize a local server.

One of the more common shells deployed is the Linux BASH shell (Bourne Again Shell). Command shell can be thought of as equivalent to the DOS command.com shell. Some other common shells include:

- **Bourne** The traditional Unix shell.

- **ksh Korn** The de facto standard shell for Unix systemsn

- **csh** The original C Shell.

- **tcsh** Extended version of the C Shell.

- **zsh** A powerful shell that integrates much of the functionality of *ksh*, *csh*, and *bash*.

The Challenges in Disk Forensics with Linux

There are a number of challenges that will be faced when Linux is used as a forensic tool to analyze a disk image. Some of these include:

- Linux is unable to identify the last sector on hard drives with an odd number of sectors.

- The majority of Linux tools either do not have a GUI interface or work better at the command line, which makes them difficult to use and increases the learning curve.

- Devices can be written to at all times. Although it is possible to mount an image as a read-only file system which will not be changed, it is still possible to write data directly to the physical drive using Linux.

- Although both commercial and open source software has bugs, Linux is often perceived as being riskier. This can influence the credibility of the tools.

Imaging Odd-Sized Drives with Linux

Although it is rare to find a tribe of an odd number of sectors, they could pose a problem for Linux. Linux cannot see the last sector of a drive with an odd number of sectors. As a result, a small amount of information may be lost in this situation.

It is recommended that either a BSD variant, commercial UNIX, or commercial Windows tool be used in this instance. Although it is unlikely that a single sector at the end of a disk will contain evidence that could sway a case, you never know.

Popular Linux Forensics Tools

Linux includes several simple utilities to make imaging and basic analysis of suspect disks and drives simpler. These include:

- **dd** Command used to copy from an input file or device to an output file or device.

- **dcfldd** A more advanced variant of *dd* that shows the progress while imaging.

- **sfdisk/fdisk** Used to determine the structure of a disk.

- **grep** Search files for instances of an expression or pattern.

- **loopback device** Allows user to mount an image without having to rewrite the image to a disk.

- **md5sum** and **sha1sum** Create and store an MD5 or SHA hash of a file or list of files (including devices).

- **file** Reads file header information in an attempt to ascertain its type, regardless of name or extension.

- **xxd** Command line hexdump tool.

- **ghex** and **khexedit** The Gnome and KDE (X Window interfaces) hex editors.

EXERCISE 6.02

STEP-BY-STEP APPROACH TO IMAGING A SYSTEM

1. Document all processes.

 1. Begin by creating a directory where all forensic activities can be completed:

```
mkdir /evidence
```

 2. It is best to create a special mount point for all physical subject disk analysis:

```
mkdir /mnt/case_1
```

2. Determine the disk structure.

 1. Create an image of the disk using the bit streaming command *dd:*

```
dd if=/dev/fd0 of=image.disk
```

2. Change the read-write permissions of the image to read-only using chmod:

```
chmod 440 image.disk
```

Setting the permissions to "440" allows read access only to the person who created the file and to the group that is assigned. If you are the only investigator working on this file, setting the permissions to "400" will allow read access only to the account which created the image.

It is generally preferable to restrict access to the file even if it is saved as a read only file. It is likely that the file will contain sensitive information and should be accessed only on a need-to-know basis.

3. Mount the restored imaged working copy and analyze the contents:

```
mount -t vfat -o ro,noexec /dev/fd0 /mnt/case_1
```

Another option is to mount a point within the image file using the loop interface rather than mounting the contents to another location:

```
mount -t vfat -o ro,noexec,loop image.disk /mnt/case_1
```

4. Verify the integrity of the data on the file image by verifying the hash of the file:

```
md5sum /evidence/md5.image.file
```

or

```
sha1sum -c /evidence/SHA.image.file
```

5. Use the ls command to view the contents of the disk. The command ls –aRl will list all files including hidden files, and list the directories recursively.

Make a list of all files along with access times:

```
ls -aiRltu > /evidence/files.list
```

6. Search for likely strings in evidence using grep:

```
grep -i porn files.list
```

7. List unknown file extensions and changed file appearances:

```
file altered_file
```

8. Files may also be analyzed using strings, cat, more or less:

 1. Keywords searches may be conducted from the entire file list.

```
cat /evidence/ files.list | grep word-list
```

 2. A systematic approach to searching for keywords can be achieved through the creation of a keywords list (for example, save a file: */evidence/key_word_list)*.

 3. Use *grep* to analyze the files for the keywords and save the results to a file:

```
grep -aibf key_word_list image.disk > search_results.txt
```

 4. Display the results:

```
cat search_results.txt
```

 5. Analyze the files at each offset using the *hexdump* tool, *xxd*:

```
xxd -s (offset) image.disk | less
```

The Sleuth Kit

The Sleuth Kit (TSK) is a collection of command line tools based on The Coroner's Toolkit (TCT). The Autopsy Browser is a graphical interface to TSK. Www.sleuthkit.org is the official website for The Sleuth Kit and Autopsy Browser. Both are open source digital forensic tools that run on UNIX systems (including Linux, OS X, FreeBSD, OpenBSD, and Solaris). These tools can be used to analyze NTFS, FAT, Ext2, Ext3, UFS1, and UFS2 file systems and several volume system types. The Sleuth Kit was developed by Brian Carrier.

The Sleuth Kit (formerly known as TASK) is a collection of UNIX-based command line file and volume system forensic analysis tools. The file system tools allow the examination of file systems associated with a suspect computer in a non-intrusive fashion. The tools do not rely on the operating system to process the file systems which means that deleted and hidden content is shown.

The volume system (media management) tools allow the examination of the disk layout and other media. The Sleuth Kit maintain support for DOS partitions, BSD partitions (disk labels), Mac partitions, Sun slices (Volume Table of Contents), and GPT disks. These tools enable the identification of a partition's location and can also extract partitions for analysis with file system analysis tools.

The Autopsy Forensic Browser is a graphical interface to the tools in The Sleuth Kit, which interfaces with the command line tools to simplify the process. Additionally, Autopsy provides case management, image integrity, keyword searching, and other automated operations that are not available in the individual tools themselves.

Tools Present in "The Sleuth Kit"

The tools in The Sleuth Kit take a disk or file system image as input. All of the file system tools support NTFS, FAT, Ext2/3, and UFS1/2 file systems. An up-to-date list is maintained at the TSK site: www.sleuthkit.org/sleuthkit/tools.php.

File system layer tools process general file system data, such as the layout, allocation structures, and boot blocks. The tool *fsstat* shows file system details and statistics including layout, sizes, and labels.

File name layer tools process the file name structures, which are typically located in the parent directory.

- **ffind** Finds allocated and unallocated file names that point to a given meta-data structure.
- **fls** Lists allocated and deleted file names in a directory.

Metadata layer tools process the metadata structures, which store the details about a file. Examples of this structure include directory entries in FAT, MFT entries in NTFS, and inodes in ExtX and UFS.

- **icat** Extracts the data units of a file, which is specified by its meta-data address (instead of the file name).
- **ifind** Finds the meta-data structure that has a given file name pointing to it or the meta-data structure that points to a given data unit.
- **ils** Lists the meta-data structures and their contents in a pipe delimited format.
- **istat** Displays the statistics and details about a given meta-data structure in an easy to read format.

Data unit layer tools process the data units where file content is stored. Examples of this layer include clusters in FAT and NTFS, and blocks and fragments in ExtX and UFS.

- **dcat** Extracts the contents of a given data unit.
- **dls** Lists the details about data units and can extract the unallocated space of the file system.
- **dstat** Displays the statistics about a given data unit in an easy to read format.
- **dcalc** Calculates where data in the unallocated space image (from dls) exists in the original image. This is used when evidence is found in unallocated space.

File system journal tools process the journal that is implemented in selected file systems. A journal records the metadata (and occasionally content) updates that are made. This may aid in the recovery of recently deleted data. Examples of file systems with journals include Ext3 and NTFS.

- **jcat** Display the contents of a specific journal block.
- **jls** List the entries in the file system journal.

Medium management tools take a disk (or other media) image as input and analyze its partition structures. Examples include DOS partitions, BSD disk labels, and the Sun Volume Table of Contents (VTOC). These can be used to find hidden data between partitions and to identify the file system offset for The Sleuth Kit tools. The media management tools support DOS partitions, BSD disk labels, Sun VTOC, and Mac partitions.

The tool *mmls* displays the layout of a disk, including the unallocated spaces. The output identifies the type of partition and its length, which makes it easy to use *dd* to extract the partitions. The output is sorted based on the starting sector so it is easy to identify gaps in the layout.

Image file tools work with the format of the image file. For instance, they can work with an image format that is a split image or a compressed image.

- **img_stat** This tool will show the details of the image format.
- **img_cat** This tool will show the raw contents of an image file.

Disk tools may be used to detect and remove a Host Protected Area (HPA) in an ATA disk. A HPA could be used to hide data so that it would not be copied during an acquisition. These tools are only available for Linux at the present time.

- **disk_sreset** This tool will temporarily remove a HPA if one exists. After the disk is reset, the HPA will return.
- **disk_stat** This tool will show if a HPA exists.

A number of other miscellaneous tools can also be found in the toolkit.

- **hfind** Uses a binary sort algorithm to look up hashes in the NIST, NSRL, Hashkeeper, and custom hash databases created by md5sum.
- **mactime** Takes input from the *fls* and *ils* tools to create a timeline of file activity.
- **sorter** Sorts files based on their file type and performs extension checking and hash database look-ups.
- **sigfind** Searches for a binary value at a given offset. Useful for recovering lost data structures.

Autopsy

The Autopsy Forensic Browser is an HTML front-end for The Sleuth Kit. As such, it provides a graphical interface to the command line digital forensic analysis tools in The Sleuth Kit. Together, they can analyze Windows and UNIX disks and file systems (NTFS, FAT, UFS1/2, Ext2/3). The Sleuth Kit and Autopsy are both Open Source and run on Linux/UNIX platforms.

The code of Autopsy is open source and all files that it uses are in a raw format. All configuration files are in ASCII text and cases are organized by directories. This makes it easy to export the data and archive it. It also does not restrict the use of other tools that may solve the particular problem better.

EXERCISE 6.03

STEP-BY-STEP APPROACH TO RUNNING AUTOPSY

1. Use the Sleuth Kit for Linux forensics investigations, and boot your computer using the Helix Bootable CD-ROM (Figure 6.10).

Figure 6.10 Helix Start Screen Under Linux

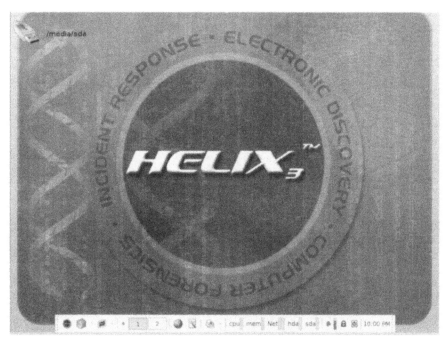

2. Choose Forensics | Forensics | Autopsy. Start the Autopsy Forensic Browser. The main screen is shown in Figure 6.11.

Figure 6.11 Step 2: Start the Autopsy Forensic Browser

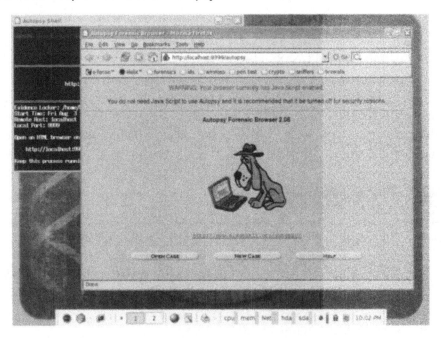

3. Click New Case, as circled in Figure 6.12.

Figure 6.12 Step 3: Start a New Case

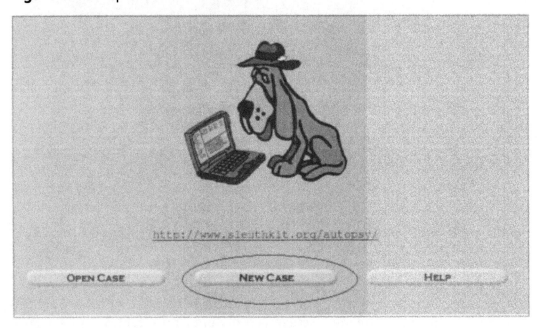

4. Enter the following details and click **New Case** (see Figure 6.13).

Figure 6.13 Step 4: Enter the Case Details

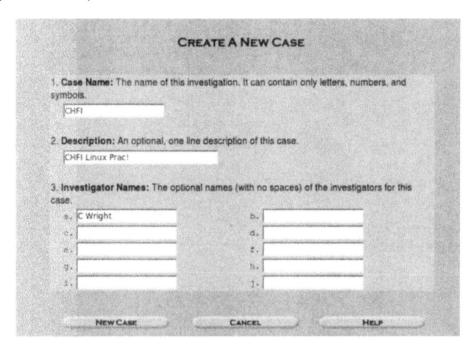

5. You will see the Creating Case screen, as shown in Figure 6.14. Don't forget to note where the evidence directory is located. You will see the following message:

Figure 6.14 Step 5: Note where the Evidence Directory is located

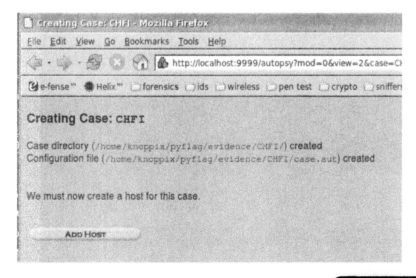

6. Click Add Host and fill in the form that appears (see Figure 6.15).

Figure 6.15 Step 6: Add a Host to the Case

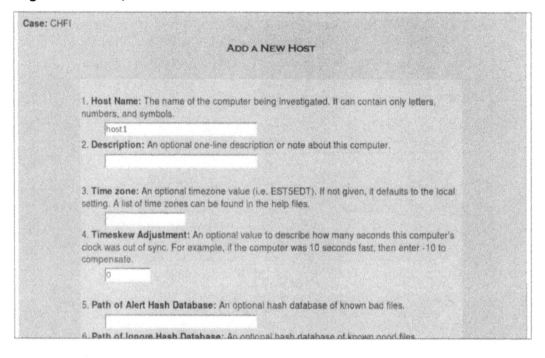

7. Note where the host is located. You will be presented with the screen in Figure 6.16:

Figure 6.16 Step 7: Note Where the Host is Located

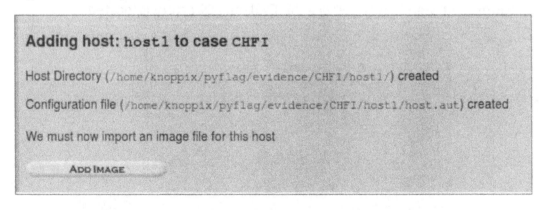

8. Add the disk image by pressing the Add Image button (Example: /home/CHFI.img. Autopsy expects that you have already captured an image of the disk using the dd command).

9. Now you will add an image to analyze from the Add a New Image screen (Figure 6.17) Select the location of the image to analyze (see Figure 6.18).

Figure 6.17 Step 8: Add an Image to Analyze

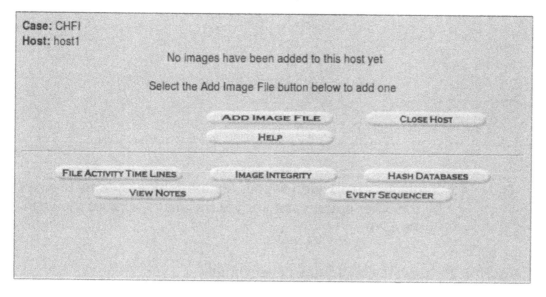

Figure 6.18 Step 9: Select the Location of the Image to Analyze

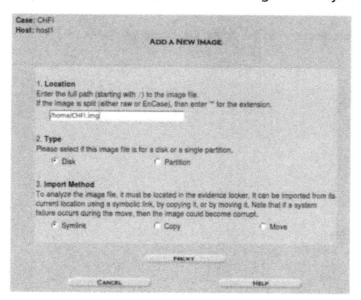

10. Go back to the Case Gallery and look at your options. You will be presented with the screen in Figure 6.19:

Figure 6.19 Step 10: The Case Gallery

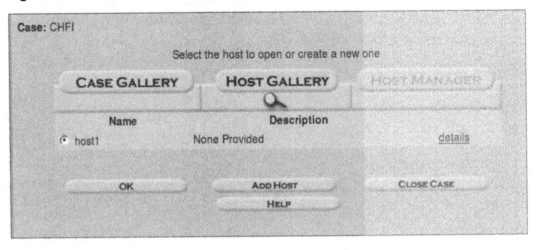

11. Continue to work with various features of the Autopsy browser. Try the other options and analyze the image (options shown in Figure 6.20).

Figure 6.20 Step 11: Now Try the Other Options

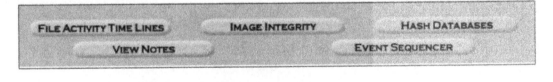

The Evidence Analysis Techniques in Autopsy

This section introduces the primary modes and functions of the Autopsy Forensic Browser. This collection of tools acts as a graphical front end to the Sleuth Kit and other related tools in order to provide the capabilities of analysis, search, and case management in a simple but comprehensive package.

A dead analysis occurs when a dedicated analysis system is used to examine the data from a suspect system. When this occurs, Autopsy and The Sleuth Kit are run in a trusted environment, typically in a lab. Autopsy and TSK provide support for raw, Expert Witness, and AFF file formats.

A live analysis occurs when the suspect system is being analyzed while it is running. In this case, Autopsy and The Sleuth Kit are run from a CD in a non-trusted environment. This is frequently used during incident response while the incident is being confirmed. Following confirmation, the system is acquired and a dead analysis performed.

The Autopsy Browser provides the following evidence search functionality:

- **File Listing** Analyze the files and directories, including the names of deleted files and files with Unicode-based names.

- **File Content** The contents of files can be viewed in raw, hex, or the ASCII strings can be extracted. When data is interpreted, Autopsy sanitizes it to prevent damage to the local analysis system. Autopsy does not use any client-side scripting languages.

- **Hash Databases** Look up unknown files in a hash database to quickly identify it as good or bad. Autopsy uses the NIST National Software Reference Library (NSRL) and user-created databases of known good and known bad files.

- **File Type Sorting** Sort the files based on their internal signatures to identify files of a known type. Autopsy can also extract only graphic images (including thumbnails). The extension of the file will also be compared to the file type to identify files that may have had their extension changed to hide them.

- **Timeline of File Activity** A timeline of file activity can help identify areas of a file system that may contain evidence. Autopsy can create timelines that contain entries for the Modified, Access, and Change (MAC) times of both allocated and unallocated files.

- **Keyword Search** Keyword searches of the file system image can be performed using ASCII strings and *grep* regular expressions. Searches can be performed on either the full file system image or just the unallocated space. An index file can be created for faster searches. Strings that are frequently searched for can be easily configured into Autopsy for automated searching.

- **Meta Data Analysis** Meta-data structures contain the details about files and directories. Autopsy allows you to view the details of any meta-data structure in the file

system. This is useful for recovering deleted content. Autopsy will search the directories to identify the full path of the file that has allocated the structure.

- **Data Unit Analysis** Data Units are where the file content is stored. Autopsy allows you to view the contents of any data unit in a variety of formats including ASCII, hexdump, and strings. The file type is also given and Autopsy will search the metadata structures to identify which has allocated the data unit.

- **Image Details** File system details can be viewed, including on-disk layout and times of activity. This mode provides information that is useful during data recovery.

Autopsy provides a number of functions that aid in case management. In particular, investigations started within Autopsy are organized by cases, which can contain one or more hosts. Each host is configured to have its own time zone setting and clock skew so that the times shown are the same as the original user would have seen. Each host can contain one or more file system images to analyze. The following functions within Autopsy are specifically designed to aid in case management:

- **Event Sequencer** Time-based events can be added from file activity or IDS and firewall logs. Autopsy sorts the events so that the sequence of incidents associated with an event can be easily determined.

- **Notes** Notes can be saved on a per-host and per-investigator basis. These allow the investigator to make quick notes about files and structures. The original location can be easily recalled with the click of a button when the notes are later reviewed. All notes are stored in an ASCII file.

- **Image Integrity** Since one of the most crucial aspects of a forensics investigation involves ensuring that data is not modified during analysis, Autopsy will generate an MD5 value for all files that are imported or created by default. The integrity of any file that Autopsy uses can be validated at any time.

- **Reports** Autopsy can create ASCII reports for files and other file system structures. This enables investigators to promptly make consistent data sheets during the course of the investigation.

- **Logging** Audit logs are created on a case, host, and investigator level so that all actions can be easily retrieved. The entire Sleuth Kit commands are logged exactly as they are executed on the system.

SMART for Linux

SMART by ASR Data is a commercial GUI forensic tool for Linux. It is a software utility that has been designed and optimized to support data forensic practitioners and Information

Security personnel in pursuit of their respective duties and goals. The SMART software and methodology have been developed with the intention of integrating technical, legal, and end-user requirements into a complete package that enables the user to perform their job most effectively and efficiently.

SMART includes a number of features that allow it to be used in a wide range of situations, including:

- "Knock-and-talk" inquiries and investigations
- On-site or remote preview of a target system
- Postmortem analysis of a dead system
- Testing and verification of other forensic programs
- Conversion of proprietary "evidence file? formats
- Baselining of a system

SMART lists the connected storage devices in its main window. Devices are listed based on the hardware connection type. Both drive partitions and unpartitioned space are listed as sub-items in the same layout as is on the device. Information such as the device make and model, storage capacity, and even partition disk usage are displayed together on a simple interface. Detailed information, such as a serial number or raw byte count, may be accessed by right clicking on the device.

Penguin Sleuth

The Penguin Sleuth Bootable CD is a forensic tool collection on CD by Ernest Bacca and is available from www.linux-forensics.com. Penguin Sleuth contains many useful tools. It is an adapted version of the Knoppix Linux Live CD that has been modified to include tools that are useful when performing a forensic computer analysis.

Tools Included in Penguin Sleuth Kit

The Penguin Sleuth Kit Base Package contains the following applications:

- **Gentoo Linux 2.6 Kernel** Optimized for Forensics Use
- **XFCE** GUI
- **Apache2** Server
- **MySQL** PHP4
- **Open Office**
- **Gimp** Graphics Program
- **KSnapshot** Screen Capture Program

- **Mozilla**

- **Gnome** CD Master

- **K3b** CD Burner

- **XMMS** Media player

- **Porthole** Gentoo Graphics Package Manager

- **Karchiver** GZIp GUI

It also includes a number of Forensics Tools, including:

- **Sleuth Kit** Forensics Kit

- **Py-Flag** Forensics Browser

- **Autopsy** Forensics Browser for Sleuth Kit

- **dcfldd** DD Imaging Tool command line tool and also works with AIR

- **foremost** Data Carver command line tool

- **Air** Forensics Imaging GUI

- **md5deep** MD5 Hashing Program

- **netcat** Command Line

- **cryptcat** Command Line

- **NTFS** Tools

- **qtparted** GUI Partitioning Tool

- **regviewer** Windows Registry Viewer

Additionally, the CD distribution also contains a number of Security Tools that may aid in incident response and investigation:

- **Etherape** GUI Network Traffic Monitor

- **Clamv** Anti Virus

- **snort** Command Line

- **John the Ripper** Command Line password cracker

- **rkhunter** Command Line

- **Ethereal** Network Traffic Analyzer

- **FWBuilder** GUI Firewall App

- **nessus** network scanner

Forensix

The goal of the Forensix Project (National Science Foundation [NSF] under Grant ANI-0230960—AKA "4N6") is to allow a system to be monitored so that, in the event of a security compromise, it is easy to track the compromise back to its source. The Forensix system requires two machines:

■ The potentially insecure "front-line" machine

■ A verified secure back-end

Forensix stores information describing system calls in a MySQL database on the back-end and is built on top of SNARE.

Forensix is designed to aid forensic examiners by increasing the efficiency, accuracy, and ease of completing an imaging and analysis assignment. The product aids in ensuring the integrity of image data and introduces a scientific process that creates reproducible analytical results with detailed documentation.

Maresware

Mares and Company (www.maresware.com/) produce a number of programs suited to computer forensics and data analysis. One forensic analyst using Linux is the software suite, Maresware: Linux Forensics.

Maresware: Linux Forensics provides tools for investigating computer records while running under the LINUX operating system on Intel processors. The software aids in the forensic discovery of evidence. Maresware: Computer Forensics software is a suite of tools designed for forensic analysis. The entire package of software applications is available together in Maresware: The Suite.

Major Programs Present in Maresware

The (F) or (D), or both (F,D), after each description designates which package the program is included in: (F)orensic or (D)ata Analysis. The programs unique to this suite, which are not contained in any other packages, include: Boot, Dater, Eventlog, Modify, and Mxcopy. These programs add several functions to your toolkit in the areas of systems maintenance, administrative tasks, and computer security. An asterisk (*) indicates that a similar program exists for LINUX.

■ **Bates_no** A unique program for adding identifying numbers to filenames in e-documents. Prepare your records for evidentiary use or simply use as a records management tool.

■ **Catalog** Catalogs every file on a Linux file system. Also identifies headers. Similar to Maresware Diskcat (which is DOS based).

- **Hash** Performs MD5 (CRC, or SHA) hash of every file on a drive.

- **Hashcmp** Compares outputs of successive hash runs.

- **Md5** Calculates MD5 hash of a file. MIT?s Linux source code for MD5 has been compiled to run on a Linux operating system.

- **Strsrch** Searches files for text strings. Similar to Maresware *Strsrch* (which is DOS based).

- **U_to_A** Converts UNIX text to DOS text.

A complete list of software available from Mares and Company may be found at www.maresware.com/maresware/suite_programs.htm.

Captain Nemo

Captain Nemo is a "Multi Platform File Manager" that allows mapping and access to Novell, NTFS, and Linux drives from any Windows computer. It consists of a file viewer, which enables viewing and access to almost any file type. It also offers a search function, which enables the capability to conduct extensive searches for specific text or files. It will also display the owners and attributes of every file to the limit of the file system that is being analyzed.

The product also allows the forensic investigator to copy files from an imaged Netware/NTFS/Linux partition to the Windows partition (see Table 6.3 for details).

Table 6.3 Supported File Systems with Captain Nemo

File System	Supported File Systems	Remarks
Novell	Netware 3.xx Netware 4.xx Netware 5.xx	File sub allocation is supported. File compression is supported. Long file names are supported. Volumes consisting of several drives aren't supported.
Microsoft Windows	NTFS 2000 XP	File compression is supported. Striping is not supported.
Linux	ext2fs ext3fs	

The Farmer's Boot CD

The Farmer's Boot CD (available for download from www.forensicbootcd.com) leads an emerging trend in Digital Forensics by allowing the previewing of a system before imaging it. This is useful with today's large hard drives because if, during the preliminary review, significant

data is discovered then the package switches modes to acquire the image. If on the other hand no data of relevance is discovered, then the forensic analyst can save time and storage space by moving on to the next system.

The primary goal of The Farmer's Boot CD (FBCD) is to provide the forensic analyst with the tools and methodology to securely and promptly sample systems (hard drives, USB drives, digital music devices, digital camera media, and anything else of interest) to aid in the identification of evidence and in making the decision whether or not to proceed to imaging.

As taken from the above Web site, The Farmer's Boot CD allows the forensic analyst to:

- Boot most x86 systems

- Mount file systems in a forensic manner

- Preview data using a single, unified graphical user interface (GUI)

- Acquire media after you?ve previewed the data and found it pertinent to your investigation

- Automatically mount file systems

- Automatically update superblocks on RAID arrays

- Preview Windows operating systems, viewing important data stores with a simple click of the mouse. This includes viewing the Recycle Bin, reading Windows Event logs, finding e-mail addresses and URLs in the *pagefile.sys* file, and reviewing web browser (Internet Explorer, Opera, and Mozilla) cache file entries (both cookies and history information).

- Preview Linux operating systems including parsing web browser activity and reviewing important log files, and collect a list of recently used files.

- Use a Windows Explorer-like file manager, point-and-clicking through the directory structure.

- Generate lists of system users and attempt to crack their passwords, for both Windows and Linux operating systems.

- Decrypt EFS-encrypted files found on some Windows operating systems.

- Convert between many different date formats with one click of your mouse: UNIX 32bit, Windows 64bit, human readable, and hexadecimal.

- Catalog a file system, searching for only those files that pertain to your case, by identifying them either by extension or by file header.

- Generate thumbnails for all graphics files on a file system either by extension or by header.

- Preview digital cameras and preview the contents of onboard memory, dumping software information as well as any graphics or video files.

- Authenticate and acquire file systems or devices in simple point-and-click GUIs.

- Generate a catalog of all hardware attached to the system, including serial numbers, make and model information, and settings and configuration information.

- Dump BIOS information of a system, providing you with a file that most practitioners never see. Information obtained is BIOS dependent, but typically includes BIOS version, vendor information, characteristics, universally unique IDs (UUID), and serial numbers.

- Obtain both hard drive and file system information by pointing-and-clicking.

- Generate a list of deleted files for FAT12/16/32, NTFS, and ext2 file system types.

- Capture network traffic and analyze with the provided tools as dictated by your case. This includes HTTP, e-mail, and messenger traffic.

- Quickly preview all sessions found on multi-session CDs.

- Identify data residing in file slack for supported file system types.

- Analyze the Windows registry using the provided tools.

Summary of Exam Objectives

There are advantages to both Linux- and Windows-based forensic processes. Ultimately, the most successful process will be a result of using each operating system based on its strengths and, where possible, aborting its weaknesses.

Windows live system analysis provides information that is volatile in nature and is lost or destroyed when analyzed off line. The analysis of file slack (the space existing at the end of the file of the last cluster), ADS (NTFS Alternate Data Streams), and system memory can aid in the identification of network logon names, passwords, and other sensitive information. This offers advantages to the forensic investigator since volatile Windows data is a vital source of evidence and leads.

The command *dir /O:d* has an important role during the investigation of a Windows system. Registry is also an important component to be examined during an investigation of a Windows system. Certain keys must be checked and given added importance as they inform the investigator on what services have been running, what services are currently running, and who has logged on to the system over a certain period of time.

Linux imparts greater control, flexibility, and power as a forensics tool than Windows, due to its ability to access devices at a physical layer. The addition of a number of simple utilities make imaging and basic analysis of suspect disks and drives easier, allowing for a simpler imaging process once the forensic analyst becomes familiar with the command-line quirks associated with Linux. To help reduce the issues associated with the Linux command-line, several popular Linux toolkits that provide a GUI interface have been developed.

The addition of NASA's loopback driver (a kernel module) introduces the ability to associate an entire disk image with a single loop device. Alternatively, devices have to be mapped partition by partition. Often raw data with valuable evidence can reside on a disk in an area outside the partition.

The main thing that you need to bring from this chapter is an understanding of the forensic process and how tools can aid you. It is important to understand that it is sometimes necessary and often rewarding to analyze live systems. The important thing to remember here is to minimize the amount of change. Volatile data needs to be collected quickly and you need to document what you have done. This chapter should have provided you with an overview of the tasks that you will need to do in order to conduct a forensic engagement on either Windows or Linux-based systems.

Exam Objectives
Frequently Asked Questions

The following Frequently Asked Questions, answered by the authors of this book, are designed to both measure your understanding of the Exam Objectives presented in this chapter, and to assist you with real-life implementation of these concepts.

Q: If live incident response and forensics always changes the system, how can I do this without corrupting the evidence?

A: This is the primary reason for collecting evidence using a document procedure and process. By maintaining a strong chain of custody over the evidence and documenting each step you take, while trying to minimize any changes you make to the system, you can demonstrate that the additional processes added value without significantly changing the system. Live systems hold valuable information and thus evidence in volatile data. It is not possible to obtain volatile data without making some changes to the system being analyzed, but the benefits far outweigh the risk of damaging the data.

Q: I know what I am doing, why do I have to write it down?

A: Often, court cases and litigation occur months or years after the analysis of the data and collection of the evidence. Keeping good notes mean that the value of the evidence you have collected will be maintained and you are less likely to forget what occurred. Tools such as the Helix Live CD for Windows aid in this process by creating automated logs of the activities that you took within them. The output from these files may then be maintained as part of the evidence.

Q: Examining Windows file slack seems like a lot of effort to get broken bits of files.

A: File fragments are admissible in court. Often, file fragments are not the only thing found in file slack. Windows file slack and RAM slack can contain entire files, e-mail, images, or information from the system memory. Of particular importance, information that is normally never stored on disk at all and is certainly never saved on the system can occasionally be found in file slack. In fact, it is possible to find both user names and passwords within file slack.

Q: I have always used Windows, why should I learn Linux?

A: Linux provides a level of access to the system that is not available on Windows. The secret is to use the tool that provides the best results. It is important to be familiar with both Windows and Linux and there are benefits to both systems.

Q: I have heard that it is always possible to write to a device on Linux. What is the purpose of the read-only option in the mount command then and does it do anything?

A: It is always possible to write to the physical device if you have the right permissions and Linux or UNIX system. An example would be writing to the */dev/hdc* physical drive. When you mount a drive on Linux, the mount point that you set it to can be configured to be read-only. The important thing to remember is not to write to the physical drive and only use the read-only mounted partition. Just because functionality is there does not mean you need to use it. Like everything in a forensic assignment, take due care and record directions.

Chapter 7

CHFI

Steganography and Application Password Crackers

Exam objectives in this chapter:

- Classification of Steganography
- Six Categories of Steganography in Forensics
- Types of Steganography
- Application of Steganography
- Hiding in Network Packets
- Issues in Information Hiding
- Steg Tools
- Steganography vs. Watermarking
- Attacking Watermarking
- Detecting and Attacking Steganography
- Application Password Cracking

Introduction

In this chapter we will discuss the technique of steganography and application password cracking. First we will discuss the concept of steganography. Steganography is defined as "hiding information in plain sight." Steganography differs from cryptography in the fact that steganography does not take a "plain" text form as input and scramble it into a "cipher" text like cryptography does. Furthermore, steganography does not alter the form of the information it is hiding. Quite simply, you use steganography to place information inside a file.

There are two types of files that are used in steganography: the file that you use to hold information that can be in the form of text or another file called the carrier file; and the file that is to be inserted into the carrier, known as the hidden file. The carrier file is also referred to as the host file in some steganography documentation. Now that we have explored what steganography is, let's take a look at some of the past history of steganography.

History of Steganography

Steganography comes from the joining of two words. These words are of Greek origin: *steganos*, meaning covert or secretive; and *graphie*, meaning writing. Putting the two words together means "*covered writing.*"

The Greeks

In *The Histories*, Herodotus documented several instances where steganography was used. One such case involved a Greek named Histaiaeus, who wanted to encourage Aristagoras of Miletus to revolt against the Persian king, and managed to do so in a rather inventive way. In order to pass these instructions securely, Histaiaeus shaved the head of his messenger, wrote the message on his bare scalp, and then waited for the hair to grow back. When the messenger reached his destination—and Aristagoras—his head was shaved and the message read. Although this certainly isn't the quickest method of communication, it was very effective since the messenger was able to pass guard inspections without harassment since he was carrying nothing suspicious.

The Chinese

The Chinese used steganography during the Yuan dynasty to revolt when China was ruled by the Mongolian people. The leaders of the time, unhappy at having to submit to foreign rule, created an inventive method of coordinating the rebellion without being discovered. The rebel leaders, knowing that the Moon Festival was drawing near, ordered the making of special cakes called "moon cakes." Baked into each moon cake was a message with the outline of the attack. On the night of the Moon Festival, the cakes were dispersed, the messages read, and the rebels successfully attacked and overthrew the government. What followed was the establishment of the Ming dynasty. Today, moon cakes are eaten to commemorate this legend.

The Culpers

Steganography played a role in the Revolutionary War and helped George Washington on many occasions. The code ring consisted of five people and used the codename Samuel Culper. Several trial and error attempts at secret communication prompted the Culpers to adopt invisible ink as one of their security precautions. The invisible ink was used on a blank piece of paper, and after the message was written, was reinserted into a ream of new, blank paper. Washington knew that by counting from the top down to a specific sheet how to find the hidden message. He would then apply a second solution to make the ink appear. A concern of Washington's was that carrying around blank sheets of paper would create suspicion, so he ordered that the invisible ink also be used on regular messages, and that the secret message be written between the lines or under the message.

Civil War Rugs

A form of steganography was used prior to the Civil War to aid slaves in escaping to freedom. In the 1800s, the underground railroad was one of the main escape routes used by slaves. Quilts, which were hung outside to dry, became an ideal way to display information inconspicuously. The quilts would have special patterns sewn into them that would convey messages to prepare or provide direction to escaping slaves who knew what to look for.

World War I

During World War I there were several periods and instances where steganography was used with success. One method was called a Turning Grille; this took Cardano's Grille method and enhanced it. The Turning Grille looked like a normal grille (a square sheet of cardboard) divided into cells, with some of the cells punched out. To use the Turning Grille, the encoder would write the first sequence of letters, and then rotate the grille 90 degrees, write the second sequence of letters, and so on, rotating the grille after each sequence.

There was also a record during the war of a cable censor who received the message "Father is dead." The censor changed the message to "Father is deceased." A reply came back: "Is Father dead or deceased?"

World War II

Steganography, and its prevention, were also prevalent in World War II. After the attack on Pearl Harbor the United States enacted a censorship organization. This organization worked to think of ways that coded messages could be passed in the open and took steps to stop them or, if there was a message, destroy the code.

Chess games were banned by mail, crossword puzzles were examined or removed from correspondence and newspaper clippings, and student's grades were removed.

Stamps were removed and replaced with ones of equal value but different denominations or numbers. Children's pictures were replaced, Xs and Os from love letters were removed, and

of course blank paper was replaced and tested for invisible ink. Mass media was censored, too. Telephone and telegraph requests for special songs were not allowed and mail-in song requests would be held for a random amount of time before being played.

The Vietnam War

Another, and well-publicized, example of steganography happened during the height of the Vietnam War. Commander Jeremiah Denton, a naval pilot who had been shot down and captured, was paraded around by the North Vietnamese in front of the news as part of a propaganda event. Knowing that he was under the proverbial microscope and unable to say anything openly critical about his captors, he blinked his eyes in Morse code, spelling out T-O-R-T-U-R-E, as he spoke to the media.

Terrorists

It is speculated that the terrorists who made up the "cell" located in the United States used steganography to communicate information between the leaders of Al-Qaeda and themselves. Part of this speculation is from captured computer files that have been found during various raids. It is really impossible to know if the "cell" did actually use steganography to communicate, but equally difficult is proving they did not.

The Future of Steganography

One powerful concept of steganography we will discuss in this chapter is the technique of hiding messages or information within a binary file. This is a powerful way to hide information, and short of reverse engineering, or disassembling the code there really is no way to tell if this technique is being used. Fortunately, the technique largely exists in the minds of a select few, and we have no indications that it is being used widespread. Refer to the sidebar, "Notes from the Underground," for more.

Classification of Steganography

There are essentially three classifications of Steganography today. The first one is the technique of inserting information inside another file. The second is the process that takes the composition of the file, and substitutes information. The third is one that uses a different model, because it creates a file with the intent of hiding information; an example of this is the capabilities you can use at the Web site www.spammimic.com.

Background Information to Image Steganography

The concept of image steganography is when a file that is some form of image like a bmp, jpg, tif, or gif file is used to hide information. The information that is hidden can be in the form of

a file or of an actual message. The process takes the user supplied message or image, and hides it in the file. There are several techniques for doing this that we will look at next. The main techniques are insertion, substitution, and creation. As we will see next, each has its own advantages and disadvantages when hiding information.

Insertion

In this method of steganography, the objective of the hiding technique is to place the information to be hidden inside the carrier or host file. This is done without any alteration of the existing information of the file. The problem with this is that when the information is inserted it increases the size of the original file, and makes it easy to detect the presence of the steg. You could use this technique if you made sure to wipe the original file once the steg file is created. As long as you did not leave a trace (hence, wipe!) of the original file on the machine it would be very difficult to determine the file had steg, because without the original file, traditional integrity checks like hashing would not have a baseline with which to compare.

Substitution

You might see some steganography references refer to this as transformation-based, but for this text we will refer to it as substitution. A popular way to hide information with this technique is to use the least significant bit (LSB) and noise manipulation method. This technique works by taking the binary data of the host, or carrier file, and changes the LSB of each pixel. The rightmost portion of the number is the LSB, and since it is the LSB, the manipulation of it has little effect on the original number or the original image; therefore, we can modify all the LSBs in the file with little or no change in the original file. The process works by taking the file that is to be hidden, and breaking it into chunks of binary data. Once the file is broken down, the resulting chunks of binary data are written to and stored in the LSBs throughout the file. The following example shows an 8-digit binary number being encoded using LSB.

Example 1

Pixel: 00 11 00 11

Insert 0010

Pixel 00 **10** 0**1** 1**0**

As you can imagine, working with 8-bit colors can be a challenge; that is why images that use 24-bit color are the ones that are preferred for the best results. With a 24-bit image, you can get usage of 3 LSBs per pixel. The reason the insertion technique works so well is the human eye can distinguish only six bits of color, and since the technique is working on the LSB of an 8-bit number. The changes are virtually undetectable.

Creation

A cover file is *generated* for the sole purpose of concealing a secret message. In this technique a picture is created of something innocent that can be passed to another person. The innocent picture is the cover that provides the mechanism for conveying the message.

Another, more modern form of generation of new files is the program Spam Mimic. Spam Mimic embeds a text message within a rather daunting piece of spam that can be e-mailed to an intended recipient. Although this generated spam doesn't make a whole lot of sense, it makes enough sense to be believable, and that's all that's needed. An excellent reference for this is the book *Disappearing Cryptography: Being and Nothingness on the Net*, by Peter Wayne (AP Professional, San Diego, 1996). The book also includes code to create this type of steganography.

Six Categories of Steganography in Forensics

In all methods of steganography, something is being done to conceal a message. Naturally, these actions or techniques can be separated and analyzed to learn what's happening during the whole process. The six categories of steganography are substitution system techniques, transform domain techniques, spread spectrum techniques, statistical method techniques, distortion techniques, and cover generation techniques. We'll look at each of these, one at a time.

Substitution System

Substitution system steganography replaces redundant or unneeded bits of a cover with the bits from the secret message. Several available steganography tools use the Least Significant Bit (LSB) method of encoding the secret message. LSB works like this. In a digital cover file, there is a tremendous amount of wasted or redundant space. It is this space that the steganography program will take advantage of and use to hide another message (on the bit level) within the digital cover.

Transform Domain Techniques

The transform domain technique is also very effective, but is a little trickier to explain. Basically, transform domain techniques hide message data in the "transform space" of a signal. If you're saying to yourself, "Huh?", hold on and I'll explain. Every day on the Internet, people send pictures back and forth, and most often they use a JPEG format. JPEGs are interesting in that they compress themselves when they close. In order for this to take place, they have to get rid of excess data (excess bits) that would otherwise prevent them from compressing. During compression, a JPEG will make an approximation of itself to become smaller. This change transforms space; thus, it can be used to hide information.

Spread Spectrum Techniques

In this section we briefly define two types of spread spectrum techniques: direct sequence and frequency hopping.

In direct sequence spread spectrum, the stream of information to be transmitted is divided into small pieces, each of which is allocated to a frequency channel spread across the spectrum. A data signal at the point of transmission is combined with a higher data-rate bit sequence (also known as a chipping code) that divides the data according to a spreading ratio. The redundant chipping code helps the signal resist interference and also enables the original data to be recovered if data bits are damaged during transmission.

Frequency hopping is when a broad slice of the bandwidth spectrum is divided into many possible broadcast frequencies. In general, frequency-hopping devices use less power and are cheaper, but the performance of direct sequence spread spectrum systems is usually better and more reliable.

Statistical Methods

Statistical methods use what's called a "1-bit" steganographic scheme. This scheme embeds one bit of information only in a digital carrier and thus creates a statistical change, even if it's only a slight one. A statistical change in the cover indicates a 1, whereas a cover left unchanged indicates a 0. This system works based on the receiver's ability to distinguish between modified and unmodified covers.

Distortion Techniques

The distortion method of steganography creates a change in a cover object to hide information. The secret message is recovered when the algorithm compares the changed and/or distorted cover with the original.

Cover Generation Methods

Cover generation methods are probably the most unique of the six types. Typically, a cover object is chosen to hide a message in, but that's not the case here. A cover generation method actually creates a cover for the sole purpose of hiding information. Spam Mimic is an excellent example of a cover generation method.

Types of Steganography

Now that we've looked at the categories of stego, let's look at the two types of stego, linguistic and technical.

Linguistic Steganography

Linguistic steganography can be described quite simply as any form of steganography that uses language in the cover. A number of forms of linguistic steganography are covered in the next sections, but the two most basic categories are open codes and text semagrams.

A program that takes advantage of linguistic steganography is NICETEXT, which uses the technique of linguistic steganography in a very inventive way. The goal of NICETEXT is to provide a program that can transform cipher text (encrypted text) into text that looks like natural language, while still providing a cover for the original cipher text. An added benefit of this type of program is that it can be applied to many different languages.

Text Semagrams

Text Semagrams work with graphical modifications of the text, such as type-spacing and offsetting. They concern details that are tiny, but nonetheless visible. Certain methods work without text as well. These are called real semagrams.

Technical Steganography

Technical steganography is a little broader in scope since it doesn't necessarily deal with the written word, even though it communicates information. Technical steganography is the method of steganography where a tool, device, or method is used to conceal the message. Let's have a look at some technical steganography methods.

Embedding Methods

The technical challenges of data hiding are formidable. Any "holes" to fill with data in a host file, either statistical or perceptual, are likely targets for removal by lossy compression. The key to successful data hiding is the finding of holes that are not suitable for exploitation by compression algorithms.

Least Significant Bit

Least Significant Bit (LSB) is the substitution method of steganography where the right-most bit in a binary notation, the bit with the least impact on the binary data, is replaced with a bit from the embedded message. This method provides "security through obscurity," a technique that can be rendered useless if an attacker knows the technique is being used.

Transform Techniques

Three main types of transform techniques can be used when embedding a message in steganography. They are the Discrete Cosine Transform (DCT), the Discrete Fourier Transform, and the Wavelet Transform, which simply embeds the secret data in the cover during the *transformation* process in various ways.

Spread Spectrum Encoding

Spread spectrum encoding is the method of hiding a small or narrow-band signal (a message) in a large or wide band cover. The foundation of this process begins with a spread spectrum encoder. The encoder works by modulating a narrow band signal over a carrier. The carrier's signal is continually shifted using a noise generator and a secret key that makes the noise seem random. The message is embedded in the existing noise of the carrier signal. This spreads the narrow signal over a wide area, decreasing the density of the hidden signal and making it much more difficult to detect within the overall carrier signal.

Perceptual Masking

This form of steganography occurs when one signal, or sound, becomes imperceptible to the observer because of the presence of another signal. This method also exploits the weaknesses of the human visual and auditory systems. A common example that almost everyone has seen is in spy films where someone is trying to communicate with someone else in a room they know is bugged. Usually the secret agent will turn up the stereo, run the shower, or do some other innocent (but noisy) task that allows a whispered conversation to take place without being heard.

Notes from the Underground...

Raising the Bar in Information Hiding

At the Blackhat USA conference in 2004 in Las Vegas, two researchers, Rakfan El Khalil and Angelos D. Keromytis, from Columbia University in New York gave a presentation based on their research, and a whitepaper that they had published. They presented an advanced concept in steganography that to date had little research published on it. Part of their presentation was the demonstration of a tool that they called "Hydan," which is an old English word that means to hide or conceal. The focus of this tool is to hide information inside of binary files. It accomplishes this by taking a binary file and analyzing the machine code of the file. Once the tool finishes the analysis, the tool will take a message, and attempt to hide it in the machine code of the file. The tool deploys a registry swapping, and instruction substitution methodology. In a registry swapping methodology, the tool will take an instruction like *mov% esi,% esi* and change it to *mov %eax, %eax,* and in an instruction substitution, the tool will take *and %esi, %esi* and change it to *or %eax, %eax.*

The last update to the Hydan tool was announced in 2004, so this powerful technique does not seem to be available today, at least not to the general public. This is a good thing, because the power of a tool like this and the implications for the governments of the world would be significant, not to mention the Department of Defense (DoD) and other organizations that rely on protecting information. There really is not a sufficient way to scan through binary types of files, and look for hidden information. So, for the time being this powerful technique seems to be a proof of concept tool, and that for most is a good thing.

Application of Steganography

When you get right down to it, digital steganography is really just the digital manipulation of 1s and 0s. This fact allows for several choices of cover media since we know that whether it be a document, picture, video, or even a file system, in the end it's all just binary. In this next section, we'll look at how stego manipulation can be applied to a wide variety of digital media.

Still Images: Pictures

The methods of steganography are quite varied. With still images, LSB insertion and spread spectrum techniques commonly are used. Texture block is another method. Texture block uses low bit-rate data hiding and is accomplished by copying a region from a random texture pattern in a picture to an area of similar texture resulting in a pair of identically "textured" regions in a picture.

Moving Images: Video

Steganography, when applied to a video file such as an .avi or .mpg, typically uses Discrete Cosine Transform (DCT) manipulation, meaning that as the video is compressed or decompressed, secret data can be added during the transformation process.

Audio Files

The following are various audio file methods:

- **LSB insertion**. The bit with the least impact on the binary data is replaced with a bit from the embedded message.

- **Differential phase variation.** The sound file is divided into blocks, and the initial phase of the sound file is modified with the secret message, preserving the following relative phase shifts. This is an effective method given it has a low signal-to-noise ratio.

- **Spread spectrum schemes.** The method of hiding a small- or narrow-band signal, the secret message, in a large- or wide-band cover.

- **Adding echo to the audio signal**. A slight echo is added to the signal using two different delays to encode the 1 and 0 bits. The echo is too slight to be perceived by the human ear.

Text Files

Three methods exist for text files:

- **Open-space**. The use of white space, between words or sentences, to hide data.

- **Syntactic**. Uses modification of the word order or punctuation to hide a message.

- **Semantic**. Uses synonyms to encode a secret message. (See the earlier example, "Is Father dead or deceased?")

Steganographic File Systems

This is another particularly interesting way of applying steganography. Let's take a closer look. A steganographic file system is a method of storing files in such a way that it encrypts data and hides it so well that it can't be proven it's there.

A steganographic file system can

- Hide users' documents in other seemingly random files.

- Allow the owner to give names and passwords for some files while keeping others secret.

- Behave like a second layer of secrecy. Encrypted files are out in the open and visible, but not understandable. Stego files aren't even visible, and an outsider can't look for files that "aren't there."

Hiding in Disk Space

Three main methods exist for hiding data in disk space: unused sectors, hidden partitions, and slack space. In this section, we'll take a closer look at how each is carried out.

Unused Sectors

Similar to the method used in the section, "Steganographic File Systems," tools that hide data in unused sectors, such as S-tools, will take the file and spread the bits out throughout the free space on the floppy. Though undetectable in the normal Windows viewer, the file is still there.

Hidden Partitions

A hidden partition on a hard drive is another way of hiding information, sometimes large amounts, in plain sight. This method isn't terribly robust since a close examination of the hard drive, independent of the operating system, will usually reveal that the drive is bigger than the OS is letting on.

Slack Space

Slack space is a type of unused space in a disk. Even if the actual data being stored requires less storage than the cluster size, an entire cluster is reserved for the file. The unused space is called

the *slack space*. If minimum space allocated is 32kb and the file is 6kb, then 26kb is left unused and considered unavailable by the operating system. This unused space (slack space) could be used to hide information without showing up in any directory or file system.

Hiding in Network Packets

A covert channel is described as "any communication channel that can be exploited by a process to transfer information in a manner that violates the systems security policy." Essentially, it is a method of communication, referred to as Internet steganography, that is not part of an actual computer system design, but can still be used to transfer information to users or system processes that normally would not have access to the information. Hiding information within network packets can be accomplished a couple of ways. One is Packet Header Manipulation, which hides data in empty fields of the packet header, and Packet "sorting," which resorts packets in such a way that their sequence carries with it a meaning of either 1 or 0, which will ultimately yield a hidden message.

Issues in Information Hiding

Most things in life require trade-offs of some sort. Something for nothing isn't the way the universe works, and information hiding is no exception. The following is a list of limitations associated with trying to hide information steganographically.

Levels of Visibility

When looking at the first issue in information hiding, determining levels of visibility can be done by asking one question: Does the embedding process distort the cover to the point where it is visually noticeable? If the image is unacceptably distorted, the carrier isn't sufficient for the payload; if it isn't distorted, the carrier is adequate.

Robustness vs. Payload

To have a robust method of embedding the message, you must have redundancy to resist changes made to the cover. This redundancy subsequently lowers the payload.

The exact opposite is also true. With little or no redundancy (robustness), the payload of the secret message can be larger.

more robust = lower payload

less robust = higher payload

File Format Dependence

Some image and sound files are either lossy or lossless. The conversion of lossless information to the compressed "lossy" information can destroy the hidden information in the cover. A good example is to think of the conversion of an uncompressed bitmap to a compressed, estimated jpeg. The compression and estimation change the bits to include the bits that might be the embedded message.

Steg Tools

There are a significant amount of tools available for creating steganographic content. These tools come in both open source and commercial versions. The majority of the tools can create steganographic content in a couple of file formats at best; this is because the tool creator wants to focus on a specific set of techniques and algorithms. You are best served to try the tools out, and see for yourself the capabilities of the tools. For this section we will discuss some of the popular tools that are used.

Snow

The tool Snow works by using whitespace to hide information. It is used to conceal text information by appending whitespace to the end of lines. Figure 7.1 shows the usage of Snow to hide a message and recover a message.

Figure 7.1 Hiding and Recovering a Message with Snow

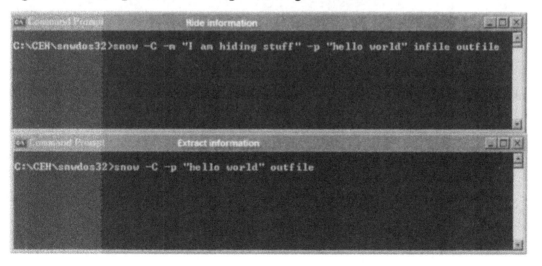

Steganos

This tool has the capability to create steganographic content, and it can encrypt the information to provide another layer of security. It can hide files inside BMP, VOC, WAV, and text files.

Gifshuffle

This program has the capability of storing messages inside GIF images; it accomplishes this by shuffling the colormap. It can work with all GIF images, even the ones that contain transparency and animation. Another feature of the tool is it provides compression and encryption. It has two modes: message concealment and message extraction. Figure 7.2 shows the usage of Gifshuffle.

Figure 7.2 Using Gifshuffle

Outguess

Outguess is a powerful tool that allows the insertion of hidden information into the redundant bits of information found in our files. The tools supports PNM and JPEG file formats. Figure 7.3 shows a screenshot of the tool.

Figure 7.3 The Outguess Tool

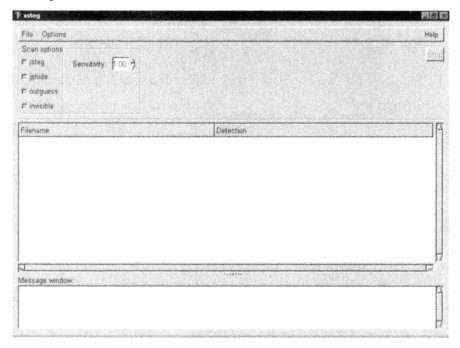

Stegomagic

This tool will hide any kind of file or message, inside of a text file, WAV, or BMP. The tool can use either 24-bit, or BMP 256-bit color files. The data to be hidden does have a size limitation in that it can be approximately only one-eighth the size of the host or carrier file.

Table 7.1 contains a brief list of steganography and steganalysis tools. Study this list to get a quick understanding of the capabilities of these tools.

Table 7.1 Steganography and Steganalysis Tools

Tool	Description
Blindside	Hides files within bitmap (BMP) images
Camera/Shy	Works with Windows and Internet Explorer Uses GIF images Provides encryption and password protection
Cloak	Compresses and encrypts documents within images
Data Stash	Hides files within other files Password protection using Blowfish

Continued

Table 7.1 contnued Steganography and Steganalysis Tools

Tool	Description
Fort Knox	Uses MD5 and Blowfish algorithms Password protection capability Hiding and securing files and folders
Gifshuffle	Used to conceal messages in GIF images by shuffling the color map Works with all GIF images, including those with transparency and animation
Hermetic Stego	Hides a message file in BMP images
Hydan	Exploits redundancy in the i386 chipset Encodes information in machine code File size remains unchanged Message is Blowfish encrypted
Image Hide	Hides text in images Simple encryption capabilities Does not increase the file size Can evade mail sniffers
Invisible Secrets 4	Encrypts information for secure transfer across the network Can hide information in JPEG, PNG, BMP, HTML and WAV
JPHIDE and JPSEEK	Allows the hiding of a file in JPEG images
Masker	Provides encryption up to 448 bits Hides information in image, video, and sound files
Mp3Stego	Hides information in MP3 files during compressions Data is first compressed and encrypted and then hidden in the bit stream
Outguess	Inserts information into the redundant bits of data sources Supports PNM and JPEG formats
Pretty Good Envelope	Hides a binary message Appends a 4-byte pointer to the location of the start of the message
Snow	A whitespace program used to conceal messages in ASCII text by appending whitespace to the end of files Has built-in encryption capabilities

Continued

Table 7.1 contnued Steganography and Steganalysis Tools

Tool	Description
S-Tools	Hides multiple applications in a single object
Steganos	Combines two technologies: encryption and steganography Works with BMP, VOC, WAV, and ASCII files
StegaNote	Hides information in images or compressed files
Steghide	Allows compression of the hidden data and encryption of the embedded information Checksum integrity checking Support for JPEG, BMP, WAV, and AU files
Stegbreak	Steganalysis tool used to launch dictionary attacks against JPHIDE and Outguess
Stegdetect	Steganalysis tool that detects hidden information in JPEG files
Stego Suite	Contains several steganalysis tools Steg Watch can extract information using a dictionary attack. Stego Break was designed to crack a passphrase used in JPHIDE and JSteg.
StegSpy	A steganalysis tool that identifies the location of hidden content Identifies Hiderman, JPHIDE, Masker, JPegX, and Invisible Secrets
wbstego	Hides files in BMP images, HTML, PDF and text files

Steganography vs. Watermarking

It is common to think of *watermarking* when we refer to steganography; there are similarities, but there are also many differences. With steganography, the intent is to hide information; the information you decide to hide is hidden in its entirety. With the concept of watermarking, the intent is to protect the material from being used in violation of the creators intellectual property rights, and in some cases the watermark is clearly visible, and in some cases it is not. Whether or not the information is visible, the main objective remains the same; that is, protect the information from being copied and used without authorization. This usually involves some form of agreement with the creator, and most likely you will pay for the usage of the material.

Digital Watermarking

Digimarc's Digital Watermarking tool allows a user to embed information into files. The information that is embedded is not visible during normal use, but it can be read by a computer or software. The information is imperceptible because the tool makes only subtle changes to the original content.

The definition of *watermarking* is "a form of marking that embeds copyright information about the artist or owner." In the traditional manufacture of paper, wet fiber is subjected to high pressure to expel the moisture. If the press's mold has a slight pattern, this pattern leaves an imprint in the paper—a watermark—which is best viewed under transmitted light. Today, the word "watermark" has been borrowed by high technology. Digital watermarks are imperceptible (or barely perceptible) transformations of digital data. Often, the digital data set is a digital multimedia object. Although digital images are most often mentioned in the same breath as digital watermarking, we note that watermarks can be applied to other forms of digital data, such as pictures, videos, and music. Now let's take a more in-depth look at the definition of, and methods used in, the technique of watermarking.

Fragile

The fragile watermark is one of the watermarking methods for authentication that has a low robustness toward modifications, where even a small change of the content will destroy embedded information, showing an attack attempt was made. In short, fragile watermarks are *supposed* to break. Think of it as a digital version of the foil put under the cap of an aspirin bottle. It's pretty hard to get by that without it looking like it's been tampered with.

Robust

A robust watermark is almost exactly the opposite of a fragile watermark. A robust watermark can be either visible or invisible, depending on its purpose. Robust watermarks are very difficult to remove or damage. The easiest example of a robust watermark can be seen any time you turn on the television. The majority if not all channels have a watermark in the lower right-hand corner, not only to let you know what station you're on, but also to let you know that what you're watching is their content. Removing a visible watermark, especially in the television example, would be very difficult to do without someone noticing after the fact.

Attacking Watermarking

There are several known attacks that try to remove the watermark in a medium.

Mosaic Attack

The mosaic attack works by splitting an image into multiple pieces, and taking the pieces and putting them back together using javascript code. The web browser displays the information by putting the pieces back together and displaying them. The attack is successful, because in small pieces the watermark is unreadable.

2Mosaic

2Mosaic is a watermark breaking tool. The tool is an attack against a digital watermarking system. The attack is carried out by chopping an image into smaller pieces and creating an image piece. The perpetrator then embeds the images into a web page, the web browser renders the small image pieces that have been placed together, and it appears to be the real and original image without the watermark.

Detecting and Attacking Steganography

Steganography detection is usually a very difficult task, especially in instances of low payloads, since fewer bits are replaced, altered, or inserted. However, there are some ways to tell. The following is a list of methods, and a partial list of tools, used for detecting steganography. One final word for you on detection of steganography: there are a significant amount of false positives when trying to search through a possible steganography file; therefore, use caution when experimenting with the detection, and validate and verify all results you find.

Detection

When it comes to detection of steganography, there are several techniques that need to be discussed. As mentioned previously, when you are trying to detect steganography there are significant factors that have to be considered. We have several types of detection that we want to discuss in the following sections. These techniques are statistical tests, stegdetect, and stegbreak.

Statistical Tests

Statistical tests can reveal that an image has been modified by determining that its statistical properties deviate from the norm. Some tests are independent of the data format and just measure the entropy of the redundant data. Expect images with hidden data to have a higher entropy than those without.

Stegdetect

Stegdetect is an automated tool for detecting steganographic content in images. It is capable of detecting several different steganographic methods to embed hidden information in JPEG images.

Stegbreak

Stegbreak is a program that uses dictionary guessing to break the encoding password. It is used to launch dictionary attacks against JSteg-Shell, JPHide, and OutGuess.

Visible Noise

Attacks and analysis on hidden information may take several forms: detecting, extracting, and disabling or destroying hidden information. Images with too large a payload may display distortions from hidden information. Selecting the proper combination of steganography tools and carriers is important to successful information hiding.

Appended Spaces and "Invisible" Characters

Appended spaces and "invisible" characters refer back to the technique of hiding data in spaces within text.

This form of text semagram uses the white space in a document to denote binary values. The white space can be between individual words, sentences, or even between paragraphs. Almost any combination is possible, but to a point, if the text appears to have too much white space, it can be subject to scrutiny. Although this form of steganography can work effectively, it has a few big drawbacks. First, if the document is digital, any modern word processor would be able to show the spacing irregularities or, worse, reformat the document and destroy the hidden information. The other drawback is that this method doesn't transmit a large amount of information easily, which can limit its practicality.

Color Palettes

Some tools have characteristics that are unique among stego tools. In some steganography programs the color palettes have unique characteristics that don't appear anywhere else. For example, the program Hide and Seek creates color palette entries that are divisible by 4 for all bit values. The palette modification creates a detectable steganography signature.

Attacking Steganography

It is usually easier to destroy than to create, and in the case of attacking steganographic files, this remains true. Since steganography is for the most part relatively fragile, a number of methods exist for attacking files that have steganographic content in them, or are suspected files that

contain steganographic content. A couple of these may actually yield the hidden message after considerable work, but most simply destroy the message, making its recovery by anyone impossible. Furthermore, if the information is encrypted, then the best result is to destroy the carrier or host, because you are not going to break strong encryption without significant time and resources.

Steg-Only Attack

In this attack only the object that contains the steganographic information is available to the attacker. This is the most common situation; you would not leave the original host or carrier file available for someone to do an integrity check on.

Known-Cover Attack

In this attack you have gotten lucky, because the suspected perpetrator has not done a good job of covering their tracks. In this attack, the object with the stegonagraphic information and the original medium are both available. This makes it a trivial process to compare the original carrier or host file to the one with the hidden information.

Known-Message Attack

In this attack you know both the hidden message, and the object that has the steganographic message, and the process to complete the attack is simple.

Known-Stego Attack

When you conduct this type of attack, you have knowledge of the algorithm that is used to create the steganographic content, and the original file, and the file that has the hidden information are available to you. Here we are trying to find the method used for embedding the content.

Chosen-Stego Attack

This attack is used when we have both the stego-medium and the steganography algorithm.

Chosen-Message Attack

The methodology of this attack is that the steganalyst generates an object containing steganographic information using some tool or algorithm of a chosen message, and looks for patterns in the created object that might lead to determining the actual tool or algorithm used to embed the steganographic content.

Disabling or Active Attacks

In this type of attack, the attackers change the carrier or host during the communication process. There are multiple techniques for doing this, as we will discuss now.

Blur

Smoothes transitions and decreases contrast by averaging the pixels next to the hard edges of defined lines and areas where there are significant color transitions.

Noise

Random noise inserts random colored pixels to an image, whereas uniform noise inserts pixels and colors that closely resemble the original pixels.

Noise Reduction

Reduces noise in the image by adjusting the colors and averaging pixel values.

Sharpen

Sharpen is the opposite of blur. It increases contrast between adjacent pixels where there are significant color contrasts, usually at the edge of objects.

Rotate

Rotation moves an image around its center point in a given plane.

Resample

Resampling involves an interpolation process to minimize the "raggedness" normally associated with expanding an image.

Soften

Soften applies a uniform blur to an image to smooth edges and reduce contrasts. It causes less distortion than blurring.

Application Password Cracking

Since the beginning of computer systems, there has always been some form of a password required for authentication into a system or network. This simple process has evolved in many ways, but it is still what we refer to as "user" controlled security. That is, the strength of this authentication method is largely in control of the user, because they are the ones selecting the password. For example, if you use a Personal Identification Number (PIN) and you select a simple PIN of all digits, that makes the PIN authentication system weak, and susceptible to

cracking. The concept of cracking passwords is taking a password and decrypting it, or disabling the password protection of a system and/or network. In this section we will take a look at the common methods of attacking passwords, and we will close with some advice on how you can make your password more secure.

Head of the Class...

Default Password Nightmare

Despite all the security training that has been given, one thing that always remain constant is no matter how much training you put in, there are always cases where someone will make a mistake. That is part of the risk that you accept when allowing users to control security. The majority of devices come with a set of default accounts. You are just an Internet search away from discovering the common default passwords that are used. It never fails, somewhere along the way you will run into a default password that has not been changed.

During a high profile assignment for a major government entity we had installed a Virtual Private Network (VPN), and one of our remote sites was an endpoint for a significant operation center. Once the site installed the VPN device we could never get the VPN to work. The contractor technical support group wanted the remote site to log into the device and check the configuration and logs. Well, the contractors passed several different passwords that they commonly used, and nothing would work, so finally the team leader said that the system never should have been placed in production with a default password, but let's check so we can rule it out. Well the password worked, so that means the system had been installed and the remote VPN endpoint still had the default password. This site was facing the Internet, and had been online for three weeks. Fortunately we never discovered a system compromise, but it goes to show you that you always have to validate and verify that the default passwords are changed. This was an embarrassing moment for the contractor group, but could have been much worse.

Types of Password Cracking

Since the first passwords were used, there have been methods to try and crack the actual text based version of the password. The reason we can crack passwords is two-fold. The users can select a weak password if the administrator has not enforced a strict password policy, and the other way is because the vendor has done a poor job with the scrambling of the password. There are several methods of attacking passwords that we will discuss. The methods are, guessing, dictionary, brute force, syllable attack, rule-based, and hybrid.

Guessing

In the guessing attack, perpetrators are successful when they are able to guess a person's password. This can be the result of selection by the user of a blank password. It can also be a result of choosing a simple password such as "password." Some users think they are smart, and will try

a word in reverse like "drowssap." Another problem is when users select a password based on their kids, spouse, relative, or other personal information that is easy to identify.

Dictionary

With this attack you load a file of dictionary words into the password cracking tool, and if the password is one of the words within the dictionary file it is cracked. It is important to note that there are dictionary files available for many languages; therefore, it is a simple process of loading your dictionary for the country you are conducting the testing in. Consultants have successfully cracked many passwords of foreign languages using this technique—a dictionary even exists for the Klingon language.

Brute Force

In the brute force method of password attacking, the concept is to try every possible combination of characters until a password is found. It is the slowest method of attack, but given enough time and resources it will discover any password.

Syllable Attack

This attack is a combination of brute force attack and dictionary attack. The technique usually is used when the password is known to be a nonexistent word.

Rule-Based

This technique is used when the perpetrator is able to get some information about the password, usually following some form of enumeration that has identified the password policy in place for an organization. For example, if the policy indicates the length of the password is not less than eight characters, and must contain at least numbers and a special character, then the perpetrator will adjust and customize the cracking tool for this.

Hybrid

A hybrid attack is used to find passwords that are a dictionary word with combinations of characters prepended or postpended to it. This attack is surprisingly successful, because in most cases users will select a password that is a dictionary word surrounded by additional characters.

Rainbow

The rainbow attack technique works by calculating all the possible hashes for a character set, and storing them in a table. The password hash is presented to the tool that uses the rainbow algorithm, and a table search is made until the password is found. This is a much quicker method than the other types of attack; however, the limitation of the rainbow technique is the size requirements for a table, so you need to think in the terms of terabytes for complex passwords.

Damage & Defense...

When You Cannot Crack the Password!

There are cases when no matter how hard you try you cannot crack the password, as more organizations implement a strong password policy, and eliminate the storage of the weak password hashes. The cumulative result of all this is, there are cases when you are not going to get the password cracked. So, what do we do? Quit? Even though you might not be able to crack the operating system password there are alternatives.

You could plant a keystroke logger, and wait for the user to login and then capture the password. The challenge of this is that in some cases, a keystroke logger will get you into possible legal trouble; therefore, you should seek legal counsel before you consider anything like this.

Another less intrusive way is to use a bootable media device like a CD-ROM or DVD, and boot from the media. Once you do this you can either change or blank the Administrator password account. It is usually easiest, and works better to blank the password. Most tools have this capability; all you need is access to the machine, and a BIOS that allows the boot from your chosen media device. We commonly do this for our own machines when we forget the password. With the auto-login that XP and other operating systems are defaulting to, it is more common that you or someone you know will forget a password. When this happens, insert the CD in and reboot, and reset or blank the password and you're in!

Password-Cracking Tools

Now that we have discussed the types of password attacks, it is time to discuss some of the tools. When it comes to cracking passwords, there are an extraordinary amount of tools that are available, so we have selected several of the most popular ones. The tools we have selected and will discuss next are cain and abel, lcp, ophcrack, john the ripper, brutus, and rock xp.

Cain and Abel

This is a Windows-based password recovery tool. It uses multiple methods to capture the password hashes. It can get the hash from the network, or dump it from the local machine. Cain and Abel uses dictionary attacks, brute force, and other cryptanalysis techniques to crack the password. This tool is much more than just a password cracking tool. The screen shot in Figure 7.4 shows the password cracking capabilities of this excellent tool.

Figure 7.4 Password Cracking with Cain and Abel

LCP

The LCP tool was developed as a free alternative to the very popular L0phtcrack tool that was the pioneer in cracking passwords on a Windows platform. L0phtcrack is no longer offered, and LCP is an excellent way to get the features that used to be available with l0phtcrack. The tool offers the ability to import from a variety of formats, and uses dictionary, hybrid, and brute force attack methodologies to discover the password. Figure 7.5 shows the LCP tool with a dump of the SAM database.

Ophcrack

Ophcrack is a Windows-based password cracker that uses the concept of the rainbow cracking methodology by conducting the crack from existing rainbow tables. The algorithm deployed is based on the time-memory trade-off technique of precomputing all possible hashes and then applying the hash to the table.

Figure 7.5 LCP with a Dump of the SAM Database

John the Ripper

John the Ripper (JTR) is a fast password cracking tool that will not only crack Windows-based passwords, but also passwords on Unix and Linux systems. The tool runs both within a Unix and a Linux environment.

Brutus

Brutus is a very fast and flexible password cracking tool that can perform the cracks remotely. It commonly is used to crack Web site passwords. It is a Windows-based tool that can support up to 60 simultaneous target connections.

Rock XP

Have you ever tried to install a copy of Windows, or a Microsoft product, but could not find the product key to do the installation? Well you are in luck—this tool excels at recovering that lost information. The tool allows you to recover your XP key, save your XP activation, and even change your XP key! Figure 7.6 shows the recovery of an XP product key.

Figure 7.6 Recovering an XP Product Key with Rock XP

Common Recommendations for Improving Passwords

As we discussed earlier, the users can assist us when it comes to making the passwords more difficult to crack. Now it is time to discuss some methods of improving your password security. There are some common-sense things to remember. The first is you cannot have a password that is a dictionary word, or a derivative of a dictionary word. There are several more we will discuss below such as no personal data and multiple character sets.

No Dictionary Words

As we just identified, the dictionary attack succeeds because users choose words that are found in the dictionary. Furthermore, there are attacks that use the hybrid approach, and append characters to the beginning or the end of a dictionary word. The safest password is one that has no resemblance to a dictionary word.

No Personal Data

As was shown in the popular 1980s movie *War Games*, a password based on the name of a child or a spouse is very weak. Additionally, a password should never be used that is known personal data like any type of identity number.

Multiple Character Sets

A password that is eight characters long, and is only alphanumeric is much easier to crack than a password that is eight characters long, but contains at least two additional character sets.

Do Not Store Weak Hashes

The Lan Man (LM) hash used in Windows systems has been shown to be susceptible to rapid cracking, and should not be stored on the machines or networks of today. There are options you can set in the Group Policy Object that will prevent the storage of these weak hashes. On Windows Server 2003, the LM hash is not stored by default.

Standard Password Advice

There are some things that you can do, and should do on a regular basis, to improve your password security. The following section highlights the recommended standards to maintain when maintaining and administering your passwords. These include changing the password, no password reuse, and selecting the right size.

Change

The most important thing is to change your password periodically, because the longer a password is around the more susceptible it is to cracking.

Not in More Than One Place

A common mistake is to use the same password in multiple areas; this is a definite "no-no" as once a perpetrator obtains the password they will have multiple access to different places. Another thing to remember is when you use protocols that are in clear text, anyone can capture your password on the network, so protocols such as Post Office Protocol (POP) reveal the password to a network capture utility; therefore, it is imperative that these passwords be unique and used only in that one place.

Size

When it comes to passwords, the size is very important, because the longer the password, the more time it will take to crack it.

Creation

One technique for creating a password is to use a phrase or saying that you know well. A popular technique is the nursery rhyme, "Twinkle, Twinkle, Little Star, How I Wonder How You Are." In this technique we take the song, and the first letter of each word, and form our password. For example, Ttl*hIwhur!. Of note, when we use more than 14 characters the LM hash is not stored.

Summary of Exam Objectives

In this chapter you have worked on the concepts tested in the Computer Hacking Forensic Investigator (CHFI) for steganography, and application password crackers. These concepts are essential to understanding the concepts of hacking, and more importantly forensics.

The chapter started with a look at the concept of steganography, and how it was defined as hiding information in plain sight. We continued the discussion with a recap of the long history of the usage of steganography, dating all the way back to the Greeks in ancient times.

Once we had covered the history of steganography, we discussed the categories of steganography and how it relates to forensics. We followed this discussion of steganography usage with the concept of detecting steganography. Once steganography has been used to hide information it can be difficult to detect. The detection is made much easier if the original file that was used to hide the information is available; however, as discussed this is rarely the case unless we are dealing with a novice hacker.

We also discussed the difference between encryption and steganography. With encryption we can see the encrypted information or data, but in steganography we are actually attempting to hide all information from view. It is important to note that some tools will combine encryption with steganography and the information or data that is hidden will still require some form of a key to allow the user to view it.

Another comparison we made was the comparison of a watermark with steganography. With a watermark we are applying a mark or code to our material to protect if from being copied illegally and in violation of intellectual property rights.

We continued in the chapter talking about passwords, and how they are attacked. We discussed the main types of password attacks that are commonly used against us. We looked at the techniques that are used within tools, and also the techniques that were of a nontechnical nature.

Our ability to crack the password relies on several factors, and we discussed how the user can select an easy-to-guess password, which would make it much easier for us to crack the password. We also discussed how if the administrator implemented strong password policies it makes cracking the password more difficult.

Within the password section we discussed that by default some operating systems store a weak version of the hash, or scrambling of the password, and when this is present it makes it much easier to crack the password.

We concluded this chapter with a discussion of proven strong password guidance, and additional guidelines for achieving a strong password policy, standard and baseline.

Exam Objectives Fast Track

Classification of Steganography

☑ Technical steganography uses scientific methods to hide messages; for example, invisible ink and microdots.

☑ Linguistic steganography hides the message in the carrier file in some nonobvious ways.

☑ Open codes uses text positioning to conceal messages; for example, vertical columns.

Six Categories of Steganography in Forensics

☑ Substitution is the process of hiding information in the redundant information of the file.

☑ Transform domain technique hides message data in the "transform space" of a signal.

☑ Spread spectrum technique uses two types: direct sequence and frequency hopping.

 a Direct sequence allocates pieces of the information to various channels.

 b Frequency hopping is when a broad slice of the bandwidth spectrum is divided into many possible broadcast frequencies.

☑ Statistical methods embed one bit of information only in a digital carrier and thus creates a statistical change.

☑ Distortion technique creates a change in a cover object to hide information.

☑ Cover generation methods actually create a cover for the sole purpose of hiding information.

Types of Steganography

☑ Linguistic steganography can be described quite simply as any form of steganography that uses language in the cover.

☑ Text semagrams work with graphical modifications of the text, such as type-spacing and offsetting.

☑ Technical steganography is the method of steganography where a tool, device, or method is used to conceal the message.

☑ Embedded methods key to successful data hiding are the finding of holes that are not suitable for exploitation by compression algorithms.

☑ Least Significant Bit (LSB) is the substitution method of steganography where the right-most bit in a binary notation, the bit with the least impact on the binary data, is replaced with a bit from the embedded message.

☑ Transform method technique embeds the secret data in the cover during the *transformation* process in various ways.

☑ Spread spectrum method encoding is the method of hiding a small or narrow-band signal (a message) in a large or wide band cover.

☑ Perpetual masking occurs when one signal, or sound, becomes imperceptible to the observer because of the presence of another signal.

Application of Steganography

☑ Still images commonly use LSB insertion and spread spectrum techniques?

☑ A moving image typically uses Discrete Cosine Transform (DCT) manipulation.

☑ Audio files use the techniques of LSB insertion, differential phrase variation, spread spectrum, and adding echo to the audio signal.

☑ Text files use the techniques of open-space, syntactic and semantic.

Hiding in Network Packets

☑ A covert channel is described as any communication channel that can be exploited by a process to transfer information in a manner that violates the systems security policy.

Issues in Information Hiding

☑ Levels of visibility refers to the embedding process and if it distorts the cover to the point where it is visually noticeable.

☑ Robustness vs payload is the redundancy to resist changes made to the cover. This redundancy subsequently lowers the payload.

☑ File format dependence comes into play if the conversion of lossless information to the compressed "lossy" information can destroy the hidden information in the cover.

Steg Tools

☑ With encryption you are not hiding anything

☑ The encrypted version of the data is always in view.

☑ With steganography, you are hiding information so that no one knows that it is there.

Steganography vs Watermarking

☑ Steganograpy is used to hide information.

☑ Watermarking might be hidden or might be visible.

☑ Watermarking is used to protect intellectual property rights.

Attacking Watermarking

☑ A Mosaic attack works by splitting an image into multiple pieces and then taking the pieces and putting them back together using javascript code.

☑ 2Mosaic is carried out by chopping an image into smaller pieces and creating an image piece.

Detecting and Attacking Steganography

☑ Statistical tests can reveal that an image has been modified by determining that its statistical properties deviate from the norm.

☑ Visible noise attacks and analysis on hidden information may take several forms: detecting, extracting, and disabling or destroying hidden information.

☑ Appended spaces and invisible characters use the white space in a document to denote binary values.

☑ Color palettes have characteristics that are unique among stego tools. In some steganography programs the color palettes have unique characteristics that don't appear anywhere else.

Application Password Cracking

☑ Programs that attempt to determine the password and gain access by decrypting or disabling the normal password protection.

☑ A technique of trying to identify encrypted passwords.

☑ Brute force attack is when every single combination of characters is attempted.

☑ A dictionary attack is when a file of dictionary words is loaded to run against the user accounts.

☑ A hybrid attack is when combinations of characters are added to dictionary words.

☑ Guessing is when the attacker attempts to guess the user password using well-known defaults or information they have about the user.

☑ A rainbow attack uses the time-memory trade-off technique and generates a table of all possible hash values, and this table is searched to find the matching value and crack the password.

☑ Cain and Abel has a password cracking capability that can de used against Windows systems.

☑ LCP works by auditing and recovering passwords on Windows systems.

☑ Ophcrack is a tool that uses the rainbow-cracking technique.

☑ John the Ripper is a fast auditing tool that can crack both Windows and UNIX/Linux passwords.

☑ Brutus is a fast remote password cracker tool that works on Windows.

☑ Rock XP allows you to retrieve your XP product key used from your Windows installation.

☑ Use strong passwords for privileged user accounts.

☑ Practice principle of least privilege and least services.

☑ Change your password on a regular basis.

☑ Never use a dictionary word to include other languages.

☑ Use a mixture of character sets.

☑ Choose a pass phrase or saying to make a password strong and easy to remember.

Exam Objectives
Frequently Asked Questions

The following Frequently Asked Questions, answered by the authors of this book, are designed to both measure your understanding of the Exam Objectives presented in this chapter, and to assist you with real-life implementation of these concepts.

Q: What type of work can someone with a Computer Hacking Forensic Investigator certification do?

A: A CHFI certification gives you the skills and knowledge to conduct forensic examinations, and gather information and evidence to prosecute in a court of law.

Q: What is the difference between the Certified Ethical Hacker (CEH) and CHFI?

A: The CEH is focused on the tools of the attacker, it gives you the outlook of what tools a hacker potentially deploys against a network. CHFI takes this baseline of knowledge and expands on it, and shows you how to identify and collect evidence left behind by the CEH types of tools.

Q: Are there any prerequisites for the CHFI exam?

A: The CHFI does not have prerequisites, but it is a natural follow-on to the CEH exam, and that level of knowledge should be obtained before doing the CHFI exam.

Q: What type of exam is given for the certification?

A: The CHFI exam is a 50-question multiple choice exam in which you have a two-hour time limit to complete the exam.

Q: I have heard of an "expert witness"; what is this?

A: An expert witness is a witness who by their education, profession, or experience is believed to have more special knowledge than the average person. This knowledge shall be sufficient so that others legally depend on that person's opinion.

Q: By using this study guide can I take the exam without going through the class?

A: The study guide is intended as a supplement to the type of material you will be expected to learn in the classroom environment. Your background, and experience in hacking and forensics will also contribute to whether or not you can take the exam without attending the class. There are ways to do this, but it is recommended that you take some practice exams, and work through the questions contained in this study guide to determine if you are ready for the exam.

CHFI

Computer-Assisted Attacks and Crimes

Exam objectives in this chapter:

- E-mail Clients and Servers
- E-mail Crimes and Violations
- Investigating E-mail Crimes and Violations
- Microsoft Outlook
- Tracing an E-mail Message
- Handling Spam

Exam Objectives Review:

- ☑ Summary of Exam Objectives
- ☑ Exam Objectives Fast Track
- ☑ Exam Objectives Frequently Asked Questions

Introduction

Everyone has heard of e-mail. It's been around for ages, and almost every corporation uses it in one way or another to conduct day-to-day business and communicate both internally and outside the company. Organizations offer e-mail as a service to their employees, and employees typically connect to a corporate mail server via a client such as Microsoft Outlook. Risks are associated with corporate mail, and far greater risks are associated with Web mail. In corporate mail environments, a user who intends to sneak data out of the company can attach a file to her outgoing message and send the file to any number of people, including competitors, ex-coworkers, or even foreign nationals. Fortunately, for us, we can track such activity via the corporate mail server.

Typically when an employee is being investigated, all of her past e-mail will be investigated to determine any wrongdoing or to build a case against her. The difficulty arises when users begin to access Web mail servers such as Yahoo! and Hotmail. These sites allow users to connect from within an organization, and attach the same file and mail it to the same people—but without leaving any sort of record of what they've done. Now, when an investigation is underway, the analyst or legal team cannot go back to the mail server and pull up records of that person's activities.

Investigators and legal teams have been using e-mail transactions as evidence of wrongdoing for years, so why is this considered a "new" data source? E-mail is considered to be a new data source because it falls outside the realm of what the typical security organization usually monitors. E-mail transactions generally have not been analyzed in real time; they have been used as part of forensic investigations. Once an employee is suspected of wrongdoing, any e-mail messages he or she has sent are questioned. Now we are trying to draw conclusions and detect early warning indicators of a potential data leakage *before* it happens, not after the fact. The information that you can gain from examining e-mail messages may surprise you.

In addition to e-mail, attackers also use the Web as a means for their attacks. These attacks include denial-of-service (DoS) attacks, cross-site scripting attacks, and buffer overflows. In the latter part of this chapter we discuss the various types of DoS attacks and then look at other Web attacks. We include examples of scripts that are used in these attacks.

E-mail Clients and Servers

An e-mail client message is composed of two parts: (1.) a header that contains information about the e-mail's origins, such as the address it came from, how it reached its destination, and who sent it, and (2.) a body, which contains the e-mail message and/or file attachments. The client connects to an e-mail server to send and receive messages. Software such as Outlook, Pine, or Eudora serve as e-mail clients.

Most organizations have a dedicated machine to handle e-mail, known as a *mail server*; it's normally not the same machine that users are looking at when they read their e-mail. In the common case of an Internet service provider (ISP) whose users dial in from their home com-

puters, the "client" computer is the user's home machine and the "server" is some machine that belongs to the ISP. When users send e-mail, they normally compose messages on their own computers and then send them to their ISP's mail servers. At this point, their computers are finished with the job, but the mail server still has to deliver the message. It does this by finding the recipient's mail server, talking to that server, and delivering the message. It then sits on that second mail server until the recipient comes along to read his mail. When he retrieves it from his own computer, this may or may not delete the e-mail from the mail server.

An e-mail server is a computer running an operating system, such as UNIX or Windows 2000, that is loaded with software to manage the transmission and holding of e-mail messages. E-mail differs based on the environment in which it is sent and received. Both the Internet and local network environments follow a client/server architecture with respect to e-mail. The server computer runs software such as Sendmail, GroupWise, or Microsoft Exchange as a message transfer agent (MTA) and Post Office or collection system.

Users log on or authenticate to the e-mail server known as a Post Office. This system authenticates the user based on their log-on information. The Post Office server is the final repository of delivered e-mail and may also act as the initial sending host. In some systems, however, it is important to note that the repository server that e-mail is delivered to will not be the same as the sending or delivery system. This type of configuration is most frequently found when investigating e-mail on an ISP. This type of configuration is rare within corporate environments and LANs (local area networks).

When you are investigating e-mail violations, internal corporate e-mail is usually simple to trace. The use of a centralized UNC (Universal Naming Convention) in most organizations, coupled with a central authentication and controls, makes it easy to recognize the senders and recipients within the e-mail. The use of authentication to both send and receive may also result in the creation of an audit trail and makes "spoofing" difficult. Internet-based e-mail accounts are more problematic due to the ease of configuring a new account, in many cases the anonymity and the international nature of the Internet.

TEST DAY TIP

E-mail crime is growing due to the ease at which it may be committed. Offenses committed using e-mail may be classified into crimes directly related to the sending of an e-mail (including phishing, spam, and mail bombs) and those that are supported through the use of e-mail (such as threats, harassment, or child pornography).

E-mail Clients

E-mail clients perform functions such as showing a list of all the messages in the mailbox by displaying the message headers, as well as the time and date of the e-mail messages, who sent them, the subject of the e-mail messages, and their size. E-mail clients select a message header and read the body of the e-mail message. An e-mail client creates new messages and sends them with attachments and saves the attachments from received messages.

E-mail Servers

E-mail servers have lists of accounts; one account for each person, with a text file for each account in the list. A person clicks a "send" button on the e-mail client to pass the e-mail server the name(s) of the recipient(s), the name of the sender, and the body of the message. The server formats the information and appends it to the bottom of the recipient's .txt file. When you want to look at e-mail, many e-mail clients connect to the server machine by sending the request via port 25 (SMTP, or Simple Mail Transfer Protocol).

Test Day Tip

SPAM is any unsolicited commercial e-mail. The act of spamming is the sending of any unsolicited commercial e-mail. This becomes a problem due to wasted network bandwidth and its associated costs, the impact on time and lost productivity, and a simple factor of annoyance. The important thing to remember is that SPAM is not just any unsolicited e-mail; it is always unsolicited commercial e-mail.

E-mail Crimes and Violations

In reality, e-mail crime is not new. Instead, the Internet has enabled many old crimes to be reborn. Many moral violations such as child pornography have become far more widespread and simpler due to the ease and reach of e-mail. Many traditional crimes such as threats and harassment, blackmail, fraud, and criminal defamation have not changed in essence, but the ease of e-mail has made them more prevalent.

Spamming

Spamming can be defined as sending unsolicited commercial e-mail messages (UCE). The more common term for spam is *junk mail*. Spammers obtain e-mail addresses by harvesting them from Usenet, bots, postings, DNS listings, and/or Web pages.

Spammers are smart, determined criminals, with a broad understanding of technology. They are willing to do anything to get access to mailing lists, vulnerable servers, and insecure routers. Spammers use their brains and well-crafted tools to make money and remain anonymous.

Spam is generally sent to a large number of e-mail addresses simultaneously. The sending address in the e-mail is generally forged, allowing spammers to hide their identities. The From and Reply To fields in an Internet e-mail header allow the spammer to provide false or otherwise misleading information designed to entice the recipient into opening the e-mail.

TEST DAY TIP

SPAM Punisher is an anti-spam tool that makes it easy for you to determine the address of a spammer's ISP and generate and send complaints. If the ISP receives a complaint generated by SPAM Punisher, the ISP usually closes Internet access to the spammer. A review of this product may be found at: http://email.about.com/cs/winspamreviews/gr/spam_punisher.htm.

SpamArrest (www.SpamArrest.com) protects an account from spam by using a challenge/response technology that blocks 100 percent of automated spam. Red Condor (www.redcondor.com) is a fully managed spam blocker with automated lists, heuristics, and live individuals that look for spam 24/7.

Mail Bombing

Mail bombing is a simple attack that has been around for a long time. It involves the intentional sending of multiple copies of an e-mail to a recipient. The objective is simply to overload the e-mail server. This is achieved by either filling the user's inbox so that he or she cannot access any more mail or flooding the server connections. Flooding server connections would be aimed at the general infrastructure, whereas flooding an inbox is aimed at an individual. Mail bombing is malicious and abusive, even when aimed at an individual to prevent other users from accessing the mail server.

Mail Storm

A mail storm is a condition that occurs when computers start communicating autonomously. This process results in a large volume of junk mail. This may happen innocently via the auto-forwarding of e-mail messages when configured to a large number of mailing lists, by using automated responses, and by using multiple e-mail addresses. Additionally, malicious software,

including the Melissa and IloveYou viruses, can result in mail storms. Mail storms interfere with the usual communication of an e-mail system.

Sexual Abuse of Children in Chat Rooms

The increasing prevalence of instant messaging, Web forums such as Facebook, and chat rooms has created a potential for sexual abuse to occur. It is common for pedophiles to use chat rooms for sexually abusing children by starting relationships with them online. This generally involves befriending the child, establishing a steady relationship, and then gradually introducing the children into pornography through images or videos that may contain sexually explicit material. Children may be exploited for cybersex initially and when the trust is gained this could lead to physical abuse.

Child Pornography

Any work that depicts the sexual behavior of children is classified as child pornography. The anonymity and ease of transfer provided through the Internet has created an international problem with child pornography. The exploitation from child pornography can lead to long-term suffering and other negative effects. Those involved in the child pornography business often target disabled children with promises of financial or other benefits. Children who are victims of sexual exploitation may suffer lifelong depression, emotional dysfunction, fear, and anxiety.

Harassment

Harassment may occur through all forms of media, and the Internet is no exception. Junk mail, sexually offensive e-mail messages, and threats delivered through online means (including both e-mail and instant messaging) are all forms of harassment. This type of harassment is a criminal action. The inappropriate accessing of sexually explicit, racist, or otherwise offensive material at the workplace is another form of harassment. This includes the sending of unwelcome messages that may contain offensive material to a coworker.

Identity Fraud

Identity theft is becoming more widespread due to the ease and profitability. This action involves the stealing of someone's identity for fraudulent financial gain. It is in effect a larceny. The sending of e-mail messages with offers that are too good to be true, fake Web sites, and other forms of phishing are all used to capture an identity. Many groups specialize in the capture of information and make financial games by selling this information to groups who will make illegitimate purchases or financial transactions.

Chain Letter

Chain letters are another form of abuse that is seamlessly migrated from the physical world to cyberspace. A chain letter is an e-mail that was sent progressively from e-mail user to e-mail user. It will generally instruct the recipient to circulate further copies of the e-mail and usually to multiple recipients. These chain letters often promise rewards or spiritual gain if the e-mail was sent and may also threaten loss or harm if the recipient does not forward it. The authenticity of a chain letter often cannot be verified because the header information from the original sender has been lost in retransmission.

Sending Fakemail

Fakemail is any e-mail that has been falsely created or altered in some manner. It is often used as a method to hide the source address in spamming. E-mail spoofing is a technique used for forged or fakemail. Fakemail can be sent by entering someone else's e-mail address in the <From> or <Reply To> fields. These may also contain information about the origin of the message.

Fakemail may be created as simply as connecting to TCP port 25 using any telnet client. Once this is done it directly connects the machine to the SMTP (Simple Mail Transfer Protocol) daemon running on that host. SMTP commands may then be written to the SMTP daemon, allowing the sending of fakemail. For example, to send fakemail to Bill.Gates@Microsoft.com, enter the message as follows:

HELO username

MAIL FROM: <president@Whitehouse.gov>

RCPT TO: < Bill.Gates@Microsoft.com>

DATA

This is a message to thank you for helping me win the election.

President Bush

QUIT.

Fakemail can be sent to anyone and it will appear to have been sent from address entered in the "MAIL FROM:" field. In effect, fakemail is used to perpetrate criminal fraud.

Investigating E-mail Crimes and Violations

To investigate e-mail crimes and violations, you must follow several steps: Examine the e-mail message, copy it, print it, view the e-mail headers, examine the e-mail headers, examine any attachments, and trace the e-mail.

The steps in the investigation process include:

1. Examining the email message
2. Copying the email message
3. Printing the email message
4. Viewing the email headers
5. Examining the e-mail headers
6. Examining any attachments
7. Tracing the email

Examining the E-mail Message

When it has been established that a crime has been committed using e-mail, it is necessary to capture and maintain the evidence that is required to prove the offense in a court of law. Evidence may be obtained through an analysis of the victim's computer. This may contain the e-mail that the victim has received.

As with all digital forensic work, it is best to first take an image of the machine's hard drive. When you are investigating the victim's machine, it is helpful to obtain any passwords needed to open protected or encrypted files. When it is not feasible to gain physical access to the victim's computer, a printed copy of the offending e-mail (including the complete header) should be made. Although the unique IP address of the server that sent the message may be falsified, this is difficult and less likely to be the case. In the majority of cases the IP address of the source post in the e-mail will relate to the host used by the offender.

Copying the E-mail Message

An investigation that involves e-mail may be initiated as soon as the offending communication is copied and printed. Any e-mail program can be used, such as Eudora or Outlook Express, and straightforward steps can be supplied in order to copy the e-mail message from the Inbox folder to a disk or other source.

The following steps may be used to copy an e-mail using Microsoft Outlook or Outlook Express:

1. Insert a formatted USB key into the machine
2. Use My Computer or Windows Explorer to access the USB key.

3. Open Microsoft Outlook.

4. Open the folder that contains the offending message, and keep Folder List open.

5. Resize the Outlook window to see both the message to be copied and the floppy disk icon.

6. Drag the message to the drive folder associated with the USB key from the Outlook window.

Command-line e-mail programs such as Pine also allow the copying of the e-mail message. The process is generally specific to the individual program.

Printing the E-mail Message

After the e-mail message has been copied, it is a good idea to print it. The main benefits of printing is that it is a simple process that may be remotely communicated to a user, and it produces results that may be used in a court of law. The ensuing steps demonstrate the method used to print an e-mail message from Outlook Express:

1. Go to My Computer or Windows Explorer and get the copy of the e-mail message received by the victim.

2. Open the message in the e-mail program.

3. Go to the File menu and click **Print**.

4. After you select the settings for printing in the dialog box, click **Print**.

5. For a command-line e-mail client like Pine or Eudora, open the e-mail message and select the Print option.

TEST DAY TIP

Internet e-mail messages are made up of two parts:

The header, which holds information about the e-mail's source, including the IP (Internet Protocol) address of the system it came from, information on how it was sent, and maybe even who sent it. Generally the header is not seen.

The body, which contains the message of the e-mail. This is what you see when you read your messages.

Viewing the E-mail Headers

An e-mail message is composed of a message header and the subject body. An investigation involving e-mail may hinge on successfully capturing the e-mail header. The e-mail header is imperative because it holds information detailing the e-mail's origin. This will include the source IP address of where it came from, the method used to send it, and potentially who sent it. The subject body of the e-mail contains the message. Subsequent to copying the e-mail message, the e-mail header can be retrieved. This process is different for each e-mail program.

Retrieving the E-mail Header (Microsoft Outlook)

1. Open Outlook and open the copied e-mail message.
2. Right-click the message and click **Options** to open the dialog box.
3. Select the header text and make a copy of it.
4. Paste the header text in any text editor and save the file with as Filename.txt.
5. Hit **<Alt-P>** and take a screen image of the header. Print this Image.
6. Save a Copy of the E-mail message as message.msg
7. Close the program.

Retrieving the E-mail Header (Outlook Express)

1. Open Outlook Express.
2. Right-click the message and click **Properties**.
3. To view the header, click Details.
4. Click **Message Source** to view the details.
5. Select the message header text and copy it.
6. Paste the text in any text editor and save the file as Filename.txt.
7. Save a copy of the e-mail (with the header) to disk.
8. Hit **<Alt-P>** and take a screen image of the header. Print this Image.
9. Close the program.

Retrieving the E-mail Header (Eudora)

1. Open Eudora.
2. Select and go to the Inbox folder.
3. Double-click the message to select and open it.

4. Select the message header text and copy it.

5. Paste the text in any text editor and save the file as Filename.txt.

6. Save a copy of the e-mail (with the header) to disk.

7. Hit **<Alt-P>** and take a screen image of the header. Print this Image.

8. Close the program.

Retrieving the E-mail Header (AOL)

1. Open AOL.

2. Open the e-mail message.

3. Click the **DETAILS** link.

4. Select the message header text and copy it.

5. Select the message header text and save the file as Filename.htm. This may also be achieved from saving the "view source" data associated with the header.

6. Hit **<Alt-P>** and take a screen image of the header. Print this Image.

7. Close the program.

Retrieving the E-mail Header (Hotmail)

1. Go to Hotmail and log in using your Web browser.

2. Open the relevant e-mail message.

3. Go to Options and click **Preferences**. For version No.8 click **Mail Display Settings**.

4. Click **Advanced Header**. For version No. 8 go to Message Headers and click **Advanced option**.

5. Select the message header text and copy it.

6. Select the message header text and save the file as Filename.htm. This may also be achieved from saving the "view source" data associated with the header.

7. Hit **<Alt-P>** and take a screen image of the header. Print this Image.

8. Close the program.

Retrieving the E-mail Header (Yahoo)

1. Open Yahoo.

2. Go to Mail Options on the right hand side.

3. Go to the General Preferences link and click **Show All Headers On Incoming Messages** and save the message.

4. Select the message header text and save the file as Filename.htm. This may also be achieved from saving the "view source" data associated with the header.

5. Hit **<Alt-P>** and take a screen image of the header. Print this Image.

6. Close the program.

Retrieving the E-mail Header (Pine for UNIX)

1. Start the e-mail client program by typing **pine** at the command prompt.

2. For setup options press **S**.

3. For the e-mail configuration press **C**.

4. Exit the mode of configuration by pressing **E**.

5. Save the changes by typing **Y**.

6. After you select the message using the arrow keys, select **O** from the lower screen.

7. View the header by typing **H**.

8. Close the program by typing **Q**.

Examining the E-mail Header

E-mail headers are a source of good information. They can tell you the e-mail sender's operating system and its version, the e-mail application used and its version, the usernames on the system used to send and receive e-mail, and the system hostname and Internet Protocol (IP) addresses.

The most effective method to obtain the pertinent e-mail for analysis is to request it from the person who received it. If feasible it is always best to have someone at the target site send an e-mail message to you. Many times, automated sales accounts and system re-mail or list functions will suffice to receive an e-mail header for comparison. Always do this for each site that you are allowed to assess. E-mail headers may also be captured by intentionally sending an invalid e-mail to the target site. This will result in a "bounce" coming back as undeliverable. The bounce may have some internal information, though this is not always the case. An analysis of the header will reveal the e-mail applications, operating systems, internal host-names, and internal system types (see Figure 8.1).

Figure 8.1 Analyzing an E-mail Message Header

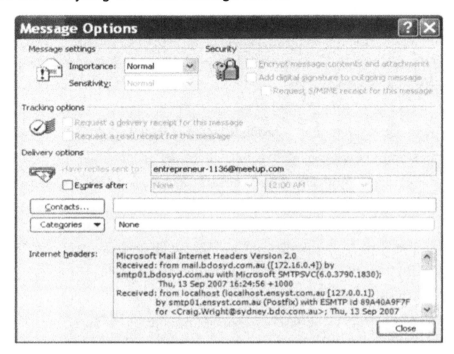

The most important information required when investigating an incident based on an e-mail is the unique sender's IP address contained within the e-mail header. The e-mail header also contains additional information, including the date and time the message was sent (a timestamp), any attachments and the format they are in, and the message body. The header may also contain information that could be used to uniquely identify the client computer.

In this section we describe the steps you need to take to examine the e-mail header. The header is captured using the steps in the preceding section.

The e-mail message header can supply significant information if examined properly. A sample e-mail header is displayed in Figure 8.2 with added line numbers to clarify the contents of the e-mail header.

Figure 8.2 An E-mail Header

1.	Microsoft Mail Internet Headers Version 2.0
2.	Received: from mail.bdosyd.com.au ([172.16.0.4]) by smtp01.bdosyd.com.au with Microsoft
3.	SMTPSVC(6.0.3790.1830);
4.	Thu, 13 Sep 2007 16:24:56 +1000
5.	Received: from localhost (localhost.ensyst.com.au [127.0.0.1])
6.	by smtp01.ensyst.com.au (Postfix) with ESMTP id 89A40A9F7F
7.	for <Craig.Wright@sydney.bdo.com.au>; Thu, 13 Sep 2007 16:24:55 +1000 (EST)
8.	Received: from smtp01.ensyst.com.au ([127.0.0.1])
9.	by localhost (smtp01.ensyst.com.au [127.0.0.1]) (amavisd-new, port 10024)
10.	with ESMTP id 11572-07 for <Craig.Wright@sydney.bdo.com.au>;
11.	Thu, 13 Sep 2007 16:24:53 +1000 (EST)
12.	Received: from wgbht002.bdo.com.au (mail.hosted-products.com [202.183.118.74])
13.	by smtp01.ensyst.com.au (Postfix) with ESMTP id 92758A9F7D
14.	for <Craig.Wright@sydney.bdo.com.au>; Thu, 13 Sep 2007 16:24:53 +1000 (EST)
15.	Received: from mail1.meetup.com (64.90.170.31) by wgbht002.bdo.com.au
16	(10.3.100.11) with Microsoft SMTP Server id 8.0.730.1; Thu, 13 Sep 2007
17.	16:24:52 +1000
18.	Received: from mail1.meetup.com (localhost [127.0.0.1]) by mail1.meetup.com
19.	(Postfix) with ESMTP id C5E3C13AC244for <craig.wright@bdo.com.au>; Thu, 13
20.	Sep 2007 02:24:50 -0400 (EDT)
21.	DomainKey-Signature: a=rsa-sha1; c=nofws; d=meetup.com; q=dns; s=meetup; b=im
22.	mj+lX7O/U7cxzO/ea0P6m/5w/qkaHf5OQCHSodhV/vDbu7OsxvA2I/pZsLV/lGL8
23.	fF+xfpgQwUHF5duaGnyLY2Odf2HayO9XYM64BWpS600Fplgb4Q77 tS9X0HVW5/o
24.	TZnSk2jv40qbA6rj6YpBzT/6S7GsJlsw7UKlRNFNo=
25.	Received: from mail.meetup.com (james1.int.meetup.com [192.168.60.31]) by

26. mail1.meetup.com (Postfix) with ESMTP id AE85613AC265 for

27. <craig.wright@bdo.com.au>; Thu, 13 Sep 2007 02:24:48 -0400 (EDT)

28. Message-ID: <1482785835.1189664682554.JavaMail.nobody@james1>

29. From: Kim H <geedot@gmail.com>

30. Sender: <entrepreneur-1136-announce@meetup.com>

31. To: <entrepreneur-1136-announce@meetup.com>

32. Subject: [entrepreneur-1136] Open Coffee Reminder

33. MIME-Version: 1.0

34. Content-Type: text/html; charset="iso-8859-1"

35. X-MEETUP-TRACK: bc1

36. Content-Transfer-Encoding: 7bit

37. Reply-To: <entrepreneur-1136@meetup.com>

38. Mailing-List: list entrepreneur-1136@meetup.com; contact postmaster@meetup.com

39. List-Id: <entrepreneur-1136.meetup.com>

40. List-Unsubscribe: <mailto: support@meetup.com>

41. Errors-To: info@meetup.com

42. Precedence: list

43. X-MEETUP-RECIP-ID: 4275355

44. X-MEETUP-MESG-ID: 825185

45. Date: Thu, 13 Sep 2007 02:24:48 -0400

46. X-Virus-Scanned: amavisd-new at ensyst.com.au

47. Return-Path: info@meetup.com

48. X-OriginalArrivalTime: 13 Sep 2007 06:24:56.0989 (UTC) FILETIME=[CDE714D0:01C7F5CE]

49. X-TM-AS-Product-Ver: SMEX-7.0.0.1345-5.0.1021-15420.002

50. X-TM-AS-Result: No—13.560300-5.000000-4

Information about the e-mail's origin can be retrieved from lines 2–20. The return path for sending a reply is indicated in line 31 and 37. Note that this is not the same as the from address (Kim H <geedot@gmail.com>) on line 30. The return path information is not reliable as it can be easily forged.

The recipient's e-mail address is specified on lines 25–27: <**craig.wright@bdo.com.au**>. Line 1 shows the type of e-mail service, such as Microsoft Mail, shown in the message header and the recognizing number, which is 12780 in the sample message. Line 19 demonstrates a server message ID (C5E3C13AC244).

Line 15 indicates the IP address of the e-mail server, 64.90.170.31 in the example, and the name of server, mail1.meetup.com, which is used to send the message.

The piece of information crucial for the tracking the of e-mail's origin is contained in line 29. Line 29 illustrates a unique message ID (1482785835.1189664682554.JavaMail.nobody@james1 in the sample header) assigned by the server while sending mail. The e-mail log should be examined to confirm the message ID.

Line 19 shows the IP address of the e-mail server along with the date and time. In the example, 10.3.100.11 is the IP address of the server that is wgbht002.bdo.com.au. Line 19 also specifies the protocol. For instance, SMTP is used to send the e-mail in the sample message.

If a message has any attachments, they will also be displayed in the header. Attachments are supporting evidence in an investigation. It is advisable to search for attachments using a search and find feature of your forensic software. A file should be copied and preserved as evidence. Internet sites such as www.whatis.com are helpful when checking an unknown file extensions and the associated programs used to create these file extensions.

Microsoft Outlook

Microsoft Outlook Mail is in effect a personal information manager (PIM), containing information related to e-mail, contacts, and calendaring. The e-mail database is generally saved in the "\user account\Local Settings\Application Data\Microsoft\Outlook" directory.

Microsoft Outlook allows the user to save e-mail messages in two different file formats based on the system configuration:

- A personal e-mail file (.pst) used for local storage. This may be used in addition to a server-based configuration (such as Microsoft Exchange) for archiving or storage (see Figure 8.3).

- An off-line e-mail file (.ost) to access Exchange e-mail messages when not connected to the server.

Files are stored by Outlook Mail as *.pst files. PST files contain archives of all PIM folders, including Outlook e-mail, the e-mail Inbox, Calendar entries, Draft e-mail messages and other files, Sent Items, and notes and journals.

Figure 8.3 The Personal Folders

PST File Location

E-mail client software enables e-mail to be opened without logging on to the user's account. All e-mail programs use a particular data file type. Microsoft Outlook opens a PST file containing archives of all folders. The following steps are used to create a .pst file:

1. Open Microsoft Outlook (this process may vary with the version of Outlook used).
2. Go to the File menu and select **Import and Export**.
3. Select **Export to file** in the Import and Export wizard.
4. Hit **Next**.
5. Select the personal folder, [file name].pst, and hit **Next**.
6. Select the folder to be exported and then hit **Next**.
7. Save the file to the chosen location and select the applicable option.
8. Select **Finish**.
9. The following steps may be used to locate the PST file:
 1. Open **My Computer** and double-click the local drive icon.
 2. Double-click **Document and Settings** and open the **User Name** folder.
 3. Click **Tools** in the menu bar.

4. Click **Folder Options** and select the View tab.

5. Click **Show Hidden Files and Folder**, click **Apply**, and then click **OK**.

6. Go to the Application data folder and Open **Microsoft**.

7. Double-click **Outlook** in the Microsoft folder and select the .pst file to retrieve the e-mail messages.

The preceding information helps in locating the .pst file location in Microsoft Outlook.

E-Mail Messages, UNIX, and More

UNIX and Linux behave differently to Microsoft in that they handle e-mail on a user-by-user basis. The system administrator creates the user accounts and groups. The members of these groups receive the same e-mail messages. If a suspect is configured using such a group, the root user or administrator can add an investigator to the group to discretely monitor and read any e-mail messages. This allows the investigator to monitor and trace an e-mail without using a suspect's e-mail or system account.

Online e-mail systems like Hotmail, and Yahoo leave files containing e-mail message information on the local computer. These files are stored in a number of folders, including Cookies, Temp, History, Cache, and the Temporary Internet Folder. Forensic tools can recover these folders for the respective e-mail clients. When folders are retrieved, e-mail files can be accessed. If the data is not readable, various tools are available such as a cookie reader used with cookies. A cookie reader is essential to examine cookies.

An additional characteristic of e-mail programs with PIM functionality (e.g., Outlook) is the personal address book (PAB). A suspect's personal address book often provides further supporting evidence and may be representative of the suspect's involvement in a crime.

Tracing an E-mail Message

The IP address of the originating host system can help you determine the owner of an e-mail address that has been used in a possible incident or crime that is being investigated. This information can be faked. Always validate any evidence that you uncover. A number of sites can help in the process of determining the owner or responsible party associated with the domain name. Some of these include:

- **www.arin.net** The American Registry for Internet Numbers (ARIN) can be used to find the domain name from an IP address. It also supplies the contact personal listed against a domain name.

- **www.freeality.com** This Web site presents various options for searching such as e-mail address, phone numbers, and names. The site allows users to do reverse e-mail searches, which may help determine the subject's real identity. This site also offers reverse phone number and address searches.

- **www.google.com** The Google search engine may be used to search for nearly any information. Google Groups and Advanced Groups Search functions allow for the searching of a single newsgroup or all newsgroups through keywords, by message ID, or author. By typing an e-mail address associated with the investigation's subject in the "AUTHOR" box, a great volume of information may be obtained, including any articles that the suspect has posted.

- **www.internic.com** This site presents the same information as www.arin.net.

These Web sites support an investigation through tracing the e-mail message and by supplying necessary evidence including a suspect's contact details.

Tools and Techniques to Investigate E-mail Messages

The forensic investigator may use a number of tools and techniques to determine the authenticity and obtain evidence related to e-mail. This section details some of these tools and techniques.

Using Logs to Analyze E-mail

In any investigation involving e-mail, it is important to validate and verify the e-mail address, source, and path. System logs are utilized to verify the path that e-mail has taken. Routers and firewalls provide valuable validation of the e-mail server and the path contained within the e-mail header through their logs. Although it is possible to easily spoof an e-mail header, it is next to impossible to also subvert all the network equipment and servers along the path of the e-mail in its transmission.

By coupling network and system logs from the source, destination and intermediate devices and servers along the path of the e-mail, you can validate the authenticity of information contained within the e-mail header. If there are any discrepancies across the systems and logs, there is good evidence that the e-mail header has been tampered with.

Examining Network Equipment Logs

Through the examination of router and firewall logs, it is possible to verify the times and the IP addresses that are contained within the e-mail header.

Both routers and firewalls may be configured to track and log ingress and egress traffic as it passes through them. In doing so, routers and firewalls generally produce log files. These log files can often provide e-mail message ID information and can also provide the source address and destination address of the servers used to send e-mail.

Examining UNIX E-mail Server Logs

Sendmail is the primary application used to transmit e-mail through a Linux or UNIX system. Both the configuration file (sendmail.cf) and the logs provide useful information. Both Linux and UNIX use syslog to maintain logs of what has occurred on the system. The configuration file, /etc/syslog.conf is used to determine where the syslog service (or daemon called Syslogd) sends its logs.

The syslog configuration file contains valuable information about the logging priority, where logs are sent, and what other actions may be taken. Sendmail can create event messages and is usually configured to record the basic information such as the source and destination addresses, the sender and recipient addresses, and the e-mail's message ID.

The syslog.conf will authoritatively display the location of the log file for e-mail. This is commonly /var/log/mailog. This file generally contains the source and destination IP addresses, date and time stamps, and other information that may be used to validate the information contained within an e-mail header.

Pine, qmail, and mailx also produce log files that may be sourced through investigating the syslog configurations.

Examining Microsoft Exchange E-mail Server Logs

Microsoft Exchange uses the Microsoft Extensible Storage Engine (ESE). When investigating e-mail that is sent using a Microsoft Exchange server, the investigator is principally concerned with EDB files STM database files, checkpoint files, and temporary files that are located on the system.

Older versions of Exchange use EDB database files. In the newer versions of Microsoft Exchange server (2000 on), both EDB and STM formats are utilized. EDB and STM database files are used to create the storage space for e-mail messages. An EDB file is utilized to save the formatted e-mail, including the MAPI (Message Application Protocol Interface) information. The STM database holds those files that are not formatted using MAPI.

Microsoft exchange uses a transaction log to maintain and process changes made to the database file. The transaction log can thus be used to determine if an e-mail has been sent or received by the e-mail server. Exchange server uses checkpoint files that are written into the transaction log to mark the preceding point that the database was last saved to disk. Checkpoints help in determining whether any loss of data has occurred since the last backup was completed, thus enabling the system administrator (and thus the forensic investigator) to recover lost or deleted messages.

Temporary files (or TMP files) are used by Microsoft exchange to store information that is received when the server is too busy to process it immediately. Database overflow information is saved using RESx.logs. These temporary files are not wiped by the system and may be recovered.

The Windows Event Viewer can be used to view a tracking log on the Exchange server. Microsoft provides a message-tracking feature with Exchange that has a verbose mode. In this mode it is possible also to view the message content associated with the e-mail. The event

viewer further supplies important information about e-mail messages that had been sent and received using the server.

The Exchange troubleshooting or diagnostic logs also provide useful information if they are enabled. These log files are read using the Window Event Viewer. There are quite a number of events that are recorded for each e-mail letter sent or received. Additionally, the Event Properties dialog box will provide additional information.

Specialized E-mail Forensic Tools

Specialized forensic tools such as FINALeMAIL, Sawmill-Group Wise, and Audimation for Logging are specifically designed to provide e-mail and attachment recovery. When used with data recovery tools (including FTK or EnCase), a process may be developed to find any log files, e-mail databases, personal e-mail storage files, and off-line storage files and then recover the e-mail messages contained within them.

E-mail recovery tools will extract information from an e-mail server or the client machine. By comparing the captured log and server information with the victim's e-mail message, you may be able to either validate an e-mail or determine that it is likely false.

E-mail Examiner

The E-mail Examiner tool aids in recovering deleted e-mail and other messages. This tool recovers deleted e-mail from the deleted items folder after it has been cleared.

E-mail Examiner has the capability to examine over 14 e-mail database formats running on Windows 95, 98, NT4, 2000, 2003, ME, and XP. It provides support for AOL, Calypso, EML Message files, Eudora, Forte Agent, Juno 3.x, Mozilla Mail, MSN Mail, Netscape Messenger, Outlook Express, Outlook Exchange, Pegasus Mail, PocoMail, USENET Groups, and a number of other formats

FINALeMAIL

FINALeMAIL is designed to scan an e-mail database to uncover deleted e-mail messages. It is particularly aimed at uncovering e-mail messages when the data location information is lost or destroyed. This includes situations when damage has caused through virus infection, deletion, and disk reformatting. This tool can be used to restore either single messages or entire database files to their original condition. FINALeMAIL provides support for Outlook Express and Eudora database formats.

Network E-mail Examiner

Network Email Examiner may be used to examine a variety of e-mail database formats. The tool displays and processes all of the e-mail accounts in the information store or database and all the associated meta-data contained within the system. The tool supports both Microsoft

Exchange and Lotus Notes data stores, including Microsoft Exchange Information Store versions 5.0, 5.5, 2000, and 2003, as well as Lotus Notes Information Store versions 4.0, 5.0, and 6.0.

The significant features of the tool include:

- A separate, simple User Interface (UI)

- Bookmarking

- Support to export data into Paraben's e-mail examiner

- An advanced search function

Network E-mail Examiner is intended to be used with Paraben's E-mail Examiner, and the output uses the same format. Network E-mail Examiner can export an entire mail store and even converted into an alternate format.

R-Mail

R-mail is an e-mail recovery tool with the capability to restore deleted e-mail messages. This tool is designed to restore Outlook Express e-mail. The tool can recover .dbx files that are broken through deletion. It uses a proprietary e-mail restoration technology called IntelligentRebuild that can rebuild damaged *.dbx files in order to recover deleted e-mail messages. The tool saves recovered e-mail messages in the .eml file format that may be imported into Outlook express. This tool is particularly useful where a suspect has deliberately deleted e-mail messages.

Tracing Back

Tracing back e-mail starts with validating the e-mail header. It is necessary to validate that the information contained within the e-mail header (including the subject, date, Sent From and Received To address) is legitimate. The Sent From line includes the source IP address of the host that was used to send the e-mail and possibly the e-mail address of the sender (which may be spoofed easily). The Received To lines point to each host that the e-mail has been processed by ending transmitted with the date and time that was processed.

Always remember that all lines in the e-mail header can be falsified except for the Received segment referencing the victim's computer. This is why it is necessary to validate the header information from external sources. The original e-mail server should be used only as the primary source to trace back to if the header information has been verified (using the techniques listed earlier in this chapter).

Once this has occurred, it is possible to approach the court and obtain a court order in order to acquire the log files from the source server. This information may be used as evidence to determine the real identity of the sender.

Tracing Back Web-Based E-mail

Web-based e-mail services (such as Hotmail or AOL) can often make it complicated to trace the sender. The services make it possible to send or access e-mail from anywhere in the world. Many of these services are free and require no authentication or proof of identity when applying for an account. Consequently organized crime groups often configure fake e-mail accounts with bogus information.

The unique IP addresses can still be obtained to locate a suspect. Most Web-based e-mail providers (including Hotmail and Yahoo) maintain a log of the IP address of each host used to access these e-mail services. Furthermore, header information from most Web-based e-mail systems will contain the unique IP address.

TEST DAY TIP

Web-based e-mail messages may also be traced back using the Multiple DNS lookup engine from www.bankes.com/nslookup.htm. This service supplies the contact details of the relevant ISP given the IP address.

Searching E-mail Addresses

Internet search engines can be used to expand the amount of information that you have on the suspect. By entering contact details (including e-mail addresses, the suspect's name, phone number, or addresses) most Internet search engines will reveal additional information on the suspect.

The following search engines are commonly utilized when searching on e-mail addresses:

- **www.altavista.com** Altavista provides a "People Finder" option at the home page. It offers two search criteria: phone and e-mail. It is possible to determine the e-mail address, phone number, and even a background report of in individual by entering the person's initial or the entire last name.

- **www.infospace.com** InfoSpace offers a reverse lookup selection that helps you trace an e-mail trail. E-mail directories and public records can be referenced as you conduct your investigation.

- **www.emailaddresses.com** This site provides a complimentary e-mail address directory. The directory consists of a variety of information and allows searching by location and even reverse lookups.

- **www.google.com** Google has become the primary search engine for many people. A whole subculture known as Google Hackers has evolved around the use of the search engine.

E-mail Search Site

The site www.EmailChange.com provides a free change of e-mail address registry and search engine. It can be used to track suspects who have changed their e-mail addresses. The suspects' new e-mail addresses can often be discovered by presenting their previous e-mail addresses into the search site.

Handling Spam

SPAM or unsolicited commercial e-mail is both annoying and wastes time, resulting in economic loss. Although it is possible to send an e-mail or note to the domain administrator responsible for the initiating IP address, this will often fail to stop the spam. Frequently, the source address that has sent the spam has been compromised or is otherwise unaware. Furthermore, sending a request to stop the spam often just validates your e-mail address to the spammer.

If you persistently get spam from an address, it may be possible to report the incident to the FTC (The U.S. Federal Trade Commission) by sending a copy of the spam message to spam@uce.gov. The FTC also provides an online complaint form at www.ftc.gov. When making a complaint, you need to include the e-mail header.

The e-mail header contains the information that is required by the consumer protection agencies in order for them to respond to a spam complaint. A copy of the spam can be forwarded to the ISP to make the ISP conscious of the spam trouble on their organization and aid them in minimizing future occurrences.

Network Abuse Clearing House

The Network Abuse Clearing House (www.abuse.net/) was started to assist Internet users in reporting abusive activities. It is designed to help control and minimize network abuse. With the rapid growth of Internet crime, the numbers of reports of abuse have also increased. The Network Abuse Clearing House maintains a master database containing all complaints it has received.

You can access this database using the following methods:

- Via an e-mail forwarding service
- Via a Web lookup page
- Via a domain name lookup
- Via a WHOIS server

Abuse.net is not a blacklist or blocking list and does not block or reject e-mail.

Protecting Your E-mail Address from Spam

E-mail spammers use a database of e-mail addresses accumulated through harvesting addresses on the Internet. The e-mail addresses can be discovered from mailing lists and Internet newsgroup postings, from Web sites, Internet chat rooms, or even an online service's membership directory. To defend e-mail addresses from spammers, it is best to minimize the number of times (if any) that they are displayed in public.

Domain keys and other encoding techniques can be used to reduce the capability of others to exploit e-mail addresses. These technologies use cryptographic procedures on the e-mail messages (such as by appending a digital signature) that help the recipient to confirm the source and legitimacy of an e-mail. They first confirm the domain and then compare it against the domain used in the sender's "From" field. If an e-mail is genuine, it is then delivered to the user's inbox. Otherwise, it is bounced. The entire procedure occurs on the server level.

Anti-Spam Tools

In this section, we'll discuss some tools that have been developed to help you minimize SPAM.

Enkoder Form

Enkoder Form is designed to prevent e-mail harvesting. It provides the capability to encrypt e-mail addresses into JavaScript code that is displayed to legitimate browsers but is hidden to many automated tools used by spammers. It aids in protecting e-mail addresses displayed on Web pages written in HTML code.

E-mail addresses may be encoded using the basic form from http://hivelogic.com/enkoder/form. Enter the information in the form and then click the **Enkode It** button. A JavaScript code is created that can be pasted directly into a Web page HTML code where the e-mail address will be displayed. The link that is created is visible in a Web browser.

eMailTrackerPro

eMailTrackerPro analyzes the e-mail header to uncover the IP address of the computer that was used to send the e-mail. It will also supply information concerning the geographical location of sender. This feature makes this tool particularly useful for preventing spamming and spoofing. This tool is available from www.emailtrackerpro.com.

An e-mail forger (spoofer) may be attempting to simply cause trouble, initiate a financial crime, or even discredit the person being spoofed by sending a falsified message to the recipient. eMailTrackerPro Advanced Edition contains an online e-mail checker that offers the capability to view all e-mail messages on the server before they are delivered to your computer.

The program's built-in location database traces e-mail messages to a country or region of the world. eMailTrackerPro further provides hyperlink assimilation using VisualRoute.

Attackers can still overcome this through using an anonymizer service for Web-based e-mail messages. Open mail relay servers may be used for normal e-mail messages. The IP address of the anonymizer company will be displayed and not the suspect's address.

SPAM Punisher

SPAM Punisher is an anti-spam tool designed to facilitate the search for a spammers' ISP address. It automatically detects fake addresses and supports a variety of e-mail client software (including AOL, Hotmail, Microsoft Outlook, and Eudora).

SPAM Punisher parses e-mail headers for IP addresses and then tries to find out which IPs are forged. It then allows you to send a complaint to the appropriate abuse address without difficulty. The templates used by Spam Punisher for complaints can be customized. Spam Punisher provides support for Windows 9x/ME/NT/2000/XP.

Investigating Denial-of-Service Attacks

A common perception is that the target of a denial-of-service (DoS) attack is a server, though this is not always the case. The fundamental objective of a DoS attack is to degrade service, whether it is hosted by a single server or delivered by an entire network infrastructure. A DoS attack attempts to reduce the ability of a site to service clients, whether those clients are physical users or logical entities such as other computer systems. This can be achieved by overloading the ability of the target network or server to handle incoming traffic, or by sending network packets that cause target systems and networks to behave unpredictably. Unfortunately for the administrator, "unpredictable" behavior usually translates into a hung or crashed system.

This section will examine the techniques, mechanisms, and implications of DoS attacks. It corresponds to module 24 in the EC-Counsel's course.

DoS Attacks

Although DoS attacks do not by definition generate a risk to confidential or sensitive data, they can act as an effective tool to mask more intrusive activities that could take place simultaneously. While administrators and security officers are attempting to rectify what they perceive to be the main problem, the real penetration could be happening elsewhere.

Some of the numerous forms of DoS attacks can be difficult to detect or deflect. Within weeks, months, or even days of the appearance of a new attack, subtle "copycat" variations begin appearing elsewhere. By this stage, defenses must be deployed not only for the primary attack, but also for its more distant cousins.

Most DoS attacks take place across a network, with the perpetrator seeking to take advantage of the lack of integrated security within the current iteration of IP (i.e., IP version 4 [IPv4]). Hackers are fully aware that security considerations have been passed on to higher-level protocols and applications. IP version 6 (IPv6), which may help to rectify some of these problems, includes a means of validating the source of packets and their integrity by using an

authentication header. Although the continuing improvement of IP is critical, it does not resolve today's problems, because IPv6 is not yet in widespread use.

DoS attacks not only originate from remote systems, but can also be launched against the local machine. Local DoS attacks are generally easier to locate and rectify, because the parameters of the problem space are well defined (local to the host). A common example of a locally based DoS attack is a fork bomb that repeatedly spawns processes to consume system resources.

Types of DoS Attacks

Denial of service as an attack vector is quite interesting because every machine ever made and most likely every machine that will ever be made is vulnerable to a denial of service in some form, and some systems are just more difficult than others to "DoS". This is because every machine has a finite set of resources that it can use to process data, by giving a machine more data than it can possibly process and in some way sustaining that you are causing a denial of service as the machine is paralyzed performing an impossible task and struggling to keep up with its other intended functions. If it helps, think of an old computer. Now think of installing a modern, resource-intensive application on that machine and trying to run it. Do you notice now how that computer is seemingly in limbo for 15–20 minutes as it tries to run that application? We are now effectively "DoS-ing" that old computer by giving it way too much to process. If after the computer catches up and becomes responsive again, we launch another such application, and another, and then another, we can keep that machine unusable for a very long time. If we keep on doing this, vital services may start to crash and the machine might become unstable and unusable until we reboot it. Whereas most of the "classic" DoS techniques that we will be discussing in this section are the result of programmatic mistakes from software vendor implementation of the IP, and other software, resource exhaustion and service termination are still the common thread for most DoS attacks.

Ping of Death

The Ping of Death DoS attack deals with IP fragmentation. When a datagram is processed from a sending to a receiving device, it may be passed through many different physical networks. Each network may have its own frame formats and specific limits that determine the maximum amount of data that can be transmitted (per datagram). For example, Ethernet limits this amount to 1,500 bytes. That is Ethernet's maximum transmission unit (MTU). If the IP must send data that exceeds a specific network's MTU, fragmentation can occur. Therefore, fragmentation is simply the process of dividing a datagram into smaller *fragments* which are each sent separately. Each fragment becomes its own datagram and is sent independent of the other fragments. They can all go their own way and take unique, separate paths to the final destination. If even one fragment does not arrive, the receiving device must discard the remaining fragments when the fragmentation timer reaches zero. As IP is a connectionless service, it's dependent on higher-layer services to force a retransmission of the datagrams. IP is dependent upon several

fields to know whether datagrams have been fragmented and how to properly reassemble them. These fields include:

- The ID field

- The more bit

- Fragmentation offset

The Ping of Death utilizes an oversized packet that is illegally fragmented. RFC 791 specifies that IP packets can be up to 65,535 octets long (2^{16} - 1), which includes the length of the IP header (usually 20 octets if no IP options are specified). An Internet Control Message Protocol (ICPM) Echo Request (ping) is carried inside an IP packet and has a header length of 8 octets followed by the length of the data octets in the ping request. So, the maximum size for the data area of a ping can be 65,507 (65,535 - 20 - 8 = 65,507). A Ping of Death carries a data payload that is greater than this maximum size (greater than 65,507 octets). Of course, as was previously mentioned, sending a ping that size will cause the packet to fragment. When the fragments are reassembled on the victim's system, it can cause a buffer overflow on older systems. As a result, the IP stack will crash and the system will become unresponsive on the network. This attack was first seen in 1996. At that time, a lot of systems were susceptible to it. Today this attack is largely of historical significance, or can perhaps be run against legacy systems.

TEST DAY TIP

You probably won't have to know things such as the maximum size of an IP packet, or which RFC dictates that size on the test. Instead, you should concentrate on the various mechanisms of DoS for the illustrated attacks. For example, a Ping of Death is made possible by sending a very large, fragmented ping; a teardrop (discussed shortly) is caused by overlapping fragments; and most of the others are a result of resource consumption.

Teardrop Attack

Fragmentation, as illustrated in the previous section, is a necessary mechanism of IP; however, overlapping fragments can also offer an attacker a means of slipping packets past an intrusion detection system and firewall. This is due to the way that different systems reassemble packets or handle them when one or more of the same fragments arrive. To better expand on the concept, consider the fact that Windows-based systems give preferential treatment to original fragments, whereas Cisco devices favor the last fragments.

Overlapping fragmentation can also be used to facilitate a denial of service. The teardrop attack is an example of this. This fragmentation attack sends packets that are malformed with the fragmentation offset value tweaked so that the receiving packets overlap. The victim does not know how to process these overlapping fragments and so they crash or lock up the receiving system, thereby causing a denial of service. This attack is also quite old and known to affect only Windows 3.1x, Windows 95, and Windows NT operating systems, as well as the Linux 2.0.32 and 2.1.63 kernels.

SYN Flooding

SYN Flooding is a DoS attack that exploits a basic weakness found in the Transmission Control Protocol/Internet Protocol (TCP/IP), and its concept is fairly simple. A standard TCP session consists of the two communicating hosts exchanging a **SYN | SYN/acknowledgment (ACK) | ACK**. The expected behavior is that the initiating host sends a SYN packet, to which the responding host will issue a SYN/ACK and wait for an ACK reply from the initiator. With a SYN attack, or SYN flood, the attacker simply sends only the SYN packet, leaving the victim waiting for a reply. The attack occurs when the attacker sends thousands and thousands of SYN packets to the victim, forcing the victim to wait for replies that never come. While the host is waiting for so many replies, it can't accept any legitimate requests, so it becomes unavailable, thus achieving the purpose of a DoS attack. Some stateful firewalls protect against SYN attacks by resetting pending connections after a specific timeout. Another protection is with the use of SYN cookies, where a computer under attack responds with a special SYN/ACK packet and does not wait for an ACK response. Only when the ACK packet in response to the SYN/ACK packet returns does the entry generate a queue entry from information within the special SYN/ACK packet.

Land Attacks

The Land attack utilized a weakness in the TCP/IP implementations of a lot of older machines. To execute the attack the attacker sends a TCP SYN packet (a connection initiation), giving the target host's address as both source and destination, and using the same port on the target host as both source and destination. Doing this would create an infinite loop on the vulnerable hosts, causing them to consume all their resources and resulting in a denial of service.

Smurf Attacks

A Smurf attack is a resource consumption attack using ICMP Echo as the mechanism. ICMP Echo attacks seek to flood the target with ping traffic and use up all available bandwidth. As a result, there is no bandwidth left for available users. Smurf is just one example of an ICMP Echo attack. Smurf exploits ICMP by sending a spoofed ping packet addressed to the network broadcast address and has the source address listed as the victim. On a multi-access network, many systems may possibly reply. The attack results in the victim being flooded with ping responses.

Fraggle Attacks

Fraggle is the same attack as a Smurf attack, only using User Datagram Protocol (UDP) Echo instead of ICMP Echo.

Snork Attacks

A Snork attack is another UDP-based DoS attack that's very similar to Smurf and Fraggle, and equally old. In this attack, a specially crafted UDP packet is sent to the Remote Procedure Call (RPC) service (UDP port 135) on a Windows NT server. This can raise the CPU utilization on the server to 100 percent for a short period. Repeated packets sent to the server can keep the utilization at 100 percent. Snork packets could also be bounced between two or more servers to cause high utilization on the network segment, DoS-ing the network as well.

DDoS Attacks

Though some forms of DoS attacks can be amplified by multiple intermediaries, the first step of a DoS exploit still originates from a single machine. However, DoS attacks have evolved beyond single-tier (SYN flood) and two-tier (Smurf) attacks. DDoS attacks advance the DoS conundrum one more painful step forward. Modern attack methodologies have now embraced the world of distributed multi-tier computing. One of the significant differences in the methodology of a DDoS attack is that it consists of two distinct phases. During the first phase, the perpetrator compromises computers scattered across the Internet and installs specialized software on these hosts to aid in the attack. In the second phase, the compromised hosts (referred to as *zombies*) are then instructed through intermediaries (called *masters*) to commence the attack. The most widely known DDoS attacks are Trinoo, Tribe Flood Network, and Stacheldracht.

Notes from the Underground...

Amplification

One of the easiest and most common ways to generate an amount of network traffic to cause a DoS condition against a specific server or network is through *amplification*. Amplification happens when an attacker can send a little bit of data to some server that will respond with a lot more data. The most common Internet servers to facilitate an amplification attack are open DNS servers. Open DNS servers will respond to DNS queries from anyone. If an attacker wants to DoS a specific machine on the Internet and knows its IP address, the attacker can send very small requests to an open DNS server, forging the source IP so that the DNS server thinks the requests are coming from the machine the attacker wishes to DoS. The server will, in turn, send a lot of data to the victim IP, much more data than the attacker ever sent to the DNS server in the first place. In some cases, when the DNS server "drone" supports the RFC 2671 extension mechanisms for DNS, a simple 122-byte query can elicit a response of 4,320 bytes. In this way, the attacker could fully saturate a 1.54Mbps T1 line when he has only a 56kbps dial-up connection.

Hundreds, possibly thousands, of zombies can be co-opted into the attack by diligent hackers. Using the control software, each zombie can then be used to mount its own DoS attack on the target. The cumulative effect of the zombie attack is to either overwhelm the victim with massive amounts of traffic or exhaust resources such as connection queues.

Additionally, this type of attack obfuscates the source of the original attacker: the commander of the zombie hordes. The multi-tier model of DDoS attacks and their ability to spoof packets and to encrypt communications can make tracking down the real offender a tortuous process.

Working of DDoS Attacks

The command structure supporting a DDoS attack can be quite convoluted, and it can be difficult to determine a terminology that describes it clearly. Let's look at one of the more understandable naming conventions for a DDoS attack structure and the components involved.

Software components involved in a DDoS attack include:

- **Client** The control software used by the hacker to launch attacks. The client directs command strings to its subordinate hosts.

- **Daemon** Software programs running on a zombie that receive incoming client command strings and act on them accordingly. The daemon is the process responsible for actually implementing the attack detailed in the command strings.

Hosts involved in a DDoS attack include:

- **Master** A computer that runs the client software
- **Zombie** A subordinate host that runs the daemon process
- **Target** The recipient of the attack

Classification of DDoS Attacks

To recruit hosts for the attack, hackers target inadequately secured machines connected in some form to the Internet. Hackers use various inspection techniques—both automated and manual—to uncover inadequately secured networks and hosts. After the insecure machines have been identified, the attacker compromises the systems through a variety of ways. The first task a thorough hacker undertakes is to erase evidence that the system has been compromised, and to ensure that the compromised host will pass a cursory examination. Some of the compromised hosts become masters, whereas others are destined to be made into zombies. Masters receive orders that they then trickle through to the zombies for which they are responsible. The master is only responsible for sending and receiving short control messages, making lower-bandwidth networks just as suitable as higher-bandwidth networks.

On the hosts not designated as zombies, the hacker installs the software (called a *daemon*) used to send out attack streams. The daemon runs in the background on the zombie, waiting for a message to activate the exploit software and launch an attack targeted at the designated victim. A daemon may be able to launch multiple types of attacks, such as UDP or SYN floods. Combined with the ability to use spoofing, the daemon can prove to be a very flexible and powerful attack tool.

NOTE

Despite its rather evil-sounding name, a daemon is defined as any program that runs on a continuous basis and handles requests for service that come in from other computers. There are many legitimate and useful daemon programs that have nothing to do with launching attacks (e.g., the line printer daemon [LPD] that runs on a remote print server to monitor for print requests). The term is more often used in reference to UNIX/Linux systems. On Windows systems, services can be considered the analogue of daemons, which run in the background waiting for requests.

After the attacker has recruited a sufficient number of zombies, he can contact the master and instruct it to launch a particular attack. The master then passes on these instructions to multiple zombies who commence the DDoS attack. After the attack network is in place, it can take only a few moments to launch a distributed attack. With similar speed, the hacker can also halt the attack.

The basic flow of the attack then becomes:

- **For Hosts** Attacker to master to zombie to target
- **For Software** Attacker to client to daemon to target

The use and development of DDoS programs have piqued the interest of governments, businesses, and security experts alike, in no small part because it is a class of attack that is extremely effective while simultaneously being hard to trace.

EXAM WARNING

Know the difference between DoS and a DDoS attacks. A DoS attack is simply any attack that makes a network or computing resource unavailable. A DDoS attack is very unique in that it orchestrates many packets to be directed to one host from multiple machines called zombies. These

are easily confused terms, stemming from the same idea, but distinct in their scope. DoS is a very general term describing any kind of attack that knocks out a service, whereas DDoS is a term that describes one specific type of DoS attack.

DoS Attack Modes

Most DoS attacks take place across a network, with the perpetrator seeking to take advantage of the lack of integrated security within the current iteration of IP (i.e., IP version 4 [IPv4]). Hackers are fully aware that security considerations have been passed on to higher-level protocols and applications. IP version 6 (IPv6), which may help to rectify some of these problems, includes a means of validating the source of packets and their integrity by using an authentication header. Although the continuing improvement of IP is critical, it does not resolve today's problems, because IPv6 is not yet in widespread use.

DoS attacks not only originate from remote systems, but can also be launched against the local machine. Local DoS attacks are generally easier to locate and rectify, because the parameters of the problem space are well defined (local to the host). A common example of a locally based DoS attack is a fork bomb that repeatedly spawns processes to consume system resources.

There are two elemental types of DoS attacks: *Resource Consumption attacks* (such as SYN flood attacks and amplification attacks) and *Malformed Packet attacks*.

Resource Consumption

Computing resources are, by their very nature, finite. Administrators around the world bemoan the fact that their infrastructures lack network bandwidth, CPU cycles, RAM, and secondary storage. Invariably, the lack of these resources leads to some form of degradation of the services the computing infrastructure delivers to clients. The reality of having finite resources is highlighted even further when an orchestrated attack consumes these precious resources.

The consumption of resources involves the reduction of available resources, whatever their nature, by using a directed attack. One of the more common forms of a DoS attack targets *network bandwidth*. In particular, Internet connections and the supporting devices are prime targets of this type of attack, due to their limited bandwidth and their visibility to the rest of the Internet community. Very few businesses are in the fortunate position of having excessive Internet bandwidth, and when a business relies on its ability to service client requests quickly and efficiently, a bandwidth consumption attack can bring the company to its knees.

Resource consumption attacks predominantly originate from outside the local network, but you should not rule out the possibility that the attack is from within. These attacks usually take the form of a large number of packets directed at the victim, a technique commonly known as *flooding*.

A target network can also be flooded when an attacker has more available bandwidth than the victim and overwhelms the victim with pure brute force. This situation is less likely to happen on a one-to-one basis if the target is a medium-size e-commerce site. Such companies generally have a larger "pipe" than their attackers. On the other hand, the availability of broadband connectivity has driven high-speed Internet access into the homes of users around the world. This has increased the likelihood of this type of attack, as home users replace their analogue modems with Digital Subscriber Line (DSL) and cable modem technologies.

Another way of consuming bandwidth is to enlist the aid of loosely configured networks, causing them to send traffic directed at the victim. If enough networks can be duped into this type of behavior, the victim's network can be flooded with relative ease. These types of attacks are often called *amplification attacks*, with a *Smurf* attack—which sends an ICMP request to a broadcast address, causing all hosts in the network to send ICMP replies to the victim—being a classic one.

Other forms of resource consumption can include the reduction of connections available to legitimate users and the reduction of system resources available to the host operating system itself. "Denial of service" is a very broad term, and consequently various types of exploits can fit the description due to the circumstances surrounding their manifestation. A classic example is the Structured Query Language (SQL) Slammer worm, which exploited a known vulnerability in Microsoft SQL Server to generate excessive amounts of network traffic in attempts to reproduce itself to other vulnerable systems, which resulted in a global slowdown of the Internet on January 25, 2003.

Another form of DoS is the now ever-present *e-mail spam*, or Unsolicited Bulk Email (UBE). Spammers can send a large amount of unwanted e-mail in a very short amount of time. If a company's mail server is bombarded with spam, it may slow down, fail to receive valid e-mail messages, or even crash entirely. Getting spammed is a very real DoS danger and e-mail protection is now high on every company's security checklist.

Malformed Packets

This attack mode deals with service termination. Some malformed packet attacks can consume resources, but most (such as fragmentation-type attacks) are aimed at crashing vital services (such as the TCP/IP stack in a target machine), or crashing the underlying operating system on the victim. These attacks are not so much concerned with consuming resources so that systems cannot function as strategically taking out vital services, producing the same result. Ping of Death and Teardrop are examples of this DoS attack mode.

Also remember that whereas many malformed packet attacks cause buffer overflows, many buffer overflow attacks are not technically caused by a malformed packet, but the result is the same.

Indications of a DoS/DDoS Attack

DoS and DDoS attacks come in many shapes and sizes, can originate locally or over the network, and have almost an infinite number of permutations in terms of how they can be executed (everything from Ping of Death to cutting the power lines outside a computing facility with no backup generator).

However, all DoS attacks have one thing in common: denial of service. Network connections become unusable, servers crash, services become unavailable, and systems become unusable. All of these things indicate that a DoS attack may have occurred.

To investigate these attacks you will want to sniff network traffic to the failing machine, look for unusual traffic spikes on Internet connections and network segments, and look for core files or crash dumps on the affected systems. All of these diagnostic procedures can help to diagnose an active DoS attack.

Challenges in the Detection of a DoS Attack

Because this attack class can present in so many ways, it can be difficult to distinguish DoS/DDoS from mere catastrophic system events. For example, you are at home; you have a DSL connection to the Internet, and you have your home computer hidden via Dynamic Network Address Translation (Dynamic NAT) from a normal consumer DSL router. You launch an application that creates a lot of IP connections to various remote systems very quickly, such as a portscan (for the sake of argument, you are authorized by your company and are checking that new network segment that was put out on the Internet to make sure all the firewall rules are implemented correctly). All of a sudden, you have no Internet connection at all! Nothing is getting out whatsoever. What happened? Are you the sudden unwitting victim of a DoS attack?

In a way you are, except you caused the DoS. You are attacking yourself! Because you are using Dynamic (Hide) NAT on that DSL router, there are a limited number of TCP ports that your router can use as source ports for NAT, and you have just used them all up very quickly with the portscan. As the portscanner runs, as soon as a port frees up, it uses another, and so on until either you stop the portscan or the application runs its course.

This is why DoS attacks can be so hard to detect. A number of normal, everyday events can go very wrong and seem like a DoS attack. Furthermore, even in legitimate scenarios in which a system has been the victim of a DoS attack, many attacks will rely on packets with forged source addresses, or innocent intermediary machines such as DDoS zombies or an open DNS server that an attacker is using for purposes of amplification. This will often make finding the original source of the DoS attack very difficult if not impossible in some cases.

Investigating Web Attacks

The topic of Web attacks is quite wide and varied, and it refers to many attack classes and attack vectors. There are typically two types of Web attacks: attacks against the Web infrastructure and attacks against the Web application. There would seem to be a subtle difference between the two, but infrastructure deals with attacks leveraged against the Web server operating system and server software itself (such as directly attacking Apache, or Microsoft IIS server). Infrastructure attacks deal with server and operating system configuration issues, buffer overflows, command injection, and protocol-based attacks. Attacks against the Web application are usually not tied to infrastructure, but rather to the actual application code of the Web site. Much can be said about Web application attacks; indeed, Web application security has become its own specialized field within the field of information security.

Types of Web Attacks

As was previously mentioned, there are many types of Web attacks, and any one type of attack could likely fill its own book. In fact, numerous books exist that detail Web attacks in depth. We will take a look at a few common Web attacks at both the application level (attacks such as cross-site scripting (XSS), cross-site request forgery (CSRF), parameter tampering, and cookie poisoning) and at the infrastructure level (with attacks such as code/command injection, buffer overflows, and protocol-based attacks).

Cross-Site Scripting

To fully understand cross-site scripting (XSS) attacks, it helps to know that attackers use several core theories and techniques to get their code into your browser. This section provides a breakdown of the many types of XSS attacks and related code injection vectors, from the basic to the more complex. As this chapter illustrates, there is a lot more to XSS attacks than most people understand. Sure, injecting a script into a search field is a valid attack vector, but what if that value is passed through a filter? Is it possible to bypass the filter?

The fact of the matter is that XSS is a wide-open field that is constantly surprising the world with new and unique methods of exploitation and injection. However, there are some foundations that need to be fully understood by Web developers, security researchers, and those IT professionals who are responsible for keeping the infrastructure together.

XSS is an attack technique that forces a Web site to display malicious code, which then executes in a user's Web browser. Consider that XSS exploit code, typically (but not always) written in Hypertext Markup Language (HTML)/JavaScript (a.k.a. JavaScript malicious software [malware]), does not execute on the server. The server is merely the host, while the attack executes within the Web browser. The hacker uses the trusted Web site only as a conduit to perform the attack. The user is the intended victim, not the server. Once an attacker has the thread of control in a user's Web browser, he can do many nefarious acts described throughout

this book, including account hijacking, keystroke recording, intranet hacking, history theft, and so on. This section describes the variety of ways in which a user may become XSS'ed and contract a JavaScript malware payload.

For a Web browser to become infected it must visit a Web page containing JavaScript malware. JavaScript malware could become resident on a Web page in many ways:

- The Web site owner may have purposefully uploaded the offending code.

- The Web page may have been defaced using a vulnerability from the network or operating system layers with JavaScript malware as part of the payload.

- A permanent XSS vulnerability could have been exploited, where JavaScript malware was injected into a public area of a Web site.

- A victim could have clicked on a specially crafted nonpersistent or Document Object Model (DOM)-based XSS link.

There are three basic types of XSS attacks: persistent, nonpersistent, and DOM based. We will take a look at each.

Persistent (or HTML Injection) XSS attacks most often occur in either community content-driven Web sites or Web mail sites, and do not require specially crafted links for execution. A hacker merely submits XSS exploit code to an area of a Web site that other users are likely to visit. These areas could be blog comments, user reviews, message board posts, chat rooms, HTML e-mail, wikis, and numerous other locations. Once a user visits the infected Web page, execution is automatic. This makes persistent XSS much more dangerous than nonpersistent or DOM-based XSS, because the user has no means of defending himself. Once a hacker has his exploit code in place, he'll again advertise the URL to the infected Web page, hoping to snare unsuspecting users. Even users who are wise to nonpersistent XSS URLs can be easily compromised.

Nonpersistent XSS is what most people think of immediately when one discusses the topic of XSS. Consider that a hacker wants to XSS a user on the *http://victim/*, a popular e-commerce Web site. First the hacker needs to identify an XSS vulnerability on *http://victim/*, and then construct a specially crafted URL. To do so, the hacker combs the Web site for any functionality where client-supplied data can be sent to the Web server and then echoed back to the screen. One of the most common vectors for this is via a search box.

DOM-based XSS is a unique form of XSS, used very similarly to nonpersistent, but where the JavaScript malware payload doesn't need to be sent or echoed by the Web site to exploit a user. DOM is a World Wide Web Consortium (W3C) specification that defines the object model for representing XML and HTML structures.

In the XML world, there are mainly two types of parsers: DOM and SAX. SAX is a parsing mechanism that is significantly faster and less memory-intensive but also not very intuitive, because it is not easy to go back to the document nodes (i.e., the parsing mechanism is one-way). On the other hand, DOM-based parsers load the entire document as an object

structure, which contains methods and variables to easily move around the document and modify nodes, values, and attributes on the fly.

Browsers work with the DOM. When a page is loaded, the browser parses the resulting page into an object structure. The *getElementsByTagName* is a standard DOM function that is used to locate XML/HTML nodes based on their tag name.

DOM-based XSS is the exploitation of an input validation vulnerability that is caused by the client, not the server. In other words, DOM-based XSS is not a result of a vulnerability within a server-side script, but rather an improper handling of user-supplied data in the client-side JavaScript. Like the other types of XSS vulnerabilities, DOM-based XSS can be used to steal confidential information or hijack the user account. However, it is essential to understand that this type of vulnerability solely relies upon JavaScript and insecure use of dynamically obtained data from the DOM structure.

Here is a simple example of a DOM-based XSS provided by Amit Klein in his paper "DOM-Based Cross-Site Scripting or XSS of the Third Kind":

```
<HTML>
<TITLE>Welcome!</TITLE>
Hi
<SCRIPT>
var pos=document.URL.indexOf("name=")+5;
document.write(document.URL.substring(pos,document.URL.length));
</SCRIPT>
<BR>
Welcome to our system
...
</HTML>
```

If we analyze the preceding code, you will see that the developer has forgotten to sanitize the value of the "name" get parameter, which is subsequently written inside the document as soon as it is retrieved. In the following section, we study a few more DOM-based XSS examples based on a fictitious application that we created.

Head of the Class…

XSS Is Everywhere

It's important to remember that XSS can lurk potentially anywhere that any form of user input is echoed back in the browser. Most people will naturally think those are limited to application variables, form fields, and other post data, but there can potentially be many more forgotten places for XSS vulnerabilities to hide.

Let's take a look at a normal HTTP request sent by a Web browser to a site such as www.example.com:

```
GET http://www.example.com HTTP/1.1

Host: www.example.com

User-Agent: Mozilla/5.0 (Windows; U; Windows NT 5.1; en-US; rv:1.8.1.4)
Gecko/20070515 Firefox/2.0.0.4 Paros/3.2.13

Accept:
text/xml,application/xml,application/xhtml+xml,text/html;q=0.9,text/pla
in;q=0.8,image/png,*/*;q=0.5

Accept-Language: en-us,en;q=0.5

Accept-Charset: ISO-8859-1,utf-8;q=0.7,*;q=0.7

Keep-Alive: 300

Proxy-Connection: keep-alive

Content-length: 0
```

Many fields are in an average HTTP request. All of these fields are controlled by the client and sent to the server.

Now let's consider a Common Gateway Interface (CGI) script, or an application error page that provides useful feedback to a developer, that is, in the error page somewhere it lists parts of the original HTTP request such as User-Agent: or Accept:.

The information that is mirrored back to the browser comes directly from the HTTP request header. That qualifies as user-supplied input. Furthermore, most developers labor under the assumption that this data is fixed and will follow an expected format, and as such even in an otherwise secure application, they do not execute routines to sanitize that input (after all, that's input from the browser, not the user, right?).

Suppose we have an error page, and as part of the error, the error page listed the full User-Agent. Also suppose we could control that User-Agent string.

Now suppose we sent an HTTP Request such as the following:

```
GET http://www.example.com HTTP/1.1

Host: www.example.com

User-Agent: <script>alert('Vulnerable to XSS');</script>

Accept:
```

Continued

```
text/xml,application/xml,application/xhtml+xml,text/html;q=0.9,text/pla
in;q=0.8,image/png,*/*;q=0.5

Accept-Language: en-us,en;q=0.5

Accept-Charset: ISO-8859-1,utf-8;q=0.7,*;q=0.7

Keep-Alive: 300

Proxy-Connection: keep-alive

Content-length: 0
```

The User-Agent: string with the HTML script tags would cause our JavaScript to execute in the browser in this example. That's why it's useful to think of XSS as client-side scripting executed from any user-supplied variable.

Investigating XSS

The Web server logs are going to be one source of information when you are investigating XSS attacks. Look at normal traffic logging and referrer information to see where the server thinks the incoming page request is originating. It is a fairly easy matter to spoof referrer information, but many times attackers take the chance that you won't see the referrer information before they have moved to the XSS site. Of primary interest are any pages that require login or authentication.

When investigating an active XSS attack, you can use a Web proxy such as Paros Proxy (www.parosproxy.org) to view the Web server transactions in real time and clearly see any communications with outside servers during the process.

Additionally, you can view the source of any HTML-formatted e-mail messages for embedded scripts or links in the URL to the victim site.

Traffic capture visualization tools may give you insight to XSS attacks, but typical traffic loads make this type of investigative tool a costly and time-consuming method.

Cross-Site Request Forgery

Compared to XSS attacks, cross-site request forgery (CSRF) or *Sea Surf* attacks are fairly new. As the name implies, this is another variation on XSS-style attacks, but with the added wrinkle of causing the victim to initiate the exploit rather than the attacker. The premise of the CSRF attack relies on the knowledge that a site has a specific trust with a user. This trust could be in the form of a session variable, cookie, or other token that is persistent longer than necessary on the victim's system.

When this attack was first seen it was assumed that the attacker had special knowledge about the victim's use of these weak sites and that is how the attack was generated. We have since learned that it is possible to interrogate for tokens, in much the same way you test for a cookie, and then launch the attack if the token is found.

There are many ways to initiate a CSRF attack. One classic method uses the image tag to post a request containing the attacker's code. This is the one we will look at in depth.

Anatomy of a CSRF Attack

In this example, we will make the following assumptions:

- The attacker wants to reduce the number of users of a competing Web site.

- The attacker has realized that the page for removing yourself from the site is vulnerable.

- The attacker has a page on his site that looks for the token and generates the attack.

When the victim last visited the target Web site www.worldofwidgets.org, the session left a valid access token on the victim's machine. The victim then visits the attacker's site. The main page of the attacker's site tested for the token and then generated the attack.

The page for removing the member from the worldofwidgets site has two fields: the e-mail address of the member and a field that requires an uppercase YES to be entered as verification that the member wants to be removed. The key parts of this form are shown here:

```
<FORM Action="Account_Close.asp" method="POST">

 E-Mail Address: <INPUT type="TEXT" Name="emailAddr"><br>
 Confirm Account Close (YES): <INPUT type="TEXT" Name="confirm"><br>

 <INPUT type="SUBMIT" value="Close Account"><p>

</FORM>
```

Armed with this information it is a simple matter for the attacker to embed the attack into an image request on one of the pages of his site. Using the get image HTML tag and appending the information for the victim is a typical method, and because the request comes from the victim's machine the token is used to verify the victim's identity and allow the removal.

```
<IMG
SRC="http://widgetworld.org/remove_member.asp?email=FredS@bignet.com&confirm=YE
S">
```

This tag sends the e-mail address of the victim, in this case FredS@bignet.com, and the confirmation field YES to the remove_member.asp page instead of fetching an image, which is what IMG SRC is supposed to be used for.

In this example, the victim may see an acknowledgment screen that would confuse him. If the worldofwidgets site designer uses security best practices, the victim would receive an e-mail letting him know this happened.

Pen-Testing CSRF Fields

The key to any testing for CSRF vulnerabilities is the token. If a site uses cookies or session variables, it is necessary to ensure that tokens expire or become invalid when they are no longer needed. In the case of cookies, it may be wise to set the expiration to a time that is reasonable depending on the type of site usage you expect. If your logs indicate that the average time a user spends on the site is 10 minutes, setting the expiration 10 minutes into the future may be a wise choice, and may negate many CSRF attacks.

Storing session variables that are no longer valid in a log may be the solution when the site is used differently, or the average user time is too varied. Having a routine set a session variable to be invalid after a logout or a period of inactivity would also work. Adding a routine to verify the session variable at the top of every page and forcing a logon if the variable is no longer valid would bring the CSRF attack to the victim's attention.

If the token is set to expire—say, in 10 minutes—you should visit the site appropriately and wait several minutes beyond the timeout and try to access an internal page on the site to which you should not have access. If the page loads or allows you access when it shouldn't, you know it has not been hardened to the CSRF attack.

Code Injection Attacks

Anytime a scripting or programming language is used in a Web page, the potential for a code injection attack exists and all the attacker needs is an opening. That opening usually comes in the form of an input field that isn't validated correctly.

The "code" part of a code injection attack doesn't have to be on the Web page either. It can be located in the back end as part of a database query or a CGI for the Web site. If any part of the server uses Java, JavaScript, C, Perl, Visual Basic, SQL, or any other code between the Internet and the data, it is vulnerable.

SQL injection attacks are popular right now and are covered in the media quite a bit, so they may be the best known type of code injection attack at the time of this writing. Yet, there are numerous attacks against Cold Fusion-, Active Server-, Java-, Perl- and Awk-based code every day as well.

Programmers that do not check every single input through which a user can possibly enter are a big part of the problem. If a programmer prepares a list of all allowed inputs and then writes input validation routines that only allow the good inputs and reject the bad inputs, most of these attacks can be stopped.

Investigating Code Injection Attacks

Evidence of a code injection attack is rarely found in the Web server logs. If the Web designer writes failed input information to a log file, you will probably see the various attempts to get the attack right. If there are no logs of incorrect attempts to fill out a form or other inputs, you may have to resort to network traffic sniffer logs.

Using an open source tool such as Wireshark to capture traffic going to the server and then searching for either all requests going to the input page or field names on the page may give you a good accounting of the malicious traffic and the IP address of the source.

You may have to gather some rather large files to catch one of the attempts. By setting the capture filter on the sniffer of your choice to just the traffic going to the server you can reduce the capture file considerably.

In Wireshark the capture filter would be *dst host xxx.xxx.xxx.xxx* (the x's are the IP address of the server). Note that you should test to see how big this file gets over the space of an hour or two and make sure you have sufficient storage space for the resulting file before you leave the sniffer running unattended for long periods.

Head of the Class…

Wireshark File Sizes

The creators of Wireshark and its predecessor, Ethereal, knew that files can get large in a hurry, so they have a few helpful items in the Capture dialog box. You can set limits to file sizes in several different ways.

You can set the maximum file size to a specific number of bytes, kilobytes, or megabytes.

You can set the maximum number of minutes or hours that the capture runs.

You can set the files to break into smaller chunks so that they fit on a CD or DVD easily.

Knowing these options and using them as you see fit during traffic capture sessions can mean the difference between having all the information you need for an investigation and exposing yourself to some serious headaches.

For more helpful hints on Wireshark, see the wiki at http://wiki.wireshark.org.

If you know that one of the input fields on a page you are investigating is labeled **homePhone**, you can use the frame contains display filter **frame contains "homePhone"**. Any packets that have information going to the input field will be shown and can be examined for proper or malicious content.

Other locations of evidence may be found in access logs or transaction data. Don't forget to look at transaction times as well. If you are seeing a large number of transactions in a short period, or at odd hours, you may be seeing signs of an attack.

Command Injection Attacks

What makes a command injection attack different from the other injection attacks is the type of payload delivered and the access level used. Command attacks will be primarily against trusted interfaces such as CGIs and deeper-level scripts or programs executed at the administrator level.

Command injection involves the passing and running of system commands at or just above the operating system level.

There have been several successful command injection attacks against Microsoft Internet Explorer, partly because of the helpful code that attempted to correct flawed Web pages. These attacks were the bane of Microsoft IE programmers for several years.

Parameter Tampering

One of the oldest types of Web-based attacks involves parameter tampering, which is the modification of unprotected data in the URL or in a hidden field of a Web page. This type of attack is traditionally aimed at a commercial site that is keeping prices or other information attached to a Web page.

For example, if the attacker is at a sporting goods Web site and is thinking of buying a tennis racket that costs $80, he might see the price reflected in the URL in this way:

http://sales.sportswidget.com/order.htm?SKU="4321A"&price=80.00

If the attacker changes the price in the URL line before pressing Enter, and the site does not verify the price, he could buy the racket for $30 this way:

http://sales.sportswidget.com/order.htm?SKU="4321A"&price=30.00

Another popular form of parameter tampering is the changing of hidden fields within the HTML itself. Here, again, if the attacker views the source of the Web page and sees the price of the racket being held in a hidden field, he could save the source code, make the modification, and then load the file and send the new price, hoping it won't be caught later. In this way, the following:

```
<input type="hidden" name="price" value="80.00">
```

could be changed to:

```
<input type="hidden" name="price" value="30.00">
```

Newer tools such as Paros Proxy are excellent for both the investigator and the attacker because it allows you to edit the received and the transmitted HTML code on your computer. This makes parameter tampering incredibly easy, and it makes testing of Web form pages easy too. Unfortunately, as is the case for many security tools, the ones that are good for the security professional are good for the attackers as well.

Cookie Poisoning

A specialized form of parameter tampering is cookie poisoning, which involves the attacker obtaining the contents of a cookie that is stored on the victim's computer. By reading the information in these cookies, the attacker can either gain sensitive information about the victim or change information for whatever purpose he wants.

A great many sites use cookies to store either session information or short-term variables that are used to track the user's progress through a site. In theory, these cookies are invisible to the end user, and in some cases, cookies are encrypted by the Web site, but many are not encrypted and are very easy to read. This makes the use of information in these cookies valuable to attackers.

If the attacker wanted to cause hate and discontent, it would be a simple matter of looking for the cookie from the sports store in the earlier example and changing the victim's cookie so that the list price of a racket is $90 instead of $80 when he checks out.

Investigating Cookie Poisoning

To detect and investigate cookie poisoning, you will need to have the cookie issuing server save session variables and cookie contents to a log file, and then compare those cookies with the transaction logs to ensure that the transaction completed with the same values stored in the original cookie.

If you then take the extra step of tracking referrer information during transactions, you may find that not only was the cookie poisoned, but also the attack may have come from an XSS attack as well.

Buffer Overflows/Cookie Snooping

One of the side benefits to the attacker that executes a buffer overflow attack on a Web page can be the direct reading of cookie information residing in memory at the time. Many programs store the cookie right next to the other variables used by the browser. Because the cookie is a variable itself, this makes sense.

By executing a buffer overflow and having the payload read the working storage area of memory, the attacker can read the unencrypted cookie data. This data can be everything from session data to Social Security numbers or bank codes.

Investigating Buffer Overflows

Evidence of buffer overflows can be found in system logs, event logs, and program logs depending on the type of overflow executed and the error recovery method the programmers used. If you are using a traffic sniffer or intrusion detection system, a buffer overflow can usually be seen fairly easily if you filter on the Web form page traffic and look at the input data. Buffer overflows are typically large packages and have repetitive data strings that jump off the screen when you see them.

When you are investigating a page that you think may be vulnerable to a buffer overflow attack, test field input routines to see whether they trim or reject inputs that are too large.

DMZ Protocol Attacks, Zero Day Attacks

Putting Internet-facing systems in a special "Demilitarized Zone" or DMZ is one of the best practices network administrators use to insulate the rest of the network from the portions that need to be available to the Internet.

There are two common types of DMZ protocol attacks: internal and external. Internal attacks use the protocols between systems in the DMZ itself. External attacks use the protocols that the DMZ uses to communicate with the internal network systems.

If an attacker can gain access to the Web server in a DMZ, he may find that the Web server talks to a database server, also in the DMZ, using a trusted Internetwork Packet Exchange (IPX) channel. By exploiting the Web server, this link can be used to then exploit the database. This is the internal attack at its best.

Once the attacker is in the DMZ, he can exploit any protocol used to go into the company's internal network or intranet. This concept of an external attack being the term for attacking the internal network can be confusing. If it helps, think of the attack from the viewpoint of standing *inside* the DMZ and attacking *outside* the DMZ into the rest of the company.

If these attacks then deliver a malicious payload that is not part of the signature database for antivirus or intrusion detection/prevention systems guarding the network, the attack is considered a Zero Day attack. This can also be considered a Zero Day attack if the attack or vulnerability has not been released to the public yet.

Example of an FTP Compromise

Attacks against FTP servers have been popular among attackers for quite a few years now. These attacks allow the attacker to transfer large amounts of data in either direction faster than other methods, and they allow attackers to steal information masked as other normal FTP traffic.

A classic example of the FTP Bounce attack is shown in the Figure 8.4. The attack uses the following steps:

1. The attacker prepares a script that logs into the victim FTP site and either requests a file or sends a file to the intermediate FTP server, typically an open server located in a public location such as a school or library.

2. The attacker then prepares a script for the intermediate FTP server that creates a port between the attacker's system (typically running an FTP server also) and the intermediate server. The attacker then logs into the intermediate server and installs the two scripts.

3. Running the scripts, the attacker creates an FTP link between his system and the intermediate system and then creates a link between the intermediate system and the victim system.

4. Once the connections are in place, the attacker can send or request FTP files or data from the victim server and all the logs on the victim server show that the attack came from the intermediate system.

Figure 8.4 An Example of FTP Bounce Attack Methods

Many different types of FTP-based attacks are used today. Depending on the age of the FTP software and the security settings used on the server, even some of the oldest attacks still work!

Intrusion Detection

The number one fallacy about intrusion detection is when people think that intrusion detection systems *prevent* intrusions. They do not prevent or deter intrusions in any way; they only report that an intrusion occurred or was attempted.

Snort is an open source intrusion detection system that has become one of the standards against which other commercial systems are compared. You can use Snort, which is available from www.snort.org, to capture network traffic and alert you of traffic analysis. You can even configure it to be a true intrusion prevention system that can stop malicious traffic.

To accomplish these tasks, Snort uses rule sets which are compared to incoming traffic. These rule sets are available from the Snort site or other security sites and are updated regularly with new attacks. If you are considering using Snort, you should definitely read and understand the documentation prior to installing. The more advanced rule sets can be quite complex and may not apply to your network configuration.

Using Snort as a live traffic analysis tool is common, and you can also use a known good Snort installation to evaluate captured traffic files. You can tell Snort to read any .cap (TCPdump-formatted) file and generate warnings from the file. Snort will typically output any warnings or alerts to the screen unless you designate an output file in which to save them.

The following code is an example of Snort alerts. As you can see, most alerts even offer links to Web sites for more information on the suspect traffic. These external references are indicated by *Xref* =>.

```
[**] [1:587:8] RPC portmap status request UDP [**]

[Classification: Decode of an RPC query] [Priority: 2]

09/15-19:06:06.81952 210.114.220.46:653 -> 192.168.1.102:111

UDP TTL:47 TOS:0x0 ID:41887 IpLen:20 DgmLen:84

Len:56

[Xref => http://www.whitehats.com/info/IDS15]

[**] [1:1971:4] FTP SITE EXEC format string attempt [**]

[Classification: Potentially bad traffic] [Priority: 2]

09/16-15:55:52.235847 207.35.251.172:2243 -> 192.168.1.102:21

TCP TTL:48 TOS:0x0 ID:16648 IpLen:20 DgmLen:76 DF

***AP*** Seq: 0xCF7869CC Ack: 0xEBCD7EC0 Win: 0x7D78 TcpLen: 32

TCP Options (3) => NOP NOP TS: 237391678 29673183
```

If you are investigating large amounts of network traffic as part of your job, you may want to set up a known good Snort environment on your examination system so that you can run traffic captures against your tested and validated rules. This method of quickly assessing network traffic for potential malicious activity is definitely one of the basic tools you will find in an experienced investigator's toolkit.

Exam Objectives Summary

In an investigation involving e-mail, it is important to appreciate how an e-mail server accounts for, logs and processes e-mail messages. E-mail servers are databases of information and e-mail messages.

- E-mail servers have log files that offer information that is valuable to the investigation of an incident or crime.

- E-mail based investigations rely heavily on message files, e-mail headers, and e-mail server logs to examine the incident.

- Spamming is irritating and wastes time – thus causing an economic loss. Countermeasures help prevent it.

- The Network Abuse Clearing House aids in registering complaints online.

- A number of tools may be used to assist in reducing SPAM.

In the second part of this chapter you learned about DoS attacks and various types of Web attacks.

Exam Objectives Fast Track

E-mail Clients and Servers

- ☑ An e-mail client message is composed of a header and a body.

- ☑ The client connects to an e-mail server to send and receive messages.

- ☑ E-mail servers have lists of accounts—one account for each person, with a text file for each account in the list.

E-mail Crimes and Violations

- ☑ The more common term for spam is junk mail.

- ☑ Mail bombing is a simple attack that involves the intentional sending of multiple copies of an e-mail to a recipient.

- ☑ A mail storm is a condition that occurs when computers start communicating autonomously.

Investigating E-mail Crimes and Violations

- ☑ When it has been established that a crime has been committed using e-mail, it is necessary to capture and maintain the evidence that is required to prove the offense in a court of law.

- ☑ As with all digital forensic work, when you are examining an e-mail message, it is best to first take an image of the machine's hard drive.

- ☑ An investigation that involves e-mail may be initiated as soon as the offending communication is copied and printed.

Microsoft Outlook

- ☑ Microsoft Outlook Mail is in effect a personal information manager (PIM).

- ☑ Microsoft Outlook allows the user to save e-mail messages in two different file formats based on the system configuration: a personal e-mail file (.pst) used for local storage and an off-line e-mail file (.ost) to access Exchange e-mail messages when not connected to the server.

- ☑ Files are stored by Outlook Mail as *.pst files.

Tracing an E-mail Message

- ☑ The IP address of the originating host system can help you determine the owner of an e-mail address that has been used in a possible incident or crime that is being investigated.

- ☑ By coupling network and system logs from the source, destination, and intermediate devices and servers along the path of the e-mail, you can validate the authenticity of information contained within the e-mail header.

- ☑ The syslog configuration file contains valuable information about the logging priority, where logs are sent, and what other actions may be taken.

Handling Spam

- ☑ Sending a request to stop the spam often just validates your e-mail address to the spammer.

- ☑ The Network Abuse Clearing House (www.abuse.net/) was started to assist Internet users in reporting abusive activities.

☑ Domain keys and other encoding techniques can be used to reduce the capability of others to exploit e-mail addresses. These technologies use cryptographic procedures on the e-mail messages (such as by appending a digital signature) that help the recipient to confirm the source and legitimacy of an e-mail.

Investigating Denial-of-Service Attacks

☑ A denial of service can mean blocking access to a server, network, or single computer.

☑ Overloading buffers, saturating network devices, and causing systems to spawn multiple time-consuming tasks are common ways to cause a denial of service.

☑ The terms indicating the roles in an attack are client, master, daemon, zombie, and target.

Investigating Web Attacks

☑ A cross-site scripting (XSS) attack is a technique that forces a Web site to display malicious code, which then executes in a user's Web browser.

☑ The "code" part of a code injection attack doesn't have to be on the Web page. It can be located in the back end as part of a database query or a CGI for the Web site.

☑ One of the oldest types of Web-based attacks involves parameter tampering, which is the modification of unprotected data in the URL or in a hidden field of a Web page. Cookie poisoning is an example of a specialized type of parameter tampering.

Exam Objectives
Frequently Asked Questions

The following Frequently Asked Questions, answered by the authors of this book, are designed to both measure your understanding of the Exam Objectives presented in this chapter, and to assist you with real-life implementation of these concepts.

Q: Is turning off HTML Preview mode in my e-mail program a good way to spot XSS attacks?

A: Yes, for two reasons. First, you will not activate any "roll-over" scripts in the HTML page that immediately activate links to malicious sites. Second, you will be able to view the text of the links and potentially see any embedded site information, or see any odd-looking links that you would want to investigate further.

Q: To stop malicious ICMP traffic such as the Ping of Death, should I block all ICMP traffic at my firewall?

A: To block ICMP or not to block ICMP is a hotly debated topic among network administrators. If you know that you have no real need for any ICMP traffic, you should block it at your firewall to help alleviate most DoS attacks based on this protocol.

Q: Wireshark looks just like another tool I have used, called Ethereal. Are they related?

A: Yes! Wireshark is based on the original Ethereal program and is written by the original author, Gerald Combs, because of contractual obligations. Technically they are the same program. Wireshark is the currently supported version.

Q: While investigating an XSS I came across a URL that had a lot of percent signs and other odd codes. How do I decode what these mean?

A: What you are seeing is URL Escaped Encoding and it is a popular obfuscation technique used by attackers. There are numerous escape sequence decoders and UU decoders on the Web. Copy and paste the URL into one of these and you can easily see the human-readable version.

Q: What services and ports should I leave running and open on my Web server?

A: It is a best practice to have only those services and ports open for the absolute minimum required for server operation. For example, if you only serve up basic Web traffic and do not need Secure Sockets Layer, only the Web services and port 80 need to be open on the server.

Q: Why don't I see evidence of an SQL injection attack in the system error log?

A: SQL injection and most command injection attacks only interact with the service and do not generate a system-level error. In the case of SQL injection, the evidence may be in the SQL Server logs if the input is detected as invalid. Otherwise, most SQL injection attacks may be seen only in access logs, because the access would be at an unusual time.

Chapter 9

CHFI

Investigating Network Traffic and Investigating Logs

Exam objectives in this chapter:

- Overview of the OSI Model
- Network Addresses and NAT
- Network Information—Gathering Tools
- Monitoring User Activity

Exam Objectives Review:

- ☑ Summary of Exam Objectives
- ☑ Exam Objectives Fast Track
- ☑ Exam Objectives Frequently Asked Questions

Introduction

Networks are exposed to an unending series of attacks and exposures. External threats usually come from the Internet and can be grouped into three broad categories such as denial of service (DoS); using the victim's network as a base of attack, to target other networks; or for threat or alteration of information. Internal threats can come from individuals with legitimate access or from those that are exceeding their level of privilege. This means that a forensic expert must understand how the network works and how to access logged data.

Monitoring for insider and outsider attacks should be a proactive activity, but many attacks may not be detected until after the attack has taken place. This will require an inspection of log files. Only by review of the audit and log files can the attack be analyzed and reconstructed. Many forensic experts don't make full use of log and audit data as they may not understand how to access this information or initially overlook it because of the extensive amount of time it takes to read through thousands upon thousands of log file entries. This chapter will look at how tools like the Log Parser can help with this task and make a tedious task easy.

Overview of the OSI Model

In 1984 the International Standards Organization developed the Open Systems Interconnect (OSI) model. The model is designed to provide order by specifying a specific hierarchy in which each layer builds upon the output of each adjacent layer. The model is still used today as a guide in describing the operation of a networking environment.

Layers of the OSI Model

The seven layers of the OSI model are the physical, data link, network transport, session, presentation, and application layers. Let's take a look at each of these layers.

The Physical Layer

Layer 1 is known as the physical Layer. At Layer 1, bit-level communication takes place. The bits have no defined meaning on the wire, but the physical layer defines how long each bit lasts and how it is transmitted and received. From a forensics standpoint a great deal of sensitive information may be available at the physical layer if no encryption is used.

The Data Link Layer

Layer 2 is known as the data link layer. The data link layer is responsible for formatting and organizing the data before sending it to the physical layer. The data link layer organizes the data into frames. A frame is a logical structure in which data can be placed. When a frame reaches the target device, the data link layer is responsible for stripping off the data frame and passing the data packet up to the network layer. The data link layer is made up of two sublayers, including the logical link control layer (LLC) and the media access control layer (MAC).

The Network Layer

Layer 3, the network layer, is concerned with logical addressing and routing. The network layer is the home of the Internet Protocol (IP), which makes a best effort at delivery of datagrams from their source to their destination.

The Transport Layer

Layer 4 is known as the transport layer, and ensures completeness by handling end-to-end error recovery and flow control. Transport-layer protocols include TCP, a connection-oriented protocol. It provides reliable communication through the use of handshaking, acknowledgments, error detection, and session teardown and User Datagram Protocol (UDP), a connectionless protocol. It offers speed and low overhead as its primary advantage.

The Session Layer

Layer 5 is known as the session layer. Its functionality is put to use when creating, controlling, or shutting down a TCP session. Items such as the TCP 3-way handshake and the TCP 4-way shutdown occur here. Session-layer protocols include items such as Remote Procedure Call and Structured Query Language.

The Presentation Layer

Layer 6, the presentation layer, is responsible for taking data that has been passed up from lower levels and put it into a format that application layer programs can understand. These common formats include ASCII, EBCDIC, and ANSI.

The Application Layer

Layer 7 is known as the application layer. Recognized as the top layer of the OSI model, this layer serves as the window for application services. The application layer is one that most users are familiar with as it is the home of e-mail programs, FTP, Telnet, web browsers, office productivity suites, and many other applications.

TEST DAY TIP

Knowing the layers of the OSI model will help you identify where key processes are located. Expect the CHFI exam to test such things as the layers of the OSI model. An easy way to help you remember the seven layers is to utilize a mnemonic device similar to the following sentence:
All
People
Seem

To
Need
Data
Processed.

Network Addresses and NAT

In networks that use TCP/IP the IP address scheme is used for logical addressing. A MAC address is considered a physical address, whereas an IP address is considered a logical address. IP addresses are configured as dotted decimal notation. The IPv4 address format is four decimal numbers that are separated by decimal points. Each of these decimal numbers is one byte in length to allow numbers to range from 0 to 255.

- **Class A Networks**. Class A networks consist of up to 16,777,214 client devices, and their address range can extend from 1 to 126.

- **Class B Networks**. Class B networks host up to 65,534 client devices and their address range can extend from 128 to 191.

- **Class C Networks**. Class C networks can have a total of 245 devices and their address range can extend from 192 to 223.

- **Class D Networks**. These addresses are reserved for multicasting and can extend from 224 to 239.

- **Class E Networks**. These addresses are reserved for experiential purposes. Their addresses range from 240 to 254

Network Address Translation (NAT) originally was developed because of the explosive growth of the Internet, and with the increase in home and business networks, the number of available IP addresses is simply not enough. Typically, Internet Service Providers (ISPs) allocate only one address to a single customer. Companies can buy lots of addresses, but they must pay for each one. Also direct connectivity to the Internet is not without its dangers. NAT is a cost-effective secure solution. NAT allows a single device, such as a router, to act as an agent between the Internet and the local network. This device or router provides a pool of addresses to be used by your local network.

EXAM WARNING

You will need to know how to describe NAT for the CHFI exam.

Network Information-Gathering Tools

Network information-gathering tools are pieces of software that can be used to obtain network data for forensic analysis. These tools generally offer the functionality of a sniffer and an intrusion detection system combined. Sniffers are powerful programs that work by placing the hosts system's network card into promiscuous mode. A network card in promiscuous mode can receive all the data it can see, not just packets addressed to it. Switches segment traffic and know which particular port to send traffic to and block it from all the rest. Although this feature adds much needed performance gains, it does raise a barrier when attempting to sniff all potential switched ports. Forensic analysis will usually require the switch to be configured to mirror a port. Some common network monitoring tools include:

- **NetWitness**. NetWitness is designed to analyze network traffic and monitor it.

- **Netresident Tool**. Considered an advanced network content monitoring program that captures, stores, analyzes, and reconstructs network events such as e-mail messages, Web pages, downloaded files, and other types of network traffic.

- **Infinistream Security Forensics**. A commercial product that builds on sniffer technology by providing high-end tracking of absolutely everything.

- **CA Network Forensics**. Allows the user to uncover and investigate network traffic. This program captures raw network data and uses forensic analysis to check for exploitation, internal data theft, and security violations.

- **Wireshark**. An open source protocol analyzer that can capture traffic in real time.

- **Snort**. A well-known open source IDS product that uses signatures to detect events.

Sniffers

Sniffers operate at the data link layer of the OSI model. This means they do not have to play by the same rules as applications and services that reside further up the stack. Sniffers can capture everything on the wire and record it for later review. They allow the user to analyze all the data that is contained in the packet. A good sniffer product is Wireshark. Not only is it free to use but it works well in both a Windows and Linux environment. You can find more details about the program at the official site, www.wireshark.com. Next, we will discuss the second category of network information-gathering tools, intrusion detection.

Intrusion Detection

Intrusion detection systems (IDS) play a second critical role in the protection of the IT infrastructure. Intrusion detection involves monitoring network traffic, detecting attempts to gain unauthorized access to a system or resource, and notifying the appropriate individuals so that counteractions can be taken. Having the ability to analyze intrusions and attacks is a powerful

tool. There are four types of logs that would be of interest during a forensic investigation—authentication, application, operating system, and network—but the IDS will be of use primarily with network logs. There are many good IDS systems available. Snort is one example of an IDS with wide industry support.

> **NOTE**
>
> Intrusion detection actually has a rather short history. In 1983 Dr. Dorothy Denning started building on the work of James Anderson and developed the first IDS system for the U.S. government. They were interested in analyzing the audit trails of government mainframe systems to determine misuse.

Snort

Snort is a freeware IDS developed by Martin Roesch and Brian Caswell. It's considered a lightweight network-based IDS that can be set up on a Linux or Windows host. The core program has a command line interface, but there are GUIs that can be used. Snort operates as a network sniffer and logs activity that matches predefined signatures. Signatures can be designed for a wide range of traffic including Internet Protocol, Transmission Control Protocol, User Datagram Protocol, and Internet Control Message Protocol. An intrusion detection system is valuable to a forensic analyst only if the data is reviewed and analyzed.

Unfortunately, sometimes an IDS will produce overwhelming amounts of data that make it difficult to process. To aid in our interpretation of the data, we can use Microsoft Log Parser to take snapshots of our IDS logs and present them in different easy-to-read reports. In this chapter, we will build an example IDS report using nothing more than the power of Log Parser.

Gathering Snort Logs

To process the alert data, we first need a consistent method for gathering the data. Log Parser is an excellent method for managing Snort logs because you can query the file while Snort still has the log open. Many administrators schedule scripts to regularly cycle the Snort logs, but this requires stopping the service to release the file so a script can move it. Using Log Parser, we can use checkpoints to read the most recent data from the file.

Although Snort supports several output formats that Log Parser could use, I have found the CSV format most flexible and consistent. To configure Snort to use the CSV output format, simply add the following line in the snort.conf file:

```
output alert_csv: alert.csv default
```

Exam Warning

To prevent attackers from modifying logs they should always be exported and written to a remote device.

This configures Snort to create a CSV log file named alert.csv in the configured logs directory using the default output fields. By default the CSV output processor includes these fields:

- timestamp
- sig_generator
- sig_id
- sig_rev
- msg
- proto
- src
- srcport
- dst
- dstport
- ethsrc
- ethdst
- ethlen
- tcpfags
- tcpseq
- tcpack
- tcplen
- tcpwindow
- ttl
- tos
- id
- dgmlen
- iplen

- icmptype
- icmpcode
- icmpid
- icmpseq

Snort CSV logs do not include a header row, so we need a separate file to name each column. To read CSV Snort alerts, you would use a command like this:

```
logparser.exe file:alert.sql -i:csv -headerRow:off -
iHeaderFile:AlertHeader.csv -iTsFormat:mm/dd/yy-hh:mm:ss
```

Note that we specify the CSV input format, but instead of using the header row, we specify a header file using the **iHeaderFile** option. We also specify the timestamp format so Log Parser can interpret that field as an actual time stamp rather than a string.

> **NOTE**
>
> All the queries in this chapter use the year in the timestamp date, which Snort does not log by default. To configure Snort to log the year, use the –y option when starting Snort. If your timestamps do not include the year, the queries in this chapter will return the error, "Semantic Error: argument of function TO_TIME must be a TIMESTAMP".

Building an Alerts Detail Report

In our IDS report we likely want to view summaries of the alert data such as:

- Most common source IP (Internet Protocol) addresses
- Most common target IP addresses

Using Log Parser's multiplex feature and template output format we can very easily create interactive HTML (Hypertext Markup Language) reports directly from the Snort logs.

Alerts by IP Address

Each IP address in the alerts report shown in Figure 9.1 is a clickable hyperlink that leads to a detail page showing all alerts for that IP address. Using a process similar to that used previously for the alert messages, we created a summary page (Figure 9.2) and detail pages (Figure 9.3) using a two-pass approach. We repeated this process for both source and destination IP addresses to produce a fully interactive HTML IDS report.

Figure 9.1 Detailed Alert Messages

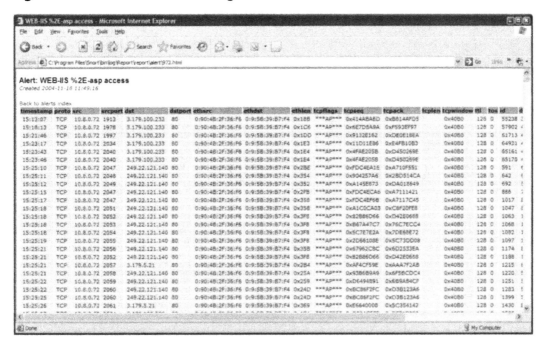

Figure 9.2 Snort Alerts by Destination IP Address

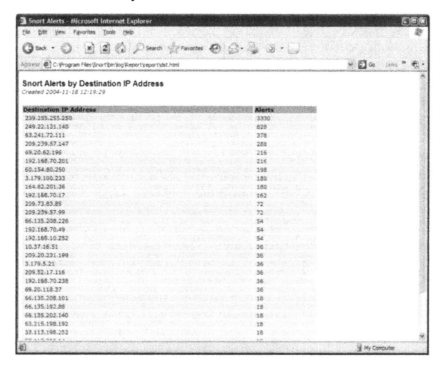

Figure 9.3 IP Address Details

At this point, you can run the entire report with these Log Parser commands:

```
logparser.exe file:Ch11Alerts-Indexsql -i:csv -iHeaderFile:AlertHeader.csv -
iTsFormat:mm/dd/yy-hh:mm:ss -headerRow:off -o:tpl -tpl:Ch11Alerts-Index.tpl
```

```
logparser.exe file:Ch11Alerts-DetailHeader.sql -i:csv -
iHeaderFile:AlertHeader.csv -iTsFormat:mm/dd/yy-hh:mm:ss -headerRow:off -o:tpl
-tpl:Ch11Alerts-DetailHeader.tpl
```

```
logparser.exe file:Ch11Alerts-Detail.sql -i:csv -iHeaderFile:AlertHeader.csv -
iTsFormat:mm/dd/yy-hh:mm:ss -headerRow:off -o:tpl -tpl:Ch11Alerts-Detail.tpl -
fileMode:0
```

```
logparser.exe file:Ch11SrcIP-Index.sql -i:csv -iHeaderFile:AlertHeader.csv -
iTsFormat:mm/dd/yy-hh:mm:ss -headerRow:off -o:tpl -tpl:Ch11SrcIP-Index.tpl
```

```
logparser.exe file:Ch11SrcIP-DetailHeader.sql -i:csv -
iHeaderFile:AlertHeader.csv -iTsFormat:mm/dd/yy-hh:mm:ss -headerRow:off -o:tpl
-tpl:Ch11SrcIP-DetailHeader.tpl
```

```
logparser.exe file:Ch11SrcIP-Detail.sql -i:csv -iHeaderFile:AlertHeader.csv -
iTsFormat:mm/dd/yy-hh:mm:ss -headerRow:off -o:tpl -tpl:Ch11SrcIP-Detail.tpl -
fileMode:0
```

```
logparser.exe file:Ch11DstIP-Index.sql -i:csv -iHeaderFile:AlertHeader.csv -
iTsFormat:mm/dd/yy-hh:mm:ss -headerRow:off -o:tpl -tpl:Ch11DstIP-Index.tpl
```

```
logparser.exe file:Ch11DstIP-DetailHeader.sql -i:csv -
iHeaderFile:AlertHeader.csv -iTsFormat:mm/dd/yy-hh:mm:ss -headerRow:off -o:tpl
-tpl:Ch11DstIP-DetailHeader.tpl
```

```
logparser.exe file:Ch11DstIP-Detail.sql -i:csv -iHeaderFile:AlertHeader.csv -
iTsFormat:mm/dd/yy-hh:mm:ss -headerRow:off -o:tpl -tpl:Ch11DstIP-Detail.tpl -
fileMode:0
```

Building an Alerts Overview Report

Now that we have a detailed alerts report, we might want to build a summary index page. This page should include links to the detailed reports and also display graphs and short summaries of the data to get a quick overview of the network

Since the summary report includes only one table of data with multiple graphs, I placed the entire HTML markup in a single template file, Ch11Summary-Index.tpl. This template creates the HTML for the report that includes references to the individual graphs. The query for the top alerts is similar to that used for the alerts index page, but includes only the top 10 records:

```
---Ch11Summary-Index.sql---
SELECT TOP 10
    sig_id,
    msg,
    Count(msg) as Alerts
INTO report\index.html
FROM alert.csv
GROUP BY msg, sig_id
ORDER BY Alerts DESC
---Ch11Summary-Index.sql---
```

The query for the pie graph is similar, but does not include the actual message, and this time processes all records:

```
---Ch11Summary-GraphTopAlerts.sql---
SELECT
    sig_id,
    Count(msg) as Alerts
INTO report\AlertsTopAlerts.gif
FROM alert.csv
GROUP BY sig_id
ORDER BY Alerts DESC
---Ch11Summary-GraphTopAlerts.sql---
```

Finally, there are three queries for the remaining graphs:

```
---Ch11Summary-GraphTopSrcIPs.sql---
SELECT
    src,
    Count(msg) as Alerts
INTO report\AlertsTopSrcIPs.gif
FROM alert.csv
GROUP BY src
ORDER BY Alerts DESC
---Ch11Summary-GraphTopSrcIPs.sql---

---Ch11Summary-GraphAlertsPerHour.sql---
SELECt
    Count(*) as Alerts
USING QUANTIZE(timestamp,360) as Hour
INTO report\AlertsByHour.gif
FROM alert.csv
GROUP BY Hour
---Ch11Summary-GraphAlertsPerHour.sql---

---Ch11Summary-GraphTopDstPorts.sql---
SELECT TOP 5
    STRCAT(STRCAT(TO_STRING(dstport),' - '), proto) AS Destination,
    Count(*) as Alerts
    USING dst as DestinationPort
INTO report\AlertsTopDstPorts.gif
FROM alert.csv
GROUP BY Destination
ORDER BY Alerts DESC
---Ch11Summary-GraphTopDstPorts.sql---
```

Finally, we can generate the entire index page with these commands:

```
logparser.exe file:Ch11Summary-Index.sql -i:csv -iHeaderFile:AlertHeader.csv -
iTsFormat:mm/dd/yy-hh:mm:ss -headerRow:off -o:tpl -tpl:Ch11Summary-Index.tpl

logparser.exe file:Ch11Summary-GraphTopAlerts.sql -i:csv -
iHeaderFile:AlertHeader.csv -iTsFormat:mm/dd/yy-hh:mm:ss -headerRow:off -
o:chart -chartType:Pie3D -groupSize:350x190 -values:OFF -chartTitle:"" -
categories:OFF
```

```
logparser.exe file:Ch11Summary-GraphTopSrcIPs.sql -i:csv -
iHeaderFile:AlertHeader.csv -iTsFormat:mm/dd/yy-hh:mm:ss -headerRow:off -
o:chart -chartType:Pie -groupSize:300x150 -values:OFF -chartTitle:"" -
categories:OFF

logparser.exe file:Ch11Summary-GraphAlertsPerHour.sql -i:csv -
iHeaderFile:AlertHeader.csv -iTsFormat:mm/dd/yy-hh:mm:ss -headerRow:off -
o:chart -chartType:smoothline -groupSize:300x150 -values:OFF -chartTitle:"" -
categories:OFF

logparser.exe file:Ch11Summary-GraphTopDstPorts.sql -i:csv -
iHeaderFile:AlertHeader.csv -iTsFormat:mm/dd/yy-hh:mm:ss -headerRow:off -
o:chart -chartType:BarStacked -groupSize:300x150 -values:OFF -chartTitle:""
```

The final result is a fully interactive IDS report using nothing more than Log Parser.

Exam Warning

For the exam you should understand that the process of analysis includes temporal analysis to uncover time and place of events, relational analysis to discover the link between the victim and the crime, and functional analysis to determine what triggered the crime.

Monitoring User Activity

Monitoring user activity is an important part of the forensic process. Unusual user activity may be just an indicator of system problems, or it may be a real security issue. By analyzing the user activity reported in your system logs, you can determine authentication problems and hacking activity.

Note

When working with older systems it is important to remember that security Auditing is not enabled on Windows 2000 systems by default.

An important aspect in determining relevant events in your system logs is determining which behavior is benign and which behavior indicates trouble. For example, if a user fails to authenticate one time in a week span, you can be pretty certain that the user simply mistyped his or her password and is not trying to hack into your system. Alternatively, if a user has two

failed authentication attempts hourly for an extended period you should look more deeply into the problem. We will be covering these types of events and going over how to make the critical determination as to whether a behavior is benign or a warning sign. Security is, and always should be, a top priority for anyone working on key infrastructure systems. Tools like Log Parser can help you identify events that could indicate a potential hack attempt or even just a user attempting to look at something he or she shouldn't be looking at. By enabling file access auditing and using Log Parser to examine the results, you can even track down potential security issues at the file level. Digging through these same log files to track down this data manually is both tedious and unnecessary with the advanced capabilities of Microsoft's Log Parser utility.

TEST DAY TIP

Even though many individuals may deal exclusively with Windows systems, you should be aware that the exam will also expect you to understand Linux logging. Linux uses Syslog; any program can generate syslog messages, which are sent to the syslogd program. It is configured from /etc/syslog.conf.

EXERCISE 9.1

MISUSE DETECTION

Mary Brown is suspected of violating the company's AUP policies. Audit logs indicate that she may be surfing unacceptable Web sites. Larry Sommers, the director of her department, would like to have her computer reviewed to help confirm or deny these allegations. If these allegations are true, Mr. Sommers would like to have Ms. Brown reprimanded and reminded of company policy.

How do you proceed? What do you look for? Where do you look? When do you perform the investigation?

Tracking Authentication Failures

When performing regular security audits of your servers, it is always important to know how many failed authentication attempts have occurred. This helps you in several ways. First, you are

able to determine specific users who may have forgotten their password and failed to request a new one. Second, and more importantly, you may be able to detect potential hacking attempts against your server by analyzing the results and noting an increase in failed logon attempts either for a single user or for multiple users. Finally, you may be able to determine problems with the system that are causing authentication failures by multiple users at a specific time. These problems could relate to network connectivity, system utilization, or a failure of an authentication server.

Listing Failed Logons

Let's return again to the Log Parser to see how easily you can use your event logs to detail out the failed logons over a specific timeframe. The following command and query can be used to list all failed logons on a specific date:

```
logparser.exe file:Ch11ListingFailedLogons.sql -i:EVT -o:datagrid
```

```
--- Ch11ListingFailedLogons.sql ---

SELECT
    timegenerated AS LogonTime,
    extract_token(strings, 0, '|') AS UserName
FROM Security
WHERE EventID IN (529;
    530;
    531;
    532;
    533;
    534;
    535;
    537;
    539)
    AND to_string(timegenerated,'yyyy-MM-dd HH:mm:ss') like '2004-09%'

--- Ch11ListingFailedLogons.sql ---
```

By running this query, you are able to see how many authentication failures have occurred on the date you specified, as well as which user IDs experienced failures.

In this query, we begin by specifying that we want to obtain the timestamp for the event from the *timegenerated* field. From there, the query gets a little trickier than usual. For failed logon events, the UserID for the event itself is always SYSTEM. In order to get the actual ID

that the logon was attempted with, we need to parse out some data from the description or *Strings* field. To do so, we use the EXTRACT_TOKEN function to tokenize the string using the pipe (|) character and specify that we want the first or 0 token, which is the UserName.

Next we specify that we wish to pull this data from the current Security log. Our WHERE clause specifies a specific range of security events that indicate logon failures, and we use this to limit our data to those specific events. A description of each of these events is detailed in Table 9.1. In the WHERE clause, we also specify the date stamp that we're looking for in the same manner as the previous query. We also need to specify the input and output format, so we add this to the end of the command line using the syntax **-i:EVT –o:datagrid**.

Table 9.1 Failed Logon EventIDs

EventID	Description
529	The logon attempt was made with an unknown username or a known username with a bad password.
530	The user account tried to log on outside the allowed time.
531	A logon attempt was made by using a disabled account.
532	A logon attempt was made by using an expired account.
533	The user is not allowed to log on at this computer.
534	The user attempted to log on with a logon type that is not allowed, such as network, interactive, batch, service, or remote interactive.
535	The password for the specified account has expired.
537	The logon attempt failed for other reasons.
539	The account was locked out at the time the logon attempt was made. This event is logged when a user or computer attempts to authenticate with an account that has been previously locked out.

EXAM WARNING

For the exam you should know common logon failures.

Identifying Single versus Multiple Failed Logons

When working with failed logons, it sometimes helps to be able to quickly determine how prevalent logon failures are over a specific time period. In the preceding section, we went over

how to list failed logons, but using this query requires manual determination of how frequently a specific user ID is experiencing problems.

You can use Log Parser to automatically tally up the number of failed logons for each user by utilizing a slightly different query. The following command and query is one example of how this can be accomplished:

```
logparser.exe file:Ch11SingleVsMltplFailedLogons.sql -i:EVT -o:datagrid
```

```
--- Ch11SingleVsMltplFailedLogons.sql ---

SELECT
    extract_token(strings, 0, '|') AS UserName,
    count(*) AS Number_of_Events
FROM Security
WHERE EventID IN (529;
    530;
    531;
    532;
    533;
    534;
    535;
    537;
    539)
    AND to_string(timegenerated,'yyyy-MM-dd HH:mm:ss') like '2004-09%'
GROUP BY UserName
HAVING Number_of_Events>2

--- Ch11SingleVsMltplFailedLogons.sql ---
```

In this query, we are doing a bit more work up front, but minimizing the manual effort required to identify multiple login failures. We start out with the EXTRACT_TOKEN function parsing out the actual userid with the failed logon. Next, we perform a count of the number of events and display that value as Number_of_Events. We then identify the Security event log as our data source and add in a WHERE clause specifying the events that we want to watch for, as well as the specific date that we want the data from.

Finally, we add a GROUP BY statement to organize our results and also add in a HAVING statement. To limit the data to show us data only from events that occur multiple times, we specify Number_of_Events>2 in the HAVING statement.

Identifying Brute Force Attacks

When dealing with system security, a major concern is the possibility of a *brute force* attack on your system. The determining factor as to whether or not an attack is a brute force attack is the manner in which the attack occurs. When attempt after attempt after attempt is made to perform a specific attack action, the overall event is considered a brute force attack because the attacker is trying to break into the system using brute force.

Log Parser can help you quickly analyze your security event logs and determine whether or not one of these brute force attacks is potentially occurring. By creating queries that watch for the behavior of a brute force attack, you may be able to stop an attack before it is successful.

Identifying a Brute Force Authentication Attack

A great example of a brute force attack is one in which someone is trying to guess the password for one of your users. Let's say that the attacker knows from previous experience that you have a policy in place that disables an account if three unsuccessful logon attempts are made within a one-hour window by the same UserID. With this in mind, the attacker is not going to risk locking out the account that he or she is trying to hack. However, the attacker will want to maximize his or her available time and attempt the maximum number of attacks that he or she can within a specific time period.

A quick way to check for this type of activity is to use the same query listed earlier for identifying multiple failed logons. With a little modification, this query can perform an intelligent scan for brute force logon attempt behavior. The original query is as follows:

```
logparser.exe file:Ch11SingleVsMltplFailedLogons.sql -i:EVT -o:datagrid

--- Ch11SingleVsMltplFailedLogons.sql ---

SELECT
    extract_token(strings, 0, '|') AS UserName,
    count(*) AS Number_of_Events
FROM Security
WHERE EventID IN (529;
    530;
    531;
    532;
    533;
    534;
    535;
    537;
```

```
539)
    AND to_string(timegenerated,'yyyy-MM-dd HH:mm:ss') like '2004-09%'
GROUP BY UserName
HAVING Number_of_Events>2
```

```
--- Ch11SingleVsMltplFailedLogons.sql ---
```

As is, this query works great for determining multiple failed logon events on the same day. However, that behavior in and of itself does not signify that a brute force attack is occurring. In order to make this query more effective, we need to add the behavior signature of a brute force attack and get a little more detail.

The best way to add that behavior search into our query is to go back to what the attacker has determined your security policy is. The account will be locked out if more than two logon attempts fail within a one-hour time period by the same UserID. So, to maximize his or her potential attack time, the attacker will probably try to perform two logon attempts, determine whether or not they fail, then wait an hour and try twice more. So what we would look for is three or more failed logon events throughout the day and obtain the timeframe in which those events occurred.

To query based on this information, we need to modify our original query as follows:

```
logparser.exe file:Ch11BruteForceAttack.sql -i:EVT -o:datagrid
--- Ch11BruteForceAttack.sql ---
```

```
SELECT
    extract_token(strings , 0, '|') AS UserName,
    quantize(timegenerated, 3600) AS TimeFrame,
    count(*) AS Number_of_Events
FROM new_security.evt
WHERE EventID IN (529;
    530;
    531;
    532;
    533;
    534;
    535;
    537;
    539)
GROUP BY UserName,
    timeframe
```

```
HAVING Number_of_Events>2
--- Ch11BruteForceAttack.sql ---
```

The only real changes in this query were the removal of the date search and the addition of a TimeFrame value based on the quantized time—generated field. When running this query, we will be presented with a datagrid showing the number of failure events for each username within a one-hour timeframe. A quick glance at the output shown in Figure 9.4 shows you the accounts that could be experiencing a brute force attack. Following up with the user to find out more detail on what is going on would be a worthwhile practice when this type of activity is found.

Figure 9.4 Brute Force Activity

Tracking Security Policy Violations

Most companies have developed some form of security policy that addresses concerns around account and password security, permissible system access, unacceptable behavior, and such. These policies dictate the specific rules that each user must follow when accessing information technology (IT) systems.

A useful activity that admins typically perform is a regular audit to ensure that corporate security policies are being adhered to. Some of the information useful for an audit of this nature can be found in the Windows event logs. A great example is tracking user logons for desktop systems. By correlating all your event log data from multiple systems and digging through them with Log Parser, you can determine whether or not users are violating a policy restricting them to log on to only one machine at a time.

Determining Logon/Logoff Behavior

Another example that requires no log correlation is determining whether users typically are logging off after their work day or leaving their systems logged in. Some companies do have this behavior documented as a violation of their corporate security policy.

To gather this data with Log Parser, first we'll need to determine all the logoff events, then check to see if there is a logon event for the same day that does not have an associated logoff event for the same SID. The following command and query can help us determine this behavior:

```
logparser.exe file:Ch11LogonLogoffBehavior.sql -i:EVT -o:datagrid
```

```
--- Ch11LogonLogoffBehavior.sql ---

SELECT
    resolve_sid(sid) AS UserName,
    eventid,
    timegenerated
FROM Security
WHERE eventid='528'
    AND to_date(timegenerated)='2004-09-06 00:00:00'
    AND sid not in
    (
    SELECT DISTINCT
        sid
    FROM Security
    WHERE eventid='538'
        AND to_date(timegenerated)='2004-09-06 00:00:00'
    )

--- Ch11LogonLogoffBehavior.sql ---
```

In this query, we need to work backward a little bit to get the information we need. First, we determine which data we want in our report. In this case, we should gather the userID, the eventID that we're working with, and the time the event occurred. Next, we'll specify the security event log as our data source.

Our creation of the WHERE clause is the more difficult part of this query. The first two items are fairly simple; the eventID has to be 528 for a successful logon and the date that we want information about has to be specified. Also, we'll need to do a *select within a select* to limit our incoming data. Specifically, we want data where the SID with the 528 event does not exist

in a query of the 538 events for the same date. You should see results similar to those shown in Figure 9.5.

Figure 9.5 Logon Events with No Logoff Event

By performing our query in this manner, we are able to isolate those users who have logged on at some point during a specific day, but do not have an associated logoff event for the same day. This will not catch all users who log on without logging off, as it does not take into account the possibility of multiple logon/logoff events for each user in a single day. However, it can help minimize the number of security policy violations of this type.

Auditing Successful and Unsuccessful File Access Attempts

Another important dataset to examine when looking at overall system security is the audit log for successful and unsuccessful file access attempts. Using NTFS (NT file system), you can enable auditing at the file system level for individual files or directories. This allows you, as an administrator, to determine whether or not someone has accessed or attempted to access critical data.

Often, file access auditing is disabled because so much data is generated out of the audit logs that it is almost impossible to sort through the information available and extract events that are important to be aware of. This is where Log Parser can help in your efforts to ensure that your systems are well secured.

TEST DAY TIP

Test candidates should understand the process of auditing for successful and unsuccessful events.

Auditing Unsuccessful File Access Attempts

When auditing is enabled for NTFS objects, Windows adds events to the Security event log to indicate the objects that are accessed. As part of this event entry, information is recorded as to the object that was accessed, the user accessing the object, and the date/time that the object was accessed. You can use Log Parser to quickly collect the events around these object access attempts.

Obviously the area more administrators are interested in is the objects that a user tries to access when they're not supposed to. With a good security implementation, this typically results in an unsuccessful file access attempt. Using Log Parser to scan through the security logs, you can quickly identify these events and export them for analysis. The command and query shown here will identify all of the unsuccessful file access events in your security log:

```
logparser.exe file:Ch11UnsuccessfulFileAccess.sql -i:EVT -o:datagrid
```

```
--- Ch11UnsuccessfulFileAccess.sql ---

SELECT
    timegenerated AS EventTime,
    extract_token(strings, 8, '|') AS UserName,
    extract_token(strings, 2, '|') AS File
FROM Security
WHERE EventID = '560'
    AND EventTypeName = 'Failure Audit event'
    AND extract_token(strings, 1, '|') like 'File'
--- Ch11UnsuccessfulFileAccess.sql ---
```

When this query runs, it looks for any events in the security log with an eventID of 560 (Success Audit), but further refines that data to events with a type of Failure Audit event. It also parses through the associated event description to ensure that we look only at files, not directories. From that subset, Log Parser extracts the time of the event, the username associated with the event, and the filename. All this data is then displayed in a datagrid format. You can take this further by having Log Parser export the data into an XML file or some other format for evidence gathering needs.

Auditing Successful File Access Attempts

Many administrators often fail to monitor successful file access attempts in addition to the unsuccessful attempts. Although the most important events to watch for are indeed failures, it is also important not to lose sight of the auditing capabilities available for successful file access attempts.

A scenario where this can be used will help. For example, let's say that you are an administrator for a large corporation with a legal department. The department currently is engaged in putting together some information around a very important case and is storing this information in the department's shared drive. In the course of events, word reaches the legal department that somehow the legal department for the other side of the case has gotten hold of the strategy that your company's legal department was going to use and is putting together a rebuttal. The only people who should have had access to the files containing this information are the members of the legal department. They ask you to track down who has accessed those files.

If you have planned ahead for this eventuality, you have already enabled successful file access auditing for the legal department's shared drive. Using Log Parser, you can easily extract the information that the legal department needs and provide it to them quickly. The following script illustrates how this is done:

```
logparser.exe file:Ch11SuccessfulFileAccess.sql -i:EVT -o:datagrid

--- Ch11SuccessfulFileAccess.sql ---

SELECT
    timegenerated AS EventTime,
    extract_token(strings, 8, '|') AS UserName,
    extract_token(strings, 2, '|') AS File
FROM Security
WHERE EventID = '560'
    AND EventTypeName = 'Success Audit event'
    AND extract_token(strings, 1, '|') like 'File'
--- Ch11SuccessfulFileAccess.sql ---
```

If you look closely at this code, you'll see that this is almost the same as the previous script you saw on auditing unsuccessful file access attempts. The only real difference is the change in the event type name. Instead of "Failure Audit event" we're now looking for "Success Audit event." Running this script will extract all the successful file access events from your security log. You could further refine this to search for events that occur with a specific directory path or filename to make the amount of data to look through smaller.

Summary of Exam Objectives

In this chapter, we have gone over many of the features available in Log Parser for working with Windows event logs. Through the sections we've covered, we have looked into the Security, System, and Application event logs and used many sample Log Parser queries to pull data from these logs for analysis.

There are a few key points you should remember when working with these logs:

- Differentiating between single and multiple events is a critical feature in Log Parser for working with the Security event log.

- Differentiating between benign events and actual errors or warnings is very important for having an accurate view of your system environment.

- When working with applications and the Application event logs, it is critical that you have a thorough understanding of the specific application you are working with.

Keeping these points in mind will help you make the most of the Log Parser utility. You'll find that as you practice using this tool, it will be a very important part of your overall systems administrator toolbox. Log Parser can help you a great deal in conserving time and effort when you need to parse through large amounts of Windows event log data.

Exam Objectives Fast Track

Overview of OSI Model

☑ The OSI model is a seven-layer model used to define how networking functions in a layered approach.

☑ Routing occurs at layer three of the OSI model.

Network Addresses and NAT

☑ NAT is used to increase the pool of usable public IP addresses.

☑ NAT masks the broadcast of private IP addresses on the public Internet.

Network Information-Gathering Tools

☑ Sniffers are a primary network information-gathering tool.

☑ Network tools are one of the best options for a CHFI to analyze traffic while an attack is occurring.

Monitoring User Activity

- ☑ Monitoring user activity is important to pick up early signs of misuse.

- ☑ Network monitoring allows repetitive mistakes to be discerned from malicious attacks.

Exam Objectives Frequently Asked Questions

The following Frequently Asked Questions, answered by the authors of this book, are designed to both measure your understanding of the Exam Objectives presented in this chapter, and to assist you with real-life implementation of these concepts.

Q: Why was the OSI model designed?

A: The OSI model was designed to bring a structured order to the world of networking.

Q: How can I easily remember the layers of the OSI model?

A: One way to remember the layers in their proper order is by **Please Don't Throw Sausage Pizza Away.**

Q: Are all layers of the OSI model designed to perform one specific function?

A: No, actually the data-link layer is composed of two sublayers that include the logical link control (LLC) and the media access control (MAC) sublayers.

Q: What is the purpose of NAT?

A: To provide multiple hosts the use of one shared public IP address.

Q: Does NAT have any role in security?

A: Yes, as NAT performs a translation between public and private addresses the internal address scheme is hidden from the public Internet.

Q: Why should CHFI candidates be concerned with network information-gathering tools?

A: Forensics is about gathering information. This means the forensic expert must have the skills to gather information from many different sources.

Q: What is one of the most widely used information-gathering tools?

A: A sniffer. Tools like Wireshark can be used to get a good view of what types of traffic are on the network.

Q: Why monitor user activity?

A: Because we must try to make the distinction between repetitive mistakes and malicious attacks.

Q: Should user activity be examined just after something has gone wrong?

A: No, the best defense is a proactive defense. This means regular periodic monitoring.

CHFI

Router Forensics
and Network Forensics

Exam objectives in this chapter:

- **Network Forensics**
- **Searching for Evidence**
- **An Overview of Routers**
- **Hacking Routers**
- **Investigating Routers**
- **Incident Response**

Exam Objectives Review:

- ☑ **Summary of Exam Objectives**
- ☑ **Exam Objectives Fast Track**
- ☑ **Exam Objectives Frequently Asked Questions**

Introduction

This chapter examines router and network forensics. This chapter is important to CHFI candidates as many attacks will require the analyst to look for information in the router or require network forensics. This requires the CHFI to have an understanding of routers and their architecture. It is important to understand where they reside within the OSI model and what role they play within network communications.

Anytime a CHFI works with forensic evidence it is critical that the concept of chain of custody be understood. How evidence is handled, stored, accessed, and transported is critical, because if basic control measures are not observed the evidence may be ruled inadmissible in court.

Network Forensics

Network forensics can best be defined as the sniffing, recording, and analysis of network traffic and events. Network forensics are performed in order to discover the source of security incidents and attacks or other potential problems. One key role of the forensic expert is to differentiate repetitive problems from malicious attacks.

The Hacking Process

The hacking process follows a fixed methodology. The steps a hacker follows can be broadly divided into six phases:

1. Reconnaissance
2. Scanning and enumeration
3. Gaining access
4. Escalation of privilege
5. Maintaining access
6. Covering tracks and placing backdoors

EXAM WARNING

You will need to know the six steps in the hacking process for the CHFI exam. You should also be aware that gaining access is the point at which the actual intrusion occurs.

The Intrusion Process

Reconnaissance is considered the first preattack phase. The hacker seeks to find out as much information as possible about the victim. The second preattack phase is scanning and enumeration. At this step in the methodology, the hacker is moving from passive information gathering to active information gathering. Access can be gained in many different ways. A hacker may exploit a router vulnerability or maybe social engineer the help desk into giving him a phone number for a modem. Access could be gained by finding vulnerability in the web server's software. Just having the access of an average user account probably won't give the attacker very much control or access to the network. Therefore, the attacker will attempt to escalate himself to administrator or root privilege. Once escalation of privilege is complete the attacker will work on ways to maintain access to the systems he or she has attacked and compromised. Hackers are much like other criminals in that they would like to make sure and remove all evidence of their activities, which might include using root kits to cover their tracks. This is the moment at which most forensic activities begin.

Searching for Evidence

A CHFI must be knowledgeable of each of the steps of the hacking process and understand the activities and motives of the hacker. CHFIs many times will be tasked with using only pieces of information and playing the role of a detective in trying to reassemble the pieces of the puzzle. Information stored within a computer can exist in only one or more predefined areas. Information can be stored as a normal file, deleted file, hidden file, or in the slack or free space. Understanding these areas, how they work, and how they can be manipulated will increase the probability that you will find or discover hidden data. Not all suspects you encounter will be super cyber criminals. Many individuals will not hide files at all; others will attempt simple file hiding techniques. You may discover cases where suspects were overcome with regret, fear, or remorse, and attempted to delete or erase incriminating evidence after the incident. Most average computer users don't understand that to drop an item in the recycle bin doesn't mean that it is permanently destroyed. Such futile attempts to avoid discovery may prevent the average user from finding data, but will not deter a CHFI.

One common hiding technique is to place the information in an obscure location such as C:\winnt\system32\os2\dll. Again, this will usually block the average user from finding the file. The technique is simply that of placing the information in an area of the drive where you would not commonly look. A system search will quickly defeat this futile attempt at data hiding. Just search for specific types of files such as bmp, tif, doc, and xls. Using the search function built into Windows will help quickly find this type of information. If you are examining a Linux computer, use the grep command to search the drive.

Another technique is using file attributes to hide the files or folders. On a Macintosh computer, you can hide a file with the ResEdit utility. In the wonderful world of Windows, file attributes can be configured to hide files at the command line with the attrib command. This

command is built into the Windows OS. It allows a user to change the properties of a file. Someone could hide a file by issuing attrib +h secret.txt. This command would render the file invisible in the command line environment. This can also be accomplished through the GUI by right-clicking on a file and choosing the hidden type.

Would the file then be invisible in the GUI? Well, that depends on the view settings that have been configured. Open a browse window and choose tools/folder options/view/show hidden files; then, make sure Show Hidden Files is selected. This will display all files and folders, even those with the +h attribute set. Another way to get a complete listing of all hidden files is to issue the command attrib /s > attributes.txt from the root directory. The attrib command lists file attributes, the /s function list all files in all the subdirectories, and > redirects the output to a text file. This text file can then be parsed and placed in a spreadsheet for further analysis. Crude attempts such as these can be quickly surmounted.

An Overview of Routers

Routers are a key piece of networking gear. Let's know the role and function of a router.

What Is a Router?

Routers can be hardware or software devices that route data from a local area network to a different network. Routers are responsible for making decisions about which of several paths network (or Internet) traffic will follow. If more than one path is available to transmit data, the router is responsible for determining which path is the best path to route the information.

The Function of a Router

Routers also act as protocol translators and bind dissimilar networks. Routers limit physical broadcast traffic as they operate at layer 3 of the OSI model. Routers typically use either link state or hop count based routing protocols to determine the best path.

The Role of a Router

Routers are found at layer three of the OSI model. This is known as the networking layer. The network layer provides routing between networks and defines logical addressing, error handling, congestion control, and packet sequencing. This layer is concerned primarily with how to get packets from network A to network B. This is where IP addresses are defined. These addresses give each device on the network a unique (logical) address. Routers organize these addresses into classes, which are used to determine how to move packets from one network to another. All types of protocols rely on routing to move information from one point to another. This includes IP, Novell's IPX, and Apple's DDP. Routing on the Internet typically is performed dynamically; however, setting up static routes is a form of basic routing. Dynamic routing protocols constantly look for the best route to move information from the source to target network.

Routing Tables

Routers are one of the basic building blocks of networks, as they connect networks together. Routers reside at layer 3 of the OSI model. Each router has two or more interfaces. These interfaces join separate networks together. When a router receives a packet, it examines the IP address and determines to which interface the packet should be forwarded. On a small or uncomplicated network, an administrator may have defined a fixed route that all traffic will follow. More complicated networks typically route packets by observing some form of metric. Routing tables include the following type of information:

- **Bandwidth** This is a common metric based on the capacity of a link. If all other metrics were equal, the router would choose the path with the highest bandwidth.

- **Cost** The organization may have a dedicated T1 and an ISDN line. If the ISDN line has a higher cost, traffic will be routed through the T1.

- **Delay** This is another common metric, as it can build on many factors including router queues, bandwidth, and congestion.

- **Distance** This metric is calculated in hops; that is, how many routers away is the destination.

- **Load** This metric is a measurement of the load that is being placed on a particular router. It can be calculated by examining the processing time or CPU utilization.

- **Reliability** This metric examines arbitrary reliability ratings. Network administrators can assign these numeric values to various links.

By applying this metric and consulting the routing table, the routing protocol can make a best path determination. At this point, the packet is forwarded to the next hop as it continues its journey toward the destination.

Router Architecture

Router architecture is designed so that routers are equipped to perform two main functions: process routable protocols and use routing protocols to determine best path. Let's start by reviewing routable protocols. The best example of a routed protocol is IP. A very basic definition of IP is that it acts as the postman of the Internet—its job is to organize data into a packet, which is then addressed for delivery. IP must place a target and source address on the packet. This is similar to addressing a package before delivering it to the post office. In the world of IP, the postage is a TTL (Time-to-Live), which keeps packets from traversing the network forever. If the recipient cannot be found, the packet can eventually be discarded.

All the computers on the Internet have an IP address. If we revert to our analogy of the postal system, an IP address can be thought of as the combination of a zip code and street address. The first half of the IP address is used to identify the proper network; the second

portion of the IP address identifies the host. Combined, this allows us to communicate with any network and any host in the world that is connected to the Internet. Now let us turn our attention to routing protocols.

Routing Protocols

Routing protocols fall into two basic categories, static and dynamic. Static, or fixed, routing is simply a table that has been developed by a network administrator mapping one network to another. Static routing works best when a network is small and the traffic is predictable. The big problem with static routing is that it cannot react to network changes. As the network grows, management of these tables can become difficult. Although this makes static routing unsuitable for use on the Internet or large networks, it can be used in special circumstances where normal routing protocols do not function well.

Dynamic routing uses metrics to determine what path a router should use to send a packet toward its destination. Dynamic routing protocols include Routing Information Protocol (RIP), Border Gateway Protocol (BGP), Interior Gateway Routing Protocol (IGRP), and Open Shortest Path First (OSPF). Dynamic routing can be divided into two broad categories: link-state or distance vector dynamic routing protocols, which are discussed in greater detail later in the chapter.

RIP

RIP is the most common routing protocol that uses a hop count as its primary routing metric. RIP is considered a distance vector protocol. The basic methodology of a distance vector protocol is to make a decision on what is the best route by determining the shortest path. The shortest path is commonly calculated by hops. Distance vector routing is also called routing by rumor.

What Is a Hop Count?

A hop count is the number of routers that a packet must pass through to reach it destination. Each time a packet passes through a router, the cost is one hop. So, if the target network you are trying to reach is two routers away, it is also two hops away. The major shortcoming of distance vector protocols is that the path with the lowest number of hops may not be the optimum route. The lower hop count path may have considerably less bandwidth than the higher hop count route.

OSPF

OSPF is the most common link state routing protocol and many times, it is used as a replacement to RIP. Link state protocols are properly called Dijkstra algorithms, as this is the computational basis of their design. Link state protocols use the Dijkstra algorithm to calculate the best path to a target network. The best path can be determined by one or more metrics such as hops, delay, or bandwidth. Once this path has been determined, the router will inform other routers as to its findings. This is how reliable routing tables are developed and routing tables reach convergence. Link state routing is considered more robust than distance vector routing protocols. One reason is because link state protocols have the ability to perform faster routing table updates.

Head of the Class…

Convergence

Convergence is the point at which routing tables have become synchronized. Each time a network is added or dropped, the routing tables must again resynchronize. Routing algorithms differ in the speed at which they can reach convergence.

Hacking Routers

Full control of a router can often lead to full control of the network. This is why many attackers will target routers and launch attacks against them. These attacks may focus on configuration errors, known vulnerabilities, or even weak passwords.

Router Attacks

Routers can be attacked by either gaining access to the router and changing the configuration file, launching DoS attacks, flooding the bandwidth, or routing table poisoning. These attacks can be either hit-and-run or persistent. Denial of Service attacks are targeted at routers. If an attacker can force a router to stop forwarding packets, then all hosts behind the router are effectively disabled.

Router Attack Topology

The router attack topology is the same as all attack topologies. The steps include:

1. Reconnaissance

2. Scanning and enumeration

3. Gaining access

4. Escalation of privilege

5. Maintaining access

6. Covering tracks and placing backdoors

Head of the Class…

Hardening Routers

The Router Audit Tool can be used to harden routers. Once downloaded, RAT checks them against the settings defined in the benchmark. Each configuration is examined and given a rated score that provides a raw overall score, a weighted overall score (1-10), and a list of IOS commands that will correct any identified problems.

Denial-of-Service Attacks

Denial-of-service (DoS) attacks fall into three categories:

- **Destruction**. Attacks that destroy the ability of the router to function.

- **Resource consumption**. Flooding the router with many open connections simultaneously.

- **Bandwidth consumption**. Attacks that attempt to consume the bandwidth capacity of the router's network.

DoS attacks may target a user or an entire organization and can affect the availability of target systems or the entire network. The impact of DoS is the disruption of normal operations and the disruption of normal communications. It's much easier for an attacker to accomplish this than it is to gain access to the network in most instances. Smurf is an example of a common DoS attack. Smurf exploits the Internet Control Message Protocol (ICMP) protocol by sending a spoofed ping packet addressed to the broadcast address and has the source address listed as the victim. On a multiaccess network, many systems may possibly reply. The attack results in the victim being flooded in ping responses. Another example of a DoS attack is a

SYN flood. A SYN flood disrupts Transmission Control Protocol (TCP) by sending a large number of fake packets with the SYN flag set. This large number of half-open TCP connections fills the buffer on victim's system and prevents it from accepting legitimate connections. Systems connected to the Internet that provide services such as HTTP or SMTP are particular vulnerable.

DDoS attacks are the second type of DoS attack and are considered multiprotocol attacks. DDoS attacks use ICMP, UDP, and TCP packets. One of the distinct differences between DoS and DDoS is that a DDoS attack consists of two distinct phases. First, during the preattack, the hacker must compromise computers scattered across the Internet and load software on these clients to aid in the attack. Targets for such an attack include broadband users, home users, poorly configured networks, colleges and universities. Script kiddies from around the world can spend countless hours scanning for the poorly protected systems. Once this step is completed the second step can commence. The second step is the actual attack. At this point the attacker instructs the masters to communicate to the zombies to launch the attack. ICMP and UDP packets can easily be blocked at the router, but TCP packets are difficult to mitigate. TCP-based DoS attacks comes in two forms:

- **Connection-oriented**. These attacks complete the 3-way handshake to establish a connection. Source IP address can be determined here.

- **Connectionless**. These packets SYN are difficult t trace because source

TEST DAY TIP

It is important to understand that EC Council divides router attacks into two broad categories: connection-oriented, which can be traced; and connectionless, which are hard to trace.

An example of a DDOS tool is Tribal Flood Network (TFN). TFN was the first publicly available UNIX-based DDoS tool. TFN can launch ICMP, Smurf, UDP, and SYN flood attacks. The master uses UDP port 31335 and TCP port 27665. TFN was followed by more advanced DDoS attacks such as Trinoo. Closely related to TFN, this DDoS allows a user to launch a coordinated UDP flood to the victim's computer, which gets overloaded with traffic. A typical Trinoo attack team includes just a few servers and a large number of client computers on which the Trinoo daemon is running. Trinoo is easy for an attacker to use and is very powerful in that one computer is instructing many Trinoo servers to launch a DoS attack against a particular computer.

Routing Table Poisoning

Routers running RIPv1 are particularly vulnerable to routing table poisoning attacks. This type of attack sends fake routing updates or modifies genuine route update packets to other nodes with which the attacker attempts to cause a denial of service. Routing table poisoning may cause a complete denial of service or result in suboptimal routing, or congestion in portions of the network.

Hit-and-Run Attacks and Persistent Attacks

Attackers can launch one of two types of attacks, either-hit and-run or persistent. A hit-and-run attack is hard to detect and isolate as the attacker injects only one or a few malformed packets. With this approach, the attacker must craft the attacks so that the results have some lasting damaging effect. A persistent attack increases the possibility for identification of the attacker as there is an ongoing stream of packets to analyze. However this attack lowers the level of complexity needed by the attacker as they can use much less sophisticated attacks. Link state routing protocols such as OSPF are more resilient to routing attacks than RIP.

Damage & Defense...

Forensic Analysis of Routing Attacks

During a forensic investigation the analyst should examine log files for evidence such as IP address and the protocol. It is a good idea to redirect logs to the syslog server. This can be accomplished as follows:

```
#config terminal
Logging 192.168.1.1
```

Investigating Routers

When investigating routers there are a series of built-in commands that can be used for analysis. It is unadvisable to reset the router as this may destroy evidence that was created by the attacker. The following show commands can be used to gather basic information and record hacker activity:

- Show access list
- Show clock
- Show ip route

- Show startup configuration

- Show users

- Show version

Chain of Custody

The chain of custody is used to prove the integrity of evidence. The chain of custody should be able to answer the following questions:

- Who collected the evidence?

- How and where is the evidence stored?

- Who took possession of the evidence?

- How was the evidence stored and how was it protected during storage?

- Who took the evidence out of storage and why?

There is no such thing as too much documentation. One good approach is to have two people work on a case. While one person performs the computer analysis, the other documents these actions. At the beginning of an investigation, a forensic analyst should prepare a log to document the systematic process of the investigation. This is required to establish the chain of custody. This chain of custody will document how the evidence is handled, how it is protected, what process is used to verify it remains unchanged, and how it is duplicated. Next, the log must address how the media is examined, what actions are taken, and what tools are used. Automated tools such as EnCase and The Forensic Toolkit compile much of this information for the investigator.

Volatility of Evidence

When responding to a network attack, obtaining volatile data should be collected as soon as possible. Although all routers are different, you will most likely be working with Cisco products as Cisco has the majority of the market share. Cisco routers store the current configuration in nonvolatile ram (NVRAM). The current configuration is considered volatile data and the data is kept in Random Access Memory (RAM). If the configuration is erased or the router powered down all information is lost. Routers typically are used as a beachhead for an attack. This means the router may play an active part in the intrusion. The attacker uses the router as a jumping off point to other network equipment.

When starting an investigation you should always move from most volatile to least volatile. The first step is to retrieve RAM and NVRAM. To accomplish this you may use a direct connection to the console port using RJ-45-RJ-45 rolled cable and an RJ-45-to-DB-9 female DTE adapter. In instances when a direct connection is not available a remoter session is the next preferred method. Insecure protocols such as FTP should not be used; an encrypted pro-

tocol Secure Shell (SSH) is preferred. The CHFI should make sure to capture both volatile and nonvolatile configuration for comparison changes and documentation purposes. Cisco routers have multiple modes, so to gain privilege mode the password must be known by the analyst.

Case Reports

Case reporting is one of the most important aspects of computer forensics. Just as with traditional forensics everything should be documented. Reporting should begin the minute you are assigned to a case. Although it may sometimes seem easier to blindly push forward, the failure to document can result in poorly written reports that will not withstand legal scrutiny.

Let's face it, not all aspects of computer forensics are exciting and fun. Most of us view paperwork as drudgery. It is a somewhat tedious process that requires an eye for detail. Don't allow yourself this fallacy. In the end, the documentation you keep and the process you follow will either validate or negate the evidence. The report is key in bringing together the three primary pieces of forensics: acquisition, authentication, and analysis.

The case report will be the key to determining one of the following actions:

- Employee remediation
- Employee termination
- Civil proceedings
- Criminal prosecution

When the investigation is complete a final written report is prepared. Some of the items found in this report will include:

- Case Summary
- Case Audit Files
- Bookmarks
- Selected Graphics
- File Location Path
- File Location Properties

Although this is not an all-inclusive list it should give you some indication of what should be included. Depending on the agency or corporation, the contents of the report will vary. What is consistent is that anyone should be able to use the logs and the report to recreate the steps performed throughout the investigation. This process of duplication should lead to identical results.

EXERCISE 10.1

CHAIN OF CUSTODY

Everyone knew Mark Reedy was a bad kid. His teachers had been having problems with him at Carson High School for several years. One day, his computer literacy teacher overheard him telling another student he could get the best Ecstasy around. He stated that all he had to do was e-mail his supplier and he could have all the "tabs" the other student wanted. Mark then was seen passing a single white tablet to the other student. At that point, the teacher intervened and school security was called.

Later, in the custody of the police, it was discovered that the single pill was indeed Ecstasy. Even though Mark refused to provide any information, a zip disk labeled "contacts" was found in his possession. The disk featured a hand-drawn picture of a marijuana leaf adorning the label. Although a search warrant of Mark's house is being executed, it is believed that they do not own a computer. However, Carson High School and the public library do have public access computers with zip disk drives. The police department has asked that you investigate the disk and provide additional information.

1. What should be your first step?
2. Should the evidence be marked? How should it be handled?
3. Should you request audit and login information from the school and library? Will these be easily obtainable?
4. Should a copy of the disk be made?
5. How should the evidence be stored?

Incident Response

Incident response is the effort of an organization to define and document the nature and scope of a computer security incident. Incident response can be broken into three broad categories that include:

- **Triage** Notification and identification
- **Action/Reaction** Containment, analysis, tracking
- **Follow up** Repair and recovery, prevention

Compromises

Before a compromise can be determined, investigators must be alerted that something has happened. It is best if the alert function is automated as much as possible. Otherwise, the sheer volume of log information would be overwhelming for an employee. Even with a high level of automation someone must still make a judgment regarding the validity of the alert. Once an attack has been validated it is important to reduce the damage of the attack as quickly as possible and work to restore normal business functions.

Summary of Exam Objectives

In this chapter, we reviewed how routers can play an important part in forensics. Readers were introduced to routed protocols such as IP and we discussed how routed protocols work. In many ways, IP acts as a "postman" since its job is to make the best effort at delivery. In a small network or those that seldom change, the route that the IP datagrams take through the network may remain static or unchanged. Larger networks use dynamic routing. Administrators use routing protocols such as RIP for dynamic routing. We also looked at how attackers attack routers and how incident response relates to routers and router compromises.

Exam Objectives Fast Track

Network Forensics

- ☑ Network forensics is the process of examining network traffic for the purpose of discovering attacks and malicious events.

- ☑ Network forensics is commonly performed with a sniffer or packet capture tool.

Overview of Routers

- ☑ Routers are designed to connect dissimilar protocols.

- ☑ Routers deal with routing protocols.

- ☑ Common routing protocols include RIP and OSPF.

Hacking Routers

- ☑ Routers can be attacked by exploiting misconfigurations or vulnerabilities.

- ☑ Routers need to have logging enabled so sufficient traffic is captured to aid in forensic investigations.

Incident Response

- ☑ Monitoring for incidents requires both passive and active tasks.

- ☑ Incident response requires development of a policy to determine the proper response.

Exam Objectives
Frequently Asked Questions

The following Frequently Asked Questions, answered by the authors of this book, are designed to both measure your understanding of the Exam Objectives presented in this chapter, and to assist you with real-life implementation of these concepts.

Q: Why is network forensics important?

A: Network forensics are important because so many common attacks entail some type of misuse of network resources.

Q: What are the different ways in which the network can be attacked?

A: Attacks typically target availability, confidentiality, and integrity. Loss of any one of these items constitutes a security breach.

Q: Where is the best place to search for information?

A: Information can be found by either doing a live analysis of the network, analyzing IDS information, or examining logs that can be found in routers and servers.

Q: How does a forensic analyst know how deeply to look for information?

A: Some amount of information can be derived from looking at the skill level of the attacker. Attackers with little skill are much less likely to use advanced hiding techniques.

Q: Where do routers reside in relationship to the OSI model?

A: Routers are a layer 3 device.

Q: Do routers pass physical addresses?

A: No, not by default since routers are layer 3 devices and physical addresses are found at layer 2.

Q: What do routers do with broadcast traffic?

A: Routers block physical broadcast traffic.

Q: Why target routers?

A: Routers can sometimes be overlooked by security professionals since so much time is placed on securing workstations and servers.

Q: What is the first thing an attacker does when targeting a router?

A: An attacker must first identify the device and be able to verify it is a router. With this done the attacker must next determine the version and model of the router.

Q: What is the most important preplanning aspect of router forensics?

A: Logging, a CHFI must make sure good policies and procedures are in place that specify adequate logging is taking place.

Q: What type of skills are required for incident response?

A: Incident response requires technical skills, investigative skills, and leadership skills.

Q: How would you best define the incident response process?

A: Incident response is the process of detecting a problem, determining its cause, minimizing the damage.

CHFI

Investigating Wireless Attacks

Exam objectives in this chapter:

- **Basics of Wireless**
- **Wireless Penetration Testing**

Exam Objectives Review:

- ☑ **Summary of Exam Objectives**
- ☑ **Exam Objectives Fast Track**
- ☑ **Exam Objectives Frequently Asked Questions**

Introduction

In many corporate networks across the country, wireless devices are extending the network perimeter beyond the confines of the office walls and into neighboring buildings and public streets. No longer do attackers need to gain network access by breaking into an office or attempting to bypass strict firewall policies. Now they can take advantage of an unsuspecting company that doesn't realize its wireless infrastructure security is so loose that it can be hacked in less than 15 minutes.

You often read stories about hackers sitting in vehicles with a laptop and a high-powered wireless antenna, scanning for insecure wireless networks to compromise. These hackers may be looking for internal corporate intellectual property to sell to a competitor or data that may be used for blackmail or extortion. The more difficult you make it for the attacker, the better chance you have that a hacker will pass on your network and go after a less secure one.

Wireless attacks are occurring! BJ's Wholesale Club, Lowe's Companies Inc., DSW, Wake Forest University School of Medicine, and TJX have all been victims of compromised wireless networks. The cost of these data breaches could be well into the millions of dollars, but their true cost remains difficult to calculate since we must take into consideration the money spent by the company to investigate the problem, provide damages to the victims, fix the vulnerabilities, and factor in loss of revenue due to low consumer confidence.

Regardless of the complexity of your design, an attacker may still attempt to compromise your wireless network. It is no longer a matter of "if" your wireless network will be attacked, but "when." External attempts to connect to your wireless network can range from simple automatic device associations to specific attacks to gain access. It can be difficult to determine whether someone is attempting to attack your network or looking for free Internet access. Regardless of their intent, every effort should be made to make your wireless network as secure as possible. Ensuring you configure strong encryption and adhere to secure wireless best practices will help minimize your risk.

As the cost to implement wireless networks continues to decrease, more and more companies are considering deploying wireless technology. Since 2006, London has seen 160 percent more wireless access points, with New York increasing a substantial 49 percent. However, you don't need to look at statistics to realize that wireless networks are becoming more popular. Open up your wireless configuration user interface and you will usually see three or four networks in the surrounding area. If you live in the city, that number can be as high as 15 to 20.

Deploying a wireless network has numerous advantages. Now, workers can access their corporate network anywhere, from the cafeteria to the conference room, without having to reconfigure their computers or plug into a wall jack. This flexibility is not only beneficial for the employee, but the employer as well. It is often much cheaper to implement a wireless solution than installing network cabling throughout the building.

This chapter discusses the basics of wireless networks and the methods hackers use to attack them. It is imperative you understand the techniques used by hackers so you can test your wireless networks for vulnerabilities. Hackers have an advantage when it comes to wireless

attacks due to anonymity and the difficulty of tracking down attacks. The attack surface is huge and the results are appealing because once a hacker gets in, they are on the internal network, bypassing many of the traditional network security barriers.

Basics of Wireless

A wireless access point connects the traditional wired network to wireless clients by transmitting network data through the air. The wireless access point acts as a relay between the wired network and wireless clients. Many companies implement many wireless access points that can hand off the wireless signal to ensure the client does not get disconnected. These access points range from home or home office devices that cost less than a hundred dollars to enterprise access points that implement complex security features and allow for specialized configuration and management.

The wireless access points themselves simply provide a means for the data to travel from the wired network to the client. The network infrastructure services must still be provided to the client. While most access points today have these features built into the device, you can also use your traditional servers to provide these services such as DHCP and routing.

Different types of wireless networks are available, the most common being 802.11 b/g. 802.11b was the first wireless standard developed for commercial use. It operates at 2.4GHz and transfers data at a rate of 11 megabits per second (Mbps). Improving data transfer to 54 Mbps, 802.11g was a welcome upgrade for consumers wanting faster throughput from their wireless infrastructure. Although the 2.4GHz band would often lead to interference problems, backwards compatibility and early adoption helped this combination become the standard for wireless devices.

For those companies that required less interference or that could not adopt the 2.4GHz band as an acceptable solution, 802.11a was released that worked on the 5GHz band. 802.11a improved on wireless stability, reducing dropped connections, while staying at the 54-Mbps transfer rate. The main downside is the expense of upgrading both the wireless access points and the client's wireless cards to devices that support this standard.

Wireless devices can also connect two remote locations by using line of sight antennas to send data from one location to another where the installation of cabling would not be feasible. A company who has a second building located less than a mile from the main building may choose to implement a line of sight wireless solution for Internet connectivity instead of spending the reoccurring cost of a traditional T1 line.

For a client to connect wirelessly to a LAN, they must have a wireless network card compatible with the wireless standard used by the target network. With the majority of laptops today including built-in network devices, wireless networks are becoming a standard with most home and corporate networks. While wireless LANs have traditionally been used for mobile devices, the ease and cost effectiveness of extending the network has some companies implementing wireless cards on their desktop machines.

Even with all the advancements in recent years, installing a wireless network on your LAN is not something you should do without careful planning. Before adding wireless connectivity to your network, you should understand the major advantages and disadvantages of introducing wireless connectivity.

Advantages of a Wireless Network

Wireless networks offer users the following advantages:

- **Ease of accessing the network** No longer are employees bound to areas where they can plug into a wall jack to connect to the network. Being able to connect your laptop to the network from anywhere in the building allows for more freedom.

- **Reduce cost of running cable** The labor cost alone of wiring an office or office building can be quite high compared to the cost of purchasing and installing a wireless device and cards. With wireless cards available for desktop computers, an office can be network available in a manner of minutes.

- **Productivity** Employees can now take their laptops with them to meetings or any other place required, and yet continue working.

Disadvantages of a Wireless Network

Wireless networks also have some disadvantages as well:

- **Security** The main disadvantage of wireless is its lack of security. If proper planning and configuration are not taken into consideration, any wireless network can be easily compromised.

- **Complexity and reliability** While adding wireless access points increases accessibility to the wired network, it can also increase the complexity of the network design. System administrators must be aware of the impact that the wireless devices have on the network and troubleshoot problems such as weak signals and dropped wireless connections.

- **Network performance** While the advertised speed of a wireless connection is 54 Mbps, the actual data throughput is often much less, especially if many computers are using the same wireless connection. A wired network drop will almost always outperform a wireless connection.

Association of Wireless AP and a Device

To transmit and receive data through a wireless connection, the client must be associated with the access point. This association connects the two devices and allows the client to obtain an IP

address and communication on the network. Signal power and security settings can interfere with the association process.

On Windows XP and Windows Server operating systems, Microsoft provides the Windows Wireless Zero Configuration (WZC) utility to assist the user with connecting to wireless networks. While it does make the association process easier, it also introduces some security concerns you should be aware of.

If a preferred network is not available, WZC will probe for networks that are already connected. This information can be viewed by anyone using a wireless analyzer and can be used to set up fake access points to lure clients to connect. WZC will also attempt to connect to the wireless network with the strongest signal. Knowing this, an attacker can create fake wireless networks with high-power antennas and cause computers to associate with their access point rather than the legitimate one. When possible, it is recommended you use the vendor-provided wireless management tool.

If you are using a wireless card from Linksys, Dell, or Netgear, you will likely have installed management software from the vendor that can control the association of the wireless device. This software has been designed by the manufacturer to work with the corresponding hardware and is typically more secure.

All wireless management software will require you to select the wireless network to which you would like to connect. You will select the Service Set Identifier (SSID). The SSID is the public name of the wireless network. If the network has security enabled, you will be prompted to enter the passphrase or encryption key. If you do not know the key, you will not be allowed access to the network. If the network is open or you enter in the correct security key, your computer will attempt to establish the connection.

Access Control

To secure the wireless network as much as possible, security controls can be implemented to minimize the ability of an attacker to gain access. These access controls can be used independently or combined to provide additional protection. The access controls available to you will depend on the type of wireless access point you are configuring. Most access points will allow the configuration of encryption and Media Access Control (MAC) filtering.

Encryption

Wireless data is being transmitted in the air that is susceptible to nonauthorized users capturing this data and reading the contents. To eliminate data being sent over the air in cleartext, wireless networks adopted encryption as part of the network standard. Unfortunately, early implementations of encryption for wireless soon became trivial to crack. As wireless networking matures, the encryption is becoming more complex and difficult to crack. Different technology is also being implemented, such as certificate-based encryption, as an alternative to preshared keys.

WEP

Wired Equivalent Privacy (WEP) is an optional security feature that was specified by the 802.11 protocol to provide authentication and confidentiality in a wireless access point. It was one of the original methods of sending secure information using a wireless network. When the IEEE committee recommended WEP be used as a mechanism, it also said WEP should not be considered an adequate security and strongly recommended it not be used without an authentication process for key management. WEP employs a symmetric key to authenticate wireless devices and guarantee the integrity of the data by encrypting the transmissions. Each wireless access point and client must share the same key in order for authentication to take place. Once WEP has been enabled, it then begins a challenge and response authentication process. WEP encrypts data before it is sent from the system, and then decrypts it at the access point. It has been shown to be severely inadequate in its security methods, and as such was replaced as the wireless encryption method of choice in 2003. It uses the stream cipher RC4 (Rivest Cipher). Its method of authentication is essentially that of Shared Key Authentication since both the access point and the wireless device possess the same key. WEP keys are always either 40 bit or 104 bit. The advertised 64-bit and 128-bit encryption results from the fact that the Initialization Vector (IV) is 24 bits. With the encryption method used by WEP, an attacker with enough IVs can crack the key used and gain full access to the network. In studies, WEP networks have been broken into extremely quickly. Recently, at an information security conference, the Federal Bureau of Investigation demonstrated how to crack WEP—and they did it in three minutes.

Overall, the use of WEP can create in the casual user a false sense of security. In the worst-case scenario, an attacker can gain full access to the network extremely quickly—as such, this should not be used to secure a sensitive network. In today's access points, WEP is not considered a secured method of securing a wireless access point.

WPA

WPA resolves the issue of weak WEP headers as explained earlier, or the IVs, and provides a way of insuring the integrity of the messages that passed the integrity check using TKIP (Temporal Key Integrity Protocol) to enhance data encryption. WPA-PSK is a special mode of WPA for home users without an enterprise authentication server and provides the same strong encryption protection. In simple terms, WPA-PSK is extra-strong encryption where encryption keys are automatically changed (called rekeying) and authenticated between devices after a specified period of time, or after a specified number of packets has been transmitted. This is called the rekey interval. WPA-PSK is far superior to WEP and provides stronger protection for the home/SOHO user for two reasons. The process used to generate the encryption key is very rigorous, and the rekeying (or key changing) is done very quickly.

WPA improves over WEP because it uses a per-session encryption key. Every time a station associates, a new encryption key is generated based on randomization and the MAC addresses of the wireless access point.

Unfortunately, though, the easiest way to use WPA actually makes it easier to crack than WEP. When 802.1X authentication is not used in WPA, a simpler system called Pre-Shared Key (PSK) is utilized instead. A pre-shared key is a password that all clients need to be configured with in order to access the access point. Most consumer routers have the capability of using the WPA with the PSK pre-shared key.

With WPA-PSK, and almost all passwords, if you make a short character password, you are susceptible to an offline dictionary attack where an attacker grabs a few packets at the time a legitimate station joins the wireless network, and then can take those packets and recover the PSK used. An attacker can get what he needs in order to guess the PSK and get out without anyone noticing. This can occur because the attacker doesn't have to be near the WLAN for more than a few seconds, and the LAN doesn't have to be very busy. This attack depends on the choice of a password, although cracking techniques get better and better. Thus, WPA has been defeated. Most wireless access points have a mechanism built into WPA, which converts an 8- to 63-character string you type in to the 64-digit or 128-digit key (as used with WEP). However, most wireless access points won't be able to use the whole 64-bit key with passphrase mode.

The innate problem is that a passphrase is easy to guess. The IEEE committee that wrote 802.11i pointed out that an eight- to ten-character passphrase actually has less than the 40 bits of security that the most basic version of WEP offers, and said that a passphrase of less than 20 characters is unlikely to deter attacks. As with WEP, wireless cracking tools exist that are specifically designed to recover the PSK from a WPA-protected network (such as Kismet) which are easily available to download.

WPA with 802.1X authentication (sometimes called WPA-Enterprise) makes for a much more secure network. 802.1X offers strong positive authentication for both the station and the WLAN infrastructure, while deriving a secure, per-session encryption key that is not vulnerable to any casual attack. This is typically used with a RADIUS server as explained earlier regarding authentication. The best wireless security mechanism out there with the most access points is 802.1X authentication, combined with WPA's improved encryption.

But instead of pointing out all of the inherent flaws in passing data over unlicensed radio frequencies, WPA, which comes with most new consumer routers, is an excellent way to keep your Internet surfing and home network as safe as it can be. Add VPN connections and MAC filtering and you basically have the same security as you do with an alarm system on your home. It deters people from getting access without considerable resolve.

MAC Filtering

With few exceptions, network devices contain a physically unique burned-in MAC address. The purpose of this is to give a unique identifier to that piece of equipment. It is pre-assigned to the devices by its manufacturer, and in theory is completely unique. In most cases, the MAC address is 48 bits long. A standard format exists for writing MAC addresses, which consist of three groups of four hexadecimal digits separated by dots. The more common method of writing is to use six groups of two hexadecimal digits, which are in turn separated by colons or hyphens—for example, 00-07-E9-E3-84-F9.

Since each MAC address is unique, it can be used to limit network access. The steps to do so will vary by access point, but will always involve the following:

- Finding the MAC address for the devices that will be allowed to access the network (this can be found either by looking on the actual device itself, or by using the *ipconfig /all* command in the Windows command console, and *ifconfig – a* for Linux and OSX consoles).

- Enter the MAC address into the configuration for the access point (this will vary by device).

In theory, once the MAC addresses are entered into the access point, they will be the only devices allowed to access the network. In practice, a number of issues can come up, including, but not limited to, the fact that any time a new system is used in conjunction with the access point (such as a visiting client who needs to connect to the network), its MAC address must be entered individually into the access point. This can pull the network administrator away from other tasks of monitoring the network. The administrator must also periodically remove the information for devices no longer being used

Another problem that exists is that of MAC address spoofing. While the address is typically encoded to the physical medium of the network device, software exists that can make a device access point have a different MAC address than it actually does. While this does have legitimate and useful purposes, including privacy and interoperability, it can also be changed to access a system illegally. Because of this large security hole, MAC address filtering should not be used by itself, and should instead be included in a wider security policy involving encryption and other authentication methods.

Cloaking the SSID

The SSID is essentially the name of the access point or wireless network seen by the user. A client can find out their SSID in only two ways: it can be told to them by the access point actively, or you can passively put it in the client's configuration. When it is given out automatically, it is called Open Network mode, but is known as Closed Network mode when "cloaking," meaning the SSID is not broadcast over the radio frequency. The automatic giving out of the SSID occurs typically every 100 milliseconds and is called a beacon, within which is contained synchronization information such as channel, speeds, timestamps, encryption status, and other information.

In Closed Network mode, the SSID is not broadcast out to the user or administrator programs. Thus, the client must probe the access point, and if the SSID matches, it will synchronize and go through the authentication process. Authentication can occur using an open system or shared key authentication. An open system does not need any credentials supplied. The SSID is used in wireless networks to identify the wireless access point and its associated network. It can be up to 32 alphanumeric characters long and is attached to all packets sent over the wireless connection. Additional access points in the area can broadcast the same SSID, so its use as a

security or authentication method is negligible. However, the SSID may be changed and cloaked (meaning it is not set to be broadcast by the AP) in an attempt to minimize the visibility of the network. By default, most APs broadcast their SSID to the surrounding area. This beacon method occurs roughly every 0.1 seconds. Most APs ship with a default SSID which are widely known and can be found on a number of Internet sites. Using a default SSID may draw malicious users who suspect that additional settings on the AP are set to default settings as well (such as the administrative password). From a security standpoint, changing the SSID may cause some possible attackers to choose a wireless network that uses default settings. Changing the SSID is reasonably simple for a nontechnical user, and though minor, is a step toward securing the AP. It is important to note that disabling the broadcast of the SSID does not completely cloak the AP. It simply makes it less visible.

Notes from the Underground…

Wigle

Wigle (Wireless Geographic Logging Engine) is the consolidation of thousands of wardriving efforts to create a database of wireless networks around the world. Wigle accepts WAP information by NetStumbler, DStumbler, Kismet, and Pocket Warrior exports. You can also use the Web site's online submission form to enter wireless networks.

In just over five years, Wigle has collected information on 10,953,561 unique wireless networks with locations. Of these networks, 44.4 percent are encrypted with WEP (which we know can be cracked in minutes) and 18.5 percent still maintain the default SSID or network name, which leads us to believe these networks may still maintain the vendor's default settings. For more information go to www.wigle.net.

The danger of so much wireless access point data being available to hackers is that by searching for APs by SSID or network name, BSSID or MAC address, longitude and latitude, or street address, anyone can find an insecure wireless network.

Wireless Penetration Testing

Many managers and system administrators never bother to learn the techniques hackers use to attack wireless networks. A negative stigma is often associated with the use of hacker tools and methodologies. They frequently consider the use of these tools as the legitimization of hacker-based tactics and strategies. This attitude can lead to an insecure wireless network that has not been tested to determine the ability to prevent a true attack from succeeding.

Conducting penetration tests to determine the security of your wireless infrastructure is essential. Through the practice of learning, understanding, and implementing the same methods of attack the intruder will use, one can better assess vulnerabilities, overcome weaknesses, and

fortify defenses. During a wireless penetration test, it is important to gather as much information about the network as possible. Most networks are discovered during wardriving (the process of scanning for insecure networks), so the attack may be targeted more towards a wireless vulnerability than a specific corporate network.

The two approaches you want to take when doing a penetration test are an internal and external attacker. The internal approach allows you to use information you already know about the network, like encryption keys, network design, and signal ranges. This type of test validates the security of the network from an internal employees point of view. External testing is done without using any knowledge of the network infrastructure. The tester uses tools an intruder would use and simulates an actual attack. It is important that a skilled security professional perform this test to ensure these tools do not negatively impact network and server systems.

The key thing to remember during a wireless penetration test is that your goal is to assess the security of the wireless network. Management approval in writing of what tests are expected and the potential impact to the network is a good way to ensure no surprises for either side.

- You should never do anything that will compromise or affect a neighboring wireless network.

- You should not try any type of Denial-of-Service attack on the network without approval.

- You will be attempting to crack the various portions of the network. Make sure to keep the result of the scan and penetration test confidential, and ensure they are stored safely.

- Report all findings to management with detailed explanations and security recommendations.

Head of the Class…

Black Hat vs White Hat

You will often hear hackers referred to as black hat or white hat. These terms describe a fundamental difference in the approach and reason that a hacker or security professional will attempt to compromise a network or computer system. White hat hackers, also referred to as ethical hackers, attempt to expose security weaknesses in systems to alert the owner or developer and assist in making the application more secure. Black hat hackers use their knowledge of security weaknesses for private gain, rather than disclosing it to the owner.

As the Internet becomes more complex, these roles have become less absolute and can be subject to interpretation. An unsolicited attack on a corporate network without permission, whether good intentioned or not, is illegal. Attempting to find exploits in Web applications without authorization is also illegal. Before attempting any security assessments, make sure you have permission from the owner.

Search Warrants

Before you can investigate on a device owned by someone else, you may be required to obtain a search warrant. You must verify that the search warrant includes the proper authorization to perform onsite examinations of computer equipment such as wireless access devices. Do not perform any forensic analysis on equipment you are not authorized to analyze.

Direct Connections to Wireless Access Point

Users that are persistent in their desire to connect to an unauthorized access point will keep an eye out for security professionals completing wireless audits and simply unplug the access point until the scan is complete. The amount of effort required for physical wireless scans can often result in less frequent scans. Detecting wireless access points from your wired network has many advantages. You can set automated scripts that search your network on a continuous basis, saving you time and money. By using tools like Network Mapper (Nmap), you can scan sections of your network not easily accessible to wireless scanning.

To perform wired network scans for access points, you must be connected to the internal network and have the ability to connect to all the subnets you want to scan.

Scanning for Wireless Access Points with Nmap

One of the more popular tools for completing network scans is the Network Mapper (Nmap), a Transmission Control Protocol (TCP) and User Datagram Protocol (UDP) Internet Protocol (IP) scanner. Nmap supports several different scanning styles, the most important being "stealth" scanning. "Flying under the radar" of the target system's administrator is crucial to the intruder's successful attack, and stealth scanning has the advantage of being able to pass through most firewall and network monitoring systems unmolested and largely unnoticed.

Using these scans, we can determine what ports are open on our network systems and identify unauthorized wireless access points. Nmap is used to identify the OS of the target system, but beware, OS fingerprinting scans are easily detectable and will be detected right away by intrusion detection systems (IDSes).

Nmap is a free open-source utility for network exploration and security auditing. It was designed to rapidly scan large networks, although it works fine against single hosts. Nmap uses raw IP packets in novel ways to determine what hosts are available on the network, what services (application name and version) those hosts are offering, what operating systems (and OS versions) they are running, what type of packet filters/firewalls are in use, and dozens of other characteristics. Nmap runs on most types of computers and both console and graphical versions are available. Nmap is free and open source

The text description, vendor name, operating system, and device type provided by Nmap during OS fingerprinting is what we will use to find wireless access points (WAPs) by scanning from the wired side of the network. Nmap fingerprinting is very effective in determining WAP

devices. To determine if an access point was connected to the network, we can run a scan of a local class c subnet using the following command:

```
nmap -A -T4 192.168.0.1/24
```

This command does a few things. The –A tells Nmap to enable operating system and version detection. The –T4 sets the timing template to 4, which speeds up the scan by setting the timeout value to 500 milliseconds. This can be extremely useful when scanning large subnets to ensure speedy results. What we are looking for in the Nmap output is Device type: WAP. This is our verification that we have scanned a wireless access point on the network.

Scanning for Wireless Access Points with Nessus

Nessus is a powerful and up-to-date open source scanner that scans the network for systems with security vulnerabilities. Nessus is very fast, reliable, and has a modular architecture that allows you to fit it to your needs. Scans can be tailored to seek out only those vulnerabilities you deem important. Each security test is written as an external plug-in. This way, you can easily add your own test without having to read the code of the Nessus engine. The Nessus scanner is made up of two parts: a server, which performs the security tests, and a client that serves as the front end. You can run the server and the client on different systems. Additionally, several clients are available: one for X11, one for Win32, and one written in Java.

Nessus plugin #11026 was written to detect the presence of wireless access points on the network using a variety of techniques. It scans the device via the TCP/IP Nmap fingerprint, analyzes the HTTP management interface, and verifies the FTP banner and SNMP information present. If any of these techniques determines that the device is a wireless access point, the scan moves on to the next device, marking this device as a WAP.

To scan using the #11026 plug-in for Nessus, complete the following steps:

- Run nessus-update-plugins to ensure the plug-ins are up-to-date.

- Start a new scan and ensure that the Access Point Detection plug-in is selected from the General plug-in section in the Plugins tab of the client.

- Make sure that the Enable Dependencies At Runtime option is checked since the plug-in requires the system info type via SNMP and HTTP Server–type dependencies to be able to scan.

Rogue Access Points

For enterprise-class access point detection, you may want to consider investing in a wireless IDS/IPS system. A wireless IDS/IPS is an intrusion detection/intrusion prevention system that provides 24/7 monitoring on the network and can dynamically respond to wireless threats.

In addition to detecting rogue devices, a wireless IDS/IPS can terminate them using air or port suppression on the switch, provide forensic analysis of packets sent and received, and provide location tracking of the device by triangulating the signal between multiple sensors.

Rogue access points represent a growing threat to network administrators because users can plug in a wireless access point with a minimal configuration and extend the network wirelessly. This creates a lack of control on where data is being sent, and worse, who is listening.

Wireless Connect to a Wireless Access Point

In this section, we are going to discuss the techniques hackers use to compromise wireless access points. Before initiating an attack, a hacker will want to know as much about the target network as possible, using various wireless tools to perform information gathering. Once the hacker feels comfortable with the information gathered, they may use injection techniques to force information across the wireless network that can be used to crack encryption schemes. Once these data have been captured, it is matter of time before the encryption key is discovered and the hacker is connected to the internal network via the wireless access point.

The tools used to perform these attacks are freely available on the Internet and included in live security distributions. We will be using many of the utilities from the Aircrack-ng suite (www.aircrack-ng.org) along with Kismet (www.kismetwireless.net) a popular wireless analyzer. While you may be able to find tools for other operating systems, most are written for Linux, so some knowledge of Unix commands will be helpful.

Notes from the Underground...

Backtrack

Getting all the tools necessary to perform penetration-testing tasks can be quite daunting. Compatibility issues with kernels and dependent drivers can have a security analyst spending most of the time getting the tools to work instead of testing the security of their applications or devices. Live CDs are bootable CDs that contain preconfigured operating systems and tools that are distributed by groups over the Internet. One of the premiere Security distributions is BackTrack (www.remote-exploit.org/backtrack.html).

The BackTrack live CD distribution comes with many security tools already installed and ready to use so that the tester can spend more time performing the penetration testing and finding security vulnerabilities in the systems. BackTrack not only contains the majority of the tools that will be discussed in this chapter, but also contains tools for Information Gathering, Network Mapping, Vulnerability Identification, Penetration Testing, Privilege Escalations, VOIP and Wireless analysis, and Digital Forensics. All you need to get started is to download the ISO image and burn it to a CD.

Information Gathering

The first thing a hacker will do when trying to gain unauthorized access to a wireless network is to do some reconnaissance and get more information on what tools will be needed next. The goal of this step is to detect rogue wireless access points, ad hoc wireless networks, and open or improperly configured access points that can be used to gain access. Hackers will want to get as much information about the wireless access points as they do the associated clients because all this information will be used to gather important connection data.

Kismet

It's time to see if our network is available. To do this, we will start by using Kismet. Kismet is a layer 2 wireless packet analyzer that works with wireless cards that support raw monitoring mode. Kismet can quickly identify wireless networks by capturing wireless packets and retrieving information such as whether they have security enabled or allow SSID cloaking. Kismet can also identify a network's channels and the SSID of a network.

This step will simulate what an attacker will look for when they are scanning for vulnerable networks. After starting Kismet, you will start to see wireless networks populate the screen. By default, Kismet sorts the network lists by Auto-fit, which can be difficult to read if there are a lot of networks available. Our first step is to sort the access points by selecting "s" to get to the sort menu, and selecting "s" again to sort by SSID. This view not only sorts the network list by SSID, but groups them into categories such as Probe Networks and Ad-hoc Networks. This will be important to know as we continue to gather information about our target wireless network. To expand/contract a grouping, highlight the group and press the **Spacebar**.

Now that we have our Network List screen sorted by SSID, let's go through the different columns.

- Name: SSID of network
- T: Type of network (A =Access Point, H = Ad-Hoc, P = Probe request, A = wireless client searching for a network, D = Data network, T = Turbocell network, and G = Group of wireless networks)
- W: Identifies if network is secured (Y = Yes, N = No)
- Ch: Channel number of network
- Packts: Number of packets captured
- Flags: Method in which IP was gathered
- IP Range: IP of the network

The Kismet colors make identifying networks easier. The following are the possible color combinations:

- Yellow: Unencrypted network

- Red: Network is using factory defaults

- Green: Secured Network

- Blue: Hidden networks that are cloaking the SSID

The information we will use in the next step from Kismet is the network channel and whether or not the network is encrypted. It will also be helpful to document if Kismet was able to determine an IP range or if the network was Red or Yellow. Both indicate that security is not configured adequately and that the network can be compromised.

Aircrack-ng

Aircrack-ng (www.aircrack-ng.org) is a suite of tools for auditing wireless networks. We will be using the *airodump-ng*, *aireplay-ng*, *aircrack-ng*, and *airdecap-ng* tools from the Aircrack-ng suite.

- *Airodump-ng* captures raw 802.11 packets to be used with *aircrack-ng*. *Airodump-ng* is also capable of logging the coordinates of access points.

- *Aireplay-ng* is primarily used to inject frames into wireless traffic, which will later be used by *aircrack-ng* to crack WEP and WPA-PSK keys. *Aireplay-ng* supports deauthentications, fake authentications, interactive packet replay and ARP request (re)injections.

- *Aircrack-ng* can recover keys once enough data packets have been captured. Optimizations to the standard attack algorithms make wireless encryption cracking with Airocrack-ng much faster compared to other WEP cracking tools.

- *Airdecap-ng* is used to decrypt encrypted capture files. It can also be used to strip wireless headers from capture files.

Our first command will begin sniffing the wireless packets using the *Airodump-ng* utility. The packets will be captured and written to a file that will later be used to crack the encryption key. From a command prompt, run the following command:

```
airodump-ng -w output -c 6 ath1
```

This command runs the *Airodump-ng* command and sets the capture file to output using the –w switch. Since we know from our Kismet scan the wireless network of interest is on channel 6, we use the –c switch to ensure that *airodump-ng* stays on that channel and captures as much data as possible. Finally, we tell the command to use the interface ath0. The interface may vary, depending on the wireless card you are using.

You should now see the Airodump-ng screen. The screen is broken into two sections: the top section shows the wireless access points; the bottom section shows the wireless clients. Now that we have *Airodump-ng* running, we will look for associated wireless clients. In the top

section, find the BSSID (MAC address) of your target network. Now look in the bottom section to see which clients are associated. We will need to document the BSSID and Station address to perform packet injection.

Injection

Wireless Packet injection allows the hacker to modify packets in the air so the wireless devices are forced to generate traffic that will be captured and used to crack the encryption key. If there is a lot of traffic on the network, the hacker will not need to perform any injections to force traffic to be generated. However, if the hacker is impatient, a quick way to generate traffic is to deauthenticate a client that is already authenticated. This deauthentication forces the client to reauthenticate, generating the handshaking packets that the hacker will use during the cracking phase.

To perform packet injection as part of our penetration test, we are going to use the *aireplay-ng* utility. This utility can perform multiple attack types. We will be testing fake authentication, ARP packet replay, and deauthentication.

First, we will associate the attacking machine with the target network. This will be done using the fake authentication method. To perform fake authentication, we will run the following command.

```
aireplay-ng -1 0 -e TestNet -a 00:0F:B5:29:8C:32 -h 06:18:4D:95:32:61 ath1
```

This command runs the *aireplay-ng* command and sets the attacktype to -1, which is fake authentication. The 0 sets the reassociation timing to 0 seconds. To set the wireless network name, the –e switch is followed by the SSID of the wireless network. Then, the –a switch is followed by the MAC address of the access point and the –h switch is followed by the MAC address of the network card used for the injection. We complete the command by adding the wireless interface name. If the command is successful, you should receive the following response:

```
Sending Authentication Request
Authentication successful
Sending Association Request
Association successful :-)
```

Your wireless network card is now associated with the target access point. The next step is to set up ARP request packet replay. This is the most effective way to generate the traffic needed to crack the encryption key. While the attack retransmits the same ARP packet, the access point responds with new IVs. These packets are the key to determining the encryption key.

We will now set up the ARP request replay using the *aireplay-ng* command. To perform this attack, we open up a new command window and run:

```
aireplay-ng -3 -b 00:0F:B5:29:8C:32 -h 00:13:CE:86:08:A6 ath1
```

This command runs the *aireplay-ng* command using the -3 attack type, standard ARP request replay. The −b switch is followed by the MAC address of the access point, and the −h switch is followed by the MAC address of the associated client. Once we initiate the following deauthentication command, the ARP request replay will start flooding the access point with the retransmitted ARP packets and create the needed IV packets.

To generate the deauthenticate attack, we will again use *aireplay-ng*. Once this process is initiated, we should see a substantial rise in traffic on our airodump-ng screen. To run the deauthenticate command, we open up a new command window and run:

```
aireplay-ng -0 5 -a  00:0F:B5:29:8C:32 -c 00:13:CE:86:08:A6 ath1
```

This command runs the *aireplay-ng* command using the -0 attack which means deauthentication. The next number sets the number of deauthentication packets to 5, setting this number to 0 sends continuous deauthentication packets. The −a switch is followed by the MAC address of the access point and the −c switch is followed by the MAC address of the client you are trying to disassociate. The final option is the wireless interface name.

Now that all the injection commands have been executed. You should see the data column for the wireless network you are testing steadily rise. You should also see that the ARP request replay is reading and retransmitting ARP packets to the access point. 40-bit WEP can be cracked with 300,000 IVs, while 128-bit WEP may require 1.5 million IVs. Once you have enough packets captured, it is time to see if the wireless encryption key is vulnerable to being cracked.

Cracking

Now that we have a capture file with the necessary data, we can test our encryption key to see if it is vulnerable to being cracked. To crack WEP keys, *aircrack-ng* uses various statistical attacks that involve brute forcing the key. Due to the complexity of WPA/WPA2 preshared keys, only a dictionary attack is available.

In a new command window, we will use the *aircrack-ng* command to attempt to crack the wireless encryption key. For a typical WEP attempt, we would use the following command.

```
aircrack-ng -m 00:11:22:33:44:55 -n 64  output.cap
```

This command runs the *aircrack-ng* command using the −m option followed by the MAC address of the access point we are trying to crack. This option is not required but helps focus the attack on our target access point. The −n switch specifies the length of the key. If you do not know the length, try both 64 or 128. Last, we will provide the capture file where the data captured from *airodump-ng* is stored.

If the command is successful, it will display the encryption key of the target network.

Passive and Active Sniffing

If you have discovered the encryption key of the target network, you will be able to associate your computer with the target network. At this point, your network has been compromised and it is a good time to reevaluate your wireless network's security controls. It is quite possible that hackers have already done what you have just done and have been trying to obtain data from your corporate network.

The first reaction most administrators have when they realize their network may be compromised is to check the logs to see if anyone who is not authorized has connected to the network. While this is a good first step when investigating whether you are actively connected, you must remember one thing, wireless data are being transmitted in the air and now that the attacker has the encryption key, they can sniff the network traffic and decrypt it passively. This means you will never see them connect to the network! To demonstrate this, let's take a look at the capture file you saved using *airodump-ng* to use with *aircrack-ng*.

The initial purpose of this file was to be used with *aircrack-ng* to discover the encryption key. Now that we know what the key is, we can use the *airdecap-ng* utility to strip the wireless headers and decrypt any encrypted packets, leaving us with a capture file that can read data from the target network in plain text with any packet analyzer, such as Wireshark.

To run the *airedecap-ng* command, we will open up a new command window and run:

```
airdecap-ng -e TestNet -w 145AA34FA1 output.cap
```

This command runs the *airdecap-ng* command and supplies the following options. The –e switch is followed by the ESSID of the target network. The –w switch is followed by the hexadecimal WEP key. Then the capture file is provided. This will decrypt the capture file and save it to a file name output-dec.cap. If the command is successful, you should see a similar result:

```
Total number of packets read          1658828
Total number of WEP data packets           255816
Total number of WPA data packets            0
Number of plaintext data packets            30
Number of decrypted WEP packets          255816
Number of decrypted WPA packets             0
```

Now you can open up decrypted captured files and read the content of the network traffic. This is a passive method of capturing data because once the encryption key is obtained; the attacker no longer must connect to the network to obtain network data. If the system administrator did not detect the initial packet injection attack on the access point and take appropriate action, the attacker will be able to continue sniffing data undetected until the key is changed.

If an attacker is not concerned with being detected on the network, they can be more aggressive and connect to try and sniff data directly from the wireless connection. While this

technique establishes a direct connection with the target network and can be logged by the access point, unless there is a wireless IDS/IPS in place or constant scanning to determine unauthorized MAC addresses on the network, it will still be difficult to detect.

One of the many dangers associated with active scanning is the hacker's ability to use more complex tools on the internal network to gather additional information. Instead of being able to only read wirelessly transmitted data, tools like Ettercap make it possible to sniff wired network traffic from a wireless connection as long as the computers are on the same subnet.

Damage & Defense…

Ettercap

Ettercap is a multipurpose suite for man-in-the-middle attacks on LAN. It provides the ability to sniff live connections, offers content filtering on-the-fly, and many other features. It supports the active and passive examination of many protocols and includes many features for network and host analysis.

With four modes of operation (IP, MAC, ARP, and public ARP), Ettercap is an extremely flexible utility that can provide a lot of information to an attacker and is difficult to detect. An attacker that uses Ettercap can use it for password collection, OS fingerprinting, ARP poisoning, and character injection.

Logging

Most wireless access points have the ability to log traffic and connections. It is important to consider logging requirements before an incident occurs. Being able to go back to a specific time when an event is thought to have occurred gives the investigator the ability to analyze and determine whether there was indeed a wireless attack on the network.

The logging on most access points does not provide the kind of granularity required for effective logging. Wireless IDS/IPS systems can be set up to monitor and log any suspicious wireless activity using wireless sensors. These sensors detect malformed wireless packets and log the data for forensic analysis later.

Investigating wireless attacks is difficult due to the nature of the technology. This is exactly the reason attackers like to use this method to gain access to corporate networks. The best solution is to configure your wireless network securely to ensure hackers will not be able to gain access easily. If a wireless incident does occur, an investigator can use the same tools the attacker used to determine how the attack was done and decide how much information may have been exposed. Proactively reviewing event logs on servers and network devices is always a good step towards identifying attacks early and handling them appropriately.

Exam Objectives Summary

To investigate attacks against your wireless network, it is important to understand the techniques and methods hackers will use to gain unauthorized access as well as the inherent vulnerabilities in the technology. Understanding the insecurities of WEP versus WPA-PSK, for example, will allow you to direct your investigation appropriately so you can determine the extent of an incident and how much data may have been compromised. Determining the extent of a damage an attack has on a company is difficult with factors such as resolving the vulnerability, legal responsibility, lost intellectual property, and lost revenue due to low consumer confidence all being part of the equation.

Unfortunately, once it is realized that the wireless network has been compromised, the damage may already have been done. The best way to prevent a wireless attack is to ensure the corporate wireless access point, wireless clients, and network configuration are as secure as possible. Using WPA-PSK is a good start, but adding additional security configurations such as MAC filtering, cloaking the SSID, 24/7 rogue access point monitoring, Nmap scans, wireless access point logging, and sound wireless policies are necessary to secure a network from hackers. These techniques by themselves are not going to stop a hacker from attacking your network, but combined they will make the task much more difficult.

Conducting scheduled penetration tests to verify the security of the wireless network are also recommended. Technology changes rapidly, as do the tools that hackers use to exploit it. A wireless network that was safe last year may not be as secure this year. Staying on top of the latest trends in wireless hacking will allow you to implement secure solutions quickly and effectively. For enterprise environments where wireless security is a top priority, a wireless IDS/IPS solution can provide an extra level of security and auditing.

Exam Objectives Fast Track

Basics of Wireless

- ☑ Wireless Access Points (WAPs) connect traditional wired networks to wireless clients. These wireless networks provide ease of access to the network for mobile users, increasing productivity while reducing infrastructure costs.

- ☑ A wireless client associates with a wireless network by connecting to the access point and providing the required encryption data if necessary. Microsoft provides a built-in wireless configuration manager called Windows Wireless Zero Configuration. Wireless device manufacturers typically provide their own wireless client manager with the hardware setup.

☑ Wired Equivalent Privacy (WEP) is an outdated encryption that, due to the ease of cracking the encryption key, is not considered a good method of securing a wireless access point. WPA-PSK is far superior to WEP and provides stronger protection for two reasons: the process used to generate the encryption key is very rigorous, and the rekeying (or key changing) is done very quickly.

☑ MAC filtering limits the allowed associations to the Wireless Access Point to only approved network cards. This provides only limited security benefits since MAC addresses can easily be spoofed.

☑ The SSID, or wireless network name, can be cloaked, which prevents it from being broadcast over the radio frequency. However, most wireless analysis tools are able to determine cloaked SSIDs, given enough time.

Wireless Penetration Testing

☑ Before performing any tests on a production system, ensure that management and the owner of the system have agreed to the penetration tests. A search warrant is required for forensic analysis on any equipment the owner does not authorize you to test.

☑ You can detect wireless access points using Nmap's OS fingerprinting techniques. These scans can be scripted for scheduled coverage of a large network. Nessus, a vulnerability scanner, can also be used to detect wireless access points on the wired network. To do so, you can use plugin #11026, which identifies WAPs by TCP/IP fingerprint, HTTP, FTP, and SNMP responses.

☑ Improperly configured rogue access points can leave your network open to attackers. Wireless IPS/IDS systems can be used to monitor the network and shut down these rogue access points by suppressing the wireless signal or shutting off the port to the switch once a rogue access point is detected.

☑ Wireless packet analyzers such as Kismet and Airodump-ng can be used to detect wireless networks and determine their security. They can also capture wireless network traffic that can be used later for encryption key cracking or viewing plaintext network data.

☑ Wireless packet injection allows attackers to generate traffic that can be used by tools to crack wireless encryption. Wireless cards must support packet injection for it to be successful.

☑ With enough data, WEP keys can be broken using brute force techniques, while WPA-PSK can only be cracked using dictionary attacks. This is why it is so important to use complex encryption keys.

☑ Sniffing wireless network traffic in the air without associating with an access point is called passive sniffing. Active sniffing is done when an attacker connects to an access point, obtains an IP address, and then sniffs traffic on the network.

☑ Investigating wireless attacks is difficult due to the immediate nature of the technology. After an attacker disassociates their connection, if logging is not enabled, forensic analysis of the wireless device after the fact may not be possible.

Exam Objectives Frequently Asked Questions

The following Frequently Asked Questions, answered by the authors of this book, are designed to both measure your understanding of the Exam Objectives presented in this chapter, and to assist you with real-life implementation of these concepts.

Q: Our company is very small. Why would an attacker want to gain access to our network?

A: Most hackers are going to go after easy-to-hack networks and try to gain as much information as possible. The motivation for many black hat hackers is financial gain. If your company uses the Internet to read corporate e-mail, access password-protected Web sites, or conduct B2B or B2C transactions, a hacker may attempt to disrupt the operation. Because one of the easiest ways to gain access to a corporate network is through wireless networks, it is important to make sure your wireless configurations are as secure as possible.

Q: To hack into a wireless network would take a highly experienced hacker and I don't think anyone in my neighborhood would be able to do it.

A: The Internet has made it possible for anyone that is curious to become a viable threat when it comes to hacking, no matter where they live or how much computer knowledge they have. Long gone are the days when a hacker would have to code an application from scratch to exploit vulnerabilities. Now, it is as simple as downloading the application and following instructions. BackTrack is security operating system distribution that provides many of the tools discussed in this book, which is available free of charge. These days, the tools that security professionals use to test systems for vulnerabilities are often the same ones hackers use for malicious intent.

Q: Which encryption should I use to protect my wireless network, WEP or WPA?

A: WEP networks have proven to have weak security and can be broken into extremely quickly. Recently, the Federal Bureau of Investigation demonstrated how to crack WEP—and they did it in three minutes. The use of WEP can create a false sense of security. WPA utilizing a preshared key is far superior to WEP and provides stronger protection for two reasons, the process used to generate the encryption key is very rigorous, and the key changing is done very quickly.

Q: How do I detect if a hacker has associated to my wireless access point?

A: The first step is to look at the management interface and determine if there are any machines that do not look familiar. Most management consoles will provide the client MAC address and computer name. Since this information can be spoofed, it should not be considered 100 percent reliable. Instability in the network may be another indication that an attacker is attempting to capture corporate data. The best solution is to implement an intrusion detection/prevention system. This system would monitor the network and search for suspicious network traffic, providing alerts to security and system administrators when an alarm is raised.

Q: Are wireless networks safe?

A: No network solution is 100 percent safe, but by taking proper precautions and using strong encryption techniques, you will be able to deter the majority of attacks. If wireless security is a top priority, investing in an IDS/IPS system that is designed for wireless networks will provide the highest level of security. Wireless IPS systems can actually intercept and suppress wireless attacks in the air, preventing many of the most common attacks from reaching your access points. They can also detect rogue access points and provide wireless packet forensic analysis.

CHFI

PDA, Blackberry, and iPod Forensics

Exam objectives in this chapter:

- PDA Forensics
- Investigative Methods of PDA Forensics
- PDA Investigative Tips
- Deploying PDA Forensic Tools
- Introduction to the Blackberry
- Operating System of the Blackberry
- Blackberry Operation and Security Capabilities
- Forensic Examination of a Blackberry
- Attacking the Blackberry

- Securing the Blackberry
- iPod Forensics
- Misuse of an iPod
- iPod Investigation
- The iPod and Windows
- The iPod and Linux
- User Accounts
- Deleted Files
- iPod Time Issues
- Registry Key Containing the iPod's USB/Firewire Serial Number
- iPod Tools

Introduction

In this chapter we will discuss the concept of conducting a forensic investigation on data that has been read, stored, or manipulated on some type of mobile device. The techniques for investigating a mobile device are similar to that of the more traditional storage devices; however, there are some notable differences that we need to be aware of while collecting potential evidence.

PDA Background Information

A personal digital assistant (PDA) is a handheld computing device that combines a multitude of functions and features including computing, telephone, fax, and Internet. Additionally, the PDA can and most often contains some form of networking or other form of connectivity capabilities. Today, a PDA is a powerful device that can function as a cellular phone, a fax sender, a Web browser, and a personal organizer. These devices have reached such a level of power and functionality that they are in essence a mini-computer.

Components of a PDA

The PDA device has several components. Our intent here is to discuss some of the more common ones. The first component of the PDA is the microprocessor, which is similar to any other microprocessor except that there is a restriction on its size. Another component of the PDA is some form of input device, such as a touch screen. In addition to these components, an essential component is the operating system that is running the software for the PDA device.

PDA Forensics

As discussed previously, the concept of PDA forensics is very similar to the procedures and methodologies that are used with any form of forensics. When we discuss PDA forensics, there are investigative methods that you should use when performing a forensic investigation of a PDA.

Investigative Methods

There are four main steps when it comes to performing a forensic investigation of a PDA. These four steps are:

1. Examination
2. Identification
3. Collection
4. Documentation

We start off by securing the evidence. It is essential that you follow a process that has been approved by legal counsel to secure the PDA. When you seize the PDA you have to ensure that you take the PDA, the docking cradle, and the external memory cards. This is probably one of the most difficult things to control and requires that you conduct a thorough search for any and all memory cards. With the size of memory cards today, there is an extensive amount of evidence that you would be missing if you missed just one memory card. Once you secure the evidence, the next step is to create an exact image to preserve the crime scene. Once you have acquired the image it is time to examine the evidence. Once you have examined the evidence, you have to present it, which is usually done by compiling an extensive report based on the investigation thus far. It is also your responsibility as the examiner to maintain the evidence, which consists of keeping it in a secure location. You also have to ensure that the PDA remains charged so that the data and information is maintained in a constant state.

Step 1: Examination

In the examination step of PDA forensics, you first need to understand the potential sources of the evidence, which can be the device, the device cradle, the power supply, and any other peripherals or media that the device being examined has came into contact with. In addition to these sources, you should also investigate any device that has synchronized with the PDA you are examining.

Step 2: Identification

In the identification step of PDA forensics, you start the process by identifying the type of device you are investigating. Once you have identified the device, you then have to identify the operating system that the device is using. It is critical to the investigative process that you determine the operating system. Furthermore, once you have identified the operating system, it is important to note that it is possible that the device could be running two operating systems. During the identification process, there are several interfaces that can assist you including the cradle interface, the manufacturer serial number, the cradle type, and the power supply itself.

Step 3: Collection

During this part of the forensic investigation, it is imperative that you collect data and potential evidence from the memory devices that are part of or suspected to be part of the PDA you are investigating. There are a multitude of these types of devices, so we will limit our discussion to just a few, including the SD, the MMC semiconductor cards, the micro-drives, and the universal serial bus (USB) tokens. The SD cards range in size from a few megabytes (MB) to several gigabytes (GB), and the USB tokens can range from a few MBs to multiple GBs. In addition to seizing and collecting the memory devices, you also have to collect the power leads, cables, and any cradles that exist for the PDA. Extending the investigation process further, it is imperative that you collect all of the types of information consisting of both volatile and dynamic infor-

mation. Consequently, it is imperative that you give the volatile information priority while you collect evidence. The reason for giving this information priority is because anything that is classified as volatile information will not survive if the machine is powered off or reset. Once the information has been captured, it is imperative that the PDA be placed into an evidence bag and maintained at stable power support throughout.

Step 4: Documentation

As with any component in the forensic process, it is critical that you maintain your documentation and "chain of custody." As you collect information and potential evidence, you need to record all visible data. Your records must document the case number and the date and time it was collected. Additionally, the entire investigation area needs to be photographed, which includes any devices that can be connected to the PDA or currently are connected to the PDA. Another part of the documentation process is to generate a report that consists of the detailed information that describes the entire forensic process that you are performing. Within this report you need to annotate the state and status of the device in question during your collection process. The final step of the collection process consists of accumulating all of the information and storing it in a secure and safe location.

PDA Investigative Tips

When it comes to the PDA device, there are several things you need to consider while carrying out an investigation. These devices can be managed and maintained at all times. Adding further complication is the fact that with PDA devices, a suspect can have immediate access 24 hours a day, 7 days a week. Another thing that makes your job as an investigator more challenging, is that PDAs are immediate boot cycle devices. Accordingly, it is important to remember these devices typically contain a plethora of information and are a vault of evidence for the forensic examiner.

Device Switched On

When you are beginning your investigation process, and discover that the PDA that you want to process for evidence is in the "on" mode, it is imperative that you act immediately and get power to the PDA, so that it will not lose the volatile information that could quite possibly be essential to your evidence collection process.

Device Switched Off

If the device is in the "off" state, you should leave the device in this state and then switch the device on and take a picture of it. Additionally, you need to note and record the current battery charge.

Device in Its Cradle

Avoid any further communication activities with the device and remove any connections from the PC device. It is important to note that there is a possibility that a sophisticated suspect might have a "tripwire" device, and once you disconnect the PC this could activate the device, which in turn could run a script that might erase potential evidence. Despite this possibility, you have to disconnect the device to continue the investigation.

Device Not in Its Cradle

If the device is not in the cradle, your investigative requirements are made much simpler, because there is no danger of a "tripwire" being triggered. With the device being out of its cradle, you simply seize the cradle and any cords associated with it.

Wireless Connection

Avoid any further communication activities if possible. Eliminate any wireless activity by placing the device into an envelope that can isolate it. This envelope also needs to provide anti-static protection so that the device is not damaged.

Expansion Card in Slot

Do not initiate any contact that requires taking components off of the device, or that requires you to open the device in any way. This includes any and all peripheral devices and/or media types of cards.

Expansion Sleeve Removed

The first thing to accomplish is to seize the sleeve itself, and also seize any and all related peripherals and media cards.

Tools of the Trade...

Impact of Mishandling PDA Devices

While conducting an investigation of a potential crime scene, our team discovered a sticky note with a password written on it. The team member entered the password, but it did not work, so he continued to try to get access, but after the tenth attempt the Blackberry did a complete data wipe, and whatever information was on that device was lost. This is because there is software that will log the attempts at entry and will do a complete wipe after a certain amount of invalid login attempts.

Deploying PDA Forensic Tools

When you are conducting a forensic investigation, there is no shortage of tools available. However, when investigating handheld or PDA devices, there are not as many tools as a typical forensic investigator has.

PDA Secure

The first tool to discuss is the PDA Secure tool. This tool offers enhanced password protection, along with encryption, device locking, and data wiping. The PDA Secure tool allows administrators greater control over how handheld devices are used on networks. Additionally, it allows you to set a time and date range to monitor information such as network login traffic, infrared transmissions, and any applications being used.

PDA Seizure

PDA Seizure is a comprehensive tool that assists in seizing the PDA. It allows the data to be acquired, viewed, and reported on. PDA Seizure works within a Windows environment and can extract the random access memory (RAM) and read only memory (ROM). It has an easy-to-use graphical user interface (GUI), and includes the tools that are needed to investigate the files that are contained within the PDA.

PDA Seizure provides multi-platform support, where the forensic examiner can acquire and examine information on PDAs for both the Pocket PC and Palm operating system (OS) platforms. The PDA Seizure tool has a significant amount of features, including forensic imaging tools, searches on data within acquired files, hashing for integrity protection of acquired files, and book-marking capability to assist the examiner in the organization of information.

EnCase

EnCase is one of the most popular commercial forensic tools available, and can be used to acquire information and evidence from a PDA. The EnCase tool can acquire images, and also consists of tools that allow you to conduct complex investigations efficiently and accurately.

Introduction to the Blackberry

The Blackberry is also known as a RIM device and is equipped with the RIM software implementation of proprietary wireless-oriented protocols. Furthermore, the device is supported by the RIM Blackberry Message Center. The Blackberry shares similarities with the PDA devices discussed earlier; however, it is always on and participating in some form of wireless push technology. As a result of this, the Blackberry does not require some form of desktop synchronization like the PDA does. This unique component of the Blackberry adds a different dimension

to the process of forensic examination, and in essence this portability can be the examiners greatest ally.

Operating System of the Blackberry

The current version of the Blackberry OS has numerous capabilities and features, including over-the-air activation, the ability to synchronize contacts and appointments with Microsoft Outlook, a password keeper program to store sensitive information, and the ability to customize your Blackberry display data.

Blackberry Operation and Security

The Blackberry device has an integrated wireless modem, which allows it to communicate over the BellSouth Intelligent Wireless Network. The Blackberry uses the Blackberry Serial Protocol, which is used to backup, restore, and synchronize the data that is communicated between the Blackberry handheld unit and the desktop software. This protocol comprises simple packets and single byte return codes. The device uses a strong encryption scheme that safeguards confidentiality and authenticity of data. It keeps data encrypted while in transit between the enterprise server and the device itself.

Wireless Security

The Blackberry has a couple of transport encryption options, which are the Triple Data Encryption Standard (DES) and the Advanced Encryption Standard (AES). Those who want to implement the most secure method will elect to encrypt with the AES algorithm. The Blackberry has another feature that is referred to as the Password Keeper, which offers the capability of securely storing password entries on the devices, which could consist of banking passwords, PINs, and so on. This important information is protected by AES encryption.

Security for Stored Data

There are several capabilities available on the Blackberry when it comes to securing the data that is stored there. The first option we will discuss is the capability to make password authentication mandatory through the customizable Information Technology (IT) policies on the Blackberry Enterprise Server. An additional method of protection from unauthorized parties is the fact that there is no staging of data between the server and the Blackberry where data is decrypted.

Forensic Examination of a Blackberry

Since the Blackberry is an always-on, push messaging device, information can be pushed to it at any time. It is important to note that the information that is pushed has the potential of

overwriting any data that was previously deleted. The problem is compounded by the fact that, without warning, there are a multitude of applications that may receive information and make the attempts by the forensic investigator to recover information and an unaltered file system much more difficult. The first step in preserving the information is to eliminate the ability of the device to receive this data push. If possible, you can turn the radio off, or a better solution is to take the device to an area where the signal cannot be received, such as putting the device inside of a filing cabinet drawer. One might think, "I'll just turn it off." This would be a serious mistake! The Blackberry is not really "off" unless power is removed for an extended period, or the unit is placed in storage mode. Furthermore, once the unit is powered back on, any items that were in the queue waiting to be pushed to the device could possibly be pushed before you could stop them. As mentioned previously, it is quite possible that a change to state such as a power-off of the Blackberry could result in a program being run on the unit that will allow the device to accept remote commands via e-mail.

Acquisition of Information Considerations

The considerations for the Blackberry are similar in some ways to the PDA devices, but there are some differences. Let's look at the considerations you have to make when acquiring evidence from the Blackberry.

Device is in the "Off" State

If the unit is off at the time of acquisition, the investigator needs to take it to a shielded location before attempting to switch it on. If a shielded location is not readily available, you might have success using a safe or other room that can block the signal well enough to prevent the data push. One thing to consider is having a unit available that you can use to walk the network and look for weak coverage areas to use.

Device is in the "On" State

If the device you are examining is in the "on" state, then as outlined and detailed above, you need to take the device to a secure location and disable or turn off the radio before beginning the examination.

Password Protected

One thing to consider when it comes to password protection is the fact that the password itself is not stored on the device. The only thing that is stored on the device is a hashing of the plain text password. This storage is similar to the storage used by the majority of operating systems.

Evidence Collection

To collect evidence from the Blackberry you have to violate the traditional forensic methods by requiring the investigator to record logs kept on the unit that will be wiped after an image is taken. There are several different log files that you want to collect evidence from, including:

- **Radio Status** This log lets you enumerate the state of the device's radio functions.
- **Roam and Radio** This log has a buffer of up to 16 entries, records information concerning the tower, channel and so on, and will not survive a reset.
- **Transmit/Receive** This log records gateway information and the type and size of data transmitted.
- **Profile String** This log contains the negotiation with the last utilized radio tower.

Once the log information is extracted and enumerated, the image will be taken. If you do not require or need the log information, the image can be acquired immediately.

Unit Control Functions

The logs are reviewed by using the unit control functions. The first function is the Mobitex2 Radio Status, which provides information on the Radio Status, Roam and Radio Transmit, or Receive and Profile String. The second control function is the Device Status, which provides information on memory allocation, port status, file system allocation, and central processing unit (CPU) WatchPuppy. The third control function is the Battery Status, which provides information on the battery type, load, status, and temperature. The last control function we will discuss is the Free Mem, which provides information on memory allocation, Common Port File System, WatchPuppy, OTA status, Halt, and Reset.

Imaging and Profiling

When you are conducting a forensic examination of a Blackberry, you need to conduct imaging and profiling. This is accomplished by extracting the logs from a developed image and acquiring an image of a bit-by-bit backup using the Blackberry Software Development Kit (SDK). The SDK is available from www.blackberry.com and is essential for the forensic examiner when investigating a Blackberry. The SDK utility dumps the contents of the Flash RAM into a file. Once the Flash RAM is dumped, it can be examined and reviewed using traditional methods with your favorite hex editor or other tool. In addition to reviewing the evidence with traditional methods, you can use the Simulator from the SDK to match the network and model of the investigated unit.

Attacking the Blackberry

There are several tools and methods available that allow you to attack a Blackberry, The first tool is the Blackberry Attack Toolkit, which along with the BBProxy software can be used to exploit Web site vulnerabilities. The second tool is the Attack Vector, which links and tricks users by downloading malicious software to the Blackberry. The last method we will discuss is the method of hijacks (or blackjacks). As the name implies, this allows someone to hijack a legal user's Blackberry and replace them on the network with potentially harmful devices.

Securing the Blackberry

There are several things you can do to secure the information on a Blackberry. The first thing you can do is clean the Blackberry memory, and protect stored messages on the messaging server. You can encrypt the application password as well as the storage of it on the Blackberry. Furthermore, you can protect storage of user data on a locked Blackberry by limiting the password authentication attempts. It is possible to set a maximum of 10 attempts to gain access to the device. Additionally, you can use AES technology to secure the storage of the password keeper and password entries on the Blackberry.

Information Hiding in a Blackberry

There are several places where you can hide information in a Blackberry. You can create hidden databases and hide information in partition gaps. Data can also be hidden in the gap between the OS/application and file partitions.

Blackberry Signing Authority Tool

The Signing Authority tool helps developers' protect data and intellectual property, and enables them to handle access to their sensitive Application Program Interfaces (APIs). The tool provides this protection by using public and private signature keys. It does this by using asymmetric cryptography to validate the authenticity of the request. Furthermore, the signing tool allows developers to exchange API information in a secure manner and environment.

iPod Forensics

Apple computers produce three separate digital media players all bearing the iPod brand. Whether the original iPod, the iPod Nano, or the iPod shuffle, all of these devices have the capability not only to play music, but also to act as a storage device. The capability to store digital data coupled with the iPod's popularity will result in the forensic analysis of these devices becoming more common.

Consequently, the National Institute of Standards and Technology (NIST) have developed guidelines for PDA forensics (Jansen & Ayers, 2004) to address this issue. The secret is to treat the iPod as you would treat any other suspect hard drive being analyzed. Treat it with the respect and care it deserves and remember that it is evidence.

The iPod

The Apple iPod family currently comprises five generations of devices for the primary units and two generations of ancillary models. These are listed below.

- **First Generation iPod** October 2001 saw the first release of the Apple iPod. This device connected using a FireWire jack and introduced the Apple physical scroll wheel. This device used the original form factor and is the classic iPod design.

- **Second Generation iPod** Implemented the large hard drive (10 GB and 20 GB), introduced the touch sensitive wheel, and put a cover on the FireWire port, but was otherwise physically the same as the first generation iPod.

- **Third Generation iPod** The third generation introduced a central row of touch sensitive buttons and a dock connector port. The primary connection was still FireWire, but USB was introduced for data syncing.

- **Fourth Generation iPod** The fourth generation of the iPod introduced the photo viewer. The color display was introduced at this stage. Either FireWire or USB could be used.

- **Fifth Generation iPod** The next generation introduced a video function and lyrics support. This version has no AC adapter universal block or A/V included, and must be purchased separately. The latest edition (generation 5.5) features a brighter display, the ability to search, and the longer video battery. Fifth generation iPods use only USB with FireWire connections relegated to charging only.

The ancillary iPods include the following models:

- **iPod Mini** The iPod Mini is a slimmer version of its original cousin. These devices use either USB or FireWire connections using either a 4 or 6 GB hard drive. This device implements a scroll wheel with integrated buttons. There are two generations of iPod Minis. iPod Mini connections are made using either USB or FireWire.

- **iPod Nano** The iPod Nano implements a flash memory storage system. These devices are otherwise similar to the fifth generation iPod in many respects. The iPod Nano uses USB connections with FireWire for charging only.

- **iPod Shuffle** There are two generations of the iPod Shuffle. All these devices implement flash memory instead of hard drive storage. The iPod Shuffle uses USB connections and the later models implement USB through the docking function alone.

iPod Features

The iPod supports a variety of file formats including Protected AAC, AIFF, MP3, WAV, M4A/AAC LC, and Apple Lossless audio file formats. From the introduction of the fifth-generation iPod, a number of video formats are also supported, including the .m4v and .mp4 MPEG-4 (H.264/MPEG-4 AVC) file formats. Additionally, iTunes has the capability to translate Windows WMA-formatted files to an iPod format as long as they are not copy protected.

The iPod is not currently able to play copy protected WMA files. Additionally, the iPod is unable to play MIDI, Ogg Vorbis, and FLAC multimedia formats. It is, however, possible to translate MIDI files to another format using iTunes. iTunes will not transfer songs from the iPod to a computer because of perceived copyright and other legal issues. A number of third-party products have been created to circumvent the iPod's copy protection.

Current iPods have the inclusion of a limited PDA functionality. Macintosh users have been altered synchronize schedules and contacts in their address book and iCal using iSync. From the release of iTunes version 5.0, Apple has integrated the ability to synchronize contacts and schedules from iTunes to the iPod. Contact maintained in either Microsoft Outlook or Outlook Express may be synchronized with the iPod in this manner. Mozilla calendar files use the same format as the iPod. So although there is no automated method to synchronize Mozilla data, these files can be copied to the iPod manually.

With this functionality, however, the inability to add or update entries on the iPod itself limits the functionality of the iPod as a PDA. From a forensic perspective, this does not diminish the ability to capture data (including calendar entries and schedules) from the device.

Damage & Defense…

Mac vs. Windows

The debate comparing Windows to Macintosh has become something of a holy war. For the most part, it comes down to personal preference. In the case of an analysis of the iPod, the Mac is definitely preferred over Windows. This is not a comparison of the OSes, but rather relates to the interaction of the iPod and the host machine.

Simply put, Apple HFS+ is superior to Windows FAT 32 from the perspective of a forensic analysis. When iPod is initially connected to a Mac, it is formatted using Apple HFS+. When it is initialized using a Windows machine, it is formatted with FAT 32. Unfortunately, the iPod doesn't come configured to support NTFS.

The Apple HFS+ format provides more detailed meta-data which supplies the forensic analyst with far greater detail than is supplied by a FAT 32 format. So it is a question of whether the Mac is better than Windows or vice versa, simply that an iPod connected to a Mac supplies more meta-data for analysis.

The iPod as Operating System

The iPod can run as a small portable computer system. iPodLinux is a μClinux-based Linux distribution (see http://ipodlinux.org/Main_Page for details). iPodLinux is a specifically designed

kernel capable of running on a number of the iPod devices. Wikipedia (http://en.wikipedia.org/wiki/IPodLinux) details a list of compatible devices and known issues.

One of the primary components of iPodLinux is podzilla and podzilla 2. The podzilla applications provide iPodLinux with an iPod like interface, video playback with sound, and the support for a large number of music file extensions. Using iPodLinux, the iPod can play AAC, MP3 and basic OGG sound file formats. Depending on the hardware capability of the specific iPod, the audio recording capabilities under iPodLinux are said to be at a much higher quality than Apple's firmware.

IPodLinux also supports the ability to play a number of games such as Doom and Doom II and many games for the Nintendo Game Boy (with the appropriate add-on software such as iBoy).

uClinux stands for "MicroController Linux," and is pronounced "you-see-Linux." uClinux supports up to the version 2.6 kernel. uClinux (http://uclinux.org/) has the support of a number of compiler programs such as the standard C++ library, which runs correctly under podzilla. As such, an attacker could create and compile middleware or some other code of interest to the forensic analyst, which can be stored on the iPod.

Drive Formats – Apple HFS+ or FAT32

The drive format used by the iPod hard drive is dependent on the computer system to which the iPod is initially synchronized. If the iPod is initially synchronized with a Mac machine, it will be formatted using the Apple HFS+ file system. If the iPod is initially connected to a Windows host, the iPod drive will be formatted with the FAT32 file system.

When conducting a forensic analysis of the iPod, it is important to know which type of system the iPod has been synchronized with. This information also provides the analyst with some background information as to the use and history of the device. Knowledge of the format used will generally make it easier to match the iPod device to the host with which it has been synchronizing. It is important to remember that just because the output has initially synchronized with either a Windows or Mac host, it may also have been used on other machines.

The iPod writes data from the beginning to the end of the drive before returning to the beginning. This is a valuable feature for the forensic analyst, as the use of this wear-levelling technique makes the overwriting of files less likely.

Being that the FAT32 file system does not maintain records of file ownership, the HFS+ file system (which maintains ownership metadata) is the preferred format from a forensic perspective. Unfortunately, the HFS+ file system is somewhat less common than the FAT32 file system.

The iPod System Partition

The System Partitions of either the Windows or Macintosh formatted iPod demonstrate that there is no user-identifiable data stored in this partition. The data contained in this partition is associated with the running of the iPod and includes:

- The iPod embedded Operating System.

- The images used during the operation of the device such as the Apple logo and the "Do Not Disconnect" screen image.

- The system fonts used for the display of the text on the device.

- Games and other applications copied to the device

Where iPodLinux has been installed, user data may exist in the system partition. Installing iPodLinux will change the hash value for the System Partition, because iPodLinux modifies the boot loader in the System Partition. The boot loader allows the iPod user to select either the official Apple embedded operating system or the iPodLinux operating system. The system files for iPodLinux are maintained in the iPod Data Partition. However, the changes to the boot loader require the System Partition to be modified by changing the hash value of the system partition.

Notes from the Underground…

Hiding the Hidden Functions

With iPodLinux, it is possible to create a dual-booted iPod that runs both the standard embedded Apple operating system and Linux. A clever attacker could partition their iPod so that the Linux partition is hidden when connected, using the default embedded system. In this manner, they could create a device that on a basic inspection would appear as an iPod with nothing to hide.

The Linux partition could be configured to be visible when booted into iPodLinux mode. A clever attacker could use this partition to smuggle data into and out of an organization, or even introduce code into a secured system. A preliminary investigation and search of the device would find only the "clean" iPod partition. Most people investigating iPod would not expect a separate Linux partition and therefore, it would be common for this to go unnoticed.

Application Formats

The standard vCard file format is used by the iPod to store contact information (see Figure 12.1).

Figure 12.1 The Standard vCard Format Used for Storing Contact Information in an iPod

vCard	
File extension:	.vcf, .vcard
MIME type:	text/directory text/x-vcard
Type code:	vCrd
Uniform Type Identifier:	public.vcard
Developed by:	Internet Mail Consortium
Type of format:	Electronic business card
Container for:	Contact information

Calendar entries are stored in the iPod using the standard vCalendar/iCalendar format (see Figure 12.2).

Figure 12.2 The vCalendar/iCalendar Format for Storing Calendar Entries in an iPod

iCalendar	
File extension:	.ical .icalendar
Type of format:	Calendar data exchange
Standard(s):	RFC 2445

Music and other file formats are stored on a variety of locations within the iPod. Accessories exist that allow the iPod to be used for a variety of functions. Applications and accessories may be loaded using either the native iPod operating system or iPodLinux. These applications allow for the storage of a variety of files including voice recordings, digital camera photo storage, and electronic games.

These files can be easily found by searching the drive for the text strings *BEGIN:VCARD* and *BEGIN:VCALENDAR*. This entry indicates the beginning of the respected file types. The data remains after the entries are deleted.

Misuse of an iPod

Like any other digital storage device, the iPod may hold incriminating evidence. In its native format, the iPod may contain calendar entries related to a crime or other event of interest. Additionally, contact information stored on the device may be relevant to an investigation. The iPod is also capable of creating voice recordings. As such, recordings of meetings may be recovered. Coupled with photographs or other substantiation, the iPod could be a rich source of evidence to the investigator.

With its large hard drive, the iPod is the ideal storage location for music that violates copyright, and with the newer devices, pornographic pictures.

iPod Investigation

When an iPod is found at a crime scene, the first respondent should wait for the advice of a forensic specialist. This is essential to ensure that the site of the evidence is documented correctly. Either explicitly document the location of the iPod and anything around it, or preferably, photograph the site. Leave the device in its current state until it is thoroughly investigated. It is possible that it could be booby-trapped with a delete command or wipe function. This is particularly relevant when the device has been configured with iPodLinux. There are tools under iPodLinux that can be set to wipe the hard drive of the iPod if it is disconnected from the charger or computer without a special code being entered.

Note the state of the iPod. If it is connected to another system, check whether it is mounted. If it is, the screen of the iPod will display a message saying "Do Not Disconnect." In this case, it is necessary to unmount the device prior to disconnecting the computer. On a Mac, this may be achieved by dragging the icon of the iPod to the trash can on the Mac desktop. Note the name of the iPod as it is displayed on the desktop before unmounting it.

Simply disconnecting or unplugging the computer could damage disk sectors on the iPod. For this reason, this should be avoided. If the iPod is connected to a Windows machine, it may be mounted by clicking the "Unplug or eject hardware" icon generally located on the task bar on the bottom right of the screen. On a Windows machine, the chances of the corruption resulting from disconnecting the iPod are less than on a Mac.

When collecting the iPod, specify the connections and cabling as well as all the details of the machine connected to it. Ensure that this information is kept with the device. The iPod should be stored like a hard drive, such as in an antistatic bag in an environment where both temperature and humidity are controlled. It should also not be exposed to excessive vibration. Never store the iPod near a magnetic source such as a speaker. It is important to maintain a strong chain of custody throughout the process.

The iPod is unlike some other embedded devices, in that it does not need to be connected to a power supply while in storage. If the battery drains over time, the information will not be lost from the hard drive. With hard drive models, it may be more effective to extract the hard

drive from the iPod for processing. This will allow the use of an external hardware write blocker. The difficulty is that imaging the hard drive correctly requires both a high level of technical skill and specialized hardware.

An iPod stores the name of the computer that it initialized with on the drive. This information may be used to link the device to other computers and consequently to suspects.

Although it is recommended that the iPod be imaged before doing any other tests, it is possible to determine the format of the drive from the iPod itself. This is achieved by selecting "Settings >", "About >". If the iPod is formatted for a Windows system, scrolling down in the "About" display will state "Format: Windows" towards the lower section of the screen. If this is not displayed, it is likely that the device has been formatted using the HFS+ format and that the iPod was initially connected to a Mac.

Timeline Generation

The iPod is designed to only be linked to one system at a time. As a result, a series of likely connection times to a system can be established. The identified times associated with connection events may also be discovered on the linked system. The times will reflect the system time of the linked system (not that as displayed on the iPod).

Time entries of primary concern to the forensic analyst may be found in the following files:

- **\iPod_Control\Device\SysInfo** The modified time of the file records when the iPod was last restored.

- **\iPod_Control\iTunes\iTunesControl** The creation time of the file records when the iPod was initialized using iTunes.

- **\iPod_Control\iTunes\DeviceInfo** The modified time of the file records when the iPod was last connected to iTunes.

- **All music files located under \iPod_Control\Music** The creation times of the files records when these files were copied from the linked system to the iPod. The modification times for these files provides further evidence linking the iPod and the Windows system and helps to create a timeline of actions/activity.

These times provide evidence of connection times to the linked system. If the Windows host is available, it may be possible to correlate these times to events on this computer.

Head of the Class....

Have You Captured All the Data?

Always check the size of the iPod's physical disk against the size of the partition. As an example, it is possible that a clever suspect could re-partition their iPod making it appear smaller than it actually is. For instance, an 80GB iPod could be formatted to appear to be a 60GB device. This would leave 20GB worth of data available. Either this hidden section of the disk could be formatted using Ext2 or another format not natively available to a Windows host, or data could be copied to the raw partition.

Using a tool such as DD, it is possible to stream data to the physical partition. In this manner, it would be possible to hide a small disk image on the physical drive. This image would be invisible to any normal scan, as no file partition would have ever been created in the disk MFT. However, an analysis of the physical disk would reveal this data.

For this reason the forensic analyst must never assume everything is at face value. Always check and ensure that everything is as it seems.

Lab Analysis

When analysing the iPod, it is important to be familiar with the tools used in the analysis. A variety of tools such as Access Data's Forensic Tool Kit (FTK), the Sleuthkit/Autopsy browser, Blackbag Technologies' Macintosh Forensic Software (MFS), or Encase forensic edition are more than adequate for this task. It must be noted, however, that the tool must be matched to the device. For instance, Blackbag MFS is designed exclusively for the Mac environment, and the Sleuthkit/Autopsy browser requires special consideration to work with the Apple file system.

It is also necessary to ensure that the necessary connectors are in place. Depending on the type of iPod, either FireWire or USB connections may be required. Ideally, the forensic analyst will disassemble the iPod and remove the hard drive for analysis. Disassembly allows for the use of a hardware write blocker.

It is generally considered best practice to disassemble the device. By activating the device, it is possible to either alter the drive thus damaging the evidence, or to set off a booby trap. It is not difficult to configure a wipe program to run on the system boot-up using iPodLinux. Such a tool could destroy valuable evidence before the forensic investigator could get to it.

Remove Device from Packaging

When receiving an iPod for forensic imaging is important to document every step. First, remove the iPod from the packaging. Carefully note the state of the machine, the model, and the interfaces. Photograph and document everything to ensure the chain of custody records are complete.

Depending on the actions that the investigator intends to take there are two possible courses:

- Work on the iPod as is (not recommended for hard drive models), or
- Disassemble the device and extract the hard drive.

It is always possible to reassemble the device after the drive has been imaged. For this reason, it is better to duplicate the hard drive first. This is a little more difficult in the non-hard drive models such as the iPod Nano, in which case it may be more practical to copy the device when assembled.

When working on an assembled device (including when the device has already been imaged and reassembled) the following steps are recommended:

1. Ensure that the battery is charged. Leave the iPod on the charger until the battery is fully charged.
2. Turn on the iPod.
3. Note any device settings and document them.
4. Based on whether the iPod has been connected to a Windows or Mac host, the subsequent stages will differ.

Exam Warning

It is important to remember that the iPod is in effect an external storage device. Although it has extra functionality (such as a limited PDA function) than a simple external hard drive, it does have the capability to act as a hard drive. Everything that applies to the forensic analysis of a hard drive also applies to an iPod.

The iPod Restore Process

The iPod Restore Process does not clear the hard drive of the iPod. Using a restore process copies new data to the iPod, which makes it appear as if it was erased and reloaded. However, only the file pointers are erased. Unless data was specifically overwritten by the restore process, it will still be available for recovery.

The Microsoft restore process is detailed in the following stages:

1. An unformatted, corrupted, or Mac HFS+-formatted iPod is connected to the Windows computer and Windows automatically loads the drivers.
2. The iPod Updater software loads and then prompts the user to format the iPod. On selecting "Restore" the following occurs:
 a. New Partition tables are written to the iPod hard drive.

b. A replacement System Partition is created on the iPod and loaded with required data.

c. A new Data Partition and File Allocation Table for the FAT32 Data Partition is created.

d. \iPod_Control and \iPod_Control\Device directories are created on the iPod hard drive.

e. The \iPod_Control\Device\Preferences file is created containing binary data.

f. · The \iPod_Control\Device\SysInfo file is created. This file contains technical data about the iPod in text format.

When the iPod is connected to the Power Adapter the operating memory is reloaded.

1. The iPod is now re-connected to the host system and either iTunes automatically loads, or it is manually run.

2. The iTunes iPod Setup Assistant will prompt the user allowing them to set the name on the iPod. If a name is set and "Next" is selected, then the name will be entered in the DeviceInfo file. If cancel is selected, the iPod Setup Assistant will then set the device name to the default, "IPOD." The file will thus contain either the name entered by the user or "IPOD." If the name is stored, it is recorded with the username and computer name used in configuring the iPod within iTunes. The following procedure then occurs:

a. The \iPod_Control\iTunes directory is made and the files DeviceInfo, iTunesControl, iTunesEQPresets, iTunesPrefs, and winPrefs are produced in this directory.

b. The \iPod_Control\Music directory is created with subdirectories named sequentially from F00 through to F49.

These entries are reflected in the \Windows\setupapi.log file on the Windows host used to configure the iPod, with a second entry from the iPodService.exe program, which also records the USB serial number of the iPod. The creation time of the \iPod_Control\iTunes\DeviceInfo on the iPod reflects the time value in the \Windows\setupapi.log file on the Windows host used to configure the iPod.

EXERCISE 12.1

ENCASE AND THE IPOD

Use the EnCase program with an iPod:

1. Install EnCase Academic Edition.

2. Connect the iPod to your computer. It is always best to ensure that you have configured read-only mode within Windows XP (SP2) by changing the registry key: *HKEY_LOCAL_MACHINE\System\CurrentControlset\Control\StorageDevicePolicies* to the hex value of 0x00000001 and restarting the computer.

3. Take an image of the iPod drive.

4. Explore various features of this program based on the EnCase information in the courseware.

The iPod and Windows

It is possible to set iPod to read-only mode within Windows XP (SP2) by changing the registry key: *HKEY_LOCAL_MACHINE\System\CurrentControlset\Control\StorageDevicePolicies*.

Setting this key to the hex value of 0x00000001 and restarting the computer will stop write access to any USB storage devices, effectively rendering them as read only. Setting the value to 0x00000000 and restarting the computer enables write access (Andersen & Abella 2004).

The Registry

The Windows registry contains significant amounts of information for the forensic analyst. Of primary concern in investigating iPods are:

- The keys created by the connection of the iPod to the Windows computer
- The last write times indicating the last time the registry keys were changed

An iPod creates a series of registry keys when it is connected to the Windows computer. These can be found under *HKEY_LOCAL_MACHINE\SYSTEM\CurrentControlSet\Enum\USBSTOR* in the registry. Located under USBSTOR will be found a key that identifies a disk device presenting the vendor identifier "Apple," the product identifier "iPod," and a revision code. This information can be used to match the host computer and the iPod being investigated.

The last write time for this key indicates the first time that the iPod connected to the Windows host. Under this in the registry, is a further key corresponding to the serial number of the iPod USB connection, followed by "&0." This value will match the value of FirewireGuid on the iPod contained in the *\iPod_Control\Device\SysInfo* file. The last write time associated with this key is the last time that the iPod connected to the Windows host.

EXAM WARNING

Remember that the iPod does not update file times and that these will reflect the create and modify timestamps of the computer to which the iPod is paired.

setupapi.log

The Windows file, *setupapi.log* (in the Windows installation directory), records all driver installations after the system has booted. The first time that an iPod is connected to a Windows system, the connection event will be recorded in this file. The information in this file will match the last write times of a series of registry keys related to the iPod.

This file is also useful in reconstructing the sequence of connection events of the iPod and the host system as it lists the driver installations. If iTunes is also installed, each occasion that an iPod connection occurs after boot will be recorded. However, if iTunes is not installed, then only the driver installation will be recorded. Also, if the iPod has been connected to the host prior to its being booted, the drivers will load during boot-up and will not be recorded even if iTunes is installed. In any event, this file provides a means to reconstruct events that have occurred on the host and also associates a particular iPod with a particular computer at a given time.

The iPod and Linux

The following procedure may be used to mount the iPod under Linux (Ubuntu used for this example):

1. Disable auto-mounting of removable media devices by selecting the **System** menu from the top of the screen, then **Preferences**, then **Removable Drives and Media**.

2. When the next window opens up click to remove the check marks by each item then select **OK**.

3. Locate the iPod within the Linux device tree as follows:

 a. Right-click in a clear area of the Linux desktop to open up a menu and select **Open New Terminal**.

 b. Enter **ls /dev/sd*** to list of all the SCSI drives on the system.

 c. Connect the iPod to the computer.

 d. Wait 20 seconds for the computer to recognize the iPod.

e. Retype **ls /dev/sd*** to get an updated list of all Small Computer System Interface (SCSI) drives on the system, and note the new listings that belong to the iPod.

4. Depending on the application, you can now mount the iPod in read-only mode.

NOTE

The Apple file system is required to be loaded into the Linux kernel in order to mount an iPod initialized using a Mac.

User Accounts

When an iPod has been set up using iTunes, a file \iPod_Control\iTunes\DeviceInfo is created which contains the user name and computer information. This information may be used to identify the user and computer that initialized the iPod. If this file contains the word "IPOD," the software was restored to the iPod without having been connected to iTunes.

Deleted Files

The iPod deletes file pointers rather than actually erasing the file. Coupled with the iPod's sequential file writing technique that starts from the beginning of the drive and adds data to the end before returning to the beginning, recovery on an iPod can be a simple process.

iPod Time Issues

The manner in which the device records time is one of the most crucial aspects of any digital forensic analysis. To be able to link the deletion, access, or alteration of the file to a particular user is necessary to be able to determine the time when the event occurred. The iPod has an internal clock, but unfortunately, the standard embedded operating system does not update file times.

On iPodLinux, however, the system clock updates file access times. It is important to remember this differentiation in times. The native iPod operating system will record the time it is associated with the computer it is connecting to. Where an alternative operating system such as iPodLinux is involved, however, the time will be set through the iPod's internal clock.

TEST DAY TIP

It is important to remember that the file create and modify times as they appear on the iPod reflect the timestamp associated with the pared computer. Although the iPod has an internal clock, it does not use this to update or modify the timestamps associated with a file that it stores. This can be useful in proving that a particular iPod was connected to a host machine.

Registry Key Containing the iPod's USB/Firewire Serial Number

The \iPod_Control\Device\SysInfo file is created on the iPod when system software is restored or the iPod is initialized. This file contains valuable data about the iPod. Another significant file, \iPod_Control\iTunes\DeviceInfo, is created after iTunes has linked the iPod with a computer. The name of the user and computer involved in linking the iPod and iTunes will be stored in this file.

Where iTunes is running on Windows, a record will be created in both the registry and *setupapi.log* file with a reference to the USB/Firewire serial number presented in the *SysInfo* file on the iPod.

iPod Tools

In addition to the standard drive imaging tools, several products specifically designed for use with the iPod have been produced. Two of the more common tools include "Music Recovery" from DiskInternals and "Recover My iPod" by GetData.

DiskInternals Music Recovery

Music Recovery from DiskInternals is designed to recover any type of music files from a hard drive, iPod, USB-flash drive, or CD/DVD. It is available in shareware format from www.diskinternals.com/music-recovery/. Music Recovery comes with an integrated media player to preview the files prior to recovery. DiskInternals provides native support for the iPod, but does not run on Mac or Linux.

The software works to recover lost files and data from damaged disks and inaccessible drives, and also works with corrupt or damaged partition tables. Although Music Recovery only runs on Windows hosts, it has support for several file systems including:

- NTFS 4 and 5,

- Linux Ext2 and Ext3,

- MacOs and Apple HFS

- Iso9660

- UDF

Recover My iPod

"Recover My iPod" allows the user to recover lost or deleted music, video, and photos including .m4a, .mp3, .mov, quicktime, and jpeg file formats. The product is available from GetData at www.recovermyipod.com/. The software supports all versions of the iPod including the iPod, iPod shuffle, iPod Mini, and iPod Nano. The product recovers data after an iPod Reset or Restore. It is important to remember that Recover My iPod will not run on a Mac.

This software will recover data and files from the iPod even when a "Drive Not Formatted" message appears, or if the iPod is not recognized by the computer. In this case, it is necessary to connect to the "Physical Drive." Although not as effective as a hardware write blocker, "Recover My iPod" mounts the iPod drive in read-only format.

"Recover My Files" is a more complete recovery tool from GetData. This tool allows for the searching of computer drives and iPods. Both products support a "deep scan" and "fast search" mode.

DD and the iPod

To image in iPod, which is mounted under Linux type *dd if=/dev/sda of=/mnt/hdb1/iPod.image* (where the iPod is connected as device */dev/sda*). This command will duplicate the entire iPod drive to the image file. If you only require a section of the drive, then substitute *sda* with the section you need. Change *iPod.image* to the filename of the image that you wish to use as evidence. Do not assume that nothing is occurring, as imaging often takes a long time.

Type **md5sum /dev/sda** to generate a checksum for the entire drive and record this value.

Summary of Exam Objectives

In this chapter, you worked on the concepts tested in the Computer Hacking Forensic Investigator (CHFI) for PDA and Blackberry forensics. These concepts are essential to understanding the concepts of hacking, and more importantly, forensics.

The chapter started with an introduction to the PDA, and how the technology of today has pretty much provided us with a handheld computer. We continued the discussion with a look at the concept of PDA forensics and how many of the same things must be considered in forensics on normal systems. We also discussed some of the differences that must be considered when performing forensics on PDA devices.

We then discussed the methods of investigating a PDA. We talked about securing the evidence, and how the PDA, docking cradle, and any external memory cards should be seized. The next method we discussed was the acquiring of the evidence. We covered how you have to create an exact image of the evidence, and once the evidence is secured and acquired, the need to go on and examine the evidence that was acquired.

We then talked about the forensic examination considerations when confronted with a Blackberry (RIM) device. We concentrated on how the Blackberry has similarities to the PDA, but one way that they differ is that the Blackberry does not require synchronization to receive a significant amount of information. The Blackberry is always on, and to make the task a little more difficult, it is in a state where it is susceptible to receiving push technology updates at any time. Therefore, we discussed how it is imperative that we take this into account when preparing to examine the Blackberry. We also discussed the software that is available to assist us when we are examining the Blackberry. One excellent package of software is the SDK from Blackberry. We also discussed some of the tools available and the ways to attack the Blackberry, including the Blackberry Attack Toolkit, the Attack Vector, and the forms of hijacking (or blackjacking). Finally, we ended this chapter by discussing the methods of securing the Blackberry. We discussed the Blackberry Signing Authority Toolkit that provides tools to help developers protect their data and intellectual property, and uses asymmetric cryptography to authenticate information.

Exam Objectives Fast Track

PDA Forensics

- ☑ PDA forensics is very similar to forensics of any system.
- ☑ Because the PDA is a handheld type of computer, you process data and information the same as you do when investigating a PC.

Investigative Methods of PDA Forensics

☑ Prior to investigating the PDA you have to secure and acquire the evidence.

☑ There are four steps to investigating a PDA:

1. Examination

2. Identification

3. Collection

4. Documentation

PDA Investigative Tips

☑ If the device is in the "on" state, you have to preserve the state by supplying adequate power.

☑ If the device is in the "off" state, leave it in that state, switch on the device, note the battery, and photograph the device.

☑ If the device is in the cradle, avoid any communication activities.

☑ If wireless is "on," eliminate any activity by placing the device in an envelope, or in an anti-static and isolation bag.

Deploying PDA Forensic Tools

☑ PDA Secure is a tool that provides enhanced password protection, encryption, and data wiping.

☑ PDA Seizure allows PDA data to be acquired, viewed, and reported on.

☑ EnCase provides many tools that allow investigators to conduct complex investigations efficiently.

Introduction to Blackberry

☑ The Blackberry is similar to the PDA when it comes to forensics.

☑ The Blackberry is a push technology device that does not require synchronization with a PC.

Operating Systems of the Blackberry

☑ The operating system of the Blackberry has multiple features such as:

- Over the air activation
- Ability to synchronize contacts and information
- Password keeper
- Customized display

Blackberry Operations and Security Capabilities

☑ The Blackberry uses the Blackberry Serial Protocol to backup, restore, and synchronize data between the Blackberry and the desktop software.

☑ The protocol comprises simple packets and single byte return codes.

☑ The Blackberry offers two encryption algorithms for protecting data:

- Triple DES
- AES

Forensic Examination of a Blackberry

☑ The Blackberry device is always-on and information can be pushed at any time.

☑ The first step in conducting an examination of a Blackberry is to isolate the device. This can be achieved by placing the Blackberry in an area where it cannot receive the push signal.

Attacking the Blackberry

☑ The "attack vector" links and tricks the users by downloading the malicious software.

☑ "Blackjack" or "hijack" programs will take over a Blackberry device and replace them with malicious devices.

Securing the Blackberry

☑ Clean the Blackberry memory.

☑ Encrypted password algorithm and storage on the device itself.

☑ Limit password authentication.

☑ Use AES to protect information

iPod Forensics

☑ iPod drives are formatted in either Mac or Windows formats (Apple HFS+ or FAT 32).

☑ iPod System Partition holds:

- The iPod embedded OS.

- The images used during the operation of the device such as the Apple logo and the "Do Not Disconnect" screen image.

- The system fonts used for the display of the text on the device.

- Games and other applications copied to the device

☑ With iPodLinux, it is possible to create a dual-booted iPod

☑ Time entries of primary concern to the forensic analyst may be found in the following files:

- **\iPod_Control\Device\SysInfo** The modified time of the file records when the iPod was last restored.

- v **\iPod_Control\iTunes\iTunesControl** The creation time of the file records when the iPod was initialized using iTunes.

- **\iPod_Control\iTunes\DeviceInfo** The modified time of the file records when the iPod was last connected to iTunes.

☑ All music files are located under \iPod_Control\Music\

Exam Objectives
Frequently Asked Questions

The following Frequently Asked Questions, answered by the authors of this book, are designed to both measure your understanding of the Exam Objectives presented in this chapter, and to assist you with real-life implementation of these concepts.

Q: When conducting a forensic investigation of a PDA, what is the first step in the process?

A: As with any forensic examination, the first step is to have permission to seize the evidence that is required for your investigation.

Q: What sort of tools do I use to conduct a forensic examination of a PDA?

A: Most of the forensic tools that work with images will create an image of a PDA file system. The commercial software product EnCase has this capability, as do many others.

Q: If I am preparing to conduct an investigation of a PDA, why must I maintain the charge to the device?

A: Similar to a regular PC, the PDA device has both volatile and non-volatile information, and if the power is not maintained, there is a possibility you could lose information.

Q: Isn't a PDA and a Blackberry the same thing?

A: It is not uncommon to make this assumption, and there are similarities, but there are also many differences. The Blackberry is an always-on device that can be pushed information at any time, and unlike the PDA, the Blackberry does not require synchronization with a PC.

Q: How would I get access to log files on the Blackberry?

A: Some of the best tools for conducting an investigation of a Blackberry come from Blackberry themselves. There is a Software Development Toolkit (SDK) that can access and collect log files and other information.

Q: What do I do if the iPod is displaying a "sad face" icon?

A: If an iPod displays a sad iPod icon, it is usually a sign of a hardware fault. If this occurs:

- Do not connect your iPod to iTunes, as the default setting in iTunes when an iPod is connected is to "auto-sync" the play list. When this occurs, iTunes will try to overwrite the list of songs to the iPod.

- When performing any forensic analysis, ensure that you do not to write new data to the drive being analysed, unless it is necessary to do so.

You can test the iPod manually by placing it in "Disk Mode." If you can force iPod into Disk Mode, it may not be a hardware problem. (In Windows, connect after changing the registry setting so that it is in read-only mode). To manually enter Disk Mode:

- Toggle the Hold switch on and off. (Set it to Hold, followed by turning it off.)

- Press and hold the Menu and Select buttons for at least 6 seconds until the Apple logo appears.

- When the Apple logo appears, release the Menu and Select buttons and immediately press and hold the Select and the Play/Pause buttons until the Disk Mode screen appears.

- When you are in Disk Mode, your iPod will display a large tick and then at the top of the LCD will be written "Disk Mode."

- If you are able to force iPod into Disk Mode, you should be able to image the drive.

Q: How do I recover a "Frozen iPod" so that I can use it?

A: If the iPod appears to freeze and no matter what you do gives no response, there are a few simple steps to try: (Important: Do not connect your iPod to iTunes)

- Check the Hold Button

- The first step is to ensure that the Hold function on iPod is not engaged. The Hold function locks the iPod buttons to stop them from being accidentally pushed.

- Slide the Hold button backward and forward and check to see if the iPod is no longer frozen. It is possible that the Hold button contacts could have fused or have dirt and grease between the contacts.

- Reset the iPod.

- Resetting an iPod is comparable to re-booting a computer. A reset should unfreeze the iPod and return it to operation.

- To reset an iPod press the Menu and Select (the center button) at the same time, and hold them down for at least 6 seconds. You should see the Apple logo appear and then the normal iPod menu display should appear.

- If you reset your iPod, the contents of the iPod should remain intact.

Q: What can't I see any files on the iPod, and why isn't it recognized as a disc?

A: The most important thing to remember when conducting a forensic analysis of any system is to minimize any change to the data. Fundamentally, the iPod is nothing more than an external disk from the perspective of a forensic analysis. It is not possible to access the data through the iPod device. It may be necessary to remove the hard drive from the iPod and connect directly to the machine that is being used to collect the disk image.

Before doing this, it is important to note that many software programs for data recovery will image the physical drive. Remember also that a high level of technical skill and specialist equipment may be required depending on the model of iPod being analyzed.

Notes

Andersen, S & Abella, V (2004), "Changes to Functionality in Microsoft Windows XP Service Pack Two," www.microsoft.com/technet/prodtechnol/winxppro/maintain/sp2otech.mspx
Knaster, S. (2004) "Hacking iPod and iTunes" John Wiley & Sons.
Jansen, W. & Ayers, R. (2004) "Guidelines on PDA Forensics (Draft Special Publication 800-72 ed)." National Institute of Standards and Technology

CHFI

Forensic Software and Hardware

Exam objectives in this chapter:

- Forensic Software Tools
- Forensic Hardware Tools

Exam Objectives Review:

- ☑ Summary of Exam Objectives
- ☑ Exam Objectives Fast Track
- ☑ Exam Objectives Frequently Asked Questions

Introduction

In this chapter we introduce to the hardware and software-based forensic tools. Due to the large number of hardware and software tools, few can be covered in great detail. We shall list the software products you will need to be familiar with to pass the exam in Part One.

The second part of this chapter introduces the physical hardware tools available to aid the forensic practitioner. Tables are included within the chapter that supply a brief description of the salient features of each tool.

Forensic Software Tools

This section summarizes the features and advantages of a large number of software forensics tools. For detailed information and technical reports it is always best to view the vendor Web sites as well as organizations that conduct technical reviews and evaluations such as National Institute of Standards and Technology (NIST). The Computer Forensic Tools Testing project (CFTT) web site contains additional valuable information:

- www.cftt.nist.gov/disk_imaging.htm

- www.cftt.nist.gov/presentations.htm

- www.cftt.nist.gov/software_write_block.htm

The information presented in this chapter is heavily based on the assertions of the various vendors who make the products listed in the chapter. Much of the information has been taken from the vendors product sheets. The Computer Forensic Tools Testing project is a good source of comparative data when deciding between these vendors.

Visual TimeAnalyzer

Visual TimeAnalyzer, shown in Figure 13.1, automatically tracks all computer usage and presents detailed, richly illustrated reports. You can easily log individual users or specific projects and compile detailed accounts of time spent within each program. The program helps track work time, pauses, projects, costs, software, and internet use and gives parents control over their children's use of the personal computer.

The software has some privacy safeguards and does not monitor all user data such as passwords and personal documents. Unlike spyware, it does not record specific keystrokes or run screen captures as a background process.

Software functions:

- **User supervision** Get detailed accounts of working hours and breaks.

- **Computer supervision** Monitor the family's PC or the company's network.

- **Software metering** Determine how often software is used and by whom.

- **Internet use** Control online time and web usage.

- **Project overview** Summarize the amount of time applied to each project milestone.

- **Compare users** See the activity of users on their computers.

Figure 13.1 Visual TimeAnalyzer in Action

X-Ways Forensics

X-Ways Forensics also is covered in further detail in Chapter 6. It is based on WinHex and is designed to be an advanced work environment for the digital forensic analyst. The product provides a number of features such as:

- Forensic cloning and imaging of sound disks

- Examination of the complete directory structure inside raw image files, even if the directory spans segments

- Native support for FAT, NTFS, Ext2, Ext3, Ext4, CDFS, and UDF file systems

- Built-in interpretation of RAID 0 and RAID 5 systems and dynamic disks

- Viewing and dumping of physical RAM and the virtual memory space of running processes

- Several data recovery techniques and file carving

- File header signature database based on flexible UNIX grep notation

- Hard disk cleansing to produce forensically sterile media

- Gathering of slack space, free space, interpartition space, and generic text from drives and images

- Creation of file and directory catalogs for all computer media

- Easy detection of and access to NTFS alternate data streams (ADS), even where other programs fail

- Calculation for mass hash file encryption (CRC32, MD5, SHA-1, and SHA-256)

- Manual decompression of NTFS volumes

- Support for the HFS, HFS+, ReiserFS, Reiser4, UFS, and UFS2 file systems

- Support for the following partition types: MBR, Windows dynamic volumes, GUID (GPT), Apple, unpartitioned (floppy/superfloppy)

- Gallery view for pictures

- Calendar view

- File preview — a seamlessly integrated viewer component for more than 400 file types

- Examination of e-mail extracted from Outlook (PST)*, Outlook Express (DBX), Mozilla (including Netscape and Thunderbird), generic mailbox (mbox, Berkeley, BSD, UNIX), Eudora, PocoMail, Barca, Opera, Forte Agent, The Bat!, Pegasus, PMMail, FoxMail, and local copies of maildir folders

- Automated check of the file signature

- Tagging of files and add them to customized report tables of notable items

- Automatic identification of encrypted Microsoft Office and PDF documents

- Automatic identification of pictures embedded in documents (for example Microsoft Word, PDF, and PowerPoint)

- Includes an internal viewer for Windows Registry files (all Windows versions) that generates an automated Registry report — works with all Windows versions

- Includes an internal viewer for Windows event log files

- Listing of the contents of archives within the directory browser, even in a recursive view

- Logical search of all or selected files and directories — following fragmented cluster chains, in compressed files, and optionally decoding text in PDF, WPD, and other file formats.

- Searches of Unicode and other types of code pages

- Skin color detection (that is, a gallery view sorted by skin color percentage that greatly accelerates searches for traces of child pornography and obscene images)

- Detection of host-protected areas (HPA) —ATA-protected areas

X-Ways Forensics can also write-protect data to ensure authenticity and integrity. It has a case management function integrated with automated activity logging (audit logs) and automated reporting. The generated reports can be imported and further processed by any application that processes HTML — for example, Microsoft Word. It also associates comments about files for inclusion in the generated reports or for filtering.

Evidor

Evidor searches for all occurrences of keywords within text files in digital media such as hard disks, and retrieves the context. It examines all files in the entire allocated space, — including Windows swap/paging and hibernate files — along with unallocated and slack space. It will find data files that have been deleted if they still physically exist on the hard disk. Evidor is a small subset of the search functionality included in in X-Ways Forensics. Evidor cannot access remote networked hard disks.

Slack Space and Data Recovery Tools

These tools aid in the recovery of deleted files and data, including file fragments in slack space on file systems supported by Windows.

Ontrack

Ontrack Data Recovery is a simple-to-use tool used to recover lost, remote, and deleted data. It is provided with a file repair capability for files in Microsoft Word and Zip format. It also recovers deleted files, folders, and entire partitions. It uses an emergency boot diskette to retrieve data from systems that cannot boot Windows. The user can start, stop, or resume the recovery process and select an FTP location as the destination for the recovered data. The user can configure the file filter for a quick or full scan.

The analyst can use this application perform an enhanced search using the options such as find, find next, and find previous. Ontrack can filter and sort data according to the file date, time, name, status, and size. It can scan the media for lost and remote data and lets the user specify the locations to copy the recovered files and folders to.

DriveSpy

DriveSpy is a modified MS-DOS shell designed to imitate and extend the potential of MS-DOS for forensic purposes. It uses a set of standard MS-DOS commands followed by commands specific to DriveSpy to process the computer during investigations.

DriveSpy can wipe an entire drive or partition, unallocated space, or slack space. It can also create an MD5 hash of an entire drive, partition, or selected files. It saves and restores compressed images of a partition for forensic use.

It can process the following:

- Hard drives with capacity of more than 8.4 GB
- Floppy drives and other removable drives
- FAT 12, FAT 16, /FAT 16x, FAT 32, and FAT 32x partitions
- Hidden MS-DOS partitions

Filters to sort the recovered files according to date, name, time, status, and size are available. DriveSpy performs the following functions for recovering data:

- Retrieve lost, remote, or deleted data and entire partitions.
- Start, stop, or resume the recovery process.
- Select an FTP location to copy the recovered files and folders to..

Data Recovery Tools

The following tools may be used to recover information from many sources including PDAs, cameras, and disk drives.

Device Seizure

Device Seizure is covert surveillance software developed by Paraben Corporation. It can aid in forensically analyzing and recovering mobile phone and PDA data including deleted text messages, photos, and call logs. It supports Palm, Windows CE, Windows Mobile, BlackBerry, and Psion devices as well as certain Nokia, Sony Ericsson, Motorola, iDen, Siemens, LG, Samsung, and Symbian-based phone models. It also supports GSM SIM card acquisition and deleted data recovery using SIMCon technology. Device Seizure is supported on Windows 98, Windows XP, and Windows Vista.

Forensic Sorter

Forensic Sorter organizes and speeds the examination of the contents of a hard drive. It sorts the contents of hard drives into categories such as video, audio, and spreadsheets so you can easily find what you're looking for. It will filter common Windows files, recover deleted files, or file fragments in slack, deleted, and unallocated space.

The application supports drive images in RAW, PFR (Forensic Replicator), Safeback, and EnCase image files and is compatible with Paraben's P2 Forensic Examination Technology. It sorts files by header rather than file extension for accuracy and sorts files located in unpartitioned space. Forensic Sorter identifies encrypted files for easy recovery using Paraben's Decryption Collection. All data output is non-proprietary so any tool can be used for analysis performed after sorting. It is designed for use with Paraben's Case Agent Companion. It supports:

- EFS file detection

- NTFS compressed file read operations

- NTFS streamoperations

- HTML reporting

- Ext 2 and Ext 3 partition operations

- Compressed archive (ZIP, RAR, etc.) sorting

- Drives with bad sectors sorting

- Unicode support

- Removable disk support

- OLE storage support

- Palm OS file detection

- Chat log file detection

- E-mail Examiner and Network E-mail Examiner-supported file detection

- XML output validation

Directory Snoop

This program is a cluster-level search tool that allows Windows users to analyze and view files in FAT- and NTFS-formatted disk drives to see what data can be recovered. It can recover deleted files or permanently erase sensitive files. Supported media include hard drives, floppy disks, Zip disks, magneto-optical drives, and flashcard devices. Its features include:

- FAT and NTFS modules

- Recovering deleted files, including those emptied from the recycle bin

- Destroying sensitive files with the secure wiping functionality, which provides up to 35 wiping passes

- Secure wiping slack and free drive space

- Purging sensitive file names left behind after normal erasing

- Copying open and locked files with the cluster copy function

- Searching, filtering, and sorting files globally by name and other parameters

- Viewing, searching, printing, and copying raw cluster data

- Dynamically linking clusters with cluster chains and the files that use them

- Examining the FAT and Master File Tables

- Viewing files through external applications

- Verifying the effectiveness of other file wiping programs

Permanent Deletion of Files

Drive wiping is a crucial component of all digital forensic examinations. Any drive that is not thoroughly wiped has to be considered suspect. The following tools aid in this goal.

PDWipe

PDWipe is capable of wiping large hard drives (in excess of 8.4 GB) in just under 11 minutes. It will perform a declassification drive wipe in accordance with the NAVSO P5239-10 security standard. This wiping algorithm exceeds that specified by the DOD 5220.22-M specification for both "clearing" and "purging" of sensitive information on hard drives.

PDWipe provides the option of specifying a character code other than 0x00 when wiping a drive. It also offers the ability to wipe the drive using a random pattern. PDWipe can also record Logical Sector Addresses, and cylinder-head-sector (CHS) addresses for Int13 and Int13x geometries at the beginning of the sectors being wiped. This is useful when diagnosing architectural discrepancies when moving a drive between systems or validating imaging utilities.

PDWipe can process all drives in a system such that *all* drives can be wiped with a single program operation. If desired, PDWipe will generate a report of the wiping activity performed on a system. PDWipe can also verify that the contents of a specified number of randomly chosen sectors have been wiped. If wipe verification is requested, PDWipe will also automatically verify the first and last sector on the drive.

PDWipe will support any drive which accessible to your system through the Int13 or the Microsoft/IBM Int13 extensions. System BIOSs typically provide this capability for all attached

IDE or EIDE devices. In addition, most SCSI adapters offer the ability to support attached devices through Int13 as well.

Darik's Boot and Nuke

Darik's Boot and Nuke (DBAN) is available from http://dban.sourceforge.net/ and is free. It is a self-contained boot floppy that securely wipes the hard disks of most computers. DBAN will automatically and completely delete the contents of any hard disk that it can detect, which makes it an appropriate utility for bulk or emergency data destruction.

DBAN can ensure due diligence in computer recycling, a way of preventing identity theft if you want to sell a computer, and a good way to totally clean a Microsoft Windows installation of viruses and spyware. DBAN prevents or thoroughly hinders all known techniques of hard disk forensic analysis.

File Integrity Checker

Failing to maintain the integrity of a file or drive image could be the end of a forensic examination. These tools help you to prove that the file you copied into evidence has not been altered subsequently. They make possible a quick and reliable diagnosis of a system image for the purpose of determining if any changes have occurred.

Filemon

Filemon and Regmon have been replaced by the Process Monitor on Windows 2000 SP4, Windows XP SP2, Windows Server 2003 SP1, and Windows Vista. Filemon and Regmon are included in these Windows versions for support of earlier Windows operating systems such as Windows 95.

Filemon monitors and displays file system activity on a system in real time. Its advanced capabilities make it a powerful tool for exploring the way Windows works, seeing how applications use the files and DLLs, or tracking down problems in system or application file configurations. Filemon's timestamping feature can show you precisely when every open, read, write, or delete operation happens, and its status column tells you the outcome. It begins monitoring when you start it, and its output window can be saved to a file for offline viewing. It has full search capability, and if you find that you're getting information overload, simply set up one or more filters.

File Date Time Extractor

File Date Time Extractor (FDTE) from Digital Detectives searches through binary files to uncover hidden, embedded, 64-bit date and time data. Windows files, such as Word documents contain several timestamp formats. It is important to note that false positives are common due to data patterns in files that look like timestamps but are not.

Decode: Forensic Data/Time Decoder

This utility was designed to decode the various date/time values found embedded within binary and other file types. It supports the following date/time formats and will allow you to specify the offset from GMT.

- Windows 64-Bit (little endian) date and time
- Windows 64-Bitan) date and time
- Windows cookie-format date and time
- Windows filetime-format date and time
- UNIX 32-Bit (little endian) date and time
- UNIX 32-Bit (big endian) date and time
- UNIX numeric date and time
- MAC absolute date and time
- MS-DOS 32-Bit date and time
- HFS 32-Bit (little endian) date and time
- HFS 32-Bit (big endian) date and time
- HFS+ 32-Bit (little endian) date and time
- HFS+ 32-Bit (big endian) date and time

Date and time values are stored within Windows in various formats.ample, Internet History – (index.dat), recycle bin (INFO) files, Windows link files, and Microsoft Office documents contain a 64-bit date/time structure. Decode can take a decimal hexadecimal value and convert it into a date and time value in a variety of formats.

Disk Imaging Tools

These tools will create a bit-image copy of a drive or other media.

Snapback DatArrest

SnapBack DatArrest can obtain the mirror images of different operating systems. It provides successful backup of data present in the hard disk of a system. It is specially designed to create backup of mission-critical data backups.

The captured image contains all system and networking software with associated drivers, software applications, and configurations, and all the files including deleted files, slack space, and data files, as well as the CMOS settings for the system.

The data gathering takes place in several modes such as copying server hard drives to tape, PC hard drives to tape, server or PC hard drives to removable media, hard drives to hard drives, or tape to tape. It obtains a bit level backup of data present in a hard disk. The DatArrest Suite provides the ability to copy:

- Server hard drive to tape
- PC hard drive to tape
- Server or PC hard drive to removable media
- Hard drive to hard drive
- Tape to tape

DatArrest backs up any hard drive (SCSI, IDE, etc.) to any SCSI tape drive, removable drive, and even a SCSI or IDE hard drive.

Partition Managers: Partimage

Partimage is a Linux utility which saves partitions with a supported file system to an image file. Most Linux and Windows file systems are supported. The image file can be compressed with the gzip or bzip2 programs to save disk space, and they can be split into multiple files to be copied on CDs or DVDs, Partitions can also be saved across the network using the Partimage network support, or using Samba or NFS. If you don't want to install Partimage, you can download and run it from a CD.

Linux/UNIX Tools: Ltools and Mtools

The Ltools application is equipped with many command-line applications, which are executed from a MS-DOSwindow in Windows 9x, Windows ME, Windows NT, Windows 2000, or Windows XP. These applications provide the same functionality as the Linux "ls", "cp", "rm", "chmod", "chown", and "ln" commands. Therefore, the MS-DOS and Windows operating systems allow users to list Linux files and directories to copy files from Linux to Windows. Supported command sets include:

1. Delete or rename files in Linux (ldel and lren)
2. Creation of symbolic links (lln)
3. Create new Linux directories (lmkdir)
4. Modify a Linux file's access rights (lchange)
5. Change the Linux default directory (lcd)
6. Set the Linux default drive (ldrive)

Many of the tools present in UNIX operating systems have functions that are built into a single executable file. These functions are called a *bundle* of command-line parameters.

The MTools application is a group of tools that can allow the user to manipulate the UNIX systems. The MTools application can perform read, write, and other operations on MS-DOS files. Each application copies the commands that are present in MS-DOS. The MTools application also allows the user to unload and mount floppy disks.

The Coroner's Toolkit and Tctutils

Dan Farmer and Wietse Venema developed The Coroner's Toolkit (TCT). This is a group of applications that can be used to aid a forensics investigation on UNIX systems. This system can be executed in most UNIX/Linux operating systems.

The Coroner's Toolkit has a collection of applications and plug-ins that give the program additional functionality. The Coroner's Toolkit was first put into use for the purpose of a post-mortem analysis of a UNIX operating system after a break-in. The application was first given to a computer forensic class for real life applications in the field in 1999. This tool is mainly designed to help in a forensic investigation and is one of the most frequently used by forensic investigators.

Password Recovery Tools

A password cracker hashes all the words in a dictionary file and compares every result with the password hash. If a match is found, the password is the dictionary word. The following are tools that may be used to file poorly configured passwords.

@Stake

The LOphtCrack application has been upgraded to version 5, which is the latest version. The LOphtCrack application is an award-wining password auditing and recovery application used by many corporate companies worldwide. The LOphtCrack application uses many methods to reduce the security risk to network administrators by:

1. Identifying and resolving security vulnerabilities.
2. Recovering Windows and UNIX account password.
3. Rapidly processing accounts by using pre-computer password tables.

LOphtCrack equipped with many additional features which include automated password scanning that can be scheduled and Windows and UNIX operating system support. The application is also equipped with a remote scanning engine for multiple domains. There are many dictionaries for constructing new and secure passwords.

Decryption Collection Enterprise

Paraben's Decryption Collection Enterprise is an advanced password recovery suite with support for Windows Vista and Server 2003, EFS, SQL, and Lotus Notes along with support for everything included in the Standard Edition of the suite. One of its most advanced features is its ability to distribute its processing on a network of up to 16 computers. This allows brute force or dictionary attacks using several computers. Its features include:

- MD5 hash verification
- Easy-to-use interface - just drag and drop file to be recovered
- Listing of the most recent files recovered
- HTML reporting of recovery results
- Password cache for quick recovery of repeat passwords
- English password recovery accuracy of 90 percent and higher

AIM Password Decoder

This utility was designed to decrypt the login password for AOL Instant Messenger version 4. Please note that version 5 of AIM uses a different encryption method so this software will not work on that version.

MS Access Database Password Decoder

This utility was designed to decrypt the master password stored in a Microsoft Access database. There are two utilities in the ZIP file for decoding Access 95, Access 97, Access 2000, and Access XP.

FavURLView: Favorite Viewer

This utility will decode Internet Shortcut (URL) files to allow you to compare a shortcut description with the associated link. It will also decode the modified time and date. The software can be run as an external viewer within Encase, iLook, or any forensic application that supports external viewers. It has also been designed to accept data from Encase through the command line.

The software will also accept drag and drop multiple files - doing it this way allows you to copy out all of the URL files from your case and examine them all at once, thereby identifying any links that have been wrongly described in an attempt to hide the true link.

NetAnalysis

This product allows for the analysis of a Web browser's history data. It is commonly used by law enforcement in child pornography cases. The forensic examination and analysis of user activity on the Internet can be the pivotal evidence in any case. With the increase in the use of computers by pedophiles and other Internet criminals, it is vital for a forensic investigator to be able to extract this data and analyze it quickly and present the evidence in an understandable format.

NetAnalysis includes the following functionality:

- Viewing Web history, manually or automatically

- Viewing browser cache data

- Extraction of browser data from unallocated space

The history extractor will also extract history records in a straightforward manner from a write-protected physical or logical device.

Multipurpose Tools

Maresware is covered in Chapter 6 in more detail. It includes the following capabilities:

- Computer forensics on Windows and Linux

- Incident response

- Computer investigations

- Data analysis and auditing

- Drive wiping for reuse, retirement, or compliance with HIPAA and other information privacy regulations

- Data, software, and hardware validation tools

- Ownership identification of hard drives for inventory or for theft or loss recovery

- Systems maintenance and IT management

- Bates numbering of filenames for e-discovery

PHOTORECOVERY by LC Technologies Software was developed for recovering images, movies, and media files from all digital media. It can be used with memory sticks, Smart Media, Connect Flash I and II, Micro Drives, SD and XD Cards, multimedia chips, floppy disks, and almost all other forms of digital film. Put the digital media in the external reading devices, run PHOTORECOVERY, and save the pictures in specified locations.

WinHex began as a disk-editing program and has developed into a forensic tool that is useful to digital evidence examiners of all skill levels. WinHex Specialist Edition can be used to

validate the results of other tools and to perform specialized tasks such as file comparison and text extraction. This program can also teach novice analysts about disk layout, file system structures, data recovery, and other fundamental concepts in digital forensics.

WinHex is a primarily a hexadecimal editor. It inspects and edits all types of files and can also recover deleted files and lost data from hard drives. It can do this on hard drives with corrupt file systems or from digital camera cards. It includes a RAM editor that provides access to the virtual memory of other processes. It is useful in concatenating and splitting files and unifying and dividing odd and even bytes and words. It also has the ability to analyze examine, and compare files. It can create a drive image and also make backups of drives. It can import all clipboard formats including ASCII hexadecimal values.

ProDiscover DFT reads the disk at the sector level, circumventing the standard file system while it recovers files, looks in slack data, the HPA section of a disk, and examines alternate data streams in Windows systems. This unique approach also allows you to examine files without altering valuable metadata such as the last-time-accessed date.

The main features include:

- Conforms to NIST's disk imaging tool specification 3.1.6 to ensure high quality
- Creates a bitstream copy of the evidence disk
- Supports FAT12, FAT16, FAT32, and NTFS file systems
- Analyzes data in a protected area (ATA) by identifying the partitions in the protected area
- Calculates the file checksum using either SHA1 or MD5
- Analyzes data in alternate data streams (ADS) of NTFS partitions
- Capable of analyzing dynamic disks

Toolkits

NTI Tools offers a compilation of software forensic tools. It is available from www.forensics-intl.com/tools.html. The products in this tool set include:

Stealth Suite

Users without a forensic background can use the Stealth Suite to assess activity on a computer hard disk. These tools can help identify whether a targeted computer system was used to access inappropriate information.

Computer Incident Response Suite

This suite of tools is often used in corporate and government investigations and security risk reviews. They are optimized for MS-DOS, which is the lowest cost forensic platform for

MS-DOS and Windows processing. Many of the tools also have Windows version. This should be one of your first forensic tool sets. It also makes an excellent set of tools to cross-validate your findings before you go before the court or the board.

Data Elimination Suite

This suite of tools performs computer data elimination and validation. It allows you to remove information from a drive and cross-validate that the information has been removed. It eliminates classified data 'leakage' and verifies that the data was properly eliminated.

TextSearch Suite

NT is used to process Windows NT/2000/XP-based computer systems from a MS-DOS command line. TextSearch Suite provides the same interface and features as its predecessor, TextSearch Plus, and also identifies many compressed and graphics files using the file header signature, giving the investigator a listing of files that could store information in a compressed or graphic format.

The HexSearch utility is also included in this suite. This tool provides a similar interface as TextSearch Plus while allowing the user to search for hexadecimal strings, such as file headers, non-printing characters, and more.

NTISecure ToolKit

This software is used to secure sensitive files stored on portable and desktop computers. Because it uses NIST- tested and approved AES 256-bit encryption, it qualifies for government use with classified *'Secret'* level data. This software exceeds commercial security requirements and it is much easier to use than Pretty Good Privacy (PGP). It includes a management tool so that corporate information is not lost to the corporation. An export license may be required for locations outside the United States.

SafeBack 3.0

This makes evidence grade bitstream backups of hard drives. NTI incorporated the NIST approved 256-bit SHA algorithm to provide greater protection against manipulation.

R-Studio

R-Studio is a family of powerful and cost-effective data recovery software. It recovers files from FAT 12, FAT 16, FAT 32, NTFS, NTFS 5 (created or updated by Windows 2000, Windows XP, Windows 2003, or Windows Vista), HFS/HFS+ (Macintosh), little- and big- endian variants of UFS1/UFS2 (FreeBSD, OpenBSD, NetBSD, and Solaris), Ext2FS (Linux), and Ext3FS (Linux) partitions. It functions on local and network disks, even if such partitions are formatted, damaged, or deleted. The suite includes the following tools:

- R-Studio
- R-Undelete
- Drive Image
- R-Firewall
- R-Guard
- R-Mail
- R-Word
- R-Excel
- R-Wipe&Clean
- R-Linux

DataLifter

DataLifter comes in two versions, DataLifter version 2.0 and DataLifter.Net Bonus Tools. Two additional packages, DataLifter - Digital Companion and DataLifter - File Extractor Pro, are add-ons. DataLifter - File Extractor Pro includes the following features:

- Multiple-thread data carving operations
- Support for source files larger than 2 GB
- Support for compressed and uncompressed Encase evidence files
- Support for logical disk access for sector-by-sector searches or searches on unallocated clusters
- An automated File Signature Builder that scans target systems so each data recovery system can be customized for the target data
- File recovery is completed through multi header points and footer values
- Twenty-three pre-configured file signatures
- File signature selection is easily organized by custom categories
- Organized recovery output
- Pausing and restarting the data carving session
- Create MD5 hash of each extracted file allowing optional deletion of duplicate files, saving you time during review
- Keyword support as a condition for reducing false positives
- Portable—can be registered and run from a thumb drive

Forensic Toolkit (FTK)

The Forensic Toolkit (FTK) is a commercial forensic software package by AccessData. FTK can parse FAT12, FAT 16, FAT 32, NTFS, NTFS Compressed, Ext2, and Ext3 file systems. It can use image files created by EnCase, SMART, Snapback, some versions of Safeback, and dd. The program allows users to search with keywords or take advantage of drive indexing using the dtSearch algorithm.

Image Master Solo and Fastbloc

Image MASSter Solo

MASSter is used as a system integration and MIS tool for system integration and system roll-outs. It is widely used for hard disk duplication. It is recommended for creating image drives. The following describes the capabilities of MASSter:

- It performs 100 percent copying of data to disk drives.
- The data transfer rate is 800 Mb/minute.
- Parallel transfer rate is 40 MB/minute.
- A sample audit trail report is available on-site with an option of a serial printer.
- It is functional for a variety of devices on the market.
- It also performs the job of wiping out unnecessary data.
- It ensures data integrity.
- MASSter is used to capture the images of affected system screens that can reveal evidence about the crime.
- It performs disk-cloning activities.
- It can perform high-speed data transfer from the affected computer to any other device.
- "Wipeout" functionality erases and sanitizes the drive you are copying.
- It comes with some external devices such as CD Writer, Serial Printer, and Battery Pack for Printer.

FastBloc

FastBloc LE (formerly FastBlocIDE) is a data acquisition and write protection device. It installs on any PC with a spare 5.25-inch drive bay.

- 40-pin IDE interface connection

- Host controller connection

- 40-pin & 44-pin IDE connection

- Suspect drive connection

- ATA-6 support

- An ATA-6-compliant host controller

FastBloc LE is a reliable solution for the forensic lab environment. FastBloc LE can be placed in a 5-inch external outlay of the forensic computer. A connection is established between FastBloc LE and other devices using a direct IDE-to-IDE device so the data can be acquired remarkably fast and does not require any other complicated or expensive hardware. This tool can be used to acquire drives without physically opening the forensic computer. When used with an ATA 6 controller, it can transfer data up to a rate of 133MB/s and can also support drives bigger than 128 GB.

The main features of FastBloc are:

- It makes use of IDE controllers and doesn't require SCSI controller card drivers.

- It has similar height and width as the internal CD-ROM drive.

- Small size (5.75"W x 3"D x 1.625"H) allows for complete portability and ease of use in the field.

- Has ports for desktop IDE as well as laptop IDE media.

Encase

Guidance Software states that, "*EnCase provides a much simpler way to conduct a search of a computer system, document the findings, and make evidentiary and discovery copies*". EnCase is a forensic data and analysis program for Windows 95 and NT that is designed to provide case management and tools for digital investigations. EnCase enables the user to understand and define the information in the system. The information collected in EnCase can be exported to several file formats.

E-mail Recovery Tools

Paraben's E-mail Examiner

This product provides forensic analysis, advanced searching, and converting and Exporting of e-mail. E-mail Examiner can examine over 16 e-mail formats, including AOL 9.0, PST files, and more than14 others. It includes the following features:

- Support for files larger than 2 GB

- Handling of bad date fields in message headers

- Handling of plain UTF-8 messages and header fields

- Handling of corrupted DBX files

- Parsing of HTML mail

- Support for maildir files

- Support for Opera 9 .mbs files

- Support for Agent 3.x and 4.x folder name conversion

- Aid4Mail console for importing, exporting, and converting

- AOL and PST Converters

- Export any e-mail format to PST

- Export to MHTML with XLS or database index

- Recovers deleted/deleted e-mail

- America Online (AOL) 9.0

- Outlook Exchange (PST)

- USENET Groups

- Eudora

- Netscape Messenger

- Pegasus Mail

- Outlook Express

- The Bat!

- Forte Agent

- PocoMail

- Barca

- Calypso

- FoxMail

- Juno 3.x

- EML message files

- Mozilla Mail

- MSN Mail
- Generic mailboxes (mbox, UNIX mail format)

Network E-mail Examiner

Network E-mail Examiner allows the examination of Microsoft Exchange (EDB), Lotus Notes (NSF), and GroupWise e-mail stores. Network E-mail Examiner is designed to work hand-in-hand with E-mail Examiner and all output is compatible and can easily be loaded for more complex tasks.

The product features include:

- Support for GroupWise information stores up to 6.5.1
- Support for Microsoft Exchange 5.0, 5.5, 2000, and 2003 SP1 information stores
- Support for Lotus Notes information stores 4.0, 5.0, 6.0
- Advanced search options
- View one or all individual e-mail accounts in the information store
- View all metadata within individual messages
- Complete bookmarking functionality
- Export data into Paraben's E-mail Examiner
- Summary HTML reporting
- Export to PST files
- Output to MSG & EML format
- Supports deleted/deleted recovery with Exchange

Oxygen Phone Manager

Oxygen Phone Manager II for Nokia phones provides a simple and convenient way to control mobile phones from a PC. Oxygen Phone Manager II offers management for the phonebook, call register, calendar, to-do lists, SMS and MMS messages, logos, tones, GPRS and WAP settings, profiles, dictaphone, FM stations, Java games, and applications.

SIM Card Seizure

Paraben acquired SIMCon and integrated it into SIM Card Seizure and Device Seizure. SIM Card Seizure can be used to recover deleted Short Message Service (SMS) messages and perform comprehensive analysis of SIM card data. It is a combination of the SIM card acquisition and analysis components in Paraben's Device Seizure utility and a specialized SIM card forensic

acquisition and analysis tool. SIM Card Seizure includes the software and a forensic SIM card reader. Its features are included in Device Seizure and the Device Seizure Toolbox.

SIM Card Seizure has Unicode support for languages such as Arabic, Chinese, and Russian, and includes the following features:

- Forensic SIM Card reader

- Calculates MD5 and SHA1 Hash Values

- Search function

- Recovers deleted SMS data

- Bookmarking options

- Report Creation wizard

- Save Workspaces for Further Review functionality

- Timestamps Calculate GMT Offset functionality

- Access to Paraben's forum

- Access to Paraben's 24-hour support

- Data acquired from SIM cards

- Phase ID

- SIM Service Table (SST)

- ICCID serial number

- Preferred Languages (LP) variable

- Service Provider Name (SPN)

- MSISDN subscriber phone number

- AND short dial number

- FDN fixed numbers

- Last Dialed Numbers (LND)

- EXT1 Dialing Extension

- EXT2 Dialing Extension

- GID1 Groups

- GID2 Groups

- SMS text messages

- SMSP Text Message parameters

- SMSS text message status

- CBMI preferred network messages

- PUCT charges per unit

- ACM charge counter

- ACMmax charge limit

- HPLMNSP HPLMN search period

- PLMNsel PLMN selector

- FPLMN forbidden PLMNs

- CCP capability configuration parameter

- ACC access control class

- IMSI

- LOCI location information

- BCCH broadcast control channels

- Kc ciphering key

Autoruns

This product is available from Microsoft at:
www.microsoft.com/technet/sysinternals/Utilities/AutoRuns.mspx.

This utility has the most comprehensive display of autostart locations of any startup monitor and displays all programs are configured to run during system boot or login. It displays the entries in the order Windows processes them. These programs include those in your startup folder, Run, RunOnce, and other Registry keys. You can configure Autoruns to show other locations, including Explorer shell extensions, toolbars, browser helper objects, Winlogon notifications, autostart services, and much more. Autoruns goes beyond the MSConfig utility bundled with Windows Me and XP.

Autoruns' Hide Signed Microsoft Entries option helps you to zoom in on third-party autostart images that have been added to your system and it has support for looking at the autostarti images configured for other accounts configured on a system. It also includes a command-line equivalent that can output in CSV format — Autorunsc.

HashDig

HashDig technology is a collection of utilities designed to help analysts automate the process of resolving MD5 and SHA1 hashes. The product site states, "In the early stages of an investigation, it is not typically possible or practical to examine all subject files. Therefore, practitioners

need reliable methods that can quickly reduce the number of files requiring examination. One such method is to group files into two general categories: known and unknown. This method can be implemented quite effectively by manipulating hashes and comparing them to one or more reference databases. Even that, however, can take a significant amount of effort. HashDig technology attempts to reduce this burden through automation and the use of lightweight, open, and verifiable techniques."

Patchit

Created for software developers, this is a two -art program used to make patches for updating software. Both the manager and the patch program are simple-to-use GUI programs. Command-line switches are also available.

PowerGREP

PowerGREP is a powerful Windows grep tool. It will search through large numbers of files on a system or network, including text and binary files, compressed archives, MS Word documents, Excel spreadsheets, and PDF files. This is done through the use of powerful text patterns (regular expressions) by specifying the form of what you want instead of literal text. It will search and replace with one or many regular expressions to comprehensively maintain web sites, source code, reports, and other sources. PowerGREP will also extract statistics and knowledge from logfiles and large data sets.

Reverse Engineering Compiler

REC is a portable reverse engineering compiler, or decompiler. It reads an executable file and attempts to produce a C-style representation of the code and data used to build the executable file. It is portable because it has been designed to read files produced for many different targets, and it has been compiled on several host systems.

RecStudio offers a modern user interface to REC's interactive mode. A command-line version is still available for Linux and Solaris hosts.

These are some of REC's features:

- Multitarget operation: REC can decompile 386, 68k, PowerPC, and MIPS R3000 programs.

- Multiformat operation: REC recognizes the following file formats:

- ELF (System V release 4, for example Linux and Sun Solaris)

- COFF (System V release 3.x, for example SCO)

- PE (Win32.exe and .dll for Windows 95 and NT)

- AOUT (BSD derivatives, for example SunOS 4.x)

- Sony PlayStation PS-X (MIPS target only)

- Raw binary data (thorough CMD files)

- Multihost operation: REC is available for Linux 3.0 (i386), Windows 95, and Sun SunOS 4.1.4.

- Supports high-level symbolic information in COFF, ELF+STAB, and AOUT+STAB.

- Scalable user interaction: From 100 percent batch mode to a full-screen, browser-like interactive mode.

- HTTP server mode allows the use of an HTML browser as the user interface.

Table 13.1 contains a list of forensic software tools.

Table 13.1 Forensic Software

Software	Description
AOL PW Extractor	Reveals all AOL passwords on your computer.
Accent Access Password Recovery	Recovers forgotten or lost passwords for Microsoft Access documents.
Accent Excel Password Recovery	Recovers forgotten or lost passwords to open for Microsoft Excel documents.
Accent Money Password Recovery	Recovers forgotten or lost passwords for Microsoft Money documents.
Accent Office Password Recovery	Recovers forgotten or lost passwords for Microsoft Office documents. If you have lost or forgotten a password for opening a Microsoft Office document (Access, Excel, and Word), or a password for saving changes to a Microsoft Word document, you can use this software. It will help you search for a password more effectively. The software offers you to choose one of the three ways: a dictionary-based attack, a brute force attack or a brute force attack with a mask.
ACDSee	Fast photo viewer and manager. Easily find, view, manage, print, edit, and share images.

Continued

Table 13.1 continued Forensic Software

Software	Description
Active Partition Recovery	Recovers deleted partitions (FAT and NTFS). Restores deleted FAT and NTFS Logical Drives. Creates –an image of a drive for backup purposes. Scans hard drives and detects deleted FAT and NTFS partitions or logical drives. Preview files and folders on a deleted partition or drive to recover data. A very small, easy to use MS-DOS program (only 150k in size)
Active Ports	Shows all open TCP/IP and UDP ports on Windows NT, Windows 2000, and Windows /XP computers and maps them to the parent application.
Active UNDELETE	Restores deleted files and directories.
Active Uneraser for MS-DOS	Data recovery (undelete) software for MS-DOS. Recovers deleted files on FAT16, FAT32, and NTFS partitions.
Adobe Reader	PDF reader.
Advanced Attachments Processor	Extracts attachments from e-mail client message databases, and makes an archive of the extracted files.
Advanced Email Extractor	Extracts e-mail addresses from web-pages on the Internet (using HTTP and HTTPS protocols) and from HTML and text files on local disks.
Advanced Mailbox Processor	Extracts owner's names and e-mail addresses from local files to creates a list.
Advanced Forensics Format (AFF)	An extensible open format for the storage of disk images and related forensic information.
Afind	Afind lists files by their last access time without altering the data the way that Windows Explorer does. Afind searches for access times between specified time frames, and coordinating the results with logon information provided from ntlast. This enables you to determine user activity even if file logging has not been enabled.
Automated Image and Restore (AIR)	A GUI front end to dd/dcfldd creates forensic bit images.
Allin1 for Sleuthkit	Runs time-consuming tasks in Sleuthkit/autopsy in batch mode.

Continued

Table 13.1 continued Forensic Software

Software	Description
APDFPRP	PDF file cracker.
ASP	Zip file cracker.
Autopsy Forensic Browser	HTML front end for TCT and TCTUtils. It has a file manager style interface, can display the contents of a file as raw data or in ASCII, and generates reports.
AutoStart Viewer	When you start Windows, dozens of programs are already running – many of them invisible and running in the background. This software identifies what is running, why it is running and determine if any are Trojans. AutoStart Viewer allows you to see every AutoStart on your system on one screen. In addition, it gives you complete control over the AutoStart references, and allows you to modify or delete them at will.
AVIPreview	A program which is capable of playing partially downloaded AVI movies.
Back2Life	Simple undelete utility for Windows
BadCopyPro	Data recovery software for floppy disk, CD, DVD, memory card, Zip disk, flash drive, and other storage media.
BCWipe	Disk wiper (DoD – 7-pass wipe tool)
Belkasoft Forensic IM Extractor	Supports various IMs: ICQ versions 99a up to ICQ5, MSN Messenger, Yahoo! Messenger, &RQ, Miranda. Supports deep ICQ analysis using different methods (with and without usage of index file) that allows user to extract even deleted and overwritten messages.
BinText	Finds ASCII, Unicode, and resource strings in a file.
BitForm Discover	Analyzes and reports information about metadata and hidden information within document collections.
Black Bag Macintosh Forensic Software	A suite of forensic solutions and a Macintosh boot CD that boots any system capable of running Mac OS X

Continued

Table 13.1 continued Forensic Software

Software	Description
bmap	Stores data in slack space on ext2 filesystems, among other features. Forensic examiners can use bmap to detect used slack space and to recover data.
Browser History Viewer	Examines the contents of web browser history files and exports the data.
BXDR	This utility will display the full sector count on a hard disk drive, including protected areas that utilities such as Safeback and Encase miss when imaging.
ByteBack	Data recovery and forensic software program that accesses media at the physical level.
Cache Reader	Reads the index.dat file in the Temporary Internet Files (TIF) folder of Internet Explorer versions 5 and 6.
Cache View	Opens cached files for viewing and copy or move them out of the cache. This will even reconstruct the names and directory paths of Web sites so you can view the HTML files. This supports all versions of Netscape, Mozilla (Gecko), and Internet Explorer.
CacheInf	Displays a browser's cache, and provides the option to delete it. Additionally, searches the cache for file names and URLs and saves the search results into a comma-separated value file.
CacheView	Cache View is a viewer for the Netscape Navigator, Mozilla, and Internet Explorer caches. It displays cached files, gives you the option to copy them or move them out of the cache. It can reconstruct the names and directory paths of the files. Cache View extracts the following information about cached files: URL, size (in bytes), MIME type, last modified date, the date the file was downloaded, and the expiration date.
CacheX for IE	CacheX displays a browser cache with a Windows-Explorer-like user interface. To view a file offline with your browser, double-click it.

Continued

Table 13.1 continued Forensic Software

Software	Description
Captain Nemo	Connects a drive containing a UNIX/Linux, Windows NT, or Novell operating system directly to a computer running the Windows operating system for accessing, viewing, printing, and copying the files as if they were on another Windows drive on the computer. This product only supports ext2 file systems on Linux.
Captive	The first free NTFS read/write file system for GNU/Linux.
Catalogue	File Metadata Miner; a file cataloging utility that enables quick creation of HTML page listing files and associated metadata, managing and updating document properties associated with such files
CD Roller	Retrieves data from a hard disk created by "drag and drop" CD and DVD writing software, such as Roxio (Adaptec) and Ahead's Nero, CeQuadrat's PacketCD, Instant Write, and B's CliP.
CD/DVD Inspector	Analyzes and extracts data on CD-R, CD-RW and DVD media. Tailored for use by professionals in data recovery, forensics, and law enforcement.
CDRoller	Toolset for CD and DVD data recovery.
Chip-it	Extracts phone numbers from a variety of mobile phones – freeware.
chrootkit	Checks for evidence of modification of the system binaries by a rootkit on a local machine.
CMOS Recovery Tools	Recovers CMOS passwords. Works with the following BIOSs: ACER/IBM, AMI, AMI WinBIOS 2.5, Award 4.5x/4.6x, Compaq (1992), Compaq (new version), IBM (PS/2, Activa, Thinkpad), Packard-Bell, Phoenix 1.00.09.AC0 (1994), Phoenix a486 1.03, Phoenix 1.04, Phoenix 1.10 A03, Phoenix 4.05 rev 1.02.943, Phoenix 4.06 rev 1.13.1107, Phoenix 4 release 6 (user), Gateway Solo, Phoenix 4.0 release 6 , Toshiba, Zenith AMI.

Continued

Table 13.1 continued Forensic Software

Software	Description
CookieView – Cookie Decoder	Decodes the internal cookie data such as the date and times and splits the data into separate cookie records. This software was originally written as an external viewer for Encase or iLook. Either drag and drop a cookie onto the main window or set it as an external viewer.
Coreography	Browses memory images. Coreography is an open-source utility.
Creed (Cisco Router Evidence Extraction Disk) - Raw Image (Freeware)	Creates and restores disk images, even non-PC formatted disks. This software was created by New Technologies Inc. Once you have downloaded the zip file, unzip it into its own directory. This is a MS-DOS application, so no further installation is required.
Crucial ADS	Finds hidden data streams in NTFS file systems.
Digital Investigation Manager (D.I.M.)	Manages incident response and forensic acquisition procedures. D.I.M. allows operations to be organized by case. Each case may contain an unlimited number of hosts (for example, workstations, servers, laptops, and PDAs). Items of evidence (hard disks, CD/DVD-ROMs, memory card, log file, network dumps) are associated with each host.
DataGrab	Investigates Internet Relay Chat (IRC) communications.
Davory	Davory recovers files from logically damaged or formatted drives. Created by the makers of WinHex.
DbExtract	Extracts mail messages from Outlook Express version 5 DBX files. It requires the existence of the Visual Basic 6 runtime DLL — msvbvm60.dll.
DBXanalyzer	Reads, analyses, and manages e-mail data files created by Microsoft Outlook Express versions 5 and 6.
DBXpress	DBXpress is a faster, more accurate, and more powerful version of DBXtract. It requires that .NET Framework version 1.1 be installed.
DBXtract	DBXtract extracts all e-mail and news messages from individual DBX files

Continued

Table 13.1 continued Forensic Software

Software	Description
DCFL-DD	An enhanced dd with MD5 hashing.
dd for Windows	Flexibly copies data within in a Win32 environ-ment.
dd rescue	Copies data from one file or block device to another.
DecExt	Recovers base 64 pictures.
Declasfy	Wipes drives according to DOD specifications. Drive wiping with Declasfy can serve many purposes where information security is a concern. For example: preparing drives for internal reuse; securing private information prior to retirement or donation of a drive; securing private information for compliance with HIPAA and other regulatory requirements.
Decode	Decodes the date/time values embedded within binary and other file types.
DFSee	Display File Systems (DFSee) is a generic partition and file system utility. It supports the following partition tables: FDISK, LVM, (V)FAT, FAT-32, HPFS, NTFS, and JFS.
Digital AudioRescue Professional	This program recovers lost data from multimedia devices including digital audio recorders, MP3 and WMA players, PDAs, and mobile phones. This program supports recovery from hard drives, CompactFlash cards, IBM Microdrives, SmartMedia cards, MultiMedia cards, Secure Digital cards, and Memory Sticks.
Digital Image Recovery	Reconstructs deleted images, videos, and audio files from formatted media, even if the media was ejected during a write process.
Directory Snoop	Snoops FAT and NTFS formatted disk drives to see what data may be hiding in the cracks. This is a cluster-level search tool. Use Directory Snoop to recover deleted files or permanently erase sensitive files. Supported media includes local hard drives, floppy disks, Zip disks, MO disks, and flashcard devices.

Continued

Table 13.1 continued Forensic Software

Software	Description
DIRV	A filter for the DIR /S command. Dirv is a program for those who still use DIR /S to obtain a recursive directory list of all the files on a system. The DIR /S program produces an output that is difficult to import into a database for additional processing. Dirv takes the output generated on file systems supported by Windows NT or Windows 9x and converts it to one-line records that contain the appropriate path and filename merged.
Disable	Disables a computer keyboard.. Best used on a boot disk for evidence protection, which isften called an evidence disk.
Disk Investigator	Disk Investigator helps you to discover all hidden data on a hard disk.
DiskCat	Catalogues all files on disks. DiskCat is short for "disk cataloguer". It creates a listing (catalogue) of all files or directories on a hard or floppy disk. It is customizable and is especially useful for forensic purposes and file maintenance. Its output is a fixed-length record and database compatible for further analysis and sorting.
DiskPatch	Repairs Master Boot Records (MBRs), partitions, and boot sectors. It also clones and wipes disks and scans for errors.
disktype	Detects the format of a disk or disk image. It detects common file systems, partition tables, and boot codes.
DivX Player	The DivX codec plays any DivX video data, including DivX VOD movies.
DNA Manager	Distributed network password cracker from Access Data. Harnesses networked PCs to do this.

Continued

Table 13.1 continued Forensic Software

Software	Description
DriveLook	DriveLook scans a drive or partition for text strings and stores them in a table. You can browse this table and view the locations where the words had been found. The search function enables fast inquiries for combinations of words. The program also enables you to index all of the text on a hard drive, browse a list of all words stored on the drive, search for words or combinations of words, view the location of words in a disk editor, switch between several views (such as hexadecimal and text), use physical drives or logical drives as an input, use image files as an input, and access remote drives over a serial cable or TCP/IP connection. DriveLook is used for forensic drive investigation and data searches.
dtSearch	Provides over two dozen indexed and unindexed text search options for all popular file types.
dumpautocomplete	Dumps Firefox AutoComplete files into XML files.
e2recover	Undeletes data on ext2 file systems.
e2Salvage	Recovers lost ext2 partitions.
Eindeutig	Parses Outlook Express DBX files.
E-Mail Detective	Extracts all email data (including graphics) from America Online's databases stored on a disk drive.
EMF Printer Spool File Viewer	Displays the contents of an EMF spool file.
Encase 4	Performs most of digital forensic analysis operations.
Ethereal	Analyzes network packets. A network packet analyzer will try to capture network packets and display that packet data in as much detail as possible. Data can be captured "off the wire" from a live network connection or read from a capture file. It runs on all major operating systems, including UNIX, Linux, and Windows. Live data can be read from the following network types: Ethernet, FDDI, PPP, Token-Ring, IEEE 802.11, Classical IP over ATM. Loopback interfaces are also supported. However, not all of these network types are supported on all operating systems.

Continued

Table 13.1 continued Forensic Software

Software	Description
Event Analysis and Reconstruction in Lisp (EARL)	Reconstructs finite state machine events. This is experimental software.
Event Log Explorer	Views, monitors, and analyzes events recorded in the security, system, application and other logs produced by the Windows operating system.
Eventlog	Takes the output of an Windows NT security eventlog and reformats it to single lines containing pipes. These can be easily imported into a database or spreadsheet.
Evidence Mover	Automates the transfer of evidentiary data from one location to another with 100 percent accuracy.
Evidor: The Evidence Collector	Retrieves the context of keyword found on computer media, Windows swap/paging files, hibernate files, and unallocated space and slack space. Created by the makers of WinHex.
EXIF Image Viewer	Reds EXIF information embedded in photos and thumbnails.
EXIF Reader	Analyzes and displays the shutter speed, flash condition, focal length, and other image information included in the EXIF image format. The EXIF image format is supported in many digital cameras.
Exifer	Recovers and displays the metadata (EXIF/IPTC) included in pictures taken by digital cameras.
EXIFRead	Utility that extracts image information from EXIF/JPG files.
Explore2fs	The Win32 explorer for Linux ex2fs partitions; reads ex2fs filesystems under NT 4.0 (and Windows 95). It is a separate program - not a file system driver.
Extract 2.10	Extracts files from a disk image created using WinImage, FDFormat, or compatible tools running under MS-MS-DOS, Windows 95, Windows 98, or the Windows NT console.
Fatback	Undeletes files from FAT file systems.

Continued

Table 13.1 continued Forensic Software

Software	Description
faust	Analyzes files found after an intrusion or the compromising of a honeypot. faust is a perl script.
File Date & Time Extractor (FDTE)	Searches binary files for hidden, embedded, 64-bit date and times.
File Disk	A virtual disk driver for Windows NT, Windows 2000, and Windows XP that uses one or more files to emulate physical disks. A console application is included for dynamically mounting and unmounting files.
File Investigator	Identifies files by content and extensions. 1,806 file formats are supported.
File Juicer	Extracts images from binary files on the Macintosh.
File Scavenger	Undeletes files on NTFS volumes. Runs on Windows NT, Windows 2000, and Windows XP. Reformatted volumes or broken hardware/software RAID volumes can also be recovered.
Filesig, Hash File, Simple Caver, Disk Map	
FileSystem Investigator	Views and extracts file system data. Platform independent.
Final E-mail	Scan Outlook Express, Eudora, and Netscape Mail e-mail database files and recovers messages. Also, locates lost emails that do not have data location information associated with them
FINAL Photo Retriever	Recovers image files, video files, and audio files from hard disks and removable media.
FinalData	Recovers data. Runs on Windows NT 4.0, Windows 2000, Windows XP.
FINALdBase 2.0 for Oracle \	Recovers Oracle databases. Runs on UNIX systems.
FinalEmail	Recovers the e-mail database file and locates lost e-mails that do not have data location information associated with them.

Continued

Table 13.1 continued Forensic Software

Software	Description
Forensic and Log Analysis GUI (FLAG)	Analyzes log files for use in forensic investigations.Often, when investigating a large case, a great deal of data needs to be analyzed and correlated. FLAG uses a database as a back-end to assist in managing the large volumes of data.
Flash Retriever Forensic	Recovers pictures, movies, and sounds from a variety of media.
Floppy Image	Create image files of floppy disks and back (for backup, shipping or transfer). Save the image file compressed, uncompressed or as a self-extracting exe. Add descriptions to or convert your old image files.
Foremost	Recovers files based on their headers and footers. Runs on Linux systems. Foremost can process image files, such as those generated by dd, Safeback, Encase.
Forensic Acquisition Utilities	A collection of utilities and libraries used in forensic-related investigations.
Forensic Analysis Toolkit (FATKit)	Analyzes volatile system memory. A cross-platform, modular, and extensible digital investigation framework.
Forensic Internet Explorer – Beta	Parses the "index.dat" file, which identifies host sites that have been visited.
Forensic Script	Modified version of a script from 'Forensic Analysis of a Live Linux System, Part One' by Mariusz Burdach, as well as a server-side script for netcat, and description of the relationship between a specified set of ports and files.
Forensic Tools on the Mac (by M Dornseif)	Compiles various forensic tools on the Macintosh.
Foundstone's Forensic Toolkit	Examines NTFS for unauthorized activity.
FSDEXT2	Transparently mounts Linux ext2fs partitions on Windows 9x systems.

Continued

Table 13.1 continued Forensic Software

Software	Description
FS-TST	Tests disk imaging tools typically used in forensic investigations. This package includes programs that use the Int13 BIOS disk interface to initialize disk drives, detect changes in disk content, compare pairs of disks, and simulate bad sectors on a disk.
FTimes	Creates system baselines and assists in collecting evidence. Its primary purpose is to gather or develops information about specified directories and files in a manner conducive to intrusion analysis.
AccessData Forensic Toolkit (FTK)	A complete forensic toolkit.
ftrace	Performs fast traceroutes Win32-based systems.
Galleta	Reconstructs a subject's Internet Explorer cookie files.
Gargoyle Forensic Pro	Determines whether malware is present on a system under investigation.
Gemulator Explorer	Reads Atari ST- and Apple Macintosh-formatted disks. Runs on Windows systems. Symantec's Norton Ghost 9.0 Performs advanced backup and recovery operations.
GNU utilities for Win32	Native Win32 ports of several GNU utilities.
gpart	Attempts to determine the primary partition table of a PC hard disk when the primary partition table in sector 0 is damaged, incorrect, or deleted. If identified, the table can be written to a file or device.
GRAB	Acquires image data. Runs on Linux systems. Created by the developers of Helix.
Handle	Displays information about open handles for any process in the system. You can use it to see the programs that have a file open, or to see the object types and names of all the handles allocated by a program.
Hard Disk Copy	Backs up and copies hard disk sectors.
Hard Drive Mechanic Deluxe	Repairs hard disk drives.

Continued

Table 13.1 continued Forensic Software

Software	Description
HD95Copy	Copies a hard drive to an image file on a network server, another hard disk, or any medium you can access using a logical drive letter. The hard disk is copied sector by sector, provided that filenames and hidden files and directories are backed up also. It also supports removable media.
HD98Copy	Same functionality as HD95Copy. Documentation in German and English
hfsutils	Manipulates HFS volumes on UNIX and other systems. HFS is the "Hierarchical File System," the native volume format used on modern Macintosh computers.
History Inspector	Reads a Internet Explorer versions 5 and 6 history database (index.dat) file and presents it as a syn-optical table. It also supports link browsing, adding Favorites, copying URLs, adding personal notes, searching and replacing text items, and printing. History Inspector for Internet Explorer Reads all of the information in the history database and presents a list in chronological or alphabetical order.
Host Protected Area (HPA)	Identifies the following information about a disk drive: the manufacturer, serial number, total number of sectors on the drive, and the number of sectors set aside in the (Host Protected Area (HPA) if one exists on the drive. HPA is very useful on a forensic boot disk because it can capture key information about any IDE drives in the system. This information can be sent to an output log file for future reference. HPA is a 16 bit program designed to work only on IDE drives.
HTTrack Website Copier	Downloads the contents of a Web site to a local directory, and recursively builds all directories, getting the HTML code, images, and all other files from the server to your computer.
Hurricane Search (formerly WinGrep)	Displays the results of a search in a hierarchical tree of the files that contain a match.

Continued

Table 13.1 continued Forensic Software

Software	Description
IE Forensic Tool	Generates an easy-to-read report showing all of the cookies, as well as the Web browsing history of the current user.
IECacheList (Lite - Free, or Pro - Commercial)	Display the contents of Internet Explorer's index.dat files, including "lost" and hidden content.
IECookiesView	IECookiesView is a small utility that displays the details of all cookies that Internet Explorer stores on your computer.
IEhist	Dumps the Web browsing history from Internet Explorer index.dat files into delimited files suitable for import into other tools.
IEHistoryView	Reads all information from a history file and generates the list of all URLs that you have visited in the last few days, and displays it.
Incident Response Collection Report (IRCR)	A collection of tools that gathers or analyzes forensic data on a Windows system. This product is similar to The Coroner's Toolkit (TCT) by Dan Farmer and Wietse Venema.
Index Dat Spy	Exposes the contents of any index.dat file, even if the file is currently in use by Windows. It translates binary data into a human-readable form.
Inforenz Forager®	Analyzes the hidden history of computer files.
Innovision USB WriteBlocker	Examines USB devices in Windows
Inquire	Issues a SCSI Inquiry command and lists any hard disk drives found along with model number, product revision level, and serial number (ESN). This is a Windows application.
Internet Cache Explorer	Displays the content of a browser cache. It comes with many additional features, like a search function that you can use to find URLs or text within visited pages and an option to save complete Web pages (including images and all) for later use.
IrfanView	Displays 32-bit image data. Many supported file formats. Can be used as an external viewer for forensic analysis.

Continued

Table 13.1 continued Forensic Software

Software	Description
JAFAT - Archive of Forensic Analysis Tools	Obtains the Safari browsing and download history on a Mac OS X system. Also, the archive contains a link parser, a cookie tool, and "dumpster dive."
Karen's Power Tools	Variety of utilities.
KaZAlyzer	Performs the following operations: lists all database entries in a tabular form, displays the file integrity tag, enables tagging and commenting on each record, identifies files that appear from title, keywords, or other evidence to be child pornography, identifies files that have a known child pornography hash value, identifies all graphics and movie files, sorts by individual columns, exports the content of a database to a CSV file, and produces summary reports. KaZAlyser can open one or more database files from any FastTrack based installation, such as KaZaA, iMesh, and Grokster, and display the contents in a tabular form. Once loaded into KaZAlyser filters can be applied to the database entries to limit the display to particular records such as 'all graphics files" or "identify known child pornography." KaZAlyser is the successor to the popular P2Pview KaZaA and Morpheus database viewer. KaZAlyser provides significant enhancements to the forensic investigation process.
KnTTools with KnTList	Acquires physical memory evidence from select Windows operating systems.
List Alternate Data Streams (LADS)	Lists all alternate data streams (ADS) of an NTFS directory. It shows the ADS of encrypted files, even when these files were encrypted with another copy of Windows 2000. It can recursively search through subdirectories and displays a byte total.
LDE	A disk editor for Linux, originally written to help recover deleted files. It is 100-percent free under the Gnu public license.
LibPST	A set of functions in library form for accessing Outlook's Personal Folders. Included with this library is the "readpst" utility that converts a PST file to mbox format. This program is part of the ol2mbox project.

Continued

Table 13.1 continued Forensic Software

Software	Description
Legal Imager and reaSsembly Application (LISA)	LISA is a MS-DOS-based disk-imaging tool, suitable for taking images of hard disk drives for the purpose of forensic analysis.
ListDLLs	Displays the full path names of loaded modules. Also, ListDLLs will flag loaded DLLs that have different version numbers from their corresponding on-disk files (which occurs when the file is updated after a program loads the DLL), and can determine which DLLs were relocated because they are not loaded at their base address.
Live View	Creates a VMware virtual machine out of a raw (dd-style) disk image or physical disk. This tool is Java-based.
Lookout	Performs lightning-fast search for e-mail and files. Works with Microsoft Outlook.
M2CFG USB WriteBlock	Toggles write protection for USB devices on and off. This utility requires Windows XP Service Pack 2
M2CFG Yahoo! Email/Text Parser	Reads a Yahoo! e-mail text file, and writes each e-mail message with its respective attachment(s) to a separate file.Yahoo! returns the contents of each screen name as one text file. This file contains all e-mail content and base64 attachments as plain text.
Mac Emulator	Macintosh emulator for Window XP.
MACMatch	Searches for files by their last write date, last access date, or creation date without changing any of this data.
MacOpener 2000	Accesses Macintosh-formatted disks from a Windows PC. Enables access to Macintosh disks form the Windows desktop. You can also format disks as Macintosh disks.
mac-robber	Collects data from allocated files in a mounted file system. The data can be used by the mactime tool in The Sleuth Kit to make a timeline of file activity.

Continued

Table 13.1 continued Forensic Software

Software	Description
Magic Rescue	Scans a block device for all recoverable file types and calls an external program to extract them. It looks at the "magic bytes" within the contents of a file, so it can be used both as an undelete utility and for recovering a corrupted drive or partition.
Mailbag Assistant	Mailbag Assistant supports Outlook Express, Eudora, Netscape, Mozilla, Pegasus, The Bat!, Forte Agent, Calypso, PocoMail, FoxMail, Juno 3.x, UNIX mail (Pine, Elm, mbox, etc.), and EML message files.
MailMeter Forensic	E-mail management and investigative solution for organizations that need to perform in-depth forensic analysis and evidentiary discovery on corporate email data
MAK_HTML	Links all files in a folder to an index.htm file that can be used to "browse" the identified files. A program from Dane Mares.
MD5	MD5 Hashing algorithm.
MD5 and Hashing Utilities	Calculates the 128-bit MD5 hash value of any file or block of text.
MD5Deep	Computes MD5 message digests on an arbitrary number of files.
md5summer	Generates and verifies MD5 checksums. md5summer is an application for Microsoft Windows 9x, Windows NT, Windows ME, Windows 2000, and Windows XP.
Media Merge/PC	Reads a tape in any format and also look at any part of the tape in unprocessed mode. In order to do forensic analysis on data from a tape, first it is essential to read the tape. Often with an investigation, tapes may be obtained but no knowledge of how they were written. With Media Merge/PC, the raw data may always be read provided a compatible tape drive is available, and the chances are extremely high that the logical tape format will automatically be detected and the files restored just as on the host system.
memdump	Dumps main memory (/dev/mem) on Solaris, BSD Unix, and Linux systems.

Continued

Table 13.1 continued Forensic Software

Software	Description
memfetch	Dumps the memory of a running process, either immediately or when an error condition occurs. It recovers information that would otherwise be lost, making it easier to check the internals of a running process.
Metadata Assistant	Analyzes Word, Excel, PowerPoint 97, PowerPoint 2000, PowerPoint 2002 (XP), and PowerPoint 2003 documents to determine what hidden metadata a client might see, display its findings, and then offer the ability to clean the document by selecting a variety of options.
MiTeC Tools	Includes an EXIF reader, Windows Registry recovery, a portable executable reader, and other utilities.
Mod Com	Alters the operating system files on a floppy boot disk so that, when booted, it will not alter any-thing on the C: drive. This is what is done manu-ally in the basic forensic classes when you alter boot disks to disable access to the C: drive. This program creates a forensically sound boot disk.
Mount Image Pro	Enables the mounting of EnCase, UNIX DD, or SMART forensic images as a drive letter on your file system.
MS Access Database Cracker	Decrypts the master password stored in a Microsoft Access database. There are two utilities in the zip for decoding Access 95, 97, 2000, and XP.
Mtools	Mtools is a collection of utilities to access MS-DOS disks from UNIX without mounting them. It sup-ports Win-95 style long file names, OS/2 XDF disks and 2m disks (store up to 1992k on a high density 3 1/2 disk).
NASA Tools	Fatback and Enhanced Loopback.
NCFS Software Write-block XP	Blocks write operations to
Nero Express	Burns CDs and DVDs.
NetAnalysis - Forensic Internet History Analyzer	Forensically analyzes Internet user activity. It can also extract Web browser history from unal-located disk space.

Continued

Table 13.1 continued Forensic Software

Software	Description
NetIntercept - Network Forensics Analysis Tool	Captures, analyzes, and discovers network traffic. The Forensic View uncovers malicious activity. It also searches connections by several customizable criteria.
Nigilant32	An incident response tool that captures as much information as possible from a running system with the smallest potential impact.
NirSoft Web site	Provides a unique collection of small and useful freeware forensic analysis utilities.
NT SAMs	Linux boot disk that accesses the Windows Partition then resets account passwords by exploiting that SAM file.
NTLast	Performs security audits on Windows NT systems. NTLast is specifically targeted for security and IIS administration. It performs scheduled reviews of NT event logs to uncover server breaches. Identifies and tracks users who have gained system access and documents the details. . It reports on the status of IIS users and well as filters Web server logons from console logons.
ntpasswd	Edits Registry entries and NT passwords. An image disk to boot in order to recover (reset) password by modifying the encrypted password in the Registry's SAM file. You'll need the rawrite to create the boot disk ou with any UNIX dd if=boot-disk.bin of=/dev/fd0 bs=1024.
ntreg	Mounts NT Registry files such as SAM and SECURITY on Linux file systems. This is a file system driver for Linux that accesses the NT registry file format. Supports only read-only mounts.
Open Digital Evidence Search and Seizure Architecture (ODESSA)	A cross-platform framework for performing computer forensics and incident response.
OE-Mail Recovery	Recovers Outlook Express e-mail.
Offline Registry Parser	A Perl script that parses the raw Registry files in binary mode, and prints out the data, to include last-write information.
Online Digital Forensic Suite (OnlineDFS)	Applies digital forensics technology to the investigation of operational computer systems.

Continued

Table 13.1 continued Forensic Software

Software	Description
Ontrack PowerControls	Copies and searches mailbox data in Microsoft Exchange Server backups, unmounted databases (EDB files), and information store files.
Open Ports	Detects all open TCP and UDP ports on a computer system, including the owner process. Using advanced port-to-process mapping technology developed for Port Explorer, OpenPorts displays results in five different styles, allowing for easy interpretation by both scripts and human eyes. This is a CLI (command line interface/console) tool.
OST to PST	Creates a PST from an orphaned OST file.
Outindex E-Discovery & Compliance	Extracts emails from Microsoft Outlook PST files and writes them to databases such as Oracle and SQL Server.
Outlook Recovery	Recovers data from corrupted Microsoft Outlook Personal Storage files (PST).
Oxygen	Forensically analyzes mobile phones. The software does not change any data on the phone. Oxygen runs on any version of the Windows operating system.
P2 Power Pack	Contains the following items from Paraben Forensics: Case Agent Companion version1.0, Decryption Collection Enterprise version 2.5, E-mail Examiner version 4.01, Forensic Replicator v3.1, Forensic Sorter version 1.0, Network E-mail Examiner version 1.9, PDA Seizure version 3.0.1.35, Text Searcher version 1.0, and Chat Examiner version1.0.
Paraben Case Agent Companion	Optimizes the time of the examiner and the agent working the case. Includes viewers for over 225 file formats and is compatible with Paraben's P2.

Continued

Table 13.1 continued Forensic Software

Software	Description
Paraben Cell Seizure	Enables the forensic acquisition of user data and portions of unallocated storage on some devices. Cellphone forensics is not to be compared with traditional bit stream forensics. Cellphone data storage is proprietary, based on the manufacturer, model, and system. Each device is unique and should be dealt with caution as each cellphone has unique considerations. Continual advances will be made to Paraben's Cell Seizure in reference to acquiring of proprietary data. Paraben's Cell Seizure currently supports certain models of Nokia, Sony-Ericcson, Motorola, and Siemens. Paraben's Cell Seizure also supports GSM SIM cards with use of a SIM card reader, which can be found in Cell Seizure Toolbox.
Paraben Decryption Collection	A suite of programs that recover passwords. Includes EFS support, Windows Server 2003 support, and Lotus Notes support along with support for everything included in our Standard Edition. It also includes QuickBooks 2003 support and Peachtree 2004 support.
Paraben E-mail Examiner	Examines e-mail messages. E-mail Examiner claims to recover more active and deleted mail messages than the leading competitor.
Paraben Forensic Replicator	Replicates exact copies of drives and media. Paraben's Forensic Replicator can acquire a wide range of electronic media, from floppies to hard disks. Forensic Replicator images can be compressed and segmented and easily read into the most popular forensic analysis programs.
Paraben Forensic Sorter	Classifies data into over 14 different categories, recovers deleted files, and filters common hashes (for example, FOCH), making examinations easier to manage and faster to process.
Paraben NetAnalysis	Interrogates Web browser cache and history data with powerful searching, filtering, and evidence identification.
Paraben Network Email Examiner	Examines a variety of network e-mail archives. Network E-mail Examiner is compatible with E-mail Examiner and can easily be configured for more complex tasks.

Continued

Table 13.1 continued Forensic Software

Software	Description
Paraben PDA Seizure	Captures data and reports on data from a PDA. Runs in a Windows environment. Includes USB support.
Paraben Text Searcher	Searches text.
Paragon Ext2FS Anywhere	Mounts Linux partitions on Windows file systems as normal logical drives with appropriate drive letters.
Partition Image	Saves partitions in many formats to an image file. Runs on Linux and other versions of UNIX.
Partition Magic	Formats and manages partitions on a hard drive.
Pasco	Examines the contents of Internet Explorer's cache files. Pasco parses the information in an index.dat file and outputs the results in a field-delimited manner so that it may be imported into your favorite spreadsheet program. Pasco runs Windows, Mac OS X, Linux, and BSD UNIX operating systems.
PC Inspector™ File Recovery	Recovers data on FAT 12, FAT16, FAT32, and NTFS file systems. Some of the features in PC INSPECTOR File Recovery 3.x include finding partitions automatically, even if the boot sector or FAT has been erased or damaged. This feature does not work with the NTFS file system.
PC Inspector™ Smart Recovery	Recovers data from Flash Card, Smart Media, SONY Memory Stick, IBM Micro Drive, Multimedia Card, Secure Digital Card, or other storage media for digital cameras.
Palm dd (pdd)	Images memory and forensically acquires data from the Palm OS family of PDAs. pdd will preserve the crime scene by obtaining a bit-for-bit image or "snapshot" of the Palm device's memory contents. Runs on all versions of the Windows operating system.
PDU spy	Another mobile phone examination program. The site has a number of interesting recovery programs and useful bits for investigating phones. Freeware.
PenguinBackup	The PalmPilot single-floppy backup system.

Continued

Table 13.1 continued Forensic Software

Software	Description
PERKEO++	Locates pornography on any type of digital media.
PFC Viewer	Displays and exports the contents of the AOL Filing Cabinet, also known as the Personal Filing Cabinet. PFC Viewer is a Java application.
Phonebase	Reports on the contents of SIM cards and phone memories. These are typically lists of phone numbers and associated names, recently made calls and text messages.
Photo Rescue	Retrieves deleted data on Compact Flash cards.
PhotoRec	Recovers lost pictures from digital camera memory.
Picalo	Forensically analyzes data. Data Analysis and Fraud Detection, a collaborative, open-source effort to produce a data analysis application suitable for auditors, fraud examiners, data miners, and other data analysts. Windows, Macintosh, and UNIX/Linux versions.
Pictuate	Finds and analyzes images for pornographic content; scans computer disks to find all image files, then scores those images as to their content. The results are sorted in descending order and viewed in a panel of thumbnail images. The user sees the images most likely to be pornographic (a target image) first and progresses to less likely candidates in subsequent panels.
Pilot-Link	Retrieves the contents of ROM and RAM from Palm devices. Additionally pilot-xfer allows acquisition
Pinpoint Labs Free Tools	Pinpoint FileMatch, Pinpoint Hash, Pinpoint Metaviewer.
Port Explorer	Displays all open ports on a system and the programs that own them — also called port-to-process mapping. Additional functionality includes packet sniffing, bandwidth throttling, and country detection. Port Explorer has an intuitive GUI that allows displays all network activity on your computer.
POSE	Emulates Palm devices on the desktop.

Continued

Table 13.1 continued Forensic Software

Software	Description
Private Eyec	Displays the entire contents of an area on your PC referred to as protected storage.
Process Dumper & Memory Parser (MMP)	Creates a dump of a running process for forensic purposes. MMP parses the metainformation stored within process dumps made with Process Dumper (pd) and extracts the different process mappings to disk.
Process Explorer	Identifies the handles and DLLs that have been opened by processes or loaded into process space. The Process Explorer display consists of two sub-windows. The top window always shows a list of the currently active processes, including the names of their owning accounts, whereas the information displayed in the bottom window depends on the mode that Process Explorer is in. If it is in handle mode you'll see the handles that the process selected in the top window has opened; if Process Explorer is in DLL mode you'll see the DLLs and memory-mapped files that the process has loaded. Process Explorer also has a powerful search capability that will quickly show you which processes have handles opened or DLLs loaded. The unique capabilities of Process Explorer make it useful for tracking down DLL-version problems or handle leaks, and provide insight into the way Windows and applications work.
Process Viewer for Windows (PrcView)	Displays detailed information about processes running under Windows.
procshow	Displays information about a running process.
Protected Storage Explorer	Displays saved data from the Protected Storage Service, including passwords for e-mail accounts in Microsoft Outlook, Microsoft Outlook Express, MSN Messenger, saved Internet Explorer form data such as phone numbers, credit card numbers, web email, search engine queries, user names and passwords on Web pages, and cached logon credentials of sites that require authentication, including FTP sites.
Password Recovery Toolkit (PRTK)	Recovers passwords. Developed by Access Data.

Continued

Table 13.1 continued Forensic Software

Software	Description
PTfinder Collection	A collection of PTfinders for Windows 2000, Windows XP, Windows XP SP1, Windows XP SP2. and Windows Server 2003.
PurgeIE	This versatile program allows you either to manage your cookies and cache files in a logical manner or, for complete privacy, to eliminate them altogether, complete with all references, tracks, trails and strays.
Putty	PuTTY is a free implementation of Telnet and SSH for Win32 and UNIX platforms, along with an xterm terminal emulator.
PyFlag	PyFlag is the Python implementation of Flag - a complete rewrite of FLAG in the much more robust python programming language. Many additional improvements were made.
QuickTime	Plays video, audio, QuickTimeVR, and graphics files. Freeware.
Remote Data Acquisition (RDA)	Remotely acquires data — such as disk cloning or disk/partition imaging data — and verifies the transfer using MD5 or CRC32 checksums. The program is both the server and the client and is a command-line tool that runs on Linux.
R-Drive Image	Creates disk image files for backup or duplication purposes. The image file contains an exact, byte-by-byte copy of a hard drive, partition, or logical disk.
RealPlayer	Plays every major media format, including DVDs.
Recover	Automates some steps of recovering deleted files on an /Ext2 filesystem.
Recover CHK Files	Renames CHK files to the correct extension.
Recover4all	After you download the utility, run the self-extracting EXE file and choose the unzip option. You should not save anything to the drive where your deleted files are to prevent the deleted files from being overwritten. For example, if your deleted files are on the C: drive, do not install any software and do not download anything to C:. Download Recover4all to A:. Recover4all does not require installation and can be run from a floppy disk.

Continued

Table 13.1 continued Forensic Software

Software	Description
Red Cliff Web Historian	Reviews Web sites stored in the history files of the most commonly used browsers, including: Microsoft Internet Explorer, Mozilla, Firefox, Netscape, Opera, and Safari.
Regdat & RegdatXP	Displays the contents of copies of the Win9x and WindowsMe Registry files System.dat, Classes.dat, and User.dat, and displays the contents in a Regedit like interface. You can search for keys and values and export them. Also functions to compare the file with the current Registry are provided as well as tools to edit the file.
Registry Information Extractor (RIE)	Extracts Registry information on Windows 95, Windows 98, Windows ME operating system. It will be updated to extract a lot more information from the Registry, including Windows NT, Windows 2000, and Windows XP support. Currently It can extract the following information: Registered Owner, Registered Organization, Windows Version, Windows Version Number, Windows Installed Date & the Computer Name. RIE can also be used as a File Viewer from within EnCase. This is a test release of a software utility that is in development and under testing.
RegMon	Determines the applications that are accessing the Windows Registry, which keys they are accessing, and the Registry data they are reading and writing – all in real-time.
RegTools	Contains the following applications: RegDACL - , a permissions manager for Registry keys; RegOwner - ownership manager for Registry keys. RegAudit - audit manager for Registry keys. RegLast - lists or queries the last write data of Registry keys.
Regviewer	
Resource Hacker	Views, modifies, renames, adds, deletes, and extracts resources in 32-bit Windows executables and resource files (RES files). Freeware.

Continued

Table 13.1 continued Forensic Software

Software	Description
Resplendent Registrar	Reviews the Registry in Windows NT, Windows 2000, Win9x, and Windows ME systems. It searches the Registry extremely fast, and presents the search results in a usable fashion.
Restorer2000	Undeletes files deleted accidentally in NTFS partitions, and recovers data on formatted or corrupted drives.
Rifiuti	Examine the contents of the INFO2 file in the Recycle Bin, and produces field-delimited output that can be imported into your favorite spreadsheet program. Rifiuti runs on Windows, Mac OS X, Linux, and BSD Unix platforms.
RKDetect	Finds services hidden by generic Windows rootkits such as Hacker Defender.
R-Linux	Recovers data on Ext2 file system partitions used in several UNIX operating systems. Supported host operating systems: Windows 9x, Windows Me, /Windows NT, Windows 2000, Windows XP. Recovered data can be written to any disk visible by the host operating system. R-Linux also can create disk images that can be later processed by more powerful R-Studio. Freeware.
R-Mail	Recovers accidentally deleted e-mail messages and recovery damaged DBX files where Outlook Express stores folders with e-mail messages. The new e-mail data recovery technology IntelligentRebuild allows R-Mail users to quickly reconstruct damaged DBX files created by Outlook Express and easily restore the lost messages. The messages are recovered in EML format and can be imported into Outlook Express e-mail and Internegt news databases.
RootkitRevealer	Detects rootkits. Processes files produced by Windows NT 4 and higher.
R-Studio	Recovers and undeletes data. Supports the FAT 12, FAT 16, FAT 32, NTFS, NTFS 5 , Ext2 file systems and recovers files both on local logical and physical disks and disks on remote computers over the networks, even if their partition structures are damaged or deleted.

Continued

Table 13.1 continued Forensic Software

Software	Description
R-Undelete	Undeletes data on the FAT, NTFS, NTFS 5, and Ext2 file systems. R-Undelete can undelete files on any valid logical disks accessible by the host OS. It cannot undelete files on damaged or deleted volumes, or if the hard drive has been repartitioned.
R-Word	Recovers MS Word documents.
SafeBack	Creates mirror-image (bitstream) backup copies of hard disks or partitions.
SagePass	Retrieves passwords from Sage Sterling, Line 100, and Instant accounting systems.
Scalpel: A Frugal, High Performance File Carver	Reads a database of header and footer definitions and extracts matching files from a set of image files or raw device files.
sdd	A replacement for a the "dd" utility.
SecCheck	Detects and removes malicious applications, back doors, Trojans, worms, and viruses.
SecReport - Click 'Toolbox'	Collects security-related information from Windows-based system (SecReport) and compares any two reports from different systems or the same system after a specified delta of time. A suite of two command-line tools.
SecretExplorer	Views, analyzes edits, imports, and exports protected storage, retrieve AutoComplete passwords and data, recovers passwords; transfer passwords and settings from one computer to another.
Secure Hash Signature Generator	Creates signatures that are unique to the data stored on a disk drive. These signatures are used to verify intentional or accidental tampering with the drive image.
SHA verify	Calculates the MD5 (128-bit), SHA1 (160-bit), SHA2 (256-bit), SHA2 (384-bit), and SHA2 (512-bit) hashes of files.

Continued

Table 13.1 continued Forensic Software

Software	Description
ShoWin	Displays information about Windows such as account passwords. ShoWin displays information a cursor is dragged over it. One of the most popular uses of this program is to display hidden password editbox fields (text behind the asterisks). This will work in many programs although Microsoft has changed the way things work in some of their applications, most notably the MS Office suite and Windows 2000. ShoWin will not work in these cases. Neither will it work for password entry boxes on Web pages, at least with most Web browsers. Additional features include the ability to enable windows that have been disabled, unhide hidden windows, and force a window to stay on top or be placed below others.
SIM Manager	Recovers phone numbers and SMS messages from a range of mobile phones
SIM Scan	Investigates the contents of SIM cards. Freeware.
SIMCon	Provides forensic imaging and analysis of the contents of SIM cards, including recovery of deleted items. Free for law enforcement.
Sleuthkit Windows Executables	Microsoft Windows executables for The Sleuth Kit. Full source code and documentation can be downloaded.
Sleuthkit/Autopsy Foremost patch	Integrates Foremost into Autopsy and enables the configuration file to be edited. Created by P. Bakker.
Sleuthkit/Autopsy Searchtools patch	Performs indexed searching capabilities for Sleuthkit/Autopsy tools. Created by P. Bakker.
SMART	Monitors hard disk drives and performs failure prediction operations. It uses S.M.A.R.T. technology to monitor the health status of hard disk drives, prevents data loss, and predicts possible drive failure.

Continued

Table 13.1 continued Forensic Software

Software	Description
SnapView HTML Viewer	Examines recovered HTML pages stored in unallocated space. This viewer is built on the same technology as used by Internet Explorer and loads pages quickly. It can also toggle between page and source view. It can use any available Internet Explorer plug-ins , giving it a large selection of supported file formats. Some of the supported file formats are : HTML, JPEG, GIF, ICO, Flash Move, Adobe Acrobat, Word, Excel, PowerPoint, Bitmap, PNG, and ART.
SNIFFER	Extracts files from the free space of computer hard disks, from a series of disk image files or directly from the hard disk device. Run on MS-DOS.
SomarSoft Utilities	Contains the following programs: DumpSec - a security auditing program for WindowsNT, and Windows 2000, DumpEvt - a Windows NT program to dump the event log in a format suitable for importing into a database, and DumpReg - a program for Windows NT and Windows 95 that dumps the contents of the Registry.
Spam CSI	Performs forensic analysis of e-mail data.
Spector CNE	Records everything employees do online, including instant messaging, chats, sending and receiving e-mails , visiting Web sites, launching applications, downloading files, and typing keys.
Spider	Displays all of the URLs and cookies stored in the index.dat file, and removes them.
ssdeep	Creates a short text signature for each input file. The signatures can be used to match other files against the original. Unlike MD5 or SHA-1, however, this algorithm can match two input files even if they are not exactly the same. Files match if they have significant homologies, or the same sequences of bytes in the same order. Functions in a similar manner to md5deep.

Continued

Table 13.1 continued Forensic Software

Software	Description
Stealer	Extracts the machine name, usernames, and dial-up user accounts and passwords. It also identifies passwords and usernames on secure web sites and password-protected shared folders on a network. Most of this information is stored within the PWL file. Stealer must be run on a restored drive if you are using it to identify information on a seized computer. One law enforcement agency used it to gain access to encrypted data as the password for the encrypted material had been duplicated. This utility can save you weeks of waiting if you are contemplating a brute force attack. Runs on Windows 9x and Windows Me.
StegAlyzerAS	Performs digital forensic analysis. This utility is designed to extend the scope of traditional digital forensic examinations by allowing the examiner to scan suspect media for artifacts of steganography applications.
StegDetect	Automatically detects steganographic content in image files. It is capable of detecting several different steganographic methods for embedding information in JPEG images. Supported methods are: jsteg, jphide (UNIX and Windows), invisible secrets, and outguess 01.3b.
StegHide	Embeds a secret message in a cover file by replacing some of the least significant bits of the cover file with parts of the secret message. After that, the secret message is imperceptible and can only be extracted with the correct pass phrase. Features include support for JPEG, BMP, WAV, and AU files; encryption of plain data before embedding (blowfish encryption algorithm); pseudo-random distribution of hidden bits in stego file; and embedding a CRC32 checksum in the data.
Stego Suite 4.1	Investigates, detects, analyzes, and recovers of digital steganography. Stego Suite 4.1 includes Stego Watch, an automated steganography investigation scanning software package; nine steganography detection algorithms covering all common digital image file types and audio WAV files; Stego Analyst, a visual image analysis package for in-depth digital image and audio file analysis; and Stego Break, an automated steganography cracking tool.

Continued

Table 13.1 continued Forensic Software

Software	Description
Stellar Phoenix FAT	Recovers data on FAT file systems. It does not to be installed prior to a data loss. Stellar Phoenix FAR provides easy recovery after the partition table, boot sector, and root directory have been corrupted and data has been lost. This software runs on MS-DOS, Windows 95, Windows 98, Windows Me, Windows NT (FAT file systems), Windows 2000 (FAT file systems). Supports all variants of FAT file system.
Stellar Phoenix Novell	Recovers vital data from corrupt volumes resulting from a crashed server. It accesses data when the volumes cannot be mounted. This software can save recovered data to a disk drive after cases of corrupt or missing volumes, deleted files, allocation errors, and partition loss.
Stellar Phoenix NTFS	Recovers data after disk crashes caused by accidental formatting, viruses , software malfunctions, file or directory deletion, or sabotage. Stellar Phoenix NT Data Recovery software examines an inaccessible hard drive and displays the stored data. The disk recovery process requires only a selection of the target files and directories to copy to a working drive.
Sterilize	Sterilizes media for use as working/examination data copies.
STG Cache Audit	Displays the contents of browswer caches, cookie, and history information.
STrace for NT	Examining the system calls made by a process running on Windows NT. It is meant to be used like the strace (or truss) UNIX operating system variants. Runs on Windows NT.
Stream Explorer	Reveals alternate file streams on NTFS file systems. Runs on Windows NT 4.0, Windows 2000, Windows XP, and Windows 2003.
Streams	Reveals NTFS alternate streams.
Strings	Searches for ANSI and Unicode strings in binary images.
SuperDIR	Lists all files and directories on FAT file systems, and dumps the results into a database. It will calculate a CRC32 for every file. Very fast.

Continued

Table 13.1 continued Forensic Software

Software	Description
SuperSCAB	Analyzes seized computers.
Swapper	Swaps all byte pairs in a file. This is required for forensic research of disks, mobile phones, and copiers.
Symantec	AV program
TAFT - The ATA Forensics Tool	Communicates directly with the ATA controller to retrieve information about a hard disk, and to examine and change HPA and DCO settings.
TaFWeb Whois	A version of the "whois" utility. It can report IP numbers as well as domain names.
TapeCat	Forensically analyzes tapes. Runs on all versions of Windows.
TASK	Performs a comprehensive forensic analysis of Windows and UNIX file systems. Open source from @stake.
Tcpflow	Captures data transmitted as part of TCP connections (flows), and stores it in a way that is convenient for protocol analysis or debugging. The "Tcpdump" utility shows a summary of the packets transmitted on the wire but usually doesn't store the data. In contrast, Tcpflow reconstructs the actual data streams and stores each flow in a separate file for later analysis. Tcpflow processes sequence numbers and correctly reconstructs data streams regardless of retransmissions or out-of-order delivery. However, it currently does not process IP fragments — flows containing IP fragments will not be recorded properly
Tcptrace	Analyzes TCP dump files. It takes as input the files produced by several popular packet-capture programs, including Tcpdump, snoop, etherpeek, HP Net Metrix, and WinDump. Tcptrace can produce several different types of output containing information on each connection seen, such as elapsed time, bytes and segments sent and received, retransmissions, round trip times, window advertisements, and throughput. It can also produce a number of graphs for further analysis.

Continued

Table 13.1 continued Forensic Software

Software	Description
TCTUtils	An enhancement to the Coroner's Toolkit (TCT) utility. TCTUtils can list directory inode contents, find the inode that is using a given block, and enables the viewing of inode and block details in various formats.
TestDisk	Checks and undeletes partitions.
Text2Hex	This utility will convert ASCII characters to hexadecimal values. This is particularly useful when performing searches using software that can accept hexadecimal values as search criteria.
ThumbsDisplay	Displays all thumbnail images with original file names and timestamps.
ThumbsPlus	Displays thumbnail images and displays, edits, and batch converts regular image files.
TNEF	Unpacks Microsoft MS-TNEF MIME attachment files.
Tree Browser (TB) / KDE Tree Browser (KTB)	Displays file hierarchies.
True Time	Prompts the user for the correct date and time, and obtains the system date and time from the system BIOS. The output can be redirected to a file for use in forensic investigations. Excellent addition to a forensic boot disk.
TULP2G	Extracts and decoding data stored in electronic devices. Based on Windows .NET technology.
UDP Cast	A Netcat substitute.
UndeleteSMS	Recovers deleted SMS messages from a GSM SIM card.
Unique	Eliminates duplicate records in a file. This program will take a sorted input file and copy records to the output for which it finds a unique occurrence of the sort key. The program passes the input file, and when it finds a new and unique sort key in a record it copies that record to the output, and disregards all subsequent records that contain that same sort key. Therefore, only a single record per sort key is copied to the output file.

Continued

Table 13.1 continued Forensic Software

Software	Description
URLSearch	Extracts web addresses and other text strings from local and remote files. Results can be edited and exported in various ways. Web addresses can be sorted by domains and exported to your browser's bookmarks (supported browsers are Netscape, Internet Explorer, and Opera). UrlSearch can also be used as a download agent and can view history and cookie files, edit typed URLs, and calculate hit rates.
USB Blocker	This application was designed to meet the needs of write blocking USB devices.
UTF-8 output patch for task-1.60/Sleuth Kit-1.6x	Displays foreign characters in the names of files located in an NTFS image. By default, Sleuth Kit converts the Unicode NTFS file system structures into ASCII. This patch changes that behavior, but doesn't change the keyword searching ability. That is still done with the "strings" and "grep" utilities, which do not easily support Unicode.
Ultimate Toolkit (UTK)	The complete AccessData software kit.
VFC - Virtual Forensic Computing	Rapidly boots a forensic image of a suspect's computer, or boots a write-blocked physical hard drive.
Viesoft Forensic Scan	Scans "index.dat" files.
vinetto	Extracts thumbnail images and associated metadata from the "thumbs.db" files generated by Windows. A console-based program that runs under Cygwin or Linux.
Vision	Reports all open TCP and UDP ports and maps them to the process or application accessing them.
VNC	Remotely accesses and views.
Web Cache Illuminator	Creates a meaningful list that displays all file names in the Web browser cache and the title of the Web page.
WebDate	Returns the last modified date and time of a Web site, Web page, or individual file.
Webtracer	Determines the owner of a Web site, the location of a server, the sender of an e-mail, and other evidence of Internet identity.

Continued

Table 13.1 continued Forensic Software

Software	Description
WhatFormat	Analyzes the first bytes of a file for signatures (or magic numbers) and determines the format of the file from this evidence.
Win32 Analyzer	Creates a forensic snapshot of a computer. Uses Windows and third-party tools.
Win32 First Responder's Analyzer Tookit	Performs basic security tasks. A self-extracting Windows executable designed to be run from a floppy disk.
Windows Forensic Toolchest (WFT)	Provides automated incident response on a Windows system and collects security-relevant information from the system.
Windows Forensics and Incident Recovery tools	A set of tools produced by the Forensic Server Project for incident response and computer forensic activities on Windows systems.
Windows Memory Forensic Toolkit (WMFT)	A collection of proof-of-concept tools, used for forensic analysis of physical memory images gathered from compromised Windows machines
Windows NT/2000 Incident Response Tools	Gathers and analyzes forensic data on a Windows system and produces snapshots of past states of system. This program is a collection of tools, and like The Coroner's Toolkit (TCT), most of the tools are oriented towards data collection rather than analysis.
WinDump	Creates dump files of network traffic data. WinDump prints the headers of packets on a network interface that match a specified boolean expression. It can also be run with the "-w" flag, which causes it to save the packet data to a file for later analysis, and with the "-b" flag, which causes it to read from a saved packet file rather than to read packets from a network interface. In all cases, only packets that match the specified expression will be processed by WinDump.
WinGREP	Searches files for specified text strings.
WinHex	Edits hexadecimal data.
WinImage	Creates disk images from a floppy and vice versa, among other functions. Developed because Windows lacks a native "dd" command.

Continued

Table 13.1 continued Forensic Software

Software	Description
Wininterrogate	Recursively scans a directory structure and obtains the following information: file name and size, complete path of files and directories, directory name, creation time, last access time, last write time, and MD5 checksum. Additional information gathered from DLL, VBX, DRV, EXE, OCX, BIN, SCR files includes CompanyName, FileDescription, FileVersion, InternalName, LegalCopyright, OriginalFilename, ProductName, ProductVersion, Comments, LegalTrademarks, PrivateBuild, and SpecialBuild.
WinOra	Converts the installation time format used in the Windows Registry.
WinPcap 3.1	Used in several network investigation tools.
WinRAR	Compresses and uncompresses RAR-format files. Also processes other compression formats. Runs on all versions of Windows.
WinZip	Compresses and uncompresses ZIP-format files. Runs on all versions of Windows.
Wipe	Securely wipes files from storage media. It is based on work by Peter Gutmann.
X1 Search	Searches for information, previews it in its native format ,and takes action on it regardless of type or location.
XANALYS Forensic Analyzer	Automatically examines an EnCase file. Extends EnCase functionality.
XnView	Views and browses multimedia files, and converts the format.
X-Ways Trace	Tracks and examines past Web browsing activity on a computer.
Yahoo Message Archive Decoder	Accesses Yahoo Messenger archive files (DAT files) and presents them in a readable format.
ZefrJPG	Recovers JPG files destroyed by the Love Letter worm and its variants on FAT or NTFS file systems (Thanks to Robert Green @ http://personal.atl.bell-south.net/~lasrpro.)
Zeitline	Edits timelines for computer forensic purposes.

Continued

Table 13.1 continued Forensic Software

Software	Description
Zero Assumption Digital Image Recovery	Recovers digital image data produced by a digital camera. digital images. It allows you to recover digital photos accidentally deleted from digital camera memory. Freeware.

Forensic Hardware Tools

The features and advantages of hardware computer forensic tools are based on techniques that substitute software for processes and the use of equipment that is compact and easy to operate.

These devices are often powered from the source or from the suspect machine. However, the forensic analyst who relies on forensic hardware must ensure that all possible connectors are available prior to starting a job. Some of the advantages include:

1. The mbedded development that has been completed, saving space and time and generally simplifying the acquisition process.

2. The greater portability of the products.

3. The increased speed of acquiring of digital data using hardware devices compared to using software.

Hard Disk Write Protection Tools

Hardware protection devices offer a simple method to acquire an image of a suspect drive with much less fiddling with the configuration settings in software. This makes the process simpler and less prone to error.

The following section introduces a number of these hardware-based forensic tools.

NOTE

NIST has a laboratory that tests and rates the various forensic tools. The reports on the results of these tests are available from www.cftt.nist.gov/hardware_write_block.htm.

NoWrite

NoWrite prevents data from being written to the hard disk. It supports hard disk drives with high capacities. It is compatible with all kinds of devices including USB or FireWire boxes, adapters, and IDE interface cables. It supports communication between common IDE interfaces.

NoWrite is only functional on native IDE devices. It supports all USB features such as plug- and-play. It is compatible with most operating systems and drive formats. NoWrite is transparent to the operating system and the application programs — MS-DOS, Windows, Linux, Sun, and Macintosh operating systems are incapable of detecting it. NoWrite maintains the image of the evidence obtained from a system and the data is able to be viewed using EnCase, FTK, and Ilook in preview modes. This product is created by MyKey Technologies, Inc.

FireWire DriveDock

Wiebetech's FireWire DriveDock is a forensic instrument designed to load hard drives on computer systems. It is a 3.5-inch hard drive that is used along with a single device to give complete FireWire desktop storage. It is a compact device of about four cubic inches that can control everything in a 3.5-inch hard drive.

At the base of the drive is a mounting plate where the power and FireWire cables are attached and an AC adapter. The drive volume does not require additional drivers. It may be used in all Macintoshes and PCs with a FireWire port. The data transfer rate is a minimum of 35 MB per second.

LockDown

Lockdown by Paraben is an advanced Firewire-to IDE or USB-to-IDE write blocker that combines speed and portability in enabling IDE media to be acquired quickly and safely in Windows-based systems. Paraben's Lockdown System includes the following equipment:

- Paraben's Lockdown
- 40-wire IDE ribbon cable for legacy desktop hard drives
- 80-wire IDE ribbon cable for newer desktop hard drives
- 44-pin-IDE-notebook-to-80-pin-IDE-desktop cable converter
- 4-pin (mini) to 6-pin FireWire (IEEE 1394a) cable
- 6-pin FireWire cable
- USB 1.0/2.0 cable
- Molex power cables for desktop hard drives
- External power supply

- User manual
- Hard carrying case

The devices feature the following capabilities:

- Connections using FireWire or USB interfaces
- Hot-swapping of suspect hard drives without restarting the computer
- Small size (4" wide, 3" deep, and 1" high) for portability and ease-of-use in the field
- IDE ports for "desktop IDE" and "laptop IDE" media, negating the need for a desktop-to-laptop IDE adapter
- Allows the reading of IDE hard drives through lightweight, portable, and common computer port interfaces (Firewire or USB)
- Can be used to acquire drives through Windows using a process that is substantially faster than MS-DOS-based acquisitions
- Easy to hook up and start an analysis

Write Protect Card Reader

The Write Protect Card Reader from *Intelligent Computer Solutions* transfers data from digital cameras, digital camcorders, PDAs, MP3 players, and digital voice recorders to a laptop or desktop computer. It can read several types of flash memory while blocking any writes to it. It is a small palm-size package with a simple USB 1.1/2.0 connection and requires no external power.

The features of the Write Protect Card Reader include:

- High-speed USB 2.0 connection
- Backward-compatible to USB 1.1
- The ability to read 12 types of digital media in a plug-and-play manner: CF-I, CF-II, Smart Media, Memory Stick™, Memory Stick PRO, Memory Stick DUO, Memory Stick PRO DUO, Micro Drive, Multimedia Card, Secure Digital Card, MINI Secure Digital Card, XDcard (using optional CF adapter)
- Can read data from four different media types simultaneously
- Maximum data throughput is 480 Mbits/sec using a USB 2.0 connection
- Unique icon for each media type in the Windows "My Computer" folder
- Small enough to fit in a jacket pocket
- Bus powered—no AC adapter needed

Drive Lock IDE

The DriveLock IDE hard drive write protection from *Intelligent Computer Solutions (ICS)* prevents write commands from being accidentally sent to hard disk drives connected through the IDE or PATA hard drive interfaces. Itdevice also blocks Serial ATA hard drives using the SATA option and blocks write commands sent to the hard drive while previewed or duplicated.

Serial-ATA DriveLock Kit

The DriveLock Serial-ATA device also from *Intelligent Computer Solutions* is a hardware write-protection device designed to prevent data writes to SATA, IDE, and PATA hard disk drives. The tool is connected to a computer's PATA interface to block write commands sent to the hard drive while the drive is being previewed or duplicated.

Wipe MASSter

Wipe MASSter from ICS is a commercial drive wiper. It has the following features:

- Wipe up to nine hard drives at speeds exceeding 2.6 GB/minute for one pass.
- Conforms to U.S. Dept. of Defense Standard DoD 5220.22-M
- Forensic audit printout after wipe
- Virtually no degradation in speed when adding drives
- Works with any IDE, EIDE, or Ultra-DMA hard drives.
- Supports 3.3-volt hard drives
- Easy firmware upgrading
- Software upgrading and saved log files using PCMCIA CompactFlash memory cards
- Automatic cable test before every run
- Locks unit setting with supervisor password
- Stores customized, predefined setting configurations
- 48-bit support for drives greater than 137 GB
- Unlocs and wipes HPA/DCO areas
- Mix different size and type of drives during the same load

ImageMASSter Solo-3 IT

Designed exclusively for forensic data acquisition, the ImageMASSter Solo-III forensics data imaging tool from ICS is a lightweight, portable handheld device that can acquire data to one or two evidence drives in high speed, with a speed exceeding 3 GB/minute.

Image MASSter Solo-3 Forensic is a complete, inclusive high-speed data acquisition tool that integrates all of the latest advanced features in data imaging. It is capable of capturing data from IDE and laptop drives, Serial ATA and SCSI drives, and Flash Cards.

With the integrated Link MASSter Option also unopened computers through both FireWire and USB2 ports.

Features of the Image MASSter SOLO 3 Forensics are the following:

- MD5 and CRC32 Hashing: Simultaneous MD5 and CRC32 hashing generation can be performed during the data capture.

- **Touchscreen user interface** The unit's advanced Touchscreen user interface and programmed keyboard provides for ease of use.

- **High-speed operation** Data acquired with a transfer rate that exceeds 3 GB/minute.

- **Built-in write protection**

- **Built-.in FireWire 1384B and USB 2.0 interface** Capture data from an unopened notebook or PC. Safely preview the drive while connected to the ImageMASSter Solo III write-protected port.

- **Capture to two evidence drives simultaneously** Capture data to two hard drives simultaneously at high speeds, without speed reduction.

- **Multiple capture methods** Acquire data using forensic sector-by-sector format or segmented file format methods (as does the "dd" utility in Linux) which enables copying multiple images to one evidence drive.

- **WipeOut** Sanitize drives and erase data at speeds greater than 3 GB/minute.

- **Biometric security** This option uses fingerprint recognition to ensure that only qualified and authorized users are allowed to operate the ImageMASSter Solo III forensics unit.

- **Audit trail and logs** Detailed operational event log information can be printed or saved to CompactFlash media.

- **Multiple media support** Supports data transfer between P-ATA, S-ATA, and SCSI hard disk drives. Also supports creating images of data on Flash Media devices and notebook computer drives.

- **Upgradable** Software and firmware upgrades performed using the supplied CompactFlash card.

ImageMASSter 4002i

The *Intelligent Computer Solutions* Image MASSter 4002 loads two IDE hard drives at speeds exceeding 1.94 GB/minute. It has the following features:

- Prints a forensic audit report after the wipe operation.

- Virtually no degradation in speed from adding drives.

- Works with any IDE, EIDE, or Ultra-DMA hard drives.

- Mix sizes and models of drives during the same load operation.

- Loads any operating system and application software, including Windows 95, Windows 98, Windows NT, Windows 2000, Windows XP, UNIX, Linux, and Mac OS.

- Full verification and error reporting: zero-defect copies.

- Automatic load size detection.

- Built-in options include NTFS-IQcopy and Wipeout.

- Supports 3.3-volt hard drives electrical interface.

- Easy Firmware upgrades.

- Software upgrading and saving log files to PCMCIA CompactFlash memory cards.

- Automatic cable test before every run.

- 48-bit addressing for drives greater than 137 GB.

- Ability to lock a unit setting with a supervisor password.

- Ability to store multiple, customized, and predefined setting configurations.

- Block-map copy mode included.

- The Image MASSter 4002 Hard Drive Duplicator includes a database option.

ImageMASSter 3002SCSI

Intelligent Computer Solutions' ImageMASSter 3002SCSI is a High Speed disk imager provides operating speeds that exceed 3.9 GB/minute. No speed degradation occurs when copying to four hard drives. It offers the capability to copy data to four target drives simultaneously with no speed degradation. It has the following features:

- Multiple Media Support: The ImageMASSter3002SCSI SCSI duplicator supports current SCSI interfaces such as Ultra-160 and Ultra-320, including SCSI Narrow (50-pin), SCSI Wide (68-pin) and SCSI-SCA80 (80-pin).hard disk drives

using optional SCSI to P-ATA converters. Also supports SCSI to S-ATA using optional SCSI to S-ATA converters.

- Multiple Copy Methods: Copy data using a sector-by-sector method, which supports copying any operating system and file system. Copy only allocated data using the ICS proprietary intelligent copy method known as "IQCOPY", which supports Windows FAT-16, F Copy only allocated data using the ICS proprietary intelligent copy method known as "IQCOPY", which supports Windows FAT-16, FAT-32, and NTFS file systems.

- Partitions and Formats Drives: Target drives are automatically partitioned and formatted during the copy process, eliminating the need to manually prepare a drive prior to usage.

- Copy between Different Drive Models and Sizes: Simultaneously copy data between different drive models and capacities of the target drive. WipeOut: Sanitize (per DoD specs) up to five SCSI drives simultaneously at speeds greater than 3.5 GB/minute.

- Bad Sector Handling: Provides flexibility in handling bad sectors found on the source drive.

- Log Information: Stores detailed operational event log information.

Image MASSter 3004 SATA

The Image MASSter 3004 SATA from *ICS* can duplicate four Serial ATA (SATA) hard drives simultaneously. It has the following specifications and features:

- Transfer rate can exceed 1.6 GB/minute depending on drive models in use. Transfer rate of 1.6 GB/minute demonstrated in a laboratory environment using Seagate ST360015AS and ST3120023AS hard drives series.

- Interface: Serial ATA data connector and Serial ATA power connector

- Mix sizes and models of drives during the same load operation

- Support for image copy and IQCOPY mode

- Support for FAT16, FAT32, and NTFS partitions using IQCOPY mode. Support for all other file systems using image copy mode

- Windows XP-based user interface

- Image MASSter 3004 SATA Hard Drive Duplicator includes built-in Wipeout option

- Built-in MultiMASSter option

- 48-bit support for hard drives with capacities greater than 137 GB

- Logs hard drives under Windows for more flexibility
- Mixes any combination of regular IDE and Serial ATA hard drives in the master and target position (which enables copying the contents of regular IDE to Serial ATA hard drives and vice versa)

Table 13.2 lists several forensic hardware tools.

Table 13.2 Forensic Hardware Devices

Hardware Device	Description
NoWrite	NoWrite prevents data from being written to the hard disk. It supports hard disk drives with high capacities. It is compatible with all kinds of devices including USB or FireWire boxes, adapters, and cables belonging to IDE. It supports communication between common IDE interfaces.
FireWire DriveDock	FireWire DriveDock is a forensic instrument designed to load hard drives on computer systems. It comprises of a 3.5-inch hard drive that is used along with a single device to give complete FireWire desktop storage. It is a compact device of about 4 cubic inches that would control everything in a 3.5-inch hard drive.
LockDown	Lockdown by Paraben is an advanced Firewire or USB to IDE write-blocker that combines swiftness and portability to allow IDE media to be acquired quickly and safely in Windows based systems.
Write Protect Card Reader	The Write Protect Card Reader transfers data to a computer system from digital cameras, digital camcorders, PDAs, MP3 players and digital voice recorders. It can read multiple types of flash memory while blocking any writes to it. It is a small palm-size package with a simple USB 2.0/1.1 connection and requires no external power.
Drive Lock IDE	The DriveLock IDE Hard Drive Write Protection is designed to completely prevent write commands from being accidentally sent to hard disk drives connected through the IDE or PATA hard drive interfaces. This write protect device also blocks Serial ATA hard drives using the SATA option. It is designed to block write commands sent to the hard drive while previewed or duplicated.

Continued

Table 13.2 continued Forensic Hardware Devices

Hardware Device	Description
Serial-ATA DriveLock Kit	The DriveLock Serial-ATA device is a hardware write protect device designed to prevent data writes to SATA, IDE and PATA hard disk drives. The tool is connected to a computer's PATA interface in order to block write commands sent to the hard drive while being previewed or duplicated.
Wipe MASSter	Wipe MASSter is a commercial drive wiper.
ImageMASSter Solo-3 IT	Designed exclusively for Forensic data acquisition, the ImageMASSter Solo-III Forensics data imaging tool is a light weight, portable hand-held device that can acquire data to one or two evidence drives in high speed, exceeding 3GB/Min.
ImageMASSter 4002i	The Image MASSter 4002 loads 2 IDE Hard drives at speeds exceeding 1.94GB/Min.
ImageMasster 3002SCSI	ImageMasster 3002SCSI is a High Speed disk imager with operating speeds that can exceed 3.9GB/min. No speed degradation occurs when copying to 4 hard drives.
Image MASSter 3004SATA	The Image MASSter 3004 SATA can duplicate 4 Serial ATA hard drives simultaneously.

Summary of Exam Objectives

The primary purpose of this chapter was to gain a level of familiarity with the wide range of hardware and software forensics tools that are available. It is not possible to detail of all the features and functions of the tools in this chapter; therefore, the student should investigate these features and functions on their own.

The two primary areas that were examined are:

- Software-based tools
- Hardware tools and write blockers

Exam Objectives Fast Track

Forensic Software Tools

- ☑ Unlike spyware, Visual TimeAnalyzer does not record specific keystrokes or run screen captures as a background process.

- ☑ Ontrack Data Recovery is a simple-to-use tool used to recover lost, remote, and deleted data.

- ☑ Forensic Sorter organizes and speeds the examination of the contents of a hard drive.

Forensic Hardware Tools

- ☑ The features and advantages of hardware computer forensic tools are based on techniques that substitute software for processes and the use of equipment that is compact and easy to operate.

- ☑ Hardware protection devices offer a simple method to acquire an image of a suspect drive with much less fiddling with the configuration settings in software.

- ☑ NoWrite prevents data from being written to the hard disk. It supports hard disk drives with high capacities.

Exam Objectives
Frequently Asked Questions

The following Frequently Asked Questions, answered by the authors of this book, are designed to both measure your understanding of the Exam Objectives presented in this chapter, and to assist you with real-life implementation of these concepts.

Q: There are so many tools. Do we need them all?

A: It is important to become familiar with a wide range of tools. It is not necessary to have all the tools.

Q: Many of the tools run on an operating system I am not familiar with. Do I need to become familiar with these operating systems?

A: Although it is good to have some level of familiarity with a wide range of systems, these tools are available for most operating systems. Whether you are familiar with Linux, Windows, or another operating system, it is likely that you will be able to find a tool that does the function you need that runs on that system.

Q: What types of evidence can digital forensics tools provide?

A: Computers store large amounts of data to a network or system of hard disks. Much of this information is stored without the user being conscious of its existence. This data may be in the form of tangible files or information that the computer used to carry out a specific task. A few examples are user files, system files, deleted files, and system data that enable the computer to perform its tasks.

Q: If I am unsure what has occurred and think that the case may never go to court. Do I still need to image the drive?

A: You never know what may occur. Imaging the drive is useful if something does turn out to be wrong. Also, being able to demonstrate that you use imaging

tools as a standard practice will make it more difficult to your procedures to be attacked in court, even on other unrelated cases.

Q: Do I need to scan a drive for malware if I have a read-only image?

A: Any forensic image file with a capture containing 100 percent of the information on a hard drive has the potential to be a virus pathway into a secure computer system. Any forensic investigation must exercise appropriate care in ensuring that none of these pathways exist.

Chapter 14

CHFI

Forensics Investigation Using EnCase

Exam objectives in this chapter:

- What Is an Evidence File?
- Hashing
- How You Acquire a File Image
- Configuring EnCase
- The Searching Ability of EnCase
- The Bookmark
- Recovering Deleted Files/Folders in a FAT Partition
- Recovering Deleted Partitions and Analyzing Media

Exam Objectives Review:

- ☑ Summary of Exam Objectives
- ☑ Exam Objectives Fast Track
- ☑ Exam Objectives Frequently Asked Questions

Introduction

Computer forensics is a relatively recent discipline that is exploding in popularity. Due to this explosion, an increasing number of forensic software and hardware tools are becoming available. Some of the most commonly used forensic software tools include EnCase, iLook (Law Enforcement Only), Forensic Toolkit (FTK), and X-Ways Forensics. EnCase, by Guidance Software, is considered by many to be the industry standard software tool for computer forensics examinations of media. Law enforcement, government agencies, and many colleges and universities have adopted EnCase Forensic Edition as their de facto software forensic tool.

Guidance Software first released EnCase Forensic edition version 1 on February 20, 1998. This first version ran only on Microsoft Windows Operating systems and was limited to reading the FAT12, FAT16, FAT32, and NTFS file systems. On January 10, 2007, Guidance Software released EnCase version 6. This latest version of EnCase runs on a variety of platforms, including Windows, Linux, and UNIX, and can read over 20 file systems, including TiVo file systems. Some of the enhanced features of this version include the ability to analyze Microsoft Virtual PC and VMware images as well some PDA (Personal Digital Assistant) platforms.

With the release of each new version of EnCase, Guidance Software continues to add features that allow computer forensic investigators to search through ever-increasing media types more efficiently. Most people in the discipline of computer forensics are familiar at some level with using EnCase Software and the various terminologies that accompany the use of this type of forensic software tool. As a person studying for EC-Council's Computer Forensic Hacking Investigator, you should become familiar with how to use the EnCase forensic software tool and be able to articulate the vocabulary used by a Computer Forensic Investigator. In order to provide testimony in a court case, or to be able to pass the Computer Forensic Hacking Investigator exam, it is essential for you to understand the language used by a computer investigators trained in the use of EnCase.

What Is an Evidence File?

In computer forensics, an evidence file is data that has been put into a special image format with a forensic software tool, such as EnCase. The purpose of creating an evidence file is to have a copy of a suspect's media so the investigator does not contaminate the original media. If the original media were investigated instead of the evidence file, a savvy attorney could argue that the investigator altered the media to incriminate their client. Creating the evidence file helps to ensure that the examined media has not been tainted by an investigator. The primary purpose of an investigator creating a separate evidence file is to ensure the original media does not become altered or contaminated when the technician conducts the forensic investigation.

TEST DAY TIP

Computer Forensic Examiners do not conduct searches or investigations on a suspect's original media. Examiners analyze a forensic copy of the original evidence so the original suspect's media is not contaminated.

An EnCase evidence file is created or "acquired" in one of several ways. An investigator can use a forensically clean DOS boot disk and boot into a DOS environment to acquire an image. A similar option will have the investigator booting to a Linux live CD, such as KNOPPIX or Helix, with a copy LinEn (Linux EnCase). Various Linux distributions can be utilized, provided they do not auto-mount media as read-write. After the computer has booted to either of these boot disks, an investigator can choose one of three methods to copy the original media file. The investigator can do a direct disk to disk copy, or use a network or parallel cable (extremely slow) to acquire the suspect's drive. For those who prefer using a GUI and Microsoft Windows, EnCase images can also be acquired by using EnCase in conjunction with FastBloc, a proprietary hardware write-blocker. A write-blocker is a hardware device, usually USB or IEEE1394 (fire-wire), that allows an investigator to connect media to a system in read-only mode. Some agencies, especially law enforcement, mandate the use of a write-blocker whenever evidence is being acquired. The Enterprise Edition of EnCase also allows an investigator to image a suspect's drive in a secure manner over the network. Regardless of how the evidence file is acquired, the original media should not be contaminated.

Notes from the Underground…

Write-Blockers

Hardware write-blockers commonly are used when acquiring a suspect's media. When a drive is connected to a Microsoft Windows operating system, changes are made to that drive. These hardware write-blockers will prevent Windows or other operating systems from writing to that drive. If a drive is connected to a system without a write-blocker and changes were written to the drive, the drive is contaminated. Any contamination could leave some doubt in a jury's mind.

The first write-blockers were connected to the IDE or SCSI cables on the motherboard. Today's write-blockers can be connected to the USB-2 or Firewire port on the motherboard. In the field, using the combination of a Linux Live CD that does not auto mount and a hardware write-blocker is an effective way to prevent the contamination of media.

An EnCase image contains a duplicate of the suspect's media, along with additional information about the case. The evidence file will contain a bit-by-bit copy of the original media copied. A bit-by bit copy is critical when creating an evidence file because it may contain items such as deleted files, folders, and slack space from the original media. The items in the evidence file could be critical in determining the outcome of a computer forensics investigation. In addition to the bit-by-bit copy of the original suspect's media, the evidence file will also contain information such as the name of the investigator, the case number, current date of acquisition, and other pertinent information about the case. This information is all relevant so that a chain of custody timeline can be established. The added information about the chain of custody is one way that the actual evidence file will differ from the actual suspect's copied media. However, because this additional information is added to the destination (evidence file) and not the source (suspect's media), the evidence file will retain its forensic integrity.

Explain Evidence File Format

When a computer forensic technician uses the EnCase imaging software, files will be saved with the extension .E##, numbered sequentially from E01 up to E99. (After E99, a system of lettering starting with EAA replaces the numbering.) In order to open and read an evidence file, a forensic software tool, such as EnCase by Guidance Software, is needed. In addition, if the evidence file was password protected for security purposes during the acquisition, the password is also required. It is important to note that an investigator can use other tools, such as Forensic Toolkit (FTK) or X-Ways forensic software, to read evidence files created with the EnCase software. The evidence file contains both the data from the suspect's original media, including deleted files, folders, and slack space, as well as information added by the investigator during the acquisition process. This could include such fields as case number, examiner name, evidence number, description, notes, and other fields that will help establish the chain of custody for this particular evidence. Because an EnCase image file contains both the suspect's media and other case-related information, it differs from an image made using dd or dcfldd. So, while Linux dd could be used to create a bit-by-bit image, that image would not have any case-related information. Using EnCase to acquire evidence files ensures that both the suspect's data as well as pertinent case information will be retained.

How Can You Verify File Integrity?

Ensuring file integrity is a critical part of the acquisition of every computer forensic investigator. For data to have integrity, it should not have been altered or corrupted. To ensure that the forensic copy of the suspect's data has integrity, EnCase forensic software does a cyclic redundancy check (CRC) for every block of 64 sectors (mandatory on all versions of EnCase prior to version 5) on the original media. A cyclic redundancy check is a mathematical check on data to ensure data has integrity. If something goes awry during the duplication process, the person doing the acquisition will receive a cyclic redundancy check error. The frequent CRC

check is one way that an investigator using EnCase to create data blocks can ensure integrity of duplicated media.

The other mechanism used in EnCase to ensure data integrity is a Message Digest 5 (MD5) hash. An MD5 hash is an algorithm applied to a data stream. When this algorithm is applied to a set of data, a MD5 hash value is generated. The possibility of two files with the same MD5 hash is very unlikely, a chance of 1 in 2^{128}. There is a better chance of someone winning the PowerBall multiple times than there is of two different files having the same MD5 hash value. There is also a greater likelihood that two different people have the same DNA or fingerprints than it is that two distinct data sets will have equivalent MD5 hash values. Even though from a mathematical standpoint it is extremely unlikely that two different files would have the same MD5 hash, recently this algorithm has come under some criticism. Due to its vulnerability to a phenomenon known as a birthday attack, some researches were able to exploit the algorithm that calculates the MD5 hash. It is also important to note that the Secure Hash Algorithm 1, or SHA-1, hash also has come under scrutiny. We have yet to see an example where someone has been able to compromise both SHA-1 and MD5 at the same time. More reliable hashes such as SHA-2 are being developed to deal with vulnerabilities that have emerged over time. Despite some criticisms, the MD5 hash value is an extremely accurate measure that two data sets are the same. EnCase software's use of both the use of CRC and MD5 will help to ensure that a suspect's original media has been duplicated properly and that the data has integrity.

Hashing

A hash uses an algorithm applied to data that will result in some type of mathematical value. When a hash is applied to two exact data sets, the expected result is the same hash value. When one data set has a slight difference or variation from another data set, the expected result would be a different hash value. There are many different hashes that can be applied to the data set. The Message Digest 5 and Secure Hash Value 1 are two of the most popular hashing algorithms used by forensic software tools. FTK and X-Ways software tools let the user choose between MD5 and SHA-1 hashes. EnCase uses a Message Digest 5 hash only on the evidence file. A computer forensic investigator will use a hash value to verify that two data are the same. On the other hand, an attorney may try to exonerate his client by explaining to a jury that data sets do not match because they have different hash values. An MD5 hash value is an extremely accurate indication that two data sets are the same.

Keep in mind that an EnCase evidence file itself will not have the same hash value as the original suspect's media. This is due to the fact that the evidence file contains additional information, including such items as examiner name, case number, CRC values, and the MD5 hash. However, the original suspect's media and the blocks of data within the evidence file will have the same hash value. When you open EnCase, start a case, and open the evidence file, the hash value in EnCase should match the hash value of the suspect's original media. The hash you see

in the EnCase program is not of the EnCase evidence file, but of the blocks of data in the evidence file. The investigator needs to be sure that the suspect's original media is the same as the data blocks contained within the evidence file. The MD5 hash allows the computer forensic investigator using EnCase to be confident that the data they are viewing is an exact match of the original suspect's media. Working on a copy of the original media allows the investigator to view and search the suspect's media without contaminating the original evidence.

Damage & Defense…

MD5

This MD5 hash is a 128-bit value generated based on the dataset and typically displayed to the investigator as a 32-character hexadecimal number. In fact, some Web sites give you an MD5 hash along with the file you download so you will be able to verify that the file did not become altered or corrupted during the download process.

Here is an example download of a MD5 hash for the English version of a KNOPPIX 5.1 ISO file:

6546a003ab532b9c0b6c142b44cf5722 *KNOPPIX_V5.1.0CD-2006-12-30-EN.iso

If someone downloads this exact file from any location in the world to any computer, when they run an MD5 hash against that file, they should expect to see that exact hash. Microsoft Windows does not have a built-in utility to do a MD5 hash on the file to verify its integrity. Linux does have an MD5 hashing tool, called md5sum. You can download this file for Windows from this Web site: www.etree.org/md5com.html. (If you do download that file, please put it in your system32 directory on Microsoft Windows.) After downloading the KNOPPIX_V5.1.0CD-2006-12-30-EN.iso, a person would type md5sum KNOPPIX_V5.1.0CD-2006-12-30-EN.iso from the directory where the file is located. By getting the same MD5 hash you see listed on the Web site, you can be confident that the file you downloaded has not been altered or corrupted during the download process. The investigator does a similar thing with the MD5 hash of a suspect's media. A computer forensic investigator will make sure that the data blocks imaged have the same MD5 hash as the original suspect media. This will give the judge, attorneys, and jury presiding over the case confidence that the investigator did not tamper with the data.

A Message Digest 5 hash, such as 6546a003ab532b9c0b6c142b44cf5722, is displayed in hexadecimal. The hexadecimal numbering system also referred to as base-16, a system of numbering that includes the numbers 0–9 and the letters A–F. The letter A in hex (hexadecimal) is equivalent to the number 10 in base 10 (decimal), and F would be equivalent to 15 in hexadecimal. The number AF47 in hexadecimal is equivalent to 44,871 as a decimal value. Here is a breakdown of the math:

Continued

A	F	4	7
10	15	4	7
10 x 163	15 x 162	4 x 161	7 x 160
10 x 4096 +	15 x 256	+ 4 x 16	+ 7 x 1
40960 +	3840	+ 64	+ 7

This can be verified in Windows by using the calculator.

EXERCISE 14.1

CONVERTING DECIMAL TO HEXADECIMAL

Requirements: Windows operating system (any)

1. Start | Programs | Accessories| Calculator
2. View | Scientific
3. Type 44871 (as seen in Figure 14.1)

Figure 14.1 Windows Calculator Displaying Decimal Numbers

4. Select the Hex radio button.
5. You should see AF47 displayed as in Figure 14.2.

Figure 14.2 Windows Calculator Displaying Hexadecimal Numbers

A hash is a mathematical algorithm applied to a set of data that results in a string of characters. That string of characters should be regenerated only when the exact same stream of data is hashed. The hashing of data is done by computer forensic investigators to ensure that the copy of the data they are working with is equivalent to the suspect's original data. That assurance, gained by an equivalent MD5 hash value, allows judges, attorneys, and juries to feel confident that the evidence that the investigator works with has integrity. EnCase uses the MD5 hash value so that the computer forensics investigator can be confident that the data blocks in the evidence file are an exact match of the data on the suspect's original media.

How You Acquire a File Image

There are several acceptable methods for a computer forensic investigator to choose from to acquire an image of a suspect's media. An investigator may boot to a DOS boot disk or Linux Live CD and acquire an image of a suspect's media. If an investigator wants to work from within a Windows environment, he or she may use EnCase with a hardware write-blocker, such as Fast-Bloc, that will prevent the alteration of the original media of the suspect. A computer forensic lab technician may also choose to acquire an image over the network in a secure manner, a process EnCase refers to as Secure Authentication for EnCase, or SAFE. The SAFE method of acquisition, however, can be used only with the Enterprise Version of EnCase. Regardless of the method the investigator chooses to acquire forensic images, they need to ensure that the suspect's original media is unaltered and that the copy of the data has integrity.

EXERCISE 14.2

CREATING AN ENCASE DOS BOOT FLOPPY

Requirements: Blank floppy

Licensed version of EnCase

Internet access

Follow these steps to make a DOS boot disk that is forensically sound (will NOT make calls to the C:\ Drive):

1. Go to the following link on the Guidance Software site: www.guidancesoftware.com/support/downloads/packets/boot-floppy.E01. Download the barebones boot floppy image to the EnCase directory in your Program Files folder.

2. To make a forensic boot floppy, insert a blank floppy into your floppy drive.

3. Start | Programs | EnCase

4. From the EnCase Menu, Tools | Create Boot Disk

5. Select the A Drive and click Next.

6. Select Overwrite diskette with a boot floppy base image, verify the path, and click Next (seen in Figure 14.3).

7. Wait for copying boot image to finish, and then click Next.

8. At the update files window, right-click in the white box and select New Insert.

9. Change the look in box to the EnCase folder in the program files directory. Find the en file and double-click it.

10. Click Finish and wait until you receive a message that says boot disk created successfully.

Figure 14.3 EnCase DOS Floppy Boot Disk Creator Program

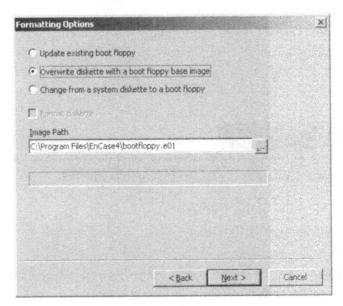

The EnCase boot floppy is a forensically clean boot disk that will not make calls to the C:\ drive. Really, the disk is nothing more than a modified Microsoft Windows 98 start-up disk. Whoever designed the disk just opened the files on the disk with a hex editor and used the Replace function to remove all references that point to the C:\ drive and replaced them with A:\ (see Figure 14.4).

Many computers do not have floppy drives.

To make this boot disk appropriate for current technology, you can use Nero Burning Rom to convert this boot floppy into a CD-ROM boot CD.

Figure 14.4 Forensically Sound EnCase DOS Floppy Boot Disk

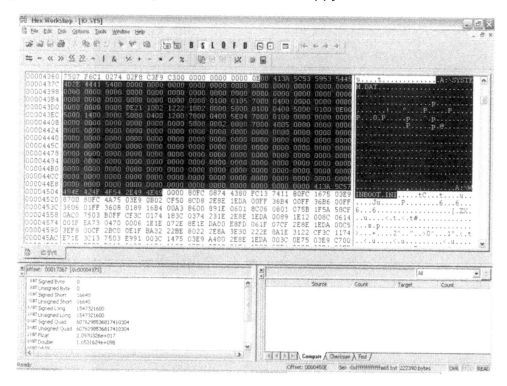

EXERCISE 14.3

MAKING AN ENCASE DOS BOOT CD-ROM

Requirements: EnCase boot floppy

Licensed version of EnCase

Nero burning ROM

Blank CD-ROM

1. Start | Programs | Nero Burning ROM| Nero

2. Select CD-ROM (boot) from the Nero menu and select New.

3. Insert your EnCase boot floppy.

4. Insert a blank CD-ROM into the CD-ROM drive.

5. Select all the files and folders on the floppy drive from the right-hand pane and drag them over to the left-hand pane (seen in Figure 14.5).

6. Choose Burn from the menu and leave the floppy in until the burn is complete.

7. When the program has finished burning, click OK. Remove the CD-ROM and floppy disk, and close the Nero program.

Figure 14.5 Using Nero Burning ROM to Convert a Boot Floppy to a Boot CD

There are many advantages to using an EnCase boot CD instead of using an EnCase boot floppy. For one, boot CDs are much quicker than their floppy counterparts. Another advantage to using a boot CD is a whopping 700MB of space to add extra utilities and features compared to the 1.44MB limitation of a floppy. Finally, there are an ever-growing number of hardware manufacturers who are choosing not to include a floppy drive with the computers they sell. (Dell is charging roughly $12 extra if you want to get a floppy drive with the purchase of your computer.) Most forensic investigators are no longer using EnCase floppy boot on a frequent basis. Even though the use of floppy boot disks is on the decline, it never hurts to have one in your toolkit in case the need arises.

On occasion, for a various number of reasons, an investigator may need to use the suspect's computer to acquire an image. If the computer was already on when the investigator arrived at the scene, first they need to follow whatever procedures their organization dictates. If a com-

puter forensics investigator is using a boot disk and not a write-blocker, he or she needs to take precautions so the suspect's computer does not unintentionally boot up to the operating system. To prevent this from happening, disconnect all cables from their IDE, SCSI, and SATA drives. Turn the computer on, and watch the splash screen for a key sequence to enter the BIOS. Often, when drives are disconnected, the BIOS will detect the removal and prompt you either accept changes or enter setup. The investigator should go into the BIOS, find the boot order selection screen, and choose CD-ROM or floppy first and disable the hard drive as a boot option. Save the changes, and place the CD floppy in the respective drive. Turn the computer off. Reconnect all disk media, then reenter the BIOS to do a final confirmation that the boot order is correct. (I have seen them change automatically when devices are added to the system. Observe carefully to make sure that the system is booting to the EnCase boot disk, not the suspect's operating system.)

Exam Warning

In the case when a suspect's computer is used for acquisition, Computer Forensic Examiners need to take every precaution possible so the computer does not boot to the operating system. Examiners initially should remove cables and find the sequence of keys used to enter the BIOS. Once in the BIOS, check the boot order, and disable the hard drive as a boot option.

Exercise 14.4

Booting to a DOS EnCase Boot Floppy or CD

Requirements: EnCase DOS boot floppy or CD

Licensed copy of EnCase

Computer with multiple drives

FAT32 partition on destination drive

1. Insert your DOS boot floppy or CD-ROM into your drive.

2. Start your computer and enter the BIOS screen. Change the boot order if necessary.

3. When you boot to either a DOS forensic boot floppy or CD, you will be provided with two initial choices once the boot disk initializes:

- Load Zip Drive Drivers

- Do Not Load Zip Drive Drivers.
 Select Do Not Load Zip Drive Drivers, unless you plan to create your evidence file on an Iomega Zip Drive.

4. Your next menu will consist of four choices (as seen in Figure 14.6):

 - UBS HDD Acquisition

 - USB HDD Destination

 - Clean Boot

 - Return to Main Menu

Figure 14.6 EnCase DOS Boot Disk Menu Choices

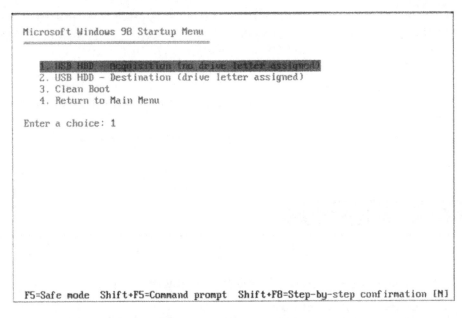

```
Microsoft Windows 98 Startup Menu

1. USB HDD - Acquisition (no drive letter assigned)
2. USB HDD - Destination (drive letter assigned)
3. Clean Boot
4. Return to Main Menu

Enter a choice: 1

F5=Safe mode  Shift+F5=Command prompt  Shift+F8=Step-by-step confirmation [N]
```

5. Choose choice #1 if you plan to acquire the data from a USB drive to one of your local disks. Choose choice #2 if you plan to acquire the data from one of your local disks to your USB mass storage device. If you have more than one physical disk in the machine, choose the third choice, clean boot, which will launch the en.exe program (see Figure 14.7).

Figure 14.7 EnCase Version 5 EN.EXE Running in DOS

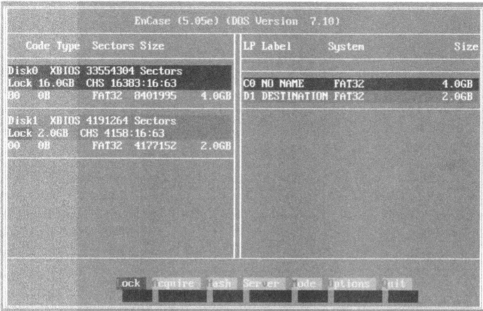

When any of the first three choices are selected from the menu option, you will eventually reach a light blue screen that specifies DOS Version 7 and the version of EnCase that you are using. The drives on your machine are all locked by default when you reach this menu. In general, you need to have a physical drive that is larger than the suspect's drive for the destination drive, because the EnCase evidence file will contain additional information, such as evidence header information, CRC values, and an MD5 hash. Before selecting the Acquire choice from the menu, properly determine which drive contains the suspect's data and which drive (should be FAT32) is your target for the evidence file. A volume label on your target drive, such as destination, could help alleviate any confusion. You can label a destination disk volume (on your own system in Windows) by right-clicking on the disk in Windows Explorer and going to properties. Or if you prefer the command line, type label X: destination, where destination is the new volume label. Never label or make any alterations to the suspect's drive. Once all drives have been properly identified, keep the suspect's drive locked and unlock all the evidence destination drives.

Once all appropriate drives have been locked and unlocked, select the mode choice from the menu selection screen. If you select ATA mode instead of BIOS, you will be able to image all portions of the hard disk, including the Host Protected Area. The Host Protected Area, or HPA, is an area of the disk, hidden from the BIOS, that contains items such as vendor restoration utilities. Most investigators want to include this part of a drive in their image because a person with advanced knowledge of hard drives might use this area to hide data. Once the

mode is selected and verified, the investigator will move on to the next step where the hash button is selected so they are able to get an MD5 hash of the suspect's drive.

> ## EXAM WARNING
>
> The HPA, or Host Protected Area, is an area of the disk set aside by manufacturers for various configurations and utilities. Be aware of the HPA for your exam and be cognizant of it when you are working in the field.

The MD5 hash of the suspect's drive is a critical step so that you can verify the integrity of your forensic copy later. Unfortunately, this step could take a number of hours or significantly longer, depending on the size of the suspect's drive you are hashing. Once the hashing process is complete, EnCase will give you the option to save the hash as a text file. Save this file to a location on your destination or evidence file media. The file will give you an output similar to this:

Name: hda

Sectors0–39102335

Hash Value: 3c4e63d51f6b9085533f7da55258c9b5

Completed on: 06/18/2007 01:23:41pm

Elapsed time: 0:17:03

Avoid trying to save this file to a floppy disk. Sometimes you get an error, and then need to restart the entire hashing process. If an investigator is in a situation where time is of the essence, one option can be to acquire now, and go back and hash the suspect's drive later when conditions are more favorable. Make sure you follow the guidelines of your agency whenever you are acquiring the evidence image.

After the suspect's media has been hashed, select the Acquire menu selection from the bottom of the screen. When asked to choose a drive, select the suspect's drive as the one you will acquire. Be sure to choose the disk number of the suspect's drive, not the logical drive letter. After selecting the drive to acquire, the investigator will be prompted for a destination path for the evidence drive. Then, the investigator will be asked a series of questions, which will be added as header information to the evidence file. This information could be relevant to the chain of custody of the evidence. The information includes such items as case number, examiner name, evidence number, description, and notes. The investigator will also be asked whether they want to compress the file. Although compression will save some disk space, it may take much longer to complete the acquisition. If time is a factor, do not choose to use compression. The investigator will also be asked if they want to generate a hash, use a password, the total sectors, and maximum file size. It is suggested that you accept the defaults, including enter

for a blank password, for all four of these values. The next step is to wait for the evidence file to be written to the destination media. Depending on the size of the original suspect's media, the writing of the evidence file could take a significant amount of time. After the evidence file is written, manually record any values, such as the MD5 hash.

EXERCISE 14.5

AQUIRING AN ENCASE IMAGE AFTER BOOTING TO AN ENCASE DOS BOOT DISK

Requirements: EnCase DOS boot Floppy or CD

Licensed copy of EnCase

Computer with multiple drives

FAT32 partition on destination drive

1. On the DOS EnCase screen, click Lock. You will be prompted to choose a disk to lock/unlock. Both disks start as locked by default, therefore selecting the destination disk will unlock that media. Verify that the suspect's drive has been locked and that the destination media is *not* locked.

2. Select Mode and press Enter and select ATA if you want to copy the HPA (recommended).

3. Click Hash, and select the suspect's disk number, not the partition. The hash can take a substantial amount of time.

4. Click Acquire, and select the suspect's drive number. You will be prompted for the path and filename (should be a FAT32 destination).

Put in the full path of the location you wish to copy your evidence file to.

5. You will be prompted to answer a series of questions relevant to the chain of custody such as case number, examiner name, evidence number, description, and notes. This information will be added as header information to the evidence file.

When a computer forensic investigator uses an EnCase boot disk, there are a number of choices for the acquisition of the evidence file. Zip drives, UBS drives, and other disk media such as IDE, SCSI, and SATA drives can all be as destination media for an investigator's evidence

files. However, there could be a situation where none of those options will be viable for the investigator. An older laptop without USB ports could be one example of a situation where additional options might be needed. If additional options were needed, an investigator could use a parallel port. If a parallel port is used, you need a special male-to-male parallel cable. The investigator will connect the parallel cable from the suspect's computer to his or her own computer running a matching version of EnCase. Once everything is connected properly, tab to the server button on the suspect's machine that has been booted to the EnCase DOS boot disk and select Server.

EXERCISE 14.6

AQUIRING AN ENCASE IMAGE VIA PARALELL CABLE AFTER BOOTING TO AN ENCASE BOOT DISK

Requirements: EnCase DOS boot floppy or CD

Licensed copy of EnCase

Two computers: One running EnCase, one booted to EnCase DOS boot disk (CD or floppy)

Male-to-male parallel cable

On the computer booted to the EnCase DOS boot disk:

1. Under Choose A Protocol, select **Parallel Port**. The machine will indicate that it is waiting (see Figure 14.8) for the investigator to add the device from the GUI in EnCase on the evidence destination machine. The investigator needs to open a matching version of EnCase on his or her system.

2. Open EnCase, Start | Programs | EnCase. Click the new button and fill in your name for the examiner.

3. File | Add Device | Parallel Port | Next (see Figure 14.9).

4. Select the drive you want to image, usually 0, and click Next. Right-click the device in the EnCase program on the investigator machine and select Hash.

5. After the hash is complete, right-click and choose Acquire. Unfortunately, though this method of acquisition can be useful in some situations, transferring an evidence image via parallel port can take an extremely long amount of time.

Figure 14.8 EnCase Version 5 EN.EXE running in DOS waiting for Parallel Connection

Figure 14.9 Adding a Machine Connected to Another Machine via Parallel Port

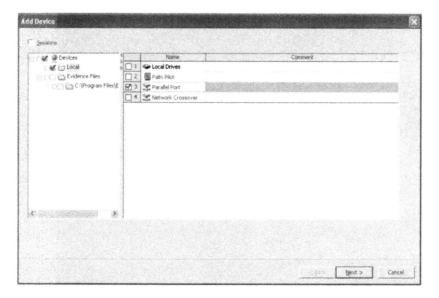

Another option for seizing an evidence image from a suspect's drive is via network and crossover cable. A yellow crossover cable comes with purchased versions of EnCase; however, any crossover cable will do. To use the crossover option, the DOS drivers for the network card are needed. Finding DOS drivers for a suspect's network card could be extremely tedious and cumbersome. It is recommended that investigators download a network boot disk with a wide range of precompiled network drivers for DOS. This site will provide EnCase users with such a disk: http://e-crime.on.ca/software/ENBD1006.exe.

Once the exe has been downloaded to the investigator's machine, he or she needs to insert a floppy in his or her drive and run the executable. Open EnCase, go to Tools, Create Boot Disk, and click Next after selecting the A drive. Select Update existing boot floppy and then select Next. Under Update files, right-click the windows pane and select New insert. Browse to the EnCase directory in your Program files and select the en file and click Finish. Label the disk EnCase network boot disk.

EXERCISE 14.7

USING A NETWORK BOOT DISK AND CROSSOVER CABLE TO AQUIRE A SUSPECT'S DRIVE

Requirements: EnCase DOS boot floppy or CD

Licensed copy of EnCase

Two computers: one running EnCase, one booted to EnCase Network boot disk

Crossover cable

1. Boot the suspect's machine up to the network boot floppy. (Follow all proper procedures for booting on a suspect's drive. This includes checking boot order and detaching and reattaching cables if possible.)

2. Select choice 1, network support at the menu list.

3. Click Auto to detect the network interface card (see Figure 14.10).

4. After detecting the card, a found message will appear and a message that states, Hit any key to continue. Press Enter.

Figure 14.10 Computer Booting to an EnCase Network Boot Disk

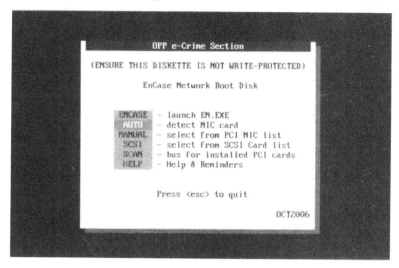

5. The machine will indicate that it is waiting for the investigator to add the device from the GUI in EnCase on the evidence destination machine.

6. The investigator needs to open matching version of EnCase on his or her system: Start | Programs | EnCase.

7. Click New and fill in your full name for the investigator.

8. Add the network crossover device by selecting File | Add Device | Network Crossover | Next (see Figure 14.11).

NOTE

If you are using a firewall, such as Windows Internet connection firewall, you will need to select Unblock at the prompt.

9. Verify that suspect machine's status changed to connected.

10. In the EnCase program, select the disk or disks you want to image, usually labeled Crossover·0, and click Next.

11. At the next screen, click Finish.

12. Right-click the device, most likely labeled Crossover·0, and choose Hash.

13. Right-click the device, most likely labeled Crossover·0, and choose Acquire.

14. After Acquisition | Select Add to Case | Next.

Your Screen should resemble Figure 14.11. The default file name is Crossover·0.E01. When the case name is changed, the case number and output fields will also change.

The default path is the location of the case and can be changed to a different logical or physical hard drive on the investigator's system if necessary. Blank fields can be filled in if necessary; any other options need to be selected before the investigator clicks Finish. All this information will be contained in the header of the evidence file. At this point, the data from suspect's drive is being copied to the data blocks of the evidence file. A flashing blue bar in the lower right-hand corner of the EnCase program will indicate progress status. The speeds of the network acquisition will vary depending on whether the systems have 10/100/or 1000 mbps network cards and whether the investigator uses a CAT3, 5, 5e, or 6 cable.

Figure 14.11 Final Screen before Hard Drive Acquisition over Network via Crossover

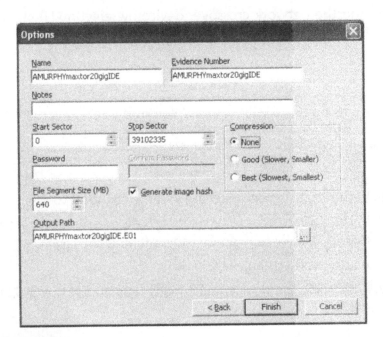

There are disadvantages to using a DOS boot disk for an acquisition of a suspect's drive. Although you can acquire disks that have various file systems including NTFS, EXT2, and EXT3, your destination drive for your evidence file needs to have a FAT partition (preferably FAT 32). Guidance software developed LinEn so that forensic investigators can use Linux Live CDs, such as Helix or KNOPPIX, in place of DOS boot CDs that have less capabilities and functionality. To obtain the LinEn file, go to the Guidance Software Web site and download it (you must read and agree to the license agreement): www.guidancesoftware.com/support/LinEn_LicenseAgreement.aspx. In order to use the LinEn tool, your company must be using at least EnCase version 5.

After the file has been downloaded, it can be added to a Linux ISO using a utility such as WinISO or UltraISO (see Figure 14.12). The KNOPPIX or HELIX ISOs can be downloaded from a variety of sites on the Web. The Web site www.distrowatch.com has active links to sites where you can download these Linux ISOs. For links to KNOPPIX ISO downloads, go to http://distrowatch.com/table.php?distribution=KNOPPIX . For links to HELIX ISO downloads, go to http://distrowatch.com/table.php?distribution=helix. Once the ISO has been downloaded, open it with a program such as UltraISO and add the LinEn file. After you add the LinEn file, save the ISO, then use Nero Burning Rom or a similar tool to burn the ISO.

Figure 14.12 Adding LinEn to a KNOPPIX ISO Using ULTRAISO

A primary reason computer forensic investigators use KNOPPIX or HELIX live CDs is because they mount drives as read-only. If the drives were not mounted as read-only, there is a danger that they could become contaminated. An investigator using a live CD needs to verify in the BIOS that the CDROM is the first boot device. Once that verification has taken place, place the CD in the drive, and boot to the live CD. Open a root shell, type cd /cdrom, then type ./linen. You should see a window pop up that says EnCase LinEn version 6.01 at the top of the screen.

Linux Partitions and Mounting

Head of the Class...

Working with partitions and mounting in Linux takes some practice. Most people are used to the drive letters associated with a Windows environment. Students often get upset when they are working with Linux distributions that do not auto mount their CD-ROMs or USB drives. Mounting devices certainly does add an extra layer of complexity to using the Linux operating system. However, the auto-mounting function has certain security risks associated with it. Once you become accustomed to mounting and unmounting devices, you will actually feel like you have greater control over your system. How many times have you been annoyed by the fact that inserting a CD-ROM caused it to auto-run or launched a box with various options?

The naming and numbering conventions that Linux uses are very straightforward. When you add devices to a Windows system, you often cannot be sure which drive letter will be associated with the device. Linux uses the HD prefix for IDE and you can have up to four IDE drives. HDA is the first IDE drive and HDD is the fourth. The SD prefix is for SATA, SCSI, and USB drives. SDC would be the third of these drives added to the system, and SDE would be the fifth. In order to do acquisitions with a Linux live CD, it is critical to understand mounting and how drives are named and numbered.

The LinEn tool appears similar to the en.exe tool designed for MS-DOS. One difference that should be noted is the naming convention for hard disks—instead of disk 0 or disk 1 and logical drives labeled as C: and D:, you will see the Linux drive naming convention (see Table 14.1). Linux uses hda-hdd for IDE devices.

Table 14.1 Linux Hard Disk Naming Conventions

Name	Type of Device
HDA	Primary Master IDE
HDB	Primary Slave IDE
HDC	Secondary Master IDE
HDD	Secondary Slave IDE

Drives that are not IDE such as SATA, SCSI, and USB are labeled SDA–SDZ. After all 26 letters have been used, the convention, SDAA–SDAZ would be followed. Any individual drive can have up to four primary partitions, or up to three primary and one extended partition. The numbers 1–4 after the letters represent partitions. Within the extended partition, you can have additional logical drives. Numbers 5 and up represent logical drives within the extended partition. Four examples are shown in Table 14.2.

Table 14.2 Linux Partition Numbering

Name	Type of Device
HDA3	Primary IDE master, third partition
HDD4	Secondary IDE slave, fourth partition
HDC5	Secondary IDE master, first logical partition
SDB9	Second SCSI device, fifth logical partition

As in the case of using EnCase in DOS, you usually acquire the drives (HDA, HDB, SDA, etc.) not the partitions or the logical drives (HDB5, SDA4, HDA2, etc.). When you are using LinEn, the work lock will not appear on the drives because Linux will not mount devices as read-write as DOS and Windows will. When investigators use LinEn in conjunction with a Linux live CD that does not auto mount (see Figure 14.13), they will be less likely to contaminate suspect's drives.

EXAM WARNING

Before you go to take the exam, make sure you have a through understanding of the way Linux partitions are lettered and numbered. Equally important, make sure that you have this concept down before you acquire a suspect's drive or you might accidentally overwrite it.

The other methods of acquiring an evidence image include using FastBloc, a proprietary hardware write-blocker. FastBloc comes in three versions: IDE, SCSI, and USB/Firewire. The suspect's drive should be connected to the FastBloc device. (Note: Other hardware write-blockers besides FastBloc can be used.) The computer forensic technician will then attach the cable of the FastBloc device to the forensic workstation. The FastBloc hardware device will prevent any changes from being made to the suspect's drive. An investigator can add the device and be confident that the original evidence is not being tainted. To add a device attached to the FastBloc controller, open EnCase and start a case. Once the case has been started, go up to File, and select Add Device. Choose Local Device and click Next. Look for the suspect's drive

that is attached to the FastBloc device, select it, and click Next. Verify that you have added the suspect's drive and click Finish. Right-click the device and choose Acquire. Select Add to case and click Next. Change any parameters if needed, and then click Finish. Once the blue bar gets to 100 percent on the lower right part of the EnCase program, the evidence file has been acquired.

Figure 14.13 Acquiring an Image Using a Linux Live CD and LinEn

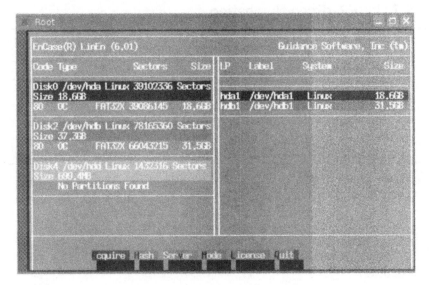

TEST DAY TIP

A hardware write-blocker is a device that allows an investigator to connect a drive to a Windows system in read-only mode to avoid any type of contamination. If a drive is connected in Windows without a write-blocker, such as FastBloc, changes to the drive will occur.

Configuring EnCase

EnCase Forensic edition has a well laid out interface that is easy to understand and relatively simple to navigate through. The EnCase program is installed very easily by clicking on the EnSetup (version#).exe executable. EnCase uses either a parallel or USB hardware dongle in an attempt to prevent users from pirating their software. Once the dongle has been connected to the forensic workstation running EnCase and the program has been installed, the program can

be launched. Clicking help | about EnCase from the menu will indicate the version of EnCase and display the license information of the software.

To utilize all the powerful functions of EnCase, an investigator should be familiar with all the panes and views that can be utilized. With every new version of EnCase, Guidance Software includes more enhanced features and capabilities. The new enhancements and features will give investigators greater ability to search through a suspect media. Knowing how to navigate through the EnCase program is critical for an investigator trying to pinpoint objects on a suspect's data sets, which are becoming increasingly larger over time.

EnCase Options Screen

When a case is created, the investigator has four fields to fill out related to the case. The case must be created in order to add existing evidence files or to acquire images using FastBloc.

The four fields at the case options screen are for the case name, examiner name, export folder, and temporary folder (see Figure 14.14). For the case name, company or organizational policy is usually followed. The investigator name is a mandatory field; an attempt to start a case without this field will result in an error. The export and temporary folders will default to the location where EnCase was installed on the hard drive. This may need to be changed if hard drive space on this partition or disk is limited.

Figure 14.14 The EnCase Case Options Screen

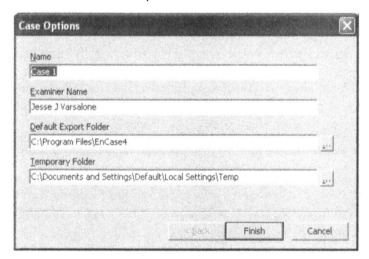

EnCase Screens

An investigator who uses EnCase needs to be comfortable with the various screens needed to properly analyze a suspect's evidence. The four main panes in EnCase are the tree, table, view, and filter pane (see Figure 14.15). It takes some practice to become comfortable with all the

panes and the subtabs within each pane. A case needs to be started or opened before all the options and subtabs become available.

Figure 14.15 The EnCase Main Panes

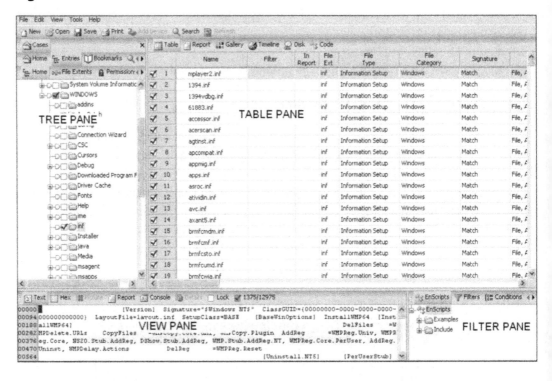

- **Tree Pane** The top left pane in EnCase. The following tabs can be accessed from the Tree pane: Cases, Home, Entries, Bookmarks, Search Hits, Email, History, WebCache, Devices, Secure Storage, and Keywords.

- **Table Pane** The top right pane in EnCase. The following tabs can be accessed from the Table pane: Table, Report, Gallery, Timeline, Disk, and Code.

- **View Pane** The bottom left pane in EnCase. The following tabs can be accessed from the View pane: Text, Hex, Picture, Report, Console, and Details.

- **Filter Pane** The bottom right pane in EnCase. The following tabs can be accessed from the View pane: EnScripts, Filters, Conditions, Queries, and Text Styles.

The Tree pane will determine what is displayed in the left screen in the EnCase program. If the EnCase user right-clicks the word cases above home and selects Auto-fit, all 10 subtabs of the Tree pane will be displayed. Or, the left pane can be expanded by moving the dividing bar from the center of the screen to the right so that all 10 Tree pane tabs can be displayed. The Tree pane subtabs include Home, Entries, Bookmarks, Search Hits, Email, history, Web cache,

Devices, Secure storage, and Keywords. The only purpose of the Home folder is for selecting a case when more than one case is open. EnCase defaults to the Entries view, which shows the disks, folders, and subfolders, in the Tree pane. Bookmark view will display items of interest flagged by investigator that are items related to the case. Search Hits view will display the results of the criteria an investigator has searched for on an evidence file. Email, History, and Web cache are views all related to e-mail and Internet browsing functions. The Secure storage view deals with the encrypted file system. The encrypted file system, or EFS, is a feature of later versions of Microsoft NTFS volumes. The Keyword searches tab or view will allow an investigator to search for keywords in the evidence file.

The right pane of the EnCase screen contains the Table, Report, Gallery, Timeline, Disk, and Code options. The right-hand pane defaults to the Table selection, which is likely why it is called Table pane. The Table pane displays the files and subfolders when the parent folder is selected in the Tree pane. The Gallery tab displays pictures within a folder. The Timeline pane has detailed information about the history of an object. Timeline categories include file creation, written, last accessed, modification, and deleted times. Clicking the Report tab on the right pane will show you the path to the file or folder on the physical disk. The Disk tab will show a colorful representation of the sectors on the disk an object occupies. The Code tab of the table pane is used to control EnScripts, the scripting language used within the EnCase program. In summary, the Table, Gallery, Timeline, Report, Disk, and Code screens are all part of the Table Screen pane.

View Menu

Select View from the top of the EnCase screen to display all of the items in the View menu. There are numerous selections including Keywords, File Signatures, Hash Sets, File Types, File Viewers, Security IDs, and App Descriptions. Keywords are for when the investigator wants to search the suspect's media for keywords. File Signatures lists a large number of known signatures, and allows the EnCase user to add new ones. File Types and Viewers deals with extensions on file types and the programs that can be used to view these files. Security IDs deals with user and group permissions on files and folders. App Descriptions has common operating system files and their corresponding hash values. The View menu also includes quick access to some of the more frequently used tabs in the four panes. The View menu also allows you to filter which subtabs will be displayed in the four panes of EnCase.

Device Tab

After a case is open, the Add Device tab becomes available. (Note: The Add Device tab is grayed out on evaluation copies of EnCase.) The Device tab in EnCase allows you to add devices to your case. Devices that can be added to your case include Local Devices, Palm Pilots, Parallel Port Devices, and Network Crossover Devices. Whenever you are adding media to your case via these four methods, you have the option to add the partitions or the disks themselves. Normally investigators are adding disks, not partitions to their evidence files.

When adding media, Local Devices include drives installed on your system and any FastBloc devices attached to the system. Normally, you do not add any suspect's devices as local devices without a write-blocker. If you attach any device to a Windows Operating system without a FastBloc or other write-blocking device, Windows will write entries to the drive and the suspect's drive will be contaminated. Palm Pilots, or PDAs, can be added through the Device tab where data can later be acquired. The Network Crossover option is for a computer connected to your workstation via crossover cable. The investigator needs to boot the suspect's computer to the EnCase network boot disk, and the computer should indicate that it is waiting to connect. The crossover acquisition could take significant time, depending on the speed of the cables and network cards. The Parallel Port Devices are added when a suspect's computer, booted to an EnCase boot disk, is connected via parallel port and using the parallel port protocol to connect to the investigators workstation. This method is extremely slow and not very practical at this point given the disk capacity of today's hard drives.

Once a device has been added, that device will appear on the screen in the left-hand pane, which is now referred to in EnCase as the Tree pane. In the Tree pane, the added device can be expanded further to allow the investigator to browse through the files and folders on a suspect's machine.

Viewing Files and Folders

Once media has been added, if you click the + sign in front of the media in the left or Tree pane, the logical drives on that disk will be displayed. As you expand the logical drives in the Tree pane, you will see the files and folders on that logical drive. The subfolders can also be expanded, and their subfolders and files will also be displayed. Before each parent, there is a small pentagon referred to as the "all files" trigger or home plate. A mouse click in the home plate area will turn home plate green, and only the folders and files within that directory will be displayed in the right-hand or Table pane. If you want to view other files and folders on the media that are not in that subfolder, just select home plate again (the icon will no longer be green) and other items can be viewed. In summary, files and folders can be displayed in the Table pane by expanding the evidence item on the left Tree pane.

Bottom Pane

The bottom pane is divided into two panes in EnCase, the View pane and the Filter pane. The View pane is on the bottom left of the EnCase screen and the Filter pane is on the bottom right. The View pane has the following six subtabs: Text, Hex, Picture, Report, Console, and Details. The Filter pane's subtabs are EnScripts, Filters, Conditions, Queries, and Text Styles. Both of these panes are accessed frequently when investigators are using EnCase.

Viewers in Bottom Pane

The six subtabs in the View pane are Text, Hex, Picture, Report, Console, and Details. Each subtab within the View pane will display an object in a different format. If a text file is selected in the Table pane, the text menu of the View pane will display the writing within the file. If the Hex tab is selected, the data of the object is displayed in hexadecimal format. The picture view of the bottom or View pane will be grayed out unless that object is a picture. The report view gives information such as when the file or folder object was created, last accessed, and information about where the object is located on the physical disk. If the object is on an NTFS partition, there will be additional information such as security identifiers (SIDS) and access control lists (ACLs). The Console tab displays output from the EnCase scripts. Finally, the Details tab displays the sectors and clusters on the disk where the object is stored. The bottom pane has a wealth of information about the file and folder objects of the suspect's media.

The other bottom pane viewer, the Filter pane, has five subtabs: EnScripts, Filters, Conditions, Queries, and Text Styles. EnScripts are scripts run within EnCase that will help search evidence files more efficiently. The Filters tab will allow you to specify parameters that will allow you to manipulate three filter pane items: filters, conditions, and queries. Conditions allow the investigator to build filters. Queries, similar to conditions, will allow the EnCase user to combine queries and conditions.

Status Bar

The status bar is gives investigators an idea of how long it will take to complete a task, such as hashing a set of data or acquiring a drive. The status bar is located in the bottom or Tree pane and is the bottommost object in the right-hand corner of the EnCase screen. The status bar will give the investigator some idea of how long it will take to finish a task, such as an acquisition or a hash (see Figure 14.16).

The Searching Ability of EnCase

One of the primary purposes of the EnCase program is to allow investigators to search through a suspect's media. After an evidence file has been added to a case or a device has been added through the add device tab, an investigator will be able to scan through the files and folders on a suspect's media. The search feature will allow an investigator to efficiently search through a suspect's media. The increasing size of today's drives will require forensic programs such as EnCase to constantly update and increase their search capabilities.

Figure 14.16 The Status Bar

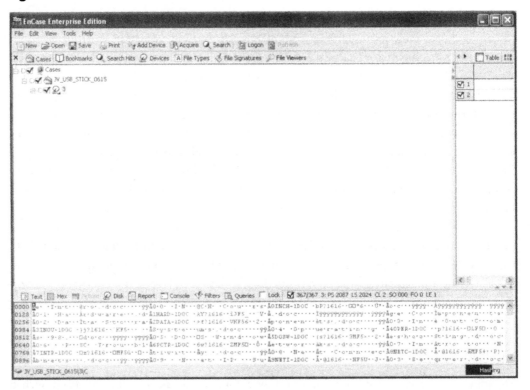

Keywords

To effectively search through a suspect's media, an investigator needs to add relevant keywords. The keywords function is a good example of a feature that has emerged over time as EnCase has become a more powerful and widely used forensic tool. In EnCase version 3, a keyword could be specific to only a single case. In EnCase version 4, keywords applied to all cases open by the investigator. EnCase 5 allows the use of both case-specific keywords, called case level keywords, or keywords that will apply to all cases, referred to as global. Keywords that are local to a specific case are saved with the case. Global keywords in EnCase are saved to an initialization file called keywords.ini. If an investigator intends to work on several cases at a time, having both global and case level keywords can be extremely useful. Keywords in EnCase, which are case sensitive, can be words, phrases or hexadecimal strings. To reach the Case keywords tab in EnCase version 5, right-click Cases in the Tree (left) pane and select Auto-fit. Global keywords can be accessed by choosing keywords from the View menu and selecting the Keyword tab to the right of Cases.

How to Add Keywords

The Keywords function in EnCase is useful because it will allow an investigator to determine if certain words, expressions, or strings exist in a suspect's media. Understanding how to use keywords is critical because when they are not turned off EnCase may not function as the investigator desires.

To add a case keyword, open the Keywords tab from the Tree pane and right-click the Keywords icon and choose New. This keyword will be applied only to the searching done within this particular case. To add a global keyword that will apply to all cases, scroll down to the keywords selection choice from the View menu. The global keyword will apply to all keywords and will be added to the keywords.ini file, which is located in the C:\Program Files\EnCase5\Config. When investigators want to search through the evidence files for a word like paypal, they need to create a new search expression. To create a new expression, the investigator will right-click Keywords and select New. The term, phrase, or string goes in the search expression field (see Figure 14.17). It is generally a good idea to name the keyword; this can be done by filling in the name field. Several other fields below the search expression and name boxes include Case Sensitive, GREP, and Unicode. Investigators may need to select or deselected these fields for each search expression to expand or further restrict their search hits.

Figure 14.17 Searching for a Keyword

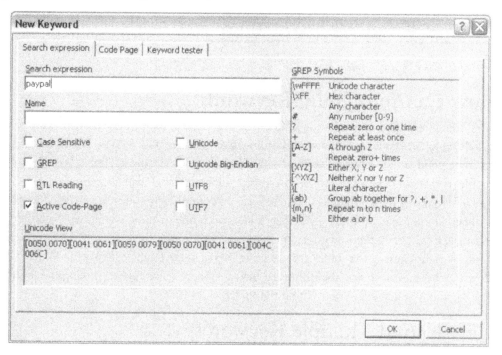

EXERCISE 14.8

ADDING A KEYWORD IN ENCASE

1. Add your evidence or FastBloc attached device to your case.

2. Select Keywords from the View menu.

3. Place a check in the box in front of Keywords, right-click Keywords and select New Keyword.

4. Type the keyword you want to look for in the search expression box and select any other options that are relevant to the criteria of your search. Click OK.

5. In the Tree pane, select the folders or drives you wish to search through.

6. From the menu bar, select Tools | Search.

7. If you do not wish to search the entire drive, mark the Selected Files Only box.

8. Check the box marked Selected Key Words only. (If that box is grayed out, you need to go back and make sure there is a blue check in front of the keywords box.)

How Can You Group Keywords?

When the global keywords tab is open from the View menu, the investigator will see two default subfolders under the Keywords heading, Examples and Global. The Examples subfolder has some good sample keyword search terms. The other default folder, Global, has additional subfolders that could be of use to an investigator, such as AIM, Email, Web Terms, and OS Artifacts. Many of these subfolders contain several keyword expressions or "grouped keywords." Grouped keywords are nothing more than folders with one or more search expressions. An investigator can group their own search expressions by creating their own subfolder under key-words by right-clicking the folder and selecting New Folder. Right-clicking the folder will allow the investigator to accomplish several tasks including renaming or deleting the folder or creating a new search expression within the folder.

How to Add Multiple Keywords

Each keyword that the investigator wants to be used in the search needs to be selected before the search begins. To select multiple keywords for a search, find the keywords you need for the

search and click the square in front of each individual keyword. A keyword search term that is turned on has a blue check in the box preceding the keyword name; an absence of the blue check means that the keyword has not been turned on. By placing a check in front of the grouped keyword folder, all the keywords within that folder will be selected. If all items within a folder have been selected, a blue check with a white background appears. A blue check with a gray background indicates that not all the items within that item's subfolders have been selected.

How to Do a Search

An investigator may choose to search for keywords within the suspect's entire media or select folders and files for the keywords. The investigator will click the Entries tab in the Tree pane and select the folders where files of interest might exist. If the investigator chooses to check the entire media for keywords, the search time will take significantly longer. If searching the whole media is not necessary, single files or folders can be selected. Blue checks with a white background in front of a folder means all subfolders and files have been selected. Blue checks with a gray background indicate only selected files and subfolders have been selected within that container. Once designated media has been selected properly, the investigator clicks the Keywords button and selects all relevant keywords. Once all keywords have been selected, the investigator conducts a search by clicking Tools and Select search. If the EnCase user wants to search through only the media highlighted in Entries, mark Selected Files Only (see Figure 14.18). At the bottom of the screen, check Selected Keywords Only. Click **Start** and watch the status bar to indicate keyword search progress.

Figure 14.18 Search Box for Selected Keyword Only

Discuss Search Hits Tab

Once EnCase finishes the keyword search, search hit results will be displayed (see Figure 14.19). The length of the search will be determined by a number of factors such as number of keywords and amount of data to be searched. The status bar will give the investigator some idea of how long the search will take to finish. Once finished, a dialog box will appear that indicates the search is complete.

Figure 14.19 Search Results

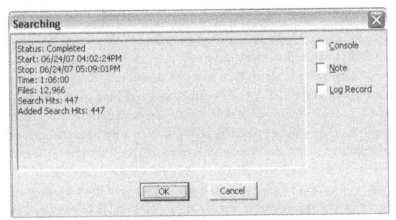

The number of hits will be displayed. The number of hits can also be displayed by clicking the Search Hits selection tab. As each keyword is selected in the left pane, the corresponding number of hits will be displayed in the right-hand pane.

The Bookmark

A bookmark in EnCase allows an investigator to highlight findings within a case. To reach the Bookmarks tab in EnCase version 5, right-click Cases in the Tree (left) pane and select Auto-fit. Investigators use bookmarks to select items pertinent to their case. These bookmarked items will, in turn, become part of the computer forensic investigator's report.

What Is a Bookmark?

Certain items in a suspect's media will warrant extra attention. The extremely relevant items need to be bookmarked so they can be included as part of the investigator's report. Investigators will place bookmarked items into one of six categories: text, picture, integers, dates, Windows, and styles. The six bookmark categories are further divided into sub-categories for each of the different data types. For example, the Windows data type is divided up into the 4 subcategories of Partition entry, Dos Directory entry, Win95 Info file Record, and Win2000

File Record. One of the subcategories must be selected; the investigator will need to select the data type to create the bookmark. It is important to note that a bookmark does not necessarily have to be a piece of evidence that incriminates a suspect. A bookmark, could in fact point to evidence on the media that helps to exonerate someone. A computer forensic investigator's job is to examine the evidence and prevent findings in an unbiased matter. In summary, bookmarks allow investigators to highlight items of interest in the case that will later become part of their report.

How to Create Bookmarks

Bookmarks are created within a case so they can be included as part of an investigator's report. Bookmarks can be created in a number of places within the EnCase program (see Figure 14.20). Bookmarks can be created from within a text file, on a picture in WebCache, on a disk structure, or in a number of other places from within the EnCase program. Investigators, however, often find it most convenient create their bookmarks from the Search Hits tab. To create a bookmark within the Search Hits tab, select the Search Hits tab within the Tree pane menu. Click one of the keywords with search hit results and select the search hit in the table pane. On the bottom or view pane, click the text box, drag your cursor over the item of interest, right-click and select Bookmark Data. Once Bookmark Data has been selected, you must choose a data type for the bookmark.

Figure 14.20 Bookmarking Data

The categories for bookmarks are text, picture, integers, dates, Windows, and styles. Once a category is selected form the menu screen, a data type subcategory must be selected. There is also an option for the investigator to add any notes about the bookmarked item.

Adding Bookmarks to a Case

Investigators often add a large number of bookmarks to their cases. If a large number of book-marked items are added to a case, an investigator may want to create several subfolders under the Bookmarks tab. For example, if the investigator was working on a case where the suspect was e-mailing four key people, he or she might want to create four folders separating the cor-respondence between each of the individuals. Once the bookmark folders have been created, the investigator will find the item of interest, usually under search hits, highlight the text in the bottom pane, and select bookmark data. Select the appropriate data type and subcategory and then select the newly created subfolder under bookmarks. Add any additional notes for the bookmarked item and click OK. Right-click the word case in the Tree pane and select Auto-fit. The bookmark will now be added to that case and should be displayed under the correct subfolder.

EXERCISE 14.9

ADDING A BOOKMARK TO A CASE IN ENCASE

1. In the Tree pane, under Entries, right-click the drive and select Bookmark Folder Structure.

2. Click bookmarks as the destination folder and select OK.

3. Click the Bookmarks tab.

4. Make sure the Table tab has been selected in the Table pane and view your bookmarked item.

Recovering Deleted Files/Folders in a FAT Partition

FAT stands for File Allocation Table, and is one of the most commonly used file systems on hard drives. There are actually three types of FAT files systems, FAT12, FAT16, and FAT32. FAT12 usually is used on floppy drives, and FAT16 has a limit of 2 gigabytes, so most of the FAT partitions will be using the FAT32 file system. In fact, many of the new thumb drives, USB, and Firewire mass storage devices come from the factory formatted with the FAT32 file system. One of the reasons it is such a popular choice for a file system is that it is compatible with almost every Microsoft operating system and other platforms outside of Microsoft as well. Every FAT file system has two FAT tables, FAT1 and FAT2, which are like a table of contents

to the locations of files. The FAT1 holds the cluster locations of the files and the FAT2 is a backup copy of FAT1. When a user deletes a file, the clusters that the file occupies are marked as available in the FAT.

Even though the file has been marked as deleted in the FAT, the file still exists on the clusters of the disk. The file will remain on the disk until new entries are added to those clusters. If the clusters have been not been reused, the data from the deleted file will most likely be recoverable by the EnCase program. If recoverable, deleted files and folders often hold a wealth of information about a case. In the Entries view of the Tree pane, deleted files that have not been overwritten are displayed with a red circle with a diagonal line in front of them. (see Figure 14.21). Deleted files where clusters have been overwritten are displayed as with red X in front of them (see Figure 14.21). The description tab in the tree pane also provides the information about whether the file has been overwritten. Deleted folders that have not been over written are yellow with a red X through them. Overwritten deleted folders also have a red X through them but are gray in color. To recover a deleted file that has not been overwritten, right-click the file and select copy/unerase (see Figure 14.22).

Figure 14.21 View of Deleted, Overwritten Files and Deleted Files Not Overwritten in EnCase

Figure 14.22 Using EnCase to Recover a Deleted File

A wizard will open and give the user several choices whether they want to recover one or more files and if they want to merge the files. After clicking Next, additional options are available, such as recovering the logical file or the entire physical file, which will include any file slack. If a cluster is 4K or 4096 bytes, and a file is 4097 bytes, is will take up two clusters on the hard drive and the remaining 4095 bytes will be called slack space. It is possible that slack space could contain valuable data from previous files occupied in a cluster. If you want to recover the file as well as the slack space, choose the entire physical file. The investigator will then be prompted for a destination where the recovered file will be placed. In summary, EnCase is able to recover deleted and folders files that have not been overwritten on FAT partitions

TEST DAY TIP

Slack space is the unused portion of a cluster on a disk. Valuable data and remnants can often reside in slack space. The EnCase Program allows you to recover the entire physical file, which includes the deleted files as well as slack space.

EXERCISE 14.10

RECOVERING A DELETED FILE

1. In the Tree pane, under Entries, click the folder where the deleted file you wish to recover is located.

2. Find the deleted file in the Table pane; right-click and select copy/unerase.

3. Select the radio button highlighted file and select Next (leave replace first character as an underscore).

4. On the Options screen, click Next.

5. Select the destination path and click Finish.

How Can You Recover Folders on an NTFS File System?

The New Technology File System was developed by Microsoft to address the many limitations of the FAT file system. The NTFS file system has file and folder level security permissions, but FAT does not. Later versions of the NTFS file system, starting with Windows 2000, include EFS. The Encrypted File System, or EFS, allows both file and folder level encryption. Unlike FAT, NTFS is a journaling file system. A journaling file system keeps a list of changes that are being made to the disk. The journal will log changes to the disk; if power is lost before the changes are made, the journal will pick up where it left off when the system comes back online. The NTFS file system uses a MFT, or Master File Table to record where data is located on a drive. The FAT table is somewhat similar to the Master File Table. However, the MFT is more efficient and provides quicker access times. Also, NTFS volumes are not subject to the many restrictions of FAT volumes, such as the 2 gigabyte file size limit of FAT 32. To recover a file on an NTFS file system, add the evidence file or device with the NTFS volume. Deleted files that have not been overwritten are displayed with a red circle with a diagonal line through them. Files that have been deleted and overwritten are displayed with a red X. Overwritten deleted folders are gray with a red X in the center; deleted folders that have not been overwritten are yellow with a red X. Before beginning the process to restore a folder, it is very important that the blue check is only in front of the folder you want to recover. If there are blue checks on folders throughout the media, the investigator may get extra data in the destination path.

EXAM WARNING

Make sure you are comfortable with the difference between FAT and NTFS file systems. Understanding the features and limitations of the file systems will allow you to eliminate "distracter answers" during your exam.

EXERCISE 14.11

RECOVERING A DELETED FOLDER

1. In the Tree pane, under Entries, select the only check box in front of the folder you wish to recover.

2. In the Tree pane, right-click the deleted folder and select Copy/Unerase (see Figure 14.23).

3. At the Copy/Unerase screen, select the tab All Selected Files in the "FROM" radio button. Select the tab Separate Files in the "TO" the radio button.

4. On the Options screen, click Next.

5. Select the destination path and click Finish.

Figure 14.23 Recovering a Deleted Partition on an NTFS Partition

Explain the Master Boot Record

Partitioning is a way of logically dividing a disk into different sections. Both Windows and Linux allow a maximum of four primary partitions on a disk or three primary partitions and one extended partition. Within an extended partition, a further logical division of the disk can exist. In order for a system to boot, one of the primary partitions must be made active. Extended partitions or the logical drives within the extended partition cannot be made active. The master boot record (MBR) is the first sector on the disk and contains the both the boot code and the drive's partitioning information. An investigator can examine the master boot record to find information on how the disk is partitioned. In EnCase, the MBR of the hard disk is displayed as a small red square at the beginning of the disk. The sector next to the MBR is labeled with all zeros (see Figure 14.24).

Figure 14.24 The Master Boot Record

TEST DAY TIP

Be aware that the master boot record is on the first sector of a hard drive. The fact that bytes 446–509 of the master boot record contain the partition tables is also noteworthy.

How Do You View Disk Geometry?

Geometry can be viewed in EnCase by using a folder information bookmark. Select the
Entries tab in the Tree pane, and locate the device for which you wish to view disk geometry
information. Right-click the device and select bookmark folder structure. Make sure the check
box that states Include Device Information is selected. Switch from the Entries tab to the
Bookmark view in the Tree pane and select Folder Information from the Table pane on the
right-hand side of the screen. On the bottom, or View pane, click the Report tab and the disk
geometry information will be displayed. One of the nice visual features is a layout of the folder
structure on the disk. This can be viewed by scrolling down below the disk geometry informa-
tion or by dragging the view pane bar higher toward the top of the EnCase program (see
Figure 14.25).

Figure 14.25 Disk Geometry Viewed in a Report

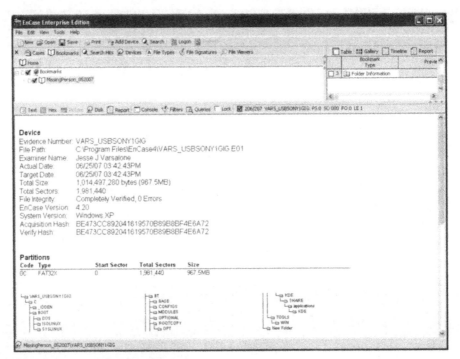

EXERCISE 14.12

VIEWING DISK GEOMETRY

1. In the Tree pane, select Entries.
2. Right-click the disk, and choose Bookmark Folder Structure.

3. Click OK to Bookmarks as the Destination folder.

4. Click the Bookmarks tab in the Tree pane.

5. Click the Report tab to view the disk geometry and folder structure.

Recovering Deleted Partitions and Analyzing Media

Some criminals will try to thwart detection by using a tool such as FDISK to delete partitions. The partition table information for the four partitions is stored in bytes 446–509 of the FDISK. On a normal partition table, bytes 446–509 will not be all zeros (see Figure 14.26). If all of the partition table information has been deleted, bytes 446–509 will be all zeros (see Figure 14.27). To try to restore the deleted partition, find the volume boot record, or VBR, usually located on sector 63 of the disk (see Figure 14.28). Even though the suspect deleted the partition information in the Master boot record successfully, the information in the VBR is often still intact. Add the evidence file with the deleted partitions or attach the disk with the FastBloc device and use the add device wizard to add the disk. Click the device in the Tree pane and click the Disk tab on the Table or right pane. You will notice that the MBR is red, followed by sectors 1–62. Most of the drives investigators work with will have 63 sectors per track, so the remaining 62 sectors in the first track should not be used. Sector 63 is usually the location of the Volume Boot Record. On a normal volume, the VBR is displayed as either a light red in EnCase 5 or pink in EnCase 4. On a volume where partition information has been altered, position the cursor over the top of sector 63. In the bottom left corner of the EnCase 5 screen, there is an indicator of sector number. To go to a specific sector on the disk, right-click the sector numbers, select Go To, and enter the sector number. Right-click the sixty-third sector and select Add Partition. Choose the file system type and click the OK tab. If the partition is restored, the files and folder will be displayed.

Figure 14.26 Normal Master Boot Record Bytes 446–509

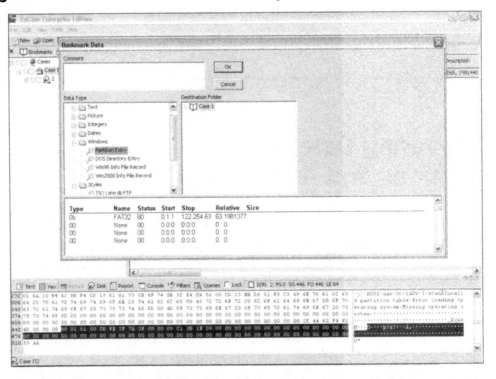

Figure 14.27 FDISKED Master Boot Record Bytes 446–509

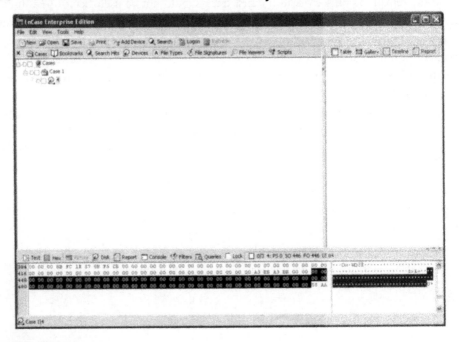

Figure 14.28 VBR Volume Boot Record, Starting at Sector 63

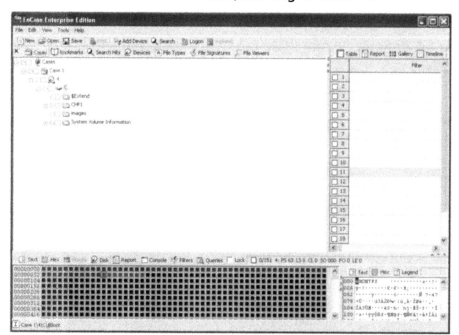

Recovering a partition when a disk has only a single partition is less difficult then recovering multiple partitions on a drive. One of the options that can be used when there are multiple partitions is using a script within EnCase to retrieve the partition information. To recover partition information in EnCase version 4, use the partition finder v4 located in the Examples folder under the Scripts category. The recovery information will be listed in the bookmarks as Highlighted Data. Recovery of partition information in EnCase version 5 is done with EnScripts, which are located in the Filter pane, or bottom right pane. Right-click Sweep Case under the Examples folder in the EnScripts menu, and select Run. Click next to the case name, select the partition finder, bookmark location, and destination, and click Finish. After an intensive search of the media, information about where the partitions are located on the disk will be displayed in the bookmarks section.

Signature Analysis

File signature analysis is an important part of analyzing a suspect's media because it allows the investigator to verify file types. A savvy suspect can change file extensions in an attempt to prevent detection (see Figure 14.29). For example the file called funding.xls could be renamed to win32db.sys. Moving this file named win32db.sys into the system32 directory would make it even harder for someone to detect. Criminals often use the technique of renaming picture files to avoid detection from other users of the computer or as an attempt to thwart law enforcement. File extensions can be changed on hundreds of files at once with the use of a one simple

DOS command. This is why a file signature analysis is so critical. Thoroughly checking through a suspect's media requires a file signature analysis.

Figure 14.29 Renaming Multiple Files with One Command in an Attempt to Hide Them

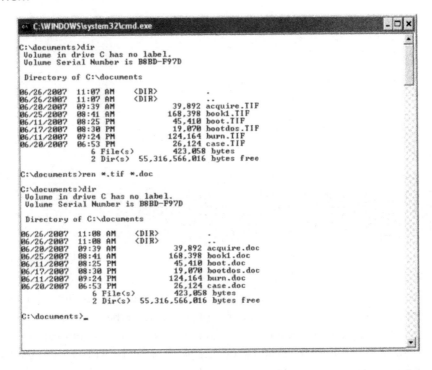

When you are examining a suspect's media, it is not enough to try to rely on the file extensions. A file signature analysis looks at the header information in a file in order to determine what type of file it actually is. The information stored in the file header is a much more accurate indicator of what the file type is than just looking for the file's extension. When the acquire.doc is opened with a hex editor such as hex workshop, the information in the file header is 49492A (see Figure 14.30), not D0CF11E0A1B11AE1, the file header information commonly found on Microsoft Office Word document (see Figure 14.31). EnCase will search for the file signatures of files and alert the user when the file extension type does not match the file signature.

Figure 14.30 A File Signature on a TIFF Document with an Incorrect File Extension

Figure 14.31 A File Signature on an Actual Microsoft Office Word Document

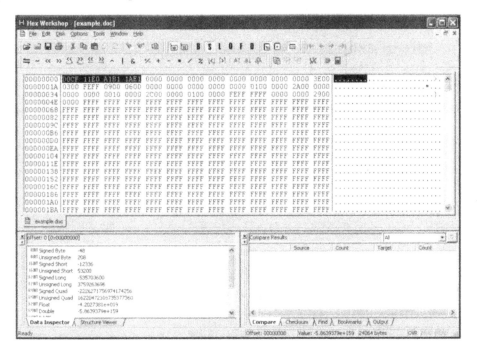

EXAM WARNING

When a File Signature Analysis is conducted on a suspect's media, this will allow the investigator to find if any files have been renamed with incorrect extensions. Although suspects may rename file extensions in an attempt to thwart detection, a file signature analysis will discover this type of activity.

How Can You View the Results of a Signature Analysis?

To do a signature analysis in EnCase, select the objects in Tree pane you wish to search through. Conducting a file signature analysis on all media within the case is recommended. From the Tools menu, select the Search button. The default is for EnCase to search all the files on the disk; the number of files on the disk is reported in the box below the word selected files only. Choose only selected files to search only objects selected in the Tree pane. When a file has an extension that does not match the file header information, EnCase will report a mismatch. In the table pane, there will be a * in the front of the signature column for that file and the correct file type will be listed (see Figure 14.32). If the mismatched files are reported to be pictures, changing the table pane to gallery view will allow you to view the images.

Figure 14.32 File Signature Search Results

Copying Files/Folders

Copying files from an evidence file or a suspect's media attached to a FastBloc device is a relatively simple process. When copying files or folders, there should be adequate space on your destination media. First, add all evidence files and FastBloc connected devices. Locate the folder to be duplicated, right-click and select Copy Folders. The full path of the folder to be copied and the destination location will appear in the dialog box. The default destination directory is in the EnCase folder in program files on the C: drive. Changing the folder from the default or verifying there is adequate space before clicking OK is advisable. It is possible to copy the entire disk or logical drives in this manner also. Copying a single file or files within a folder is a similar process. Find the parent folder the file is located in, and double-click it in the Tree pane. Select the file or files you would like to copy within that folder. Right-click the parent folder and select Copy Folders. Mark the box that states Copy Only Selected Files inside each folder. Verify source and destination path and click OK.

E-mail Recovery

Evidence that either incriminates or exonerates suspects can often be retrieved in e-mail messages. EnCase has powerful e-mail recovery tools that allow investigators to view various formats of e-mail messages. EnCase can recover e-mail messages from the two most popular Microsoft Window's e-mail clients, Outlook (.pst files) and Outlook Express (.dbx files), as well as the Linux/Unix mbox format. Webmail messages from such companies as Yahoo, AOL, and Hotmail can also be recovered. To locate the E-mail tab in EnCase, right-click Cases in the Tree pane and select Auto-fit. The e-mail subtab under Cases is a new feature that started with EnCase version 5.

To search for e-mail on a suspect's media, place a check in the box in front of email, right-click Email, and select Email/Internet Search. Keeping both selections checked is advisable; however, there is an option to look on the media only for certain types of e-mail. The Internet subcategory has the four main browsers as selection choices: Internet Explorer, Mozilla, Opera, and Safari. The e-mail category has seven subcategories: Hotmail, Yahoo!, AOL, Outlook Express, Outlook, Netscape, and Mbox. Once the desired selections have been made, click Search. If any e-mail messages are found on the suspect's media, they will be displayed in an easy-to-read column format. There are 15 columns related to the displayed e-mail messages including Subject, To, From, CC, BCC, Attachments, Sent, and Received. In summary, EnCase, beginning with version 5, has very powerful and easy-to-use e-mail recovery tool.

Reporting

After a computer forensic investigator has finished searching through a suspect's media, he or she needs to generate a report in order to present his or her finding. EnCase has a robust reporting feature that allows the investigator to generate either hardcopies or softcopies of the

findings. Reports can either be generated from bookmarks made in a case or by using the case initialization script feature of EnCase. An EnCase script, or EnScript, can be used to generate report items. This script, known as the Initialize Case, will allow the user to fill in information about the name and agency of the investigator, the agency, and other chain of custody. The script will allow investigators to sweep the media for a wealth of information such as drive geometry, volume information, Windows users, services, software, and shared folders.

In order to effectively generate reports, an investigator must be comfortable with the bookmark interface. The items that have been bookmarked throughout the case can be included as part of the report. To decide which bookmarked items to include in your report, right-click the Cases tab in the Tree pane menu and select Auto-Fit. Select the Bookmarks subtab; you will notice all items that have been bookmarked during the case are displayed in the Table pane. If you click the Report tab (next to table), you will see a preview of the items that will be included in the report. If you are happy with the report as it stands, you may print a hard copy by selecting File, **Print**. If a soft copy of the report is required, right-click and select Export. Choose a destination path and file name for the report and choose OK.

If you wish to exclude certain items from the report, click back on the Table tab in the Table pane. Click the item you wish to exclude and select Delete. As long as the check Show Deleted has not been selected, the deleted item will no longer be included in the report. If you change your mind, and wish to include the deleted item, the bookmarked item can be restored by clicking Show Deleted Items, selecting the deleted item and choosing Delete again. Deleting a deleted bookmark item will restore it and the item will once again be included in the report.

What Are IE Cache Images?

Many computer-related crimes deal with images found on a suspect's media. Often these images have been downloaded and placed in folders on a suspect's drive. There are other incidents when a suspect has not directly downloaded images, but they have visited Web sites with illegal content. When people browse the Internet, Microsoft's Internet Explorer (as well as other browsers) cache web images in order to speed up the browsing process. Those images from Internet browsing at times can still be on a suspect's computer. EnCase will find these images from Internet Explorer and they can be displayed in the gallery. To search a suspect's media for IE Cache Images, right-click Cases and choose Auto-fit. Select the WebCache tab button; right-click this button and select Email/Internet search. Click OK and wait for the search to finish. After the search has concluded, the WebCache items will be displayed in the Table pane. Clicking on the Gallery tab will allow you to view these images. Right-click and select Bookmark Data on any images that are pertinent to the case. Any of the images that were bookmarked can then be included as part of the investigator's report.

Summary of Exam Objectives

EnCase is one of the most widely used and respected tools in the emerging discipline of computer forensics. When an investigation begins, a chain of custody needs to be maintained so the evidence can be tracked throughout the investigation process. Computer Forensic professionals do not use the suspect's media when they are conducting their examinations. Rather, they make bit stream copies of the original evidence using EnCase tools. There are several methods that can be used to acquire a suspect's image, depending on the equipment in the lab and the circumstances surrounding the acquisition.

A DOS EnCase boot disk can be used to acquire a suspect's drive to a zip drive, USB drive, or another hard drive. Other options from the DOS boot disk include a parallel or network acquisition. LinEn, a newer tool from Guidance Software, makers of EnCase, allows similar acquisition options from a Linux environment. If investigators prefer working in a Microsoft Windows environment, they can purchase a FastBloc hardware write-blocker that will keep any suspect's media free from contamination. Once a method of acquisition has been decided upon, the investigator will create the evidence file.

A hash is conducted on the original media and the copied data blocks to ensure that the examiner is working with an exact copy of the suspect's media. The investigator will then search the media for keywords, pictures, e-mails, web history, and other evidence artifacts. Features of EnCase, such as signature analysis, will allow the investigator to further determine if the suspect was attempting to conceal information. After all the evidence has been bookmarked, it is organized into a report. The report will be turned over to the proper authorities or officials. The examiner should always act in an ethical manner, reporting all findings whether they exonerate or incriminate the person being investigated. In Summary, EnCase is a series of computer forensic tools that can be utilized throughout the investigation process by computer forensic examiners.

Exam Objectives Fast Track

What Is an Evidence File?

- ☑ An evidence file contains data blocks, CRC values, MD5, case header information.
- ☑ Extensions range from .E01 to .E99 and then start at EAA.
- ☑ Extension files contain bit-by-bit copies of the data blocks of the imaged drive.

Hashing

- ☑ Hashing is a process used to determine that two data sets are exact.

☑ EnCase uses the MD5 hash values.

☑ The possibility that two files have the same MD5 hash is very unlikely, a chance of 1 in 2^{128}.

How You Acquire a File Image

☑ FastBloc, a hardware write-blocker, can be used to acquire file images.

☑ You can also use a forensically sound DOS boot disk to acquire file images.

☑ Another method for acquiring file images is using LinEn on a live CD that does not auto mount.

☑ You can also acquire file images over a network or through a crossover cable.

Configuring EnCase

☑ The four main panes are View, Table, Tree, and Filter.

☑ Devices are added through the Add Device tab.

☑ A case must be started, with an investigator name, for most options and tab to become available.

☑ The status bar will indicate when items are still processing.

☑ Files that do not match their extensions can be displayed in the EnCase Program.

☑ The EnCase program can read e-mail messages from Outlook, Outlook Express, and Mbox.

☑ Signature Analysis can be configured in EnCase to use file headers to determine if a file has been renamed with an incorrect extension.

The Searching Ability of EnCase

☑ The increasing size of today's drives will require forensic programs such as EnCase to constantly update and increase their search capabilities.

☑ Understanding how to use keywords is critical because when they are not turned off EnCase might not function as the investigator desires.

☑ An investigator may choose to search for keywords within the suspect's entire media or select folders and files for the keywords.

The Bookmark

- ☑ Bookmarks can be created in several places throughout EnCase.

- ☑ Bookmarks are often created from the Search Hits tab.

- ☑ Pictures, folder structure, text, and a variety of items can be bookmarked.

- ☑ Bookmarks can be used in the investigator's final report.

- ☑ IE cache images can be bookmarked and placed into a report.

- ☑ Web Mail messages, such as Yahoo, AOL, and hotmail, can be detected and bookmarked.

Recovering Deleted Files/Folders in a FAT Partition

- ☑ The FAT file system has no security or permissions on files and folders.

- ☑ FAT1 is the primary file allocation table and FAT2 is the backup.

- ☑ When a file is initially deleted, the entry is removed from the FAT table; however, that file still remains in the clusters.

- ☑ Folders on suspects' drives can be copied to destination media.

- ☑ Slack space from the sectors where a file is located can be recovered.

- ☑ Deleted folders and files that have not been overwritten can be recovered.

Recovering Deleted Partitions and Analyzing Media

- ☑ The volume boot record can be used to recover partition information.

- ☑ The master boot record is located on the first sector of the hard drive.

- ☑ The partition table is located in bytes 446–509 of the master boot record.

Exam Objectives
Frequently Asked Questions

The following Frequently Asked Questions, answered by the authors of this book, are designed to both measure your understanding of the Exam Objectives presented in this chapter, and to assist you with real-life implementation of these concepts.

Q: What is an evidence file and why does one need to be created?

A: An evidence file has a bit-by-bit copy of the suspect's original evidence. An evidence file is created so that the original suspect's evidence is not contaminated.

Q: What is signature analysis?

A: Criminals will often rename the file extensions on their files to thwart detection. For example, a savvy criminal might change all bitmap picture files from .bmp to .doc to avoid someone detecting the illegal images. A signature analysis will look at the file headers to verify if files actually have the correct extension.

Q: Why is a hardware write-block device used?

A: When a drive is added to a Microsoft Windows operating system, changes are made to that drive. A hardware write-blocker is a device that will allow an investigator to connect a drive to a Windows operating system without fear that the disk will be written to and contaminated. To avoid the normal contamination that occurs when a drive is added to a system, a hardware write-blocker can be utilized.

Q: What are the options for acquiring evidence files in EnCase?

A: Drives can be acquired in one of several ways using EnCase. A forensically clean EnCase DOS boot disk can be used to acquire a disk to a zip drive, a USB drive, or another hard drive. Drives can also be acquired by using a crossover or parallel cable between two computers. A Linux live CD with LinEn will allow investigators to acquire a disk to another drive. If an investigator prefers using Microsoft Windows, he or she can acquire images by using FastBloc, a proprietary hardware write-blocker that works in conjunction with EnCase.

Q: If a file is deleted, is it really gone from the hard drive?

A: If a file is deleted from a hard drive, the cluster location or locations of the file is marked as being available. If those clusters are not written to, the file is likely recoverable. If another file is written to those clusters, the previous file is over-written. Parts of that file possibly could remain in slack space and still be recovered.

Q: What is the Chain of Custody?

A: The location of the suspect's media needs to be accounted for at all times. If, at any time, the whereabouts of the suspect's drive cannot be accounted for, that could leave some reasonable doubt in a jury's mind. The Chain of Custody will establish a timeline and document who was in possession of the suspect's drive, and where it was located. This timeline is critical so that juries can be confident that the drive was not altered or tampered with since it was seized.

CHFI

Incident Response

Exam objectives in this chapter:

- Preventing Incidents
- Incident Response, Incident Handling, and Incident Management
- Categories of Incidents
- Risk Assessment
- Staffing the Team
- Steps of Incident Response
- First Responder Procedures
- First Responder Roles

Introduction

In this chapter we discuss the role of the Computer Security Incident Response Team (CSIRT). The CSIRT is best compared to the emergency response services that are deployed after a 911 call. When a 911 call comes in, different groups are deployed, including emergency medical services, fire and rescue, and law enforcement. Usually more than one group is deployed to an incident and often, little information is known about the incident before the team responds. Incident response teams need to have the wherewithal to perform with the available resources, which are often limited. Therefore, the mantra "Proper Planning Prevents Poor Performance" should be followed at all times.

We also discuss first responder procedures, including guidelines, a definition of electronic evidence, chain of custody, and issues pertaining to the handling and transporting of evidence.

Preventing Incidents

No matter how good an incident response team is, it is always better to be prepared *before* an incident happens. Several defensive measures should be used through the use of controls, which can be as complex as firewalls and intrusion prevention systems (IPSes), or as simple as logging all access to critical systems. In the following section, we look at the preventive controls that can deter an incident.

Firewalls

Firewalls are often the first and in some cases, the only line of defense against an incident occurring. There are three primary types of firewalls: *packet filter, stateful inspection,* and *proxy.* Each type of firewall has strengths and weaknesses.

The *packet filter firewall* provides limited protection, but is often the fastest of the firewall types and also the least expensive. Packet filter firewalls are often included with other network devices such as routers, wireless access points (WAPs), and network switches. Packet filter firewalls provide a better level of protection for outgoing packets as opposed to incoming packets. Because of the necessary configuration of the packet filter firewall response (those which are returning to an outbound request), packets are statically configured to allow the response to enter without being subject to additional filtering. This means that to allow Web or Hypertext Transfer Protocol (HTTP) traffic for an organization, all high ports (Transmission Control Protocol [TCP] ports 1025–65535) must be open for response. Thus, an attacker can use these open ports as a potential attack vector.

The next type of firewall is the *stateful inspection firewall*. The stateful inspection firewall builds on packet-filtering technology with one key advantage: the stateful inspection firewall uses dynamic rules to allow response packets back into an organization. This means there is no statically configured rule, which opens all TCP high ports to an organization. Rather these response rules are opened dynamically for a brief period and provide protection for incoming

packets. The stateful inspection firewall provides benefits to the CSIRT in that it usually has increased logging capability, which may be useful in determining the source of an incident. Other advantages of the stateful inspection firewall is speed, which rivals that of packet filter firewalls, and often the stateful inspection firewall is a dedicated device, which is not part of another network device. The stateful inspection firewall tends to cost more than packet filter devices.

The final type of firewall is the *proxy-based firewall*. One of the strengths of the proxy-based firewall is that they read more of the packet than the other types of firewalls, to determine filtering approval or denial. The proxy firewall is often slower than the other types of firewalls and does not often understand all applications that pass through the firewall. The proxy device has exemplary logging, which is often useful to the incident response team. The proxy firewall functions by maintaining two separate conversations, one between the client and the firewall, and one between the firewall and the end server. Organizations should have one or more proxy firewalls that should be configured for logging all accesses and blocked attempts.

Intrusion Prevention Systems

IPSes are used to provide additional protection beyond the protection of a firewall. These devices can protect an organization by looking for network attacks that may have bypassed the firewall and entered the network. They are dedicated devices that are separate from other network devices, and often provide the greatest detail of logging.

Other Controls

While firewalls and IPSes are some of the more common security controls that can prevent an incident, there are also other types of controls, such as routers with access control lists (ACLs), virtual local area networks (VLANs), two-factor authentication, and services such as vulnerability assessment and penetration testing. These last two examples mimic the attacks performed by an attacker to ascertain where an organization's weaknesses are and how they might be compromised. Regular testing using either vulnerability assessment or penetration testing can help reduce the likelihood that an incident will happen. Often best practice standards require these services as part of an overall system development life cycle (SDLC). An example of these standards is the PCI-DSS standard used for e-commerce sites to secure payment transactions. An important key to remember is that incident prevention is most often less costly than incident response.

Incident Response, Incident Handling, and Incident Management

There is a close relationship between *incident response*, *incident handling*, and *incident management*. Incident response is the practice of detecting a problem, determining its cause, minimizing the

damage it causes, resolving the problem, and documenting each step of the response for future reference. Incident handling's primary goal is to contain and repair any damage caused by an event and to prevent any further damage. Incident management is the overall process of management of the incident from declaring the incident, to documentation, to post-mortem reviews after the incident has occurred. As you can see, each incident will require all three of these components.

Incident Response Planning

In incident response, one of the primary goals is to "freeze the scene." This process is used to keep the area and systems that are part of the incident from being modified in order to protect and preserve the evidence that will be used in future forensics. Since computer forensics will be built upon the results of the incident response team, it is critically important to plan for incident response. This is where creating an incident response checklist comes in. The checklist will contain key components of the overall incident response plan, including logging all access physically and electronically to the incident scene. Scene documentation includes sketches, photographs, video recordings, and audio recordings. While these examples are by no means a complete list, the best resource for developing your own incident response checklist is the National Institute of Justice (NIJ) First Responder Guide available at www.ncjrs.gov/pdf-files1/nij/187736.pdf.

Computer Crime Reporting

Many organizations do not report computer crime to the authorities for a number of reasons. One of the most popular reasons is because of the loss an organization will take financially if news of the incident is reported. This can come from fines, loss of reputation affecting stock price, and lack of customer confidence, thereby reducing overall sales. Prior to legislation such as the Gramm-Leach-Bliley Act (GLBA) and the Health Information Portability and Accountability Act (HIPAA), disclosure of incidents was not required by law. Today there are many pieces of legislation, both on a federal and state level, which require disclosure. Still, many organizations use loopholes in these laws in an attempt to not disclose the breach. The annual CSI/FBI study shows the rate of crimes disclosed, the types of crimes, and the loss due to those crimes. Recently, this study has shown a decrease in the number of crimes occurring and an increase in the cost per incident.

Vulnerability Resources

There are many resources available to provide the incident response team with details about common vulnerabilities. The best resources include sites such as:

- www.securityfocus.com
- www.milw0rm.com

- www.frsirt.com/english/
- www.packetstormsecurity.nl/
- www.astalavista.box.sk/

In addition to these Web sites, the next best source for vulnerability information is to collect vulnerabilities about the target organization itself. To do this, a vulnerability scanner should be used. The best-known vulnerability scanner is the Nessus scanner available from Tenable Security at www.tenablesecurity.com (see Figure 15.1). All of these resources will inform both the incident response team and the organization about holes in controls as well as potential attack vectors.

Figure 15.1 The Nessus Scanner

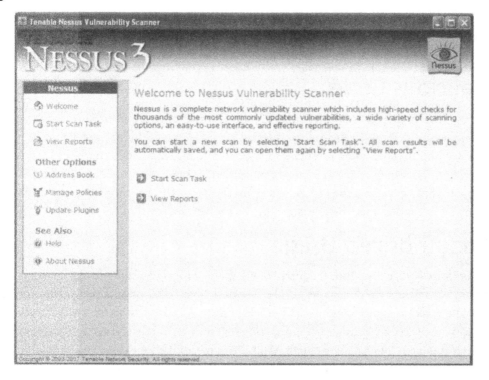

Categories of Incidents

One of the toughest components of incident response is the need to respond to different types of incidents. Each type of incident has unique requirements. This means each type of incident requires its own procedures to adequately respond.

Denial of Service

Denial-of-service (DoS) incidents stop legitimate access to the required resource. There are several examples of DoS attacks, but the most popular are the buffer overflow attack, which does not produce a remote command execution, and the resource starvation attack. The buffer overflow attack usually allows the attacker to control what is going to be run on the central processing unit (CPU), but in the DoS buffer overflow the attack simply points the CPU to a non-existent memory address causing the process to end. Resource starvation attacks work by robbing the system of some needed resource such as CPU cycles, available memory, or network bandwidth. These attacks consume all of the resources until there is none available for the legitimate application. These incidents were very popular until February 2000, when the traditional DoS attack was replaced with the distributed denial-of-service (DDoS) attack. These newer attacks use zombie servers, which are controlled by a master system. Since all packets originate from the zombies, it is difficult to track the attack back to the master machine. When it comes to responding to a DoS incident, the first priority is usually to restore access to the process if it is business critical.

Malicious Code

Virus and worm attacks are malicious code attacks, which often leave evidence only in the random access memory (RAM) of the infected host. Because of this, the incident response team needs to have separate procedures to respond to a malicious code attack than for a DoS or system compromise. A key component of incident response for malicious code is the containment of the malicious code so more systems are spared the infection. This leads to the four tenants of information security: *prevent*, *detect*, *contain*, and *recover*.

Unauthorized Usage

Unauthorized usage is perhaps the most common type of incident that requires incident response. In unauthorized usage, an attacker "owns the box." This means the attacker can control what the system is going to process and in what order, as well as having the ability to gain continued remote access even after the initial compromise. A term often related to unauthorized usage is Remote Command Execution (RCE). This means the attacker can run code, usually from a shell prompt on the attacked system. This allows the attacker to take complete control.

Inappropriate Usage

Inappropriate usage incidents generally occur in one of two forms. Inappropriate usage can be the installing of pirated software on the organization's machines, or it can be abusing the intended use of a resource. For example, inappropriate usage of the e-mail system may be sending threatening e-mails to a coworker or using the Internet to view adult content. These types of incidents happen often and need to be addressed in the risk assessment portion of incident management.

Risk Assessment

One of the most important components of incident response is incident management, which has the responsibility to perform risk assessment. A risk assessment will sort risks into high risk, medium risk, and low risk. Usually this is determined by evaluating each risk using probability (likelihood the event will happen) and impact (the overall effect to the organization). Many organizations use a classification chart like the one shown in Figure 15.2 to determine where a risk falls on the spectrum.

Figure 15.2 A Risk Assessment Chart

		Impact to the Organization		
		Low	Medium	High
Probability	Low	1	4	7
	Medium	2	5	8
	High	3	6	9

These risk charts help to prioritize which events are going to need the greatest number of controls and the more detailed incident response planning. Once the risk assessment is completed, the organization should have a list of risks, a ranking of how dangerous the risk is, and controls or safeguards that can help mitigate these risks. This helps the organization to focus on which types of incidents should be planned for first and the corresponding procedures developed.

Staffing the Team

The skill sets of incident response team members will vary greatly. Since incident response can comprise everything from keeping management updated on the progress to taking forensic images of hard drives from compromised machines, no one person can do it all. This is why a team is needed. Typically, an incident response team will need representatives to perform the following roles:

- **Lead investigator** The lead investigator is the manager of the incident response team. Duties include keeping management updated and ensuring that the incident response moves smoothly and efficiently. The lead investigator also interviews and interrogates suspects and witnesses. In addition, the lead investigator is usually involved in the creation of the incident response plan.

- **Information security representative** The information security representative alerts the team to possible security safeguards that may impact their ability to respond to the incident. An example of this is hard drive encryption, which could slow down the processing of the hard drive significantly. In addition, the IS representative can provide information about the system's configuration and help document the incident scene.

- **Legal representative** The legal representative ensures that the process does not break any laws during the response to an incident.

- **Technical representatives** Technical representatives perform forensic backups of the systems that are the focus of the incident, and provide more information about the configuration of the network or target system. Usually there is more than one technician deployed to an incident.

- **Human resources** Human resources personnel are usually involved to ensure the policies of the organization are enforced during the incident response, and also to suspend access to a suspect if needed. Human Resources personnel often work closely with legal to ensure the incident response is lawful and to help cover the organization's liability.

Steps of Incident Response

When it comes to incident response, each organization will have a slightly different approach as to how to respond to an incident. Some organizations prefer to outsource this function to a specialized company. However, the skill set needed for incident response is difficult to find, and in some cases, less than qualified incident responders may be deployed. Outsourced providers also are at a disadvantage, because they have less information on how the network and systems are architected. Because of this, many organizations are now choosing to have an internal CSIRT. The biggest problem with using an internal team is the potential conflict of interest or a member of the team may be a potential witness or suspect. Regardless of whether the CSIRT is internal or external, a process similar to the steps outlined in Figure 15.3 will be used. Table 15.1 shows the strengths and weaknesses of using different types of incident response teams.

Figure 15.3 Incident Response Steps

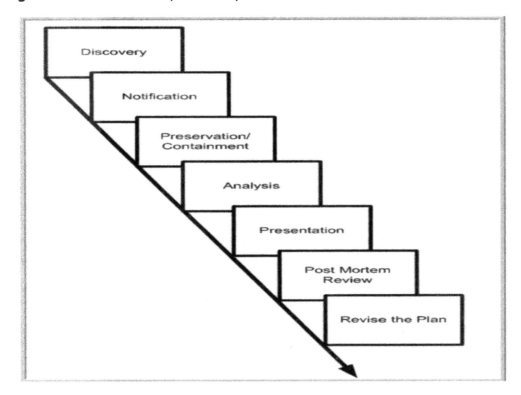

Table 15.1 Strengths and Weaknesses of Different Incident Response Teams

Group	Strengths	Weaknesses
Internal security team	1. Understanding of the systems and personnel	1. May be suspect or perpetrator 2. Potential conflict of interest
External consultants	1. No conflict of interest	1. High costs 2. Difficult to find highly trained consultants 3. Lack of prior intimate knowledge of systems
Law enforcement	1. No conflict of interest 2. Less cost	1. Lack of investigative control

Preparation

Before you respond to an incident, it is important to have the structure in place for incident response. Since building the team, creating policies, and creating procedures are all time-consuming activities, it is essential to prepare before an incident occurs. This is largely due to the time-sensitive nature of incidents, which do not allow for extensive breaks for management or committee approval for each new procedure or for each staffing appointment to the CSIRT.

Identification

How are incidents discovered? There are a number of different ways, but in large part, a user or administrator notices incidents accidentally. Proper training and procedures are necessary to ensure that the person noticing the incident understands the proper reporting channel. Incidents can also be discovered during the course of a log review. These logs can exist in many different places, such as the firewall, intrusion detection systems (IDSes), IPSes, routers, and servers. A somewhat recent development is the Security Incident Management (SIM) device. SIM devices correlate the logs from all of these different sources and many look for hidden patterns in the log data. A SIM device may one day be the most effective device for detecting incidents.

Usually the discovery phase uses a preliminary investigation to verify that an incident has occurred. This can be a little tricky because of the need to preserve evidence. Typically, the preliminary investigation is as follows:

- **Determine if a crime has occurred** The goal of the preliminary investigation,

- **Review complaint** If accidental discovery has occurred, this is the verification that the event is truly an incident.

- **Inspect damage** This happens most often in malicious code incidents where an outbreak has occurred and there are multiple infected machines. In the event of unauthorized access, inspecting the damage on the compromised machine may possibly overwrite evidence or damage the evidence left behind.

- **Interview witnesses** This is usually performed by the lead investigator. The goal here is to verify that other people have seen the incident.

- **Examine logs** As covered above, logs may be rich sources of information (assuming logging is enabled).

- **Identify investigation requirements** The last phase of the preliminary investigation happens only when the event has now become an incident. In this phase, the lead investigator meets with senior management to determine the goals for the investigation.

Notification

As information security professionals, our primary job is to alert senior management to the event and the possibility for the event to turn into an incident. Senior management (usually with the help of legal staff) will determine if notification needs to be made to the media, law enforcement, business partners, or customers. This decision should be made by senior management and is not usually the responsibility of the incident response team.

Preservation and Containment

My mentor gave me a line from Sun Tzu's "The Art of War," to help guide me through the incident response process. The quote is "Ponder and deliberate before you move." Since we are dealing with both transient data (information that will be lost at shutdown, such as open network connections, memory resident programs, and so on), and fragile data (data that is stored on the hard disk, but can easily be altered, such as the last accessed time stamps), we have to try our best to preserve the evidence during the incident response phase. This is where the procedures of an organization's CSIRT can really become important. The preservation of evidence is often called "freezing the scene".

Alongside preservation is containment. Containment is the process of trying to keep the incident from affecting more systems on the network. This may mean removing the infected or compromised system from the network, the Internet, or both.

Analysis

During this phase, the scene is documented, serial numbers are recorded, and machines are moved to the forensic processing stage. In some cases, incident response may be required to perform the forensic or bit-stream back up of the drives, but often it is performed by the forensic team instead of the CSIRT. Figure 15.4 includes an example of a form that is used for analysis.

The CSIRT incident reporting form from CERT is available at www.cert.org/reporting/incident_form.txt.

Figure 15.4 An Incident Analysis Form

KNOPPIX EVIDENCE INVENTORY WORKSHEET
Original Media Access Worksheet

TO DOCUMENT EACH ACCESS TO ORIGINAL MEDIA	Date:		Time:
	Accessed by:		
	Computer ID:		

Location of Computer:

BIOS SETTINGS

Access Date:	System Date:	
Access Time:	System Time:	
BIOS Set to Boot to CD ROM	YES	NO
BIOS Settings Modified to Boot to CD ROM	YES	NO

SEARCH

Following files extensions were searched for:

JPG	JPEG	GIF	BMP	OTHER:
PNG	AVI	MPEG	MPG	

Following text and/or file names were searched for:

During search the following directories were examined:

Search revealed following:

Results documented to media	YES	NO
Computer Seized	YES	NO
Special Notes:	Time Ended	

Eradication and Recovery

Once the scene is frozen it is sometimes necessary for the CSIRT to fix the underlying problem that caused the incident. However, many organizations employ a separation of duties where a group such as computer operations or information security will fix the problem. If the responsibility does fall with the CSIRT, the goal is to stop the current incident, and then stop the incident from occurring again. This is most often the case with a malicious code attack, since the initial outbreak at the organization will need to be addressed to stop more infections from happening, followed by an update on anti-virus software to stop future virus outbreaks from occurring. If a system is damaged beyond repair, they may need to be recovered from backup. If backup copies of the systems do not exist, then the systems may need to be reinstalled to ensure that the system in uninfected before a return to production.

Presentation

During presentation the incident response team turns over the investigation to the forensics team. Incident response sheets (see Figure 15.4) are turned over as well as the target systems

and forensic back-ups of those systems. Any evidence discovered during the incident response is presented to the incident response team and from this point on the forensic team handles the investigation. If your organization is a small- to medium-size enterprise, your incident response team and your forensic team may be one and the same. In this case, the presentation may only need to be made to senior management.

Post Mortem Review

After the incident response team has turned the evidence over to the forensic team, it is time to begin looking for ways to improve the incident response process for next time. Typical areas for improvement are:

- **Incident response plan** The plan itself will probably need at least some tweaking to make the process smoother the next time around.

- **Information dissemination policy** If information was leaked to the media or if a team member relayed sensitive information, it might be necessary to create an information dissemination policy.

- **Incident reporting policy** Did the end user who accidentally discovered the incident know who to call or where to go when he or she uncovered the incident? If not, training and an incident reporting policy may need to be created.

- **Electronic monitoring statement** There is great debate as to who owns the information sent on the network unless it is set by policy. An electric monitoring statement such as "This system is for authorized users only. All access is logged. By accessing this system you agree to the monitoring" reinforces the policy and reminds employees of the security measures in place.

- **Audit trail policy** If no policy exists, a policy may need to be created to inform users of logging taking place. This works with the above statement.

- **Additional personnel security controls** If physical access to your building is not controlled, it is much harder to determine possible inside threats. A physical card reader with logging may be a control, which can help eliminate the general public as a suspect.

Revise the Plan or Follow Up

When it comes to incident response, there is always room for improvement. The output of a post mortem review should provide the possible changes to the plan to make responding to the next incident smoother. If the incident response when out without a need for updating the plan, look to see if the plan would still perform as well in the event of a different sort of attack. For example, if the plan performed well with a virus outbreak, consider a system compromise or a DoS attack.

International CSIRTS

In September 2000, a group known as Trusted Introducer started to certify European CSIRTs using a documented procedure to evaluate CSIRTs. Several organizations have been classified as listed, accreditation candidate, or accredited. This information as well as other resources can be found at www.trusted-introducer.nl/index.html.

First Responder Procedures

Imagine if we could go back in time and examine some of the most famous crimes. If only we could freeze time to the instant those crimes took place. We would be able to examine each case with near perfect evidence. We could disprove all the conspiracy theories of the past. In the world of computer forensics investigation, we almost have that luxury.

The first response is the most critical part of a computer crime investigation. If done correctly with forensically sound practices, it is a solid building block to any investigation. In this section, we discuss sound incident response procedures and the role of first responders.

Damage & Defense...

Consent

It is critical that you consult your legal counsel on corporate, local, state, national, and international laws that may apply to any investigation. Consent allows a first responder to conduct incident response and forensics procedures. Consent is usually granted by the owner of the assets. This is the most highly contested area of computer forensics. Does the owner of the system own the information on it? Work closely with attorneys to clarify rules on consent as it applies to your job function. Consent can be a legal nightmare if you are not careful. If you don't have consent, you can't do incident response.

The Forensic Process

Every incident should be treated as if it will end up in court. This is why the forensics process should be followed for every incident. The forensics process includes and is not limited to preparation, collection, examination, analysis, and reporting (see Figure 15.5). Each phase feeds the next phase in the process. The first responder is an integral part of the collection phase.

Figure 15.5 The Forensic Process

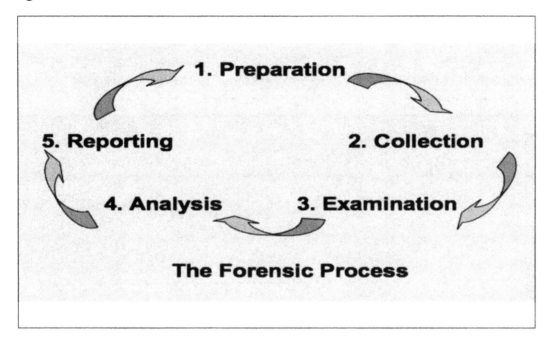

Preparation

Prior planning and preparation prevent poor performance. An organization must come up with policies and procedures to support a sound forensics process. Software licensing is a major consideration, because law enforcement cannot use evidence collected with pirated software. There should be an organized life cycle based on emerging technologies and personnel working the collection, examination, analysis, and reporting. This ensures that organization forensics practice is scalable for emerging issues and technology.

- Policy
- Procedures
- Standards
- Software licensing
- Training for personnel
- Forensically clean media
- Response workstations
- Collection hardware
- Collection software

Collection

The collection phase of forensics is the phase where first responders are handling incidents. As mentioned before, the collection phase is critical to any investigation. The first responder should minimize any loss of electronic evidence (see the Damage & Defense sidebar for a definition of electronic evidence). All procedures completed by the first responder should be documented. All data should be verified and hashed for integrity.

Electronic Evidence

Electronic evidence is any data stored or transmitted with electronic devices. As a first responder, it is imperative to understand the types of information devices can hold.

Before we move on to the next step, we'll briefly discuss the various electronic devices from which evidence might need to be collected. Although it is impossible to list all forms of electronic devices that may hold evidence, we will discuss the most common devices (see Figure 15.6). Table 15.2 lists several types of devices and media and the evidence that each of these devices contains. Responders must be careful because of the volatile nature of electronic devices, in order to maintain the integrity of the evidence.

Figure 15.6 Various Types of Potential Evidence

Table 15.2 Devices and Media

Device or Media	Potential Evidence
Computer System	Computer files, video, audio, e-mail, images, notes, documents, contacts
Routers	Logs, ACLs, routing tables
Switches	MAC address, security violation logs
Firewalls	Logs, ACLs, configuration information
Servers	Computer files
Network Traffic Sniffers	Binary log captures
Intrusion Detection Systems	Intrusion alert logs
MP3 Players	Computer files, video and audio recordings
Smart Cards	Identification, credentials, access information,
Smart Phones	Computer files, video, audio, e-mail, images, notes, contacts
Digital Cameras	Internal Memory, video, audio, computer files
Personal Digital Assistant (PDA)	Computer files, agenda, notes, audio,
Hard Drives	Computer files, video, audio, e-mail, logs
Memory Cards	Computer files, video, audio,
Global Positioning Systems (GPS)	Logs for tracking suspect movement
Digital Video Recorders (DVR)	Computer files, video, audio,

Figure 15.7 shows an example of a DVR with a 40GB hard drive.

Figure 15.7 A DVR with a 40GB Hard Drive

Examination

During the examination phase, forensics practitioners perform a holistic examination of the evidence collected by the first responders. Contrary to popular belief, the forensics practitioner's function is to take an impartial look at the evidence provided to them. The examiner tries to detect hidden, obscured, and encrypted data. The forensics practitioner should provide an unbiased examination report.

Analysis

The analysis phase is utilized to determine the who, what, when, and where of an incident. The evidence is scrutinized to determine its value to a case. At this stage, it may be determined that there is nothing of evidentiary value.

Reporting

The examination report should contain only relevant information for the requested services. All procedures used and notes taken during the examination are preserved for discovery and testimony. The examiner must articulate the findings.

First Responder Roles

Identifying and understanding the roles of First Responders are crucial steps in the development of an Incident Response Program. The first responders are just that, the first members to identify and address an incident. More often than not, they are system and network administrators that are not trained in forensics. This is why it is crucial for an organization to have policies and procedures in place, so they have a written guideline to follow for each type of incident, they know what *not* to do, and they know whom to contact before contaminating evidence. The team should include representatives from legal counsel and Human Resources. They should be consulted on all policies and procedures before implementation. Additionally, their expertise will be invaluable once the data is collected and examined. These may be considered liaison roles in some organizations (e.g., legal counsel would not likely be member of the forensic incident response team; however, they are a necessary component of the entire process.)

System Administrator

System Administrators are critical to any computer crime investigation. It is the system administrator that discovers anomalies during their daily operations. Unfortunately, most system administrators are concerned more with system availability than forensic practices. It is important that all organizations and agencies indoctrinate their system administrator on incident response procedures. During a response, the system administrator can provide system configuration, network topology, logs, and other critical information.

Forensics Personnel

Forensics personnel are ideal personnel to respond to a suspected incident. Forensics personnel are trained to preserve and collect electronic evidence. They usually have a selection of tools and software to support system administrators who suspect their systems are compromised. The role of forensics personnel is to provide an unbiased forensic analysis to determine the evidentiary value of electronic evidence.

Non-forensics Personnel

Since computers are a part of everyone's home and work environment, this raises the possibility that anyone can be a first responder. Organizational management should take steps to ensure that all personnel are aware of what steps to take should an incident occur. Training should be given informing all non-forensics personnel on policy to ensure that incidents can be processed with forensics practice. Figure 15.8 shows the FCC's Computer Security Incident Form. This type of form should be available to all organizations to record accurate and detailed information of computer systems incidents.

Figure 15.8 FCC Computer System Incident Report Form

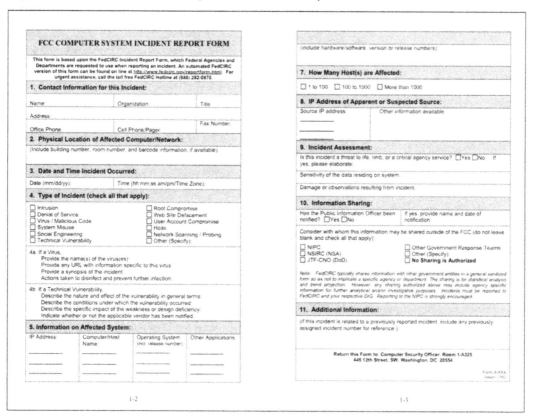

Securing Electronic Crime Scene

The number one rule of incident response is to preserve as much evidence as possible. It is important to quickly establish a cordial relationship to gain maximum cooperation from personnel, especially management, in the response environment. Management typically assigns someone as the DAA who will work with the incident responder on making decisions affecting the organization's assets.

The responder must work efficiently and document all events that occur. The responder should immediately start taking notes with dates and times using a known good time source, such as a cell phone. Prosecution could take years in some cases, and notes could refresh a responder's memory for testimony. All of your actions, including your notes, are subject to discovery in a criminal case.

Initially the responder should take steps to secure the safety of all personnel present. Generally, no personnel should be able to take materials away from the crime scene. It is important to treat other areas outside the proximity of a workstation as a crime scene. Once the area is secured from all personnel, the responder can proceed with collection. If you are responding to an unfamiliar environment, as is the case with many law enforcement and corporate investigators, you will need some help.

Health and Safety Personnel

In incident response, it important to remember the safety of everyone involved. Sometimes in a high-pressure situation this is forgotten. Due to the nature of "electronic" evidence, there are natural causes for concern. It is in everyone's best interest to preserve personnel as well as electronic evidence. Some safety items to consider are:

- Unplug the power before working on internal components
- Some equipment may hold an electric charge after unplugging
- Liquids and electricity
- Beware of dangerous radio waves (i.e., microwave transmissions)
- Lasers components on equipment could damage eyesight

Collecting and Preserving Evidence

In a business environment, first responders must locate system administrators or other personnel with knowledge of the computer and network setup. Once the computers involved in the incident are identified, the responder should take an initial look at the workstation to verify if any destructive activity is occurring. The suspect may try to cover their tracks by executing utilities that can destroy electronic evidence. If an incident responder notices such behavior, they should immediately pull the plug on the equipment.

Identifying Potential Evidence

The responder should look for all identifying markings on the system. The best information to obtain is a serial number. If a serial number is not present, the responder should record all possible identifying properties of the equipment. When seizing computers, all connections are labeled for reassembly at a forensics lab (see Figure 15.9). All of the cables and the corresponding ports should be labeled.

Figure 15.9 Labeling Computer Cables

Collecting Volatile Data

When the first responder arrives, they can attempt to collect volatile data from the powered-on machine. Volatile data is information that is only present when the machine is turned on. If a network intrusion has occurred, the attacker may still have connections established. Many organizations have their own trusted toolset for collecting volatile data. Once you have collected volatile data, you should hash the files and record the hash values in your notes. All collected data must be put on forensically clean media. The netcat tool is often used to collect volatile data over a network.

Responder Computer: Setting up Netcat Listener

Starting on the incident responder's collection computer, we will start a Netcat listener. The first command sets up a Netcat listener on TCP port 4444. Data received will be redirected to forensically clean media on the G: drive.

```
H:\IR\bin>nc.exe -l -p 4444 > g:\ipconfig.txt
```

Victim Computer: Sending Volatile Data with Netcat

The next command is issued from the victim computer. This step sends Internet Protocol (IP) configuration data to the first responder's workstation.

```
H:\IR\bin>ipconfig | nc 192.168.1.254 4444
```

Responder Computer: Verifying and Hashing

Next we verify and then hash the information. The *type* command is used to verify the results from the Netcat transfer and *MD5deep* is utilized to hash the information. The *type* command is also used to verify the hash value. It is important to redirect the hash output to a new file. In the example below, *ipconfig.txt* was hashed and the results were redirected to *ipconfig.md5*.

```
H:\IR\bin>type g:\ipconfig.txt
Windows IP Configuration
Ethernet adapter Wireless Network Connection 2:
     Connection-specific DNS Suffix . : cwd.superchimp.net.
     IP Address. . . . . . . . . . . : 192.168.1.101
     Subnet Mask . . . . . . . . . . : 255.255.255.0
     Default Gateway . . . . . . . . : 192.168.1.1
H:\IR\bin>
H:\IR\bin>md5deep.exe g:\ipconfig.txt
H:\IR\bin>md5deep.exe g:\ipconfig.txt > ipconfig.md5
H:\IR\bin>type g:\ipconfig.md5
3d9b58dda0f6a14e0d0016fd28f8fcce g:\ipconfig.txt
```

Automated Volatile Data Collection Tools

Automated incident response scripts offer a speed advantage over manually typing in commands. Many organizations have a custom software tool belt for incident response. Many of the tools contain static binaries, which are compiled to be totally self contained when operating. The static binaries are preferred because they tend not to trample on evidence. There are many tools, such as E-Fense's live CD Helix, that an organization may use as an incident response tool to collect volatile data (see Figure 15.10).

Figure 15.10 Efense's Helix Incident Response CD

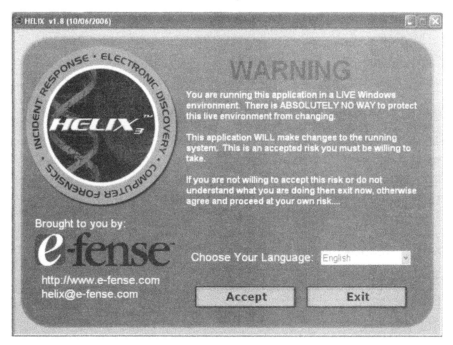

The Initial Interview

First responders must utilize the initial interview to obtain information that may not be available in the future. System Administrators and potential suspects may be willing to give up more information in an initial interview. As mentioned earlier, the legal system's wheels turn slowly in some cases. If information is stored in notes, it can be retrieved for later testimony and examination. The following is some of the information you should try to collect during an initial interview:

- Signed statements
- Owner information
- All users
- Contact information
- Passwords
- Encryption keys
- Internet aliases
- E-mail addresses
- Internet Service Provider (ISP)

- Purpose of the system
- Remote backups or storage
- Media storage
- Removable media

Documenting the Electronic Crime Scene

Documenting the crime scene must be done meticulously. This process creates a historical document of the crime scene. Each crime scene tells a story. When first responders document a crime scene, they should take 360-degree pictures of the entire room and any rooms related to the crime. If a video camera is available, it should be utilized as well. Pictures of the active programs should be taken to help profile the user (see Figure 15.11).

Figure 15.11 Capturing the Screen Can Profile the User

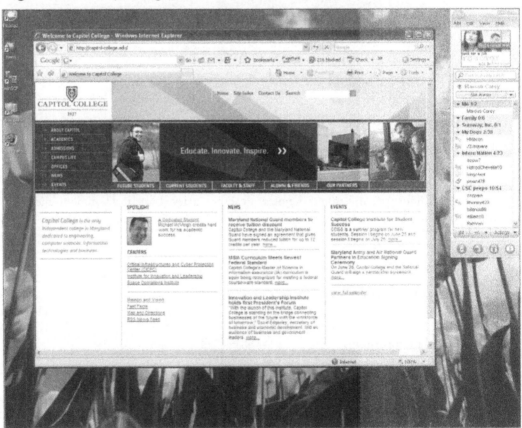

In Figure 15.11, the incident responder was able to get a screenshot of the user's activity. We see that the user has the homepage of a college open as well as a chat program. The chat program reveals the user's online alias. Further inspection of the desktop (see Figure 15.12) reveals that the user has a secure file transfer program, WinSCP, which shows a more advanced computer user who encrypts file transfers.

Figure 15.12 WinSCP Icon

In Figure 15.13, we see the suspect's tower computer case. In the next image (see Figure 15.14) we can see that the user has a KVM switch under the desk. This usually means that there was more than one computer connected under the desk. This may prompt the responder to inquire about the whereabouts of a second computer.

Figure 15.13 Suspect's Computer

Figure 15.14 Suspect's KVM Switch

Evidence Collection Tools and Equipment

As part of the preparation phase, organizations should have a toolkit ready for action. In short, first responders need to be prepared for any situation. With the vast amount of electronic equipment available today, it is best to plan for versatility. Instead of taking four different card readers for flash memory imaging, take one multi-card reader similar to the one shown in Figure 15.15. Some of the tools in the following list should be included in the responses.

General Equipment and Tools

- Forensically clean media for imaging
- Flashlight
- Camera
- Video recorder
- Voice recorder
- Write blocker
- Responder laptop
- Multicard reader

Figure 15.15 Products Like a Multicard Reader Have Versatility

Hardware Tools

- Various size screwdrivers (flat-head and Phillips)
- Precision toolset
- Various pliers
- Wire cutters
- Hex-nut tools
- Tweezers

Chain of Custody

To ensure the integrity of electronic evidence, a chain of custody should be established. The chain of custody should be documented in writing to include all handlers from seizure, transfer, storage, examination, analysis, and disposition of electronic evidence, and must be done in accordance with corporate, local, state, national, and international jurisdictions and other policies. Once the evidence is collected, it must be accounted for in documents literally during every stage of the investigation. Evidence can be thrown out at court if it not handled properly. Figure 15.16 shows the electronic evidence chain of custody form that comes with Helix. This form covers the key needs of most chain of custody cases. Each organization should create forms and chain-of-custody procedures specific to it. The typical chain-of-custody form should include the case number, evidence details, handler names, signatures, dates, and relevant location information.

Figure 15.16 Helix Chain of Custody Form

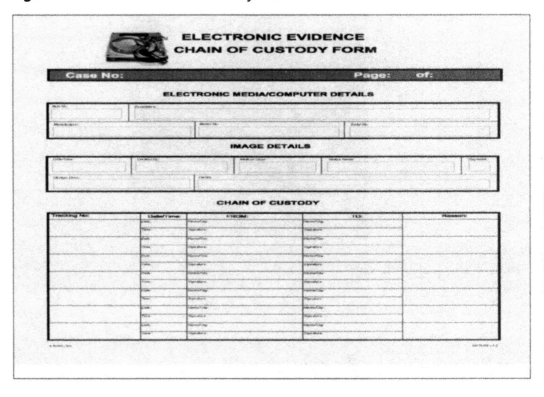

Transporting Electronic Evidence

The delicate nature of electronic equipment requires extra attention. When leaving a scene, electronic evidence should always be packed and labeled along with the chain of custody forms. Ideally, electronic media should be placed in an anti-static bag and then wrapped in anti-static wrap or bubble wrap. First responders should transport the material in sturdy boxes or cases until arriving at a designated evidence room. Once the material arrives safely to the evidence room, the chain of custody documents can be appropriately documented and turned over to the evidence custodian. If acceptable by your organization, you may be able to use mail services to transport evidence.

It is important to consider the environment in which the devices are placed. Electronic evidence is susceptible to damage by extreme cold or heat. If you are transporting evidence by vehicle or air delivery, you should consider the extremities of each environment.

Materials Needed for Transporting Evidence

The following is a list of equipment and materials needed for transporting materials:

- Antistatic bags
- Antistatic bubble wrap
- Cable ties
- Evidence forms
- Cable tags
- Scissors
- Felt tip markers
- Self-adhesive labels
- White masking tape
- Evidence bags
- Evidence tape
- Packing tape
- Cardboard boxes (various sizes)

Forensics by Crime Category

It is impossible to definitively profile the electronic evidence that will be recovered from each crime. The following outline attempts to place potential evidence in the different crime categories.

General Crimes

- E-mail
- Images
- Internet browser history
- User information

Network and Computer Intrusions

- System logs
- Binary captures
- Configuration files
- Detailed system information

Child Exploitation or Abuse

- Images
- Video files
- Digital camera
- Details directory conventions for illegal content
- Internet browser history

Summary

CSIRTs are complex groups that are the first line of response when an event is detected. These teams need to have a wide range of skill sets. Incident Management is a key process that performs risk assessments to determine the most likely types of incidents, and also devises the policies and procedures for the CSIRT to follow. Typically, the CSIRT follows a process of discovery, notification, preservation and containment, analysis, presentation, port-mortem reviews, and CSIRT plan revisions. Each incident is unique and common incidents include DoS, unauthorized usage, malicious code, and inappropriate usage. Each type of incident requires a unique response from the CSIRT. There are many resources available for the CSIRT, including vulnerability Web sites (listed above), www.cert.org/csirts/Creating-A-CSIRT.html (the home of the US Cert), the FCC incident response guide at http://csrc.nist.gov/fasp/FASPDocs/incident-response/Incident-Response-Guide.pdf, the NIST national guideline on incident management at http://csrc.nist.gov/publications/nistpubs/800-61/sp800-61.pdf, as well as the international list of accredited teams (listed in the previous section).

Exam Objectives
Frequently Asked Questions

The following Frequently Asked Questions, answered by the authors of this book, are designed to both measure your understanding of the Exam Objectives presented in this chapter, and to assist you with real-life implementation of these concepts.

Q: What can a first responder do when they forget to hash and record evidence on the scene?

A: Create a document stating the error, then hash the evidence and document accordingly.

Q: Can system administrators collect evidence on their network with management approval?

A: Laws vary vastly on the expectation of privacy. Consult an attorney.

Q: What do I do if I can't log on to a system to collect volatile data?

A: Even though volatile data can't be taken in all cases, a thorough forensics examination can still be done.

CHFI

Types of Investigations

Exam objectives in this chapter:

- **Investigating Corporate Espionage**
- **Investigating Trademark and Copyright Infringement**
- **Writing Investigative Reports**
- **Investigating Child Pornography**
- **Investigating Sexual Harassment**

Exam Objectives Review:

- ☑ **Summary of Exam Objectives**
- ☑ **Exam Objectives Fast Track**
- ☑ **Exam Objectives Frequently Asked Questions**

Introduction

This chapter introduces the student to the main types of forensic investigations that you're likely to encounter. It is important to both understand the nature of the incident being investigated as well as to be able to report it effectively. After all, it is of little use uncovering evidence if you are unable to report it in a suitable format. Always keep in mind that any evidence you uncover may end up subject to scrutiny within the court room.

The most effective investigators understand the nature of the incidents they work with. You should become familiar with the various types of investigations and the peculiarities of each.

Investigating Corporate Espionage

This section explores corporate espionage and the methods used to combat it. The questions we have to ask include:

- Why does corporate espionage occur?

- Who are these 21st century techno-spies?

- How do they go about stealing?

- What do they really take?

- What can we do about it?

To fully understand corporate espionage in the 21st century requires an understanding of the Information Age or Age of Technology. Modern espionage does not concern only the government and is more than spies stealing military secrets. Corporate espionage in the new global business environment is emerging as the primary 21st century means for creating a competitive advantage, whether as a country, organization, business, or military power.

What Is Corporate Espionage?

Corporate espionage is defined under "theft of trade secrets" and "economic espionage" by the U.S. Economic Espionage Act of 1996 (Title 18 UCS 1831). It is a federal criminal offense.

The Economic Espionage Act became effective October 11, 1996. It was originally aimed at ending the foreign theft of U.S. information. It criminalizes on a federal level the theft of trade secrets. It has two main provisions that cover state-sponsored (1831) and commercial (1832) thefts.

TITLE 18, PART I, CHAPTER 90, PROTECTION OF TRADE SECRETS

This U.S. Act covers the primary legislative elements of economic espionage and the theft of trade secrets. Of particular concern to the forensic investigator are sections § 1831. Economic Espionage and § 1832. Theft of Trade Secrets. This legislation makes the theft or attempt to steal any trade secret a felony offense. See www4.law.cornell.edu/uscode/html/uscode18/usc_sup_01_18_10_I_20_90.html for details.

EXAM WARNING

Take the time to review the following U.S. acts:
- Wiretap Act, 18 U.S.C. 2511
- Access to Stored Electronic Communications, 18 U.S.C. 2701
- Wire Fraud Act, 18 U.S.C. 1343
- Trafficking in Fraudulent Access Devices, 18 U.S.C 1029
- Computer Fraud and Abuse Act, 18 U.S.C. 1030

The Motives Behind Corporate Espionage

The primary motivations for corporate espionage include:

- Theft of trade secrets for economic gain
- Attempting to monopolize a product or other offering in a selected market
- Acquiring competitive advantage in domestic and global markets
- Threats of computer technology
- Privacy violations

Basically, the threats are the same as they have always been; only the media have evolved to make it easier to commit the crime.

Information: What Do Corporate Spies Seek?

The corporate spy will seek anything that provides him or her with an advantage or profit. Some of the possible sources of information include:

- Documents, whether completed or still in draft, and working notes or scrap paper
- Computer-based information
- Photographs, maps, and charts

- Internal correspondence and e-mail
- Legal and regulatory filings
- Company intranet access and publications
- Formal meeting minutes or transcripts
- Casual conservations
- Conversations at trade shows and events

A competitive organization may also be able to use and gain an advantage using:

- Marketing and product plans (especially prior to release)
- Source code
- Corporate strategies and plans
- Marketing, advertising, and packaging expenditures
- Pricing issues, strategies, and lists
- R&D, manufacturing processes, and technological operations
- Target markets and prospect information
- Plant closures and development
- Product designs, development, and costs
- Staffing, operations, organization charts, and wage/salary information
- Partner and contract arrangements (including delivery, pricing, and terms)
- Customer and supplier information
- Merger and acquisition plans
- Financials, revenues, P&L, and R&D budgets

With the rise of identity fraud and other related offenses, the theft of proprietary company information and private personnel records is also increasing. The records sought include:

- Home addresses
- Home phone numbers
- Names of spouses and children
- Employees' salary
- Social Security numbers
- Medical records

- Credit records or credit union account information
- Performance reviews

Corporate Espionage Threats

The threat agents exist in several general categories. Any of the following may be a source of threat to your organization:

- Accidental antagonists, who cause you harm through ignorance or by negligence

- Incidental antagonists, who seek another target but attack because you are there and obtainable

- Insiders, who may compromise or steal information assets because of motivations from dissatisfaction to economic gain

- Competitors, who may attack to gain a benefit or to achieve market dominance

- Cyber vandals, who could attack because you are there or you have a product they do not like

- Hackers and crackers, who may attack in an attempt to obtain information concerning everything that is denied to them or who might be offering their technical proficiency to another with motives of their own

- Thieves, who may attack to further their own financial well-being

- Terrorists, who can attack to disrupt the connection linking the general public and critical infrastructure

- The military, who are involved in information warfare actions.

In particular, the threats may be summarized as:

- Third world countries
- Organized crime
- Hackers
- Terrorist organizations
- Internal competitors (within a nation)
- Foreign competitors
- Foreign intelligence agencies

Hostile nations such as China, North Korea, Cuba, and Iran are only one source of remote threat. Friendly nations have been known (and caught) in these activities in the past.

The Various Techniques of Spying

There are four primary methods of obtaining information illegally. These are hacking, social engineering, dumpster diving, and ease dropping. In addition to these there are "white" and "gray" areas. The white areas are activities that are legal (if unethical). The gray areas (such as Google hacking) are legally unclear but rarely ethical.

Hacking

Computer hacking/cracking is becoming one of the most utilized and effective techniques for acquiring trade secrets. This is growing. The availability and simplicity of tools and the commercialization of spyware and zombie networks is only adding to the threat. Hacking can be separated into local system, remote network, and physical attacks.

Social Engineering

The common techniques associated with social engineering include pretexting, phishing, distributing Trojan horses, and "road apples." Social engineering is simply a means to commit fraud on another through a confidence trick or other means of disseminating false information. Social engineering is used to manipulate an innocent victim into performing an action they normally would not do. This includes giving out information such as their username and passwords. Is generally much simpler to convince another person to give up information then it is to find a vulnerability in a system or crack a password.

The U.S. Gramm-Leach-Bliley Act (GLBA) of 1999 expressly addresses pretexting of banking records as an illegal act punishable under federal statutes. Pretexting is an invasion of privacy tort of appropriation in common law terms (Restatement 2d of Torts § 652C).

Dumpster Diving

Dumpster diving is a very successful technique used to obtain trade secrets and other important information. Dumpster diving is even legal in some cases. If there is no signage or other form of trespass notification and the bin is located in a public street or alley, case law dictates that if materials or property are left to be accessed by commercial carters, it is no longer private property.

Ease Dropping

"Ease dropping" involves using a digital recording tool to monitor a fax line and record a fax transmission and reception. Replaying the soundtrack into a modified Group III or Group IV fax machine allows the creation of an accurate copy of a message. This attack is passive and is thus extremely difficult to detect.

Google Hacking

Google hacking is a term defined by Jonny Long, the maintainer of the Google hacking database see, http://johnny.ihackstuff.com/ghdb.php). This technique uses a series of complex search engine queries to find vulnerabilities on the Web. In the process of indexing Web servers, Google will inadvertently capture sensitive information from poorly configured systems. This could be through buffer overflows, poor passwords, or the default configurations. The end result is the googledork. These are those people whose systems have been inadvertently indexed exposing their vulnerabilities.

This is a no-tech method of breaking into systems. These techniques may further be used to capture sensitive information including credit card numbers, Social Security numbers, and passwords.

Espionage and Spying Countermeasures

The primary countermeasures to espionage and spying are achieved through the introduction of effective controls. Technical controls are useful, but people are often the biggest risk. Involving human resources and adding awareness training will greatly aid in minimizing the risk associated with espionage.

An organization's human resources department should instigate the following controls:

- Proper position descriptions
- Pre-employment investigations
- Periodic investigations
- Nondisclosure/competitive agreements
- Effective exit interviews
- Benefits achieved through awareness training
- Prevention of accidental disclosures
- Predictability
- Conversations
- Reporting contacts and activity

Netspionage

Netspionage is network-enabled espionage. Netspionage is a type of infocrime (i.e., a crime in which the criminal targets information). Netspionage is the specific-intent information crime of attacking, by means of a computerized or networked system, information systems and assets with the express intention to commit theft, misappropriation, destruction, or a disinformation attack.

The growth of the Internet has fueled this class of crimes. Netspionage is, in effect, a family of specific-intent information crimes. Corporate management has been slow to recognize and react to the specter of digital espionage. Most existing security systems reflect a concern for short-term profit or reaction to a specific breach of security in the past. The need to educate employees about the protection of intellectual property is rarely seen as a high-priority item.

A WarRoom Research survey of 236 respondents showed major underreporting of security incidences related to computers:

- 6.8 percent always reported intrusion.

- 30.2 percent report only if they can remain anonymous.

- 21.7 percent report only if everyone else did.

- 37.4 percent report only if they are required to by law.

- 3.9 percent report only for other reasons, including to protect themselves.

How to Investigate Corporate Espionage Cases

Corporate spies come in two categories: the skilled attacker (this person is proficient in scripting/programming new automated attack tools) and the unskilled attacker (this person has a basic ability to use tools, whether publically available or underground). Corporate spies may be further divided into professional and armature attackers. A professional will be difficult to discover and uses only the "hacker underground" for his personal means without truly becoming involved. He does the job at hand, covers his tracks, and does not generally return to the scene of the crime. The nonprofessional will generally access e-mail or files, use the system as an attack platform, share information with others in his peer group or underground, and create back doors as well as install Trojan horses or other malware, and sniffers.

Investigators can acquire evidence about an attack using a number of methods. These include:

- Real-time interception from monitoring the network and systems

- Keystroke recorders

- E-mail monitoring

- Court order

- Court-issued subpoena

- Review of log files

- Transactional data

- System usage history

- Intrusion detection systems and firewalls

In the United States, searches and interceptions may be augmented with a "Reasonable and Articulable Facts Order" (18 U.S.C. 2703).

To successfully prosecute corporate espionage, it is necessary to prove that the information has value. This can be a monetary value, a hidden value, or an economic advantage to an adversary/competitor. You also need to demonstrate that the information was protected and properly marked for protection, that policies and procedures were in place, and that awareness training was instituted.

The forensic analyst will be searching for evidence of access and, using the other techniques in this book, will be able to create a timeline of actions on the system to reconstruct the actions of a corporate spy or other related threat.

Features and Functions of Monitoring Tools

This section introduces a couple of tools that are commonly used to engage in monitoring and corporate espionage. The key features of each have been listed.

Employee Monitoring: Activity Monitor

Activity Monitor allows you to track any LAN, giving the administrator detailed information on what, how and when all network users and their actions. The product is available at www.softactivity.com/employee-monitoring.asp.

The application consists of server and client parts. You can install the Activity Monitor server on any computer in the entire LAN. Remote spy software (Agent) is a small client program that is installed on all computers on the network to be monitored. You can even install it remotely from the PC with Activity Monitor on it.

Any computer in the network under control can be spied on remotely and discretely. The software provides the capability to tune itself so that it will record activity on all networked computers. This information can be later used for deeper analysis and advanced report generation.

Activity Monitor includes the following functionality:

- View remote desktops without the other party knowing.

- Monitor Internet usage.

- Monitor software usage activity in real time. With this feature you know what programs users are using, and how long they are using them.

- Record activity for all workplaces in one centralized location on the main computer with Activity Monitor installed.

- Track any user's keystrokes on your screen in real-time mode, including passwords, e-mail, and chat conversations.

- Take snapshots of the remote PC screen on a scheduled basis.

- Create a time-sorted history of the activity in compressed JPEGs on your computer.

- Gain total control over the networked computers. You can start or terminate remote processes, run commands, and copy files from remote systems. You can even turn the computer off or restart it, as well as log off the current user.

- Deploy the Activity Monitor Agent (the client part of the software) remotely from the administrator's PC to all computers in your network.

- Auto-detect all networked computers with the Agent installed.

- View logs and export reports to HTML, Excel, and CSV.

Spy Tool: SpyBuddy

SpyBuddy offers the ability to record every action on a computer system (including keystroke monitoring) on which it is installed. It includes the capability to record all e-mails sent and received, all AOL, ICQ, MSN, AIM, Yahoo!, and Trillian chat conversations, all Web sites visited, all windows opened and interacted with, every application executed, every document printed, every file or folder renamed and/or modified, all text and images sent to the clipboard, every keystroke pressed, every password typed, and more!

SpyBuddy's surveillance and logging features include:

- **Internet Conversation Logging** SpyBuddy will log and record both sides of all chat and instant message conversations for most of the popular chat platforms.

- **E-Mail Message Logging (POP3/SMTP)** SpyBuddy can record and save all e-mail messages sent and received from the monitored system for POP3- and SMTP-supported e-mail clients.

- **Disk Activity Logging** This can record all changes made to the monitored system's hard drive and external media.

- **Window Activity Logging** This will capture information on every window that was viewed and interacted with.

- **Application Activity Logging** This tracks every application/executable as it is executed and interacted with.

- **Clipboard Activity Logging** This enables you to capture every text and image item that is copied to the monitored system's clipboard.

- **AOL/Internet Explorer History** This enables you to view all AOL and Internet Explorer Web sites visited before SpyBuddy was installed, and when SpyBuddy was not recording on the targeted system.

- **Printed Documents Logging** This allows you to log specific information on all documents that were sent to the printer spool.

- **Files/Documents Accessed** With this you can log all files and documents that were viewed from inside Windows Explorer (text files, videos, images, etc.).

- **Keystroke Monitoring [before | after]** This lets you track all keystrokes pressed (including hidden system keys) and which windows they were pressed in on the monitored system. Keystrokes can also be passed through a formatter for easy viewing/exporting.

- **Website Activity Logging** This lets you record all Web site URLs that are accessed on the system.

- **Screen Shot Capturing** The program can automatically capture screen shots of the desktop on the monitored system (or the active window) at set times.

- **SpyBuddy Activity Logging** SpyBuddy will keep track of all user shutdowns, SpyBuddy interaction, e-mail deliveries, and invalid password attempts for later review.

Investigating Trademark and Copyright Infringement

The primary goal of this section is to impart the required knowledge of trademark and copyright issues and investigative techniques to the reader. This section addresses how trademark and copyright infringement happens and how to stop it. It also discusses the laws and definitions of patent and domain name infringement.

Defining the Term "Trademark"

The U.S. Patent and Trademark Office (USPTO; www.uspto.gov) states that "a trademark is a word, phrase, symbol or design, or a combination of words, phrases, symbols or designs, which identifies and distinguishes the source of the goods of one party from those of others." This definition includes brand names, symbols, slogans, and design of merchandise. Even the packaging style, specific words, smell, specific color, or an amalgamation of any of the these which could aid the consumer in differentiating a particular product or service from others in an equivalent trade are categorized as trademarks. Trademarks can fall into three primary categories: service marks, collective marks, and certification marks.

EXAM WARNING: TRADEMARK SEARCH

Using a number of online Web sites (e.g., www.uspto.gov, www.google.com, and www.thomasregister.com) can greatly aid in any trademark search. Internet search engines can be used to extend the

online search. Best practice dictates using more than one search engine for a trademark search. As a digital forensic investigator, remain conscious of other Web sites that may aid in conducting a trademark search.

Service Mark

The USPTO defines a service mark as "any word, name, symbol, device, or any combination, used, or intended to be used, in commerce, to identify and distinguish the services of one provider from services provided by others, and to indicate the source of the services." A service mark is comparable to a trademark, with the single distinction being that a service mark is used to identify and differentiate the service of an organization from others in the equivalent field of trade.

Collective Mark

The USPTO defines a collective mark as "a trademark or service mark used or intended to be used, in commerce, by the members of a cooperative, an association, or other collective group or organization, including a mark, which indicates membership in a union, an association, or other organization."

Certification Mark

The USPTO defines a certification mark as "any word, name, symbol, device, or any combination, used, or intended to be used, in commerce with the owner's permission by someone other than its owner, to certify regional or other geographic origin, material, mode of manufacture, quality, accuracy, or other characteristics of someone's goods or services, or that the work or labor on the goods or services was performed by members of a union or other organization."

Service Mark and Trade Dress

The difference between a trademark and a service mark is minor. Primarily, the differentiation occurs as one of product and service. A trademark (™ is used to represent an unregistered trademark) differentiates products of the same trade. A service mark (using the symbol ᔆᴹ for an unregistered service mark) differentiates services of the same trade. A trademark does not consist only of a label, logo, or other identifying symbol. It may also cover the distinctive packaging belonging to a particular product (e.g., the shape of a Coke bottle).

This is called trade dress. Color, pattern, shape, design, arrangement of letters/words, packaging style, and graphical presentation form a part of trade dress. In the early days, trade dress referred to the way a product was packaged to be launched in the market, but now even the

product design is an inclusion element of trade dress. Elements of trade dress for a particular product do not affect the way in which the product is used. Federal law for trademark applies to trade dress also. There is no distinction between trade dress and trademark, as the Lanham Act (also known as the Trademark Act of 1946) does not provide any distinction between the two.

TEST DAY TIP

The site www.legal-definitions.com defines an infringement to be "the authorized use of another's right or privilege, usually an intellectual property right, such as a patent, copyright, or trademark."

Trademark Eligibility and the Benefits of Registering

Any individual or organization that wishes to use a unique identifier to categorize its goods or services can qualify for a trademark. The trademark needs to be unique and not misleading. To register a trademark, you should fill out an application form at the USPTO.

Before the USPTO will accept an application to register a trademark, the application must detail the following:

- The applicant's name

- A name and address required for correspondence

- An apparent depiction of the mark

- A list of the goods or services provided

The applicant must also pay the application filing fee for one or more sets of goods or services. The following points cover the benefits of registering a trademark:

- It protects an organization's name/logo.

- The registered owner attains exclusive rights of the mark and gains protection against trademark infringement.

- The mark may be used to differentiate the product from other products in the same trade.

- Following the trademark registration, it is updated in the trademark search database, which aids in discouraging other applicants from filing a comparable variety of trademark.

- If a registered trademark is infringed, the titleholder of the registered trademark can request that the infringing party pay damages.

- It provides a foundation for filing the registration for the specific trademark in a foreign country.

Trademark Infringement

A trademark infringement refers to the unauthorized use of a protected trademark or service mark, or the use of something very similar to a protected mark. The success of any legal action to stop (or injunct) the infringement is directly related to whether the defendant's use of the mark causes a likelihood of confusion on the part of the average consumer. If a court determines that a reasonable average consumer would be confused, the owner of the original mark can prevent the other party from using the infringing mark and even possibly collect damages. A party that holds the legal rights to a particular trademark can sue other parties for trademark infringement based on the standard "likelihood of confusion."

In the United States, the Trademark Act of 1946, statutes § 1114 and § 1125, are specific to trademark infringement. The Lanham (Trademark) Act (15 U.S.C.) is available online from www.bitlaw.com/source/15usc/.

EXAM WARNING

Read the following legislation online before your test:
 Trademark Act of 1946 (Lanham Act) as amended
 PUBLIC LAW 79-489, CHAPTER 540, APPROVED JULY 5, 1946; 60 STAT. 427
 § 32 (15 U.S.C. §1114). Remedies; infringement; innocent infringers
 TITLE 15 > CHAPTER 22 > SUBCHAPTER III > § 1125
 § 1125. False designations of origin, false descriptions, and dilution forbidden

Investigating Copyright Violations

The U.S. Copyright Office Web site (www.copyright.gov) defines copyright as being "a form of protection provided by the laws of the United States (title 17, U. S. Code) to the authors of 'original works of authorship,' including literary, dramatic, musical, artistic, and certain other intellectual works." The first copyright goes back to 1476 and the introduction of the movable type printing press into England by William Caxton. The crown recognized the immense opportunity offered to authors and created an official register for all works. These days, copyright is a means of protecting the author's investment of time and effort in creating a new work.

Investigating Copyright Status

Here are three fundamental methods that you can use to investigate the copyright status of a particular work include:

1. Examine the copy of a work to uncover any elements that necessitate it being included in the copyright notice. Works published after March 1, 1989 do not need to have a copyright notice incorporated with the copyrighted work. As a result, the investigator must research the work to determine its copyright status. Research can be conducted online, through various search engines.

2. The investigator can search the U.S Copyright office's online database (www.copyright.gov/records). The record search page is classified into three categories (see Figure 16.1):

 a. Books, Music, etc.

 b. Serials

 c. Documents

 You can search a particular document after selecting the appropriate tab. An advanced search is best conducted using the Library of Congress Information System (LOCIS). You should read the LOCIS usage guide (www.copyright.gov/records/guide.html) before connecting to LOCIS. LOCIS runs on a command prompt using either the TN3270 or Telnet protocol.

Figure 16.1 The Search Options on the U.S Copyright Office's Online Web Site and Database

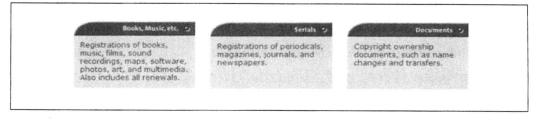

3. Request that the U.S. Copyright Office run a search against the specified category. Officials will search the records for a fee of $75 per hour if a request is lodged for a copyright search. They will create either a typewritten or an oral report based on the selected preference made when requesting the search.

Consider the changes to the status of copyright materials made under the Copyright Act of 1976, the Berne Convention Implementation Act of 1988, the Copyright Renewal Act of 1992, and the Sonny Bono Copyright Term Extension Act of 1998 whenever you investigate copyright infringements in the United States.

How Long Does a Copyright Last?

As with all things, copyright protection eventually ends; it is only a "limited monopoly." When copyrights expire, they fall into the public domain. With a number of exceptions, public domain works may be unreservedly copied or used in the production of derivative works without either the permission or the authorization of the former copyright holder. At some stage in the Clinton administration, the contentious Sonny Bono Copyright Term Extension Act (CTEA) passed into law. This Act added 20 years to most copyright terms. It also created a moratorium that in effect stops any new works from entering the public domain until 2019. The bill was enacted to ensure protection for U.S. works in the foreign market. The CTEA includes access restrictions over works published later than 1922. The U.S. Supreme Court rejected (Eldred et al. v. Ashcroft, Attorney General 537 U.S. 186) a popular challenge to the CTEA.

Validity of Copyright for Joint Works

Works completed by multiple (two or more) authors are called joint works. The validity of copyright for a joint work remains pending the demise of the last surviving author of the work plus an additional 70 years.

Validity of Copyright for Anonymous Work, Pseudonymous Works, and "Made for Hire" Works

A copyright will remain enforced for a period of 95 years commencing in the year when the work was originally published or for a term of 120 years since the year when the work was produced. Renewal and extension of copyrights for "work for hire" works cover a term of 67 years when the owner of that particular class of work requests the extension.

The Mission of the U.S. Copyright Office

The U.S. Copyright Office is run by the Library of Congress. It is tasked with providing "factual information about copyright owners and related matters in the catalog records, finding aids and other texts that accompany collections."

The Doctrine of "Fair Use"

Section 107 of the U.S. Copyright Act details the doctrine of fair use. This doctrine has evolved through the decisions of a number of court cases over time. Reproduction of a selected work for criticism, news reporting, comment, teaching, scholarship, and research are included within the provisions of fair use as defined in Section 107 of the Act. The Copyright Office does not provide the authorization to use copyrighted works. You need to seek permission from the owner of a particular copyrighted work in order to use it.

Section 107 of the Act sets out four factors used in determining fair use:

1. The purpose and character of the use, as well as whether such use is of commercial nature or is for nonprofit educational intentions

2. The nature of the copyrighted work

3. The degree and substantiality of the section used in relation to the copyrighted work as a whole

4. The effect of the use upon the potential market for or value of the copyrighted work

It is difficult to distinguish among use that is covered by "fair use" provisions and copyright infringement. There is no mention of the number of lines, words, and notes that may be taken from a copyrighted work before it constitutes an infringement.

Investigating Copyright Violations

Copyright infringements and violations are investigated through the following:

1. Explanations of parties and third persons

2. Testimonial evidence

3. Written and material evidence

4. Audio and video records

5. Conclusions of experts

The following points list the types of evidence used to determine whether a copyright violation has occurred:

■ Any documents received by law enforcement agencies from the tests they completed either as a result of their own initiative or by complaints of the rights holder

■ Record of checking and searches

■ Records from the forensic examination of computer systems and software

■ Record of examination of a material carrier where the installation of software products was executed

- Expert reports where a conclusion has been made following the assessment of the seized computer system

- The account of the employees of the vendor company; the account of the customer

- Delivery note or invoice for the purchased computer system

- Any statutory documents of a legal body

- Job positions from the vendor selling computer facilities and software

- Advertising materials, price lists, and catalogs that provide substantiation of alleged actions

- Warranty declaration on the purchased computer system,

- Other documents connected to the illegal sale or distribution in any form of a copyrighted work

At some stage in an investigation, it is essential to ascertain an estimate of the revenue obtained from an infringement or violation of a copyright and the contiguous rights.

The following financial documents should be maintained as evidence:

- Reports of checks and inspections

- Delivery notes, invoices, pick slips, and other documents related to the distribution of products as well as any proof of payment

- Financial statements and accounts

- Agreements covering any particulars of suspected criminal activity

How Copyright Is Enforced

The Uruguay Round Agreements Act (URAA) came into force December 8, 1994. This agreement introduced the Notice of Intent to Enforce (NIE). According to the URAA, the copyright holder of a restored work needs to inform the reliance parties if preparations to enforce copyrights for a particular work are commenced. A reliance party is an individual or organization that used the copyrighted work through its status in the public domain for the period preceding the URAA agreement.

The URAA instructs the holder of the restored work to notify the reliance party directly through the supply of a tangible notice or to present a constructive notice by filing an NIE that is lodged with the U.S. Copyright Office.

A legal action may be filed against any party that is involved with a violation of the rights of the copyright holder. A party that infringes these rights but prevails upon the fair use doctrine to attempt to commercialize the work of a copyright holder by representing it as their own will often face legal action.

The holder of a copyright that has been infringed may:

- Seek orders from a court to prevent or injunct against an escalation of infringements

- Request compensation from the infringing party for damages

- Request that the infringing party pay the legal fees

Copyright Infringement: Plagiarism

Webster's New World Dictionary describes plagiarism as taking the ideas of another and passing them as "one's own." This section details the tools and detection factors involved when investigating plagiarism. A common misconception is that plagiarism hurts nobody. The reality is that it is a fraud and thus a criminal offense (see § 1341; frauds and swindles). Plagiarism takes away from the effort of the author and society suffers as a consequence.

The Various Plagiarism Detection Factors

Konstantinos Tripolitis, in his 2002 dissertation, "Automated Detection of Plagiarism" (University of Sheffield, UK), addresses the various plagiarism detection factors that commonly occur. He includes the following as possible detection factors:

- Changes of vocabulary When the vocabulary an author uses varies significantly in the text under consideration, there is a great possibility that the author has committed plagiarism.

- Incoherent text Inconsistency in the style of a text, such that parts of the text seem to be written by different people, can imply plagiarism.

- Punctuation When two texts exhibit extremely similar punctuation, plagiarism can be implied, as it is not possible that two authors could use punctuation in the same way.

- Dependence on certain words and phrases If particular words or phrases used by a certain author in a customary way are used consistently by another author, plagiarism is possible, as authors tend to have different word preferences.

- Amount of similarity between texts Texts written by different people and sharing a great amount of similar text should be checked more thoroughly for plagiarism. This is a fundamental idea for a detection tool and is the one mainly used in the present work. A reliable detection tool should be able to provide a fairly accurate similarity measure to be useful.

- Long sequences of common text Lengthy sequences of successive common characters or words found in the texts under test exhibit a fair possibility that plagiarism may have been committed. It is also known as the sequence comparison approach.

- Order of similarity between texts If two texts have the same order of matching words or phrases, plagiarism is a possibility.

- Frequency of words Finally, words used in the same frequency in two texts written by different authors suggest potential plagiarism.

Features and Functions of Plagiarism Detection Tools

The following utilities are designed to aid in the detection of plagiarism in documents.

Turnitin

Turnitin (www.turnitin.com) is an online plagiarism detection tool that focuses on the educational market. It distinguishes plagiarized entries in a document by conducting a proportional revision of the document using submission pages available on the Internet and in its database.

CopyCatch

CopyCatch is a tool designed to detect plagiarism in text. Available from www.copycatchgold.com, CopyCatch uses no keywords, no proximity setting, and no "ANDs" or "ORs". It takes a whole document or set of documents for the search entry. The investigator does the rest by identifying similar sentences in the documents.

CopyCatch is available free for higher-educational institutions in the UK. This utility aids in checking for plagiarism in works submitted in Microsoft Word and Corel WordPerfect, as well as documents in text format.

Eve2

The Essay Verification Engine, or EVE2 (www.canexus.com), accepts essays in plain text, Microsoft Word, or Corel WordPerfect format and returns links to Web pages from which a student may have plagiarized. EVE2 has been developed to be powerful enough to find plagiarized material while not overwhelming the professor with false links.

The tool performs a large number of complex searches to find material from any Internet site. It does a direct comparison of the submitted essay to the text appearing on suspect sites. If it finds evidence of plagiarism, the URL is recorded. Once the search has completed, the teacher is given a full report on each paper that contained plagiarism, including the percent of the essay plagiarized, and an annotated copy of the paper showing all plagiarism highlighted in red.

Copy Protection System

The Copy Protection System (COPS) is a series of products designed to reduce data piracy. The product range includes:

- CDR-Cops
- DVD-Cops
- WebCops

The COPS product range is designed to protect information on CDs, DVDs, and Web pages. These programs provide cryptographic controls which are designed to stop unauthorized copying.

SCAM

The Stanford Copy Analysis Mechanism (SCAM) crawls the Web, compares the Web content with the registered content, and notifies the content owners of illegal copies. It was designed with the following points in mind:

- Accuracy, in terms of high precision and recall

- Scalability, in terms of coping (such as crawling, comparing, and indexing) with several terabytes of data (or several tens of millions of Web pages)

- Resiliency to "attacks'" (such as audio clipping, and perceptual attacks)

Information on SCAM is available at http://infolab.stanford.edu/~shiva/SCAM/scamInfo.html.

www.plagiarismchecker.com

The Web site www.plagiarismchecker.com provides free checks for plagiarism online. The site provides a check service for Web sites, documents, and blogs. The site also provides handouts, FAQs, and general information on plagiarism and the methods to report it.

Jplag

JPlag, available at www.ipd.uni-karlsruhe.de/jplag/, finds similarities among multiple sets of source code files to detect software plagiarism. This program analyzes the programming language syntax and program structure to detect many attempts to disguise similarities between plagiarized files. JPlag currently supports Java, C#, C, C++, Scheme, and natural language text.

VAST

Visualization and Analysis of Similarity Tool (VAST) presents a visual representation of the similarity between two documents. A user can quickly select the areas of interest and view the associated sections of the documents to verify whether they represent plagiarism. VAST is available from http://cise.lsbu.ac.uk/orcheck/vast.html.

SIM

The software and text similarity tester SIM tests lexical similarity in texts in C, Java, Pascal, Modula-2, Lisp, Miranda, and natural language. It is used to detect potentially duplicated code fragments in large software projects, in program text, in shell scripts, and in documentation to detect plagiarism in software projects, educational and otherwise. Sim is available from: www.cs.vu.nl/~dick/sim.html.

YAP

Yet Another Plague (YAP) is a series of systems that follow a common pattern. YAP3 is the current version. In the first stage, which is common to all three systems, source texts are tokenized. In particular:

- Comments and string-constants are removed.
- Uppercase letters are translated to lowercase.
- A range of synonyms are mapped to a common form.
- If possible, the functions/procedures are expanded in calling order.
- All tokens that are not in the lexicon for the language are removed.

YAP is available from http://luggage.bcs.uwa.edu.au/~michaelw/YAP.html.

SPlaT

The SPlaT tool is available at http://splat.cs.arizona.edu/. SplaT is designed to uncover self-plagiarism. This occurs when an author recycles portions of his earlier writings in successive research papers. The SPlaT tool has three approaches to detect self-plagiarism:

1. The web spider mode checks research papers published by Computer Science departments.
2. The reviewer's workbench mode conducts an evaluation of an author's prior works to a new publication.
3. The author mode enables authors to check their latest papers against earlier publications in order to ensure that they have not inadvertently duplicated prior works.

Sherlock

Sherlock is a C program that uses digital signatures to find similarities between textual documents. A digital signature is a number which is formed by turning several words in the input into a series of bits and joining those bits into a number. Sherlock works on text files such as essays, computer source code files, and other assignments in digital form. It is available for download at www.cs.usyd.edu.au/~scilect/sherlock/.

Urkund

Urkund (www.urkund.com) offers an automated system designed to deal with the problem of plagiarism. It requires only a minimal effort from the user to help prevent plagiarism by checking from three man source areas: the Internet, published material, and student material.

FreestylerIII

Freestyler is stated to be a "graphical stylistic metrics tool." It presents rolling average graphs of various metrics (reading age, sentence length, voice and punctuation) to assist in providing an evidential indication that a document supposedly written by a single individual may have been written by two or more. It is available at http://cise.lsbu.ac.uk/orcheck/freestyler.html.

SafeAssignment

The SafeAssignment plagiarism detection system integrates with a number of educational suites (such as Blackboard). It matches using sentence matching scores and an overall matching score. The scoring is defined as follows:

1. Scores below 15 percent—low scores such as these indicate little evidence of plagiarism.

2. Scores between 15 percent and 40 percent—at this level it is likely that the paper being analyzed contains plagiarism or can have just too much quoted material. We usually recommend reviewing the reports with such scores before making any judgments about the papers.

3. Scores over 40 percent—with such scores, there is almost 100 percent probability that the papers contains some text copied from elsewhere, and, even if this text is properly cited, such amount of cited material is considered excessive in most cases. Therefore, such scores give a clear warning to instructors. However, there are few cases when such scores can be given to authentic papers, for example, when the paper was legitimately published online before it was sent for processing (instructors have just to "Delete" the source pointing to the legitimate copy), or when the same student has already submitted this paper or a similar paper to another class (it is not plagiarism, but such practice is not allowed in some institutions).

TEST DAY TIP

The following Internet sites provide a good overview of the available antiplagiarism tools:

> www.shambles.net/pages/staff/ptools/
> wwwlb.aub.edu.lb/~eplagio/Anti_plag.htm
> http://plagiarism.phys.virginia.edu/links.html

Patents and Patent Infringement

A patent is a right granted for any device, substance, method, or process which is new, inventive, and useful. It is essentially a monopoly right over a registered invention or discovery that is legally enforceable and provides the holder the exclusive right to commercially exploit the invention for the life of the patent. A patent is not automatic and it must be applied for and registered in each country to which it is to apply (there is no such thing as an international patent). Patents give effective protection if you have invented new technology that will lead to a product, composition, or process with significant long-term commercial gain.

In the United States, the USPTO issues patents. Patents are effective for up to 20 years from the date on which the application is filed. In Australia and many other countries, two types of patents in operation:

- A standard patent gives long-term protection and control over an invention for up to 20 years.

- An innovation patent is a relatively fast, inexpensive protection option, lasting a maximum of eight years. The Australian innovation patent replaced the petty patent May 24, 2001.

Patent laws allow for the granting of a patent on the new article, not on the propositions that claim to put into practice those ideas to make the article. You cannot patent an idea.

Any article, process, or manufacturing technique that asserts a right to a patent is required to prove its utility. 35 U.S.C. § 102, (www.uspto.gov/web/offices/pac/mpep/documents/appxl_35_U_S_C_102.htm) details the conditions in patent law covering when an invention cannot be patented.

The primary types of patents include:

- Utility patents These are granted to an individual who invents a new device, process, useful composition of matter, or product. Some examples include:

 A new process for the fraction distillation of petroleum

 A novel manufacturing method for paper

 A machine such as a motorbike or car

 A previously undiscovered composition of matter, including a drug

- Design patents These are granted to an individual who creates a new, innovative design for an article of manufacture. It guards the look of an article; for example, the shape of the Apple iPod.

- Plant patents or breeders rights These are granted to an individual who conceives, discovers, or asexually reproduces a distinctive variety of plant.

■ An innovation patent This is a fast and inexpensive but limited protection option in they have an eight-year term (unlike the 20-year term for a standard patent).

Patent Infringement

Patent infringement is governed in the United States by federal law 35 U.S.C. 271. This defines infringement as "whoever without authority makes, uses, or sells any patented invention, within the United States during the term of the patent therefore, infringes the patent." This is available online at www.uspto.gov/web/offices/pac/mpep/documents/appxl_35_U_S_C_271.htm.

There are three primary categories of patent infringement:

■ Direct infringement This occurs whenever any individual constructs, uses, offers to sell, sells, or imports into the country where the patent is held any patented invention, without authority, during the term of the patent.

■ Indirect infringement A person who instigates another person to sell, make, or use a patented invention is liable to fall under the category of indirect infringer.

■ Contributory infringement Also known as an "active inducement to infringement," a contributory infringement occurs when someone actively induces infringement of a patent .

Resolving patent infringement is a two-step process:

1. Analyze claims by going through all patented documents.

2. Verify the claim for its authenticity. In this step, devices or processes, which are claimed, are validated to establish the accuracy of the claim.

The Strategy for Conducting a Patent Search

The USPTO has formulated the following seven-step strategy for conducting a patent search:

1. Search the Index to the U.S. Patent Classification Begin with this alphabetical subject index to the Manual of Classification. This is an alphabetical index containing general terms depicting the invention and its function, effect, end product, structure, and use.

2. Search the Manual of Classification This also contains an outline of all patentable technologies (both new and old) where the class and subclass numbers may be referenced. It is used to locate word classes in the U.S. Patent Classification System.

3. Research the Classification Definitions This holds detailed definitions of the subject matter in each class and subclass of the U.S. Patent Classification system and includes valuable search notes and suggestions for other classifications to consider not found anywhere else. Go through the definitions to ascertain the relevancy of class(es) and

subclass(es) to the investigation. These definitions include essential search notes and suggestions that can be referred to in supplementary searches.

4. Browse Patent Titles and Abstracts Inspect whether the search is proving fruitful. If not, alter the search to discover lists of patents and published applications containing the keywords and begin the search again.

5. Retrieve a Subclass Listing Once you have identified relevant classes and subclasses, obtain a list of all patent numbers granted from 1790 to the present for every class and subclass to be searched.

6. Research the Official Gazette Go to the Official Gazette (Patent Section) and look up summaries and a representative drawing for every patent on your subclass list to eliminate those patents clearly unrelated to your invention. It is possible to view published applications online.

7. Complete the Patent Document Examine full-text U.S. patent copies online and note the "U.S. Cl." and "Field of Search" designations as these will provide additional search information.

DVD-ROMs with all registered patients from 1790 to present are available and can be checked against any potential ideas or infringements. This will assist in determining any similarities and dissimilarities in your innovation and published patents.

Test Day Tip

IP.com is in the business of processing and authenticating its clients' intellectual property. Its registry service provides the following:

Irrefutable proof of the date and content of your work
The ability to upload documents to a personal registry
Simple retrieval of intellectual property

Domain Name Infringement and How to Check for It

Before registering a domain name, it is always prudent to engage in a thorough investigation. Doing so will help minimize the risk of domain name and trademark infringement with the associated risk of litigation. The following sections present a few recommended steps to take to minimize this risk.

Step 1

Use a number of search engines similar to Google to determine whether a particular domain name is already in use. In Google, using the search term "site:domain.com" will display all pages associated with "domain.com". This will aid you in determining whether a domain name is already in use. Use the Google "link:domain.com" filter to display all links that could contain the domain names identical to the desired name. Using a search to display all businesses or services that have similar names to that of the domain you wish to register is also effective. If the desired domain name has already been registered, seek another domain name.

Step 2

Conduct searches on sites such as www.completewhois.com and www.whois.net to determine whether another domain contains text identical to your domain name or business name. You can also use Internet sites such as InterNIC (www.internic.net) to conduct text string searches. This site is dedicated to helping the trademark owner or other registered domain owners to maintain the integrity of their intellectual property.

Step 3

The Trademark Electronic Search System (TESS) is a database that contains all federally registered trademarks and service marks in the United States (http://tess2.uspto.gov/). Additionally, it maintains a record of all formerly registered trademarks and service marks and all pending applications for trademark registration.

Step 4

If you are still unsure, appoint a dedicated search firm to do a national trademark, service mark, and domain name search. These firms, including Thomson & Thomson (www.thomson-thomson.com), offer an all-inclusive search and present all results in a formal written report. Additionally, by using these firms you lower your risk due to professional indemnity clauses.

Step 5

Finally, in larger cases it is wise to hire a specialized intellectual property and trademark attorney who can perform all of the preceding steps. Appointing a specialist intellectual property lawyer will help to circumvent a lot of confusion, as he or she is able to establish whether any infringement issues are likely to come about based on the facts and circumstances of a prospective domain name that is being sought.

Laws Related to Trademark and Copyright

Before your exam, ensure that you are familiar with the following U.S. federal statutes:

U.S. Title 18, Part 1, Chapter 25—Counterfeiting and Forgery:
www4.law.cornell.edu/uscode/html/uscode18/usc_sup_01_18_10_I_20_47.html

- § 497: Letters Patent

- § 1030 Fraud and related activity in connection with computers

U.S. Title 18, Part 1, Chapter 47—Fraud and False Statements:
www4.law.cornell.edu/uscode/html/uscode18/usc_sup_01_18_10_I_20_47.html

- § 1030 Fraud and related activity in connection with computers

U.S. Title 18, Part 1, Chapter 63—Mail Fraud:
www.law.cornell.edu/uscode/html/uscode18/usc_sup_01_18_10_I_20_63.html

- § 1341: Frauds and Swindles

- § 1343: Fraud by Wire, Radio, or Television

- § 1361 Injury to government property

- § 1362 Government communication systems

U.S. Title 18, Part 1, Chapter 90 – Protection of Trade Secrets:
www.law.cornell.edu/uscode/html/uscode18/usc_sup_01_18_10_I_20_90notes.html

- 18 U.S.C. 1831 Economic Espionage Act

- 18 U.S.C. 1832 Theft of trade secrets

U.S. Title 18, Part 1, Chapter 113 – Stolen Property:
www4.law.cornell.edu/uscode/html/uscode18/usc_sup_01_18_10_I_20_113.html

- § 2319A: Unauthorized Fixation of and Trafficking in Sound Recordings and Music Videos of Live Musical Performances

- § 2320: Trafficking in Counterfeit Goods or Services

U.S. Title 18, Part 1, Chapter 119 – Stolen Property:
www4.law.cornell.edu/uscode/html/uscode18/usc_sup_01_18_10_I_20_119.html

- § 2512: Manufacture, Distribution, Possession, and Advertising of Wire, Oral, or Electronic Communication-Intercepting Devices Prohibited

U.S. Title 47, Chapter 5, Sub-Chapter V-A – Part IV - Miscellaneous Provisions:

- www4.law.cornell.edu/uscode/html/uscode47/usc_sup_01_47_10_5_20_V-A_30_IV.html

- § 553: Unauthorized Reception of Cable Service

U.S. Title 47, Chapter 5, Sub-Chapter VI – Part IV - Miscellaneous Provisions: www4.law.cornell.edu/uscode/html/uscode47/usc_sup_01_47_10_5_20_VI.html

- § 605: Unauthorized Publication or Use of Communications

Writing Investigative Reports

One of the most crucial aspects of any forensic engagement is the production of an investigative report. This document is written to communicate the outcome of digital forensic analysis and examination. If you cannot report your findings, no one will know or understand what you have found or its importance.

Understanding the Importance of Reports

In forensic investigations, the investigative report is of essential importance. In most cases, report writing skills are overlooked. Producing a well-structured and logical investigative report improves the chances that a jury will be convinced that you know what you're doing and that the evidence is valid. A report should not only communicate the facts, but also present expert opinion. During a criminal investigation, the reports also become the source for the preparation and presentation of the investigation for trial. The intention of any investigative report is to document the facts and evidence. If you find evidence that does not help your case you still need to report it. Related exhibits such as diagrams and pictures must be included for the report to be effective.

Investigative reports must stipulate the fees paid for the expert's services and list all the civil or criminal cases in which the expert has testified for the preceding four years. The report should not include the cases in which the expert acted as a lay witness. A lay witness is a witness who is not testifying in the capacity of an expert witness. Always include exhibits such as the CV of the investigator acting as a witness that lists all publications that the witness has written during the preceding 10 years. Ensure that you maintain the highest standards for writing and testifying. Not only will reports be stored in a deposition bank or library and even be available on the Internet, but also your testimony is generally conducted under oath.

The Requirements of an Investigative Report

An investigative report is created with the intent that it may be used in a court of law. It should be succinct and focus on the mission or goal of the investigation. The investigator's primary purpose is to locate information and, thus, evidence on a precise matter, to recover significant documents, or recover certain file types and any date and timestamps. The goal of the investigation will be defined by your client. Your client could be internal to the organization you work for or another investigator or lawyer. Spending time documenting the objective will generally

save time and reduce the cost of the examination. Always ensure that the investigative report specifies the mission of an investigation.

Your report should flow in a matching order, reflecting that of the facts as they were discovered during the investigation. An outline or an arrangement based on appendices and an exhibit is suggested to assist in assembling substance for the report. The report should be written in a logical manner that states the problem, presents the results of the investigation, and sets forth the conclusions and recommendations. A coherent presentation should be used to assemble the facts and evidence.

Report Classification

Your first step in writing a report should be to identify the report's intended audience and purpose. The investigative report should be structured so that people who don't have a high level of technical knowledge can understand it. When reading this document a nontechnical reader should be able to understand the findings and proceedings of the case.

Reports are generally categorized into:

- Verbal reports
- Written reports

Reports may also be categorized as being:

- Formal in nature
- Informal

When you deliver a formal report verbally it should be structured for presentation orally to a board of directors, managers, or a jury. Always organize the report to fit within the time frame given. A supplementary document that contains anticipated questions and relevant answers needs to be prepared for the people to whom you are presenting and to aid your presentation. This document is called the examination plan and is created by the lawyer for the investigator's benefit. Changes to the examination plan such as those involving clarification or definition can be requested by the investigator for action by the attorney if an expression or term is misused. Do not include items that are not related to the testimony.

An informal verbal report is less structured than a formal report and is delivered in person (most often in an attorney's office). This report is designed to be a preliminary report and it needs to be strictly controlled to stop inadvertent release. It should contain the aspects of the investigation that have not been completed, including any tests or analysis that has not been concluded, interrogatories, document production, and depositions.

An informal written report is also a preliminary report. This type of report is a high-risk document that contains sensitive information which could prove beneficial for the opposing party. The opposing party may receive the document in discovery. Discovery is the attempt

made to obtain evidence prior to a trial. The information may be a written request for admissions of fact, deposition, or questions and answers written under oath.

A formal written report is a report sworn under oath (including an affidavit or declaration). Always ensure that your word usage, grammar, spelling, and details are correct when writing formal reports. As this report is formal in nature, the preferred style will use first-person narratives with a natural language style. An affidavit may be used to sustain the issuing of a warrant or be presented as evidence in a formal court hearing. Always give your full attention to writing a document in the formal written style.

It is prudent to incorporate the substance of written, informal reports in an informal, verbal report. Summarize the process and methodology including the subject system, tool used, and findings, in the verbal, informal report. Never destroy a written, informal report without formal written guidance from an attorney, as this action may be considered as the destruction or concealing of evidence.

EXAM WARNING

In legal terms, the destruction or concealing of evidence is known as spoliation.

A Sample Investigative Report Format

The following section presents a possible layout of an investigative report. The presentation of accurate text is equivalent to being able to speak clearly. As such, always give your full attention to layout and presentation of information in a report when you are writing. It is further advisable to consistently adhere to a single layout throughout the report. This creates consistency. Two main methods exist for creating a layout structure: decimal numbering and legal-sequential numbering.

Here is an example of the decimal numbering system:

1.0 Introduction

1.1 The Nature of the Incident

1.1.1 The Details of the Victim

2.0 First Incident

2.1 The First Witness

2.1.1 Witness Testimony – Witness No. 1

3.0 Location of Evidence

3.1 Seizure of Evidence

3.1.1 Transportation of Evidence

4.0 Analysis of Evidence

4.1 Chain of Evidence

4.1.1 Extraction of Data

5.0 Conclusion

5.1 Results

5.1.1 Expert Opinion

Legal-sequential numbering uses this format:

I. Introduction

 1. Nature of the Incident

 2. The Victim

 3. Witness to the Event

 4. Location of Evidence

II. Examination

 5. Chain of evidence

 6. Extraction of Evidence

 7. The Analysis of Evidence

The legal-sequential numbering system is used in pleadings and is popular among lawyers. Roman numerals are used for the foremost aspect of the report and Arabic numbering supports the information detail.

The most vital component of any investigative report is the use of effective language to communicate the information clearly. To do this, signposts should be included within the report. A signpost serves as a guide to the readers of the document that focuses their thought on a point or sequence of a process. Signposts highlight the main points that you wish to convey by creating a logical development of the information within the report. This makes it easier for the reader to comprehend the document.

For instance, the steps within the document could be introduced using a signpost such as "The first step in this section," or "The second step in the examination". These act as the signposts for the sequence of information.

Try to steer clear of redundant statements such as "This report is submitted", or "As the result of the investigation, I have to report as follows". The use of proper style and tone and thought concerning the use of correct format, punctuation, vocabulary, and grammar is essential when you're writing a report.

Test Day Tip

You should use the following guidelines to write an investigative report for expressing an opinion:

The report should be communicable. Any reader (even a novice), with no knowledge of the case, should be able to comprehend what is written.

Ensure that all ideas flow logically. The information from facts to conclusions should be stated in precise and unbiased terms.

Never make an assumption about any facts while writing the report. For example, if an e-mail address is discovered to be jake11@gmail.com, it is does not necessarily mean that the person's name is Jake.

Refrain from specifying the leads. If something significant is discovered, include it in the report without emphasizing the facts.

Always check the document for spelling errors and poor grammar. Grammar and spellcheck tools can be used to avoid mistakes.

When writing, use active voice. Emotional, judgmental, or value-laden words and phrases should be avoided when describing events.

Keep your writing brief. Including too much irrelevant data obscures the important matters and makes the report unclear.

Avoid the repetition of words and unnecessary descriptions of documents and evidence.

Always follow a simple and direct approach to report writing. Concentrate on using the correct format, punctuation, vocabulary, and grammar.

Report Writing Guidelines

Whatever you write in your report, you should remember that its presentation needs to flow in a logical order if it is to convey the information you have collected in the manner that you desire. To achieve this it is necessary to plan the report before writing it. This enables you to

create your argument piece by piece. The report should contain a proper flow of sentences which are arranged to aid the progress of thought in a clear and unambiguous manner from the start to the end of the document. Each paragraph should be correlated to reflect the aims of the entire document and provides the reader with an impression of unique relation.

The use of headings with details underneath is recommended. These details should be set in paragraphs, each restricted to a particular topic. Any use of jargon, slang, or technical terms should be avoided where possible. If necessary, prepare a glossary containing slang or technical terms.

When writing, employ active voice rather than passive voice. Active voice encourages conciseness and accuracy in writing and comes across as being more forceful. Always avoid trite and superlative phrases.

When a particular abbreviation is used for the first time in the report it is advisable to write the full form of the same. Comprise acronyms in the Glossary included at the end of the report.

Most lawyers do not have a detailed technical knowledge. As a result, it is possible to confuse them when using of acronyms.

Using Supporting Material

A well-written investigative report tells a story in which one has to answer various questions such as who, when, where, why, and how. While answering these questions, supporting materials such as figures, tables, data, and equations are required if they help the story unfold in an effective form.

The supporting material can be referred to directly in the text and integrated in the writing to enhance the impact. It is advisable to number figures and tables in the same order as they are introduced in the report. For example, tables can be numbered as Table 1, Table 2, and so on. In the same way, figures can be labeled as Figure 1, Figure 2, and so on. Numbering the material avoids confusion and makes it easier to understand.

To reduce narration and emphasize important facts, put tables and schedules in appendices.

Captions are preferred over simple titles, as the complete information adds to the conciseness of the presentation. If charts are used, they should be labeled, including axes and units. In a paragraph, if any table or figure is mentioned, that figure or table should be inserted after the paragraph. One could also gather all supporting material after the reference section.

Consistency and Other Important Aspects of a Good Report

Whenever you are writing a report remember that consistency is important. Create and maintain document templates to aid you. A good investigative report format should include the following sections:

- Abstract or summary

- Table of contents

- Body of report

- Conclusions

- References

- Glossary

- Acknowledgments

These sections may be adjusted to suit the purpose of the report. The abstract or summary should present the essence of the report as an abbreviated or condensed form of the investigation. That is, it should present the key ideas expressed within the report. A well-designed table of contents should provide quick reference to all important features of the investigation.

Any appendices included within the report need to be listed and described in the table of contents. The report body should contain the main points that you wish to convey. It should refer to the purpose of the report. References and appendices list the substance referred to in the report, including output from tools and interview notes. A presentation can follow any format that you and the other parties are comfortable with.

The Main Features and Aspects of a Good Report

A good report will generally have the following features:

- It will provide a detailed explanation of the methods, examination procedures, materials, or equipment used. It will further detail any analytical or statistical techniques, data/collection, or sources within a variety of subsections that aid the reader in developing an understanding of the investigation process.

- Any good report provides a well-organized presentation of the data collected. The data collection process is a critical component of an effectively conducted forensic examination. In preparing the lab report, data such as observations should be recorded in a laboratory notebook for later reference. All the tables used for presenting data should be labeled.

- Include any calculations that you make. It is good practice to summarize the common name of the calculations (e.g. Secure Hashing Algorithm for SHA-1) used to ensure the integrity of the evidence and the dates that these where completed during the investigation within the report. Briefly describe the standard tools and their cited source that have been used for this calculation.

- List a statement detailing any provision for uncertainty and error analysis. There are always limitations of knowledge and there is no foolproof way to protect the integrity of data. For instance, when retrieving a timestamp from a computer system

you should state that the timestamp can be reset easily and that this information alone should not be relied upon.

- Give detailed explanations for your results. These should be listed in a logical order using subheadings containing text which addresses the purpose of the report. Where possible, use tables and figures within the text to enhance its presentation. Ensure that any reader with no knowledge of the case can understand the investigation and the results solely on this report.

- Present a discussion of the results and conclusion. Discussing results and conclusions is essential. The significance of the research should be established in this section of the report. Provide answers to questions such as how the case progressed, what problems occurred, and any problems that were addressed.

- List your references. Include the people and publications cited in the report. Plagiarism will destroy the credibility of your report. Site all source material, Web sites, the opinions of others, and any works that are not your own.

- Include any required appendices. An appendix should be used to reference any extra material that is referenced in the report. You should include charts, diagrams, graphs, transcripts, and copies of tool output. Arrange the appendices in the order that they appear in the report.

- Provide acknowledgment where it is warranted. Thanking those people who helped during the creation of a report will make it more likely that they will help you in the future. List people who have contributed to the analysis of data, proofreading, or any other useful activity. Acknowledgment is optional, but recommended.

The Investigative Report Format

There are as many report writing formats as there are companies or organizations. When a prior report is available that is acceptable to the parties, follow the format it used rather than re-creating one. Review the facts to determine the relevancy and thus what facts to include and which to eliminate prior to writing the report. Carefully examine any facts and ensure that they are relevant. The report must include all the relevant evidence. This includes evidence that does not support the report's conclusion. You should maintain your objectivity in the report and document the findings in an impartial and accurate manner. Try to find flaws in thinking or examination, as it is likely that if you don't, someone else will. Do not develop an agenda except for finding the truth during report writing.

There are basically four sections to an investigative report. These are:

- **Section 1** This section includes the administrative details such as the investigating officials, how to contact them, and the location of the working papers.

- **Section 2** This section covers the background and summary of the report. It consists of a summary of the complainant's allegations, discretionary information that may aid the reader in understanding the case, the outcome of the case, and the list of allegations.

- **Section 3** This section introduces the first allegation. It presents the facts, provides an analysis and discussion of the facts, and, where suitable, provides a recommendation. Conclusions can be declared in this section, and this section may include the disposition to document any remedial actions that the responsible authority took concerning any substantiated allegations. In this section, you should attend to each allegation in the equivalent format if one exists. Further sections can be introduced to the document at this point, depending on the allegations.

- **Section 4** The concluding section lists and describes the interviewees, the documents reviewed, and all other evidence that has been collected.

Before writing the report, remember that various forensic software tools, such as Forensic Toolkit (FTK), DriveSpy, ILook, and EnCase, can generate reports. These tools can create reports in text format, a word processor format, or HTML format. The final document is the combination of the report generated using forensic tools and the official investigative report.

The Dos and Don'ts of Forensic Computer Investigations

The seven most crucial dos and don'ts that will apply to any forensic investigation are:

1. Ask questions Inquire as to the nature of the request. The more knowledge you have regarding the investigation, the more effective you can be.

2. Document methodically No matter how simple the demand, write it down—even if you feel that you will not perform that portion of work.

3. Operate in good faith Generally, you should follow instructions from your superior or legal counsel in the course of an investigation. It may be possible that some investigative actions could be illegal. Bring this to the other parties' attention.

4. Don't get in too deep If any of the following conditions are true, you may need to make an important determination as to whether to continue on your own or to call in other parties (such as law enforcement):

 a. The investigation involves a crime.

 b. The investigation is expected to result in serious discipline or termination of an employee.

 c. The investigation requires that documents are prepared and maintained for a court or a government investigative body, and follow legal discovery rules.

d. Large-scale investigations over multiple jurisdictions should be conducted by experienced investigators.

5. Decide to investigate Involve people who are necessary to the investigation and don't make all the decisions yourself.

6. Treat everything as confidential Regardless of who knows—or the rumors that surface—keep all information confidential and disclose the information only to those who need to know.

7. File it Keep your documentation and store it safely. Always file it in a controlled manner.

Best Practice for Investigation and Reporting

Any good report will answer the five Ws: who, what, why, when, and where. Remember to document who was involved in the case and who requested it. Document what was done and why. When and where did it occur? A good report should explain the computer and network processes and document all salient aspects of the system.

A well-conducted investigation should also follow the SMART methodology. This is:

- Specific Detail each component.

- Measurable Ensure that you log record sizes, times, and other relevant material.

- Achievable Ensure that you have the resources to achieve your objectives.

- Realistic Report the facts, don't speculate.

- Time-based Work to time constraints and deadlines, and ensure that you recorded all the events as they have occurred on the system.

Reports are critical to an investigation as they provide the means to exchange the findings and other evidence to the necessary people. A report may be formal or informal, verbal or written, but it always needs to be grammatically sound, so ensure that you use the correct spelling and avoid any grammatical errors. When writing the report, avoid using jargon, slang, or colloquial terms and ensure the clarity of writing, as this is critical to the success of a report.

Writing a report is like thinking. The presentation of the report must flow logically to convey the information in a structured form. Discuss the results and conclusions. Remember that the final document is a combination generated using forensic tools and the official investigative report.

Also, when conducting the investigation, remember: Document everything! In digital investigations, the most critical thing to remember is documentation, or maintaining chain of custody. Documentation must be maintained from the beginning to the end of the engagement. Having an improper chain of evidence is worse than having no evidence at all!

Document the system's hardware configuration. After you have moved the system to a secure location where an appropriate chain of custody can be maintained, it is crucial to take as documentation pictures of the system hardware components and how the connections and cables are arranged.

Also, document the system date and time. This is extremely important. An incorrect date and timestamp can allow the refuting of evidence and call into question the integrity of the findings. Even if everything else occurs perfectly, the mere fact that it got to this point will impact the entire investigation.

Document filenames, dates, and times on the system and create a timeline. The filename, creation date, and last modified date and time are of vital importance from an evidentiary standpoint when admitting digital evidence. The filename, size, content, and creation and modified dates have to be documented.

Finally, you should document all of the findings. It is important to document the findings sequentially as the issues are identified and evidence is found. A proper record of all the software employed in evaluation of the evidence should be prepared. One should be legally licensed to use the software because pirated software is of no use in a trial of the case. Document can also include the software license and screen shots to show how software was used in the evidence collection process.

Investigating Child Pornography

No matter how safe you feel in an environment, there are always those who may be victimized. The Internet is widely used as a source of information and enjoyment, but it also contains online predators who attempt to coerce or seduce children into having sex, and child pornography is rampantly downloaded and traded online. These images may be acquired using home or work computers. Although the workplace should be a safe environment, sometimes employees will display pornography, bully others, and create a hostile environment where others find it difficult to function.

Because of how common these issues are, there is always a chance that you may be required to participate in a computer investigation that involves these illegal activities. In doing so, you should follow the forensic procedures that have been described throughout this book, and become aware of laws, tools, and initiatives that may be available.

Investigating Child Pornography

Child pornography is the sexually explicit depiction of anyone under the age of legal consent. When most people think of child pornography, which is also called kiddie porn, they think it relates to photos of prepubescent children involved in sexual activity. Although this is an example of child pornography, it can also include stories and other written passages, drawings, digitally manipulated images, video, or any number of other media. Also, because the legal definitions of a child and laws related to consent vary, a picture may be legal in one region or country and illegal in another.

As we'll see in the sections that follow, a number of laws have been developed in different countries to protect children from exploitation. Because the Internet allows distribution of these materials across jurisdictions, this often requires law enforcement to work together and may require joint operations that are coordinated by government agencies or special projects that focus on eliminating child pornography, prosecuting offenders, and rescuing children.

Defining Child Pornography

There are challenges in controlling child pornography at every level of government and society, inclusive to defining it in a way that will control illegal activity. Before you balk at this statement, consider that to first create effective laws dealing with child pornography, you need to define two things:

- What is a child?
- What is pornography?

What Is a Child?

The age that a person progresses from childhood to adulthood varies depending on culture, religion, and legal designations. For example, in Jewish law, the age of maturity is 13 for boys and 12 for girls. However, Israeli law dictates that children cannot have consensual sex until age 16, marry until age 17, or reach the age of majority until age 18. In the United States, the age of adulthood in many states is 18, as this is the age when someone can legally enter into a contract, although the child is not considered an adult in terms of legal drinking age until 21. In looking at these ages, the differential of a child and adult varies dramatically. In terms of determining an age of consent for sexual activities, it can be even more convoluted.

In looking at the ages of consent shown in Table 16.1, you can see that the legal age for sex varies from country to country. Many people believe that the age of consent for sex is the same age used to determine whether a person is of legal age to pose for or perform sexual acts in pornography. However, separate ages are often set for exploitive situations, such as prostitution or pornography. For example, although the legal age for consensual sex in Canada is 14, it is illegal to be in pornography until 18. Similarly, although 12 is the minimum age for consensual sex in Mexico, a prostitute is underage if he or she is less than 16 years of age. As you can see, the age in which a child is considered to be mature enough to handle sex or participate in sexually exploitive situations is neither agreed upon nor internationally recognized.

Table 16.1 Ages of Consent for Sex by Country

Country	Age of Consent
Namibia (16 for girls)	7
Mexico	12
Burkina Faso, Japan, Nigeria, South Korea, Spain, Syria, Thailand	13
Albania, Bolivia (16 for boys), Bosnia Herzegovina, Brazil (no set age for boys), Bulgaria, Canada, Chile, Columbia, Croatia, Cuba, Ecuador, Estonia, Germany, Georgia, Guatemala (16 for boys), Honduras, Hungary, Iceland, Italy, Lesotho (16 for girls), Liechtenstein, Madagascar, Montenegro, Myanmar (Burma), Nicaragua, Papua New Guinea (16 for girls), Paraguay, Peru, People's Republic of China, Portugal, Puerto Rico, Serbia, Togo	14
Andorra, Argentina, Costa Rica, Cote d'Ivoire, Czech Republic, Denmark, Ethiopia, France, French Guiana, French Polynesia (Tahiti), Guadeloupe, Guinea, Greece, Jordan, Laos, Lebanon, Monaco, Morocco, Poland, Slovakia, Slovenia, Sweden, Turkey, Uruguay	15
Algeria, Antigua (Barbuda), Armenia, Aruba, Australia, Azerbaijan, Bahamas, Bahrain, Barbados, Bolivia (14 for girls), Belize, Belgium, Bermuda, Botswana, Brunei, Cook Islands (male only), Cambodia, Cape Verde, Dominica, Falkland Islands (Malvinas), Fiji, Finland, Gibraltar, Grenada, Guatemala (14 for girls), Guyana, Hong Kong (SAR - China), Indonesia (boys at 18), Israel, Jamaica, Kenya, Kyrgyzstan, Latvia, Lesotho (14 for boys), Liberia, Luxemburg, Macao (China), Macedonia, Malaysia, Mali, Mauritania, Mauritius, Moldova, Mongolia, Namibia (7 for boys), Nepal, Netherland Antilles, Netherlands, New Zealand, Norway, Pakistan (boys at 18), Papua New Guinea (14 for boys), Russia, Samoa (male only), Senegal, Singapore, St. Kitts & Nevis, South Africa, Sri Lanka, Suriname, Swaziland, Switzerland, Taiwan, Trinidad & Tobago, Turkmenistan, Ukraine, United Kingdom, Uzbekistan, Venezuela, Zimbabwe	16
Cyprus, Ireland, Tajikistan, Tasmania (Australia), South Australia	17
Austria, Belarus, Bhutan, Burundi, Djibouti, Dominican Republic, Egypt, El Salvador, Eritrea, Gabon, Haiti, India, Kazakhstan, Malta, Martinique, Pakistan (girls at 16), Panama, Philippines, Romania, Rwanda, Seychelles, Sudan, Tanzania, United States of America (Federal – State legislation varies between 14 to 18), Uganda, Vanuatu, Vietnam	18

Continued

Table 16.1 continued Ages of Consent for Sex by Country

Country	Age of Consent
Indonesia (girls at 16)	19
Tunisia	20
Cameroon	21
Iran (girl can marry at 9), Oman, Qatar, Saudi Arabia, United Arab Emirates	Marriage only

NOTE

In looking at the ages shown in Table 16.1, it is important to realize that these ages may change as laws change. You can view the latest information on ages of sexual consent at the World Ages of Consent for Sex and Marriage Web site, at http://aoc.puellula.com/, or by visiting the Interpol Web page on sexual offenses against children, at www.interpol.int/Public/Children/SexualAbuse/NationalLaws/.

The varying ages of sexual consent have also caused another problem: child sex tourism, in which pedophiles travel to countries with low ages of consent to have sex with children, who are under the age of 18. A pedophile is someone whose primary sexual interest is in children. Some professionals make the distinction that pedophiles are interested in children, and hebophiles are interested in adolescents; however, for the purposes of this chapter, we will use the term pedophile to refer to a person whose sexual interest is with a minor (i.e., someone below the age of legal consent). Because such individuals are fearful of being arrested in their own country, they will travel to countries such as Thailand, where the legal age of consent is 13 and child prostitutes are plentiful. Even if a person is arrested in this country, often he or she can avoid prosecution by bribing officials.

Child sex tourism is a major problem in many areas of the world. According to a report issued by the United Nations International Children's Educational Fund (UNICEF) in 1997, more than 1 million children are forced into prostitution every year in Asia. Also, increasing numbers of children are being exploited by foreigners and aid workers in Russia, Romania, the Czech Republic, and Poland. According to the group End Child Prostitution, Child Pornography, and Trafficking of Children for Sexual Purposes (ECPAT), these children are trafficked to Western European brothels, where a proportion of their customers are child sex tourists.

The child sex industry generates billions of dollars, and the commercial exploitation of children under the age of 18 extends to photos and videos taken of child prostitutes and those hired as "models." A report released in 2006 (www.state.gov/g/drl/rls/hrrpt/2005/61682.htm) stated: "According to domestic and foreign law enforcement officials, a significant portion of the child pornography available on the Internet continued to originate in Ukraine." In fact, in one case, a child pornography studio that was closed down reportedly used approximately 1,500 girls between the ages of 8 and 16 for pornographic images sold over the Internet.

Over the past few years, reforms in child exploitation laws throughout the world have established higher ages of consent, or in some cases helped to establish an age of consent where there was none before. However, the need to establish an international standard age of consent for areas of sexual consent, pornography, and other sexually exploitive activities is needed.

Head of the Class…

Evolution in Ages of Consent

The age of consent often changes over the years, with different ages being attributed to different acts and genders. To illustrate this, consider that in Canada, until the later part of the 19th century, only girls who were under the age of 12 were unable to consent to sexual intercourse. In 1890, the legal age of consent for girls was raised to 14, and when the Criminal Code of Canada was established in 1892, it retained this age. In 1886, it was also illegal to seduce a female under 18 "under promise of marriage," with this age being raised to females under 21 in 1887. This continued to be an offence until 1920, when the offense of seduction became limited to those between the ages of 16 and 18 who were of "previously chaste character."

In looking at these laws, you'll notice that they were sexually discriminatory, and applied only to protecting girls who were under the age of 21. In 1988, previous laws were repealed and replaced by Bill C-15, which prohibited adults from sexual contact with boys or girls under the age of 14, and included a sexual exploitation offense that further prohibited an adult in a position of trust or authority from having sex with anyone over 14 but under 18. Not only did the changes in law protect both boys and girls, but also the wording changed to prevent any kind of sexual contact, whereas the wording of previous laws prohibited only intercourse.

There are still a number of exceptions to age of consent in Canada. If a person is under 16 and less than two years older than someone over 12 and under 14, it is also not illegal to have consensual sex. Also, a person who is under 18 cannot legally consent to anal intercourse, although both the Ontario Court of Appeal and Quebec Court of Appeal have struck down relevant sections of the Criminal Code pertaining to this. Finally, sexual exploitation legislation prevents someone under the age of 18 from consenting to exploitive activities. This means someone under 18 cannot consent to sexual activity in acts of prostitution, pornography, or with an adult with whom there is a relationship of trust, authority, or dependency.

What Is Pornography?

The definition of pornography has varied over the years. Pornography comes from the Greek word pronographos, meaning the "writing of prostitutes," and is derived from porne, which originally meant bought or purchased, as in a slave or prostitute. A variation of this appeared in the French language as pornographie, meaning a "description of prostitutes," but didn't appear in the English language until the 19th century. In 1864, it first appeared in Webster's Dictionary as "licentious painting employed to decorate the walls of rooms sacred to bacchanalian orgies, examples of which exist in Pompeii." However, although the erotic art of Pompeii that had been recovered in excavations had a dramatic impact on Victorian culture, it doesn't exactly capture what we think of as pornographic today.

Whether something is considered pornographic is often related to the social mores of the time, the content, and the medium used to create it. Today, a painting or sculpture with nudity or sexually explicit content is generally considered art, although this isn't necessarily the case. Michelangelo's David has on numerous occasions been considered pornographic and had its genitalia covered, inclusive to a 1995 incident in which Jerusalem rejected a gift of a replica statue due to its nudity. Even literary works such as Shakespeare's Romeo and Juliet has been subject to controversy, considering that Juliet was 13 and was portrayed in the 1968 film version by Olivia Hussey, who appears topless at the age of 16. In truth, there are many incidents in which underage actresses have appeared nude in mainstream films, or in sexual situations in popular literary or artistic works.

Many countries do not consider the nudity of an underage person illegal. For example, in the Western world, it is common for parents to take a picture of their child's first bath or the traditional bare-bottom photo of their baby on a rug. In advertising, there are images of child nudity such as the famous Coppertone ad that depicted a young girl's bathing suit being pulled down by a puppy. To use an example that is more widely distributed on the Internet, there are also photos of nudists and art photos. In North America, a distinction of whether a picture of a child is illegal is whether there is lascivious exhibition of the pubic area or genitalia, and what is occurring in the image. In other words, what the person is doing or having done to him or her is a major factor in determining whether it is pornographic.

Part of what defines pornography is that it is sexually arousing to those viewing it, and considered obscene to a portion of society. By being obscene, it is generally considered to be without artistic merit. An image or literary work that is sexually arousing for artistic purposes is considered erotica, and attempts to constrain or ban it are widely viewed as censorship. The distinction can create legal and social disputes. Although the First Amendment may protect artistic expression, obscene work is not protected, and determining whether an image, film, or other item is pornographic or artistic is subjective. n 1964, Justice Potter Stewart perhaps best explained the distinction between the two by saying, "I shall not today attempt further to define the kinds of material I understand to be embraced . . . [b]ut I know it when I see it."

To define pornography, you have to realize that there are different kinds of pornography. The two main types of pornography include:

- Softcore This depicts people in various levels of nudity, and/or sexual activities that are not graphically depicted nor show sexual penetration.

- Hardcore This depicts sexual acts in an extremely explicit or graphic manner. This type of pornography will show such things as genital touching and masturbation, and will generally depict oral, vaginal, and/or anal penetration.

Pornography is banned in a number of countries, including the People's Republic of China, India, Indonesia, Iran, Malaysia, Norway, Pakistan, Sri Lanka, and Vietnam. In countries where it is banned, child pornography laws may not exist because all pornography is illegal. Of course, whether anti-pornography laws are actively enforced is another issue. In other countries where pornography is legal, there may be laws that prohibit certain content or genres, such as that containing violence, or sex with children or animals (i.e., bestiality). For example, in 2006, the Netherlands instituted new animal welfare laws in which bestiality became illegal. In looking at these laws, you can see that although pornography isn't limited to adults having consensual sex, the tolerance for what's acceptable often has very clear boundaries.

A final aspect of pornography is that the sexual activities or nudity must be captured in some form of media. Pornography includes photographs, film, literature, sculpture, paintings, animation, video games, digital images, and other media. If a sexual act or nudity is not captured or reproduced using some form of media, it is considered an act. In terms of filming or photographing children, this is the difference between sexual abuse and child pornography.

What Is Child Pornography?

By putting together what we've previously discussed, you can see that the specific details regarding what defines a child and pornography can vary from country to country. In North America, child pornography can be simply defined as any sexually explicit depiction of a person less than 18 years of age. However, the ages for consent to pose for and/or perform in pornography are not universal, and in many cases are nonexistent.

In a report developed by the International Centre for Missing and Exploited Children in 2006 (www.icmec.org/en_X1/pdf/ModelLegislationFINAL.pdf), a review of 184 countries that were members of Interpol found that 95 countries had no legislation specifically addressing child pornography. Of those that did:

- Fifty-four countries had no definition of child pornography in their legislation.

- Twenty-seven countries didn't provide for computer-facilitated offenses (i.e., digital images and media, and the downloading or distributing of such media over the Internet).

- Forty-one countries didn't criminalize the possession of child pornography.

As we'll see in later sections of this chapter, of the countries that do have laws which address these issues, child pornography is generally defined as having sexually explicit content. This may include such acts as lascivious exhibition of genitals, masturbation, fellatio and/or cunnilingus (oral sex), intercourse, anal sex, or other graphic content. In countries where child pornography laws exist, it is generally illegal to possess, distribute, or produce such images or depictions. However, exceptions may exist if it is for specific circumstances, such as artistic or medical purposes. For example, a photo in a medical book may show a child's genitals, but would not be considered child pornography.

Child pornography may consist of any number of different people of different ages. Images may consist of a single child, a child being abused by an adult or group of adults, or children with other children. The ages of the child may range from a baby of a few months of age up to the legal age of consent.

In addition to this are genres of child pornography that are created for specific audiences. For example, incest pornography will portray a familial relationship between those being filmed or photographed. The images may depict an uncle, father, or brother having sex with a niece, daughter, or sister. Although in many of these images there is actually no relationship, in many others a family member documenting the act is sexually abusing a child. In addition to this is child pornography that may also involve bestiality (sex with animals) or sadomasochistic sex (S&M), where people are aroused either by inflicting pain on others (sadists) or by having pain inflicted on them (masochists). Essentially, for any type of pornography depicting adults, there is an equivalent depicting children.

Child Pornography without the Pornography

Because of wordings in the law, some photos and depictions of children don't meet the legal definitions of child pornography. These photos are widely available on the Internet, as well as in art books and other media. In some cases, they are even available in mainstream bookstores.

Child erotica is a term applied to photos or depictions of naked children, which may or may not be also categorized as art. The images don't fall under standard definitions of pornography, as the photos of the children are natural poses and are not sexually explicit. In other words, there is no lascivious exhibition of genitalia, such as a child spreading his or her legs or posing lewdly. In many cases, the distinction between whether it is deemed as art is in the way it's presented.

In the 1996 case United States v. Dost, a federal judge suggested a six-step method of evaluating images to determine whether the nude image of a child could be considered legal or illegal. The criteria were:

1. If the focal point was the child's genitalia or public area

2. If the setting of the visual depiction was sexually suggestive

3. If the child was in inappropriate attire or an unnatural pose

4. If the child was fully, partially, or completely nude

5. If the visual depiction suggested coyness or a willingness to engage in sexual activity

6. If the visual depiction was intended or designed to elicit a sexual response from the person viewing it

Although the list of factors isn't comprehensive, and other aspects of an image may be relevant, the Dost factors do provide a good measurement in determining whether an image is illegal. They address the fact that just because nudity is present, labeling it as child pornography may not be applicable.

TEST DAY TIP

Remembering the six-step method for evaluating images can help you identify whether a picture is considered to be child pornography.

Photographs may involve nude subjects who are under 18, but are professionally taken for the purpose of art rather than sexual arousal. In such cases, the photos are available for viewing in art galleries and other venues. A number of photographers have published books and have their photos available on the Internet, including David Hamilton, Jock Sturges, and Sally Mann. These photographers' books are available on sites such as Amazon and may be sold in local bookstores. Such photos have obvious qualities that differentiate them from raw images of naked children.

There are also many sites on the Internet that operate under the thin guise of promoting nudism, even though the predominant number of images are those of teenage or prepubescent children. Many sites operate by charging money for access to more revealing images of children or the bulk of their photos. The photos are often taken at nudist resorts or other locations where nudity is legal, allowing amateur photographers to take photos of naked boys and girls without worry of immediate repercussions. These sites are able to operate by skirting the line between what is legal and illegal.

Another type of photography that skirts the issue of child pornography is Web sites featuring child models. These child model or glamour sites feature young girls posing in bikinis, miniskirts, sheer lingerie, and other outfits. An example of such as site is True TeenBabes (www.trueteenbabes.com), which features models between the ages of 13 and 18, and charges an access fee of $29.95 per month. According to information on the site, once the models turn 18, their images are then used on another Web site. The photos of girls on such sites may not contain any nudity, but they are provocative and show scantily clad girls in suggestive poses. For good reason, such sites have undergone serious scrutiny over the past few years, with many being shut down.

As with most child modeling sites, children appear with permission of their parent or legal guardian, because the children are too young to consent. The rationale for parents allowing the

photographs has ranged from raising money for college (as in the case of the now defunct Lil' Amber site that featured a 9-year-old girl) to gaining exposure for legitimate modeling jobs—neither being particularly good reasons for creating sexualized images of a child. In 2002, Representative Mark Foley took on combating this type of exploitation and introduced a bill called the Child Modeling Exploitation Prevention Act, which would ban selling photographs of minors. Needless to say, doing so would impact legitimate modeling companies and other businesses, and due to opposition the bill never left committee. As for Rep. Mark Foley himself, he resigned in 2006 after ABC News reported on his inappropriate e-mails and sexually explicit instant messages to teenaged pages.

Head of the Class…

Censorship vs. Pornography

An issue that often arises in the topic of laws dealing with pornographic or nude imagery is the issue of censorship. This argument may even arise when the topic involves children, as child nudity is often equated with child pornography. The fear is that legislation will impact the availability and freedom of creating art.

Nude art has often involved children, in a variety of media. Paintings by Raphael included images of nude children as cherubs, whereas other paintings such as those by Henry Scott Tuke featured naked adolescent boys. As mentioned earlier, books and film have also featured nude children, as in the case of 12-year-old Brooke Shields posing naked in Pretty Baby. Although the formats are different, child nudity is present in each medium.

Laws protecting minors under a legal age of consent are a necessary component of any society. When addressing the issue of children abused in pornography, strict laws must be created and re-created to keep up-to-date with changes in technology and media. However, such laws should not be pushed through without considering the wide-reaching implications on areas where abuse is neither present nor presented.

Child Pornography without the Child

Laws against child pornography are based on the assumption that children are harmed in the making of the pictures. The pornography laws generally apply to visual depictions only, with the written word (stories about child sex) being protected by the First Amendment in the United States. However, even though no child is harmed in the generation of certain types of pornography, it is viewed by those who abuse children sexually or are intrigued by the idea of having sex with a child. Many different types of child pornography don't involve actual children.

Virtual child pornography is a type of digital fakery in which the images appear to be of children having sex or posing nude, but they are actually digitally manipulated or morphed images. It can be as simple as a cut and paste of a child onto another image, or extensive digital editing. Superimposing the child's face on a body of a minor, or someone with a body type similar to an underage child, gives the illusion that the child is actually posing nude or having sex.

The issue of "virtual child pornography" that uses high-quality, computer-generated images instead of real photographs is a matter of intense debate. It is illegal in some countries such as Germany, where it is punishable by up to five years imprisonment, but legal in other countries such as the United States. In April 2002, the Supreme Court struck down federal laws making this form of kiddie porn illegal. At the time of this writing, the Justice Department and members of Congress were intent on rewriting those laws more narrowly, in a way that would outlaw virtual child pornography that is indistinguishable from the real thing while still allowing the law to pass constitutional muster.

NOTE

In the United Kingdom, under the Protection of Children Act (1978) and Section 160 of the Criminal Justice Act of 1988, it is a criminal offense for a person to possess either a photograph or a "pseudophotograph" of a child that is considered indecent. The term pseudophotograph is defined as an image made by computer graphics or that otherwise appears to be a photograph. Typically this is a photograph that is created using a graphics manipulation software program such as Adobe Photoshop to superimpose a child's head on a different body (the same type of "virtual child pornography" addressed by the U.S. Supreme Court in an April 2002 decision).

A variation of virtual child pornography involves virtual communities, in which people can chat and interact with one another using alter egos called avatars. Similar to using a character to move around a video game, virtual communities such as Second Life allow characters to have sex with one another. This leads to a problem where some people were using avatars of children to have sex, or were selling them for virtual profits. They were also using it as a forum to connect with others so that real child pornography could be traded.

Another type of child pornography that has no children in it is lollipop or Lolita pornography. The genre gets its name from the 1955 novel by Vladimir Nabokov, which is about an older man's obsession with a sexually precocious 12-year-old girl, and has been adapted into film twice. With this type of pornography, girls who are just above the legal age will have hairstyles and accoutrements to make them appear younger than they are. They will wear pigtails or have their hair done up in a child-like fashion, shave pubic hair, wear school uniforms or childish clothes, and pose in a childish fashion. Doing so provides the illusion or fantasy role-play of being a child, even though the models are not underage.

Similar to lollipop porn are the depictions of children in sexually orientated Japanese cartoons and comics, which are referred to as Lolicon (a slang combination of the phrase Lolita complex). The Japanese style of animation is commonly referred to as Japanimation or anime,

whereas comic books (and sometimes mistakenly cartoons) are referred to as manga. These cartoons and comics feature characters that are children or are childlike, and sexually orientated versions of this genre involve the characters in sexual activities. The female characters are commonly drawn to resemble prepubescent girls, and may appear bound and gagged, raped, or having exaggerated sexual exploits. Although child pornography is illegal in Japan, this type of pornography is freely available and considered legal. Because it doesn't involve flesh-and-blood actresses, many other countries are also slow in recognizing issues in such cartoon pornography.

NOTE

Even though the term Lolita is used to describe this type of role-play pornography, it is also commonly used to refer to underage girls on various sites and newsgroups. Many of these sources of child pornography will use the term, because Western culture relates it to a sexualized underage girl.

The Motives Behind Child Pornography

Child pornography involves a number of aspects: people who create pornographic materials using minors, those who distribute these materials, and those who access them. When computers and networks are used for any of these activities, child pornography becomes a cybercrime.

The reasons child pornography is manufactured and distributed are as diverse as the people involved. You might initially think of child pornographers as being creepy little men in dirty raincoats, but you'd be surprised to find that many of them are individuals running a business, people like your neighbor, and sometimes individuals who are taking pictures of themselves. Their reasons for creating child pornography may be for personal or commercial gain.

The Manufacture and Distribution of Child Pornography for Personal Reasons

Since the early days of photography, photographers have taken pictures of people in various states of undress and/or sexual situations. As video cameras and Polaroid cameras became available for home use, couples began filming themselves or taking instant photos of themselves having sex or in sexually appealing poses. Although images such as these are legal in many places throughout the world, consider that we are now living in a digital world.

Many children and teenagers have computers with Web cams, access to digital cameras and camcorders, and cameras on their mobile phones. Unfortunately, the availability of technology has also added to the increase in child pornography. A teenage boy or girl may photograph him or herself and send it as a gift to a boyfriend or girlfriend. As an added kick to having sex, a

teenage couple may take digital pictures or video of themselves engaging in various sex acts. Because these children are under the age of 18, they are manufacturing and distributing child pornography. Even if it's a picture of you, it is the age of the person depicted that makes it child porn, not whether permission was given.

Because the ability to take digital images and video is readily available, online predators that prey on children will often try to get a child they're chatting with to send a photo. At first it may be a request for an innocuous picture, but the pedophile will then try to convince the child to take more salacious pictures, getting the child to pose nude, masturbate, or perform other sex acts. The process of asking for a nonsexual picture to convincing the child to take sexual pictures may take hours or several online chats over a period of days or weeks. By repeatedly asking for the pictures, and slowly wearing down the child's resolve, predators will work to eventually get what they want.

The best way to think of the Internet is that once a picture is sent, it is available for everyone to see. Even though a teenager may send a picture to one person, there is no guarantee that other people won't see it. Multiple people may use the computer, find the picture, and send it to their friends. Also, never underestimate the cyber equivalent of locker room talk, where a person will brag about having sex with a girl or boy, and then send out the picture as proof. In the same vein, if a teenage couple broke up, there is no guarantee that one of the two may exact a little revenge by posting the picture online. Once the image is online, the distribution of it proportionally increases, with each person acquiring it possibly posting it on other sites or sharing it with other individuals.

Another common way in which pornography is manufactured for personal reasons is in cases of child abuse. In most cases of sexual child abuse, the abuser is known or related to the child. This may be the father, uncle, brother, a boyfriend of the mother, or friend of the family. Because the abuser may have unfettered access to the child, there is no difficulty in filming or photographing pornographic images, and thereby documenting the abuse. The reasoning may be to create a souvenir or trophy of the sexual experience(s), allowing the abuser to revisit and fantasize over it again in the future. As we'll see later in this chapter, once a video or photo is taken of the child, it may be shared with others over the Internet, or traded to acquire a larger collection of child pornography.

The Commercial Manufacture and Distribution of Child Pornography

Although producing kiddie porn for personal use is primarily for sexual gratification, the commercial manufacture and distribution of child pornography is predominantly based on financial gain. Top Ten Reviews (http://internet-filter-review.toptenreviews.com/internet-pornography-statistics.html) states that in 2006 there were 100,000 Web sites offering child pornography. Because Internet pornography sales for 2006 were $4.9 billion, you can see that selling pornography is a lucrative business. Although exact numbers aren't available due to it being illegal, the business of child pornography has generated billions of dollars at the expense of its victims.

Online credit card billing has made it easier for people to pay for access to these sites. By providing a credit card number, a person can gain access to areas of the site that require a subscription that costs a specified number of dollars every month. These "members only" sections may provide series of images featuring different girls, and often more graphic photos than nonmembers can view.

Because of advances in technology, the ability to produce commercial pornography is easier than ever before. As seen through the adult entertainment market, amateur pornography has become a growing industry with couples making their own videos that are sold over the Internet. The same applies to child pornography. By using digital editing software, videos and photos are created on home computers, and then distributed over the Internet or by mail order. Photos and video can be produced and distributed using various technologies, including using streaming video to create interactive Web sites that offer live performances.

In stating that financial gain is a primary motivation of commercial child pornography, it is important not to lose sight of the fact that it is not a legitimate business. It is a systematic abuse of children for a monetary return. Children may pose nude, masturbate, or perform other sex acts with other children and/or adults. In certain situations, the pornographer will have sex with the child but be careful not to have his or her face shown on camera. In other situations, the pornographer will not appear on film, but will still have sex off camera. In doing so, he or she may believe there is less likelihood of being incriminated in the actual abuse of the child.

Although the profits from child pornography continue to make commercial producers a growing threat, most of it is created, distributed, and collected on a noncommercial basis. The children appearing in most of the images and video available on the Internet are photographed by individuals they know, or others who have targeted them for abuse. Regardless of their purpose for manufacturing the images and/or video, these are dangerous individuals. Internet child pornographers are usually classified as sex offenders (pedophiles) and regarded as violent or potentially violent criminals.

NOTE

Because it is an illegal activity, the revenue generated by producing and distributing child pornography is difficult to determine. However, the U.S. Department of Justice estimates it to generate between $2 billion and $3 billion per year.

The Motives of People Accessing Child Pornography

Sex is one of the strongest instincts in any animal, including humans. Psychologists and psychiatrists argue over what causes normal sexual feelings to become perverted, but there is no ques-

tion that sexual deviance (defined as sexual behavior that is out of the norm or breaks societal rules) is common among certain types of criminals. Although not all sexually deviant behavior is illegal or considered harmful, when sexual arousal becomes associated with violence or with inappropriate objects of desire, such as children, serious harm and criminal activity can result.

People view child pornography with different intentions or purposes. Although women do access or produce child pornography, most people who create, access, and disseminate this type of material are male. Those who are sexually attracted to this type of pornography will often fall into one of these categories:

- Passive pedophiles These people use the Internet to access and download kiddie porn and use photos and stories of children engaging in sex (usually with adults) to feed their own fantasies. Even if they never act out those fantasies in real life, in the United States and many other countries, it is illegal to even possess child pornography in photographic form.

- Active pedophiles These people use the Internet to find their victims. These criminals usually also collect child pornography, but they don't stop at fantasies. They often hang out in chat rooms that are frequented by children and engage them in virtual conversations, attempting to gain their trust and lure them into an in-person meeting. They might then rape the children, or they could simply "court" them, preferring to gradually seduce them into sexual relationships. Because children under a certain age (which varies from one state to another) are not considered capable of consenting to sex, sexual conduct with a minor is still a crime, even if the child agrees to it. Usually the offense is defined as statutory rape or some category of sexual assault.

- Sexually indiscriminate These people are looking for new kinds of sexual stimuli.

- Sexually curious These people are accessing the images out of curiosity. For example, people under the age of 18 may access child pornography to view people within their own age range, whereas adults may visit a site because they are curious as to what kiddie porn is.

As we'll discuss further when we discuss victims of child pornography, it is possible to become desensitized to pornography. In some cases, people have viewed a considerable amount of pornography, and move on to forms of pornography that would initially have offended them. In other words, they have viewed so much porn that they have become desensitized to it. Such people will visit sites and possibly download images with little regard to its implications, because to them, porn is porn. When analyzing a computer, it is easy to identify such people because there is a diverse range of different types of pornography. For example, images may include erotic images from men's magazines, amateur adult porn, images of older women or men (possibly even senior citizens) posing or engaged in sex, as well as a number of other genres. Regardless of whether there is a prevalent amount of child pornography, it is important to remember that even a single image of child pornography can result in criminal charges.

EXAM WARNING

Remember that people who access child pornography may be active or passive pedophiles. Passive pedophiles will download child pornography, but won't act on their sexual attraction to children. Active pedophiles will also collect child pornography, but will abuse children sexually. This latter type also includes predators who will try to engage children in conversations over the Internet, and attempt to meet with them for purposes of sex.

In addition to the types of people we've discussed so far, there are those who may access pornography, and may have an added attraction to violent types of pornographic material. Although rarer than those previously mentioned, they include:

- Fans of S&M, or sadomasochistic sex, who are aroused either by inflicting pain on others (sadists) or by having pain inflicted on them (masochists). Although S&M behavior between consenting adults is generally not considered a crime, some sadistic individuals hunt for partners on the Internet and then take the activities beyond the level that the partner bargained for or consented to, seriously injuring or sometimes even killing their victims. As with the remaining types of cybercriminals discussed here, in some situations, the partners or victims may also be underage.

- Serial rapists, who develop relationships (hetero- or homosexual) online, and then invite their victims to meet in real life, only to rape them. Serial rapists often have problems performing sexually in a normal, loving situation. They are able to become aroused only when the sex is violent and forced. Psychologists call rape an anger-motivated or powermotivated crime rather than a sexually motivated one, but sex is certainly an important element, if only as the "tool of the crime."

- Sexual serial killers, who—like serial rapists—cruise Internet chat rooms and forums looking for victims. Psychiatric literature recognizes two types of serial killers: organized and disorganized. The organized killer is often of above-average intelligence, is socially gregarious and charming, and is usually married or living with a partner. Disorganized killers are almost exactly the opposite; their IQ is usually below average, and they are socially inadequate loners and are anxious during the commission of the crime. Organized killers tend to be very controlled and unemotional and are often diagnosed (as was Ted Bundy, one of the country's most famous sexual serial killers) as sociopathic. In fact, sexual serial killers, despite the sexual motivation for their crimes, belong in the next category of motivation: serious psychiatric illness.

Regardless of the motives, child pornography is generally considered a violent crime, even if some of the people involved have had no physical contact with children. This is the case because sexual abuse of children is required to produce pornographic materials and because people who are interested in viewing these types of materials often do not confine their interest to pictures and fantasies but are instead practicing pedophiles, or aspire to be, in real life.

Types of Pornography Accessed

In the report "Child Pornography Possessors Arrested in Internet-Related Crimes: Findings from the National Juvenile Online Victimization Study," which was created by the National Center for Missing & Exploited Children (www.missingkids.com/en_US/publications/NC144.pdf), information was reported on the types of images that people who were arrested for possession of child pornography had on their computer. Of those studied:

- People generally had images of prepubescent children and adolescents. However, 17 percent had images that were just of children 12 and under, and 8 percent had images that were just of adolescents aged 13–17.

- Of the pictures that people were in possession of, most were of girls. Sixty-two percent had mostly images of girls, 14 percent had mostly pictures of boys, and 15 percent had pictures of boys and girls in roughly equal numbers.

- Ninety-two percent had images that focused on genitals or sexual activity by children.

- Eighty percent had images showing sexual penetration (i.e., vaginal, anal, oral) of children.

- Seventy-nine percent had images showing minors who were nude or semi-nude but were not graphic. However, it is important to note that 99 percent possessed other types of images in addition to these.

- Seventy-one percent had images that showed sexual contact between adults and minors.

- Twenty-one percent had images showing sexual violence. This included bondage, rape, torture, and other types of sadistic sex in which the child was gagged, blindfolded, and/or tied up.

- Three percent had images that were digitally manipulated or morphed.

In looking at these figures, you can see that most of the images found on the computers and removable media were graphic in nature. In addition to this, large numbers of images were found, with 39 percent also having child pornography on videos. Of those who possessed child pornography, 37 percent possessed 1–100 images, 34 percent had 101–999 images, and 14 percent possessed more than 1,000 images. In looking at this, you can see that most people who

possess child pornography don't simply access it; they collect it in the form of downloaded files saved to their hard disk or other media.

Victims of Child Pornography

The primary victims of child pornography are the children who are abused in the photos and videos. According to the National Center for Missing & Exploited Children's report mentioned previously, of those arrested for possession of child pornography:

- Eighty-three percent had images involving children between ages 6 and 12.

- Thirty-nine percent had images involving children between ages 3 and 5.

- Nineteen percent had images of infants and toddlers under age 3.

As previously mentioned, most of the children used in child pornography are female victims, and although these figures do not account for adolescents, you can see that most of the children involved in child pornography are between the ages of 6 and 12. Although the gender is agreed upon by most studies, an article available from the Computer Crime Research Center (www.crime-research.org/articles/536/) states that "Federal Bureau of Investigation (FBI) personnel estimate that over 50 percent of all child pornography seized in the United States depicts boys rather than girls. Canadian Customs puts that figure at 75 percent for Canada." Regardless of gender, the children may be required to pose nude for softcore images, or may be used for hardcore pictures and video in which they perform various sex acts.

How they become victims of this crime varies, but there is sufficient information to show it is an international problem. Children may be exploited in countries with low ages of consent, where there are no child pornography laws, or where existing laws aren't enforced. Poverty is also an issue, as children who are impoverished and/or living on the street are often targeted for prostitution or pornography.

As mentioned earlier in this chapter, countries with low ages of consent for exploitive activities such as prostitution, or where underage prostitution is not enforced, can be destinations for child sex tourism and child pornography. In a report from Save the Children titled "Position paper on child pornography and Internet-related sexual exploitation of children" (www.inhope.org/doc/stc-pp-cp.pdf), it was reported that up to 50 percent of child prostitutes were also subjects of child pornography. By being used as prostitutes and in kiddie porn, it shows that child prostitution provides an avenue for pedophiles and pornographers to acquire children to abuse.

The areas of the world where the production of child pornography is most prevalent have changed over the years, ranging from Japan, Taiwan, Russia, and other countries. According to a 2004 report by the Russian National Consultation on the Commercial Sexual Exploitation of Children (www.ecpat.net/eng/Russia.asp), child pornography makes up 25 percent of the pornography on Internet Web sites, and more than 50 percent of these contain child pornog-

raphy from Russia. It is estimated that pornography from this country involves tens of thousands of children being exploited.

Child pornography created in Russia, the Ukraine, and other areas of the former Eastern Europe has also become a problem over the past number of years. Although not limited to these parts of the world, young women or girls may be offered modeling jobs that are actually child pornography. They may be required to pose nude or in sex acts. The images are then sold over the Internet or through various magazines in countries where the legal age is low enough to make publishing legal.

In some cases, the levels in which children are procured are highly organized and insidious. In Russia, businesses involved in child pornography will pose as modeling and fitness schools, where children are actually groomed for participation in pornographic films. One such institution was the Aphrodite School which operated as a school for young models. It had an enrollment procedure that should have seemed odd to parents, where the girls had to show themselves naked before they were accepted. This may seem inconceivable to most people, unless they're living in destitution with no chance for a better life. Poverty mixed with opportunity can create an atmosphere where children appear in pornography with their parents' permission or endorsement.

Regardless of the situation, a child is powerless and cannot give consent to appearing in pornography, and thereby doesn't have a choice. As stated in the Save the Children report mentioned previously, "German police estimate that 130,000 children in 1993 were forced by parents or other acquaintances to participate in the production of pornography." Beyond commercial pornographers and child sex tourists, children may become victims of the very people they believe are there to protect them.

The Effects of Pornography on Children

A common source of child pornography is people who are related to or acquainted with the victim. An abuser may be in an incestuous relationship with the child, or a pedophile that seduced or coerced the child into performing sexual acts and/or posing naked. In having pictures taken while being abused, the child is victimized twice; first by the sexual abuse, and second by the permanent record of the abuse that may be distributed over the Internet for years.

It's important to remember that when a child has pictures taken of him or her, it isn't a single picture and it's over. A child will generally have entire sets of pictures taken, in a variety of poses and performing different sexual acts on an adult or with other children. To illustrate this, we only need to look at the work of the COPINE (Combating Paedophile Information Networks in Europe) Project, which has studied the exploitation of children on the Internet and can be visited at www.copine.ie. The project is based in the Department of Applied Psychology at University College Cork in Ireland, and has conducted significant research on child pornography. In the university's database of 50,000 pictures, 2,000 individual children were depicted in these photos.

To groom the child into performing sex acts, it is common for abusers to use pornography to make the child more comfortable with what will occur. The abuser uses the pornography to not only seduce or raise the child's interest in sex, but also to get the child to overcome any inhibitions he or she might have. When children view pornography, it may first appear shocking to them, but they become desensitized to it. In viewing the images and films depicting adults and children having sex, the child is made to believe that it is normal for adults and children to have sex.

Although this may be done in the confines of a home, online predators also use pornography to seduce or groom potential victims. Once they are in a chat or interacting with a child online, images or video is then sent to the child. This leads the conversation into specific discussions about sex, and provides an avenue for the pedophile to ask what the child has done, whether the child would like to try something in the picture, or other questions. In the National Center for Missing & Exploited Children's report mentioned previously, it was found that 27 percent of those who possessed child pornography had also shown or given it to identified victims, and 25 percent of them had done it to groom the child into having sex.

Exchanging images in this way also provides a way to get the child to send pictures of himself or herself to the predator. Because images have been exchanged, the pedophile will beleaguer or coerce the child. In some situations, a pedophile will threaten to tell the children's parents about what they've done. Once the child actually sends a picture, the pedophile can more easily convince the child to do or reveal more in additional pictures, or threaten to show the image he or she has sent to the parents if the child doesn't do what's asked.

By using pornography as a tool, pedophiles are better able to convince a child to perform acts depicted in the images or video. Once the child is seduced or groomed, additional images can be taken of the child. In doing so, the use of pornography allows the predator to create more pornography. It is a vicious circle that victimizes the child, and embarrasses the child into doing more.

Damage & Defense…

Paying for Pornography

Many victims are involved in child pornography, including those who pay for it. In saying this, we're not saying those who view it, but people who have been scammed into paying for subscription fees.

Operation Ore was an investigation conducted in 1999 that was intended to arrest users of Web sites that offered child pornography. The operation resulted from computers seized by U.S. federal agents, who took computers from Landslide Productions, which provided a payment system that allowed people to sign up and pay for access to affiliated porn sites. Data on the hard disks seized found accounts around the world, resulting in Operation Ore. The United Kingdom operation resulted in thousands of suspects, arrests, and homes being searched. What it didn't take into account was credit card fraud.

Landslide had been targeted by a number of credit card fraud rackets, in which criminal organizations used credit card information to purchase online

Continued

services through Landslide. Web sites in Indonesia, Russia, and Brazil would use lists of stolen card numbers to charge for access to their own sites. Because the amounts were small, they usually went unnoticed by the owners of the card. That is, until the police investigated the use of these cards to access child porn sites and began searching homes, handing out indictments, and arresting people. According to the Guardian (http://money.guardian.co.uk/scamsand-fraud/story/0,,2059878,00.html), 90 percent of those whose cards had been used never noticed the charges or never complained.

Although every year you hear that credit card fraud is an important issue, and you should check any charges on your monthly statement, this case gives a new reason for doing so. In addition to fake charges on your card, you could also become involved in criminal actions taken with the card. At least by calling your credit card company and contesting the charges, you'll have some proof that you weren't involved.

The Role of the Internet in Promoting Child Pornography

When the Internet began to become popular in the mid-1990s, child pornography began to appear on various sites. In these early years, most of the pornography came in the form of photographs or pictures from magazines that were converted into an electronic format using scanners. These were often photographs of children taken by child abusers, or magazines from the Netherlands featuring adolescent girls. Another common source was nudist magazines, showing naked minors playing sports or other activities. In some cases, these scanned images were more than a decade old, but the amateur production of child porn soon increased with newer photos. Once digital cameras become more affordable, higher-quality images began to appear more frequently on Web sites located in countries where child pornography laws were nonexistent or not enforced.

The Internet has created a new marketplace that makes the distribution of child pornography easier. As mentioned in the Save the Children report "Position paper on child pornography and Internet-related sexual exploitation of Children" (www.inhope.org/doc/stc-pp-cp.pdf), "Child pornography on the Internet has expanded dramatically in recent years and appears to have largely overtaken and absorbed previous production and distribution methods of child pornographic material." As with any other kind of pornography, anything a pedophile wants is just a mouse-click away.

By being part of the global village, pedophiles have been able to establish international child pornography rings. The Internet can be used to make connections with others who possess child pornography, allowing them to trade and sell it with one another, and also learn the dos and don'ts to avoid getting caught. Not only is the Internet a resource for porn, it is also an educational tool.

Driven from Back Alleys to the Information Superhighway

The Internet provided a relative safe haven for those seeking child pornography. Previous to the Internet, the availability of child porn was often limited to behind-the-counter purchases at adult bookstores or ordering magazines and films from other countries and receiving them through the mail. In the 1970s, adult bookstores began selling them openly, which incited new laws and police crackdowns, making the availability of these items more difficult to purchase. This lasted until the 1980s, when computers provided a new method of exchanging data. Bulletin Board Systems (BBSs) are programs that can be installed on a computer, allowing other computers to dial in and access e-mail, exchange messages, download files, and perform other functions that became commonplace on the Internet. During the 1980s, those seeking child pornography no longer had to travel to unsafe neighborhoods; they could now download the pornography to a computer.

Because BBSs were privately run, what was allowed on the board depended on the person who owned the computer on which the BBS was installed. Individuals could start their own BBSs, and create private areas that limited access to anything they wanted, ranging from illegal software to child pornography. However, although BBSs did exist that provided access to folders filled with child pornography, many of those who ran these boards discouraged such activities and commonly banned people from their BBS. Another reason they were self-policed was because most of those in law enforcement were computer-illiterate—remember that computers were relatively new at this time. By the time the police took a serious interest in BBSs, many of them were shutting down from lack of use, because most people had discovered the Internet.

Whereas BBSs provided access to a local community of computer users, the Internet provided availability to international sources. In terms of child pornography, it opened up the market. It allowed pedophiles from around the world the chance to communicate with one another and share pictures and video, with a greater degree of anonymity than they'd ever had before.

The ability to download more pornography and save it to a computer also stemmed from advances in connectivity and storage media. The sizes of hard disks on computers increased and their prices dropped during the early 1990s, allowing them to acquire more files in less time. As seen in Table 16.2, a 500KB file would have taken more than 35 minutes to download from a BBS using a 2400-baud modem. When the Internet became popular, Internet service providers (ISPs) required people to have a modem that could connect at 28.8- or 33.6Kbps. This same 500KB file now took less than 3 minutes to download. Today, people commonly have high-speed connections to the Internet, meaning it now takes a few seconds to download this same file. The advances in speed and storage made it possible for higher-quality images and full videos to be distributed over the Internet.

Table 16.2 Differences in Time to Download a 500KB File at Different Speeds

Transfer Speed	Estimated Time
300bps	4 hrs. 44 min. 26 sec.
1200bps	1 hr. 11 min. 6 sec.
2400bps	35 min. 33 sec.
9600bps	8 min. 53 sec.
14.4Kbps	5 min. 55 sec.
28.8Kbps	2 min. 57 sec.
33.6Kbps	2 min. 32 sec.
57.6Kbps	1 min. 13 sec.
128Kbps (ISDN)	32 sec.
256Kbps	16 sec.
512Kbps	8 sec.
728Kbps	5.33 sec.
1.544Mbps (T1/DS1)	2.65 sec.
2.048Mbps	2 sec.
10Mbps (10Base-T)	0.41 sec.
44.736Mbps (T3/DS3)	0.09 sec.
100Mbps (Fast Ethernet)	0.04 sec.

As we'll see in the next section, the Internet provided a number of features and areas where child porn could easily be obtained. In many cases, the pornography could be acquired at no additional cost, making it significantly cheaper than previous methods. Consider that in the 1970s, kiddie porn would have to be ordered through the mail. The postal service was the main distribution source for child pornography at that time. Whenever it was identified, the package would be delivered to the person, meaning he or she would have to sign for it. Postal inspectors and police would execute a search warrant and arrest the person who signed. Using information associated with the order, the evidence in a single case could include the order form, check or money order to pay for the porn, the signature provided by the person who accepted the order, and the porn itself. The paper trail was easy to follow, making the risks associated with manufacturing and possessing child pornography extreme. The risks were less so with the Internet, and because the costs of those risks weren't passed on to the consumer, it was cheap to pay for the porn when required to do so.

Tools of the Trade

A number of tools and services are used to acquire child pornography. Basically, any Internet tool that has the capability of sending and receiving a file can be used to exchange images, video, and other files containing pornographic images. If these tools also have the capability to communicate with other people, online predators may use it to meet children online.

E-mail

Because e-mail allows you to attach files to a message, any images, video, audio, or other files can be sent with a message. E-mail is used to distribute child pornography in small quantities, attaching one or a few files to any message. A person may send child pornography to others who have an interest, or a pedophile may send messages to a child with these images attached to seduce or groom the child into having sex or sending back pictures of him or herself. Because a message can be associated with the image, the predator can tell the child that this is what he'd like to do, and possibly pique the child's interest or desensitize him or her and loosen any inhibitions.

Mailing Lists

Mailing lists are lists of e-mail addresses that are subscribed to, allowing you to join a group that shares a common interest or need to exchange information with one another. By sending an e-mail to the group's e-mail address, everyone in the group receives it. Numerous mailing lists are available on the Internet, and you subscribe to them by sending an e-mail to either an automated program or a moderator. The moderator's purpose is to ensure that any rules pertaining to the group are observed, and also facilitates adding new members to the list. Because mailing lists may consist of any type of group with a shared interest, it follows suit that there are those available for sharing child pornography, or information on how to obtain it (i.e., lists of sites, etc.).

E-Groups

An e-group is a service that allows users to send e-mails to members, post messages, share pictures, chat with other members, and access other features. One popular site for e-groups is Yahoo! Groups (groups.yahoo.com). By searching such sites, you can find groups dealing with everything you can imagine, and a number of things you can't. Once you find a site, you sub-

scribe to it much like a message list. Certain people can even have different access than others, controlling whether certain trusted users have access to specific photos or other items that the rest of the group can't see.

Newsgroups

Newsgroups or discussion groups are used to exchange messages and files through Usenet, which was established in 1980 and continues as one of the oldest computer networks. These groups allow people to post publicly accessible messages, which are distributed across news servers over the Internet. Each group may contain thousands of messages from people, and there are tens of thousands of newsgroups that you can view or subscribe to. Newsgroups are accessed using a newsreader or features in e-mail programs such as Outlook Express, which connect to the news server to download groups and their messages.

There are newsgroups that address specific interests and topics, which may or may not be monitored by a moderator. By accessing a group, you can post text or binary files, including images, video, audio, software, and other files. This makes it one of the largest possible sources of pornography on the Internet, with specific groups geared toward child porn. As seen in Figure 16.2, some of the newsreaders allow you to filter the listing of groups (which in this case exceeded 60,000) so that you can find ones with specific subject matter. The names of these groups reflect their content, with some of them providing free downloads of pornographic images and video featuring adolescents and prepubescent children.

Figure 16.2 Listing of Available Newsgroups Using Forte Agent Newsreader

TEST DAY TIP

Remember the different methods used to distribute and acquire pornography over the Internet. Although newsgroups are often over-looked or unknown to many users of the Internet, they are also the largest resource for pornographic images on the Internet.

Peer-to-Peer

Peer-to-peer (P2P) applications are used to network different computers together over the Internet so that they can share files on one another's hard drives. Examples of P2P networks include KaZaA, Morpheus, FreeNet, and Gnutella. Users access the distributed network of computers using P2P software, which allows them to share files and have a shared directory on their hard drive searched. As seen in Figure 16.3, tools such as LimeWire can then be used to search the computers making up the network for specific types of files or files that match a certain criterion.

Figure 16.3 LimeWire

When you've heard of file sharing, you've probably heard it in the context of people sharing copies of music files with one another, as in the case of Napster. However, more than simply music is available on these networks. Using them, you can download literature, programs, video, images, and other items. However, although the music industry has made an issue of file sharing, a more important issue of P2P is that it is also used to exchange child pornography. In fact, on the Internet Pornography Statistics Web page at Top Ten Reviews (http://internet-filter-review.toptenreviews.com/internet-pornography-statistics.html), it is shown that in 2006 there were 116,000 Gnutella requests daily for child pornography.

Web Sites

As we've discussed throughout this chapter, Web sites are a popular method of providing access to child pornography. A Web site's Web pages may consist of text, pictures, audio, video, or other content that Internet users can access using Web browsers such as Internet Explorer, Opera, Safari, and Firefox. These browsers access the site and their pages using a unique address, called a Uniform Resource Locator (URL). As mentioned, many of the sites providing access to child pornography may also charge a fee. The owners of these sites may create their own porn to sell online, or collect it from other sources on the Internet.

A new twist to being able to find such sites are the image search features in search engines. Search engines are used to find specific sites based on keywords or phrases that you enter. Sites such as Google also have features to look for images that are on sites, allowing you to find ones that have specific names or content. For example, by going to http://images.google.ca, you could type in "child porn" and preview images from sites around the world. By clicking on one of these images, you are then taken to the site. Not only is this useful to pedophiles interested in child pornography, but it can also be a useful tool for investigators trying to find these sites.

Chat Rooms and Instant Messaging

Chat rooms are Web sites or programs that allow you to send text messages to one another in real time. The chat room works as a virtual room, where groups of people send messages that can be read instantaneously by others. Often, the chat rooms will use aliases or nicknames to provide some anonymity, and are used to meet others. If individual visitors to the chat room wish to talk privately, they can enter a private chat room, which allows two or more people to send messages privately to one another. Some examples of chat rooms are Internet Relay Chat (IRC) and Web sites such as Talk City (www.talkcity.com).

Among other groups, chat rooms appeal to adolescents and teenagers, who communicate with others and use features to send files to one another online. Because of this, online predators will use chat rooms to meet young people and attempt to engage in sex chat, where individuals in a private chat room will tell one another what they would like to do sexually to one another. Basically, sex chat is the textual equivalent of a dirty phone call. In addition to this, features in chat programs allow pictures to be sent to one another, enabling pedophiles to exchange child pornography with one another, or groom potential victims with pictures.

Instant Messaging (IM) is similar to the function of a private chat room. It is a service that allows two or more clients to send messages to one another in real time using IM software. Generally, each of these IM clients ties into a service that transfers messages between other users with the same client software. However, programs such as Trillian allow users to consolidate their accounts on different IM networks and connect to AIM, Yahoo Messenger, Windows Live Messenger, ICQ (I Seek You), and Internet Relay Chat, all within a single interface. In recent years, such features have also been folded into other IM software, such as Windows Live Messenger supporting messages exchanged with Yahoo! Messenger clients.

Because so many young people enjoy chat rooms and instant messaging, these features are also being incorporated into other tools. For example, a game used on an Xbox or PlayStation may provides features so that you can chat with people you're playing against online. Although this can be fun for those with a real interest in the game, it can also be used by pedophiles to connect with children and adolescents who are trying to connect with young people in new ways.

Investigating Child Pornography Cases

When investigating an incident involving child pornography, the tasks you perform will often involve the role you play in the investigation. If you are the person who identified the presence of child pornography on a machine, your role may be as a complainant who simply informs authorities. For example, if you were repairing a computer and noticed there were pornographic files depicting children on the hard drive, you would call police and wait for them to arrive and take over the investigation. If, however, you were involved in other ways in the investigation, you would need to follow the procedures outlined in Chapter 4 of this book for performing a computer forensic investigation.

Regardless of your role, it is important that every step taken should be documented. This may be used as evidence, and can be used to assist you in preparing a statement of what you saw, heard, and did. This can help to ensure the validity of the evidence, and establish that nothing was done to alter the data on the computer.

In Chapter 3, we discussed in detail the methods and guidelines for performing a computer forensic investigation. In this chapter, we discussed how it is important to preserve the crime scene, and thereby preserve any evidence. Because of the type of evidence involved in a child pornography investigation, it is important that you don't show the material to anyone, except authorized personnel and (of course) the authorities. Even as a member of the investigation, you should limit access to viewing the material, as it may compromise the investigation, your credibility, and the credibility of those you showed it to. The investigation should be kept as confidential as possible, with information about it restricted on a need-to-know basis.

You also shouldn't open any files on the computer, or make copies of them. This can alter the timestamp of when the file was last accessed. Not only can this destroy evidence regarding when the suspect last viewed the data, but it also can compromise your credibility and bring into question why you were viewing these files. To view the files, you should first make an

image of the hard drive using forensic software so that the data can be analyzed properly without fear of altering it in any way.

Different Sources of Digital Evidence

In performing a computer forensic analysis of a machine, a number of sources for digital evidence that apply to pictures, video, and other files may contain child pornography. In addition to this, certain tools should also be checked for evidence or leads to other sources. Previously in this chapter we looked at the tools and services that may be used to acquire child pornography. Because they're used, it follows suit that they can also serve as sources of evidence.

E-mail can be a useful source of evidence for several reasons. The e-mail may provide information on children that a pedophile communicated with, may provide information on others who are involved in possessing or distributing kiddie porn, or may have file attachments that contain child pornography. It may also provide information on mailing lists that the person subscribed to, allowing a simple investigation to reveal a ring of people involved in exchanging illegal material.

Searching for log files is also an important step when examining a computer. Many tools such as chat and instant messaging applications provide features to log what occurs in an online conversation. If a chat has been logged, you can read line by line what the conversation entailed.

Information from Web browsers can also provide a wealth of information on what a suspect did. History information in the Web browser will show which sites a person visited and when. This can be used to identify different sites where child pornography was acquired, and matching image files stored on the person's hard drive to those on a site can show where a particular image was acquired. However, checking the history of URLs visited is often enough to confirm whether sites were visited, and copies of Web pages and their content may still be available in the Temporary Internet Files directory on the machine.

If you are part of an Incident Response Team, you should limit following up on evidence you've found. For example, you may have checked the firewall logs and found that a particular employee was visiting sites or newsgroups with names that indicate child pornography. Unless you are law enforcement, you should avoid visiting these sites. Doing so could put you in danger of prosecution as well as cause you embarrassment, so visit the sites only as a last resort.

When analyzing computers containing child pornography, it's not uncommon in a single case to go through thousands of images stored in directories on hard disks. These images may be a mixture of legal adult pornography in addition to videos, photographs, drawings, and other media of child pornography. These files may be stored on hard disks, floppy disks, CDs, DVDs, USB Flash Drives, and other media. In many cases, the numbers of pornographic images can grow in proportion to the available storage space.

In reviewing a system, you will often find that the images are clustered in certain areas of the disk. People who collect child pornography can be meticulous with their pictures and videos, and organize them on the hard disk. You may find that a case you're working on has the

files catalogued under different directories, with titles that reflect their content. For example, you may find a directory named Child Erotica, or the person may use a simple code to identify the folder's contents, such as naming the directory "Y" for "Young."

Even when the suspect uses a home computer, it's worth checking for the existence of backups. Many computer hobbyists, having been the victims of system failure in the past and having lost valuable data because of it, regularly back up their important files. Child pornographers often are emotionally attached to their kiddie porn collections and might have made extra copies in case of a disk failure. If a tape drive is attached to the system, there's a good chance it's used for backups. If a CD or DVD writer is installed, the suspect might have used it for archiving. As such, you should request that the search warrant specify seizure of any tapes, disks, CD-ROMs, or other media commonly used to back up files, in addition to the computer equipment itself. Backups have saved the day in many cases when no evidence could be found on the computer's hard disk.

Laws Related to Child Pornography

When investigating child pornography cases, the content may be incredibly disturbing. During the course of a person's career in computer forensics or working with cases involving child pornography, hundreds of hours can be spent looking at hundreds of thousands of images. Although certain tasks in acquiring data can be automated to limit the amount of material you'll need to sift through, ultimately the human eye must evaluate the images to determine whether they're illegal. Of course, what's legal will depend on where the investigation takes place.

A number of sources on the Internet provide information on legislation dealing with child pornography around the world. One such site is Interpol's sexual offences Web site, at www.interpol.int/Public/Children/SexualAbuse/NationalLaws/, which provides up-to-date information on the child pornography laws of countries that are members of Interpol. Additional information may also be acquired by contacting the consulate of the country in question.

U.S. Laws

In the United States, it is a federal crime (18 USC 2251 and 2252) to advertise or knowingly receive child pornography. The Child Pornography Prevention Act (CPPA) of 1996 expanded the definition of child pornography to any visual depiction of sexually explicit conduct in which the production involved the use of a minor engaging in sexually explicit behavior, even if the visual depiction only appears to be of a minor engaging in such conduct or is advertised or presented to convey the impression that it is of a minor engaging in such conduct. The Free Speech Coalition sued to have the law struck down as unconstitutional, and a federal appellate court did strike down the statute. In October 2001, the Supreme Court heard arguments in the case Ashcroft v. The Free Speech Coalition on the constitutionality of the CPPA. In April 2002, the Supreme Court ruled that the provisions of U.S.C. 2256 that prohibit "virtual child pornography" (computer-generated images of children engaging in sexual conduct) are overly broad and unconstitutional.

In 1998, the Protection of Children from Sexual Predators Act (Sexual Predators Act) was also enacted, and made it illegal for an ISP to knowingly allow child pornography to exist on Web sites. The ISP is required to notify law enforcement upon learning that a Web site hosted on its server contains child pornography. Once the ISP has cooperated with police or other law enforcement agency in the investigation, it must remove the site or pornography from the server as soon as instructed to do so.

Australia Laws

In Australia, laws dealing with child pornography are mainly handled at the state level. Australian law defines child pornography as involving a subject who appears to be under the age of 16. By qualifying child pornography in this way, law enforcement is relieved of the burden of proving the exact age of a subject during the time when the pornography was produced. If the person looks to be underage, the material is considered kiddie porn.

The states of Victoria and Queensland use the Classification of Films and Publications Act as a source of legislation to deal with child pornography. Under this Act, procuring a child to be part of an "objectionable film" (such as that involving sexual penetration) could result in up to five years' imprisonment. Possession of child pornography could result in up to a year in prison. Each state has additional laws to deal with this crime.

Australia's legal system also has provisions that a citizen can be punished even if the crime occurred in a foreign country. The Child Sex Tourism Act also makes it illegal for Australian citizens to have sex with children overseas, and provides a maximum sentence of 17 years' imprisonment.

NOTE

For more information on computer crimes laws in Australia, see the Web site of Baker & McKenzie at www.bmck.com/Australia/australia_crime.htm.

Austria Laws

Austria is one of the countries that have no set age for legal consent for sexual activity, although it does consider a minor to be anyone under the age of 18. The Penal Code specifies that in terms of child pornography, a minor is anyone under 14 years of age. According to the Austrian Penal Code § 207a StGB, child pornography is defined by sexual intercourse with a minor, or by focusing on the genitals of minors. It doesn't consider photos of naked children (such as those on nudist beaches) to be illegal, nor texts that describe sex with children. Other media, such as comics, paintings, or drawings, are a gray area of the law.

Under the Austrian Penal Code, anyone who produces or distributes child pornography can be sentenced to up to three years' imprisonment. If you possess child pornography in which the child is under 14 years of age, you can be sentenced for up to two years' imprisonment. If, however, you produce or possess pornography in which the child is over 14, and you have his or her consent and/or don't distribute it, there is no punishment. Otherwise, possessing an image of a minor who is over 14 can result in up to one year in prison.

Under Austrian law, any citizen can be punished even if the crime did not take place in Austria. If the person produced, distributed, or possessed child pornography in a foreign country, he or she could still be punished under Austrian law, even if it isn't punishable in the country in which the violation took place.

Austria also requires that ISPs report any suspected child pornography. Any found on the ISP servers must be reported to law enforcement immediately.

Belgium Laws

Although other pornography is legal in Belgium, child pornography is considered to be material that shows positions or sexual acts that are pornographic in nature, involving or presenting minors. Under Article 383bis of the Penal Code, it is illegal to produce, distribute, or possess "emblems, objects, films, photos, slides or other visual media" of anyone under the age of 18. This was increased from the age of 16 in 2000.

In looking at this wording, you may find it strange that emblems or symbols are included in the law. However, symbolic images can include comics and virtual pornography. This means that any images created using tools to insert a child or morph the image is considered child porn. In addition to this, the visual media described in the law provide exemptions where certain images of naked children aren't considered illegal. Images of a child where the genitals aren't visible in detail, or images created for teaching, artistic, or scientific purposes, aren't viewed as child porn.

Possessing child pornography can result in up to a year's imprisonment and a fine of 100–1,000 francs, and distributing it can result in up to two years' imprisonment and a 100–1,000-franc fine. In 2005, Belgium expanded its laws regarding child pornography, and made it illegal to recruit, transport, and/or shelter people for purposes of prostitution and/or child pornography. It also requires that ISPs report any suspected child pornography. Any found on the ISP servers must be reported to law enforcement immediately.

Belgian law also allows a citizen to be punished for child pornography crimes committed in foreign countries. Even if the foreign country doesn't have laws making child pornography illegal, a citizen or resident of Belgium could still be charged upon returning home. It also provides that anyone convicted of sexually abusing children can't receive parole without first undergoing treatment and counseling, which they must continue after being released from prison.

NOTE

> Only six countries have legislation that requires ISPs to report suspected child pornography to law enforcement. They are Australia, Belgium, Colombia, France, South Africa, and the United States. Other countries rely on self-regulation or voluntary action to report sites containing child pornography.

Cyprus Laws

Cyprus defines a child in terms of child pornography as anyone under the age of 18. The age is the result of an agreement between European countries at the 2001 Budapest Convention on Cybercrime, which set that any minor under the age of 18 depicted in sexually explicit acts is banned as child pornography. Although the agreement sets the age at 18, it also gives countries the right to set a lower age limit, as long as it isn't under 16.

Under the Convention on Cybercrime, it is illegal to produce, distribute, transmit, procure, offer, or make child pornography available through a computer system. The other law dealing with child pornography is the Combating Trafficking in Human Beings and Sexual Abuse of Minors Law, which also addresses the sexual exploitation of children. This law prohibits anyone who trades children or creates, possesses, carries, imports, or exports child pornography. Under this law, these actions are punishable by up to 10 years' imprisonment.

Japan Laws

Under Japanese law, the age of sexual consent is 13, although a minor in terms of child pornography is anyone under the age of 18. It is illegal to produce, distribute, transport, import, or export child pornography, and any cases involving the Internet are punished under existing laws dealing with this material. Once convicted, an offender could face imprisonment of up to three years and a fine of more than 3 million yen.

The amount of child pornography originating or being distributed from Japan has decreased in recent years, although Japan at one point had the highest number of child pornography sites in the world. A study conducted by the University of Cork in Ireland found that between June and November 1997, 73 percent of the sites providing child pornography and sexualized images of children originated in Japan. The next highest was the United States at 14 percent, with most of the images from these countries' Web sites consisting of pictures of boys. A year later, Interpol estimated that 80 percent of sites with child pornography originated in Japan, and the National Police Agency also stated that in 2002, 40 percent of Japan's 3,000 pornographic Web sites contained images of children (www.japantoday.com/news/jp/e/tools/print.asp?content=news&id=245192). When laws in Japan were implemented making child pornography illegal, the number of sites decreased dramatically.

Challenges in Controlling Child Pornography

Cybercrime cases often have more challenges that other, more traditional types of crime. To effectively combat computer-related crimes, those directly involved in investigating these crimes need specialized training and equipment, which (as with anything dealing with computers) needs to be upgraded every few years, at least. This can be difficult for many police organizations, as the budgets for implementing specialized units can be quite limited. This can limit the ability to investigate computer crimes at its most basic level.

In many cases, the source of a crime might originate in one country where legislation differs from that of your own country or where the act is not a crime at all. For example, although child pornography might be defined as pornographic images of persons under 18 years of age in North America, the legal age to pose for such images in other countries might be considerably younger. This difference can cause a dilemma for law enforcement officers, because it is legal for a Web site in one country to distribute the images but illegal for people in other countries to download them. Investigators can arrest people in possession of the pornographic files, but they might be powerless to shut down the Web site distributing the pornography.

In Cyprus, police face the obstacle of conflicting laws. As with most European countries, the Cypriot government signed the Budapest Convention on Cybercrime in 2001, and agreed to take action against such crimes as child pornography. However, there are existing laws that protect privacy, and state that communication services are prohibited from disclosing personal information. Under Chapter 17 of the Cyprus Constitution, a person's right to privacy can't be infringed upon by listening in on private telephone conversations, which means that any data transmitted over the phone line (such as child pornography) also can't be used as evidence. Unless the material is found on the hard disk of a computer or other media, Cypriot authorities can't investigate incidences in which a person is downloading or distributing child porn.

Not all countries view a child in the same way, such as Norway, which considers that child pornography is sexually explicit material with a child under the age of 16, but if the child's sexual maturity is obviously at its peak, under paragraph 204 of the Penal Code, he or she isn't considered a minor in terms of child pornography. Whether a child has reached a certain level of sexual maturity is determined on a case-by-case basis by the court. This doesn't mean that a

person can't be punished in such situations, as charges against someone producing child pornography could still be laid under other laws dealing with assault or exploitation.

The ability to perform investigations that go outside of jurisdictional boundaries almost always relies on cooperation with law enforcement entities in those areas. Police in one country generally have no official jurisdiction in other countries. However, when police in different countries work together, the impact on crime can be significant. This impact is seen in a number of collaborative efforts between police and other law enforcement agencies in various countries.

A major achievement in international policing was seen in the British-led Operation Cathedral, which focused on the pedophile network called Wonderland that provided kiddie porn to its members over the Internet. To become a member of Wonderland and participate in the exchange of child porn, a person had to show that he or she possessed at least 10,000 images depicting child pornography. In September 1998, 100 raids in Britain, Australia, Austria, Belgium, Finland, France, Germany, Italy, Norway, Portugal, Sweden, and the United States were carried out. The cooperation of police in all these countries resulted in effectively shutting down this massive cybercrime operation.

Joint Operations and International Cooperation

Law enforcement groups in various countries are also working together to attack the threat of Internet-related criminal activity. Because such activities can cross international jurisdictions, such cooperation is vital to combating cybercrime. In December 2000, a joint effort between Russia's Moscow City Police and the United States Customs CyberSmuggling Center resulted in the shutdown of Blue Orchid, a Russian Web site that featured images and videos of children being physically and sexually abused. As a result of this and other operations, many hundreds of videocassettes and DVDs and more than 1,000 pornographic pictures were seized. Arrests in both countries resulted from the operations.

Even corporations can assist in combating international computer crimes, as seen in the case that culminated in nearly 1,500 arrests in 2000. Italian police sought the assistance of Microsoft to create a fake pedophile Web site called amantideibambini ("Lovers of Children"). This site specifically stated that the content was illegal, but despite the warnings, 1,032 people subscribed to the site. Italian police raided 600 residences, arrested 831 Italians, and attempted to extradite another 660 from various other countries.

As nations cooperate with one another in various endeavors, a global vision of what is considered right and wrong has been established on a variety of subjects. Because numerous countries don't have laws or adequate legislation dealing with child pornography, cyber terrorism, and other activities related to cybercrime, international consortiums saw a need to provide a legal framework for updating the laws of these countries. International organizations and political coalitions have influenced legal changes in many countries, pressuring some countries to create new laws or revise existing ones to deal with crimes that the majority of the world considers abhorrent or potentially devastating.

With the intervention of the United Nations (U.N.) and the International Labor Organization (ILO), many countries that previously didn't have laws dealing with child pornography have changed existing legislation or created new laws criminalizing this offense. In doing so, they have made it illegal to distribute or obtain child pornography through such sources as the Internet, allowing law enforcement to shut down pedophile Web sites, arrest owners of these sites, and arrest Internet users acquiring such digital images and movies. For example, in the summer of 2002, Europol (the European Union's police agency) reported that European police conducted child porn raids as part of Operation Twins in seven countries, seizing equipment and arresting suspects in Belgium, Britain, Germany, Italy, the Netherlands, Spain, and Sweden. Twelve countries were involved in the operation, including the United States and Canada.

The U.N. Convention on the Rights of the Child (CRC), which includes an Optional Protocol on child prostitution and child pornography, has been ratified by almost 200 countries, and more than 100 of them have signed the Protocol. (For more information, see www.unicef.org/crc/crc.htm.) The ILO has been fighting child pornography since the 1930s and, at the International Labor Conference of 1997, extended its pressure on member nations to pass strong laws against child pornography "whatever the technical method used," thus ensuring that such activities using the Internet (or other, future technologies) would be addressed. In 1999, the European Parliament and the Council of the European Union adopted a multiannual action plan devoted to promoting safer use of the Internet by combating illegal and harmful content on global networks. The plan, managed by the European Commission (EC), ran through December 2002 and provided 25 million euro in funding.

The impact of such agreements between countries has significantly changed laws around the world. For example, child pornography laws are a recent addition to Mexico's legal framework. In January 1999, the Mexican Congress amended the country's criminal code to categorize child pornography and child prostitution as "grievous crimes." Before this time, no law dealt with such activity.

Anti-Child Pornography Initiatives and Organizations

Because a simple cybercrime case can quickly expand to involve law enforcement in other areas, there is a need for initiatives and organizations to assist in coordinating and assisting in these investigations. A number of organizations on the Internet provide information on child pornography and child exploitation, as well as online reporting of Web sites distributing this material. With the number of local, regional, state, national, and international investigations that occur, there is also a need to train those who may be involved in investigations, as well as provide educational materials that will train children on how to avoid online predators. In the sections that follow, we'll look at a few of these initiatives and organizations, including:

- Innocent Images National Initiative
- Internet Crimes Against Children
- Project Safe Childhood
- Anti-Child Porn.org

EXAM WARNING

Before taking the CHFI exam, make sure you understand the missions of the organizations discussed in this section, and what their purpose and functions are in terms of child pornography and exploitation.

Innocent Images National Initiative

The FBI developed the Innocent Images National Initiative (IINI) as part of its Cyber Crimes Program for the purpose of identifying, investigating, and prosecuting those who use computers for child sexual exploitation and child pornography. In performing these tasks, they also attempt to identify and rescue children being exploited or who appear in these images.

Originally, the IINI provided one of the few online presences of law enforcement, although this is no longer the case due to the volume of police and other agencies that pose undercover in chat rooms and other forums, attempt to identify online predators, or are involved in cybercrime investigations. Because of the involvement of local, state, and international law enforcement in these endeavors, the IINI provides training and assistance, as well as coordinating national or international investigations.

Over the years, the IINI has expanded its mission to include sexual tourism, in which American citizens or residents travel for the purpose of having sex with minors. Several federal statutes in the United States deal with sex tourism and trafficking (18 U.S.C. §§ 1591, 2421, 2422, and 2423), which make interstate and international sex tourism and sex trafficking within a state illegal. Although their focus now includes these types of illegal activities, this hasn't deterred the IINI from attempting to identify, investigate, and prosecute those who produce, distribute, or possess child pornography.

Additional information on the Innocent Images National Initiative is available on the FBI's Web site, at www.fbi.gov/publications/innocent.htm. By visiting this Web page, you can view the latest statistics on the IINI, and view information on individuals they've added to the FBI's Ten Most Wanted Fugitives.

Internet Crimes Against Children

The Internet Crimes Against Children (ICAC) program is a network of 46 regional task forces that are funded by the U.S. Department of Justice. It was created to provide federal assistance to state and local law enforcement so that they could better investigate computer- and Internet-based crimes that sexually exploit children.

The program is funded through the U.S. Office of Juvenile Justice and Delinquency Prevention, and provides a variety of different resources that are useful to organizations and law enforcement dealing with crimes against children, including the following:

- The Training and Technical Assistance program provided by ICAC (www.icac-training.org) provides information and resources for training ICAC initiatives, as well as contact information for technical support. This trains law enforcement on how to perform undercover chats, investigative techniques, and a variety of other topics and technologies. They also provide presentation material to teach students ranging from kindergarten to high school, parents, and other interested parties.

- The ICAC Research Center (www.unh.edu/ccrc/) provides up-to-date statistics, publications, and other resources on sexual abuse, exploitation, and other crimes and issues dealing with children.

- The e-mail distribution list provided by ICAC allows individuals affiliated with ICAC to communicate with one another and share information.

- Conferences are available to facilitate networking and additional training.

Project Safe Childhood

Project Safe Childhood (PSC) is an initiative developed by the U.S. Department of Justice to provide a coordinated effort in combating child pornography and sexual exploitation. It is designed to help local communities create programs and develop strategies to investigate child exploitation, and identify and rescue victims. PSC is based on Project Safe Neighborhoods, and focuses on providing a framework to better investigate and prosecute crimes that involve and target children through the Internet and other methods of communication and media. It involves U.S. attorneys partnering with ICAC task forces, nonprofit organizations, and federal, state and local law enforcement to develop strategies to combat these issues and assist child victims.

By coordinating efforts, local law enforcement is better able to access services provided at a federal level. PSC works in conjunction with the Innocent Images National Initiative so that PSC task forces can pursue local leads. Once an arrest is made, the involvement of federal agencies can then charge the person under federal law, which generally involves harsher penalties than laws at the state level.

Part of the PSC initiative involves developing programs to provide training and education, and promote awareness. This includes educating not only communities, but also law enforcement. Training programs are provided through a variety of programs, including ICAC and the

National Center for Missing and Exploited Children (www.missingkids.com), who provide information about missing children on their Web site, online resources, and a CyberTipline to report child pornography and sexual exploitation.

The PSC Web site at www.projectsafechildhood.gov provides information on legislation that is used to prosecute offenders, as well as online resources such as publications, links to related Web sites, and information on training and technical assistance.

Anti-Child Porn.org

Anti-Child Porn.org (ACPO) is a volunteer organization that has members worldwide, focusing on issues related to child exploitation, online predators, and child pornography. Its Web site, at www.antichildporn.org, provides information for law enforcement, parents, and other interested parties, including brochures, multimedia presentations, survivor stories, and other resources. As we'll see in the next section, it also provides software such as Reveal, which can be downloaded and used to evaluate files on a computer for objectionable or illegal material.

The ACPO Web site also provides an online reporting feature, in which you can report Web sites and FTP sites that contain child pornography. As seen in Figure 16.4, entering information on this site consists of entering the URL and any additional information you can provide. You can enter four Web sites and four FTP sites at a time on the Reporting Web page. No information about yourself is required, making it completely anonymous.

Figure 16.4 Anti-Child Porn.org Child Pornography Reporting

Anti-Child Pornography Tools

As we saw in Chapter 4, many different tools are used to analyze computers that may contain child pornography. However, all of these tools will only tell you whether there is information on the computer after the fact, rather than preventing it from getting there in the first place. If a parent wanted to keep a child from accessing such data to begin with, or employers wanted to prevent employees from downloading child porn or accessing questionable sites, they would need other types of software.

Censorware is a term applied to tools that will filter or block certain content from being accessed over the Internet. For example, if you entered the term "child porn" into a search engine or visited a site containing child pornography, the software would block that site from being displayed. In addition to this, the software may prevent e-mails containing certain words from being sent or received, prohibit accessing certain newsgroups, and limit access to programs that allow access to Internet data. By censoring what data is accessible, the possibility of downloading porn, sexually harassing fellow employees, or meeting people online for possible sex is removed.

Because forensic analysis is overkill for most parents and employers who want to see what has been downloaded or accessed over the Internet, tools are available for scanning a computer and revealing its contents. This will allow you to view a person's browsing behavior, objectionable e-mails or communications, and other content on the computer. Such tools should never be used as forensic software, however, as they can alter the data on a machine. Although this is an important issue for a forensic examiner or investigator, this may not be a priority for parents and employers who simply want to see how a computer is being used.

Finally, in the sections that follow, we'll look at how anti-child pornography tools can assist in investigations, and identify offenders and victims involved in child pornography or other exploitive acts. By linking different cases together, police have a better chance of investigating cybercrimes and rescuing victims.

TEST DAY TIP

Although many different tools are available to filter content, block sites, and display what actions a person has taken on a computer, you are not expected to know all of them for the test. The ones discussed in the sections that follow should be understood before test day, as questions regarding them may appear on the test.

Reveal

Reveal is an application developed by Protect Your Family (www.protectyourfamily.net), and is used to identify objectionable material on hard disks and other storage media. It is not forensic software, but is designed for parents and other concerned parties to scan files on a computer containing certain keywords, compile a list of multimedia files, and generate thumbnails of any images on the storage media. By viewing the report created at the end, you can determine whether there are any files that are illegal or offensive.

As seen in Figure 16.5, Reveal allows you to select which dictionaries to search with. The dictionaries are lists of words that the program will try to find in files. Several different dictionaries are available that contain words used by certain groups or related to specific topics. These include:

- Pornography
- Violence/hate
- Drugs
- Cults
- Occult

In addition to this, you can add different words to search for. For example, if you were concerned that your child was talking to or about a certain person, you could type the name in the field under Customize Dictionary, and then click the Add Word button (see Figure 16.5).

Figure 16.5 Reveal

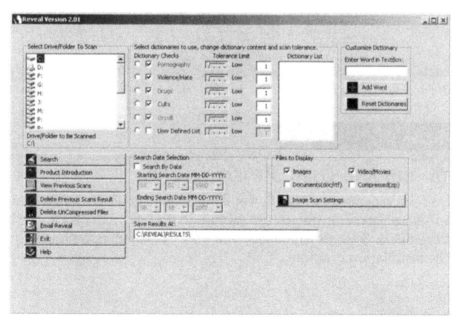

As seen in Figure 16.6, once a scan is complete, a detailed report is provided, allowing you to view thumbnails of images found in the search, a summary of suspect files, multimedia files, and other information. Because the report is an HTML document, any of these files can be opened and reviewed by simply clicking on the link for a particular file. Because the results of scans are stored in the directory you specify in the Save Results At field, you can view previous results at any time by clicking the View Previous Scans button.

Figure 16.6 Reveal Results

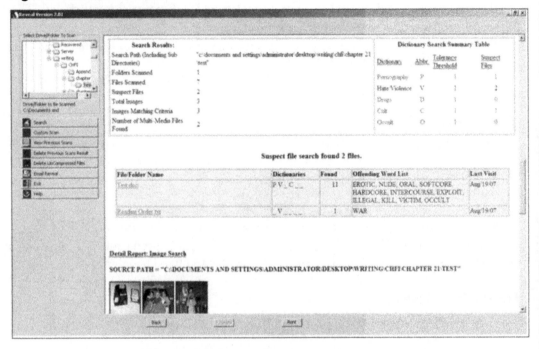

Now that we've looked at some of the features of Reveal and what it can do, let's go through the steps of using the software to scan a hard disk and what's on your own computer.

EXERCISE 16.1

INSTALLING AND USING REVEAL

Visit www.protectyourfamily.net, and download a copy of the Reveal software. Reveal is free to use (although donations are accepted by the developer). Once downloaded, open the ZIP compressed folder, and run the installation program.

1. When the Welcome screen appears, click Next.

2. When the Select Destination Directory screen appears, accept the default installation folder, and click Next.

3. When the Select Start Menu Folder screen appears, accept the default folder name, and click Next.

4. When the Select Additional Tasks screen appears, check the checkboxes indicating whether you would like to Create a desktop icon and Create a Quick Launch icon. Click Next.

5. Review your installation settings, and then click Install.

6. The installation will then install the program based on your settings. When it has completed, click Finish.

7. From the Windows Start menu, select Programs | Reveal, and then click on the Reveal menu item.

8. When the Reveal program opens, click on the drive you would like to check in the Select Drive\Folder To Scan list.

9. Click the Search button, and wait for the scan to finish.

10. When the scan has finished, a report of results from searching the hard disk will be displayed. Review the results about keywords that have been found in files, thumbnails of images, listings of multimedia files, and other information discovered on the drive.

iProtectYou

iProtectYou is parental control and filtering software that was developed by SoftForYou (www.softforyou.com), and is intended to control what users on a computer are allowed to access over the Internet. Using this tool, you can specify what programs certain users and groups on a computer can and cannot use, block certain communications, and schedule when the Internet can be used.

You can use default settings or specify words or phrases that will determine whether an e-mail, Instant Message, Web site, or other media is blocked. If an inappropriate word is used in the communiqué or Web site, the message is blocked or the Web page will not display. You can also block other sites that you specify or that fall into specific categories, such as pornography, violence, or weapons. Even certain newsgroups can be blocked if they aren't included in the database of child-safe groups.

iProtectYou logs any activity, allowing you to view what sites were visited. You can save content in a directory you specify, or have the program automatically send a screenshot at regular intervals to an e-mail address that you specify. As seen in Figure 16.7, by viewing the Logs and Statistics feature, you can view which sites or other Internet content was blocked, online activity, programs that were used, and the dates and times these events occurred.

Figure 16.7 iProtectYou Logs and Statistics

Child Exploitation Tracking System

The Child Exploitation Tracking System (CETS) is a tool developed for law enforcement to organize, analyze, share, and search information related to child exploitation cases, such as those involving child pornography. Developed as a partnership project between Canadian police services, the NCECC (www.ncecc.ca), and Microsoft, CETS is used to track cases and reveal common factors between them. Using this tool, links between different cases can be identified, even if they're being investigated by law enforcement in different jurisdictions.

The success of CETS was seen even before it was officially unveiled in April 2005. An example of how well it works is a 2004 arrest of a man who sexually assaulted a four-year-old girl, took photographs of the crime, and distributed them on the Internet. The man was identified by CETS linking information in Operation Falcon (a U.S. Department of Homeland Security investigation) to an FBI investigation. This link was discovered while the program was

still in its Beta version, and since then has been used to assist in the arrests of dozens of other people, including the March 2006 arrests of 27 people located in four different countries who ran a private chat room designed to groom children.

CETS works by allowing different police to access a centralized database, which is located at the National Child Exploitation Coordination Centre (NCECC) in Ottawa, Ontario. By entering information into CETS, an investigator can then determine whether aspects of his or her case match with other investigations that involve the same people. It will search for similar e-mail addresses, online identities (i.e., aliases, nicknames, etc.), or other aspects that can match a person to multiple cases. By finding matches between such information, law enforcement is better able to make arrests and identify victims.

Although CETS was initially available to Canadian law enforcement, it is now used in other countries, with additional ones looking to deploy CETS in the future. It is used in the United Kingdom, and in October 2006 it assisted police in identifying and arresting 37 suspects and rescuing five children. Indonesia, Italy, and Brazil also began using CETS in 2006, with 13 other countries planning on deploying it as well.

Investigating Sexual Harassment

Sexual harassment is any repeated, unwanted behavior of a sexual nature. It can occur between individuals who are of different genders or of the same sex, and often occurs when there is an imbalance of power between two people. For example, an employer may seek sexual favors as a condition of employment. However, sexual harassment may also occur in situations where two people are peers, as when a colleague repeatedly makes unwelcome sexual advances. The aspect that makes it sexual harassment in all of these cases is that the conduct is unwelcome, and doesn't stop when asked.

There are different ways in which a person may be sexually harassed, including:

- Verbal, which is the most common form of sexual harassment. Verbal harassment involves a harasser making unwelcome comments or demands. This may include someone telling offensive jokes, discussing subjects that are sexual in nature, name-calling, or commenting on a person's body shape or size. It may also involve a harasser asking someone on a date after being turned down or asking for sexual favors.

- Visual, which can consist of any item, object, or gesture that can be sexual in nature. This may include displaying pornography, leaving sex toys or other paraphernalia on a person's desk, making gestures (such as gyrating hips, mimicking sex acts, etc.), or bringing attention to a person's body parts.

- Written, which can include notes or documents that contain sexual content. This can include notes left on a desk, locker, or other areas to seduce, hurt, or taunt a person. Because of text messaging, instant messaging, chat programs, e-mail, and other electronic methods of communication, a person can be sexually harassed throughout

the day and night, regardless of whether he or she is in the presence of a harasser or the workplace.

■ Physical, which consists of any unwanted touching or invasion of personal space. This may involve a harasser blocking another person's path, pretending to grab or reaching for a person's body part, pinching, caressing, or touching in a sexual manner. Other common examples include unwanted hugging, kissing, or touching, as when a harasser rubs another person's shoulder, arm, or other areas.

These actions can be perpetrated by anyone, and they have serious consequences on everyone involved. As we'll see in the sections that follow, laws and policies can result in a harasser being disciplined or even terminated from their position. In certain cases, the person may even face criminal action, and harassers and employers alike could be involved in civil litigation, requiring them to pay damages for allowing this conduct in a workplace.

Types of Sexual Harassment

Although the details of sexual harassment may vary from one situation to another, the courts have recognized two different types of sexual harassment that may occur in and out of a workplace. These are:

■ **Quid pro quo sexual harassment**, in which a person is offered some kind of benefit in exchange for sexual favors, or is threatened to lose something if he or she doesn't give in.

■ **Hostile environment sexual harassment**, in which the conduct is such that it has created an unpleasant or offensive environment. In this type, sexual harassment is determined on the basis of whether a reasonable person would consider the workplace to be hostile.

Quid pro quo is an easily identifiable form of sexual harassment, because it involves an offer or threat: Have sex with me, and/or this will happen. In this type of harassment, a person may be offered a job, salary increase, promotion, better performance evaluation, or some other benefit in exchange for sexual favors. In other words, you give me something; I'll give you something. Alternatively, a person whose sexual advances have been rejected may punish the victim by terminating the victim's employment, assigning different shift or work assignments, giving a bad performance evaluation, or costing the person some other benefit.

Although this type of sexual harassment is commonly associated with an employer and an employee, it can also occur in other areas of life. For example, a teacher may offer a passing grade, or a consultant may threaten to dissolve the victim's position or cause other problems unless a sexual request is fulfilled. Sexual harassment may also occur if the person turns down a proposition, and then faces retaliation.

Whereas quid pro quo can be sexual harassment on the basis of a single sexual advance, hostile environment sexual harassment generally involves a pattern of behavior. It is the ongoing conduct of an individual or members of an organization, and is established through a series of incidents. For example, in the case of Clark County School District v. Breeden, Shirley Breeden claimed retaliation for reporting sexual harassment. The allegations of harassment stemmed from an October 21, 1994 incident in which she, her male supervisor, and another male coworker were meeting to review the psychological evaluations of job applicants. One of these reports stated that an applicant had once commented to a coworker, "I hear making love to you is like making love to the Grand Canyon." The comment was read aloud by Breeden's supervisor, who said, "I don't know what that means." Breeden's coworker responded by saying, "Well, I'll tell you later," and both men "chuckled." Breeden complained about the men's comments to the employee who made the remark, his supervisor, and another assistant superintendent. She claimed that she was punished for reporting the men, and filing charges against the Clark County School District with the Nevada Equal Rights Commission and the Equal Employment Opportunity Commission (EEOC). She contended that a lateral transfer made by her supervisor before even hearing of the lawsuit was evidence of this retaliation. In a unanimous decision of the U.S. Supreme Court in April 2001, it was decided that a hostile environment refers to a pattern of "severe and pervasive" abuse, and that an offhand remark, simple teasing, or an isolated incident (unless it was extremely serious) didn't constitute as sexual harassment.

As you can see from this, it is the ongoing conduct of employees, employers, or others in an organization that can determine whether sexual harassment exists. A hostile environment can be identified when any of the forms of harassment discussed earlier are perpetrated on a person, and which continue to occur after it has been made clear that the behavior is unwelcome. Even if these actions cease, any subsequent actions that a reasonable person would consider retaliation could still make it a hostile environment. For example, if you complained that people in the office had pornography on their desk, it would still be considered hostile if people in the office started calling you a snitch, or you received a demotion or were laid off for causing trouble. The factors that make a hostile environment can be varied in this regard, and need to be evaluated based on the merits of complaints on a case-by-case basis.

EXAM WARNING

Work environments are considered hostile when the conduct of employees, management, or nonemployees becomes a hindrance to an employee's job performance. A hostile work environment may exist when situations occur involving sexual harassment, discrimination, or other events that offend someone in the workplace. In terms of computers and the Internet, such situations may involve downloading and

viewing pornographic or other offensive materials on company computers. If these materials are accessed through company computers and printed or distributed in the workplace, the company can be sued for creating a hostile work environment.

Consequences of Sexual Harassment

Sexual harassment has a destructive effect on the person being harassed, but can also have a wider impact on the organization as a whole. The influence of events can affect the victim, others in the organization, and the company itself. The consequences of sexual harassment can affect people's work, result in litigation, and cause other problems that should be identified as a serious risk to any organization.

When a person is sexually harassed, it can affect his or her performance at work, and create a work environment that is intimidating, hostile, and/or offensive to function in. Because physical contact may be involved, this can be perceived as a forerunner to other unwanted contact (such as sexual assault), making the person fearful and anxious. The effects of the event(s) can be incredibly stressful, and can impact a person in the following ways:

- Physically, such as experiencing headaches, changes in appetite, decreased energy, sleep disturbances, and/or other stress-related ailments

- Emotionally, such as feeling guilt, anxiety, self-doubt, depression, inability to concentrate, loss of ambition, mood swings, and/or other psychological symptoms

- Socially, such as by withdrawing from others, self-isolation, being dependant on others, and/or difficulty interacting with superiors and coworkers, superiors, and peers

The consequences of the event and its subsequent effects can influence a person's ability to function in his or her job. The victim's interest in performing duties may decrease, and the quality of work may suffer. If working in this environment becomes too much, he or she may eventually quit the job. This could result in a loss of wages, future income, or other benefits.

Sexual harassment can affect more than the intended target. Others in a workplace may be affected by the sexual harassment, even though they weren't the one directly being harassed. For example, if the friend or coworker was being sexually harassed and you were aware of it, you might feel helpless to assist him or her or worried that you'll be the next one treated this way. Because the workplace is hostile, you might even experience the same stress-related symptoms as the person being harassed.

Although sexual harassment is commonly associated with conduct in the workplace, it may also occur in work-like environments, such as schools or universities. In such institutions, the effect on a student may result in decreased grades and academic performance, and may even

result in the person dropping out of school. As in the workplace, the harassment can also have an impact on other students, instructors, departments, or the wider school community. When someone sexually harasses a student or staff member in a school environment, the punishment can be severe, and can result in a reprimand, suspension, expulsion, or (in the case of staff) transfers or dismissal.

The impact of sexual harassment can have a dramatic effect on the organization as a whole. The effect on the victim and coworkers can result in increased absenteeism, reduced productivity, and valuable employees quitting. Low morale may also impact the productivity of entire departments or larger portions of the company. Each of these consequences can cost the company a considerable amount of money. The business may have to pay for sick time, increasing staff or paying another employee to pick up the slack, or delays in projects being completed. If the employee quits, the company will also have to pay to train a new employee. This doesn't even begin to cover the costs of civil litigation, if the company is sued for allowing the sexual harassment to take place.

When a supervisor or person in a position of power uses quid pro quo sexual harassment to acquire something from another person, the organization is generally considered responsible. The abuse of power could result in criminal charges against the person, but the company may be held responsible for sexual discrimination or violations of labor or tort law. This is because supervisors, managers, and other agents of the company are representatives of the company, and act on their behalf. This could mean that the organization may be responsible for compensating the victim for such things as loss of wages, future financial loss, medical expenses (such as counseling or therapy), loss of enjoyment of life, and punitive damages.

When sexual harassment occurs in an organization and it isn't handled responsibility, the effects can also result in a loss of reputation. Because the business is now perceived as not being able to conduct its affairs and handle employees responsibly, customers may no longer wish to do business with them. The future loss of business can be considerable, and can influence the company's practices and feasibility for years to come.

Responsibilities in an Organization

Because of the consequences associated with sexual harassment, it makes sense that it is in the best interests of both the employees and the employer of a company to take responsibility as soon as possible. For an employee, this means that he or she should report the incident and perform other tasks that will benefit the case. For the employer, it can involve implementing policies and procedures that will assist the company in handling the risk of a sexual harassment incident before it actually occurs. In the sections that follow, we'll discuss these and other measures so that each party in a sexual harassment incident is best protected and able the handle the situation.

Responsibilities of Employees

For any conduct to be considered as sexual harassment, the harasser's behavior, comments, and actions must be unwelcome. Any sexual advances or conduct of a sexual nature must be unacceptable, meaning the person making these advances or exhibiting this behavior must be aware of this. This may be indicated by telling the harasser, but may also be indicated by other indications, such as a physical reaction. For example, if a man touched a woman's shoulder and she cringed or brushed the hand off her shoulder, a court may consider this as an indication that the action was unwelcome. To be clear, however, it is generally best to indicate verbally or in writing that the behavior isn't acceptable. Unless the person's actions are so grievous that a reasonable person would know it is unacceptable, the victim must indicate that it is unwanted and/or offensive.

There should be a certain consistency to indicating whether certain language, jokes, actions, or comments are unwelcome. For example, if a person made an off-color joke one day and you laughed, told him the next day that you found such jokes obscene, and then asked later whether the person heard any more dirty jokes, you are sending a mixed message. The same can occur when an employee asks a coworker out and is rejected, and then the coworker begins flirting with the employee who was rebuffed. The lack of consistency doesn't send a clear message as to whether certain behavior is acceptable. Once you've indicated that the conduct is unwelcome, it is important to remain consistent.

When sexual harassment occurs, it is important that records are maintained of the incidents. These may be used later in an investigation or as evidence in court. The documentation should include:

- The date and time of each incident.

- The location of each incident, including stating the address, which floor of the building, or whether it occurred in a particular room or at a specific person's desk.

- The names of those involved. This should include the name(s) of offender(s), and any witnesses that may have been present or nearby and saw or heard what occurred.

- Details of the incident, including what was said or done.

Once you've told someone to stop harassing you, it is important to notify supervisors or other management immediately. Procedures on how to make a complaint of sexual harassment may be included in internal policies, or may simply require informing an employer. If the employer allows the conduct to continue, the company may be found liable and forced to pay damages if you pursue a civil law suit.

Exam Warning

Because sexual advances or other behavior must be unwanted, it is important that a victim informs a harasser that the behavior is unwanted or unacceptable. If the behavior continues, the victim should document the activities and pursue making a complaint of sexual harassment.

Responsibilities of Supervisors and Employers

When a supervisor or employer becomes aware of sexual harassment, it is crucial that he or she take action immediately. If no action is taken to correct the problem, the company can be held liable, because the company implied or explicitly condoned the activities involved in the sexual harassment. If, however, the employer is unaware of the situation, or has made an effort to correct the problem, the company will generally not be held liable for a hostile environment.

It is different when quid pro quo sexual harassment occurs. If a supervisor makes unwelcome sexual advances, requests sexual favors as a basis for employment decisions, or harasses an employee through verbal or physical conduct of a sexual nature, the company is generally liable. This is because the supervisor acts as a representative of the company, and thereby acts on the company's behalf.

Additional problems may occur if the sexual harassment involved computers used by the company, and entailed illegal materials that are accessed, printed, or distributed within the company. For example, as we discussed thoroughly in this chapter, it is illegal to produce, possess, send, or receive child pornography. If someone downloaded such material and showed it to others in the company, not only could this result in sexual harassment, but it would also involve other criminal charges. This means the computer equipment could be subject to seizure and forfeiture because it was used in the commission of the crime.

Employers can take a number of preventive steps to avoid or eliminate sexual harassment in a workplace, including:

- Communicating to employees that certain behavior will not be tolerated
- Establishing a complaint mechanism or grievance process
- Taking appropriate action immediately after a complaint is made

These steps can be outlined in policies and procedures that state the company's position on sexual harassment and provide information on what to do regarding allegations of sexual harassment.

Policies and Procedures

A policy is used to address concerns and identify risks. For example, as we'll see in the sections that follow, a sexual harassment policy may be created to deal with the potential problem of an employee's conduct creating a hostile environment or infringing on the rights of another employee. Through the policy, an issue that is pertinent to the organization is explained and dealt with.

Procedures consist of a series of steps that inform someone how to perform a task and/or deal with a problem. For example, a procedure may be established that outlines what steps are performed when a complaint of sexual harassment is made. It may outline who is to be notified, disciplinary measures, and other tasks that need to be performed to effectively deal with the situation. By following these instructions, the supervisor or other employees can effectively deal with a problem or crisis.

Sexual Harassment Policy

Sexual harassment policies are used to encourage the reporting of such incidents, and outline the procedures to follow when sexual harassment occurs. The policy should begin by defining what sexual harassment is, and provide a summary of what types of actions are considered to be sexual harassment. This will limit any confusion regarding the types of behavior or comments that won't be tolerated by the organization. The policy should state that it can include, but is not limited to:

- Unwanted sexual advances, propositions, or threats. This includes subtle or overt pressure for sexual favors.

- Coerced sexual acts, such as in the case of being a condition of employment.

- Romantic displays or overtures that are persistent and unwanted.

- Repeated comments that may make other employees uncomfortable, such as sexual innuendo, obscene or lewd remarks, slurs or insults, off-color jokes, profanity, or other sexual comments.

- Name-calling, such as using sexually orientated demeaning names.

- Sexually suggestive sounds, such as whistling or cat calls.

- Sexually suggestive gestures, including leering, winking, or sexualized body movements.

- Unwelcome or coerced touching, such as kissing, massaging, squeezing, patting, fondling, or other physical contact that could be considered sexual.

- Correspondence or other written communication (including e-mail, notes, faxes, text messages, etc.) that are of a sexual nature.

- Pornographic material, including displaying calendars, cartoons, or other material of a sexual nature, and pornography on computers.

The policy should also indicate the procedure for notifying employers of a problem. This may be a specific individual, such as a supervisor, or a group of individuals, such as the human resources department or senior staff. Because it is possible that a supervisor or another person who is part of this grievance process may be accused of sexual harassment, contingencies should be made as to whom an employee may report an incident.

Once the complaint has been made, the policy should also accommodate what procedures are involved in investigating the matter. It may involve appointing an investigator to review the claim, or selecting a panel that will review the accusations. Regardless of the internal mechanisms in place, this doesn't mean that the employee can't pursue civil litigation outside this process, or in some cases press criminal charges.

The policy should also outline how sexual harassment incidents may be resolved. This may include sanctions against the harasser or possible dismissal. It should also specify that retaliation against an employee for making a complaint will not be tolerated. Because it is also possible that an employee may make a false accusation, the policy should also address this risk, and state that false accusations may be met with immediate disciplinary action.

Acceptable Use Policy

An acceptable use policy establishes guidelines on the appropriate use of technology. It is used to outline what types of activities are permissible when using a computer or network, and what an organization considers proper behavior. Acceptable use policies not only protect an organization from liability, but also provide employees with an understanding of what they can and cannot do using company resources.

In an organization, employees act as representatives of the company to the public. How they conduct themselves, and the actions they perform, reflect upon the organization and can either enhance or damage the reputation of the company. Because employees have greater access to clients and other members of the public through e-mail, Web pages, and other technologies, acceptable use policies are used to ensure that users conduct themselves appropriately. Acceptable use policies restrict users from making threatening, racist, sexist, or offensive comments. In many cases, companies fortify this position by providing empathy training.

Acceptable use policies also restrict the types of Web sites or e-mail an employee is allowed to access on the Internet. When employees access pornography over the Internet, not only does it use up bandwidth and fill hard-disk space on non-work-related activities, but it also creates an uncomfortable work environment for the other employees. Because a company can be liable for creating or allowing a hostile work environment, businesses commonly include sections in their acceptable use policies that deal with these issues.

Many organizations implement acceptable use policies as contracts between the company and the employee, and require workers to sign a copy of the policy to show that they agree to

abide by it. Through these contracts, organizations have justifiable reason to fire employees or (in the case of schools) expel students who violate the agreement. In extreme cases, it can be used as evidence for prosecution. Because the responsibility of adhering to the policy is placed on the person signing it, organizations can also use the signed acceptable use policy as part of their defense from litigation. For example, if an employee sent e-mail of a sexual nature to another employee, a company could use the signed policy to show the onus of responsibility rests with the employee and not the company itself.

What is the best way to enforce an acceptable use policy? Audits should be conducted on a regular basis, including audits of data stored in personal directories and local hard disks, and audits of firewall and system logs, to determine what has been accessed. In cases where suspected breaches of policy have occurred, e-mail messages may also be audited. Because courts have generally held that employees have no reasonable expectation to privacy regarding data stored on computers belonging to a company, such audits can occur regularly and without warning. To ensure that users are aware that these audits occur, and to inform them that the organization takes its acceptable use policy seriously, mention of such measures should be included in the policy.

Exam Warning

Whereas a sexual harassment policy will focus on different kinds of sexual discrimination and unacceptable behavior of a sexual nature in the workplace, an acceptable use policy focuses on the proper usage of technology.

Investigating Sexual Harassment

Investigating sexual harassment can be a difficult process, because in many cases it may be the word of the employee against a coworker, supervisor, or other members of an organization. It is up to the investigator to seek out any existing evidence and evaluate it to determine what has actually occurred. When electronic or physical evidence is present, such as written notes or e-mail, this can make determining what happened considerably easier, as the evidence will help explain what events transpired.

Determining whether comments or actions are considered harassment is subjective, and varies from one person to another. What is offensive, abusive, or unwelcome to one person may not be to another. Because of this, many people may have some difficulty determining whether they are risking sexual harassment, or whether they have been harassed. Many states determine this boundary on the basis of whether a reasonable person would consider it to be sexual harassment.

As we'll see in the sections that follow, under the law, a primary consideration of whether someone was sexually harassed is how a person perceived the behavior, and not how the harasser meant it to be received. In other words, it is the person receiving the comments or treatment that determines whether they are unwelcome. If your comments or actions were of a sexual nature, weren't well received, and had a negative impact on a person, it could be considered sexual harassment. If the law weren't concerned with the impact of the behavior rather than the intent, it would be a simple defense for someone who's sexually harassing another person to simply claim he or she was joking or didn't mean it.

During an investigation, a number of aspects dealing with the incident are examined. For example, in cases of hostile environment sexual harassment, an investigator may look at the following factors:

- Was the conduct verbal, physical, or both?

- How often did it occur (i.e., the frequency with which it was repeated)?

- Was the conduct hostile or patently offensive?

- Was the person who was accused of sexual harassment a supervisor or a coworker?

- Did others join in when the person was harassed?

- Was the harassment focused on one or more individuals?

- What happened when senior management was made aware of the situation?

This final point has a specific focus on the employer's involvement in perpetrating the harassment, as it determines whether the organization dealt with the conduct, if it was immediately ended, or if it was explicitly or implicitly condoned. As we discussed earlier, it is important for employers to investigate and take action immediately when sexual harassment allegations arise or are suspected.

If the allegations involve computers or other devices owned by the company, they should be analyzed for evidence. Because they are the property of the organization, you don't need a warrant to seize them, because the computer and any data on it belong to the company. You only need the permission of an authorized person in the company, such as senior management, or another person who can authorize the search. As we discussed in Chapter 3, however, warning banners and policies should indicate this fact so that the employees know that any information on their computer isn't private and is the property of the company.

To narrow the search, you should use information acquired from statements or interviews with the complainant to determine what devices or data were involved. For example, the person may have sent e-mail, but not messages through a Blackberry device, meaning you would need to check only e-mail on the computer. Similarly, if the harasser showed pornography on only his computer, you wouldn't need to check every workstation in the office. By narrowing the search, less time is required to investigate the matter.

It is also advisable to check both the victim's and the harasser's computers. Because an e-mail must be sent by one computer and received by another, copies of the e-mail should be available on both machines, verifying that the harasser did send the e-mail. In addition to this, you may find additional victims in searching the harasser's machine, finding that other people received harassing e-mail as well. By checking only the victim's computer, you are limiting what information may be available to you.

Head of the Class…

Two Computers Are Better Than One

Never underestimate the benefits of checking the victim's and the suspect's computers if both are available to you. An example of this was a case I worked on, in which the complainant said she received harassing and threatening e-mails from another woman. The officer who was investigating the matter showed me the e-mail, and said that the suspect claimed she had never made such threats, and wasn't harassing anyone. I told the officer that I could check her computer to see whether a copy of the e-mail on her machine matched what the other person received. To my surprise, the suspect volunteered her machine.

After making an image of the suspect's hard disk, I checked the e-mail on her machine found that the copy of the e-mail received by the victim was different from what had been sent. Although the two were similar, the copy on the suspect's machine was a pleasant message, and didn't contain any threats, name-calling, or derogatory remarks. The complainant had modified her copy of the e-mail before printing it, making it appear that the suspect was threatening her. The complainant was trying to get the suspect in trouble, and in the end was the person who was arrested.

Sexual harassment may also involve other crimes. For example, if a person was physically harassed and someone grabbed her body parts, the harasser could also be charged with sexual assault. Similarly, if a person was told or received a note stating that she's have to perform some sex act or the harasser would reveal embarrassing or damaging information about the person, the harasser could also be charged with blackmail.

It is also important to realize that no one factor makes a hostile environment, and many contributing factors can work together to create an atmosphere in which sexual harassment exists. The severity of each of these components can play together so that any reasonable person in the victim's position would consider the environment to be hostile. Because of this, sexual harassment cases that involve hostile environments should always be evaluated on a case-by-case basis.

Once evidence has been acquired and a case has been established, a hearing may be conducted to evaluate the case. Sexual harassment cases are different from many others in that the burden of proof is on the employer and/or harasser to show that the harassment didn't occur. Once a person establishes a case of sexual harassment that meets legal standards, the harasser is essentially considered guilty until proven innocent. The organization must show that a hostile environment did not exist and/or that its actions (or lack of them) didn't impact on the

employee's rights, allowed quid pro quo harassment to occur, or any cost of benefits to an employee didn't involve discriminatory reasons.

Sexual Harassment Laws

To address the serious issue of sexual harassment in the workplace and other environments, a number of laws have been established to deal with victims' rights and punish offenders appropriately. Although internal policies may handle such problems internally, a victim may seek making complaints to the Equal Employment Opportunity Commission, or other agencies that have been established to accept and investigate complaints. In the United States, there are a number of laws on sexual harassment, including:

- 1964 Civil Rights Act, Title VII

- Civil Rights Act of 1991

- Equal Protection Clause of the 14th Amendment

- Common Law Torts

- State and Municipal Laws

Title VII of the 1964 Civil Rights Act

Title VII of the 1964 Civil Rights Act was developed to protect an employee from discrimination on the basis of race, color, religion, sex, and national origin. By specifying that protection from discrimination is based on gender, this means that sexual discrimination is prohibited for both males and females, even though the emphasis of the Act was originally to protect women in the workplace.

Although this Act wasn't originally designed to deal with sexual harassment, courts began to use this Act as the basis for sexual harassment cases. In 1986, the U.S. Supreme Court used Title VII as the basis for determining that sexual harassment is sex discrimination. In the case of Meritor Savings Bank v. Vinson, (477 U.S. 57 (1986)), Mechelle Vinson alleged that Sidney Taylor, the vice president of the bank she was fired from, had coerced her into having sex at work and forcibly raped her on several occasions. The court agreed with her that this created a hostile environment (to say the least), and determined that Title VII was "not limited to 'economic' or 'tangible' discrimination." It found that the objective of the law was to address the disparate treatment of men and women in the workplace, and found that sexual discrimination can create a hostile work environment.

In the same year that this Act was passed, Congress created the Equal Employment Opportunity Commission (EEOC). Six years later, Congress also passed the Equal Employment Opportunity Act, which gave the EEOC authority to enforce Title VII.

The Civil Rights Act of 1991

The Civil Rights Act of 1991 was enacted to amend parts of the Civil Rights Act of 1964 and "to restore and strengthen civil rights laws that ban discrimination in employment, and for other purposes." It amends a number of sections in Title VII of the 1964 Civil Rights Act, and applies changes that allow certain actions, such as a trial by jury, as well as provides for damages in cases where there is intentional employment discrimination. Although many other federal laws applied to employers with 15 or more employees, the Civil Rights Act of 1991 made no such distinctions and applied to all employers.

Equal Protection Clause of the 14th Amendment

The Equal Protection Clause of the 14th Amendment states that state governments must provide equal protection to all persons. It provides a constitutional guarantee that the government can't deny equal protection under the law, as shown in Section 1 of this amendment:

> **"All persons born or naturalized in the United States, and subject to the jurisdiction thereof, are citizens of the United States and of the State wherein they reside. No State shall make or enforce any law which shall abridge the privileges or immunities of citizens of the United States; nor shall any State deprive any person of life, liberty, or property, without due process of law; nor deny to any person within its jurisdiction the equal protection of the laws."**

Common Law Torts

A tort is a wrong committed to a person or property, in which the injured party can seek damages or legal remedies in civil court. Tort is a legal term that is used to refer to a civil wrong that has occurred, and which the court can find as grounds for a lawsuit. By pursuing civil litigation, the victim attempts to show liability, and can claim compensation for damages. In the United States, torts generally fall into one of three categories:

- **Intentional torts**, which include acts that were deliberate, such as sexual assault, defamation of character, invasion of privacy, and other acts.

- **Negligence**, which results from a lack of due care, or wanton, reckless, or despicable conduct. If an employer showed intentional misconduct or liability in not avoiding the act from occurring, the employer could be considered negligent.

- **Strict liability**, which results from a person being directly responsible for damage or loss.

As we stated earlier, when an employer fails to take any action to deal with acts or events that create a hostile environment, it is possible that the employer may be liable for civil damages.

State and Municipal Laws

In addition to federal laws, statutes may also be enacted at the state and municipal levels, allowing legal actions within those jurisdictions. Many states and municipalities have their own legislation related to employment, labor, safety, and other issues that may be related to incidents regarding sexual discrimination. Equal protection under these laws is protection under the 14th Amendment, meaning that individuals pursuing action under these laws cannot be discriminated against. These laws can vary from state to state, and are limited to events or citizens of those jurisdictions.

Summary of Exam Objectives

Modern espionage does not concern only the government, and encompasses more than spies stealing military secrets. Corporate espionage in the new global business environment is emerging as the primary 21st century means for creating a competitive advantage, whether as a country, organization, business, or military power.

One of the most crucial aspects of any forensic engagement is the production of an investigative report. This document is written to communicate the outcome of digital forensic analysis and examination. If you cannot report your findings, no one will know or understand what you have found or its importance.

The safety and security of people in the workplace and online are important issues that have been heavily discussed in the media. Legislation has been created to protect those who are the targets of unwanted sexual conduct in the workplace or work-like environments, and policies may be enacted to prevent or eliminate sexual harassment. If this conduct is ongoing, the organization could be deemed a hostile environment and be subject to civil litigation.

Although the Internet is commonly used for legal purposes, there are those who seek to abuse others online, or access images and other media depicting those who have been previously abused. Child pornography involves minors posing or performing in pornographic depictions, and is the subject of a number of initiatives and laws that are designed to help law enforcement investigate and arrest offenders, and rescue those who are the subjects of this type of pornography.

Law enforcement can use a number of tools to track and investigate child pornography. Parents can use tools to block certain sites or messages, or review material on their child's hard disk. Similarly, initiatives and tools are available to help coordinate investigations and detect common factors in cases that may help identify those who produce, distribute, or collect child pornography.

Exam Objectives Fast Track

Investigating Corporate Espionage

☑ Modern espionage does not concern only the government and is more than spies stealing military secrets. Corporate espionage in the new global business environment is emerging as the primary 21st century means for creating a competitive advantage.

☑ Corporate espionage is defined under "theft of trade secrets" and "economic espionage" by the U.S. Economic Espionage Act of 1996 (Title 18 UCS 1831). It is a federal criminal offense.

☑ The primary motivations for corporate espionage includes the theft of trade secrets for economic gain, acquiring competitive advantage in domestic and global markets, and privacy violations.

☑ Hostile nations such as China, North Korea, Cuba, and Iran are only one source of remote threat. Friendly nations have been known (and caught) in these activities in the past.

☑ Netspionage is network-enabled espionage.

☑ Corporate spies come in two categories: the skilled attacker (this person is proficient in scripting/programming new automated attack tools) and the unskilled attacker.

☑ SpyBuddy offers the ability to record every action on a computer system.

☑ Activity Monitor allows you to track any LAN.

Investigating Trademark and Copyright Infringement

☑ The aim of this module is to learn about the investigation of both trademark and copyright infringements. This section covers:

☑ The eligibility to obtain a trademark and the benefits gained through registering.

☑ The definitions of service marks and trade dress.

☑ The interaction between trademarks and Internet domain names.

☑ Trademark infringements and searches.

☑ Copyright, copyright registrations and copyright notices.

☑ The doctrine of fair use.

☑ The U.S. Copyright office.

☑ Trademarks are categorized into three types: service marks, collective marks, and certification marks.

☑ In the United States, applications for renewal and extension of a copyright covering a "work for hire" creation is for a period of 67 years when the possessor of that particular type of work requests the same.

☑ The standard "likelihood of confusion" acts as the basis to allow the trademark owner to take legal action against (sue) another party for trademark infringement.

☑ The online utility LOCIS helps an investigator when searching for copyright records.

☑ The CTEA amended the Copyright Act by extending the term of protection for works currently in their renewal term from 75 years to 95 years. Under the new law, any work published in 1923 (which would have otherwise fallen into the public domain on January 1, 1999) will now be protected until January 1, 2019.

☑ Paraphrasing is an act of plagiarism.

☑ Paper mills are online Web sites that offer students with papers, assignment answers, completed reports, and essays.

☑ There are three types of plagiarism tools: tools for text, tools for code, and tools for data collection/submission.

Writing Investigative Reports

☑ The section on investigated reports covers:

☑ Why an investigated report is required.

☑ Report classifications and specifications.

☑ What is opinion and its place in a forensic report.

☑ How to write a forensic investigative report in what must contain.

☑ The features of a good report.

☑ The purpose of an investigative report is to communicate the results of the examination. It enables the presentation of evidence as testimony and aids in the expression of expert opinion.

Investigating Child Pornography

☑ In North America, child pornography can be simply defined as any sexually explicit depiction of a person less than 18 years of age.

- ☑ Child pornography laws vary from country to country, with numerous countries developing no definition of what child pornography is.

- ☑ Child sex tourism is the practice of (pedophiles) traveling to countries with low ages of consent to have sex with children.

- ☑ A pedophile is someone whose primary sexual interest is in children. Some professions make a distinction that pedophiles are interested in prepubescent children, whereas hebophiles are interested in adolescents.

- ☑ Virtual child pornography involves the digital manipulation or creation of images in which the pictures appear to be of children having sex or posing nude, but are actually digitally manipulated images.

- ☑ Lollipop or Lolita pornography involves girls who are just above the legal age who are made to appear younger.

- ☑ Lolicon is a slang combination of the phrase Lolita complex, and depicts children or childlike characters in sexually orientated cartoons and comics. The Japanese style of animation is commonly referred to as Japanimation or anime, and comic books (and sometimes mistakenly cartoons) are referred to as manga.

- ☑ Child erotica is a term applied to photos or depictions of naked children, which may or may not be also categorized as art.

- ☑ Passive pedophiles will access child pornography out of a sexual interest in the material, and to feed fantasies.

- ☑ Active pedophiles will access child pornography and use the Internet to find victims.

- ☑ Online predators use child pornography to seduce or groom children into having sex, and to get the child to send images of him or herself to the pedophile.

- ☑ Advances in technology and the Internet have increased the amount and availability of child pornography.

- ☑ Child pornography is obtained on the Internet from a variety of sources, and using a number of different tools. Common methods of acquiring and distributing child pornography over the Internet include Web sites, e-mail, mailing lists, e-groups, newsgroups, peer-to-peer, chat rooms, and instant messaging.

- ☑ The FBI's Innocent Images National Initiative (IINI) attempts to reduce the sexual exploitation of children by identifying, investigating, and prosecuting those who use computers for child sexual exploitation and child pornography. Its mission also includes identifying and rescuing victims, providing training and assistance to other law enforcement, and coordinating efforts in cases involving local, state, and international governments.

☑ Internet Crimes Against Children (ICAC) is a network of task forces that provide assistance to law enforcement in computer- and Internet-based crimes that sexually exploit children.

☑ Project Safe Childhood is an initiative developed by the U.S. Department of Justice to provide a coordinated effort in combating child pornography and sexual exploitation. It is designed to help local communities create programs and develop strategies to investigate child exploitation, and identify and rescue victims.

☑ Reveal is an application used to identify objectionable material on hard disks and other storage media.

☑ iProtectYou is parental control and filtering software that controls what a computer user is allowed to access over the Internet.

☑ The Child Exploitation Tracking System (CETS) is a tool developed for law enforcement to organize, analyze, share, and search information related to child exploitation cases, such as those involving child pornography.

Investigating Sexual Harassment

☑ Sexual harassment is any repeated, unwanted behavior of a sexual nature. It can occur between individuals who are of different genders or of the same sex, and often occurs when there is an imbalance of power between two people.

☑ Quid pro quo sexual harassment occurs when a person is offered some kind of benefit in exchange for sexual favors, or is threatened to lose something if he or she doesn't give in.

☑ Hostile environment sexual harassment occurs when conduct in the workplace is such that it has created an unpleasant or offensive environment. In this type, sexual harassment is determined on the basis of whether a reasonable person would consider the workplace to be hostile.

☑ Employees are responsible for informing a person that specific conduct is not welcome or acceptable.

☑ Employers may be held accountable for the actions of supervisors who sexually harass employees, or for condoning a hostile environment.

☑ A policy is used to address concerns and identify risks.

☑ Procedures consist of a series of steps that inform someone how to perform a task and/or deal with a problem.

☑ Sexual harassment policies are used to encourage the reporting of such incidents, and outline the procedures to follow when sexual harassment occurs.

☑ The Equal Protection Clause of the 14th Amendment states that state governments must provide equal protection to all persons.

☑ Title VII of the 1964 Civil Rights Act was developed to protect an employee from discrimination on the basis of race, color, religion, sex, and national origin.

☑ The Civil Rights Act of 1991 was enacted to amend parts of the Civil Rights Act of 1964.

☑ A tort is a wrong committed to a person or property, in which the injured party can seek damages or legal remedies in civil court.

Exam Objectives
Frequently Asked Questions

The following Frequently Asked Questions, answered by the authors of this book, are designed to both measure your understanding of the Exam Objectives presented in this chapter, and to assist you with real-life implementation of these concepts.

Q: What do I need to do if I what to commence legal action for corporate espionage?

A: To successfully prosecute corporate espionage, it is necessary to prove that the information has value. This can be a monetary value, a hidden value, or an economic advantage to an adversary/competitor. You also need to demonstrate that the information was protected and properly marked for protection, that policies and procedures were in place, and that awareness training was instituted.

Q: Why shouldn't I use passive voice when writing my reports?

A: "The author wrote the words in his diary" employs active voice. "The words in the diary were written by the author" illustrates passive voice. When writing a report, avoid any form of the verb to be, such as is, are, was, and were. Read your writing aloud; you'll find that passive voice can lead you to lapse into a sing-song schoolchild reading his "what I did last summer" essay out loud. It is much more difficult to take passive voice seriously.

Q: What is considered public domain?

A: Like all things, copyright protection eventually ends; it is only a "limited monopoly." When copyrights expire, they fall into the public domain. With a number of exceptions, public domain works may be unreservedly copied or used in the production of derivative works without either the permission or the authorization of the former copyright holder. At some stage in the Clinton administration, the contentious Sonny Bono Copyright Term Extension Act (CTEA) passed into law. This Act added 20 years to most copyright terms. It also created a moratorium that, in effect, stops any new works from entering the public domain until 2019. The bill was enacted to ensure protection for U.S. works in the foreign market.

Q: What is wrong with using acronyms in my reports?

A: TLAs are the bane of all good reports. Acronyms often conflict within similar spheres. However, when you take a range of different occupations and knowledge fields, people start to read different meaning into this technical jargon. The result is that the report is less clear to the average reader.

Q: I am investigating an incident where child pornography was found on a computer. The person who used the computer claims he received a pop up containing a link to child pornography and clicked on it. How can I determine whether the person's story is true?

A: Always remember that just because a questionable site or image is found on a computer, it doesn't mean the person is surfing for kiddie porn. E-mail messages and pop ups are distributed with images and links to child pornography Web sites, and because the pop up, e-mail, or Web site contained images of child pornography, this means they are also on the person's hard drive. When analyzing a computer, it is easy to identify such situations as there are only images and Web site history relating to an e-mail, pop up, or Web page that was visited. In other words, the person's browsing behavior doesn't indicate that he was trolling for kiddie porn sites. In addition, firewall logs may show that the person accessed the site or pop up for only a moment, indicating he closed the pop up or Web browser immediately after identifying the illegal material.

Q: I work for an ISP in the United States, and have discovered child pornography on a Web site we host. What should I do?

A: Under the Protection of Children from Sexual Predators Act of 1998 (Sexual Predators Act), ISPs are required to notify law enforcement of Web sites containing child pornography on their server(s). Failing to report it could mean that the ISP will be fined.

Q: I'm curious whether someone in my organization may be downloading child pornography. Because CETS is a Microsoft product, can I get a copy and use it to view information about a particular person?

A: No. The Child Exploitation Tracking System is a law enforcement tool, and is not available to the general public. It is designed to link cases involving child exploitation so that police can identify and investigate individuals involved in such activities, and rescue children who may be exploited.

Q: A coworker showed me a child pornography picture he downloaded, and after I complained about it, this person was arrested. Other coworkers also have legal sexual images in calendars on their walls and as wallpaper on their desktops. Even though the person was arrested, could I still sue the company for providing a hostile environment?

A: Although it's always best to consult with a lawyer, the environment could be considered hostile because the company allows employees to have sexual images displayed. Just because a person was arrested for a criminal act related to this activity doesn't mean a civil recourse isn't also available to you.

Q: A coworker is always brushing past me in the hall, even though there is room to get by. Is this sexual harassment?

A: This may be considered sexual harassment, as the person is brushing against you, possibly to touch you for sexual reasons. If it is unwanted, you should inform the person, and if it continues, make a complaint of sexual harassment.

References

Boni, William, and Gerald L. Kovacich. Netspionage: The Global Threat to Information (Butterworth-Heinemann: 2000).

CSI, the Computer Security Institute; www.gocsi.com/.

Mokhiber, Russell, and Robert Weissman. "Corporate Spooks." March 6, 2001; www.commondreams.org/views01/0306-03.htm (accessed August 2, 2007).

Nichols, Randall K., Daniel J. Ryan, and Julie J.C.H. Ryan. Introduction to Digital Espionage: Defending Your Digital Assets Against Hackers, Crackers, Spies & Thieves (McGraw-Hill: 2000).

WarRoom (1996). "1996 Information Systems Security Survey," WarRoom Research, LLC, available at www.infowar.com/.

Zwillinger, Marc J. "Investigation and Prosecution of Computer Crime." Computer Crime and Intellectual Property Section Criminal Division, U.S. Department of Justice, November 4, 1998.

Notes

1. http://en.wikipedia.org/wiki/Patent_infringement

CHFI

Becoming an Expert Witness

Exam objectives in this appendix:

- **Understanding the Expert Witness**
- **Testifying As an Expert Witness**

Exam Objectives Review:

- ☑ **Summary of Exam Objectives**
- ☑ **Exam Objectives Fast Track**
- ☑ **Exam Objectives Frequently Asked Questions**

Introduction

A cybercrime investigation and building of the case file is aimed toward one end result: obtaining a conviction of the cyber criminal in a court of law. No matter how good the evidence you obtain—log files showing unauthorized access to the network, hard disks seized from the suspect's computer containing clear-cut indications of the criminal activity, network records tracking the intruder back through Internet servers to his or her computer—none of this evidence can stand alone. Under most judicial systems, physical and intangible evidence must be supported by testimony. Someone must testify as to when, where, and how the evidence was obtained and verify that it is the same when it is presented in court as it was when it was collected.

Even though you should treat every case as though you were expecting it to go to court, actually testifying in court can be a stressful experience. If you've never been in a courtroom before, it can feel similar to your first day at a new school. You're unfamiliar with the environment, don't know the procedures, and may even make mistakes that will cause you to cringe later. Even when you know what to expect, it can still feel like you're walking into the principal's office (or at times like you're walking onto the playground to be beaten up). Testifying generally isn't a pleasant experience, although it can be made easier through knowledge and experience. With enough preparation, the occasion can even be something you'll remember with pride.

Understanding the Expert Witness

Testimony in court is provided by witnesses, which are people who have firsthand knowledge of a crime or incident, or whom offer evidence during a trial, tribunal, or hearing. When evidence is technical in nature and difficult for laypeople to understand, experts may be required to testify to explain the nature of the evidence and what it means to the case. In a cybercrime case, police investigators and IT personnel may be required to take the witness stand. Two types of witnesses can be called to testify in criminal actions:

- Evidentiary witnesses
- Expert witnesses

An *evidentiary witness* is someone who has direct knowledge of the case. For example, a network administrator might be called to testify as to what he or she observed during an attack on the network, or an investigator might be called to testify as to the evidence that he or she observed on a computer that was seized pursuant to a search warrant. An evidentiary witness can only testify as to facts (what he or she saw, heard, or did) but cannot give authoritative opinions or draw conclusions.

An *expert witness* is different from an evidentiary witness in that he or she can give opinions and draw conclusions about facts in the case. The *expert witness* may have no direct

involvement in the case but has special technical knowledge or expertise that qualifies him or her to give professional opinions on technical matters. Expert witnesses sometimes prepare reports that outline their opinions and give reasons for each opinion.

Exam Warning

Differences exist in the types of witnesses that may be used in a trial. An evidentiary witness is limited to presenting facts of the case, even if those facts contain technical testimony. An expert witness can testify to the same events and evidence that an evidentiary witness can, but has the benefit of making opinions that are based on scientific, technical, or other fields of knowledge in which he or she has expertise. The framework of what a witness can and cannot discuss is outlined in the Rules of Evidence, which we'll discuss later in this chapter.

Even though an expert witness can present conclusions, he or she is limited in the opinions that can be expressed. For example, an expert in computer technology may testify that a threatening e-mail was traced to an account that was owned by the defendant, and how analysis of the defendant's computer showed that it was in fact sent from that machine. The witness cannot present a conclusion that the defendant is thereby guilty as sin. After all, a person is considered innocent until proven guilty, and the neutrality of the expert witness should follow that philosophy. The expert in computers also couldn't speak about the mindset of the defendant as it was being sent, as psychology isn't the witness's expertise. A witness is limited to testifying about what he or she saw, heard, or did, and expert witnesses can speak only to this and/or about information that is within the scope of their knowledge and experience.

The prosecution and defense attorneys are permitted to have expert witnesses testify in a case, although they aren't always deemed necessary by one or either side. As such, experts aren't used in most trials. In many cases, the weight of evidence is evaluated and a plea bargain is reached. A *plea bargain* is an agreement in which the defendant pleads guilty to a lesser crime to have more severe charges dropped. Even when a case does go to trial, often the evidentiary testimony is all that a prosecutor or defense attorney needs to argue the guilt or innocence of a defendant. For each case going to trial, an attorney must determine whether the facts would benefit from an expert opinion, or whether the evidentiary testimony and evidence can stand on its own.

The expert witness should also not be confused with experts that serve as consultants, which both sides may use to understand different types of evidence. For example, in a trial involving a car accident, the defense lawyer may contact an expert in safety standards to understand issues related to the air bags used in a particular make and model of car. Although the expert can provide clarity in understanding aspects of the case, he or she isn't an expert witness because:

- The person hasn't been subpoenaed or sworn in as a witness.

- No testimony has been given in court.

- The court hasn't recognized the person as an expert.

As we'll see in the next section, whether someone is designated as an expert witness is primarily at the discretion of the judge hearing the case. The expert witness provides information about his or her qualifications, and both the prosecution and the defense review the person's education, experience, and other credentials. Either side may challenge the person's qualifications in court, or they will both agree that the person is an expert in a particular field. Ultimately, however, it is up to the judge to recognize the person as an expert.

Qualifying As an Expert Witness

The standards for qualifying as an expert witness vary around the world. In some countries, expert witnesses must be registered as experts in a particular field. In the United States and Canada, experts must generally prove their expertise by presenting their credentials in court.

To determine whether a person qualifies as an expert witness, and whether their testimony is admissible, involves a process of examination, cross-examination, and being recognized by the court. The attorney calling the potential expert witness will generally read his or her qualifications into the record, and/or may ask a series of questions. These questions are designed to show the person's credentials as an expert. Such questions might include:

- What degrees, diplomas, or certificates do you have?

- What positions have you held in the field?

- What lectures or courses have you taught in this field?

- What additional training or courses related to this field have you taken?

- What memberships in organizations related to this field do you have?

- What books or papers have you written pertaining to the field?

- What is your past experience as an expert witness in this field?

The quality of your answers to these questions will help to determine whether you'll be recognized as an expert in a particular area. However, in looking at these questions, don't feel that you have to have a positive answer to every one. For example, if you had education and experience but didn't have any teaching experience, you might still be declared an expert. The key factor is the overall expertise, not whether you have an impressive answer to each and every one of these questions. After all, the first time anyone testifies in court, the answer to whether you have testified before is a resounding "no."

Once the witness has been called to the stand and examined, the court will be asked to accept him or her as an expert. The opposing side will then have the opportunity to accept the

witness as an expert or challenge its admissibility. If a challenge is made, the opposing side can cross-examine the witness on his or her qualifications.

The opposing side may challenge the expert witness's credentials in an attempt to have that person's testimony deemed inadmissible, or prevent him or her from stating opinions and conclusions about the evidence. The attorney making this challenge has a heavy burden in attempting to exclude evidence or testimony at any stage of litigation. Not only must he or she attack the credibility of such witnesses, their testimony, and any evidence they've provided, but also must do so with limited knowledge. The attorney may be an expert in law, but have minimal or no expertise in the field of the witness.

As we'll see in later sections of this appendix, an attorney may use a number of tactics and resources when cross-examining a witness and challenging him or her as an expert. Such tactics can include ways of asking questions, and tricks that are often successful in tripping up a witness's testimony. To understand technical aspects of the case and ask more effective questions, the attorney may hire his or her own expert, who can be consulted before the trial and/or during the proceedings. Because the challenging side's expert is never sworn in as a witness, the identity of the expert may never be known to the opposing side, and will never be cross-examined. Although this can help a lawyer's case a great deal, costs involved with hiring an expert can be prohibitive, so they aren't used in most cases.

Once the opposing side has cross-examined the witness, the court will hear arguments from both sides on the issue of whether the person should be recognized as an expert. In addition to challenging that the expertise of a witness hasn't been established, and that the person is thereby unqualified to give opinions on subject matter, arguments may be made that the person's expertise is limited. Challenging the limited expertise of a witness can be done during cross-examination. If the person's expertise is deemed limited, he or she may still be able to give opinions, but the person's testimony will be given little weight.

Regardless of whether the witness's qualifications are challenged, the final decision rests with the judge. If the judge is satisfied that the witness has sufficient education and experience to testify and form opinions on subject matter related to the case, the court will recognize that the person is an expert. The area of expertise that's recognized may be broad (such as being an expert in computer technology) or limited to a narrow field of knowledge (such as being an expert on a particular piece of software).

Just because a person is an expert in one trial, doesn't necessarily mean that he or she will be recognized in another trial. Being declared an expert applies only to that particular case, and doesn't carry forward to any other cases in which you might testify in the future. For each trial, the process of being recognized as an expert must begin again.

Curriculum Vitae

Curriculum vitae is a Latin term meaning "course of life," used to refer to a document that outlines a person's education, experience, and other credentials. A curriculum vitae (CV) is

commonly referred to as a resume, although there are a number of differences between them. CVs are used in court cases to state the qualifications of a prospective expert witness, and one should be submitted to the attorney you'll be working with before going to court to qualify as an expert. Once the attorney receives this information, he or she can then forward a copy to the opposing counsel. By allowing both the prosecution and defense attorneys to review your CV before attending court, the number of questions they will need to ask about your qualifications can be minimized.

A CV can easily be compared to a resume, but in doing so you will see a great number of disparities. A resume provides an overview of your abilities and achievements and serves as your introduction to a prospective employer. It may include information on why you left a previous employer, your salary history, and a list of personal references. A CV contains none of these elements. It is a detailed synopsis of the qualifications that make you an expert in a particular field. A CV is also generally longer than a resume. Although the recommended length of a resume is no more than one or two pages, a CV can be two or more pages in length. Because it is used to showcase your credentials, it is important that it contains all of the education and experiences you've had that correspond to a particular area of expertise.

NOTE

Just as many people searching for employment have different resumes that correspond to different types of jobs, many people who serve as experts also have several CVs prepared. For example, you might have one that focuses on computer forensics, and another that stresses your education and experience with networks. When a case requires a particular expertise, you can then use the CV that is best suited for that particular case.

Writing a CV

You can use a number of different formats to write a CV, but most of them contain the same elements and perform the same purpose: They describe who you are as a professional. The CV should identify who you are and how to contact you, and describe what qualifications you can bring to a case to bring a better understanding of evidence.

Writing a CV begins by providing your name at the top of the document. The attorney who will call you to the stand will need the correct spelling of your name, so you can be added to the witness list. As such, the CV should have your full legal name, as it would be read into the official record when qualifying as a witness.

A CV can also include a line at the top of the document that specifies in what field you're an expert. In doing so, the type of testimony you can provide is easily identifiable to those

reading it. For example, a line might be included stating "Specialist in Computer Forensics, Computer Technology, and Information Systems" or "Computer Expert Witness with Emphasis in the Areas of…." This is not required, but the latter example commonly appears on CVs belonging to expert witnesses that are hired to testify.

Below this, you would type your contact information. This includes not only a phone number, P.O. box, and/or other addresses, but also any electronic methods of contacting you, such as an e-mail address and Web site. Contact information is important, as the attorney you're working with will want to be able to reach you as needed. In addition to this, a current address is needed so that the court can notify you of a court date by having you subpoenaed (as we'll explain later in this appendix).

In writing your contact information, you should refrain from using a home address. Doing so can impact your personal safety. After all, if the case involved a violent offender or someone who possessed child pornography on his or her computer, you wouldn't want this person knowing where you lived. If you are creating a CV because of a case you were involved with at work, whether your involvement was as part of an incident response team or an agent of law enforcement, you could use your employer's address. Alternatively, if you've been hired as an expert, you should buy a P.O. box and then use the P.O. box number in your contact information.

Below the contact information, you should also include a brief biography, which serves as a summary of your qualifications. Essentially, this captures the highlights of the CV within a few short paragraphs. It should provide a brief overview of education and key points relating to your experience within the field.

The bulk of the CV appears under this information, as this is where your education and experience are listed. The CV should be organized into categories, with qualifications related to each category listed and/or described underneath. Some of the categories under which you could organize your background information might include:

- Formal education, inclusive to degrees, diplomas, and certifications. You should also include any additional courses, conferences, or workshops you've attended, and list the number of hours of training involved in taking these courses.

- Related employment.

- Teaching and research experience.

- Grants and fellowships.

- Licenses and memberships in professional associations.

- Publications you've written or contributed to. For each item under this category, you should identify the publisher, name of the publication, and publication dates.

- Awards and honors.

- Previous testimony experience, with specific reference to any cases in which you were previously recognized as an expert witness.

Any information appearing under these categories should be related to the field of knowledge to which you'll be testifying. In other words, limit your information to what's pertinent. Even though you probably graduated high school, it can generally be omitted from the CV because it's irrelevant. What lawyers will be looking for is any post-secondary education related to this field. Similarly, unlike a resume, you wouldn't include information about your interests, hobbies, or anything else that doesn't reflect the scope of your expertise in the area in which you'll be testifying.

EXERCISE A.1

WRITING A CURRICULUM VITAE

The following exercise requires you to open a new document in word processing software on your computer. In the new document, follow these steps:

1. On the first line of the document, type your full name.

2. On the next line, specify the area to which you are a specialist.

3. On the lines below this, type any contact information you feel comfortable with releasing. This could include a P.O. box number or other address, as well as e-mail, Web site, or other methods of contacting you. At this point, your CV should have a format similar to the following:

<div align="center">

Kevin Smith

Computer Forensic Expert

P.O. Box 1234, Los Angeles, CA 54321 USA

Phone: 555-289-1234 - Fax: 555-289-4321 – E-mail
ksmith@mooby.com

</div>

4. Below this, write a category title called "Summary and Highlights of Experience".

5. On the next few lines, write a brief summary of what you are an expert in, and what knowledge and experience you can bring to the trial. For example:

I specialize in the areas of computer forensics, information technology, and password and e-mail recovery for evidentiary purposes. My prior education and work experience is in the areas of information technology and computer forensics, and I have worked in the field of computers for more than 20 years.

6. Below this, write a category titled "Formal Education".

7. On the next lines, add pertinent information on your education, including any courses, conferences, or workshops you may have attended. In doing so, specify the year you graduated or took the course. For training workshops, specify the number of hours. For example:

 2007: 12 hours accredited training in computer forensics, Institute for Computer Professionals, Portland, Oregon

 2002: Bachelor of computer science, Whatsamatta University, Thorold, Ontario

8. Below this, write a category titled "Related Employment".

9. On the lines after this, type information regarding any employment that is related to your area of expertise. In doing so, specify the years you worked in this position, the employer, position held, and a brief synopsis of the work performed. For example:

 1987 to Present: Drug Enforcement Agency, Information Technology – Duties include performing forensic examinations on suspect computers, recovering deleted and encrypted files, recovery of passwords and e-mail. Provide briefings on technology-related issues and results of examination to law enforcement and government executives.

10. Below this, write a category titled "Previous Testimony Experience."

11. On the lines after this, list any cases in which you have been a witness, and specify which ones you were recognized as an expert. In doing so, specify the name of the case, case number, type of court, and information regarding what you testified to. For ones in which you were an expert, specify what you were deemed an expert in. For example:

 Garner v. Affleck - Family law (computer forensics), LA County Superior Court, CA (June 2001) – Identification of hidden assets and community property assets.

 New York v. Grimm - Criminal law (computer forensics), Supreme Court of the United States (January 2000) – Identification of hidden assets and homicide – Court Recognized as an 'Expert in Computer Technology.'

12. Repeat the process of writing categories related to your credentials and list your qualifications and experience beneath each category. For example, categories could include Awards, Publications, Teaching Experience, Grants and Fellowships,

Licenses and Memberships, and any other categories that relate to your experience or achievements. In writing these points, specify dates and other pertinent information.

Falsifying Credentials

In writing the CV, you should be absolutely honest. Although some people will pad their resume with useless and fraudulent information, lying on a CV used to qualify you as an expert witness could lead to perjury charges against you. Remember that any information appearing on the CV may be verified when questioning you in court, so you'll be faced with either the embarrassing situation of coming clean under oath, or continuing the lie and possibly going to jail later.

An example of bogus credentials putting an "expert" on the wrong side of the law is James Earl Edmiston, who admitted to committing perjury in two cases in which he falsified his qualifications as an expert witness. In declarations prepared between April 3, 2006 and July 19, 2006, he falsely claimed to have had a master's degree from California Institute of Technology, and degrees from University of California or University of Las Vegas. Not only did he lie about this, but he also neglected to mention a prior criminal record for forgery convictions that had included a prison term. In May 2007, Edmiston pleaded guilty to two counts of perjury, which carries a maximum penalty of 10 years in prison and a $500,000 fine.

Experts Who Are Not Witnesses

Lawyers are taught never to ask a question that they don't know the answer to. However, even though he or she has expertise in practicing law, the lawyer will have limited knowledge of technology or other specialized fields. To compensate for this lack of knowledge, experts may be used as consultants.

Regardless of whether a professional consulting with the lawyer testifies in court, the prosecution or defense attorneys may use him or her to provide greater insight to a case throughout the course of a trial. The attorney may consult with experts prior to a trial and/or during proceedings. In many cases, the expert will write reports that explain technical aspects of a case in layman's terms, and report any mistakes apparent in witness statements that contain technical information or in the processing of evidence. Because of the information provided by the expert, the attorney can better prepare for the potential testimony of witnesses, and cross-examine them on technical aspects of a case. Because the consultant is never formally used in court (i.e., sworn in to provide testimony), one side might never know the name or existence of a consultant being used by the other side.

In some cases, experts may also be present in court. The expert will listen to testimony, provide information on technical anomalies or other facts in what a witness testifies to, and may even provide some follow-up questions that the attorney can use. When the opposing side attempts to qualify a witness as an expert, the consultant can assist in clarifying areas of the witness testimony, and suggest questions for cross-examination that may disqualify the witness as being an expert.

Experts in various fields are also used for the purpose of testing evidence that will be used in the case. For example, DNA evidence may play a key role in a murder trial, or one involving sexual assault or paternity. A DNA expert might be hired to test blood or semen samples. Through the testing, the validity of this evidence can be determined, and can show that it matches a defendant or has been tainted in some way. Through such tests, the guilt or innocence of a person may be established, and can help to determine whether the case should be dismissed. Needless to say, if any of the results were used in court the person would then be called as a witness, and probably go through the process of being qualified as an expert witness.

Although experts may be used in a case without ever appearing as a witness, expert witnesses are also commonly used in the capacity of a consult. The attorney who called the witness may request the person remain in the courtroom to provide insight into technical issues, or assist in other ways. Because the court has already recognized the person as an expert, there is an advantage of being able to re-call the witness to the stand to provide further testimony on facts as they arise during the trial.

Types of Expert Witnesses

An expert witness testifies in relation to subject matter in which he or she has expertise, so it should come as no surprise that because there are so many different subjects, there are many different types of expert witnesses. Although experts exist in many fields, some of the more common ones used in trials include:

- Civil litigation experts
- Criminal litigation experts
- Computer forensic experts
- Medical and psychological experts
- Construction and architecture experts

Criminal Litigation Experts

Criminal litigation experts are used to assist in the prosecution and defense of individuals involved in a crime. Criminal litigation involves actions against individuals who have committed illegal acts, who are brought to court by the government to address charges of breaking specific laws. To assist in understanding technical details of a case, evaluate and present evidence,

and perform other functions that can best be addressed by an expert in a related field of knowledge, expert witnesses are used.

The specialties of criminal litigation experts used in court vary greatly. There are experts in almost any field you can think of who may be used to explain any type of evidence or aspect of a case. In criminal cases, the majority of experts used by the prosecution will be members of the police, or others involved in the investigation. As we've discussed, the person who performed a computer forensic examination will often be called as a witness, and may be qualified as an expert in a particular area of technology. Similarly, in a case involving a car accident, a police officer trained as an accident reconstructionist will collect evidence at the scene of a traffic accident, and reconstruct the cause, effects, and other events that led to the accident from these clues. The defense may also use experts to support their position in the trial. These experts may be used to perform tests and review facts of the case, as well as provide alternative interpretations of the evidence. By providing this expertise to a case, the facts of the case become clearer to the judge, jury, and other parties involved in the case.

As we mentioned previously, experts are also used to provide technical consulting to legal counsel, and they serve as a resource for explaining technical details. This insight will prove useful not only during the trial, but also during discovery and depositions, which we'll discuss later in this appendix.

Head of the Class…

Hiring Experts

In looking at the kinds of professions in which expert witnessed have education and experience, you might wonder why they would be so willing to testify in court. In many cases, the expert witnesses used in a trial are paid for their time and expenses. Payment is usually on a *per diem* basis and may include travel expenses and accommodations during the trial. Many people hire themselves out as expert witnesses, specializing in many different technical or scientific fields, including computer forensics. Although it's more common to hear of people trying to get out of court duties or of being anxious to testify only if they have a vested interest, many such expert witnesses advertise their services on the Internet. For example, The Expert Pages (www.expertpages.com/experts/computers.htm) is a database listing expert witnesses in many fields, available throughout the United States and Canada.

Civil Litigation Experts

In addition to criminal cases, experts are used in civil litigation in which one party sues another to reclaim what they feel is owed them. In doing so, civil litigation courts provide a forum for resolving these disputes. Different types of civil litigation can include any number of lawsuits between individuals and/or businesses, including:

- Libel and slander
- Land disputes

- Probate of wills

- Wrongful dismissal

- Malpractice

- Personal injury

- Wrongful death

- Contract disputes

- Other disputes between individuals and/or businesses

In looking at the various legal actions that may occur in civil court, you can see that not all of them involve suing for monetary settlements. In many cases, civil litigation attempts to determine the rights of an individual, the scope of an agreement, or the intention of a contract. For example, if a person died without a will, the court may be required to determine the wishes of the deceased, and how to best divide the estate between the person's wife, children, and other interested parties. To determine the facts of a case, and come to an equitable decision, expert witnesses may be used to evaluate and assist in understanding the details of the case. These experts are often the same types as those that may be used in a criminal trial, including forensic accountants, medical experts, and other professionals who specialize in any field that could provide insight to aspects of the case.

Even though civil court is different from criminal court, the two often overlap. In addition to using the same types of experts in both areas of law, a case that is held in criminal court may later appear in civil court. A popular example of this is the O.J. Simpson trial in which he was acquitted of the murders of two people, but was later found responsible in civil court and ordered to pay damages in a wrongful death suit. Just because an individual is tried in criminal court doesn't mean he or she can't be sued later in civil court.

Computer Forensic Experts

As you well know from reading this book, computer forensics is the collection, examination, preservation, and presentation of digital evidence. Computer forensic experts acquire and examine potential evidence during an investigation, including data that's been deleted, encrypted, or damaged. Any steps taken during this process are documented, and methodologies are used to prevent the evidence from being altered, corrupted, or destroyed. As we've stressed throughout this book, any case involving computer forensics should always be treated as though it were going to court, and that any documentation and evidence will eventually be turned over to a prosecuting attorney.

In criminal cases, the defense attorney may also hire his or her own expert to review the evidence, and determine whether any errors were made during the examination of the computer. The expert will also document the actions he or she took, which will generally be incorporated into a final report that's submitted to the lawyer. This expert may also be required to testify in court, but this time on behalf of the defense attorney.

While serving as an expert for the defense, the computer forensic expert should remain impartial and perform many of the same functions as that of the prosecution. Any examinations he or she performs would involve examining, preserving, and presenting evidence, and could also require collecting additional evidence that was missed during the investigation. In doing so, the expert would attempt to find alternative reasons for the presence of data, such as identifying whether a Trojan horse, botnet, or other malicious software was present on the machine. Because he or she is working on behalf of the defense, it is important that any client–attorney information that is inadvertently acquired is kept private and not divulged without consent of the attorney or under order of the judge.

Computer forensic experts may also be used in civil litigations. Because information dealing with a case may be stored on computers or other devices, computer forensic experts may be used to search for data such as e-mail, text messages, chat logs, Web site history, calendar files, spreadsheets, documents, images, and other files on a machine. Examining this data may reveal facts that uncover an adulterous affair, fraud, malfeasance, downloading or visiting illegal or disturbing material (such as pornography), or other activities that could determine the outcome of a lawsuit.

Because the data acquired through computer forensics includes documents, spreadsheets, and other files that contain information outside of the computer expert's scope of knowledge, additional experts will be used to explain what has been found. In such situations, the investigation and ensuing criminal or civil litigations will often use other experts that are suited to the evidence.

TEST DAY TIP

Although after reading this book, you'll be familiar with the role of a computer forensic expert, you will also need to be aware of other types of expert witnesses that may be used in a trial. Before the exam, quickly review the information on medical and psychological experts and construction and architecture experts, and know the differences between civil and criminal litigation experts.

Medical and Psychological Experts

Like computer forensic experts, medical and psychological expert witnesses can be used in both civil and criminal litigation. Medical and psychological experts respectively provide insight and assistance in physical and mental issues that may be involved in a court case. They may be used by either side in a court case to perform tests, evaluate existing diagnoses, or testify about technical details related to evidence.

Medical experts are doctors or health professionals that are dedicated to specialized fields of medicine. They may be used to perform DNA or toxicology tests, testify to the extent of injuries suffered by a victim or plaintiff, or provide information on diseases, disabilities, practices, and/or procedures. Some of the other areas in which they provide specialized assistance include:

- Dentistry, which can include forensic dentistry and bite marks

- Drugs, which may involve testifying about prescription medication or illegal drugs taken by an individual. This type of expert can testify about different types of drugs and their effects, or perform and evaluate drug tests on an accused person or individuals involved in a case.

- Malpractice, in which errors made by doctors or medical professionals are evaluated, reported, and presented in court.

Psychological experts are doctors and medical professionals who specialize in areas of mental health, psychological, and psychiatric fields. They may be used to evaluate and testify to the competency of an accused person or individual involved in the case, such as when it needs to be determined whether a person is fit to stand trial, or to establish the mental state of a person when a crime took place. In hearings involving children, they may also be used to establish whether a parent is unfit, or should be allowed to have unsupervised access to children. Some of the areas in which they provide specialized assistance include:

- Diagnosis and treatment of mental illnesses

- Medications and psychotropic drugs

- Standards of care

- Emotional distress and effects of a crime or event

Because medical and psychiatric experts may be used during an investigation, they may be required to testify in relation to information they provided earlier or evidence acquired by them. For example, if a forensic or behavioral psychologist were used to develop a profile of a serial killer and victims associated with the case, the information previously provided to police would appear as evidence in a trial. The expert would then need to testify, to explain the techniques that were used, and explain details that may not be clearly understood to the court.

Construction and Architecture Experts

Criminal and civil litigation can also involve issues that deal with real estate and the way in which a building or structure was constructed or designed. To provide insight and services in these cases, construction and architecture expert witnesses may be used. Some of the other areas in which they provide specialized assistance include:

- Building and fire codes
- Project management
- Defects in construction or design
- Accidents and safety

Construction and architecture experts can also provide information on how incidents involving properties occurred. For example, if a building was bombed, experts could be used to explain how the bomb was placed in a location that would bring down the building. In criminal and civil litigations, experts can also provide insight as to how various types of damage were caused by poor construction, errors in how the building was designed, or other issues that resulted in financial loss, injury, or death.

Testimony and Evidence

Testimony and evidence fall hand in hand with one another in a court case. Evidence often needs some narrative to put it into the context of the case, and relies on witness testimony to do that. When someone providing technical details of a case gives testimony, it can fall into one of two categories:

- Technical testimony
- Expert testimony

Technical testimonies are statements given under oath that present facts of a technical nature. In presenting the information, the witness must be technically accurate while translating complex and scientific issues to simple terms and concepts. In other words, in addition to testifying about the case, he or she must also teach the jury and/or judge so that they understand the relevance of these technical facts. Because it is vital that those in the court understand what is being discussed on the stand, there are a number of elements you can add to your testimony to make it more understandable to laymen, including:

- Refrain from using jargon.
- Explain the meaning and relevance of terms and acronyms. For example, "EnCase is forensic software that was used to acquire data from the computer. It's a proven product which the FBI has used for many years."
- Provide a glossary of technical terms and concepts to legal counsel. This may also be used by the court reporter when transcribing your testimony.
- Provide diagrams and pictures that will allow the jury and/or judge to better understand what's being talked about.

It is often useful when relating technical information to speak in a slow, gentle tone of voice. Although you should talk slow enough that the court reporter can effectively transcribe

your statement, and the judge and jury can follow the progression of your testimony, you shouldn't talk so slow that it appears you're patronizing those in the room. Practicing the pace and timber of your voice on friends and family before testifying can help in identifying the best way of speaking clearly.

Because many people may not understand certain technologies being discussed, and will find it difficult relating to your testimony, you should try to use analogies when explaining difficult concepts. For example, "IP addresses are similar to street addresses. The same way your home address lets other people know where you live, IP addresses are also unique addresses that identify one computer to others on a network." By using a familiar concept, people can more easily relate to what's being said.

Unless you are qualified as an expert, you should refrain from offering any opinions about the case, as they will be deemed inadmissible. You should state the facts, and answer questions without providing any personal or professional conclusions.

Expert witnesses also commonly give technical testimony, but are able to expand on their comments by expressing opinions and conclusions. *Expert testimony* is statements given under oath by a witness who's been recognized as an expert in a particular field. In providing facts that will help a jury and/or judge better understand the case, the witness may express an educated opinion related to his or her area of technical or specialized knowledge. The scope of this knowledge is established when qualifying the witness as an expert, and determines what the witness is and isn't allowed to express during the trial. Any opinions that are outside of the person's expertise are considered inadmissible.

Rules of Evidence

The guidelines that dictate whether a person can be recognized as an expert witness, and the admissibility of evidence, are governed by the laws of the jurisdiction of the court in which the evidence will be introduced. Thus, it is extremely important for investigators to become familiar with the applicable laws. These rules are adopted by statute and are usually codified into a document titled *Rules of Evidence*.

In the United States, Congress adopted the Federal Rules of Evidence (FRE) as a set of standards that determine how evidence is presented and deemed admissible in court. Because state and federal laws are different, many states have also adopted their own sets of rules, some of which are identical to those in the Federal Rules. The FRE contains a considerable number of rules, but those dealing with opinions and expert testimony are explained under Article VII. The rules under this Article consist of:

- Rule 701, Opinion Testimony by Lay Witnesses
- Rule 702, Testimony by Experts
- Rule 703, Basis of Opinion Testimony by Experts
- Rule 704, Opinion on Ultimate Issue

- Rule 705, Disclosure of Facts or Data Underlying Expert Opinion

- Rule 706, Court Appointed Experts

EXAM WARNING

On the exam, you will be expected to know the rules pertaining to expert witnesses testifying in court. You should pay particular attention and know the details of Rule 702 (Testimony by Experts) and Rule 703 (Basis of Opinion Testimony by Experts). The latest version of the Federal Rules of Evidence (at the time of this writing) is available on the U.S. House of Representatives Committee on the Judiciary Web site, at http://judiciary.house.gov/media/pdfs/printers/109th/31310.pdf.

Rule 701, Opinion Testimony by Lay Witnesses

Rule 701 addresses evidentiary witnesses who are not in court to provide expert testimony. Because of this, the scope of testimony is limited to events that transpired, and to what a person saw, heard, or did. Any opinions and inferences that the witness does make are limited to the following criteria:

- They must be rationally based on their perception.

- They are helpful to achieving a clear understanding of the testimony or determination of a fact in issue.

- They are not based on scientific, technical or specialized knowledge.

Although this rule enables the witness to have an opinion on the events he or she witnessed, it does limit the opinion to a narrow scope. For example, if a mugger held a gun to your head and said, "Give me all your money. You don't want to die," a rational perception of this event would be that he was going to kill you if you didn't give him your money. Such opinions are void of any specialized knowledge and deal only with clarifying the event, and what you believed was occurring.

Rule 702, Testimony by Experts

Rule 702 addresses testimony by expert witnesses who can have opinions based on scientific, technical, or specialized knowledge. As we discussed earlier, for this rule to apply, the witness must be qualified as an expert before he or she testifies in court. Rule 702 states the following:

"If scientific, technical, or other specialized knowledge will assist the trier of fact to understand the evidence or to determine a fact in issue, a witness qualified as an expert by knowledge, skill, experience, training, or education, may testify thereto in the form of an opinion or otherwise, if (1) the testimony is based upon sufficient facts or data, (2) the testimony is the product of reliable principles and methods, and (3) the witness has applied the principles and methods reliably to the facts of the case."

In looking at this rule, you will see that the function of providing expert testimony is to assist in understanding, determining, and relating to evidence and facts presented in the case. The information the expert provides must be based on facts or data and must use reliable principles and methods. In other words, any methods used can be reproduced.

Scientific methods that not accepted also cannot be used for expert testimony. For example, let's say an expert based his conclusions that the defendant was guilty on *physiognomy*, which is a pseudoscience in which criminal behavior can be determined based on a defendant's facial appearance, head shape, and other physical features. Because this isn't a reliable or accepted science, the opinions, conclusions, and possibly the defendant's entire testimony would be inadmissible.

Rule 703, Basis of Opinion Testimony by Experts

Rule 703 is another major rule for expert witnesses and the opinions they may express in testifying. This rule states:

"The facts or data in the particular case upon which an expert bases an opinion or inference may be those perceived by or made known to the expert at or before the hearing. If of a type reasonably relied upon by experts in the particular field in forming opinions or inferences upon the subject, the facts or data need not be admissible in evidence in order for the opinion or inference to be admitted. Facts or data that are otherwise inadmissible shall not be disclosed to the jury by the proponent of the opinion or inference unless the Court determines that their probative value in assisting the jury to evaluate the expert's opinion substantially outweighs their prejudicial effect."

The basis of this rule is that experts have access to evidence or information prior to a trial. In such cases, the expert may form an opinion on these facts, even if they are not used or are inadmissible in court. For example, a psychological expert might be aware that a defendant on trial for possession of child pornography had prior convictions for child molestation. Even if the jury isn't allowed to hear about these prior convictions, the psychologist could use this information to form an educated opinion that the defendant is a pedophile. The expert

couldn't mention the prior convictions in court, but could state an opinion that was formed by this information.

Rule 703 is controversial to some, as evidence that can't be used in court is being used in an indirect manner. The evidence the expert used doesn't completely provide a backdoor to submitting evidence, although there is some validity to this argument. If the jury has difficulty evaluating the expert's opinions, the judge could provide them with information and evidence that the expert used, even if it was otherwise inadmissible.

Even though the expert's opinion is considered vital to a trial, and can even outweigh the prejudicial effect of certain evidence, this isn't to say that opposing sides are powerless to an expert's conclusions. The witness can still be cross-examined to challenge the validity of his or her opinions, and the opposing side can call their own expert witnesses to provide alternative conclusions and opinions on the facts of the case. However, a problem with this tactic is that when experts are called to challenge or provide conflicting opinions to a previous expert, the end result is that the jury can become confused and even disinterested. Because the opinions expressed can ultimately be discarded, it is known as junk testimony.

TEST DAY TIP

Rules 702 and 703 are considered the main rules regarding expert testimony, and you should review them on exam day. By understanding these rules, you'll be in a better position to answer questions regarding who can qualify as an expert witness, and what opinions they can give.

Rule 704, Opinion on Ultimate Issue

Rule 704 deals with the ability of legal counsel to object to opinions made by an expert, and what an expert can testify to in certain situations. In most cases, an attorney cannot object to an opinion made by an expert, because its validity should be decided by the facts of the case. In other words, cross-examination and evidence in the case should help evolve a decision regarding whether the expert is correct. However, an objection can be made if the expert testifies about the mental state of a defendant in a criminal case, and whether the defendant had this mental condition while committing the crime or when using it as a defense. The expert isn't permitted to make such a conclusion, as the facts of the case should decide this issue, not the opinions of a witness.

Rule 705, Disclosure of Facts or Data Underlying Expert Opinion

Rule 705 addresses issues raised in Rule 703 regarding facts and data that were used to form an expert opinion being disclosed to the jury. In this rule, the expert may provide an opinion

without releasing information or evidence that helped to form that opinion. He or she may be able to disclose these facts if the judge instructs him or her to do so, or may be required to disclose certain facts during cross-examination. This rule states that "the expert may testify in terms of opinion or inference and give reasons therefore without first testifying to the underlying facts or data, unless the Court requires otherwise. The expert may in any event be required to disclose the underlying facts or data on cross-examination."

Rule 706, Court Appointed Experts

Rule 706 provides guidelines on how experts should be appointed by the court. The rule provides information dealing with:

- How they are appointed

- The monetary compensation they receive

- Disclosure, which simply states that the court may inform the jury that the court appointed an expert witness

- That legal counsel (i.e., the prosecution and defense) may also call their own expert witnesses

Authentication of Evidence

The rules of state courts may differ from those of the federal courts, and the rules for evidence in criminal trials may differ from those for civil trials. Generally, evidence must be *authenticated*, which in this context usually means that some witness must testify to its authenticity. In the case of digital evidence, this could be a witness who has personal knowledge of the evidence (e.g., a person who shared the computer with the accused and observed the document or file in question on the computer). It could also be the first responder who saw the evidence on-screen when responding to the incident, or an expert who examined the computer and evidence after it was seized. In terms of when a duplicate of the data was made using forensic software, testifying about how the software authenticates a data image is generally all that's necessary. One of the most important aspects of preparing to introduce evidence in court is determining which witnesses will testify as to its existence and validity, describe the circumstances of its discovery, and verify that it has not been tampered with.

Certain types of evidence are sometimes held by the Rules of Evidence to be self-authenticating. This means testimony as to authenticity isn't required and usually refers to such things as public documents under seal, certified copies of public records, official publications, and the like. It is also possible for both sides at trial to agree to *stipulate* as to the authenticity of a piece of evidence, in which case it does not have to be authenticated through testimony. When both sides agree to the stipulation of a fact (such as the fact that the evidence is authentic), the judge will advise the jury that they are to presume that the fact is true and it is not a matter that has to be proved or disproved at trial.

Evidence Processing

Computer forensic standards have been developed that apply to the collection and preservation of digital evidence, which differs in nature from most other types of evidence and thus requires different methods of handling. Following procedures that are proper, accepted, and, in some cases, prescribed by law in dealing with evidence is vital to the successful prosecution of a cybercrime case. The proper handling of these procedures comes into play at two different points in a trial:

- If evidence is not collected and handled according to the proper standards, the judge may deem the evidence inadmissible when it is presented (usually based on the opposing attorney's *motion to suppress*) and the jury members will never get a chance to evaluate it or consider it in making their decision.

- If the evidence is admitted, the opposing attorney will attack its credibility during questioning of the witnesses who testify regarding it. Such an attack can create doubt in jury members' minds that will cause them to disregard the evidence in making their decision—and perhaps even taint the credibility of the entire case.

The entire investigation will be of little value if the evidence that shows the defendant's guilt is not allowed into the trial or if the jury gives it no weight. Thus, proper handling of evidence is one of the most important issues facing all criminal investigators and, because of the intangible nature of digital evidence, cybercrime investigators in particular. Because this is such an important topic—not only for investigators, but also for prosecutors, judges, and justice system professionals involved in cybercrime cases—many organizations and publications are devoted solely to issues concerning digital evidence:

- The International Organization of Computer Evidence (IOCE) was established in 1995 to provide a forum for law enforcement agencies around the world to exchange information about computer forensic issues; its U.S. component is the Scientific Working Group on Digital Evidence (SWGDE).

- The International Association of Computer Investigative Specialists (IACIS; www.cops.org) is a nonprofit organization that is dedicated to educating law enforcement professionals in the area of computer forensics.

- *The International Journal of Digital Evidence* (www.ijde.org) is an online publication devoted to discussions of the theory and practice of handling digital evidence.

- *Computer Forensics Magazine* is published by DIBS, a maker of computer forensic equipment. *Computer Forensics Online* (www.shk-dplc.com/cfo) is a Webzine that is run by attorneys and technical professionals specializing in computer law.

Many other similar resources that focus on computer forensics are available, and more broad-based organizations such as the American Academy of Forensic Sciences (www.aafs.org) address computer crimes and digital evidence along with other forensic topics. A glance at any of these resources will reveal that digital evidence handling is a huge topic that could easily fill several books (and already has). It is far beyond the scope of this appendix to cover every aspect of collecting and preserving digital evidence.

Admissibility of Evidence

There are a number of requirements for evidence to be admissible in court. The evidence must be *competent* (i.e., reliable and credible), it must be *relevant* (it tends to prove a fact of the case), and it must be *material* (it substantiates an issue that is in question in the case).

In addition, to be admissible in U.S. courts, evidence must be obtained legally. That is, it must be obtained in accordance with the laws governing search and seizure, including laws expressed in the U.S. and state constitutions. If evidence is obtained through an illegal search, even though it proves the guilt of the defendant, the evidence is considered to be "tainted." This is known as the "fruits of the poisonous tree" doctrine, or the *exclusionary rule*. Case law in some jurisdictions sets special rules for the admissibility of scientific evidence. Under the Federal Rules of Evidence, Rule 402, all relevant evidence is admissible except as otherwise provided under the U.S. Constitution, by Act of Congress, or under the Federal Rules of Evidence themselves (e.g., evidence obtained in violation of a suspect's constitutional rights). Rule 401 defines relevant evidence as "any evidence having a tendency to make the existence of any fact that is of consequence to the determination of the action more probable or less probable than it would be without the evidence." This is known as the *relevancy test*. Another standard sometimes applied to scientific evidence is the *general acceptance test*, also known as the *Frye standard*, which holds that a scientific technique must be generally accepted in the field before the results of the technique can be admitted as evidence.

EXAM WARNING

Don't confuse Rule 401 with the Frye standard. Although both deal with the admissibility of evidence, Rule 401 addresses the relevance of evidence to a trial, whereas the Frye standard speaks to whether the techniques in obtaining that evidence or information are accepted.

Digital Evidence

Although the rules of evidence regarding digital data are not clear-cut, it is always safest to exceed the minimum requirements for admissibility. When investigators take extra precautions

to ensure the integrity of evidence, above and beyond what the court might find acceptable, not only will the possibility of having the evidence excluded by the judge be avoided, but also the impression on the jury will be more favorable. Organizations such as the IACIS provide standards governing forensic examination procedures for their members. Showing in court that you adhered to such high standards in conducting the investigation will enhance your case. Most computer forensic organizations and experts agree on some basic standards regarding the handling of digital evidence, which can be summarized as follows:

- The original evidence should be preserved in a state as close as possible to the state it was in when found.

- If at all possible, an exact copy (image) of the original should be made to be used for examination so as not to damage the integrity of the original.

- Copies of data made for examination should be made on media that are *forensically sterile* that is, there must be no preexisting data on the disk or other media; it should be completely "clean" and checked for freedom from viruses and defects.

- All evidence should be properly tagged and documented and the chain of custody preserved, and each step of the forensic examination should be documented in detail.

TEST DAY TIP

Preservation of data is a primary component of computer forensic practices, and you should understand it when taking the test. It is important that any evidence that is obtained from a computer isn't tainted, damaged, or destroyed as this can affect its admissibility in court.

Testifying As an Expert Witness

Testifying as an expert witness can be an intimidating and stressful experience, especially if it's your first time. You may be unfamiliar with the courtroom, its layout, what's expected of you, and what will happen in court. Although you may receive some preparation from the attorney who will call you as a witness, often you receive little to no preparation and feel like you're simply thrown in the lion's den.

Although the courtroom can appear professional and reverent, the moments between cases and breaks in court can be absolutely chaotic. Paperwork needs to be processed, exhibits need to be prepared, witnesses need to be organized and updated, and those involved in a trial become embroiled in a flurry of activity behind the scenes. Although this chaos can filter into

the trial, what most people see when entering a courtroom is an ordered and sober environment. Each person involved in a trial have his or her own place in the room and his or her own tasks to perform, including the following:

- **Judge** This is a court official that's either appointed or elected to preside over the court, and make judgments on issues in trials and hearings.

- **Court reporter** This is a court officer that transcribes the testimony and arguments made in the trial, which will become an official record of the proceedings.

- **Court clerk** This is a court officer that performs administrative duties, such as swearing in witnesses, handling exhibits, and performing other duties for the court.

- **Bailiff** This is a court officer that's responsible for maintaining order and decorum in the courtroom. In some jurisdictions and countries, the bailiff may instead be court security, and be designated as a special constable of the police. The bailiff has custody of the jury and will escort them in and out of the courtroom, and may also perform other duties, such as calling in witnesses waiting outside the courtroom.

- **Prosecutor** This is the lawyer representing the state (or the Crown in Canada and the United Kingdom) in criminal court cases. In doing so, the prosecutor represents the people and is responsible for taking legal action against the defendant and putting him, her, or them on trial.

- **Defense attorney** This is the lawyer representing the defendant in a criminal court case.

- **Plaintiff** This is the person suing a defendant in civil litigation. In civil litigation, both the plaintiff and the defendant may also have their own legal counsel.

- **Defendant** This is the person charged with a crime (in criminal court) or the person being sued (in civil court).

- **Jury** This is a group of citizens that have been selected to hear evidence and render a verdict.

- **Witnesses** These are individuals testifying to events that occurred or evidence presented as exhibits in the trial.

- **Spectators** These are members of the public and/or media watching the trial. They may consist of friends and family of the defendant, or interested parties who have come to watch the proceedings.

Of these roles, serving as a witness can be one of the most demanding to fulfill. Without the testimony and evidence a witness provides, it would be impossible to achieve a conviction. Although testifying can be uncomfortable even if you have years of experience as an evidentiary or expert witness, knowing about the process relieves much of the stress. In the sections that follow, we'll discuss aspects of the courtroom, trial proceedings, the tactics that prosecutors

and defense attorneys may use, and what you can expect when testifying. The fewer surprises and the more prepared you are, the fewer problems you'll encounter on the stand.

Layout of a Courtroom

Courtrooms are traditionally laid out in a specific manner, with seating arrangements and furniture arranged for special purposes. Dissimilarities may be apparent when comparing courtrooms that are used for different purposes or judicial systems, such as when comparing family court to a military court martial, or those of different countries. However, even when these differences are seen, similarities in functionality can usually be recognized.

As shown in Figure A.1, a courtroom layout can consist of numerous individual components, including the following:

- **Judge's bench** This is a desk area where the judge is seated to preside over the trial.

- **Witness stand** This is an enclosed seating area where the witness gives testimony.

- **Court reporter's desk** This is where the sworn proceedings of the trial are transcribed.

- **Court clerk's desk** This is where court records are maintained.

- **Jury box** This is seating for members of the jury.

- **Prosecution's table** This is where the prosecutor is seated. In a civil litigation, this would be the plaintiff's table.

- **Defendant's table** This is where the defendant and his or her legal council (i.e., defense attorney) is seated.

- **Podium** This is where the prosecutor and defense attorneys will stand when formally addressing the court and examining/cross-examining witnesses.

- **Well of the courtroom** This is the main area of the courtroom where proceedings of the trial take place.

- **Bar** This is a railing separating the gallery from the well of the courtroom.

- **Gallery** This is an area where members of the public, media, and other spectators are seated.

Figure A.1 Sample Layout of a Courtroom

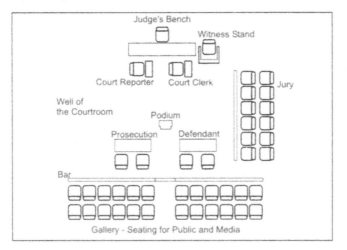

A courtroom serves as the staging area of a trial, and has a theatrical design. When looking at Figure A.1, you can see that it is intended to accommodate an audience, as most trials are open to public spectators. Although public trials provide accountability regarding how they are conducted, the design of a courtroom is also influenced by the centuries-old practice of it being a form of public entertainment. The layout of a courtroom is designed to give maximum visibility to those watching the trial (whether they be judge, jury, or spectators), and to focus their attention on the actions and actors involved in the courtroom process.

To help achieve this, the components of a courtroom are layered to varying heights. The judge's bench is positioned higher than other seating areas in the room. It allows him or her to rule over the court from a vantage point that overlooks everything, but it also conveys that the judge is an authoritative and imposing figure that has control over the room. The witness stand may also be raised but is lower than that of the judge's bench, forcing anyone giving testimony to look up at the judge, but remain at eye level with the lawyers who stand at a podium in the well of the courtroom when examining and cross-examining witnesses. Less visible are the court officers who sit at the foot of the judge's bench. Although the court reporter generally remains unnoticed during the trial while transcribing the proceedings, the court clerk is generally noticed only when swearing in witnesses or performing other court functions. To the side of the judge, a jury box provides the next best possible seats. In a jury trial, the jurors will be able to see and hear everything in the trial as it plays out in front of them, much like the spectators who sit in the gallery to the backs of the lawyers and the accused.

Technology in the Courtroom

Although tradition has dictated the design, technology has also influenced the courtroom. Newer courtrooms are often built with technology in mind, whereas older ones may be retrofitted to accommodate computers and display digital evidence more easily. Because there

are no standards for the availability of technology, what you may see can vary greatly between courtrooms.

Even in older courthouses, a certain amount of technology will be present. Microphones are used in the witness box, judge's bench, and podium to allow voices to be heard throughout the courtroom, and lawyers will often use laptop computers to maintain their notes and other information brought to court. Although newer courtrooms are designed to have a sufficient number of electrical outlets, this generally isn't the case in older courthouses. As such, these and any other devices brought to court may require extension cords and/or power bars to be taped or draped across the floor. This can be a little surprising to see when walking to the witness stand, and having to step over a mat or duct tape covering electrical cords.

In newer or retrofitted courtrooms, there is a greater integration between technology and the justice system. Some of the advanced technology you may find in these courtrooms may include the following:

- **Document camera** This is a device on which documents or a small to medium-size object can be placed so that an overhead camera can capture its image. The camera may project the image to a screen (much like an overhead projector would) or transmit it to monitors networked together in the room.

- **Display monitors** These are used to display images, multimedia presentations, or other output from a computer or a document camera. These can be flat panel displays that are located on the judge's bench, on the witness box, on the court officer's table(s) (i.e., court clerk, court reporter), on legal counsel's tables, and between pairs of jurors in the jury box.

- **Annotation monitors** These are monitors located at the podium and witness box that allow on-screen drawings to be made, such as diagrams or other information that enhance what is displayed on other monitors in the courtroom.

- **Real-time transcription** This allows transcribed testimony to be directed to the judge's bench and counsel tables.

- **Translation and listening devices** These allow any testimony in another language to be spoken into a microphone, translated by another person, and then broadcast via infrared or other technologies to listening devices (i.e., headsets, etc.) that are worn by the judge, jurors, legal counsel, court officers, and others directly related to the trial.

- **Videoconferencing** This involves cameras fixed in the courtroom that are focused on the judge, witness, and legal counsel at the podium. Other cameras may also be set up in other rooms of the courthouse, such as the judge's chamber or a room used for testimony by individuals who have been excused from testifying in the courtroom. Using the images captured by these cameras, video conferencing can then be used for pretrial conferences, remote witness testimony, or other proceedings. For

example, a child who was sexually abused might be excused from facing his or her abuser in the courtroom, and be able to testify from a remote location.

- **Computer-ready counsel tables** These are tables used by the prosecution and defense attorneys. These may be discretely fitted with electrical outlets and ports that allow connections to display monitors or other features available through the courtroom.

- **Printers** These allow information displayed on monitors to be printed, as well as data from any or specific computers in the courtroom.

Because the level of technology available in a courtroom may vary, you may need to confer with the prosecution regarding whether certain equipment will be accessible for your testimony. For example, if your testimony relies on showing the images or other files found on a hard disk, it would be beneficial to know whether they can be displayed on monitors already in the courtroom, if a computer projector and screen are available, or if you will need to bring your own equipment. By being prepared and understanding what's available to present your testimony, you can avoid situations that make testifying chaotic and stressful.

Order of Trial Proceedings

The trial process actually begins when a suspect is arrested or a warrant is issued for a suspect's arrest. After the arrest, the defendant is taken before a magistrate (a judge or, in some cases, the mayor of a city or town) within a specified period—usually within 48 hours—and *arraigned*. This arraignment is an informal process whereby the magistrate tells the defendant what charges have been filed against him or her, Mirandizes the defendant, and sets or denies bail.

A preliminary hearing usually takes place within a few days. In this hearing, the prosecution must present enough evidence to convince the judge that the defendant should go to trial. In some cases, the defendant goes before a grand jury instead of a judge. This is a secret proceeding in which the grand jury decides whether to hand down an *indictment*. Next, a formal arraignment may be held, at which the defendant can enter a plea for the charges against him or her.

Before the actual trial, there is usually a pretrial conference or hearing at which motions can be filed (e.g., asking for a change of venue). Finally, the case goes to trial. If the defendant pleads not guilty to the charges, a jury is selected through the *voir dire* process, during which each side gets to question potential jurors and *strike*, or exclude, a certain number. The judge instructs the jury on the applicable law, and then the attorneys each give an opening statement.

Because the burden of proof is on the prosecution, the prosecuting attorney gets to go first with an opening statement. After the defense attorney's opening statement, the prosecution calls witnesses. With each witness, the prosecution asks questions; this process is called *direct examination*. Then the defense attorney is allowed to question the witness about the matters that were brought up during direct examination. Afterward, the prosecution can *redirect*, after which the

defense can *recross*. This process occurs with each witness until both attorneys are finished questioning that witness.

An investigator or IT professional testifying as to personal knowledge of the evidence in the case (an evidentiary witness) will be testifying as a prosecution witness and thus will be directly examined by the prosecutor and cross-examined by the defense attorney. Expert witnesses may testify for either side, but must be qualified as experts prior to testifying so that any opinions they have may be included in the testimony.

When the prosecution has presented all its witnesses and evidence, the defense attorney usually makes a motion to dismiss the case due to lack of evidence. If this motion is granted, the trial is over and the defendant goes free. If not, the defense presents its case, calling witnesses to testify. These witnesses are cross-examined by the prosecutor, and so forth, in the same manner as the prosecution witnesses. After the defense has presented its case, the prosecution is allowed to call rebuttal witnesses, and the defense can rebut those witnesses.

Finally, when all the rebuttals are done, the attorneys make their closing statements (which side goes first depends on the court) and the judge gives more instructions to the jurors, who are then sent out to reach a verdict.

Subpoenas

A *subpoena* is a legal document that is issued by the court to notify you that you are required to attend court to give evidence as a witness. The court may subpoena you on behalf of the prosecution, the defense, or both. In looking at the subpoena shown in Figure A.2, which is an actual subpoena with the pertinent data removed, you will see that it contains a considerable amount of information regarding a trial, including the following:

- The name and address of the person being summoned to court
- The date and time you are required to attend court
- The name of the defendant
- What the defendant is charged with
- The address where the trial will take place
- The name and contact information of the officer in charge of the case
- The name of the attorney subpoenaing you
- Instructions to bring any books, documents, writing, or other exhibits related to this case with you

Figure A.2 A Subpoena

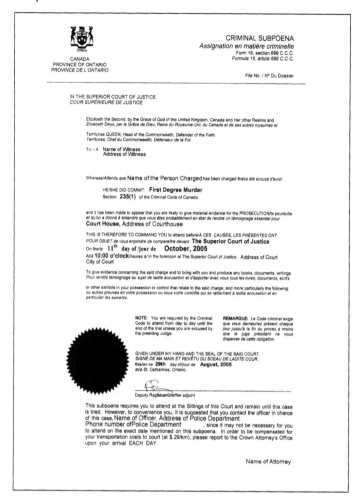

The subpoena is hand-delivered to you by a summons officer or other court officer, who will use information on the subpoena and other contact information that you may have previously supplied to the investigator or attorney. Once you have been served with the summons to appear in court as a witness, you are required to attend. If you fail to attend, criminal charges may be pressed against you, and if you are convicted you could face imprisonment and/or a fine.

Not Appearing in Court

Sometimes attending court is not possible. When there is a good reason not to attend court, you should notify the attorney who subpoenaed you and the officer in charge of the case as soon as possible. If a reason is good enough, you may be rescheduled, or (in cases where your testimony is pivotal to the case) the trial itself may be rescheduled.

An example of not being able to attend court occurred the first time I was subpoenaed to appear as an expert witness in a trial. When I saw the date of the case, I realized it was the due date that my wife was to give birth. I informed the investigator and attorney, and mentioned that the chances of my wife actually giving birth on that date were slim. As fate would have it, my son was right on time, born on the day I was scheduled to testify.

Although I had warned those involved of this possibility, I was on the phone in the delivery room explaining how I wouldn't be able to attend court. I should also mention that I had the good sense to call *after* my wife had delivered our son. The attorney prosecuting the case offered congratulations and I was rescheduled to testify the next day. The thought was that I would be the first to testify, and then could return to the hospital to bring my wife and son home after they were discharged.

Although I generally recommend a witness getting a good night's sleep, I managed to get three hours of rest before dropping off my daughter at a babysitter, and showing up in court the next day. Upon arriving at court first thing in the morning, I found that my scheduled testimony had been delayed due to another witness needing to complete her testimony from the previous day. I waited for the other witness's testimony and cross-examination to be completed, and then found that another witness was being moved ahead of me to offer his testimony. By that afternoon, I was wondering whether I was even going to be called to the stand, or whether I would be rescheduled to the next day. I explained that my wife and newborn son had been discharged from the hospital, but were waiting for me to pick them up. Although my wife was patiently waiting for me to be finished, she had now been waiting all day in the maternity ward for a ride home. The attorney who called me as a witness told me to leave court, pick her up from the hospital, and bring my family home … then rush back and testify.

After unceremoniously dropping my wife and newborn son off at home, I returned to court, where other witnesses were still being examined and cross-examined. When I was finally called to the witness stand, I received congratulations from the judge and court officers, gave my testimony, and then proceeded to be grilled by the defense lawyer until the day concluded. Few witnesses ever remember one of the most stressful times testifying in court as also being one of the happiest days of their life.

Depositions

A *deposition* is the process of questioning witnesses prior to a trial, and it is used in the pretrial stages of both civil and criminal cases. In a deposition, the witness is under oath and is required to tell the truth as though in the trial. Legal counsel can examine and cross-examine the witness, and may even use this as an opportunity to discover information that may be used in the later trial. Because the deposition doesn't require a public forum, it may not necessarily be held in the courtroom, but instead in a meeting room or another venue that's been agreed upon.

Throughout the deposition, a court reporter or a stenographer documents the questions and statements made, so they can be preserved for future reference. Although the deposition doesn't replace testifying during the trial, unless there are exceptional circumstances for why the witness is unable to attend (such as dying before the trial starts), the information gathered in the deposition can later be used in trial. Attorneys may use statements made in a deposition to show contradictions in later testimony, thereby discrediting the witness by showing inaccuracies between incongruous statements made under oath.

Testifying in a deposition is generally less formal than the trial itself, although the same etiquette of showing respect for the court and those involved in the process applies. Because of this, requests for a break can be made whenever needed. Although it can be less formal, you should never assume anything is off the record. Any remarks made during the deposition will be recorded, so you should refrain from saying anything you don't want preserved for posterity until you are away from the court reporter and the location where the deposition is held.

Once a deposition has been transcribed, a witness is given the opportunity to review its contents for any inaccuracies and to make corrections. It is important that you read the transcription thoroughly, because once you read and sign it, it becomes an official record. When reviewing the document, you should look for mistakes in dates, times, quantities, or technical details that may appear later during the trial as evidence. The more accurate it is the less chance a mistake will be used to contradict truthful statements made later in court.

TIP

When testifying in a deposition or trial, you are generally given a glass of water immediately upon taking the witness stand. This is because your mouth and throat can get parched because you're talking so much, because you're nervous, and (especially in older courthouses) because of the dry environment of the courtroom. Just as you should go to the washroom before going on the witness stand (no pun intended), you should be careful how much water you drink, or your testimony may take on an untended urgency from needing a recess.

Swearing vs. Affirming

When serving as a witness, you are obviously expected to tell the truth. To declare that you will do so, one of two brief formal procedures is performed in which you promise to be honest. They are:

- Swearing in
- Affirming

For various reasons, most witnesses in the Western World are sworn in. This involves either holding your right hand on the Bible or taking a Bible in your right hand and holding up your left hand. After doing so, you are then asked whether you swear to tell the truth "so help you God." In some courts, the mention of God isn't used, although most continue to do so. In swearing to tell the truth, you are now a witness and can continue the task of providing testimony.

If you are an atheist or have religious beliefs that prohibit you from swearing to God, there is also the option of affirming. When you affirm, you may be asked to raise your hand while making an oath to promise to tell the truth. In doing so, no Bible or mention of God is used. Once this is done, you are affirmed, and you have completed a declaration of honesty that carries the same weight as being sworn in.

Affirming or swearing to tell the truth occurs immediately after you've been called as a witness and taken the stand. Once you've entered the witness box, the judge or court clerk will ask whether you would like to be sworn in or affirmed. Which you choose is entirely up to you, and has no effect or bias in the events that follow, while you're testifying. Regardless of whether you've been sworn in or affirmed, if you lie you can be charged with perjury.

Being affirmed or sworn in can occur in either civil or criminal proceedings, as well as depositions and affidavits (which we'll discuss next). The reason they are used in so many areas of law is simple: It is crucial for the witness to tell the truth. If the truth wasn't presented to the court, an accurate determination of events cannot be made, and a proper ruling cannot be made.

Affidavits

An *affidavit* is a formal statement of facts. When you are a witness in a criminal trial or civil dispute you may be required to provide an affidavit that outlines the facts as you know them. This provides a written version of your formal statement. This written document states what you saw, heard, or otherwise know to be the truth. In terms of an expert witness, this would be information that is within your area of expertise. It is signed by you to validate that everything you have written is true, and by another person who has you take an oath. The oath is that you either swear or affirm that everything stated in the document is true. The oath is taken by someone authorized by the court, such as a notary public or a court officer, which formalizes the document as being true and legal.

Legal Etiquette and Ethics

As with any official gathering, there are certain codes of conduct that should be followed. In accordance with legal etiquette and ethics, you are expected to conduct yourself with a specific level of professionalism when attending court. *Etiquette* is the rules of socially acceptable behavior and courtesy, whereas *ethics* are moral principles or values. Together, they define how a person behaves in the courtroom.

Courtrooms are intended to be solemn, reflecting the serious nature of the forum they provide. Conducting yourself in a manner that maintains this atmosphere shows respect not only to the court itself, but also to those who must attend and have their fates decided in trials. Just as you would behave in a serious and thoughtful manner at a memorial service, ceremony, or other formal event, you should show the same level of respect in the courtroom. Some of the ways to show this respect include:

- Dress conservatively in business attire (such as a suit, dress, or other conservative clothing you might wear to a business meeting or solemn occasion).

- Arrive early and be available to testify when called.

- When speaking to the judge, refer to him or her as "your honor."

- Do not whisper or talk in the courtroom unless it is absolutely necessary. If information must be exchanged, it is better to pass a note to the attorney or other person you are conferring with.

- Bring only the notes you will use on the stand. Do not bring magazines or other reading material to pass the time.

The legal etiquette and ethical behavior you show in a courtroom applies not only to those attending as jurors and legal counsel, but also (and especially) to witnesses. The way you behave in the courtroom and on the witness stand will be observed by others in the courtroom, and will affect the way they perceive your credibility as a witness under direct and cross-examinations.

TIP

If you are testifying as an expert witness, you may not see the defendant until you are called as a witness. Because of this, avoid talking to others about the case, and limit your contact with other people who may be waiting outside the courtroom. You don't want to accidentally get into a discussion with someone against whom you'll later be giving testimony.

Direct Examination

Direct examination refers to the process of a witness being questioned by the attorney who called him or her to the stand. Because the attorney who called you to the stand wants you to give good testimony, any questions that are asked are for the purpose of eliciting facts about the case. In other words, the lawyer asks these questions to help you provide evidence.

The first rule for giving direct testimony (or any sworn testimony) is to always tell the truth. Witnesses should not be afraid to say "I don't know" or "I don't remember" when that's the truth. Telling the truth is vital to providing facts to the case, and failing to tell the truth is a serious matter. Lying under oath is a criminal offence called *perjury*, and it can result in imprisonment and fines being imposed on you.

In addition to this most important and basic element of being a witness, there are a number of best practices for testifying in court. Remember that the jury will evaluate the credibility of each witness and decide whether to believe the testimony based on that evaluation. Here are some ways to enhance your credibility as a witness:

- **Be on time or slightly early for court** Although we discussed this and the following point in the preceding section, attending court early allows you time to prepare and scope out the layout of the courtroom, the route you'll walk from your seat in the courtroom to the witness stand, and so on. Arriving late makes a bad impression on the jury and detracts from your credibility.

- **Dress professionally** Appearance does count, and your credibility will be enhanced by conservative business attire.

- **Don't appear to be nervous** Juries expect people to act nervous when they're lying. You might not be able to control how you feel, but with practice you can control any visible manifestations of nervousness, such as repetitive gestures.

- **Keep a good posture** Juries will look at a person's body language when approaching, leaving, or sitting in the witness box. Standing and sitting up straight convey confidence, whereas slouching can appear as though you're uncomfortable and are trying to hide something. Although you want to be relaxed on the stand, don't forget what your mother told you about sitting up straight.

- **Remain calm and don't get angry** The opposing attorney might try to make you lose your temper; doing so will damage your credibility with the jury. Witnesses should never argue or be sarcastic in response to an attorney's questions. Similarly, you should refrain from showing hostility toward the defendant, as this can make it seem like you have a personal agenda against the person. Remaining calm and professional will strengthen the case.

- **When applicable, answer with "yes" or "no"** Although this goes hand in hand with our next point, when answering a question to the affirmative or negative, you

should always use the word "yes" or "no." On the stand, people often make the mistake of nodding or shaking their head to answer, grunting answers, or using terms such as uh-huh, yep, nope, or similar phrases. Whenever this occurs, the attorney questioning you must correct you and tell you to answer with yes or no, which can get monotonous and irritate everyone very quickly.

- **Don't volunteer extra information** Answer the questions you are asked, but don't provide more information or veer off the topic. Don't provide hearsay evidence (what other people said to you), because it's generally inadmissible.

- **Avoid making absolutes in your statements** Making an absolute statement such as "I always …" or "I never …" can create an adversarial situation in later cross-examination, which may be used to prove you wrong. After all, very little is absolute. Even saying "the sun always shines in the sky" is incorrect when you consider eclipses and nighttime.

- **Don't discuss the case with anyone but the attorney** When attending court as a witness, you may spend little time in the actual courtroom. You'll generally be restricted from entering the courtroom until being called, and adjournments and recesses will allow you to leave court for a period. During these moments, you'll be exposed to others who may testify; victims and defendants in a case; and possibly even the media. Because you probably won't know who most of these people are, you should never discuss the case with anyone. Doing so can taint the testimony of others or provide sensitive information to the wrong people.

- **Consider the question carefully before you answer** Be sure you understand the question, and if you don't, ask the attorney to repeat it. Don't start answering until you're sure that the attorney is finished asking the question.

- **Speak clearly and confidently** An effective witness doesn't shout, but speaks loudly enough to be heard by the judge, jury, and attorneys. Testimony as an evidentiary witness should be limited to "just the facts, ma'am, just the facts." Don't offer opinion or speculation; in an impartial, objective manner, simply tell what you did or observed.

- **If the judge or attorney begins to speak, stop talking** When you are testifying, attorneys or the judge may interject to obtain a better understanding of a particular point, or stop you from revealing information that is inadmissible. When either of them speaks, immediately stop your testimony and listen to what they are saying.

- **Avoid memorizing answers** Although it's important that you review the notes and fully understand specifics of your testimony beforehand, preparing answers to anticipated questions can make your testimony appear scripted and unreliable.

- **Remain impartial and speak to the facts** Remember that as a witness, you are presenting facts of the case. Never exaggerate, never guess, and never manipulate answers to an attorney's question to favor one side or the other. Simply tell the truth, regardless of whose side the answer may benefit.

Exam Warning

Expect questions that deal with testifying as an expert witness to directly or indirectly deal with direct testimony and/or cross-examination. Ensure that you understand the differences between the two before taking the test.

Cross-Examination

Cross-examination is the process of providing the opposing side in a trial the opportunity to question a witness. In any trial, the prosecution has the right to question witnesses called by the defense, and defense has the right to question witnesses called by the prosecution. It is the job of the cross-examining attorney to discredit the opposing side's witness. Attorneys may use psychological techniques to attempt to discredit witnesses. When testifying, be careful not to fall into their traps. Be prepared for and ready to avoid such cross-examination tactics as:

- Rapid-fire questions with no time to answer between questions

- Leading questions ("Isn't it true that what you saw was …?")

- Repeating your words with a twist that changes their meaning

- Pretending to be friendly, then turning against you suddenly

- Feigning bewilderment, outrage, or shock at what you've said

- Prolonged silence designed to cause discomfort in hopes you'll say more

The most important thing for you to remember when subjected to these tactics is this: Don't take the attorney's tactics personally; he or she is just doing a job. Our advice to the witness is to just do *your* job; keep your cool and state the facts.

You can use a number of tricks to deal with an attorney's tactics during cross-examination. Lawyers will often attempt to gain a pace to their questions, starting by asking questions with some time between them, and then shortening the time between questions until they're being fired off in quick succession. This limits the time you have to think of an answer, and it increases the possibility of being caught in a trap. Many times, a question will be asked one way, and then asked a different way later. If you change your answer, the lawyer will use this to

discredit your testimony. A simple way to defuse these rapid-fire questions is to force a delay before answering. By quietly tapping your foot three times before giving an answer, you give yourself a moment to think, and you control the pace of the questions and answers being given. Because you are sitting in an enclosed witness box, no one can see you discretely tapping your foot and defusing the attorney's attempt at rapid-fire questioning.

It is important to always listen to the questions being asked, and be ready to respond. A lawyer may ask a question, wait for an answer, and then repeat what you've said but twist the words. Doing so can change the meaning of your statement and can twist what you've said to the lawyer's favor. If the lawyer restates it as a question (such as by beginning with "So, you're saying that …") and you're not paying attention, you could actually agree with something you never said. Never be afraid to say, "That's not what I said" in these situations, and reiterate your previous statement.

TIP

The way to answer questions when testifying is to stop, think, and then answer. Always consider what is being said, and the way it is asked. If you don't understand the question, say so, and the attorney will attempt to rephrase it.

Another common method is to start questioning you with points of agreement. In doing so, the lawyer conducting the cross-examination appears friendly and brings the witness's guard down. The witness will generally be more cooperative, and the lawyer can then either dismantle previous statements by asking follow-up questions, or ask leading questions that may cause the witness to make statements that will be positive to the opposing side's position. Often, once your guard is down, the lawyer will turn from being friendly to suddenly attacking what you've said or becoming confrontational. This can confuse you and leave you feeling a little betrayed the first time it happens, and it allows the attorney to take the upper hand in questioning you.

Other psychological ploys can involve saying very little or nothing at all. Once you've finished answering, the attorney may delay asking the next question, choosing instead to pause for a long period. Because the prolonged silence can be uncomfortable, the witness may feel that he or she should say more. If nothing is added, the lawyer will undermine your comments by saying, "Oh, I'm sorry, are you done?"

Many of the methods attorneys use are implemented throughout the trial process, including when a witness is being qualified as an expert. When challenging a witness, the attorney will ask a series of questions to probe details of the witness's qualifications and evaluate his or her level of knowledge. In general, the challenging party is given a fairly loose reign in the questions asked about a person's credentials, and judges and attorneys calling you may

allow a line of questioning to continue until it appears the witness is being unfairly attacked. How legal counsel undercuts the witness's authority will vary, as lawyers have different styles of cross-examining witnesses.

One method that is used to varying degrees is to review your credentials, and then undermine them by repeating facts in a snide tone of voice. For example, if a computer technician graduated from community college, the lawyer might repeat the name of the school in a sarcastic tone, and then ask, "So, you never went to a university?" Similarly, if you had a CompTIA certification, the lawyer would repeat "CompTIA?" as if you were making it up. It is a simple tactic that requires little to no knowledge about a subject.

Because there is an element of theatre to court, lawyers will often act a part. They may pretend to be an avid proponent of justice, or someone who actually cares and believes in their client's innocence. Although this may be true of some court officers, the fact is that lawyers will defend clients regardless of whether they are guilty or innocent. Despite this, they will use a tactic of pretending to be morally outraged, baffled, or shocked by a statement. Because lawyers are also generally bad actors, this can be more annoying than surprising when it occurs. The attempt is made to play into the hands of the jury, and make themselves look good by making you look bad.

NOTE

After a cross-examination, the attorney who initially examined the witness will have the opportunity to redirect the witness. After this, the attorney who conducted the cross-examination will have the opportunity to recross. This gives both sides the chance to clarify and ask any questions that may have arisen during the preceding testimony.

Refusing to Answer

While serving as an expert witness, you might be asked a question which you do not want to answer. A lawyer may ask a question that is embarrassing to you, or that you find irrelevant to the case. In such situations, you can ask the judge whether you're required to answer the question. If the judge agrees that the question isn't relevant to the case or necessary to answer, he or she will instruct you not to answer if you don't wish to. If the judge instructs you to answer the question, however, you have no real choice but to comply, or risk being cited with contempt of court.

Another situation in which you may refuse to answer is when doing so would cause you to confess to a crime. Under the 5[th] Amendment of the U.S. Constitution, and under the protection of the Charter of Rights and Freedoms in Canada, you do not need to testify if your

testimony will incriminate you. This is because by answering in a way that isn't incriminating, you are essentially forced to commit perjury.

Using Notes and Visual Aids

What if you're required to testify as a witness, but your memory isn't so great? What if you're afraid of forgetting important facts, especially information that's difficult to remember, such as numbers? Is it legal for you as a witness to take notes with you to use as a reference when testifying?

Police officers and other witnesses use notes as a memory aid during court testimony all the time. There are advantages and disadvantages in doing so. Some jurors might be impressed by the fact that you're reading from notes, because they might trust the written word more than someone who relies on memory alone. On the other hand, others might think you're being coached or prompted if you refer to notes; they believe that if what you're saying is the truth, you would remember it without notes.

Test Day Tip

Just as you should review your notes before testifying, you should review your notes before taking the exam. However, do not take your notes with you into the exam room, as this could be considered cheating and disqualify you from taking the exam. A good idea is to review the notes outside the test center (such as in a coffee shop or park), and then leave them in your car before going in.

A very important consideration in deciding whether to use notes is the fact that if a witness does so, the notes will be entered into evidence and taken into the custody of the court for the duration of the trial. If you do choose to use notes, therefore, it's important to be sure that the notebook or paper on which they're written doesn't have other notes that refer to matters not related to the case, because the opposing attorney can question you about anything in the notes.

Visual aids are another common element, especially in cases that involve evidence such as digital images, or require maps of a location. When referring to visual aids, such as photographs or diagrams, it is important to be as descriptive as possible. Rather than raising your hand and saying, "Here we see," you should try to focus the attention on what you're talking about, such as by saying "In the lower right-hand corner." Not only does this make it easier for those watching your testimony to understand what you're talking about, but it also makes it easier to understand in the transcription of the testimony.

Damage & Defense...

Notes As Evidence and Witness Resources

Anyone involved in an incident, including investigators and computer forensic examiners, may be called to testify in court if criminal charges or civil lawsuits are brought in relation to the incident. In addition to documentation being used as evidence, the ability to use notes as a resource is another reason to create extensive documentation that can be reviewed prior to giving testimony. Often, a case doesn't come to trial until months or years after the incident took place, and the human memory often isn't reliable after so long a time without a little help. In situations where an incident response team or group responded to an incident, the person who creates the documentation should be the one to testify to its authenticity if it is to be entered into evidence.

It is important for team members to understand that their reports regarding the incident may end up being entered into evidence at trial. For this reason, such documentation should be kept in a special notebook with numbered pages, and the notebook should not contain any personal information, becayse the entire notebook may become part of the official record.

Summary of Exam Objectives

When most people think of a witness, they often think of a person who actually saw the crime take place. However, many witnesses in cybercrime cases offer information about the effects of a crime, or facts about evidence that was obtained during an investigation. Testimony explaining this evidence is used to show when, where, and how a crime occurred, what was affected, and who was identified as being responsible.

Testimony may be given in civil court (where one person or organization sues another), or criminal court (where the government brings the person to court for breaking the law). The person giving testimony may be an evidentiary witness, who can speak about evidence and events that occurred, or an expert witness who can also provide opinions based on knowledge and experience in a particular field. There are many different types of expert witnesses, including those specializing in computer forensics, medical, psychological, construction, architecture, and other fields. The Rules of Evidence, which is a set of rules set at the state or federal level that dictates what and how evidence can be presented in court, regulates any testimony and evidence that may be presented in court.

In being a witness, you will be called to the stand and given the option of swearing in or affirming to tell the truth. Upon doing so, you will then be given the chance to give direct testimony, where the attorney who called you will ask a series of questions. The opposing attorney can then cross-examine you, in which he or she will then ask his or her own questions. After this, the attorney who called you has the option of redirecting you (asking questions to clarify information given under cross-examination), and after this the opposing attorney can recross. Once this process has completed, you're excused and can leave the courtroom, but you should remain in the courthouse in case you're re-called to the stand.

Exam Objectives Fast Track

Understanding the Expert Witness

- Witnesses are people who have firsthand knowledge of a crime or incident, or who offer evidence during a trial, tribunal, or hearing.

- An evidentiary witness can only testify as to facts (what he or she saw or heard) and cannot give opinions or draw conclusions.

- An expert witness may have no direct involvement in the case, but has special technical knowledge or expertise that qualifies him or her to give professional opinions on technical matters.

- To qualify as an expert witness, the witness will have his or her credentials reviewed by the court, and entered into the record after being sworn in. If the opposing side

wishes to challenge, the witness is cross-examined. The judge evaluates the information acquired through this process, and can then recognize or reject the witness as an expert in a particular field.

- A plea bargain is an agreement in which the defendant pleads guilty to a lesser crime to have more severe charges dropped.

- A curriculum vitae is a document that outlines a person's education, experience, and other credentials. It is a detailed synopsis of the qualifications that make you an expert in a particular field.

- Criminal litigation expert witnesses are used to assist in the prosecution and defense of individuals involved in a crime.

- Civil litigation expert witnesses are used to assist in civil court cases where one individual and/or business sues to resolve a dispute and reclaim what they feel is owed them.

- Computer forensic experts acquire and examine potential evidence during an investigation, including data that's been deleted, encrypted, or damaged.

- Medical and psychological experts respectively provide insight and assistance in physical and mental issues that may be involved in a court case. They may be used by either side in a court case to perform tests, evaluate existing diagnoses, or testify about technical details related to evidence.

- Construction and architecture experts can provide insight and assistance in issues involving real estate, building and fire codes, errors in construction and design, and other issues involving properties.

- Technical testimony is statements given under oath that present facts of a technical nature.

- Whether a person can be recognized as an expert witness, and the admissibility of evidence, are both governed by the laws of the court's jurisdiction (i.e., state or federal). These rules are adopted by statute and are usually codified into a document titled *Rules of Evidence*.

- Under Rules of Evidence, evidence presented in court must be authenticated, meaning that a witness must testify to its authenticity.

- If evidence is not collected and handled according to the proper standards, the judge may deem the evidence inadmissible when it is presented. This may be based on a motion to suppress from the opposing attorney so that members of the jury will never get a chance to evaluate it or consider it in making their decision.

Testifying As an Expert Witness

- A courtroom is where a trial takes place, and it consists of a judge's bench, witness stand, court reporter's desk, court clerk's desk, jury box, podium, and tables for the prosecution and defense. A bar (which is a railing) is used to separate the gallery where spectators sit from the well of the courtroom.

- Technology in courtrooms can vary, so you should identify what equipment is available and whether you will need to provide any equipment of your own to display exhibits.

- A subpoena is a legal document that is issued by the court to notify you that you are required to attend court on a set date and time to give evidence as a witness.

- Being sworn in requires that you place your hand on a Bible and swear to God that you'll tell the truth in your testimony, whereas affirming simply involves a promise that you'll tell the truth.

- Depositions are a process of questioning witnesses prior to a trial, and are used in the pretrial stages of both civil and criminal cases.

- Courtroom etiquette should always be followed, including treating everyone in the courtroom with respect and referring to the judge as "your honor."

- Direct examination refers to the process of a witness being questioned by the attorney who called him or her to the stand.

- Cross-examination is the second line of questioning a witness faces, in which the opposing side in a trial or hearing has the opportunity to ask questions.

- Once a witness is cross-examined, the attorney who called the witness has the opportunity to redirect, and ask further questions. The opposing attorney can then recross, and also ask additional questions.

- Witnesses are not required to answer a question under oath if doing so will incriminate them. If this doesn't apply, and the witness still doesn't want to answer, he or she should ask the judge if it is necessary to answer the question, and then abide by the judge's decision.

- Notes that are used as reference material when testifying under oath are entered into evidence.

Exam Objectives
Frequently Asked Questions

The following Frequently Asked Questions, answered by the authors of this book, are designed to both measure your understanding of the Exam Objectives presented in this chapter, and to assist you with real-life implementation of these concepts.

Q: I'm a witness in a criminal case, and have discovered that a friend of mine has been called as a juror to the same case. What should I do?

A: Tell your friend to inform the court that he or she knows one of the witnesses. During the jury selection process, jurors are asked if there's any reason(s) that should prevent them from being a juror. This could include knowing the defendant, being involved in the investigation, knowing witnesses, or other issues that would affect the outcome of the trial. By having a relationship to one of the witnesses, a person could be released from jury duty.

Q: I'm part of an incident response team, and I have become involved in an incident that will probably go to court. Who can I talk to about this?

A: Although you could talk generically about the case to anyone, you should try to avoid having any conversations about it with anyone who isn't connected to the case. In other words, although you can talk to the attorney in charge of the case, you shouldn't talk to friends, significant others, or coworkers about the specifics of the case. By telling someone who isn't involved, there is a chance this information could be passed on to others, including members of the media. In addition, you could inadvertently talk to someone who knows or is related to the defendant, or may be a potential juror.

Q: How do I know when and where I'm supposed to testify in a case?

A: When you're summoned to be a witness, you'll be served with a subpoena by an officer of the court. The subpoena has information on the location of the trial, and when you're to attend court to testify. Unless the attorney who has called you indicates otherwise, you will need to attend the courthouse every day that the trial continues in case you're re-called to the stand.

Q: My religious beliefs prohibit me from the practice of placing my hand on the Bible and swearing to God that I'll tell the truth. When being called to testify, what should I do?

A: When you are called to the stand, you have the option of swearing or affirming. When sworn in, you will hold your hand on a Bible and swear to God that you'll tell the truth. Affirming doesn't require this. When being affirmed, you simply promise that any testimony you give will be truthful.

Q: Why is it important that all the software used by law enforcement officers be licensed and registered? Law enforcement budgets are often tight; why not use freeware as much as possible?

A: Some freeware and shareware tools that are available on the Internet are good tools, and the price is certainly right. However, there are some dangers in using these programs for forensic purposes. First, you never know exactly what you're getting when you download a free program (and you certainly can't ask for your money back if it doesn't work properly). Downloads can be infected with viruses or Trojans that can damage the systems on which you use them. Using unlicensed software (illegal copies) is even worse. The opposing attorney(s) will have a field day if they discover that the police used pirated or "borrowed" software in the investigation. This behavior can destroy the credibility of the people who conducted the forensic examination and even result in losing the case. In addition, with properly purchased and registered software, you will be able to get technical support from the vendor if necessary. Makers of computer forensic software often offer discounts to law enforcement agencies, making it easier to afford the proper tools for the job. After all, officers and agencies probably wouldn't suggest saving money by buying their duty weapons from a pawnshop; that's because these are essential tools of the trade and must be as reliable as possible. For the cybercrime investigator or technician, the same is true of the forensic software that is used to collect and preserve evidence that can make or break a criminal case.

Q: On my statement, I wrote an incorrect date and didn't realize my mistake until after the statement was sent to the prosecutor. Now I've been subpoenaed to testify about the facts. What should I do?

A: Notify the investigator and prosecutor immediately about the mistake before any depositions and before the trial begins. By being honest and pointing out

the mistake early, you can avoid any unnecessary questions during the trial about inconsistencies in the information you've presented.

Q: Why is documentation so important? Doesn't the evidence speak for itself?

A: In many computer-related criminal cases, the evidence speaks a language that most of the members of the jury (and often the judge, prosecutor, and law enforcement officers) don't understand. At one time, juries were likely to accept the testimony of expert witnesses without question, but as the public has become more technically sophisticated and expert testimony has been called into question in high-profile cases such as the O. J. Simpson case, juries have become more skeptical of experts' infallibility and are more likely to accept the opposing attorney's challenges which raise doubts about evidence-processing methods and forensic techniques. This is the reason it is so important to document the actions of law enforcement officers and technicians every step of the way. Documentation is also important to refresh the memories of people who must testify in the case. Often, trials are delayed for months or even years, and by the time an officer or technician is required to take the stand, he or she has handled many other cases.

Appendix B

CHFI

Worldwide Forensic Acts and Laws

Exam objectives in this chapter:

- Civil and Criminal Law
- Jurisdiction
- Defamation and Injurious Falsehood
- Harassment and Cyber Stalking
- Pornography and Obscenity
- Privacy
- Searches (and the Fourth Amendment)
- Authorization
- Intellectual Property
- Evidence Law
- Interpol: Information Technology Crime
- The Council of Europe's Convention on Cybercrime
- The G8 Countries: Action Plan to Combat High-Tech Crime

Introduction

The foremost dilemma with the study of electronic law is that it is very complicated to confine its study within simple parameters. Internet and e-commerce do not define a distinct area of law as with contract and tort law. Electronic law crosses many legal disciplines, each of which can be studied individually. Examples of a range of areas of law that electronic, e-commerce, and Internet law touch upon can be seen in the following pages.

In fact, existing laws already address the majority of cybercrimes. In most cases, cybercrimes are just age-old crimes committed using a new technology. Identity theft, for instance, has existed for hundreds of years, only now the speed and volume, and hence the effect, of the crime has increased.

New challenges do arise through the nature of widely distributed networks such as the Internet. Some legal jurisdictions have addressed this issue through the mending of existing laws. Most however, have adopted an approach where they define solutions to a perceived unique legal problem through the creation of separate digital laws. In particular, these are manifest in the numerous additions to computer crime statutes in their criminal codes.

Of particular confusion to many people is the distinction between what is illegal and what is criminal. This, however, is not a distinction solely confined to electronic law. It is important to note that although many actions are illegal, they may not be criminal in nature. This is important as the evidentiary requirements in criminal cases are far stricter than in civil litigation. It needs to be noted that the level of professionalism and standards attached to handling evidence should be maintained equally in both civil and criminal cases.

This section will endeavor to summarize the primary areas of electronic law that the forensic practitioner is likely to encounter.

Civil and Criminal Law

One of the key distinctions between all legal cases concerned is the distinction between what is criminal and civil in a legal nature. Generally, a criminal case consists of one where the state is punishing a person due to their undesired behavior. A civil case revolves around a person or company bringing action to recover damages or stop some behavior (for example, through an injunction). The forensic practitioner, depending on who they work for, is likely to encounter either type of case.

Criminal or penal law concerns those issues believed to affect the whole of the population. The fundamentals of criminal law are known as the *actus reus* (or the guilty act) and the *mens rea* (the guilty mind) of the crime. The *actus reus* covers the actual act of having committed the crime. This is the physical element. In hacking, the physical act could be sitting at the offender's computer and starting an attack script.

The *mens rea* of an act is the mental element associated with the deed. This is more commonly known as intent. In some instances, recklessness may suffice to cover the element of intent. An example of intent could come from something like bragging. A hacker who

announces over IRC the intent to break into a site could be said to have intent. Conversely, a penetration tester who unknowingly attacks sites belonging to someone else under the honest belief that the site belonged to their client would either be at worst reckless, if they had not checked the address, or could be shown to not have intent if they are acting in good faith.

A variety of civil actions exist, which are primarily contract or tort actions.

A contract is any agreement where there is offer, acceptance, and consideration. Consideration may be of a monetary nature or anything else of value. Torts are civil wrongs that involve violations of the personal, business, or property interests of persons whom a reasonable person ought to have foreseen would be impacted by their actions, if they were not prudently carried out.

As an example of a tort, if you allow Bob to run his Web site on your server but do not give him any permission to do anything else and then he subsequently uses the server to send large volumes of unsolicited e-mail having your site blacklisted, you could recover damages. The rule is, if you let somebody use your property, and they use it in a way you did not anticipate or give authorization (license) for, you may recover for this *tort of conversion*. On the other hand, if you had offered the site to Bob for a monthly fee which he accepted, the action would be for breach of contract.

At times, the forensics professional will be involved in gathering information that is not strictly attached to a legal action. Some examples include cases where the material is:

- Highly offensive but not unlawful

- A breach of procedure, policy, and so on

- Inappropriate only

In "at will" employment situations, no legal wrong may have been committed. However, an employer may seek to minimize risk by removing the party who is the source of a risk.

Contracts

A simple definition of e-commerce is the creation of a contract electronically. It should come as a modest revelation that the law of contract is relevant to the study of e-commerce and hence will relate to the forensic analysis of computers. Questions can be posed of contract law. For instance, do the common principles of contract formation concern transactions over the Internet? Conversely, do problems arise because of this new media?

The forensic practitioner may be called in to determine the origins and scope of contractual dealing. In particular, e-mail conversations and saved copies of contracts and associated documents may often be recovered.

Crime (Cybercrime)

There will always be those in the world who wish to gain some benefit without actually paying for it. As a result the electronic law will also cross over certain aspects of criminal law. Whether by an outsider or through the actions of disloyal employees, crime is something that is likely to remain with us for the foreseeable future. The Internet and digital networks create new vulnerabilities and methods that criminals can exploit for their own gain.

Most of the existing crimes can be replicated and transacted with the aid of an online environment. Further, novel new crimes designed to exploit the features and advantages of the Internet and other digital networks have emerged and are likely to continue to emerge in the future. Some example criminal activities that have benefited from the advances in digital technology include:

- Computer break-ins (or trespass) including illegal access to the whole or any part of a computer system without right

- Illegal interception without right, made by technical means, of nonpublic transmissions of computer data to, from, or within a computer system

- Data interference, or the damaging, deletion, deterioration, alteration, or suppression of computer data without authorization

- Interfering with a system or seriously hindering the same without the right of the functioning computer system by inputting, transmitting, damaging, deleting, deteriorating, altering, or suppressing computer data

- Possession of obscenity/prohibited pornography (for example, child pornography and bestiality)

- Industrial espionage

- E-mail fraud

- Harassment

- Web page defacements (cyber vandalism)

- Theft of company documents

While none of these crimes is wholly new, the ease in which they may be committed, and the difficulty in capturing the offender, has added a new dimension to crime. For instance, it is unlikely law enforcement officials will be able to take action against many cybercriminals unless the majority of countries first enact laws that criminalize the behavior of the offenders.

Some of the primary issues facing law enforcement in cybercrime cases include:

- Increased investigative costs due to the need for high-priced specialists

- The difficulties of conducting "real time" investigations

- The ease of anonymity on the Internet

- Difficulties with jurisdictional issues

- The rate at which technology is evolving

- The irrelevance of geographic distance

Jurisdiction

Jurisdiction addresses the question, "Where should the case be heard?" in many places, including the U.S. This is further complicated by the requirement that the court have two types of jurisdiction in order to hear a case—in other words, the court needs both subject matter jurisdiction and personal jurisdiction.

Subject matter jurisdiction is the power of the court to hear the particular type of dispute being brought before it. For example, criminal courts concern actual crimes; family court addresses matters such as divorce; and a number of civil courts take on tortuous and contractual matters.

Personal jurisdiction is related to the power to enforce a judgment over a defendant. This is often a question that is difficult to answer. A jurisdiction will define in statute how far it believes it can reasonably assert personal jurisdiction over another. In some cases, this may only extend locally. In others, the perceived jurisdiction may encompass the entire globe. The difficulty arises when these jurisdictional boundaries conflict.

A variety of fundamental challenges have been imposed by the borderless nature of the Internet and electronic networks. In everything from electronic commerce to cybercrime, domestic law has been fundamentally challenged. The issue of jurisdiction in electronic law concerns both the location of the parties to the matter and the location of the computers or other systems.

This matter can be complicated due to one party impacting a computer in another jurisdiction that is owned or controlled by a separate party in a third jurisdiction. In these cases, the difficulty of international law and treaty conventions becomes critical in handling data.

Defamation and Injurious Falsehood

Even in the U.S., with strictly defined protections of free speech in the Constitution, there is no overriding right of free speech. You can, no doubt, defame someone using an electronic message, and the publication of a statement about a person is by definition defamatory if it is likely to result in the loss of reputation as viewed by a reasonable person.

Generally the following must be present to establish defamation:

- A defamatory statement (or material) or imputation

- The statement (or material) identifies the plaintiff

- The statement (or material) is published to a third person—that is, at least one person supplementary to the plaintiff

Where an attack is made against the offerings of an organization, it may be possible to establish that there has been an injurious falsehood. In this case, the organization may be able to obtain damages compensated for the damage suffered. In injurious falsehood cases, it is required that the plaintiff prove the matter was maliciously published and that damage resulted. Digital forensic methods are utilized in tracing compensations that may offer proof of malicious intent.

In defamation cases, the plaintiff does not need to prove that the statement against them was false. It is up to the defendant to prove the nature of their claim.

The primary defenses to defamation include:

- The imputation is true or substantially true.

- In many jurisdictions, the doctrine of absolute privilege will protect anything said in court or Parliament. This is also extended to transcripts of these proceedings as qualified privilege as long as the statements are accurately reported.

- There is a requirement to divulge (for example, reporting crimes to authorities)

- Specific jurisdictional projections or statues exist (for instance, whistleblower laws)

- Political debate and discussion

- Fair comment

- Consent

Defamatory statements or material must be published to at least one person. If a single person views information that has been uploaded onto the Internet, then that information is taken to have been published. Traditionally, verbal and published imputations have been distinguished respectively as slander (in cases of verbal abuse) and libel (in cases of published materials).

The digital forensic practitioner will primarily become involved in defamation in civil cases. This may be from either the perspective of the defendant or the plaintiff. An example of such involvement would include determining the source of an anonymous e-mail or the author of a comment on a Web page. Even where e-mail has been through anonymous accounts, traces may exist on an offender's computer.

Harassment and Cyberstalking

Whether it is racial or sexual harassment, stalking, bullying at work, or neighbors from hell, harassment is a form of discrimination that is generally prohibited by legislation. Harassment in the workplace is something employers must not tolerate, and includes any form of unwelcome, unsolicited, or unreciprocated behavior that a reasonable person would consider offensive, humiliating, or intimidating.

Harassment includes behavior that has this effect because it is of a sexual nature or it targets a person due to a particular characteristic (such as race, sexuality, disability, age, national origin, or gender). Included as harassment are obscene communications, derogatory remarks or slurs, communications (such as jokes or visual images) designed to ridicule, demean, or torment another individual by focusing on a personal characteristic, and stalking (whether physically or via cyberstalking).

It is worth noting that a single incident can constitute harassment. The intentions of the person who did the harassing are irrelevant. An employer will also become liable if an employee commits an act of harassment and the employer cannot prove that it took reasonable steps to prevent it.

Sexual harassment is the most common form that comes before a court, and doesn't just include sexual harassment of women by men. There is female harassment of males, same-sex harassment, and harassment that occurs through the publication of images or statements of a sexual nature.

Cyberstalking is the distribution of malicious communication through e-mail and the Internet. Although based on new technology, it is in principle precisely the same as any other form of malicious communication and can be dealt with through the usual civil and criminal law methods. The distribution of offensive e-mails through the Internet and such communication will also constitute an offense under a variety of statutes (such as the *Malicious Communications Act* in the U.K.).

Pornography and Obscenity

Pornography is big business on the Internet and has even been seen by some as its foundation. In the U.S., pornography is protected as speech under the First Amendment of the Constitution. Obscenity, on the other hand, is not protected. Obscenity may be legally possessed in an individual's private home, but generally its distribution is illegal. The Miller test, as articulated by the Supreme Court in the 1973 case of *Miller v. California* is used in the U.S. to determine whether expression has crossed the line from being pornography to obscenity.

The test was defined in the case as:

- Would the average person, applying contemporary community standards, find that the work, taken as a whole, appeals to the prudent interest?

- Does the work depict or describe, in a patently offensive way, sexual conduct specifically defined by applicable state law?

- Does the work, taken as a whole, lack serious literary, artistic, political, or scientific value?

The U.S. Congress tried to address the problem of the ease of access to this type of material by children through the Telecommunications Act of 1996. Title V of the act (commonly known as the Communications Decency Act [CDA]) included provisions with the intent to

regulate the dissemination on the Internet of material deemed to be inappropriate to minors. Shortly afterward, however, the Supreme Court struck down sections 223 (a) and (d) in *Reno v. American Civil Liberties Union et. al.* As a result of these and subsequent cases, no clear "community standard" defines obscenity.

In cases such as child pornography, this is clearly not held as an expression protected by the First Amendment. The Internet has provided offenders with greater access to obscene materials and even aids in the solicitation of children by pedophiles.

Privacy

U.S. Justice Cooley defined privacy as the right to be left alone. Others see privacy as the right to be anonymous. These different definitions imply different implications.

In legal terms, privacy is a two-headed coin. On one side is the right to be free from government intrusion. On the other is the right to be free from intrusions from private individuals. The nature of this right is the protection of our private lives.

The right of privacy comes from the common law. In particular, four pillars have been created through tort. These are:

- The right to stop another from appropriating your name or likeness.

- The right to be free from unreasonable intrusion through intentional interference with another person's interests in solitude and seclusion.

- Freedom from false light. This is freedom from publicity which presents a person to the public in a manner that damages their reputation (see defamation).

- And freedom from public disclosure of private facts.

In addition, governments have imposed statutes aimed at further increasing the rights to privacy. In Europe, the right to privacy has been integrated into European Treaty convention.

- The primary statutes enacted in the U.S. to protect privacy include:

- The Electronic Communications Privacy Act of 2000, which was designed to regulate the interception of electronic indications such as e-mail.

- The Privacy Act of 1974, 5 U.S.C. § 552a, which has imposed limits on the amount of personal information that can be collected by federal agencies.

- The Fair Credit Reporting Act (FCRA), as amended on October 13, 2006, regulates the collection and use of personal data credit reporting agencies.

- The Federal Right to Privacy Act (1978) limits the amount of information from customer files that financial institutions may disclose to the U.S. federal government.

- The Video Privacy Protection Act of 1988, which prohibits movie rental companies from disclosing customer names and addresses on the subject matter of their purchases for marketing use.

- The Cable Communications Policy Act of 1984, which prohibits cable television companies from using their systems to collect personal data concerning their subscribers without their express consent.

- The Equal Credit Opportunity Act (ECOA) prohibits creditors from collecting data from applicants, such as gender, race, religion, birth control practices, national origin, and similar information.

- The Family Educational Rights and Privacy Act (FERPA) of 1974 allows students to examine and challenge their educational transcripts and other records.

The word *privacy* appears at no point in the U.S. Constitution. The result is that the right to privacy has developed as a separate body of law. In the U.S., the Fourth Amendment to the Constitution, with its prohibition of "unreasonable searches and seizures," has built the foundation for many of these rights.

Searches (and the Fourth Amendment)

In much of the common law world (including the USA, UK, Canada, NZ, and Australia), law enforcement needs to obtain a legal authorization in order to search and seize evidence. Generally, this power is granted through a request for a search warrant that states the grounds for the application, including the law that has been broken. In the United States and the United Kingdom, the requirements further require that the application describes the specific premises to be searched, as well as the items being sought.

In the U.S., the Fourth Amendment and the Electronic Communications Privacy Act (ECPA) determine the lawfulness of a search. The Fourth Amendment only applies to government searches (such as those conducted by law enforcement officials), while the ECPA applies to everyone (whether government or private) and prohibits the unlawful interception or access to electronic communications.

In the physical world, there is a real limit on the length of time during which a search can be conducted. This rule does not impose much of a limit on electronic searches. Since the investigator is able to make a copy of the digital evidence (such as a hard drive), they are able to continue to search these files both for "strings," which are beyond the scope of the original warrant, and do so at their leisure.

Neither the Fourth Amendment nor federal rules of criminal procedure required the investigator to promptly search the evidence. In fact, U.S. federal law provides little other than the return of property seized pursuant to warrant. The suspect must file a motion in court in which it is proven that the seizure was illegal or that the investigator no longer has any need to retain the evidence and that the digital evidence should be either returned or destroyed.

As a result, law enforcement officials can keep a copy of any digital evidence they seized under a warrant and continue to search it without any effective time limit. Fourth Amendment rules do not provide useful guidelines for investigators' conduct in digital forensic labs. There are no limitations as to the regions of a hard drive that a forensic computer analyst may examine for evidence, and whether the analyst may continue to look for evidence of other crimes.

The Fourth Amendment rule is that an investigator executing a warrant is able to look in any place listed on the warrant where evidence might conceivably be concealed. Traditionally, an investigator was precluded from looking into any location beyond the area of the evidence they wished to seize. Electronic evidence, however, may be stored anywhere. The result is that an investigator can electronically look anywhere in search of digital evidence.

Katz v. United States[1] stated that "the Fourth Amendment protects people, not places." The result is that the Fourth Amendment continues to be deeply tied to physical places.

Warrants

To be accepted as evidence in court, a warrant is generally required for law enforcement to search and seize evidence. Exceptions to this include:

- When the evidence is in plain view

- Where consent to search has been granted

- Situations involving some exigency, such as an emergency that threatens life or may cause bodily harm

- To obtain a search warrant, an investigator must convince the court of the following three points:

 Some criminal act has been committed.

 Evidence of a crime exists and is available.

 It is probable the evidence will be found at the place being searched.

Anton Piller (Civil Search)

An Anton Piller order is a civil court order providing for the right to search premises and seize evidence without prior warning. In the U.S., the Business Software Alliance has used these orders as a remedy when they are attempting to stop illegal software use (termed software piracy) and copyright infringement to achieve the recovery of property.

Ormrod LJ in Anton Piller *KG v. Manufacturing Processes Limited* in 1976 (UK) defined the three-step test for granting this order:

- There is an extremely strong prima facie case against the respondent.

- The damage, potential or actual, must be very serious for the applicant.

- There must be clear evidence that the respondents have in their possession incriminating documents or items and there is a real possibility they may destroy such material before an inter partes application reaches the court.

In the UK, Anton Piller orders have been (for the most part) outmoded by the introduction of a statutory search order under the Civil Procedure Act of 1997. These applications are still common in many places, such as Canada and France.

Authorization

In legal terms, authorization is defined as the right to use a product or service within the agreed upon terms. Authorization may be implied (such as when using a public Web site for the purposes to which the site owner designed it) or explicit (such as occurs when using Internet banking after having authenticated one's valid credentials).

In legal terms, the granting of permissions through authorization is in effect the granting of a license.

License

To license or grant a license is to give permission or authorization. A license is the demonstration of that permission. In cases of software, for instance, the license is the right to use the software as long as the user agrees to the terms of the license. Licenses may be granted by a party ("licensor") to another party ("licensee") as a constituent of an agreement between those parties. A simple explanation of a license is "a promise by the licensor not to sue the licensee."

In intellectual property law, a licensor grants the licensee the rights to do some action (such as install software, make use of a patented invention, or even watch a movie) without fear of retribution through an intellectual property infringement.

Intellectual Property

Intellectual property laws concern the protection of another's intellectual designs and works. It is important to understand that when surfing the Internet, what is seen is protected by copyright. In addition, the actual Web site visited, along with the domain and host address, is often the subject of trademark or passing off litigation.

The law of intellectual property is aimed at safeguarding people's ideas. Intellectual property is an expanse of law that deals with the protection of intangible items such as ideas and creativity that exist in some tangible form (such as a movie, music CD, name, or design). Many separate subject areas exist in intellectual property law, including:

- Copyright
- Confidence
- Design rights
- Domain names
- Moral rights
- Performance rights
- Patents
- Passing off
- Trademarks

Evidence Law

Electronic evidence in law is the legal recognition and evidential value in litigation of evidence in digital format. Of particular importance are the U.S. Federal Rules of Evidence, the UK Police and Criminal Evidence Act (PACE), and the UK Civil Evidence Act. Similar rules of evidence apply in other jurisdictions.

Before admitting evidence, a court will generally ensure it is both relevant to the case and also evaluate it to ensure it satisfactorily fulfills what it is claimed to provide. A court needs to determine whether the evidence is hearsay and otherwise determine its admissibility.

The primary issues concerning digital evidence are associated with the ease to which documents may be copied or altered and the resultant effect on its value as evidence in court, as well as the impact on civil liberties. The nature of digital technologies has compounded the amount of information available. As a consequence, it is far easier to violate the privacy rights and other civil rights of the individual in this digital age.

The most common mistake made in obtaining digital evidence occurs when it has been taken without authorization. Generally, a warrant or court order must be granted for the collection of the evidence before it will be admissible. Exceptions exist to this rule, which were listed in the earlier section on warrants.

For the evidence to be admissible, it must go through a process known as authentication, which is designed to determine whether the evidence meets what its proponent claims, and subsequently determine its probative weight. Even in cases where reasonable doubt exists as to the reliability of electronic evidence, this may not make it inadmissible in court. It will, however, reduce the weight it is given by the court.

Rules of *Best Evidence* were originally introduced to prevent a party from misrepresenting materials (such as written documents, photographs, or recordings) by simply accepting the testimony regarding the contents. With digital evidence, an exact duplicate can generally be made. The result is that a copy is generally acceptable in court. In fact, statutory provisions

(such as the Electronic Transactions Act, 1999 Australia) may determine that a digital copy or extraction of a physical document is equivalent to the original printed form. Further, due to the nature of embedded materials (such as macros in Microsoft Word), the digital format may even be preferable.

The distinction between correct and circumstantial evidence is that direct evidence categorically establishes the fact. Circumstantial evidence, on the other hand, is only suggestive of the fact. Authentication logs are generally accepted as direct evidence short of proof that another party used the access account.

The rules of *Scientific Evidence* apply to digital forensics. The U.S. case, *Daubert v. Merrell Dow Pharmaceuticals*, [509 U.S. 579 (1993)], set the standard for evaluating scientific evidence. The test developed in this case consists of:

- A determination of what the theory or technique is capable of, and whether it has been tested.

- The existence and maintenance of standards controlling techniques of operation and whether these are likely to result in a high known or potential error rate.

- Determining whether the theory or technique has been rigorously subjected to peer review and publication.

- Determining whether the theory or technique is subject to "general acceptance" within the relevant scientific community.

For the most part (and even though error rates have not been established for most digital forensic tools), electronic evidence has been accepted by the courts as scientific evidence. Currently, the most effective approach to validating the methodologies and approach used by an investigator remains peer review. For this reason, it remains good practice to have another investigator double-check any findings using multiple tools or techniques to ensure the reliability and repeatability of the process.

"Evidence is hearsay where a statement in court repeats a statement made out of court in order to prove the truth of the content of the out-of-court statement."[2] An example of hearsay evidence would apply where a suspect has sent an e-mail purporting to have committed a crime. Law enforcement officials would still need other evidence (such as a confession) to prove this fact.

Interpol: Information Technology Crime

The Interpol General Secretariat acts as a regional coordinating body between its members in the field of Information Technology Crime (ITC). Interpol coordinates a number of working parties consisting of representatives from various national computer crime units. Interpol has set up working parties in Europe, Asia, North and South America, and Africa.

Interpol has worked to develop Information security, crime prevention research, and whitepapers that are available to both law enforcement and the public. This research investigates both the current state of technology and its possible criminal implications.

More information on how Interpol is helping combat Information Technology Crime (ITC) is available from their site at www.interpol.int/Public/TechnologyCrime/default.asp.

The Council of Europe's Convention on Cybercrime

The Convention on Cybercrime CETS No.: 1852.[3] (the CoE Convention) was opened for signature in Budapest on November 23, 2001. By means of decision CDPC/103/211196, the European Committee on Crime Problems (CDPC) determined to implement a committee of specialists to prepare a solution to the issues of cybercrime.

The Committee of Experts on Crime in Cyber-space (PC-CY) was created by decision CM/Del/Dec(97)583 at the 583rd meeting of the Ministers' Deputies (4 February 1997). This committee was specifically tasked with the following terms of reference:[4]

i. Examine, in the light of Recommendations No R (89) 9 on computer-related crime and No R (95) 13 concerning problems of criminal procedural law connected with information technology, in particular the following subjects:

ii. cyber-space offences, in particular those committed through the use of telecommunication networks, e.g. the Internet, such as illegal money transactions, offering illegal services, violation of copyright, as well as those which violate human dignity and the protection of minors;

iii. other substantive criminal law issues where a common approach may be necessary for the purposes of international co-operation such as definitions, sanctions and responsibility of the actors in cyber-space, including Internet service providers;

iv. the use, including the possibility of transborder use, and the applicability of coercive powers in a technological environment, e.g. interception of telecommunications and electronic surveillance of information networks, e.g. via the Internet, search and seizure in information-processing systems (including Internet sites), rendering illegal material inaccessible and requiring service providers to comply with special obligations, taking into account the prob-

lems caused by particular measures of information security, e.g. encryption;

v. the question of jurisdiction in relation to information technology offences, e.g. to determine the place where the offence was committed (locus delicti) and which law should accordingly apply, including the problem of ne bis idem in the case of multiple jurisdictions and the question how to solve positive jurisdiction conflicts and how to avoid negative jurisdiction conflicts;

vi. questions of international co-operation in the investigation of cyber-space offences, in close co-operation with the Committee of Experts on the Operation of European Conventions in the Penal Field (PC-OC).

The Committee should draft a binding legal instrument, as far as possible, on the items i) – v), with particular emphasis on international questions and, if appropriate, accessory recommendations regarding specific issues. The Committee may make suggestions on other issues in the light of technological developments.

The convention is primarily a framework that creates a standardized approach to the implementation of cybercrime statutes within Europe and acts as a guideline for other non-member states. This document has been created in four chapters:

- Use of terms
- Measures to be taken at a domestic level—substantive law and procedural law
- International cooperation
- Final clauses

Chapter (II) is divided into two main sections. The first section, substantive law issues, covers the criminalization provisions and related requirements to cybercrime, and defines the types of offenses, which are grouped into four categories. The offenses in this section include: illegal access, illegal interception, data interference, system interference misuse of devices, computer-related forgery, computer-related fraud, child pornography, and breaches of copyright and neighboring rights.

The second section of chapter (II) goes beyond the offenses previously listed and applies to any and all offenses committed by means of a computer. In this manner, it applies to any traditional crime that has been committed in an electronic form. Chapter (II) ends with the jurisdictional provisos and procedural powers (such as the interception of content data).

Chapter (III) contains provisions for mutual assistance and extradition rules related to cybercrime. Mutual assistance covers situations where there is no legal basis between the party states and where such an agreement exists. This chapter also contains the requirements for transborder access to stored computer data not requiring mutual assistance.

The G8 Countries: An Action Plan to Combat High-Tech Crime

The G8 has its origin at an economic summit in 1975 convened by President Valery Giscard d'Estaing of France and attended by leaders from Germany, Japan, the United Kingdom, and the United States. In 1996, a working group of ITC experts (which has become known as the "Lyon Group") produced Forty Recommendations to combat trans-national organized crime. These recommendations were endorsed by the G8 Heads of State during the Summit Meeting in Lyon in June 1996.

The G8's Subgroup on High-Tech Crime was formed to address issues raised by the "Lyon Group." Its mission was to enhance the capability of G8 countries to *"prevent, investigate, and prosecute crimes involving computers, networked communications, and other new technologies."* This mission has expanded to include work with third-world countries and has expanded to contain topics such as combating terrorist uses of the Internet and protection of critical information infrastructures.

The Subgroup on High-Tech Crime has completed:

- The creation of a network allowing 24-hour points of contact for high-tech crime, currently with 40 members, and an international Critical Information Infrastructure Protection Directory

- The negotiation of widely accepted principles and an action plan to combat high-tech crime

- Published a variety of best practices documents, including security guides for computer networks, international requests for assistance, legislative drafting, and tracing networked communications across borders

- Conducted threat and impact assessments for law enforcement in regards to the impact of new wireless technologies, encryption, viruses, worms, and other malicious code

- Conducted training conferences for cybercrime agencies from every continent (save Antarctica)

- Holds conferences for law enforcement and industry on improved cooperation and tracing criminal and terrorist communications, and for all stakeholders in protection of critical information infrastructures

Principles and Action Plan to Combat High-Tech Crime[5.]

Investigations into trans-national organized crime face uncharacteristic difficulties related not only to the high latency of organized crime generally, but also to the trans-boundary-based dealings of organized criminal groups. Organized criminal groups have expanded beyond their former frontiers and make use of the potential accessible by the Internet. This has resulted in an interrelated process of economic and criminal globalization. In an attempt to combat this trend, the Principles and Action Plan to Combat High-Tech Crime were formulated.

Statement of Principles (TC \14 Statement of Principles)

We hereby endorse the following PRINCIPLES, which should be supported by all countries:

I. There must be no safe havens for those who abuse information technologies.

II. Investigation and prosecution of international high-tech crimes must be coordinated among all concerned states, regardless of where harm has occurred.

III. Law enforcement personnel must be trained and equipped to address high-tech crimes.

IV. Legal systems must protect the confidentiality, integrity, and availability of data and systems from unauthorized impairment and ensure that serious abuse is penalized.

V. Legal systems should permit the preservation of, and quick access to, electronic data, which are often critical to the successful investigation of crime.

VI. Mutual assistance regimes must ensure the timely gathering and exchange of evidence in cases involving international high-tech crime.

VII. Transborder electronic access by law enforcement to publicly available (open-source) information does not require authorization from the state where the data resides.

VIII. Forensic standards for retrieving and authenticating electronic data for use in criminal investigations and prosecutions must be developed and employed.

IX. To the extent practicable, information and telecommunications systems should be designed to help prevent and detect network abuse, and should also facilitate the tracing of criminals and the collection of evidence.

X. Work in this area should be coordinated with the work of other relevant international fora to ensure against duplication of efforts.

Action Plan (TC \13 "Action Plan)

In support of these PRINCIPLES, we are directing our officials to:

1. Use our established network of knowledgeable personnel to ensure a timely, effective response to trans-national high-tech cases and designate a point-of-contact who is available on a 24-hour basis.

2. Take appropriate steps to ensure that a sufficient number of trained and equipped law enforcement personnel are allocated to the task of combating high-tech crime and assisting law enforcement agencies of other states.

3. Review our legal systems to ensure that they appropriately criminalize abuses of telecommunications and computer systems and promote the investigation of high-tech crimes.

4. Consider issues raised by high-tech crimes, where relevant, when negotiating mutual assistance agreements or arrangements.

5. Continue to examine and develop workable solutions regarding: the preservation of evidence prior to the execution of a request for mutual assistance; transborder searches; and computer searches of data where the location of that data is unknown.

6. Develop expedited procedures for obtaining traffic data from all communications carriers in the chain of a communication and to study ways to expedite the passing of this data internationally.

7. Work jointly with industry to ensure that new technologies facilitate our effort to combat high-tech crime by preserving and collecting critical evidence.

8. Ensure that we can, in urgent and appropriate cases, accept and respond to mutual assistance requests relating to high-tech crime by expedited but reliable means of communications, including voice, fax, or e-mail, with written confirmation to follow where required.

9. Encourage internationally recognized standards-making bodies in the fields of telecommunications and information technologies to continue providing the public and private sectors with standards for reliable and secure telecommunications and data processing technologies.

10. Develop and employ compatible forensic standards for retrieving and authenticating electronic data for use in criminal investigations and prosecutions.

A Summary of Contacts and Statutes by Country

Australia

Federal Laws

The Electronic Transactions Act of 1999 and the Privacy Amendment (Private Sector) Act of 2000 legislate for e-security and authentication, while the Cybercrime Act of 2001 penalizes cybercrime.

The Cybercrime Act of 2001[6]

The Cybercrime Bill implements the substantive law provisions of Articles 2-6 of the CoE Convention, and the search and seizure provisions of Article 19.

The Cybercrime Act of 2001 introduces the following new offenses to the Criminal Code Act of 1995.

The serious offenses are under Division 477, being:

> Section 477.1 Unauthorized access, modification, or impairment with intent to commit a serious offense.

> Section 477.2 Unauthorized modifications of data to cause impairment.

> Section 477.3 Unauthorized impairment of electronic communication.

The other offenses are under Division 478 and include:

1. Section 478.1 Unauthorized access to, or modification of, restricted data.
2. Section 478.2 Unauthorized impairment of data in a computer disk, and so on.
3. Section 478.3 Possession or control of data with intent to commit a computer offense.
4. Section 478.4 Producing, supplying, or obtaining data with intent to commit a computer offense.

Restricted Data

For data to be defined as restricted, it must be held in a computer that uses an access control system. It is not required for the data itself to be protected by an access control system, only the computer. Such a control would include a password. To be in breach of s 478.1, an individual must at least view data without authorization, whether or not that particular data was secured.[7] This is further complicated by the lack of explanation as to what constitutes "authorization."

Authorization

A critical condition for conviction in any of the Division 477 offenses, and many of the Division 478 offenses, is that access, modification, or impairment is "undertaken without authorization."

Powers Granted Under the Act

Powers granted to law enforcement include:

1. The power to take away "a thing" to a different place for assessment or processing in order to establish whether it may be "seized under a warrant" if more practical, or there is reasonable justification that the "thing" contains, or is, evidence. (Paragraph 3K)

2. The power to "operate electronic equipment at the warrant premises to access data (including data not held at the premises)" if law enforcement personnel consider that the data holds evidentiary material. (Paragraph 3L1A)

3. The power to necessitate a person "to provide any information or assistance that is reasonable and necessary to allow the officer to" create a copy of data from equipment that might hold evidential material.

4. The power to necessitate a "person with knowledge of a computer or a computer system to assist access etc." (Paragraph 3LA)

The Telecommunications (Fraud) Act 1997

The Telecommunications (Fraud) Act 1997 was an amendment to the Telecommunications Act 1984 to make further provision for the prevention of fraud in connection with use of a telecommunication system.

The Privacy Act 1988 (Cth) and the Privacy Amendment (Private Sector) Act 2000[8]

The Privacy Act contains 11 Information Privacy Principles (IPPs) that apply to Commonwealth and ACT government agencies. It has a further 10 National Privacy Principles[9] (NPPs) that apply to parts of the private sector and all health service providers. Credit providers and credit reporting agencies are regulated through Part IIIA of the Act.

The Privacy Commissioner additionally has regulatory functions under other enactments, including the *Telecommunications Act of 1997* (Cth), the *National Health Act of 1953* (Cth), the *Data Matching Program (Assistance and Tax) Act of 1990* (Cth), and the *Crimes Act of 1914* (Cth).

The Electronic Transactions Act 1999 (ETA)

ETA allows businesses to fulfill, in electronic form, any of the following requirements under a law of the Commonwealth:

- Giving information in writing

- Providing a signature

- Producing a document in material form

- Recording or retaining information

The ETA is based on two principles:

- Functional equivalence (or media neutrality), which means that paper documents and electronic transactions are treated equally by the law

- Technology neutrality, which means the law does not discriminate between different forms of technology

At the time of publication, all states and territories, with the exception of Western Australia, have passed Electronic Transactions Acts that complement the Commonwealth's ETA.

State Laws

All Australian State and Territory Governments either have or are intending to implement the computer-related offenses of the Australian Model Criminal Code (see Chapter 4). The NSW Crimes Amendment (Computer Offenses) Act of 2001 was passed by the NSW Parliament in April 2001 and received Royal Assent in June 2001.

Further Information

For additional information, visit the following Web sites:

The Office of the Federal Privacy Commissioner

The Privacy Amendment (Private Sector Act) 2000

Information Sheets

www.privacy.gov.au

The Trade Practices Act of 1974

Cybercrime Act of 2001

The Australian Securities and Investments Commission Act 1989

www.law.gov.au

The Electronic Transactions Act 1999

http://scaleplus.law.gov.au/html/comact/10/6074/pdf/162of99.pdf

Australia's Legal Framework for Electronic Commerce

www.ag.gov.au/agd/www/Securitylawhome.nsf/Page/38A611AD4AB77CB0CA256
B9D00182477?OpenDocument

Contacts

The Australian High Tech Crime Centre (AHTCC)

URL: www.afp.gov.au/email_forms/contact
The Australian High Tech Crime Centre (AHTCC) provides a nationally coordinated approach
to technology enabled crime.

Australian Federal Police

URL: www.afp.gov.au
"The Australian Federal Police Online Child Sex Exploitation Team (OCSET) performs an
investigative and coordination role within Australia for multi-jurisdictional and international
online child sex exploitation matters. The AFP is responsible for the investigation of online
child exploitation including pornography, abuse, grooming, and procurement of children."
Electronic data recovery for law enforcement agencies
Computer Forensics National Coordinator
GPO Box 401
Canberra City 2614
Ph: (02) 6223 3279

NSW Police

URL: police.nsw.gov.au
E-Crime Unit
Phone: (02) 9269 3795
Fax: (02) 9269 9797
Child Exploitation Internet Unit
Team Leader
Phone: (02) 9690 4199
Fax: (02) 9690 4111
E-mail: cpeaint@police.nsw.gov.au

Northern Territory Police

URL: www.nt.gov.au/pfes/police/index.html
Phone: (08) 8922 3611
Fax: (08) 8922 3596
E-mail: computer.crime@nt.gov.au

Queensland Police Service

URL: www.police.qld.gov.au
Major Fraud Investigation Group
Queensland Police Service
200 Roma Street, Brisbane, Qld 4000
Phone: (07) 3364 6622
Fax: (07) 3364 6549

South Australia Police

URL: www.police.sa.gov.au
Commercial & Electronic Crime Branch
GPO Box 1539
Adelaide SA 5001
Phone: (08) 846 37430
Fax: (08) 846 37460

Tasmania Police

URL: www.police.tas.gov.au
Fraud Investigation Services
Tasmania Police
Phone: (03) 6230 2661
Fax: (03) 6230 2288
Post: GPO Box 308
Hobart TAS 7001

Victoria Police

URL: www.police.vic.gov.au
Victoria Police Computer Crime Squad
Level 19/412 St.Kilda Rd.,
Melbourne, Victoria, 3004
Phone: (03) 9865-2757
Fax: (03) 9865-5031

Western Australia Police

URL: www.police.wa.gov.au
Officer in Charge
Computer Crime Investigation
Commercial Crime Division
Western Australia Police Service
Phone: +61 8 9220 0700
Fax: +61 8 9225 4489
E-mail: computer.crime@police.wa.gov.au

Albania

LAW No. 8888, date 25.4.2002
For ratification of "convention for crime in the cybernetic area"

Contacts

The name and address of the authorities responsible for making or receiving requests for extradition or provisional arrest in the absence of a treaty are:

> Ministry of Justice, Bulevardi Zog. I., Tirana
>
> National Central Office of Interpol, Bulevardi Deshmoret e Kombit, Tirana.

The contact information for the central authority responsible for sending and answering requests for mutual assistance, the execution of such requests, or their transmission to the authorities competent for their execution is:

> Ministry of Justice, Bulevardi Zog. I., Tirana
>
> The 24/7 network point of contact designated by Albania is the:
>
> Police of State
>
> Ministry of Interior
>
> Bulevardi Deshmoret e Kombit
>
> Tirana
>
> Albania

Austria

The Austrian Privacy Act of 2000 became effective January 1, 2000. This statute establishes penalties for unlawful acts directed at data.

Strafrechtsanderungsgesetz 2002 (1166 d.B.)

§ 118a: Widerrechtlicher Zugriff auf ein Computersystem

§ 119: Verletzung des Telekommunikationsgeheimnisses

§ 119a: Missbrauchliches Abfangen von Daten

§ 126b: Storung der Funktionsfahigkeit des Computersystems

§ 126c: Missbrauch von Computerprogrammen oder Zugangsdaten

An amendment to the Austrian Criminal Code, which went into force on May 1, 2004 (BGBl. I 15/2004, "Strafrechtsänderungsgesetz 2004"), reorganized in particular sexual offenses (especially child pornography, § 207 a StGB) and offenses regarding non-cash means of payment (§§ 241 a – g StGB).

Contacts

Bundesministerium für Inneres (Austrian Federal Ministry of the Interior)

Generaldirektion für die öffentliche Sicherheit (Directorate-General for Public Security)

Bundeskriminalamt (Federal Criminal Office)

Meldestelle Kinderpornographie

Josef Holaubek Platz 1

A-1090 Wien

Tel: +43 (0)1 53126-0

Fax: +43 (0)1 31345-85190

E-mail: meldestelle@interpol.at

Bulgaria

The National Assembly implemented amendments in the Penal Code on September 13, 2002. The new Chapter on Cybercrime included:

Art. 319a (1) A person who obtains unauthorized access to the resources of a computer and copies or uses computer data without permission, when such one is required shall be punished with a fine of up to 3,000 levs.

(2) In case the act under para one has been committed by two or more persons that have conspired to commit the act, the punishment shall be imprisonment of up to one year, or a fine of up to 3,000 levs.

(3) In case the act under para one is committed repeatedly, the punishment shall be imprisonment of up to three years or a fine of up to 5,000 levs.

(4) If the acts under the previous items 1 thru 3 are committed concerning information qualified as government secret, the punishment shall be imprisonment from one to three years, provided there is no heavier punishment prescribed.

(5) If the act under item four causes grave consequences, the punishment shall be imprisonment from one to eight years.

Art. 319b (1) A person who, without the permission of the administrator or the user of the computer, adds, changes, deletes, or destroys a computer program or data when the impact is significant shall be punished with imprisonment of up to one year or a fine of up to 2,000 levs.

(2) In case the act under the previous paragraph has caused significant damage or other grave consequences, the punishment shall be imprisonment of up to two years or a fine of up to 3,000 levs.

(3) In case the act under para one has been committed with the purpose of obtaining material benefit, the punishment shall be imprisonment from of up to three years or a fine of 5,000 levs.

Art. 319c (1) A person who commits an act under the previous article with regard to data that by virtue of a law are provided through electronic means or through a magnetic carrier shall be punished by imprisonment of up to two years and a fine of up to 3,000 levs.

(2) If the act under the previous para has been committed for the purpose of frustrating the execution of duties, the punishment shall be imprisonment of up to three years and a fine of up to 5,000 levs.

Art. 319d (1) A person who brings a computer virus into a computer or the information network shall be punished with a fine of up to 3,000 levs.

(2) If significant damage has been caused by the act under the previous paragraph, or it has been committed repeatedly, the punishment shall be imprisonment of up to three years and a fine of up to 1,000 levs.

Art. 319e (1) A person who distributes computer or system passwords that result in disclosure of personal data or a government secret shall be punished with imprisonment of up to one year.

(2) If the act under the previous paragraph has been committed for material advantage or has caused significant damage, the punishment shall be imprisonment of up to three years.

Art. 319f A service provider who violates the provisions of Art. 6, para 2, item 5 of the Electronic Document and Electronic Signature Act shall be punished with a fine of up to 5,000 levs, provided a heavier punishment is not warranted.

Contacts

The Ministry of Justice is the Central Authority responsible for making or receiving requests for extradition, and the Supreme Cassation Prosecutor's Office is the Central Authority responsible for making and receiving requests for provisional arrest.

In accordance with Article 27, paragraph 2.c, of the Convention, the Republic of Bulgaria has designated the following central authorities as being responsible for sending and answering requests for mutual assistance:

The Supreme Cassation Prosecutor's Office In respect of requests for mutual assistance at the stage of pre-trial proceeding.

The Ministry of Justice In respect of requests for mutual assistance at the stage of the trial.

In accordance with Article 35, paragraph 1, of the Convention, the Republic of Bulgaria has designated the National Service for Combating Organized Crime under the Ministry of Interior to perform the functions of point of contact for the purpose of investigations concerning cybercrime.

Brazil

The National Congress approved the General Telecommunications Law (LGT) No. 9.472 on July 16, 1997, which authorized the privatization of state-controlled telecom companies and created a regulatory agency (the National Telecommunications Agency, or ANATEL).

Brazil has also implemented Law No. 9,983 on July 7, 2000 which covers the "Insertion of fake data into systems of information" and the "Non-authorized modification or alteration of systems of information," respectively.

Article 313-A. An authorized public servant must not insert or facilitate the insertion of fake data, or alter systems of information, or improperly exclude correct data from these systems, or from any data banks of Public Administration, with the purpose of obtaining undue advantages, for himself or for other people, or causing any harm

Sentence: Prison, 2 (two) up to 12 (twelve) years, and fine.

Article 313-B. A public servant must not modify or alter systems of information, or computer software, without authorization or by order of a competent authority.

Sentence: Prison, 3 (three) months up to 2 (two) years, and fine.

The sentences are increased by one third up to half of the total value if the modification or alteration performed resulted in harm to the Public Management or to any of its assets.

Contacts

URL: www.policia-civ.sp.gov.br/
The Brazilian Police handle matters of cybercrime.

Belgium

In November, 2001, the Belgian Parliament adopted new legislation that inserted a series of articles (Computer forgery, Article 210(b); Computer fraud, Article 504(4), Computer sabotage, Article 550[3]) into the Belgian Criminal Code to deal with cyber crime. These articles make "computer forgery, computer fraud, hacking, and sabotage . . . criminal offenses in their own right."[10.]

The Belgian Parliament adopted new articles into the Criminal Code covering computer crime that went into effect on February 13, 2001.

IV. COMPUTER HACKING

Article 550(b) of the Criminal Code states:

§1. Any person who, aware that he is not authorized, accesses or maintains his access to a computer system, may be sentenced to a term of imprisonment of 3 months to 1 year and to a fine of (BFr 5,200-5m) or to one of these sentences.

If the offense specified in §1 above is committed with intention to defraud, the term of imprisonment may be from 6 months to 2 years.

§2. Any person who, with the intention to defraud or with the intention to cause harm, exceeds his power of access to a computer system, may be sentenced to a term of imprisonment of 6 months to 2 years and to a fine of (BFr 5,200-20m) or to one of these sentences.

§3. Any person finding himself in one of the situations specified in §§ 1 and 2 and who either: accesses data which is stored, processed, or transmitted by a computer system, or procures such data in any way whatsoever, or makes any use whatsoever of a computer system, or causes any damage, even unintentionally, to a computer system or to data which is stored, processed, or transmitted by such a system, may be sentenced to a term of imprisonment of 1 to 3 years and to a fine of (BFr 5,200-10m) or to one of these sentences.

§4. The attempt to commit one of the offenses specified in §§ 1 and 2 is sanctioned by the same sentences as the offense itself.

§5. Any person who, with intention to defraud or with the intention to cause harm, seeks, assembles, supplies, diffuses, or commercializes data which is stored, processed, or transmitted by a computer system and by means of which the offenses specified in §§1-4 may be committed, may be sentenced to a term of imprisonment of 6 months to 3 years and to a fine of (BFr 5,200-20m) or to one of these sentences.

§6. Any person who orders or incites one of the offenses specified in §§ 1-5 to be committed may be sentenced to a term of imprisonment of 6 months to 5 years and to a fine of (BFr 5,200-40m) or to one of these sentences.

§7. Any person who, aware that data has been obtained by the commission of one of the offenses specified in §§1-3, holds, reveals, or divulges to another person, or makes any use whatsoever of data thus obtained, may be sentenced to a term of imprisonment of 6 months to 3 years and to a fine of (BFr 5,200-20m) or to one of these sentences.

§8. The sentence carried by §§1-7 are doubled if an offense under one of these provisions is committed within 5 years of a judgment or decision of condemnation for one of these offenses (or for computer fraud, forgery, sabotage, or illegal interception of telecommunications).

Contacts

The FCCU should be alerted in all cases of computer crime, such as Denial-of-Service attacks, hacking, fraud, and any major computer crime incidents. Smaller computer crime that has no impact on the safety of citizens or where the financial impact is low will be given a lesser

degree of priority and should be dealt with by the local and federal police as part of their general duties.

Federal Computer Crime Unit

Notelaarstraat 211 rue du Noyer
B – 1000 Brussel / Bruxelles
T : +32 2 743 74 74
F : +32 2 743 74 19
E-mail: contact@fccu.be
URL: www.fedpol
Languages: French, Dutch, German, English

National Privacy Protection Commission

(Commissie voor de bescherming van de persoonlijke levenssfeer/Commission de la protection de la vie privée)
Hoogstraat 139 rue Haute
B – 1000 Brussel / Bruxelles
T: +32 2 213 85 40
F: +32 2 213 85 65
E-mail: commission@privacy.fgov.be
URL: www.privacy.fgov.be
Languages: French, Dutch, German, English

Canada

The Canadian Criminal Code includes Sections:

342.1 (1) Everyone who, fraudulently and without color of right,

(a) obtains, directly or indirectly, any computer service,

(b) by means of an electromagnetic, acoustic, mechanical, or other device, intercepts or causes to be intercepted, directly or indirectly, any function of a computer system.

(c) uses or causes to be used, directly or indirectly, a computer system with intent to commit an offense under paragraph (a) or (b) or an offense under section 430 in relation to data or a computer system, or

(d) uses, possesses, traffics in, or permits another person to have access to a computer password that would enable a person to commit an offense under paragraph (a), (b) or (c)

is guilty of an indictable offense and liable to imprisonment for a term not exceeding ten years, or is guilty of an offense punishable on summary conviction.

342.2(1) Every person who, without lawful justification or excuse, makes, possesses, sells, offers for sale, or distributes any instrument or device or any component thereof, the design of which renders it primarily useful for committing an offense under section 342.1, under cir-

cumstances that give rise to a reasonable inference that the instrument, device, or component has been used, or is or was intended to be used, to commit an offense contrary to that section,

(a) is guilty of an indictable offense and liable to imprisonment for a term not exceeding two years; or

(b) is guilty of an offense punishable on summary conviction.

430. (1.1) Everyone commits mischief who willfully

(a) destroys or alters data;

(b) renders data meaningless, useless, or ineffective;

(c) obstructs, interrupts, or interferes with the lawful use of data; or

(d) obstructs, intercepts, or interferes with any person in the lawful use of data or denies access to data to any person who is entitled to access thereto.

Contacts

Canadian Anti-fraud Call Centre "PhoneBusters" coordinate the reporting of computer fraud. Phone: 1-888-495-8501.

Reporting Illegal and Offensive Content on the Internet – The Government of Canada Strategy to promote Safe, Wise, and Responsible Internet Use.

http://cyberwise.gc.ca/english/home.html

Information Technology Association of Canada site on Cyber Security:

URL:

www.itac.ca/client/ITAC/ITAC_UW_MainEngine.nsf/ALL/6192EB38740F6B7E852569A50 002AB3F?OpenDocument

Alternatively, the Royal Canadian Mounted Police Force (RCMP) may be contacted in your local area.

Denmark

Denmark's Cybercrime Bill was adopted by Parliament on May 19, 2004. The bill contains the following provisions:

Penal Code

§ 263.

(2) Any person who, in an unlawful manner, obtains access to another person's information or programs which are meant to be used in a data processing system, shall be liable to a fine, or to imprisonment not exceeding 1 year and 6 months.

(3) If an act of the kind described in subsection 1 or 2 is committed with the intent to procure or make oneself acquainted with information concerning trade secrets of a company or under other extraordinary aggravating circumstances, the punishment shall be increased to imprisonment not exceeding 6 years. Conducts described in subsection 2 are punished in the same manner, whenever perpetrations of more systematic or organized character occur.

§ 193.

(1) Any person who, in an unlawful manner, causes major disturbances in the operation of public means of communication, of the public mail service, of publicly used telegraph or telephone services, of radio and television installations, of information systems, or of installations for public supply of water, gas, electricity, or heating shall be liable to imprisonment not exceeding 6 years or to a fine.

Contacts

In accordance with Article 27, paragraph 2, and Article 24, paragraph 7, of the Convention, the Government of the Kingdom of Denmark has designated the Ministry of Justice, Slotsholmsgade 10, DK-1216 Copenhagen K, Denmark, as a competent authority.

In accordance with Article 35, paragraph 1, of the Convention, the Government of the Kingdom of Denmark has designated the Danish National Police, Police Department, Polititorvet 14, DK-1780 Copenhagen V, Denmark, as a competent authority.

Estonia

In order to ratify the Council of Europe Cybercrime Convention (effective May 12, 2003), Estonia updated its Penal Code as follows:

§ 206. Computer sabotage

(1) Unlawful replacement, deletion, damaging, or blocking of data or programs in a computer, if significant damage is thereby caused, or unlawful entry of data or programs in a computer, if significant damage is thereby caused, is punishable by a pecuniary punishment or up to 1 year of imprisonment.

(2) The same act, if committed with the intention to interfere with the work of a computer or telecommunications system, is punishable by a pecuniary punishment or up to 3 years' imprisonment.

§ 207. Damaging of connection to computer network

Damaging or obstructing a connection to a computer network or computer system is punishable by a pecuniary punishment.

§ 208. Spreading of computer viruses

(1) Spreading of a computer virus is punishable by a pecuniary punishment or up to 1 year of imprisonment.

(2) The same act, if committed:

1) at least twice, or

2) in a manner which causes significant damage,

is punishable by a pecuniary punishment or up to 3 years imprisonment.

§ 217. Unlawful use of computer, computer system, or computer network

(1) Unlawful use of a computer, computer system, or computer network by way of removing a code, password, or other protective measure is punishable by a pecuniary punishment.

(2) The same act, if it:

1) causes significant damage, or

2) is committed by using a state secret or a computer, computer system, or computer network containing information prescribed for official use only,

is punishable by a pecuniary punishment or up to 3 years imprisonment.

§ 284. Handing over protection codes

Unlawfully handing over the protection codes of a computer, computer system, or computer network, if committed for the purpose of personal gain and in a manner which causes significant damage or results in other serious consequences is punishable by a pecuniary punishment or up to 3 years' imprisonment.

Computer-related offenses are covered by computer-related fraud (§ 213).

Contacts

The Republic of Estonia designates the Ministry of Justice, in the absence of an extradition treaty, as the authority responsible for making or receiving requests for extradition or provisional arrest.

The Ministry of Justice is designated as the central authority responsible for sending and answering requests for mutual assistance, the execution of such requests, or their transmission to those authorities deemed competent for their execution.

Pursuant to Article 35, paragraph 1, of the Convention, the Republic of Estonia designates the Central Criminal Police as the point of contact.

Finland

The Finish Penal Code (Chapter 38 Section 8) contains a section covering "Data trespass":

Any person who, by using an identification code that does not belong to him, or by breaking through a corresponding protective system unjustifiable, breaks into a computer system where data are processed, stored, or transmitted by electronic or other technical methods or into a separately protected part of such a system, shall be sentenced for data trespass to fines or imprisonment not exceeding 1 year.

For data trespass is also sentenced any person without breaking into a computer system or a part thereof, uses a special technical device to unjustifiably obtain information that is stored in such a computer system.

Attempts are also punishable.

This Section will only be applied if the act is not punishable as a more severe offense.

Contacts

Pursuant to Article 35, paragraph 1, of the Convention, the Republic of Finland designates the National Bureau of Investigation, Criminal Intelligence Division / Communications Centre as the point of contact available on a 24-hour, 7-day-a-week basis.

Pursuant to Article 24, paragraph 7, of the Convention, the Republic of Finland declares that the authority responsible for making and receiving requests in Finland is:

> for requests for extradition, the Ministry of Justice, Eteläesplanadi 10, FIN-00130 Helsinki, and

> for requests for provisional arrest, the National Bureau of Investigation, Jokiniemenkuja 4, FIN-01370 Vantaa, fax: +358-983.886.299, e-mail: KRP-RTP-VLP@krp.poliisi.fi

Pursuant to Article 27, paragraph 2.a, of the Convention, the Republic of Finland declares that the central authority who is responsible for sending and answering requests for mutual assistance, the execution of such requests, or their transmission to the authorities competent for their execution is the Ministry of Justice, Eteläesplanadi 10, FIN-00130 Helsinki.

France

France ratified the Council of Europe Convention on Cybercrime on January 10, 2006. French Penal Code was amended as Law No. 2004-575 on June 21, 2004, which went into effect on June 23, 2004. This code contains the following provisions:

> Article 323-1 Fraudulent accessing or remaining within all or part of an automated data processing system is punished by a sentence not exceeding two years' imprisonment and a fine of 30,000 Euro.

> Where this behavior causes the suppression or modification of data contained in that system, or any alteration of the functioning of that system, the sentence is not exceeding three years' imprisonment and a fine of 45,000 Euro.

> Article 323-2 Obstruction or interference with the functioning of an automated data processing system is punished by a sentence not exceeding five years' imprisonment and a fine of 75,000 Euro.

> Article 323-3 The fraudulent introduction of data into an automated data processing system or the fraudulent suppression or modification of the data that it contains is punished by a sentence not exceeding five years' imprisonment and a fine of 75,000 Euro.

> Article 323-3-1 Fraudulently, and without legitimate motive, importing, holding, offering, selling, or making available any equipment, tool, computer program, or any data designed or particularly adapted to commit one or more offenses provided for

by articles 323-1 to 323-3, is punishable by the sentences prescribed for offenses in preparation or the one that carries the heaviest penalty.

Article 323-4 The participation in a group or conspiracy established with a view to the preparation of one or more offenses set out under articles 323-1 to 323-3, and demonstrated by one or more material actions, is punished by the penalties prescribed for offenses in preparation or one that carries the heaviest penalty.

Contacts

In accordance with Article 24 of the Convention, France declares that:

- the Ministry for Foreign Affairs is the authority responsible for making or receiving requests for extradition in the absence of a treaty (*Ministère des Affaires étrangères, 37, Quai d'Orsay, 75700 Paris 07 SP*);

- the territorially competent State Prosecutor shall be the authority responsible for making or receiving requests for provisional arrest in the absence of a treaty.

In accordance with Article 35 of the Convention, France designates as point of contact the *"Office central de lutte contre la criminalité liée aux technologies de l'information et de la communication"* (*11, Rue des Saussaies, 75800 Paris*).

Hungary

Additions have been introduced to the Hungarian penal code concerning Criminal Conduct for Breaching Computer Systems and Computer Data (in Section 300/C) and for Compromising or Defrauding the Integrity of the Computer Protection System or Device (in Section 300/E):

Section 300/C

(1) Any person who gains unauthorized entry to a computer system or network by compromising or defrauding the integrity of the computer protection system or device, or overrides or infringes his user privileges, is guilty of a misdemeanor punishable by imprisonment not to exceed one year, work in community service, or a fine.

(2) Any person who

a) without permission alters, damages, or deletes data stored, processed, or transmitted in a computer system or network or denies access to the legitimate users,

b) without permission adds, transmits, alters, damages, deletes any data, or uses any other means to disrupt use of the computer system or network is guilty of a misdemeanor punishable by imprisonment not to exceed two years, work in community service, or a fine.

(3) Any person who, for financial gain or advantage,

a) alters, damages, or deletes data stored, processed, or transmitted in a computer system or network or denies access to the legitimate users,

b) adds, transmits, alters, damages, deletes data, or uses any other means to disrupt use of the computer system or network,

is guilty of a felony punishable by imprisonment not to exceed three years.

(4) The punishment for the criminal act defined in Subsection (3) shall be

a) imprisonment between 1 to 5 years if it causes considerable damage,

b) imprisonment between 2 to 8 years if it causes substantial damage,

c) imprisonment between 5 to 10 years if it causes particularly substantial damage.

Section 300/E

(1) Any person who, for the commission of the criminal activities defined in Section 300/C,

a) creates,

b) obtains,

c) distributes or trades, or otherwise makes available computer software, passwords, entry codes, or other data with which to gain access to a computer system or network is guilty of a misdemeanor punishable by imprisonment not to exceed two years, work in community service, or a fine.

(2) Any person who, for the commission of the criminal activities defined in Section 300/C, conveys his economic, technical, and/or organizational expertise to another person for the creation of computer software, passwords, entry codes, or other data with which to gain access to a computer system or network shall be punished according to Subsection (1).

(3) In the case of Paragraph a) of Subsection (1), any person who confesses to the authorities his involvement in the creation of any software, passwords, entry code, or other data with which to gain access to a computer system or entire computer network before the authorities learned of such activities through their own efforts, and if the person surrenders such produced things to the authorities and assists in the efforts to identify the other persons involved, shall be exonerated from punishment.

Contacts

In accordance with Article 24, paragraph 7, subparagraph a, of the Convention, the Republic of Hungary communicates that the Ministry of Justice is responsible for making or receiving requests for extradition or provisional arrest in the absence of a treaty. The National Central Bureau of Interpol is only responsible for making or receiving requests for provisional arrest.

In accordance with Article 27, paragraph 2, subparagraphs a and c, the Republic of Hungary communicates that, regarding requests delivered before starting the criminal procedure, the designated central authority is:

> The Hungarian National Police International Implementing Co-operation Centre
>
> Budapest, Teve u. 4-6
>
> 1139 – Hungary

Regarding requests delivered after starting the criminal procedure, the designated central authority is:

The General Prosecutor's Office of the Republic of Hungary

Budapest, Markó u. 4-6

1055 - Hungary

In accordance with Article 35, the Republic of Hungary communicates that the designated point of contact available on a 24-hour, 7-days-a-week basis is the Hungarian National Police International Implementing Co-operation Centre.

Iceland

On June 3, 2006, Iceland enacted legislation on cybercrime and on January 29, 2007, ratified the Council of Europe Convention on Cybercrime. The legislation is available at: www.althingi.is/altext/stjt/2006.074.html

Penal Code § 228 Section 1 has been updated to include the following provision:

> **The same penalty shall apply on any person who by unlawful manner obtains access to data or programs stored as data.**

Contacts

In accordance with Article 24, paragraph 7, of the Convention, the Government of Iceland has designated the Ministry of Justice, Skuggasundi, 150 Reykjavík, Iceland, as the authority responsible for the making or receipt of a request for extradition or provisional arrest in the absence of a treaty.

In accordance with Article 27, paragraph 2.c, of the Convention, the Government of Iceland has designated the Ministry of Justice, Skuggasundi, 150 Reykjavík, Iceland, as the authority responsible for sending and answering requests for mutual assistance, the execution of such requests, or the transmission of them to the authorities competent for their execution.

In accordance with Article 35 of the Convention, the Government of Iceland has designated the National Commissioner of the Icelandic Police (Ríkislögreglustjórinn), Skúlagata 21, 101 Reykjavík, Iceland, as the point of contact available on a 24-hour, 7-days-per-week basis in order to ensure the provision of immediate assistance for the purpose of investigations or proceedings concerning criminal offenses related to computer systems and data, or for the collection of evidence in electronic form of a criminal offense.

India

The Indian government is in the process of updating what it terms a "comprehensible for cybercrimes." Currently, the Information Technology Act, 2000 (No. 21 of 2000) details the provisions associated with computer hacking.

CHAPTER XI - Offenses

66. Hacking with a computer system.

(1) Whoever with the intent to cause or knowing that he is likely to cause wrongful loss or damage to the public or any person destroys or deletes or alters any information residing in a computer resource or diminishes its value or utility or affects it injuriously by any means, commits a hack.

(2) Whoever commits hacking shall be punished with imprisonment up to 3 years, or with a fine which may extend up to two lakh rupees, or with both.

Contacts

The Computer Emergency Response Team of the Asian School of Cyber Laws (ASCL-CERT)
Head Office
6th Floor, Pride Senate,
 Opp International Convention Center,
 Senapati Bapat Road,
 Pune - 411016.
 India
Contact Numbers:
+91-20-25667148
+91-20-40033365
+91-20-65206029
+91-20-6400 0000
+91-20-6400 6464
Fax: +91-20-25884192
E-mail: info@asianlaws.org
URL: www.asianlaws.org

Mumbai
9225548601
9324602256
Pune
9225548604
Bangalore
9243490885
Delhi

9212227459
Chennai
9282349290
Ernakulum
9249425022

Latvia

Latvia adopted a new Criminal code as of June 17, 1998. The provisions concerning cyber crime are contained in Chapter XX: "Criminal Offenses against General Safety and Public Order"

Section 241. Arbitrarily Accessing Computer Systems

(1) For a person who commits arbitrarily accessing an automated computer system, if opportunity for an outsider to acquire the information entered into the system is caused thereby, the applicable sentence is custodial arrest, or a fine not exceeding 80 times the minimum monthly wage.

(2) For a person who commits the same acts, if breaching of computer software protective systems or accessing of communications lines is associated therewith, the applicable sentence is deprivation of liberty for a term not exceeding one year, or a fine not exceeding 150 times the minimum monthly wage.

Section 242. Unauthorized Acquisition of Computer Software

(1) For a person who commits unauthorized copying of computer software, files, or databases stored in the memory of a computer system, if substantial harm is caused thereby, the applicable sentence is custodial arrest, or a fine not exceeding 80 times the minimum monthly wage. For a person who commits the same acts, if commission thereof is repeated or breaching of computer software protection systems or accessing of communications lines is associated therewith, the applicable sentence is deprivation of liberty for a term not exceeding two years, or a fine not exceeding 150 times the minimum monthly wage.

Section 243. Damaging of Computer Software

For a person who commits modifying, altering, damaging, or destroying, without authorization, information stored in an automated computer-based system, or knowingly enters false information into an automated system, or knowingly damages or destroys information-bearing devices, computer software, or protection systems, if substantial harm is caused thereby, the applicable sentence is deprivation of liberty for a term not exceeding 5 years, or a fine not exceeding 150 times the minimum monthly wage.

Section 244. Disseminating a Computer Virus

(1) For a person who commits disseminating a computer virus, that is, the disseminating knowingly of such means of programming as causes unsanctioned destruction or alteration of computer software or information, or damages information equipment, or destroys protection systems, or who commits the introduction of a new kind of virus into the computer software

environment, the applicable sentence is deprivation of liberty for a term not exceeding 4 years, or a fine not exceeding 200 times the minimum monthly wage.

(2) For a person who commits the same acts, if substantial harm is caused thereby, the applicable sentence is deprivation of liberty for a term not exceeding 10 years.

Section 245. Violation of Safety Provisions Regarding Information Systems

For a person who commits a violation of provisions regarding information storage and processing, which have been formulated in accordance with an information system or the protection thereof, or a violation of other safety provisions regarding computerized information systems, where committed by a person responsible for compliance with these provisions, if such has been a cause of theft, destruction, or damage of the information, or other substantial harm has been caused thereby, the applicable sentence is deprivation of liberty for a term not exceeding two years, or community service, or a fine not exceeding 40 times the minimum monthly wage.

Contacts

In accordance with Article 24, paragraph 7.a, of the Convention, the Republic of Latvia declares that the authority responsible for making or receiving requests for extradition or provisional arrest in the absence of a treaty is:

Prosecutor General Office
Kalpaka Blvd. 6, Riga
LV-1801, Latvia
Phone: +371 7044400 - Fax: +371 7044449
E-mail: webmaster@lrp.gov.lv

In accordance with Article 27, paragraph 2.c, of the Convention, the Republic of Latvia declares that the authority responsible for sending and answering requests for mutual assistance, the execution of such requests, or their transmission to the authorities competent for their execution is:

Ministry of Justice
Brivibas Blvd. 36, Riga
LV-1536, Latvia
Phone: +371 7036801 - Fax: +371 7285575
E-mail: tm.kanceleja@tm.gov.lv

In accordance with Article 35, paragraph 1, of the Convention, the Republic of Latvia has declared that the point of contact is:

International Cooperation Department of Central Criminal Police Department of State Police
Brivibas Str. 61, Riga
LV-1010, Latvia
Phone: +371 7075031 - Fax: +371 7075053
E-mail: kanc@vp.gov.lv

Germany

German penal code contains the following provisions concerning cybercrime:

Section 202a. Data Espionage:

(1) Any person who obtains without authorization, for himself or for another, data which are not meant for him and which are specially protected against unauthorized access, shall be liable to imprisonment for a term not exceeding 3 years or to a fine .

(2) Data within the meaning of subsection 1 are only such as are stored or transmitted electronically or magnetically or in any form not directly visible.

Section 303a. Alteration of Data

(1) Any person who unlawfully erases, suppresses, renders useless, or alters data (section 202a[2]) shall be liable to imprisonment for a term not exceeding 2 years or to a fine.

(2) The attempt shall be punishable.

Section 303b. Computer Sabotage

(1) Imprisonment not exceeding 5 years or a fine shall be imposed on any person who interferes with data processing which is of essential importance to another business, another's enterprise, or an administrative authority by:

1. Committing an offense under section 300a(1) or

2. Destroying, damaging, rendering useless, removing, or altering a computer system or a data carrier.

(2) The attempt shall be punishable.

Italy

Cyber crime divisions are detailed in Italian Penal Code Article 615

- 615 ter: Unauthorized access into a computer or telecommunication systems:

Anyone who enters unauthorized into a computer or telecommunication system protected by security measures, or remains in it against the expressed or implied will of the one who has the right to exclude him, shall be sentenced to imprisonment not exceeding 3 years.

The imprisonment is from one until 5 years:

1) if the crime is committed by a public official or by an officer of a public service, through abuse of power or through violation of the duties concerning the function or the service, or by a person who practices—even without a license—the profession of a private investigator, or with abuse of the capacity of a system operator.

2) if to commit the crime, the culprit uses violence upon things or people, or if he is manifestly armed.

3) if the deed causes the destruction or the damage of the system or the partial or total interruption of its working, or rather the destruction or damage of the data, the information or the programs contained in it.

Should the deeds of the 1st and 2nd paragraphs concern computer or telecommunication systems of military interest or (concerning) public order or public security or civil defense or

whatsoever public interest, the penalty is—respectively—1 to 5 years or 3 to 8 years' imprisonment. In the case provided for in the first paragraph, the crime is liable to punishment only after an action by the plaintiff; the other cases are prosecuted "ex-officio."

-615 quater: Illegal Possession and Diffusion of Access Codes to Computer or Telecommunication Systems:

Whoever, in order to obtain a profit for himself or for another or to cause damage to others, illegally gets hold of, reproduces, propagates, transmits, or deliver codes, keywords or other means for the access to a computer or telecommunication system protected by safety measures, or however provides information or instructions fit to the above purpose, is punished with the imprisonment not exceeding 1 year and a fine not exceeding 10 million liras.

The penalty is imprisonment from 1 until 2 years and a fine from 10 until 20 million liras in the case of one of the circumstances numbered in 1 and 2 in the fourth paragraph of article 617-quater.

-615 quinquies: Diffusion of Programs Aimed to Damage or to Interrupt a Computer System:

Whoever propagates, transmits, or delivers a computer program—edited by himself or by another—with the aim and the effect to damage a computer or telecommunication system, the data or the programs contained or pertinent to it, or rather the partial or total interruption or an alteration in its working, is punished with imprisonment not exceeding 2 years and fined not exceeding 20 million liras.

Greece

The Greek public order Law No. 1805/1988 covers cybercrime. This code includes Penal Code Article 370C §2:

> Everyone who obtains access to data recorded in a computer or in the external memory of a computer or transmitted by telecommunication systems shall be punished by imprisonment for up to 3 months or by a pecuniary penalty not less than 10,000 drachmas, under condition that these acts have been committed without right, especially in violation of prohibitions or of security measures taken by the legal holder. If the act concerns the international relations or the security of the state, he shall be punished according to Art. 148.
>
> If the offender is in the service of the legal holder of the data, the act of the preceding paragraph shall be punished only if it has been explicitly prohibited by internal regulations or by a written decision of the holder or of a competent employee of his.

Lithuania

In order to ratify the Council of Europe Cybercrime Convention, the Lithuanian government made the following additions to the penal code:

Article 196: Destruction or interference of computer data

Article 197: Destruction or interference of a computer program

Article 198: Interception and distribution of computer data

Contacts

Pursuant to Article 24, paragraph 7, subparagraph a, of the Convention, the Republic of Lithuania declares that the Ministry of Justice and the General Prosecutor's Office of the Republic of Lithuania are designated as responsible authorities to perform the functions mentioned in Article 24, paragraph 7, subparagraph a.

Pursuant to Article 27, paragraph 2, subparagraph a, of the Convention, the Republic of Lithuania declares that the Ministry of Justice and the General Prosecutor's Office of the Republic of Lithuania are designated as central authorities to perform the functions mentioned in Article 27.

Pursuant to Article 35, paragraph 1, of the Convention, the Republic of Lithuania declares that the Police Department under the Ministry of the Interior of the Republic of Lithuania is designated as a competent authority to perform the functions mentioned in Article 35.

Netherlands

Dutch parliament has enacted Article 138a to address cybercrime:

Article 138a Any person who intentionally and unlawfully accesses an automated system for the storage or processing of data, or part of such a system, shall be liable, as guilty of breach of computer peace, to a term of imprisonment not exceeding 6 months or a fine of 10,000 guilders.

In addition, Article 138b covers the unlawful serious hindering of data processing, and Article 232 applies to the forgery of any electronic token that has evidentiary value and the usage of such tokens as if they were genuine.

The Council of Europe Convention on Cybercrime Article 6 has been fully implemented.

Contacts

In accordance with Article 24, paragraph 7, of the Convention, the authority designated by the Netherlands is:

The Ministry of JusticeOffice of International Legal Assistance in Criminal Matters

P.O. Box 20301

2500 EH THE HAGUE

Tel. +31 (0)70-3707911

Fax +31 (0)70-3707945

In accordance with Article 27, paragraph 2.c, of the Convention, the central authority designated by the Netherlands is:

Landelijk Parket van het openbaar ministerie

(National office of the public prosecution service)

Postbus 395

3000 AJ ROTTERDAM

Tel. +31 (0)10-496-69-66

Fax +31 (0)10-484-69-78

In accordance with Article 35 of the Convention, the point of contact designated by the Netherlands is:

Landelijk Parket van het openbaar ministerie

(National office of the public prosecution service)

Postbus 395

3000 AJ ROTTERDAM

Tel. +31 (0)10-496-69-66

Fax +31 (0)10-484-69-78

Norway

The Norwegian government has ratified the Council of Europe convention on cybercrime and has enacted the following penal codes:

Penal Code § 145

> Any person who unlawfully opens a letter or other closed document or in a similar manner gains access to its contents, or who breaks into another person's locked depository shall be liable to fines or to imprisonment for a term not exceeding 6 months. The same penalty shall apply to any person who unlawfully obtains access to data or programs that are stored or transferred by electronic or other technical means.
> If damage is caused by the acquisition or use of such unauthorized knowledge, or if the felony is committed for the purpose of obtaining for any person an unlawful gain, imprisonment for a

term not exceeding 2 years may be imposed.

Accomplices shall be liable to the same penalty.

Public prosecution will only be instituted when the public interest so requires.

Penal Code § 145b

Any person who unlawfully makes available a computer password or similar data, by which the whole or any part of a computer system is capable of being accessed, shall be sentenced for spreading of access data, to a fine or imprisonment not exceeding 6 months or both.

Serious spreading of access data shall be sentenced to imprisonment not exceeding 2 years. In deciding whether the spreading is serious, special regard shall be paid to whether the data may access sensitive information, whether the spreading is extensive, or whether the conduct in other respects causes a danger for considerable damage.

An accomplice shall be liable to the same penalty.

Penal Code § 151b

Any person who by destroying, damaging, or putting out of action any data collection or any installation for supplying power, broadcasting, telecommunication, or transport causes comprehensive disturbance in the public administration or in community life in general shall be liable to imprisonment for a term not exceeding 10 years.

Negligent acts of the kind mentioned in the first paragraph shall be punishable by fines or imprisonment for a term not exceeding one year.

Accomplices shall be liable to the same penalty.

Contacts

In accordance with Article 24 of the Convention, the Norwegian authority responsible for making or receiving requests for extradition is The Royal Ministry of Justice and the Police, P.O. Box 8005, N-0030 OSLO.

In accordance with Article 27 of the Convention, the Norwegian authority designated is the National Criminal Investigation Service (KRIPOS). Direct telephone number for 24/7 (The High Tech Crime Division) contact is: + 47 23 20 88 88.

Romania

Romania has enacted a model national cybercrime legislation based on the Convention through its anticorruption law. In particular, Title III (On preventing and fighting cyber crime) addresses these issues:

Chapter III

Crimes and contraventions

Section 1

Offenses against the confidentiality and integrity of data and computer systems

Art.42 – (1) The illegal access to a computer system is a crime and is punished with imprisonment from 6 months to 3 years.

(2) If the fact mentioned at item (1) is performed by infringing the security measures, the punishment is imprisonment from 3 to 12 years.

Art.43 – (1) The illegal interception of any transmission of computer data that is not published to, from, or within a computer system is a criminal offense and is punished with imprisonment from 2 to 7 years.
(2) The same punishment is applied also for the illegal interception of electromagnetic emissions from a computer system carrying non-public computer data.

Art.44 – (1) The illegal alteration, deletion, or deterioration of computer data of the access restriction to such data is considered a criminal offense and is punished with imprisonment from 2 to 7 years.

(2) The unauthorized data transfer from a computer system is punished with imprisonment from 3 to 12 years.

(3) The unauthorized data transfer by means of an information data storing mean is also punished as in paragraph (2).

Art.45 – The serious hindering, without right, of a computer system operation, by the introducing, transmitting, altering, deleting, or deteriorating of computer data or by restricting the access to these data is considered a criminal offense and is punished with imprisonment from 3 to 15 years.

Art.46 – (1) The following are considered criminal offenses and punished with imprisonment from 1 to 6 years.

a) the production, sale, import, distribution, or making available, in any other form, without right, of a device or a computer program designed or adapted for the purpose of committing one of the offenses established in accordance with arts.42-45;
b) the production, sale, import, distribution or making available, in any other form, without right, of a password, access code, or other such computer data allowing total or partial access to a computer system for the purpose of one of the offenses established in accordance with arts.42-45;

(2) The possession, without right, of a device, computer program, password, access code, or computer data referred to at paragraph (1) for the purpose of one of the offenses established in accordance with arts.942-45 is also punished similarly.

Contacts

In accordance with Article 24, paragraph 7.a, of the Convention, Romania declares that the central authority responsible for making or receiving requests for extradition or provisional arrest is the Ministry of Justice (address: Str. Apollodor nr. 17, sector 5, Bucuresti).

In accordance with Article 27, paragraph 2.c, of the Convention, Romania declares that the central authorities responsible for sending and answering requests for mutual assistance are:

a) the Prosecutor's Office to the High Court of Cassation and Justice for the requests of judicial assistance formulated in pretrial investigation (address: Blvd. Libertatii nr. 12-14, sector 5, Bucuresti);

b) the Ministry of Justice for the requests of judicial assistance formulated during the trial or execution of punishment.

In accordance with Article 35, paragraph 1, of the Convention, Romania declares that the point of contact designated to ensure the immediate and permanent international cooperation in the field of combating cybercrime is the Service of Combating Cybercrime within the Section for Combating Organized Crime and Drugs Trafficking to the High Court of Cassation and Justice (address: Blvd. Libertatii nr. 12-14, sector 5, Bucuresti).

Slovenia

The Slovenian government has ratified the Council of Europe Cybercrime Convention.

Contacts

In accordance with Article 24, paragraph 7, of the Convention, the Republic of Slovenia declares that the Ministry of Foreign Affairs is the authority responsible for making or receiving requests for extradition in the absence of a treaty:

> Ministry of Foreign Affairs of the Republic of Slovenia
>
> Presernova 25
>
> SI - 1000 Ljubljana
>
> Tel. +386 1 478 2000

The Ministry of the Interior, Criminal Investigation Police Directorate, International Police Cooperation Section, is the authority responsible for making or receiving requests for provisional arrests in the absence of a treaty:

> Ministry of the Interior
>
> Criminal Investigation Police Directorate
>
> International Police Cooperation Section
>
> Tel. +386 1 428 4780
>
> Fax +386 1 251 75 16
>
> Mobile phone (officer on duty): +386 41 713 680 ; +386 41 713 699
>
> E-mail : interpol.ljubljana@policija.si

In accordance with Article 27, paragraph 2, of the Convention, the Republic of Slovenia designates the Ministry of Justice as the central authority responsible for sending and answering requests for mutual assistance:

> Ministry of Justice
>
> Zupanciceva 3
>
> SI - 1000 Ljubljana

In accordance with Article 35 of the Convention, the Republic of Slovenia designates as point of contact available on a 24/7 basis, the Ministry of the Interior, Criminal Investigation Police Directorate, International Police Cooperation Section:

Ministry of the Interior

Criminal Investigation Police Directorate

International Police Cooperation Section

Tel. +386 1 428 4780

Fax +386 1 251 75 16

Mobile phone (officer on duty): +386 41 713 680; +386 41 713 699

E-mail: interpol.ljubljana@policija.si

The Former Yugoslav Republic of Macedonia

The government of the Former Yugoslav Republic of Macedonia has ratified the Council of Europe Cybercrime Convention.

Contacts

In accordance with Article 24, paragraph 7, subparagraph a, of the Convention, the Republic of Macedonia declares that the Ministry of Justice of the Republic of Macedonia is designated as responsible authority to perform the functions mentioned in Article 24, paragraph 7, subparagraph a.

In accordance with Article 27, paragraph 2, subparagraph a, of the Convention, the Republic of Macedonia declares that the Ministry of Justice of the Republic of Macedonia is designated as a central authority to perform the functions mentioned in Article 27.

The 24/7 Network point of contact designated by the Republic of Macedonia is:

Mr. Marko Zvrlevski

Deputy Public Prosecutor

Department for Fight against Crime and Corruption

Office of Public Prosecutor

ul. Krste Misirkov bb

1000 SKOPJE

Mob phone : 0038970.397849

E-mail: office@zjorm.org.mk

Ukraine

Article 163 (Illegal Breach of Communications, Including by Means of Computer)

1. A person charged for illegal access to personal communications, telephone conversations, telegraph or any other correspondence, transmitted by means of electric communications or computers, faces either penalty ranging from 50 to 100 minimal wages, or up to 2 years of penitential labor, or up to three years of deprivation of liberty.

2. Same regarding public servants, or involving special monitoring equipment results in deprivation of liberty from 3 to 7 years.

Article 361 (Illegal Interference with Computers, Computer Systems and Networks)

1. Illegal intrusion into computer systems, networks, resulting in deletion or damaging of information contained therein, or information carriers; spreading of computer viruses results in either a penalty ranging up to 70 minimal wages, or deprivation of liberty or penitential labor of up to 2 years.

2. Same actions resulting in serious damage, or conducted repeatedly, or upon previous arrangement by a group of persons results in restriction of liberty up to 3 years or deprivation of liberty from 3 to 5 years.

Article 362 (Obtaining of Information without Right)

1. Stealing, obtaining or requesting of computer information or acquiring it by means of fraud or abuse by a public servant of one's position results in penalty ranging from 50 to 200 minimal wages or penitential labor of up to 2 years.

2. Same actions, conducted repeatedly or upon previous arrangement by a group of persons, result in a penalty ranging from 100 to 400 minimal wages or restriction of liberty up to 3 years or deprivation of liberty for the same time period.

3. Same actions named under either of previous paragraphs and resulting in serious damage result in deprivation of liberty for a time period from 2 to 5 years.

Article 363 (Failure to Follow the Rules of Operating Automated Data-Processing Systems)

1 Failure to comply with the rules of operating automated data-processing machines, systems, and/or computerized networks by a person, responsible for operation of the latter, resulting in a security breach, loss, or deterioration or deletion of information contained therein, or damage to the means of information security, unauthorized copying of information, or obvious malfunctions in operations of such a machine and/or system of machines or computer networks, results in a penalty of up to 50 minimal wages, or deprivation of the right to occupy certain positions or indulge in certain activities for the time period of up to 5 years, or penitential labor for up to two years.

2 Same actions causing serious damage result in a penalty of up to 100 minimal wages, or penitential labor of up to two years, or deprivation of liberty for up to 5 years, may be accompanied by deprivation of the right to occupy certain positions or indulge in certain activities for the time period of up to 3 years.

Contacts

In accordance with Article 24, subparagraph 7.a, of the Convention, Ukraine declares that the authorities empowered to perform the functions mentioned in paragraph 7 of Article 24 of the Convention shall be the Ministry of Justice of Ukraine (concerning court's inquiries) and the General Prosecutor's Office of Ukraine (concerning inquiries of bodies of prejudicial inquiry).

In accordance with Article 27, subparagraph 2.c, of the Convention, Ukraine declares that the authorities responsible for sending requests for mutual assistance, answering them, their execution, or their transfer to the empowered authorities shall be the Ministry of Justice of Ukraine (concerning courts' commission) and the General Prosecutor's Office of Ukraine (concerning commissions of bodies of prejudicial inquiry).

United Kingdom

The Police and Justice Act of 2006[11.]

35 Unauthorized access to computer material
(1) In the Computer Misuse Act 1990 (c. 18) ("the 1990 Act"), section 1 (offense of unauthorized access to computer material) is amended as follows.
(2) In subsection (1)
(a) in paragraph (a), after "any computer" there is inserted ", or to enable any such access to be secured";
(b) in paragraph (b), after "secure" there is inserted ", or to enable to be secured,".

(3) For subsection (3) there is substituted—

"(3) A person guilty of an offense under this section shall be liable—

(a) on summary conviction in England and Wales, to imprisonment for a term not exceeding 12 months or to a fine not exceeding the statutory maximum or to both;

(b) on summary conviction in Scotland, to imprisonment for a term not exceeding 6 months or to a fine not exceeding the statutory maximum or to both;

(c) on conviction on indictment, to imprisonment for a term not exceeding 2 years or to a fine or to both."

36 Unauthorized acts with intent to impair operation of computer, etc.

For section 3 of the 1990 Act (unauthorized modification of computer material) there is substituted—

"3 Unauthorized acts with intent to impair, or with recklessness as to impairing, operation of computer, etc.

(1) A person is guilty of an offense if—

(a) he does any unauthorized act in relation to a computer;

(b) at the time when he does the act he knows that it is unauthorized; and

 (c) either subsection (2) or subsection (3) below applies.

(2) This subsection applies if the person intends by doing the act—

(a) to impair the operation of any computer;

(b) to prevent or hinder access to any program or data held in any computer;

(c) to impair the operation of any such program or the reliability of any such data; or

(d) to enable any of the things mentioned in paragraphs (a) to (c) above to be done.

(3) This subsection applies if the person is reckless as to whether the act will do any of the things mentioned in paragraphs (a) to (d) of subsection (2) above.

(4) The intention referred to in subsection (2) above, or the recklessness referred to in subsection (3) above, need not relate to—

(a) any particular computer;

(b) any particular program or data; or

(c) a program or data of any particular kind.

(5) In this section—

(a) a reference to doing an act includes a reference to causing an act to be done;

(b) "act" includes a series of acts;

(c) a reference to impairing, preventing, or hindering something includes a reference to doing so temporarily.

(6) A person guilty of an offense under this section shall be liable—

(a) on summary conviction in England and Wales, to imprisonment for a term not exceeding 12 months or to a fine not exceeding the statutory maximum or to both;

(b) on summary conviction in Scotland, to imprisonment for a term not exceeding 6 months or to a fine not exceeding the statutory maximum or to both;

(c) on conviction on indictment, to imprisonment for a term not exceeding 10 years or to a fine or to both."

37 Making, supplying, or obtaining articles for use in computer misuse offenses

After section 3 of the 1990 Act there is inserted—

"3A Making, supplying, or obtaining articles for use in offense under section 1 or 3

(1) A person is guilty of an offense if he makes, adapts, supplies, or offers to supply any article intending it to be used to commit, or to assist in the commission of, an offense under section 1 or 3.

(2) A person is guilty of an offense if he supplies or offers to supply any article believing that it is likely to be used to commit, or to assist in the commission of, an offense under section 1 or 3.

(3) A person is guilty of an offense if he obtains any article with a view to its being supplied for use to commit, or to assist in the commission of, an offense under section 1 or 3.

(4) In this section, "article" includes any program or data held in electronic form.

(5) A person guilty of an offense under this section shall be liable—

(a) on summary conviction in England and Wales, to imprisonment for a term not exceeding 12 months or to a fine not exceeding the statutory maximum or to both;

(b) on summary conviction in Scotland, to imprisonment for a term not exceeding 6 months or to a fine not exceeding the statutory maximum or to both;

(c) on conviction on indictment, to imprisonment for a term not exceeding 2 years or to a fine or to both."

38 Transitional and saving provision

(1) The amendments made by—

(a) subsection (2) of section 35, and

(b) paragraphs 19(2), 25(2), and 29(2) of Schedule 14,

 apply only where every act or other event proof of which is required for conviction of an offense under section 1 of the 1990 Act takes place after that subsection comes into force.

(2) The amendments made by—

(a) subsection (3) of section 35, and

(b) paragraphs 23, 24, 25(4) and (5), 26, 27(2) and (7), and 28 of Schedule 14,

do not apply in relation to an offense committed before that subsection comes into force.

(3) An offense is not committed under the new section 3 unless every act or other event proof of which is required for conviction of the offense takes place after section 36 above comes into force.

(4) In relation to a case where, by reason of subsection (3), an offense is not committed under the new section 3—

(a) section 3 of the 1990 Act has effect in the form in which it was enacted;

 (b) paragraphs 19(3), 25(3) to (5), 27(4) and (5), and 29(3) and (4) of Schedule 14 do not apply.

(5) An offense is not committed under the new section 3A unless every act or other event proof of which is required for conviction of the offense takes place after section 37 above comes into force.

(6) In the case of an offense committed before section 154(1) of the Criminal Justice Act 2003 (c. 44) comes into force, the following provisions have effect as if for "12 months" there were substituted "six months"—

(a) paragraph (a) of the new section 1(3);

(b) paragraph (a) of the new section 2(5);

(c) subsection (6)(a) of the new section 3;

(d) subsection (5)(a) of the new section 3A.

(7) In this section—

(a) "the new section 1(3)" means the subsection (3) substituted in section 1 of the 1990 Act by section 35 above;

(b) "the new section 2(5)" means the subsection (5) substituted in section 2 of the 1990 Act by paragraph 17 of Schedule 14 to this Act;

(c) "the new section 3" means the section 3 substituted in the 1990 Act by section 36 above;

(d) "the new section 3A" means the section 3A inserted in the 1990 Act by section 37 above.

The Computer Misuse Act 1990 (Chapter 18)

1. Unauthorized access to computer material:

(1) A person is guilty of an offense if—

(a) he causes a computer to perform any function with the intent to secure access to any program or data held in any computer, or to enable any such access to be secured,

(b) the access he intends to secure, or to enable to be secured, is unauthorized, and

 (c) he knows at the time when he causes the computer to perform the function that that is the case.

(2) The intent a person has to have to commit an offense under this section need not to be directed at:

(a) any particular program or data,

(b) a program or data of any particular kind, or

(c) a program or data held in any particular computer.

(3) A person guilty of an offense under this section shall be liable—

(a) on summary conviction in England and Wales, to imprisonment for a term not exceeding 12 months or to a fine not exceeding the statutory maximum or to both;

(b) on summary conviction in Scotland, to imprisonment for a term not exceeding 6 months or to a fine not exceeding the statutory maximum or to both;

(c) on conviction on indictment, to imprisonment for a term not exceeding 2 years or to a fine or to both.

2. Unauthorized access with intent to commit or facilitate commission for further offenses.

(1) A person is guilty of an offense under this section if he commits an offense under section 1 above ("the unauthorized access offense") with intent

(a) to commit an offense to which this section applies; or

(b) to facilitate the commission of such an offense (whether by himself or by any other person); and the offense he intends to commit or facilitate is referred to below in this section as the further offense.

(2) This section applies to offenses

(a) for which the sentence is fixed by law; or

(b) for which a person of 21 years of age or over (not previously convicted) may be sentenced to imprisonment for a term of five years (or, in England and Wales, might be so sentenced but for the restrictions imposed by section 33 of the Magistrates Courts Act 1980).

(3) It is immaterial for the purposes of this section whether the further offense is to be committed on the same occasion as the unauthorized access offense or on any future occasion.

(4) A person may be guilty of an offense under this section even though the facts are such that the commission of the further offense is impossible.

(5) A person guilty of an offense under this section shall be liable—

(a) on summary conviction, to imprisonment for a term not exceeding the statutory maximum or to both; and

(b) on conviction on indictment, to imprisonment for a term not exceeding 5 years or to a fine or to both.

3. Unauthorized acts with intent to impair, or with recklessness as to impairing, operation of computer, etc.

(1) A person is guilty of an offense if—

(a) he does any unauthorized act in relation to a computer;

(b) at the time when he does the act he knows that it is unauthorized; and

(c) either subsection (2) or subsection (3) below applies.

(2) This subsection applies if the person intends by doing the act—

(a) to impair the operation of any computer;

(b) to prevent or hinder access to any program or data held in any computer;

(c) to impair the operation of any such program or the reliability of any such data; or

(d) to enable any of the things mentioned in paragraphs (a) to (c) above to be done.

(3) This subsection applies if the person is reckless as to whether the act will do any of the things mentioned in paragraphs (a) to (d) of subsection (2) above.

(4) The intention referred to in subsection (2) above, or the recklessness referred to in subsection (3) above, need not relate to—

(a) any particular computer;

(b) any particular program or data; or

(c) a program or data of any particular kind.

(5) In this section—

(a) a reference to doing an act includes a reference to causing an act to be done;

(b) "act" includes a series of acts;

(c) a reference to impairing, preventing, or hindering something includes a reference to doing so temporarily.

(6) A person guilty of an offense under this section shall be liable—

(a) on summary conviction in England and Wales, to imprisonment for a term not exceeding 12 months or to a fine not exceeding the statutory maximum or to both;

(b) on summary conviction in Scotland, to imprisonment for a term not exceeding 6 months or to a fine not exceeding the statutory maximum or to both;

(c) on conviction on indictment, to imprisonment for a term not exceeding 10 years or to a fine or to both.

3A. Making, supplying, or obtaining articles for use in an offense under section 1 or 3

(1) A person is guilty of an offense if he makes, adapts, supplies, or offers to supply any article intending it to be used to commit, or to assist in the commission of, an offense under section 1 or 3.

(2) A person is guilty of an offense if he supplies or offers to supply any article believing that it is likely to be used to commit, or to assist in the commission of, an offense under section 1 or 3.

(3) A person is guilty of an offense if he obtains any article with a view to its being supplied for use to commit, or to assist in the commission of, an offense under section 1 or 3.

(4) In this section, "article" includes any program or data held in electronic form.

(5) A person guilty of an offense under this section shall be liable—

(a) on summary conviction in England and Wales, to imprisonment for a term not exceeding 12 months or to a fine not exceeding the statutory maximum or to both;

(b) on summary conviction in Scotland, to imprisonment for a term not exceeding 6 months or to a fine not exceeding the statutory maximum or to both;

(c) on conviction on indictment, to imprisonment for a term not exceeding 2 years or to a fine or to both.

Contacts

SCD6 Economic and Specialist Crime OCU
Wellington House
67-73 Buckingham Gate
London
SW1E 6BE
E-mail: fraud.alert@met.police.uk.

United States of America (USA)

The United States has a wide coverage of both the Federal and State legislation including:

Prosecutorial Remedies and Tools Against the Exploitation of Children Today Act (PROTECT Act)

The Homeland Security Act of 2002 (Amendments)

Cyber Security Enhancement Act of 2002

The USA Patriot Act of 2001

Federal Criminal Code Related to Computer Intrusions

- 18 U.S.C. § 1029. Fraud and Related Activity in Connection with Access Devices

- 18 U.S.C. § 1030. Fraud and Related Activity in Connection with Computers

- 18 U.S.C. § 1362. Communication Lines, Stations, or Systems

- 18 U.S.C. § 2510 et seq. Wire and Electronic Communications Interception and Interception of Oral Communications

- 18 U.S.C. § 2701 et seq. Stored Wire and Electronic Communications and Transactional Records Access

- 18 U.S.C. § 3121 et seq. Recording of Dialing, Routing, Addressing, and Signaling Information

A Small Selection of U.S. State Computer Law

Each U.S. state has enacted a variety of codified legislation covering electronic, e-commerce, and other aspects of digital law.

The Computer Crime & Intellectual Property Section of the United States Department of Justice (www.usdoj.gov/criminal/cybercrime/) has links to both state and federal legislation as well as contact points. As may be seen from the small selection shown in Table B1, U.S. cyber law has developed extensively. The primary difficulty, however, is that the volume of law in the U.S. makes analysis of the requirements difficult for nonlawyers.

Table B1 U.S. Cyber Laws

State	Bill or Law
Alabama	Regulations § 810-14-1-.33.01
Alaska	Alaska House Bill 345 of 1997
	Alaska Senate Bill 232 of 1997
	Alaska House Bill 415 of 1997
Arizona	Arizona House Bill 2518 of 1998
California	California *has adopted* the UETA.
	California SB 820 of 1999
	California SB 1124 of 1999
	California AB 374 of 1999
	Online Disclosure Act of 1997; California
Senate Bill 49 of 1997	
Colorado	Colorado House Bill 1043 of 1998
	Colorado Senate Bill 155 of 1997

Contacts

Pursuant to Article 24, paragraph 7, of the Convention, the United States of America has not designated an authority responsible for extradition or provisional arrest in the absence of a treaty, as the United States will continue to rely on bilateral extradition treaties, and the authority responsible for making or receiving extradition requests on behalf of the United States is set forth in the applicable bilateral extradition treaties.

Pursuant to Article 27, paragraph 2, of the Convention, the Office of International Affairs, United States Department of Justice, Criminal Division, Washington, D.C., 20530, is designated as the central authority of the United States of America for mutual assistance under the Convention.

Pursuant to Article 35, paragraph 1, of the Convention, the Computer Crime and Intellectual Property Section, United States Department of Justice, Criminal Division, Washington, D.C., 20530, is designated as the point of contact available on a 24/7 basis to ensure the provision of immediate assistance under the Convention. Contact Information for the Computer Crime and Intellectual Property Section is given in the following: 24/7 Contact: United States of America.

Contact and Telephone Number

Computer Crime and Intellectual Property Section (CCIPS)

U.S. Department of Justice, Washington, DC

Tel: +1-202-514-1026 / Monday to Friday 0900 to 1800 hrs

Tel: +1-202-353-5216 / Mon to Fri after hours, Saturdays, Sundays, holidays

Tel: +1-202-514-6113 / Always on, but only monitored Monday to Friday 0900 to 1800 hrs

Description of Contact

CCIPS is a section of the Criminal Division of the U.S. Department of Justice that has 40 lawyers with responsibilities for combating cybercrime and theft of intellectual property, and with expertise in obtaining electronic evidence. Many CCIPS lawyers also have expertise in international assistance. CCIPS has "duty attorneys" available 24/7 to respond to urgent requests for assistance.

The language capabilities of the contact: English.

What to Say When Calling Contact Number

During business hours, call +1-202-514-1026. Tell the receptionist:

1. That you have "a cybercrime 24/7 request"

2. From what country you are calling

3. That you want to be connected to "a duty attorney"

After business hours and on Saturdays, Sundays, and holidays, call +1-202-353-5216. Your call will be connected directly to a duty attorney.

The fax number is +1-202-514-6113. This fax machine operates 24 by 7, but faxes sent outside of normal working hours will not receive attention until the next business day.

Exam Objectives Summary

Although these questions are more difficult than what you should experience on the exam, they have been designed to ensure your understanding of the concepts discussed in this section of the book and thus adequately prepare you to complete the exam. It is essential that the digital forensic practitioner has at least a basic understanding of the legislative framework that applies to them. Although each jurisdiction varies in its application of laws and statute, many of the fundamentals remain the same.

To answer the questions in this objective, you should be familiar with the basics of IT law as it applies to forensic practice. In addition, you should know how to search for the relevant legislation and understand the key terms.

References

Allison, Arthur, Currall, James, Moss, Michael, and Stuart, Susan (2003), *Digital Identity Matters*, University of Glasgow, UK.

Bainbridge, D. (2000), *Introduction to Computer Law*, Longman/Pearson Education: Harlow.

Hoey, A. (1996), "Analysis of the Police and Criminal Evidence Act, s69 – Computer-Generated Evidence," *Web Journal of Current Legal Issues*, in association with Blackstone press Ltd.

Leroux, Olivier (2004), "Legal admissibility of electronic evidence 1," *International Review of Law, Computers & Technology*; Volume 18, Number 2 / July 2004; pp 193–220.

Lim, Yee Fen (2002), *Cyberspace Law, Commentaries and Materials*, Oxford University Press UK.

Martin Donaghy, Stanbrook & Hooper, International Centre for Commercial Law.

Reed, Chris (2004), *Internet Law Text and Materials*, 2nd edition, Cambridge University Press, UK.

Roe, Michael (1997), *Cryptography and Evidence*, A dissertation submitted for the degree of Doctor of Philosophy at the University of Cambridge.

Schu, Reinhard (1997), "Consumer protection and private international law in internet contracts," *International Journal of Law and Information Technology*, 5 Int J L & IT 192.

Notes

1. 389 US 347, 351 (1967)

2. Hoey, 1996

3. This document is available from http://conventions.coe.int/Treaty/Commun/QueVoulezVous.asp?NT=185&CM=8&DF=06/02/04&CL=ENG. This site links into the full text of the treaty, an explanatory report, summary, and the chart of signatures.

4. Committee of Experts on Crime in Cyber-space (PC-CY): www.coe.int/t/e/legal_affairs/legal_co-operation/combating_economic_crime/6_cyber-crime/documents/1Terms%20of%20reference%20PC-CY.asp.

5. This document is available online at www.npa.go.jp/cyber/english/policy/hightech_prog.htm.

6. The home page of the Act is www.comlaw.gov.au/comlaw/management.nsf/lookupindex-pagesbyid/IP200402692?OpenDocument.

7. Cybercrime act. Commonwealth of Australia, 2001

8. The Act is available from: www.austlii.edu.au/au/legis/cth/num_act/pasa2000n1552000373/.

9. NPPs are available at www.privacy.gov.au/publications/npps01.html.

10. Donaghy, Stanbrook & Hooper

11. www.opsi.gov.uk/acts/acts2006/20060048.htm

Index

Licensed Penetration Tester

Earn the Most Prestigious
Certification for Penetration Testers.

Licensed Penetration Tester

EC-Council's Licensed Penetration Tester (LPT) is a natural evolution and extended value addition to its series of security related professional certifications. The Licensed Penetration Tester standardizes the knowledge base for penetration testing professionals by incorporating the best practices followed by experienced experts in the field.

The objective of a Licensed Penetration Tester is to ensure that each professional licensed by EC-Council follow a strict code of ethics, is exposed to the best practices in the domain of penetration testing and aware of all compliance requirements required by the industry.

Unlike a normal security certification, the licensed penetration tester is a program which trains security professionals to analyze the security posture of a network exhaustively and recommend corrective measures authoritatively. EC-Council's license vouches for their professionalism and expertise thereby making these professionals more sought after by organizations and consulting firms globally.

Benefits

EC-Council's endorsement as a licensed penetration testing professional and allows them to practice as penetration testing consultant internationally.
Industry acceptance as a legal and ethical security professional
Access to proprietary EC-Council software, templates and penetration testing methodologies.
License to practice and conduct security testing in organizations accredited by EC-Council.
Acquire knowledge from experienced hands, on penetration testing methodologies and latest penetration testing practices.

Requirements

1. Achieve Certified Ethical Hacker (CEH) Certification.
2. Achieve EC-Council Certified Security Analyst (ECSA) certification.
3. Complete LPT Training Criteria
4. Fill up and submit LPT Application form with payment of USD 500.00.
5. Documentation on criminal background check, or an authentication from an investigation agency absolving a criminal history.
6. Resume with detailed professional experience, previous certification /certificates and references for verification to be submitted.
8. Agree to EC-Council Code of Ethics.

For additional information, please visit
http://www.eccouncil.org/lpt.htm

L|P T ™
Licensed Penetration Tester

http://www.eccouncil.org EC-Council

Master | of Security Science™

escription

ie Master of Security Science (MSS) is part of a nested suite of programs, which includes an EC-Council certification, ist Graduate Diploma and a Master's degree with different entry points depending upon previous academic studies. ie program is intended both for new graduates and for experienced graduates who wish to update their skills or change eir area of specialization. It is concerned with the design, management and implementation of network security in rporations and public networks, or service provision to public and private networks.

ie focus of the course is to provide students with a wide understanding of Security Science. The course is sufficiently tailed to give an excellent background for a professional career in industrial or commercial organizations, and the quired background in security science to enable the student to undertake further study leading to the specializations eded for a research career. The MSS course is suitable for students with a wide range of previous security experience.

rofessional Recognition

he CEH, CHFI, ECSA and LPT certifications are widely recognized and valued in the security industry. EC-Council rtification exam credits can be applied towards the MSS program.

uration

 months part-time

ourse Structure

his program prepares students to manage computer security and incidence response. The courses include computer vestigations, security planning etc. Total of 42 semester credits . Plan B oral presentation and research development redits are required to complete this program.

ntry Requirements

pplicants will be expected to have a degree or equivalent in any discipline. Applicants with at least two years of xperience in the IT industry will be given preference.

ward

he Master of Security Science degree will be awarded by EC-Council University.

For additional information, please visit

http://www.eccuni.us/mss.htm

CPSIA information can be obtained
at www.ICGtesting.com
Printed in the USA
BVHW090233010222
627651BV00011B/671

9 781597 491976